Using Excel 3 for the Macintosh®

Christopher Van Buren

Using Excel 3 for the Macintosh

Library of Congress Catalog No.: 91-61978

ISBN 0-88022-715-X

94 93 92 91   4 3

Interpretation of the printing code: the rightmost double-digit number is the year of the book's printing; the rightmost single-digit number, the number of the book's printing. For example, a printing code of 91-1 shows that the first printing of the book occurred in 1991.

Using Excel 3 for the Macintosh is based on Microsoft Excel Version 3.0.

Publisher: Lloyd J. Short

Associate Publisher: Karen A. Bluestein

Acquisitions Manager: Terrie Lynn Solomon

Product Development Manager: Mary Bednarek

Managing Editor: Paul Boger

Book Designer: Scott Cook

Production Team: Claudia Bell, Jeanne Clark, Kimberly Mays, Denny Hager, Joe Ramon, Tad Ringo, Bruce D. Steed

For my father, Robert Van Buren

Product Director
Shelley O'Hara

Production Editor
Fran Blauw

Editors
Sara Allaei
Sharon Boller
Lori Lyons
Cindy Morrow
Daniel Schnake
Susan Shaw
Heidi Weas Muller

Technical Editor
Daniel Zoller
softDev, Inc.

Composed in Garamond and Macmillan

by Que Corporation

Christopher Van Buren

C hristopher Van Buren is a veteran computer book author, having written over a dozen books on such subjects as spreadsheets, integrated packages, and desktop publishing. He was a writer/editor for a major computer book publisher, and then went on to become a software marketing manager for a software publishing company in San Diego. Van Buren also was editor and publisher of several computer newsletters involving desktop publishing, Microsoft Works, and AppleWorks. Besides writing books, Van Buren consults in marketing communications and publication design.

For a disk of sample files, macros, and utilities, contact Chris Van Buren at:

Box 117144
Burlingame, California 94010

TRADEMARK ACKNOWLEDGMENTS

Que Corporation has made every effort to supply trademark information about company names, products, and services mentioned in this book. Trademarks indicated below were derived from various sources. Que Corporation cannot attest to the accuracy of this information.

1-2-3, DIF, Lotus, and Symphony are registered trademarks of Lotus Development Corporation.

Adobe Illustrator is a trademark and Postscript is a registered trademark of Adobe Systems Incorporated.

ANSI is a registered trademark of American National Standards Institute.

Apple Computer, Inc., ImageWriter, LaserWriter, MacDraw, and Macintosh are registered trademarks and MultiFinder is a trademark of Apple Computer, Inc.

dBASE II and dBASE III are registered trademarks, and dBASE IV is a trademark of Ashton-Tate Corporation.

Helvetica is a registered trademark of Allied Corporation.

Microsoft is a registered trademark of Microsoft Corporation.

Rolodex is a registered trademark of Rolodex Corporation.

ACKNOWLEDGMENTS ▼

Many thanks go to my agents Bill Gladstone and Matt Wagner at Waterside Productions for constant support and representation. Thanks to my brother, Alexander, for truth and inspiration and to my father for suggestions and corrections to the first edition. Thanks to Microsoft for providing the software, and to Daniel Zoller for providing a thorough technical review. Most of all, thanks to Trudy for helping me make decisions throughout this book and for everything.

CONTENTS AT A GLANCE

TABLE OF CONTENTS ▼

II   Excel Charts

III Excel Databases

IV Excel Macros

Introduction

There certainly are a lot of spreadsheets on the market today, but Microsoft Excel is on top with its attention to detail, its flawless operation, and its powerful features. Also, because Excel has become the standard on the Macintosh, it comes with a vast network of support systems, such as ready-made Excel worksheets (templates), instructional videos, and user groups. Some companies have published ready-made macros and add-in utilities for Excel that make your applications easier to manage. Another plus is that Excel is a Microsoft product; Microsoft offers some of the best technical support in the industry, as well as excellent upgrade policies.

What Is a Spreadsheet Program?

A *spreadsheet program* is an electronic version of the familiar columnar pad used for accounting, bookkeeping, and business analysis. When VisiCalc introduced the world to electronic spreadsheets in 1978, it created a reason to buy a computer. With VisiCalc, a computer could be used to speed up common business accounting and number-crunching. Moreover, you could use an electronic spreadsheet to perform "what if" tests instantly—merely by changing variable information. The electronic spreadsheet used custom-made formulas to total columns, calculate averages, perform cost analysis, and more. You even could store the results on disk for later use.

Of course, there has been a host of spreadsheet products since VisiCalc, most significantly Lotus 1-2-3, which appeared in 1983. Lotus 1-2-3 took the

1

electronic spreadsheet to the next level by adding not only larger capacities than VisiCalc offered but also built-in graphing and tools for sorting and extracting spreadsheet information—much like the tools used in a database. Thus, the three components of 1-2-3 are worksheet, database, and graphing capabilities.

The *Lotus 1-2-3 macro language*, a set of commands that could be combined to perform tasks automatically, quickly became the most popular programming language of all time. Because of the complexity that could be programmed into a spreadsheet, an entire industry of "template" products emerged. A *spreadsheet template* is a predesigned and preprogrammed spreadsheet file—a file that already contains the text, formulas, functions, and macros in it. Without knowing much about spreadsheets, a computer user can buy a template, enter his own data, and get the results.

When the Macintosh had gained some popularity in business, Microsoft introduced Excel. The original version of Excel, first available in September 1985, was the most powerful spreadsheet available for a microcomputer. It included similar but vastly superior spreadsheet, database, and graphics, as in Lotus 1-2-3, and improved dramatically on the user interface, offering the best the Macintosh had to offer. In addition, Excel included a significant number of spreadsheet functions not found in Lotus 1-2-3. The Excel macro language was equally impressive and easy to use.

Excel Version 2.2 introduced many new features. Fast graphing made it easy to produce graphs. Excel also gave you total control over the formatting of graphs, including changing the graph type, adding titles and legends, changing colors and patterns, and much more. Excel's macro language was updated to offer some of the most sophisticated commands available in spreadsheets.

Since Version 2.2 appeared, spreadsheet users have come to expect a new level of sophistication from their spreadsheets. Drawing and graph-annotation features are what users want in spreadsheet products, for example. So Microsoft responded with Version 3.0.

What's New in Version 3.0?

Version 3.0 provides everything you want in a spreadsheet. And, it does not sacrifice ease of use to do so. If you are familiar with Version 2.2, review the following list for a summary of new features in Version 3.0:

Worksheets

- *Placing Charts onto the Worksheet:* You can create charts directly on the worksheet and merge them with your worksheet data. You also can create charts and save them separately, as in older versions.

- *Drawing on the Worksheet:* New drawing tools enable you to create graphical objects on the worksheet. These tools are excellent for annotating worksheets and charts. Objects include lines, rectangles, ovals, arcs, and pictures.

- *Using Color:* The new color palette enables you to customize colors for use in your worksheets and charts. Choose 16 of these colors for any worksheet.

- *Using the Toolbar:* The new Toolbar offers point-and-click buttons for commonly used features, such as alignment, formatting, and drawing.

- *Outlining Data:* Use worksheet outlining tools to view various levels of your worksheet data. Outlining is useful for charting and getting an overview of your worksheet.

- *Consolidating Data:* Consolidation options enable you to merge data from several worksheets into one worksheet. You can perform mathematical functions on the data as it is merged—or create links between the various worksheets.

- *Using Templates:* You can save a worksheet as a template and use it over and over as a starting point for other worksheets. You cannot change templates accidentally.

- *Printing:* You can adjust print margins and column widths in the updated preview screen. By dragging the margin and column indicators, you can control the information on the page.

- *Using Workgroups:* By establishing a set of worksheets as a workgroup, you can enter and format information on all worksheets simultaneously by changing only the main worksheet.

- *Formatting Cells:* You can change the color and pattern of worksheet cells for color printouts and various effects.

- *Using Arrays:* You now can include up to 6,500 elements in an array.

- *Using the Solver:* The Solver add-in can help you find financial goals and seek particular values by solving models backward. Use the Solver as an extended "what if" tool.

- *System 7 Support:* Excel 3.0 supports the new capabilities of Macintosh System 7 including linking data with Publish/Subscribe, Balloon Help, and controlling external programs with Macintosh Events.

Charts

- *Using worksheet charts:* You can draw charts right onto the worksheet and save them with the worksheet data. Charts act like other worksheet objects; you can move them and size them at any time.

- *Using 3-D Charts:* You can select from several 3-D chart types, including 3-D line, 3-D column, 3-D area, and 3-D pie. You also can change the perspective of 3-D charts.

- *Creating Picture Charts:* You can use graphic objects—including clip art images—as pictures for picture charts, or pictographs. Various styles of pictographs are available.

- *Editing Data Series:* You now can change the values and references in a data series by using a simple command, rather than by editing the SERIES formula.

- *Editing Chart Values:* You can change chart values by dragging on the plot points inside the chart itself. Excel automatically enters a corresponding value into the worksheet. This enables you to change a chart's values visually rather than numerically.

- *Formatting Charts:* New chart formatting options enable you to position legends anywhere in the chart, change the patterns of individual plot points (even when they are part of a data series), and select from more line styles and colors.

Macros

- *Creating Add-ins:* You can create your own add-in macros that operate like Excel commands or pop-up utilities. These add-ins are useful for creating custom applications or commercial products.

- *Creating Dialog Boxes:* You now can add several types of list boxes to your custom dialog boxes. You also can use macro commands to disable and enable portions of a dialog box based on dialog-box selections.

- *Debugging Macros:* The macro debugger add-in can help you find and correct macro errors in large macro worksheets.

- *Programming Macros:* New macro commands make it easy to control any aspect of Excel or your worksheet. You can manipulate objects or get information about any aspect of the worksheet. A new programmer's IF-THEN-ELSE logic makes decision-making macros easier to create.

With Excel, you can design forms that practically fill themselves out. You can create custom applications that are self-documenting, password-protected, and self-modifying. You can perform financial analysis and chart the results, using presentation-quality graphs. Excel's possibilities are endless, including checkbook balancing, general ledger accounting, loan analysis, financial projections, break-even analysis, business statistics with charts, forms generation and printing, tax preparation, marketing and sales analysis, and payroll operations.

What's in This Book?

You certainly have chosen the right spreadsheet for your computer. Now you're ready to get down to work, and that's what this book is all about. You will find this book to be a valuable companion to your Excel program. This book covers all of Excel's commands, options, and special features, and is designed to enable you to begin using Excel quickly and with as few problems as possible.

Using Excel 3 for the Macintosh documents each new command and feature with examples and steps. It contains step-by-step procedures, tips, and advanced sections. The book fully explains regression analysis, the Excel Solver, and worksheet analysis and auditing. You also learn techniques for developing custom applications.

Although the book follows a natural progression, feel free to skip around. If you're eager to get a total picture of Excel, try the four quick start chapters (Chapters 2, 10, 14, and 17) at or near the beginning of each section. These quick starts provide step-by-step instructions for each of the main parts of the program: worksheet, charts and graphics, databases, and macros.

Although the quick start chapters give little explanation of commands and functions, they cover a slew of features in a short time; if you're able to pick up unfamiliar programs quickly, these chapters will involve you deeply in Excel. The following sections summarize the chapters in this book.

Part I: Excel Worksheets

This section of the book covers the Excel worksheet—the electronic version of a columnar accounting sheet. Using this electronic worksheet consists of entering numbers, formulas, and text onto the "page." All Excel worksheet features are covered in this section.

Chapter 1, "Getting Started," gives full details about the Excel worksheet tools, commands, and menu options. This chapter introduces you to Excel and what you can expect to see as you progress through the book.

Chapter 2, "Creating Worksheets: A Quick Start," provides a step-by-step overview of the worksheet. It takes you through the process of building a basic worksheet, formatting the information, and entering formulas that calculate results. You will use several features of the worksheet, but Chapter 3 provides a more complete explanation of features.

Chapter 3, "Creating Worksheets," shows you how to open an Excel worksheet, how to save your work, and how to enter three types of information into Excel: numbers, text, and formulas. The chapter also presents some details about formulas.

Chapter 4, "Editing Worksheets," describes how to make changes to your worksheets. You can change the information in the worksheet, copy and move information, and remove parts of the worksheet.

Chapter 5, "Formatting Worksheets," shows you how to enhance your worksheets by using numeric and text formatting. Such enhancements include the use of fonts, type styles, and color.

Chapter 6, "Using Worksheet Functions," provides descriptions and examples of each worksheet function. Worksheet functions offer special calculations for your applications and can save you a lot of time when you create a worksheet. This chapter is useful as a reference even after you have read the entire book and are familiar with Excel.

Chapter 7, "Using Multiple Worksheets and Linking Worksheets," shows you how to use more than one Excel worksheet at a time. As you use the more advanced features of Excel, you will want to start using several applications at once. This chapter shows you how to link worksheets and use consolidation to combine worksheets.

Chapter 8, "Using Advanced Worksheet Features," contains information about some special worksheet features. You will find this information useful after you become familiar with Excel. Features include working with lookup tables, creating data tables, performing date math, outlining worksheets, and using the new Solver utility.

Chapter 9, "Printing Worksheets," shows you how to create various reports from worksheet information and how to use the options available for formatting the reports. These options include page numbering, margin settings, font manipulation, headers, footers, and borders.

Part II: Excel Charts

This section covers Excel's special charting capabilities. Excel offers a host of tools for graphing your worksheet data, and Version 2.2 offers some important new charting capabilities—all of which are explained in this section.

Chapter 10, "Charting and Drawing: A Quick Start," provides step-by-step instructions on using Excel's charting features. You will create various types of charts and edit the information in those charts.

Chapter 11, "Creating Charts," provides complete instructions for creating and editing charts in Excel. All chart types are explained, including 3-D charts and combination charts.

Chapter 12, "Customizing Charts," covers options for customizing charts. Here, you learn how to add and remove elements from existing charts, change axis scales, customize chart text, and more.

Chapter 13, "Drawing," explains the new drawing capabilities of Excel 3.0. You learn how to use the drawing tools to annotate worksheets and charts. The chapter also discusses using images created from other programs.

Part III: Excel Databases

Part III explains how to use Excel's database features to manage large amounts of data. Database management includes sorting, searching, extracting, and manipulating data. Although Excel is no match for a large relational database, it is ideal for storing financial data and creating simple databases.

Chapter 14, "Using Databases: A Quick Start," shows you how to set up a database in Excel. You create a database and extract information from it. These exercises prepare you for the details covered in Chapter 15.

Chapter 15, "Creating and Manipulating Databases," provides details about using Excel for database manipulation. You discover how to set up a database, enter information into it, and locate information in it—either manually or with the Automatic Data form.

Chapter 16, "Using Advanced Database Techniques," shows you how to build your own custom data forms for Excel databases. This process involves using the Dialog Editor program, which comes with Excel. You also discover how to manipulate several databases on one worksheet and databases contained on external worksheets.

Part IV: Excel Macros

Macros enable you to perform complex or repetitive tasks with a single command or option. In addition to simplifying your work by performing lengthy tasks automatically, macros can be useful in worksheets that you create for others to use. This section provides complete details about macros, starting with the basics.

Chapter 17, "Using Macros: A Quick Start," provides a step-by-step guide to using macros in Excel. You create basic macros that automate commands and operations. This chapter also includes an exercise on using the macro-recording feature.

Chapter 18, "Creating Macros," provides details about the macro language and its uses in a worksheet. You learn how to create macros and what types of commands to use in a macro. You also learn how to enter and store macros for use in any worksheet.

Chapter 19, "Using Advanced Macro Techniques," shows you how to use simple programming techniques in your macros to make them more powerful. Here you learn about variables, loops, and program logic. You also learn how to use all kinds of cell references in your macro commands and functions.

Chapter 20, "Building Custom Applications," explains some useful techniques for creating larger, more complex applications. The chapter shows how to create custom menus, options, and dialog boxes. You also learn some useful techniques, such as error-trapping and auto-startup control.

Appendixes

Appendix A, "Installing Excel," provides the essential information for installing Excel on your computer. Whether you use a hard disk or floppy disks, this appendix gets you started.

Appendix B, "Using Excel's Macro Commands," explains the dozens of macro commands available for use in your custom macros, and provides details about how to use the commands. Use this appendix as a reference while you create new macros.

Appendix C, "Excel Command Guide," groups the various menu commands by function, lists key combinations that are command equivalents, and lists shortcut keys for moving the pointer and selecting.

What Are the Conventions in This Book?

Special Typefaces

Words that you are to type are presented in *italics*. For example, type *Advertising* in column 1.

Formulas or commands are indented on a separate line in regular typeface. For example, enter the following formula:

=A5+A6+A7+A8+A9

Commands or functions that you are to type are presented in capital letters, with the arguments in lowercase italics. Words in italics represent the *type* of information that you are to type, but not the exact wording. For example, type

SAVE.WORKSPACE(*name_text*)

Words or prompts that appear on-screen are in a `special computer typeface`. For example, Excel then presents you with the message

`Error in formula.`

Menu, Screen, and Option Names

Menu, Screen, and Option Names appear in headline-style type. For example, choose the Column Width command from the Format menu.

Many times, if you are to choose a command such as the Paste Special command from the Edit menu, the book simply tells you to choose the Edit Paste Special command; the name of the pull-down menu is the first word in the command.

Key Combinations

If you are to press a key and hold it down while pressing one or two other keys, a hyphen connects those keys that you press. For example, if you are to press the Shift key and then press the Option key at the same time, Excel tells you to press Shift-Option. If you are to press the Command key with another key, Excel tells you to press ⌘-Option-Shift.

Part I

Excel Worksheets

Getting Started
with Excel

E xcel is an electronic version of a columnar pad. This spreadsheet program is a powerful tool for such financial functions as general accounting, projections, budgets, and tax planning. In addition, Excel provides tools for creating business charts and storing database information. With the introduction of Version 3.0, you now can enhance your worksheets and graphs with illustrations and simple graphic enhancements.

This chapter offers an overview of Excel and its features. First is a brief discussion of the three basic keyboard styles, then an introduction to Excel worksheets, databases, charts, graphics, macros, and icons. Next, the chapter describes the various parts of the Excel worksheet screen—such as the title bar, Toolbar, formula bar, and status line—and introduces the program's menus and Help feature. Even if you are familiar with other spreadsheets, you should find this chapter helpful because of its overall look at Excel features. The next chapter takes you through a step-by-step example of how to use Excel's basic worksheet tools.

Understanding Your Keyboard

Before using Excel, you should be aware of the type of keyboard you have. Two basic keyboard models are prevalent for the Macintosh: the standard and extended keyboard (actually, you can find many different styles made by third-party manufacturers, but these are the most common). Figure 1.1 shows these keyboards.

13

Macintosh Standard Keyboard

Macintosh Extended Keyboard

Fig. 1.1. The two types of Macintosh keyboards.

Special Keys

A few keys are common to all types of keyboards, while others are available on the Extended keyboard only. In addition to the typical alphabetic and numeric keys (at the top of the keyboard), your keyboard may include the keys shown in table 1.1, which perform special functions.

Table 1.1
Special Macintosh Keys

Key	Function
Return	Accepts an entry or command selection. After you type information into a cell and press Return, Excel moves the pointer down one cell. You also can move the pointer down after pressing Return by choosing the Workspace command from the Options menu.
Enter	Works like Return except that Enter leaves the pointer in place.
Shift	Creates uppercase letters when used with alphabetic keys; creates symbols when used with numeric keys. You also can use the Shift key in combination with special command keys to issue alternative commands. Used with direction keys, Shift moves in the opposite direction. If you press Shift while accessing a menu, Excel presents alternative menu options.
⌘	Invokes Excel's special commands when pressed with a character key. Pressing ⌘-Q, for example, invokes the Quit command.
Option (Alt)	Used with the alphabetic and numeric keys, the Option key accesses special characters within the active font. When used with the Command key and a character key, Option activates or runs your custom macros.
Tab	Moves the cell pointer and menu highlight bar.
←, →, ↑, ↓	Moves the cell pointer in the direction of the arrow. These keys also perform other direction-oriented actions.
Caps Lock	Turns on capital (uppercase) letters until you press Caps Lock again.
Backspace (Delete)	Erases the character to the left of the cursor. When the cursor is not present, you can use Backspace to "blank" a cell. You also can press ⌘-B to blank a cell.

Table 1.1 *(continued)*

Key	Function
Clear	Clears the information in a cell or erases selected text. When used with the Shift key (that is, when you press Shift-Clear), Clear toggles the numeric keypad on or off.

Tip: Using the Command, Shift, and Option Keys
By holding down Command or Option and pressing other keys, you can perform operations similar to those of the function keys. These combinations, such as ⌘-V, ⌘-Option-PgUp, and ⌘-Shift-→, are described in Appendix C.

Key	Function
Control (Ctrl)	Works with other keys to enable you to perform special actions much like the Command key.
Esc	Cancels an action. Pressing Esc is identical to pressing ⌘-. (period).
Print Screen (PrtSc)	Prints a copy of the screen. This key is present on the extended keyboard only. Use the equivalent version, ⌘-Shift-4, on the other keyboards. Note that this feature is not available under MultiFinder.
Scroll Lock	Changes the way scrolling operates within a worksheet. When scroll lock is "active," the arrow keys scroll the screen without moving the cell pointer. The Scroll Lock key is present on the extended keyboard only. Press the key again to deactivate scroll lock.
Pause	Pauses macros and presents options for continuing or stopping.
F1	Available on the extended keyboard. F1 and the other function keys perform special functions that you often can duplicate with ⌘-*key* combinations. See Appendix C for a list of these keys.

The Numeric Keypad

Both keyboards contain a numeric keypad—a set of numbers to the right of the main keys. The numeric keypad has two purposes: to serve as a 10-key pad for numeric entry and to serve as directional keys for moving around inside Excel. All numeric keypads can serve as numeral keys or directional keys. When you first start Excel, the numeric keys are active on the keypad. Table 1.2 shows the numeric and direction keys.

Table 1.2
Macintosh Direction Keys

Key	Function
1 (End)	Moves the cell pointer to the last column that contains information. The pointer remains in the same row.
2 ($\downarrow$)	Moves the cell pointer down one cell.
3 (PgDn)	Moves the worksheet down one screen.
4 ($\leftarrow$)	Moves the cell pointer left one cell.
6 ($\rightarrow$)	Moves the cell pointer right one cell.
7 (Home)	Moves the cell pointer to the first column in the same row.
8 ($\uparrow$)	Moves the cell pointer up one cell.
9 (PgUp)	Moves the worksheet up one screen.

In other words, when you press the 4 key, you get the left-arrow action, not the numeral 4. You can combine these numeric-keypad keys with Command and Shift to produce various effects. To make these keys represent their respective numbers, press Shift-Clear, which is called the Num Lock toggle (because that key combination "locks" the numbers into place). Press Shift-Clear again to switch back to the directional keys. As you will see later in this book, the directional keys 2, 4, 6, and 8 on the numeric keypad are not identical to the four arrow keys on the main part of the keyboard. Also, remember that you have a set of number keys in the usual "typewriter" position above the main keys.

Function Keys

Function keys, available only on the extended keyboard, are labeled F1 through F15. These keys are assigned special purposes by the software package you are using. Excel uses function keys for single-key equivalents of the numerous Command-key combinations available throughout the program. Pressing F4 or ⌘-V, for example, invokes the Paste command (which also is available from a menu). Used with the Shift key, the Command key, or the key combination Shift-⌘, the function keys provide more than 30 possible actions for Excel. Note that some keyboards offer only 10 function keys. If you have one of these keyboards, use Alt-F1 for F11, Alt-F2 for F12, and so on. The effects of pressing these keys in Excel are described throughout this book. A summary of function keys and other special commands appears in Appendix C.

Understanding the Excel Worksheet

The Excel worksheet is a grid of 256 columns and 16,384 rows into which you can enter numbers and labels. A *cell*—the basic unit in any worksheet—is the intersection of a row and a column (see fig. 1.2). All worksheet information is entered into cells. You can create formulas that automatically add columns and rows, calculate averages, perform statistical analysis, and do other functions. By moving to the various cells and entering text (such as headings and titles), numbers, or formulas, you build a worksheet. The worksheets you can design include those for budgets, income projections, expense projections, travel expenses, checkbook balancing, and loan analysis.

The power of a worksheet comes from the formulas you can enter into the cells. Formulas enable you to calculate information for a cell so that you don't have to enter the information directly. The formula can calculate its result by using information from other cells of the worksheet (and even from other worksheets). The benefit of this capability is that you can change the data at any time and have the formulas recalculate their totals to account for the changes.

In addition to calculating data found elsewhere in the worksheet, formulas can access a host of special functions. One function, for example, computes the square root of any number. Worksheet functions are not much different from the functions on a hand-held calculator. See Chapter 6 for details about these functions.

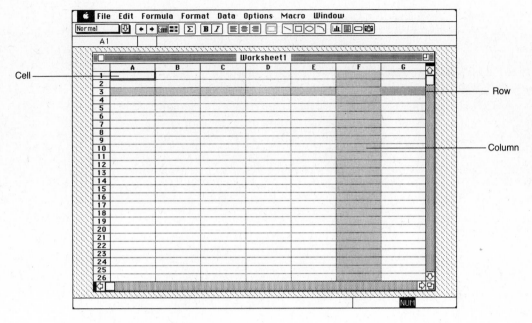

Cell — Row — Column

Fig. 1.2. The Excel Worksheet.

Understanding the Excel Database

A *database*—the electronic version of a file cabinet—stores data for reference and makes that data easily accessible. With a database, you also can rearrange easily the data and create reports based on information contained throughout the file. With Excel, you can set up a database within a worksheet. The Excel database is simply an area of the worksheet that contains data repeatedly accessed and extracted for reference. When a database section is established, it inherits numerous extra features that help you to retrieve information. Many commands in the Data menu, for example, become "active" when you establish a database section; these commands operate only on that section.

The database capabilities of the worksheet are useful when numeric or financial calculations—such as those for general ledger tasks, payroll tasks, and employee record-keeping—require data storage and retrieval. See Chapter 15 for details on Excel's database features.

Understanding Excel Charts

Chart is Excel's term for a graphic representation of a set of numbers (commonly called a *graph*). Types of charts include bar, line, pie, scatter (also known as XY), and a host of 3-D charts. Figure 1.3 shows you an Excel bar chart. Excel gives you total control over each element of the chart. You can adjust the scale, add titles, change the type of chart, stack the chart (stacked charts are discussed in Chapter 11), change the fonts used for the labels, and so on. With 3-D charts, Excel gives you control over the chart's perspective and proportions. When a chart's underlying values (contained on the worksheet) change, the chart adjusts to reflect this change. Charts are the most powerful way to express numeric data, and with Excel, chart-building is easy.

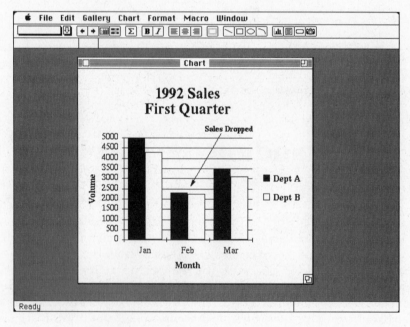

Fig. 1.3. *An Excel bar chart.*

With all these charting variations, you may think charting is complicated. Not at all. Excel offers over 50 predesigned charts in each of the main categories: line, bar, pie, scatter, column, area, 3-D line, 3-D pie, 3-D column, and 3-D area. All you have to do is select one of the predesigned charts for your data. You also can create your own chart designs. Furthermore, Excel offers a host of combination charts, which are like two different charts in one. Combination charts are explained in detail in Chapter 12.

Understanding Excel's Object-Oriented Drawing

Excel offers basic object-oriented drawing capabilities. This means that you can draw objects such as ovals, rectangles, lines, and arcs onto the worksheet. You can use these capabilities to embellish worksheet data and charts. You also can use this feature to draw simple graphics for your reports, such as logos.

Drawn objects are not actually drawn onto the worksheet itself. They are, technically, drawn *above* the worksheet onto an invisible layer, called the *graphics layer*. This is like a sheet of glass placed over the worksheet. Actually, each drawn object appears on its own layer above the worksheet. For this reason, drawings cover up worksheet data—and each other. For details about Excel's drawing tools, see Chapter 13.

Understanding Excel Macros

Macros are little programs, or lists of instructions, that can control any aspect of Excel. Macros are useful for automating worksheet tasks—the same tasks that you may perform manually by using basic Excel commands and options. By building a macro, you can perform complex or repetitive tasks with a simple keystroke. This capability is especially valuable when you build a worksheet that will be used by others. Macros can control the information entered, check that the information is correct, and even control where the user can move within the worksheet.

Macros consist of a series of macro commands. Like the commands in any programming language, macro commands must be combined in specific ways, but macros are simple to create and use. This book shows you the basics of building macros in Excel and provides techniques that you can use to make macros more powerful. A macro commonly serves one of two purposes: it automates a lengthy or complex task or provides controls for making a worksheet easier to use by others.

The most common reason for building a macro is to automate a lengthy task. Using a macro, you can take a series of commands, options, and keystrokes and perform them with a single command. This command can take the form of a menu option, a keyboard command, a button, or one of many different action commands. Macros commonly are used to set up and print portions of the worksheet; alter data; format numbers and charts; change charts from one type to another, using the same data; and move information between worksheets.

Excel Version 3.0 also enables you to attach a macro to a button so that you can invoke your macro instructions by clicking on the button. You can place this button anywhere in a worksheet. See Chapter 19 for details on macros and buttons.

In addition to using macros to automate complex or repetitive tasks in Excel, you can use macros to produce interactive screens and to control the actions available in a worksheet. You can develop your own on-line help screens that are displayed at the touch of a button, for example. You can create macros that check the accuracy of data entered into a worksheet. You even can develop macros that prompt for information to be entered into the worksheet and then place the information in the correct cells so that the user never really manipulates the worksheet itself. Such macros enable someone else to more easily use a worksheet you have built; the worksheet becomes a kind of self-running program. These types of macros can become extremely involved. See Chapter 21 for details about these types of macros.

Starting Excel

When you insert the Excel disks into your disk drive and examine their "desktop," you notice several types of icons. Excel has unique icons for worksheet files, macro files, charts, and the Excel program itself. Figure 1.4 shows examples of these icons.

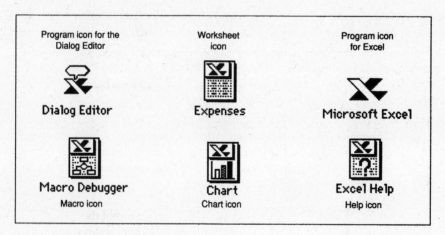

Fig. 1.4. Examples of Excel's Icons.

To start Excel and open a new, blank worksheet, double-click on the program icon for Excel. When you create worksheets with Excel, you can save them for future use. Saved worksheets are called data files, or *worksheet files*. Worksheet files are stored on disk and are assigned the worksheet icon. When you double-click on the icon for a particular worksheet, you start Excel with that worksheet already open and in view.

Charts rely on the data in specific worksheets, but when you save a chart, Excel stores it in a special file on disk and assigns the chart a Chart icon. You can double-click on a Chart icon to start Excel with the chart in view on-screen. The worksheet to which the chart applies, however, will not be open.

Macros created for Excel worksheets are stored in special files marked by a Macro icon. Do not start Excel by double-clicking on a Macro icon, unless the macro is built specifically for that purpose or unless you have a specific reason for doing so. See Chapter 19 for more information.

Another icon you notice when using Excel is the Help icon, which represents the Excel on-line help information that you can access while you are using the program. When you click on this icon, Excel starts up with the Help dialog box in view. Other icons, such as the Macro Debugger and the Dialog Editor, represent special utility programs that work with Excel. These programs are explained in Chapter 20.

Examining the Excel Screen

Excel has all the basic elements found in any worksheet, such as rows, columns, and menu options, and also contains special tools particular to Excel. Figure 1.5 shows the Excel screen, which includes a blank worksheet, the Toolbar, and the Excel worksheet menus.

The following sections describe each element shown in figure 1.5.

Menu Bar

A *menu bar* is a group of individual menus along the top of the screen. The bar displays only the name of each menu. From this bar, you can select one of the menus to view (so that you can choose one of a menu's options). In Excel, one of three menu bars (that is, one of three different groups of menus) may appear on-screen: one containing basic worksheet menus, one containing chart menus, and one containing the info-screen menu. The reasons for these three groupings will become clear as you progress through this chapter.

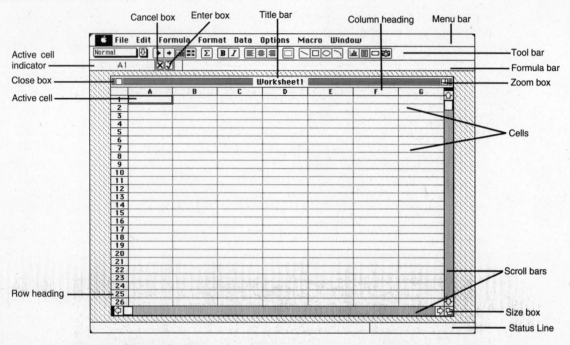

Fig. 1.5. The Excel screen.

When you enter Excel but remove all worksheets from the screen, Excel presents a fourth menu bar, which is really just a subset of the worksheet menu bar. All the menus and options of this fourth menu bar are covered in "Worksheet Menus," later in this chapter.

Title Bar, Close Box, and Zoom Box

Each worksheet created with Excel has a title bar. The *title bar* displays the name of the worksheet and contains the *close box* and *zoom box*, which are common to most Macintosh windows. Clicking on the close box closes the worksheet (or removes it from the desktop) and enables you to save any changes made. The zoom box toggles between a full-screen window and a modified window size. If you have shrunk the window by using the size box, you can use the zoom box to return the window to its full size.

Size Box

The *size box*, located in the bottom right corner of the window, enables you to change the size and shape of the active window. Figure 1.6 shows an example of the effects of using the size box.

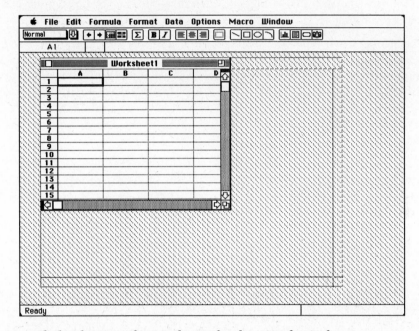

Fig. 1.6. Shrinking or enlarging the window by using the size box.

To shrink or enlarge the window, click on the size box and drag the mouse pointer to another location on-screen; then release the mouse button. Of course, if the window is already the size of the screen, you cannot enlarge the window further.

Column and Row Headings

Column and *row headings* are simply the names of the various columns and rows in the worksheet. Rows are numbered, and columns can be numbered or lettered. The column heading displays the style you chose by using the Options Workspace command.

Column headings normally are given letters, beginning with A. The column fifth from the left, for example, is column E. After labeling the columns A through Z, Excel begins with AA and continues through AZ, then begins with BA, and so on. The final column is IV, making a total of 256 columns.

Cells

As explained earlier, a worksheet *cell* is the intersection of a row and a column. All information in a worksheet is entered into cells. You can change the width of cells in a column or the height of cells in a row, and you can perform calculations by using cell references—that is, by having one cell refer to another. A *cell reference*, or *cell address*, is simply the name of a cell.

Excel offers two types of addresses for each cell. One type—the *R1C1 format*—uses numbers for both rows and columns. The cell at the intersection of row 4 and column 3, for example, is called R4C3. The second type of cell address—the *A1 style*—is the default; it uses numbers for rows and letters for columns. The cell at the intersection of row 4 and column C, for example, is called C4. This book uses the second type of cell address—the A1 style.

To change the format in which the column and row headings appear, select the Workspace option from the Options menu. After the dialog box appears, check the R1C1 box in the set of display options. Doing so switches the headings to the R1C1 format. Return to this dialog box and remove the check mark to change the format back to the A1-style headings. Figure 1.7 shows the A1-style headings, and figure 1.8 shows the R1C1 format.

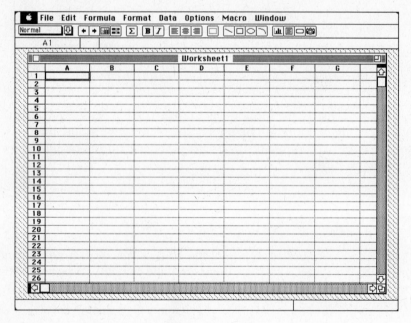

Fig. 1.7. The A1-style cell addresses.

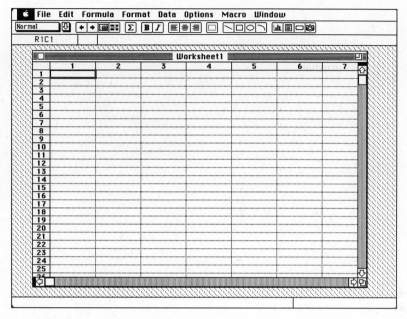

Fig. 1.8. *The R1C1-style cell addresses.*

Active Cell, Active-Cell Indicator, and Cell Pointer

The *active cell* is the cell in which the pointer is currently located. The *cell pointer* (or pointer) is a sort of highlighter that can rest on any worksheet cell. You can reposition the cell pointer by using the mouse, the arrow keys, the Tab key, the Return key, the Shift-Tab combination, the Shift-Return combination, and a host of automatic "find" options. The *active-cell indicator*, in the upper left corner of the screen, displays the address of the current cell. The contents of the active cell are displayed in the formula bar, discussed in the next section.

Formula Bar

As just mentioned, the *formula bar* displays the information contained in the active cell. The formula bar also is the place where you enter information into a cell; when you move to a cell and begin typing information, that information appears in the formula bar. The formula bar can contain more than one line of information, and automatically wraps your entry onto several lines as you type. Figure 1.9 shows what the screen looks like when the pointer is on a cell that already contains information.

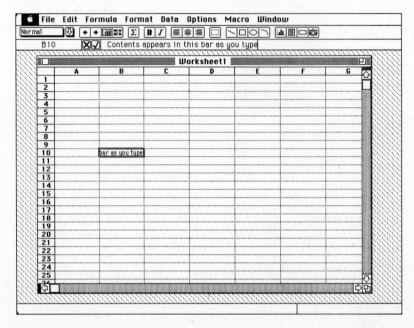

Fig. 1.9. The cell contents displayed in the formula bar.

Toolbar

The *Toolbar* contains special tools (primarily buttons) that you can select with the mouse. These tools generally are provided to reduce common commands and actions down to a simple mouse click. A few tools provide special features for your worksheets, however, that you can apply only by using the Toolbar. Figure 1.10 shows all the tools.

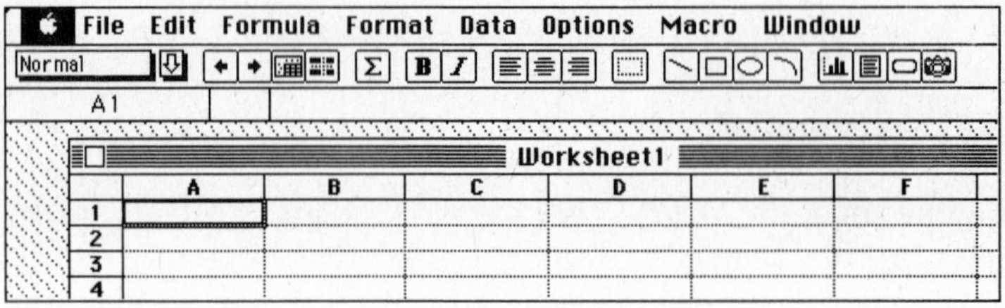

Fig. 1.10. The Toolbar contains several buttons.

Descriptions of the Toolbar buttons follow, in the order that they appear on-screen:

- *Style List:* Stores formatting options in named sets. You can apply a set of formats to a cell or range by selecting the name from the style list. See Chapter 5 for more information on this tool.

- *Promote and Demote Buttons:* Establishes levels for sections of a worksheet. You can use this for worksheet outlining, which is discussed in Chapter 9.

- *Outline Symbols Tool:* Displays the outline symbols on the worksheet. This reveals the outlining selections you've made. See Chapter 9 for more details.

- *Select Visible Cells Tool:* Selects all cells on the worksheet containing data that is not "hidden." This button applies to outlining and is discussed in Chapter 9.

- *Auto Sum Tool:* Automatically sums a range, row, or column. Highlight the data you want to sum, including an extra cell for the total. Make sure that you select the extra cell in the highlighted range and click the Auto Sum button. Excel automatically enters the SUM function into the cell.

- *Bold or Italic Tool:* Applies boldface or italic print to the selected cell or range. This is a shortcut to the Font command in the Format menu. You also can apply bold and italic by using the keyboard shortcuts Shift-⌘-B and Shift- ⌘-I. See Chapter 5 for more formatting options.

- *Alignment Tool:* Aligns the selected data. Choose left-align, center, or right-align buttons. This is equivalent to the Alignment options in the Format menu.

- *Selection Tool:* Selects objects drawn on the worksheet and enables you to move, resize, or copy them. See Chapter 14 for more information about drawing and manipulating objects on the worksheet.

- *Drawing Tools:* Creates lines, boxes, ovals, or arcs on the worksheet. Click on the tool you want and then click and drag on the worksheet to draw the object. You then can edit the object in many ways. See Chapter 14 for more details.

- *Chart Tool:* Creates a chart on your worksheet using the currently highlighted data. You then can customize the chart in many ways. See Chapter 11 for more information.

- *Text Box Tool:* Creates a text box on the worksheet. A text box can hold any text you want and can be moved around the worksheet independent of cells. You can format the text inside the text box by using fonts and styles. See Chapter 9 for more information.

- *Button Tool:* Creates buttons to which you can link a macro. The button, when linked to a macro, invokes (or runs) the macro. See Chapter 19 for more information.

- *Camera Tool:* Takes a *picture* (a graphical representation of the data and the worksheet) of the selected range. You can use this picture as a graphic object in Excel or any other program. Excel maintains links to the picture, however, so that changes to the original worksheet will update the picture. See Chapter 7 for more information on this tool and linking between Excel and other programs.

Scroll Bars

When you look at the worksheet screen, you see only a fraction of the entire "page" available for your work. Imagine that the worksheet rows and columns continue past the edge of the screen and that the screen is a window revealing about 20 rows and 8 columns at a time. You can move the screen across and down the entire page area to reveal other sections of the worksheet. Figure 1.11 illustrates this concept.

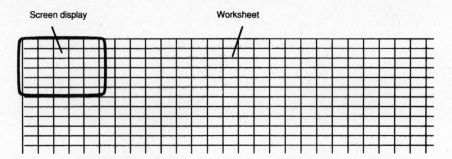

Fig. 1.11. Your view of the worksheet is a portion of the entire worksheet.

The *vertical scroll bar* at the right side of the screen and the *horizontal scroll bar* at the bottom of the screen enable you to move the screen's view (which is your view also) around the entire page. As in all normal Macintosh applications, you can click on the scroll bar arrows to move slowly around the worksheet, or you can hold down the mouse button with the pointer on the arrows to move quickly around the worksheet.

You also can click on the scroll box and drag it to another location on the bar to jump to various locations on the worksheet. Moving the box up on the vertical bar advances you to the lower row numbers; moving the box down advances you to the higher rows. Moving the box to the left on the horizontal bar advances you to the lower column numbers (or letters); moving the box to the right advances you to the higher column numbers (or letters).

You also can click in the gray portion of the scroll bar (that is, on the bar itself) to jump one screen at a time. You can click above or below the scroll box on the vertical scroll bar to move up or down on the screen, or you can click to the left or right of the scroll box to move the screen to the left or right.

Note: You can use the arrow keys, Tab, and Return to move around the worksheet. Details about moving through the worksheet are covered in the next chapter.

As you drag the scroll box to a new location on the bar, Excel displays in the active-cell indicator box the column (if you are using the horizontal bar) or row (if you are using the vertical bar) to which you are moving. Before releasing the mouse button, you can determine the destination by glancing at this indicator (see fig. 1.12). If the worksheet is empty or new, you are able to scroll only a short distance by using this method.

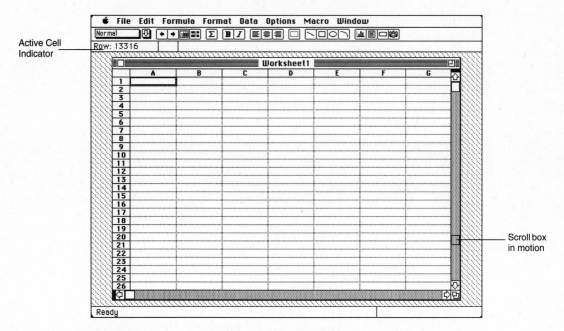

Fig. 1.12. When you use the scroll bars, Excel displays the column or row to which you are moving.

Enter and Cancel Boxes

When you enter information into a cell, you must either accept or reject your entry. Clicking on the appropriate box informs Excel of your decision. These boxes appear in the formula-bar area when you begin typing into a cell. If you accept an entry, it remains on the worksheet, becoming part of the worksheet. If you reject (or cancel) an entry, it disappears, as if you never entered the entry.

Excel offers keyboard equivalents for both the enter box and cancel box. Pressing Return is the same as clicking on the enter box; pressing ⌘-. is the same as clicking on the cancel box.

Status Line

The status line displays information about menu options and Excel's modes. When you highlight, or select, a menu option, Excel displays a brief explanation of that option on the status line. Each menu option displays such a message when highlighted. In addition to this information, the status line shows which mode Excel is in at any given time and indicates what you must do after you initiate your command. Table 1.3 explains the various modes you may see listed on the status line.

Table 1.3
Excel Modes

Mode Indicator	Meaning
Calculate	Worksheet needs to be recalculated. Calculation has been set to manual, and changes have been made that affect worksheet formulas.
Circular:*cell ref*	Excel found a circular reference in the worksheet indicated by the cell address listed.
Copy	Excel expects you to complete the Copy operation that has been started.
Cut	Excel expects you to complete the Cut operation that has been started.
Edit	Excel is in Edit mode, and a cursor is active in the formula bar. You use the cursor-movement keys to navigate within the formula bar.

Mode Indicator	Meaning
Enter	Excel is in Enter mode; you can enter information into the active cell.
Find	Excel is in the middle of the Find operation.
Help	Excel is in the middle of the Help operation.
Point	Enter a cell or range reference. You can point to the cell or range or just type the reference.
Ready	Excel is waiting for an action. You can select a command, move the pointer, or perform any number of operations.
Recording	Excel is recording a macro.

The far right portion of the status line displays the keyboard indicator codes. These codes inform you of active keyboard settings, such as Num Lock. Table 1.4 summarizes these indicators.

Table 1.4
Active Keyboard Settings

Keyboard Indicator	Meaning
EXT	The F8 key on the extended keyboard has been activated. You now do not have to press Shift to extend a selection of cells.
FIX	A fixed number of decimal places is active for the worksheet. You choose the Workspace command from the Options menu so that all numbers entered into the worksheet will contain the fixed number of places.
NUM	The Num Lock option is active, which means that you can use the numeric keypad for numbers rather than as directional keys. You activate and deactivate this option by pressing Shift-Clear.

continues

Table 1.4 *(continued)*

Keyboard Indicator	Meaning
SCRL	The Scroll Lock key is active. This changes the way Excel scrolls through the worksheet by moving the screen instead of the pointer. Press the Scroll Lock key to deactivate this option.
CAPS	The Caps Lock key is active; all uppercase letters are being used. Press Caps Lock again to return to normal.

Selecting Menu and Dialog Box Options

Excel uses the standard Macintosh interface for menus and dialog box options. (A *dialog box* contains a number of options or settings from which you can choose.) Learning Excel therefore is easy if you already know how to use other Macintosh products. You also can use the keyboard to select options from menus and dialog boxes. The following two sections describe how to use the mouse and the keyboard interfaces in Excel.

Selecting Options with the Mouse

If you are familiar with the Macintosh, you probably know how to use the mouse to select menu options. Just press the mouse button with the pointer positioned on any of the menu titles and hold down the button. This action pulls down the appropriate menu, as shown in figure 1.13.

While still pressing the mouse button, drag the mouse to point to the option in the menu list that you want to select. When that option is highlighted, release the button to invoke that option.

Menu options often produce dialog boxes. In some cases, pressing the Tab key moves the highlight bar from option to option in the dialog box, but you always can click on any option name or button shown in the box. Figure 1.14 shows a typical dialog box.

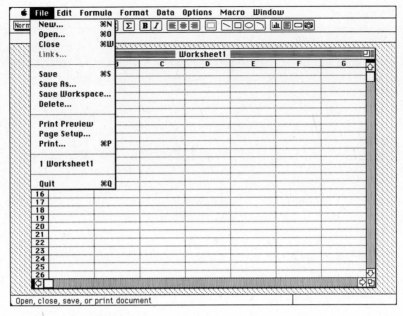

Fig. 1.13. *A pull-down menu.*

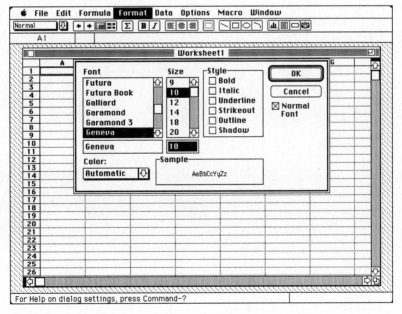

Fig. 1.14. *A dialog box.*

Clicking on the OK button marks your acceptance of the changes made in the dialog box; clicking on Cancel returns the box to its prior state. Both buttons remove the box from view. One of the two buttons, OK or Cancel, will have a thick border around it. This border indicates that you can press the Return key to select the option instead of using the mouse. Press ⌘-. to cancel the dialog box.

Selecting Options with the Keyboard

If you prefer to use the keyboard instead of the mouse, you can take advantage of the complete keyboard interface provided by Excel. To select a menu option by using the keyboard, follow these steps:

1. Press the slash (/) key to activate the menu bar. Key letters within each menu name are underlined.

2. Press the letter associated with the option you want (the underlined letter) to pull down the menu. Alternatively, use the right-arrow and left-arrow keys to move to the menu option you want and then press Return.

3. With the menu active, press the letter associated with the menu option (the underlined letter). Alternatively, press the down-arrow and up-arrow keys to move to the option you want and press Return.

To cancel your selection at any time, press ⌘-. (period).

> **Tip: Viewing Alternative Menu Options**
> When you select a menu with the keyboard or mouse, you see various options within that menu. Excel also offers a set of alternative options throughout the menus. You can view these by holding down the Shift key before selecting the menu you want. (Using the keyboard, press the Shift key while you press the letter of the menu you want.) For details about each alternative option, see the listing of menu options in the following section, "Introducing Excel's Menus."

Excel also provides an alternate menu activation key for your convenience. This is set automatically to the slash (/) key for compatibility with other spreadsheet programs. You can change the key used as the menu-activation key. Select the Workspace command from the Options menu, and the dialog box shown in figure 1.15 appears.

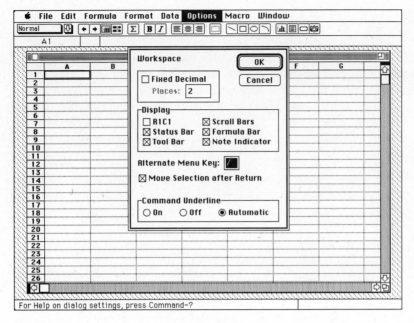

Fig. 1.15. *The Options Workspace dialog box.*

In the Alternate Menu Key box, press the key that you want as the menu-activation key. Press one key only (from the main keyboard). The Command Underline options control whether underlines appear on the command names. The On choice turns the underlines on for all situations; the Off choice turns the underlines off for all situations; the Automatic choice turns the underlines on when you invoke the menus with the menu-activation key but leaves them off otherwise. Click on the OK button to accept the changes you make in this dialog box. Note that these changes apply to Excel in general and will affect all your Excel worksheets.

To select dialog box options with the keyboard, press Tab to move from option to option. If several options appear in a group, you sometimes can move to the group using the Tab key and then use the arrow keys to move to specific options. Press the Command key with the underlined letter of the dialog option you want to select. Press Return to close the dialog box.

Introducing Excel's Menus

Menus organize Excel's many worksheet features according to function. Menus appear at the top of the screen in sets. One of three sets of menus appears at the top of the screen at any given time: one set for general worksheet needs, one for chart needs, or one for tasks involving Info windows (see figs 1.16 – 1.18). This section provides an overview of Excel's menus. You can find details about these options throughout the rest of the book.

Actually, Excel presents a fourth set of menus when you have no worksheets open. This set, called the *null menu*, contains a subset of the general worksheet menus.

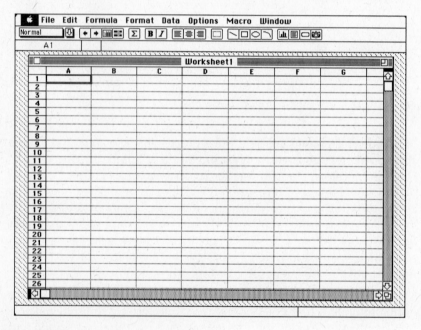

Fig. 1.16. The general worksheet menu bar.

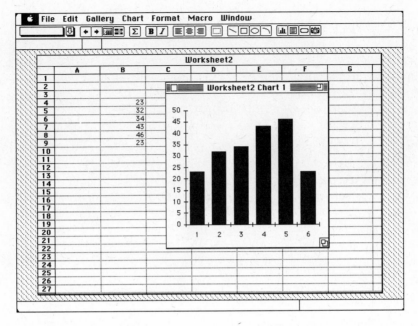

Fig. 1.17. *The chart menu bar.*

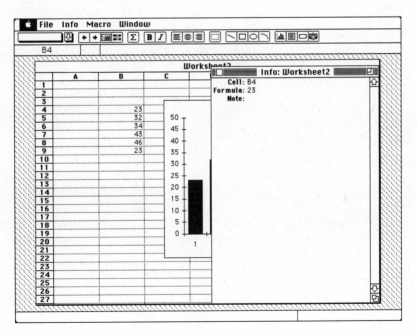

Fig. 1.18. *The Info window menu bar.*

Tip: Your Menus Don't Necessarily Show All the Options
If your menus do not match those in the figures, you probably have short menus active. *Short menus* do not show all the options available; they are designed to be easier to use for beginners. To activate full menus, select the Full Menus command from the Options menu. Options affected by these commands are shown in bold in the following lists.

Note that many menu commands offer shortcut versions that involve pressing the Command key with another key. These shortcuts enable you to bypass the menu. Most shortcuts appear to the right of commands that offer them. Appendix C contains a complete list of shortcut keys.

Note that if you select a menu command that ends in an ellipse (...), a dialog box with further options appears.

Worksheet Menus

The worksheet menus are the File, Edit, Formula, Format, Data, Options, Macro, and Window menus. These menus apply when a new or existing worksheet window is open and in view. When you close all worksheet windows, Excel removes most of these menus. The following sections discuss these menus.

Saving and Opening Files

The File Menu

The File menu contains options common to all Macintosh applications, such as options for opening new and existing files, saving files, setting up the printer, and printing (see fig. 1.19). Each worksheet is an independent file which you can manipulate independently by using the File menu options. Table 1.5 describes the File menu options.

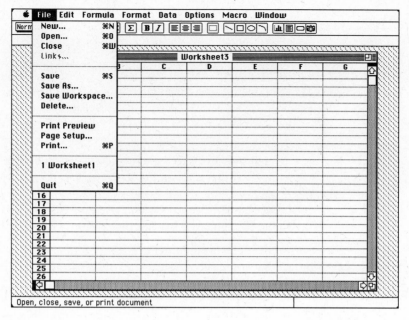

Fig. 1.19. The File menu.

Table 1.5
File Menu Options

Option	Function
New	Opens a new, blank worksheet, chart, or macro sheet. You can choose the New command even if an existing worksheet, chart, or macro sheet is open.
Open	Presents a selection box from which you can open a worksheet that has been saved to disk.
Close	Removes the current worksheet from the screen. If you have made changes, Excel gives you the opportunity to save them. This option changes to Close All when you use the Shift key when selecting the menu. Close All closes all open worksheets, charts, or macro sheets at once.

continues

Table 1.5 *(continued)*

Option	Function
Links	Opens files that are linked to the current file.
Save	Saves the worksheet currently in view. If you have not saved the worksheet before, you are given the opportunity to enter a name for the saved file.
Save As	Enables you to save a worksheet under a name different from the worksheet's current name, as if you had never saved the worksheet previously. You also can save the file by using one of the nonstandard formats.
Save Workspace	Saves the arrangement of all open files so that you easily can open all of them again by using the Open command. Using the Save Workspace command is helpful when several files are linked.
Delete	Removes files permanently that have been saved on disk. You can select from a list the files you want to delete, including non-Excel files.
Print Preview	Displays the active print area on-screen as it will appear on your printer. You can make adjustments to the page margins by using this preview.
Page Setup	Presents options for changing the page dimensions, the alignment of printed information, and other page-oriented matters.
Print	Presents printing options, such as the number of copies to print and the specific pages to print.
Quit	Enables you to leave Excel and return to the Macintosh system. If you have not saved changes to the open file, Excel gives you the opportunity to do so before you quit.

Changing the Worksheet

The Edit Menu

Options in the Edit menu, which are common to most Macintosh applications, enable you to cut and paste information within a worksheet or between worksheets. You also can insert and delete information by using these options. Figure 1.20 shows the Edit menu. Table 1.6 describes the Edit menu options.

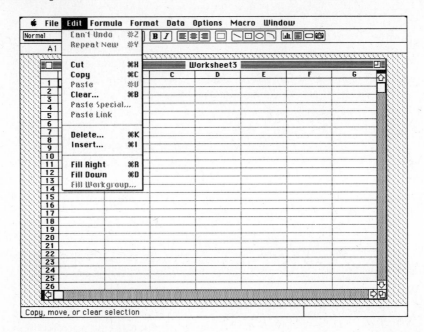

Fig. 1.20. The Edit menu.

Controlling Formulas

The Formula Menu

The Formula menu contains options that apply to constructing formulas (see fig. 1.21). Such options include those for naming cells, ranges, and formulas; finding specific information in formulas; and selecting cells according to the information in them. Table 1.7 lists the Formula menu options.

Table 1.6
Edit Menu Options

Option	Function
Undo	Revokes your last action in Excel, leaving the worksheet as it was before the action. The Undo option will include a message to describe what will be undone, such as `Undo Paste`.
	Some limits to this feature apply (not all actions can be undone). Excel displays `Can't Undo` for this option if an action cannot be revoked. Often, when you undo an action, you can use the Undo command again to redo the action.
Repeat	Repeats your last command or action. The Repeat option works only for commands or actions that are capable of being repeated. The Repeat option will include a word to describe what will be repeated, such as `Repeat New`.
Cut	Removes selected data when used with the Paste command. Must be used with the Paste command to move data.
Copy	Copies the selected object or data to the clipboard. This option changes to Copy Picture when you use the Shift key to select it. Copy Picture copies charts to the clipboard or copies the currently selected worksheet area to the clipboard as a picture.
Paste	Copies whatever is currently on the clipboard to the current location on the worksheet.
Clear	Clears selected cells of any information, leaving them blank.
Paste Special	Performs various paste functions that apply the contents of the clipboard to the currently selected cells.

Option	Function
Paste Link	Copies whatever is currently on the clipboard to the current location on the worksheet and establishes a link to the source of that data.
Delete	Deletes the currently selected cell, range, row, or column. This feature also can delete more than one row, column, or cell.
Insert	Inserts a cell, range, row, or column at the currently selected location. This feature also can insert more than one row, column, or cell.
Fill Right	Copies data from the leftmost column in a selected block of cells into the remaining portion of the block. If a single row is selected, only one cell is copied to the right. If more than one row is selected, each cell in the first column is copied to the right. If only one column is selected, nothing happens. This option changes to Fill Left when you use the Shift key to select it. Fill Left works like Fill Right but copies to the left.
Fill Down	Copies data from the top row in a selected block of cells into the remaining portion of the block. If a single column is selected, only one cell is copied down. If more than one column is selected, each cell in the first row is copied down. If only one row is selected, nothing happens. This option changes to Fill Up when you use the Shift key to select it. Fill Up works like Fill Down but copies upward.
Fill Workgroup	Copies data into all worksheets in the current workgroup. This saves data-entry time when managing multiple worksheets. See Chapter 7 for more information on using workgroups.

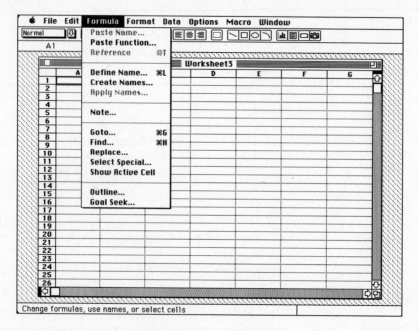

Fig. 1.21. The Formula menu.

Table 1.7
Formula Menu Options

Option	Function
Paste Name	Provides a list of currently defined names and enables you to select a name to paste into the current location.
Paste Function	Provides a list of Excel functions and enables you to select a function to paste into the current location. You also can paste arguments with the Paste Function.
Reference	Automatically changes selected cell references in formulas to absolute, relative, or mixed references. You choose the reference option you want. The Reference option is available only when you are editing a formula.
Define Name	Enables you to define a name for a cell or range of cells.

Option	Function
Create Names	Automatically creates a series of names, using information from a selected block of data. You can use labels in the top row, left column, right column, or bottom row (or any combination) for range names.
Apply Names	Automatically replaces range references throughout the worksheet with the corresponding range name (if defined). This command applies to selected cells or to the entire worksheet.
Note	Enables you to attach a note to a cell. The note can contain any text you want. Cells with notes attached are marked in the upper right corner.
Goto	Moves the cell pointer to any specified cell or range.
Find	Locates information in the worksheet by using specified criteria.
Replace	Locates information in the worksheet by using specified criteria; then replaces the information with your specified replacement text.
Select Special	Highlights worksheet data that has attributes specified in the dialog box. This command is useful for debugging worksheets.
Show Active Cell	Brings the active cell into view on-screen.
Outline	Designates the selected block of data as part of the worksheet outline.
Goal Seek	Calculates the variable needed to reach a particular result for the currently selected formula. This is useful for what-if analysis.

Dressing Up the Presentation

The Format Menu

The Format menu options enable you to spruce up the information in a worksheet (see fig. 1.22). You can select particular fonts, sizes, and styles to create more impact, and you can alter the color and texture of objects that are on-screen. Table 1.8 lists the Format menu options.

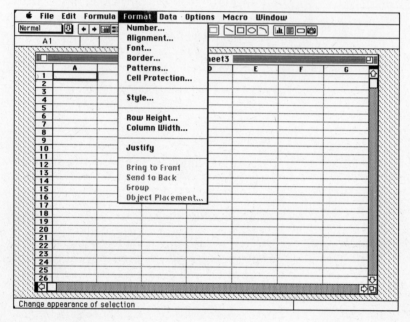

Fig. 1.22. The Format Menu.

Using Databases

The Data Menu

The options on the Data menu control the database features of Excel (see fig. 1.23). You can set up a database, specify search criteria, and extract information from a database by using these options. Table 1.9 describes the Data menu options.

**Table 1.8
Format Menu Options**

Option	Function
Number	Displays a set of options for changing the number formats. These options include adding dollar signs, displaying numbers as percentages, and so on. Options for date and time formats are included in this menu as well. You also can create custom formats by using this command.
Alignment	Changes the alignment of selected data. The alignment of a piece of information is relative to the cell it occupies. Alignment options include center, flush right, flush left, text wrapping, and other special alignments.
Font	Lists the fonts available to Excel for formatting worksheet information.
Border	Adds border lines to selected cells. The Border option is useful for creating boxes, lines, and other graphic elements on the worksheet. This option also can shade highlighted areas.
Patterns	Provides interior pattern choices for worksheet objects and cells. Each object or cell can have a different interior pattern.
Cell Protection	Provides options for protecting information in the worksheet. This protection can consist of preventing changes to the data or hiding the contents of the cells. You also must use the Options Protect Document command to invoke the protection.
Style	Creates a style set and adds it to the styles list in the Toolbar. All Format menu options currently set are applied to the style. The option asks you to name the style set.
Row Height	Controls the height of the selected rows. You can enter the height in points.

continues

Table 1.8 *(continued)*

Option	Function
Column Width	Controls the width of the selected columns. You can enter a column width in number of characters.
Justify	Reformats a block of text so that it fits into a highlighted block of cells. This option is useful for creating uniform columns of text.
Bring to Front	Moves an object to the top layer, making it overlap objects below it.
Send to Back	Moves an object to the bottom layer.
Group	Combines several objects so that you can manipulate them as one object.
Object Placement	Provides options for linking objects with the worksheet cells. Normally, changing cell widths and heights affects objects that are placed in those cells.

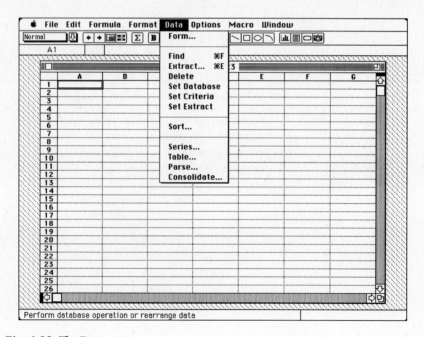

Fig. 1.23. The Data menu.

Table 1.9
Data Menu Options

Option	Function
Form	Presents options for creating a database entry form. This option is useful for making data entry easier. Use this command after you activate a database with the Set Database command.
Find	Locates and highlights database records that match the currently defined criteria. Use this command after defining the database and criteria ranges.
Extract	Extracts database records that match the currently defined criteria. Extracted records are placed in the specified extract range. Use this command after defining a database and criteria range.
Delete	Removes database records that match the currently defined criteria.
Set Database	Determines the active database according to the selected range of cells. You can use the active database with other database commands.
Set Criteria	Determines the active criteria range. The criteria range contains the conditions on which Excel finds information in the active database. The criteria range is essential for database extractions and statistical analysis.
Set Extract	Determines the active extract range for the database extract procedure.
Sort	Sorts a selected range of cells, using an ascending or descending key as a basis.
Series	Enters special information into a selected range. The fill information is determined by the first entry of the selected range and can include numbers or dates.

continues

Table 1.9 *(continued)*

Option	Function
Table	Contains options for table calculations, including options for recalculating the table, selecting the table range, and determining the database range and extract range. Table calculations can be somewhat advanced (see Chapter 8).
Parse	Divides a single block of text into individual cells with each word placed into a different cell. Useful for formatting tables imported from other programs.
Consolidate	Consolidates values contained in several related worksheets for quick summation reports.

Using Other Worksheet Options

The Options Menu

You can find miscellaneous options—such as those for printing and displaying worksheets—on the Options menu (see fig. 1.24). Table 1.10 lists the Options menu options.

Creating Macros

The Macro Menu

You use the Macro menu to create and manipulate macros in Excel (see fig. 1.25). You can create and edit macros, open specific macros, run macros, and more. Table 1.11 lists the Macro menu options.

Table 1.10
Options Menu Options

Option	Function
Set Print Area	Determines the exact worksheet area that prints when you use the Print option. You can change the print area at any time.
Set Print Titles	Determines the information that is printed at the top of each page.
Set Page Break	Forces a new page at the position of the cell pointer. When printing, Excel starts a new page at the specified point.
Display	Offers options for changing the basic Excel display. These options include removing or changing the color of the cell grid and removing the column and row headings.
Color Palette	Provides options for creating your own colors. You can mix primary colors to create almost any color you choose and then use your custom colors on the worksheet.
Freeze Panes	Applies when you have split the screen into halves or quarters by using the split-screen markers. Normally, each half (pane) of a split screen can be scrolled independently. This command freezes the contents in one or more of the panes.
Protect Document	Determines whether a document's cell protection is active or inactive. This command acts like a master switch for cell protection.

continues

Table 1.10 *(continued)*

Option	Function
Calculation	Offers various kinds of recalculation options for the worksheet. You can specify that manual recalculation be used so that the worksheet is calculated only when you choose the Calculate Now option.
Calculate Now	Recalculates the formulas in all open worksheets. This option is most useful if you set calculation to Manual by using the Calculation option. Calculate Now changes to Calculate Document when you use the Shift key.
Calculate Document	Calculates only the active worksheet, whereas Calculate Now calculates all open worksheets.
Workspace	Provides options for changing some attributes of Excel's worksheet. These options include those for handling decimal points and determining the style of cell addresses.
Short Menus	Removes many of the advanced menu options from Excel's menus. The Short Menus option appears on the Options menu when you are using full menus.
Full Menus	Makes all menus show all the available commands. The Full Menus option appears on the Options menu when you are using short menus.

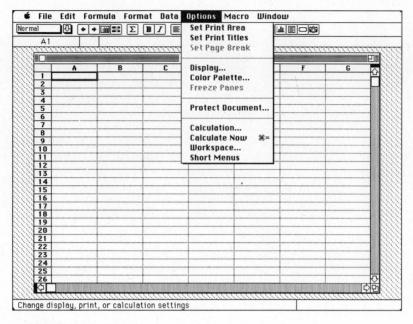

Fig. 1.24 *The Options Menu*

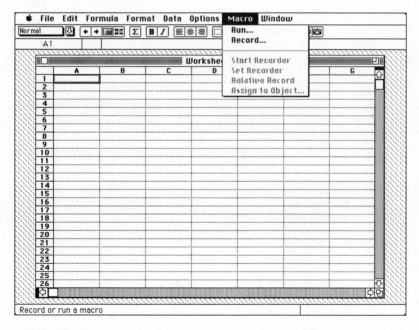

Fig. 1.25. *The Macro menu.*

Table 1.11
Macro Menu Options

Key	Function
Run	Lists available macros from which you can choose. The macro you choose will be run on the current worksheet.
Record	Begins recording your keystrokes as a macro. If a macro sheet is not already open, this command also opens a macro sheet and lists the finished macro on the sheet.
Start Recorder	Begins recording your keystrokes and lists the macro in the range set with the Set Recorder command.
Set Recorder	Determines where a recorded macro is listed.
Absolute Record	Records cell addresses in a macro as absolute references. The Absolute Record option appears on the full Macro menu if you chose the Relative Record option.
Relative Record	Records cell addresses in a macro as relative references. The Relative Record option appears on the full Macro menu if you chose the Absolute Record option.
Assign to Object	Attaches a macro to a worksheet object, such as a box, button, or graphic image. After you click on the object, Excel runs the attached macro.

Arranging Windows

The Window Menu

Most Macintosh applications present information in windows. You can move, resize, and reshape a standard Macintosh window. Also, you can view several windows on-screen at one time. In Excel, the capability to see several windows at once means that you can look at several worksheets simultaneously or that you can look at one worksheet through several windows. The Window menu options enable you to create new windows for a worksheet, bring particular windows into view, and arrange windows on-screen (see fig. 1.26). Table 1.12 lists the Window menu options.

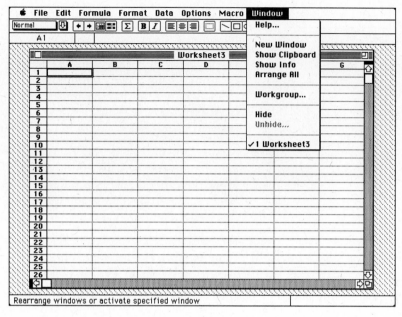

Fig. 1.26. *The Window menu.*

Table 1.12
Window Menu Options

Key	Function
Help	Displays Excel's help window, which you can use to get information on commands and options in the program.
New Window	Opens a new window for the active worksheet. This window can display any of the information in the original worksheet.
Show Clipboard	Displays the contents of the clipboard. Excel places data onto the clipboard that is copied or deleted. You can paste data from the Clipboard into a worksheet.

continues

Table 1.12 *(continued)*

Key	Function
Show Info	Displays the Info window for the active document. This option and the Show Document option enable you to toggle between the Info window and the relevant document.
Show Document	Displays the document related to the active Info window. This option and the Show Info option enable you to toggle between the Info window and the relevant document.
Arrange All	Arranges windows on-screen when two or more windows are open. This command brings all windows into view.
Workgroup	Creates a workgroup from various open windows. You can choose the worksheets you want to place into the current workgroup. Special workgroup features are available for grouped worksheets, such as consolidation.
Hide	Hides the active window from view but leaves it open for access by other sheets.
Unhide	Displays hidden windows.

Chart Menus

The chart menus—Gallery, Chart, and Format—appear when you create a new chart or activate an existing chart. Certain original worksheet menus are available as well: File, Edit, Macro, and Window. These four menus are the same as those described in "Worksheet Menus," earlier in this chapter, except that some unusable options have been removed or deactivated. The Gallery, Chart, and Format menus are shown in figures 1.27 through 1.29.

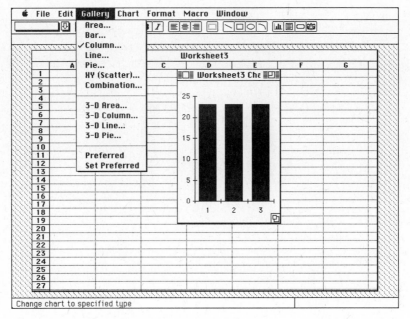

Fig. 1.27. *The Gallery menu.*

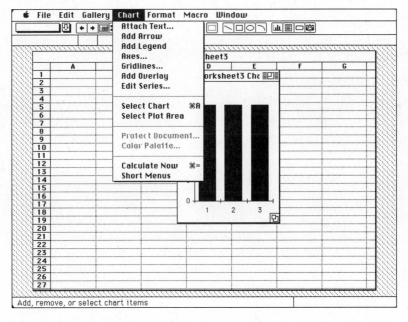

Fig. 1.28. *The Chart menu.*

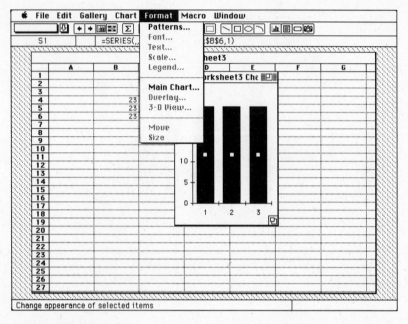

Fig. 1.29. The Format menu.

Selecting a Chart

The Gallery Menu

From the Gallery menu, you select one of the various chart types available in Excel. You can change the type of a chart after you create it. Table 1.13 lists the Gallery menu options.

Table 1.13
Gallery Menu Options

Key	Use
Area	Area charts are good for showing how the total of several items changes over time.
Bar	Bar charts (horizontal bars) are good for comparing items over several different categories, such as sales of two items over four years.

Key	Use
Column	Column charts (vertical bars) are good for showing performance or progress.
Line	Line charts are good for comparing several items over time.
Pie	Pie charts are good for showing how individual items contribute to a total.
XY (Scatter)	Scatter charts are good for plotting x and y values in a grid.
Combination	A combination chart combines many of the other chart types. Combination charts are good for contrasting two types of data.
3-D Area, Column, Line, Pie	The 3-D versions of these charts are good for showing the performance of several items.
Preferred	Specifies the chart type chosen with the Set Preferred command.
Set Preferred	Specifies any of the preceding chart types as the default for new charts.

Manipulating Charts

The Chart Menu

The Chart menu provides options for creating and manipulating charts. You can control the legend, change the axes, and change the data being referenced by the chart. Other options in this menu include Protect Document, Calculate Now, and Short Menus—all of which are available in the standard worksheet menus. Table 1.14 lists the Chart menu options.

Table 1.14
Chart Menu Options

Key	Function
Attach Text	Adds labels to various elements of the chart.
Add Arrow	Places an arrow on the chart in a specified location.
Add Legend	Creates a legend for the chart.
Axes	Determines whether either or both of the chart axes are visible.
Gridlines	Determines whether grid lines are visible on the chart.
Add Overlay	Creates an overlay chart, splitting the main chart into two separate charts superimposed on each other.
Edit Series	Provides options for changing the series in a chart. This includes changing its placement and the data used to create the series.
Select Chart	Activates the chart. This command is useful with formatting commands.
Select Plot Area	Activates the current chart's plot area for formatting.
Protect Document	Determines whether a document's cell protection is active or inactive. This command acts like a master switch for cell protection.
Color Palette	Enables you to create custom colors for use in your charts.
Calculate Now	Recalculates the formulas in the worksheet. Calculate Now is most useful when you have set calculation to Manual by using the Calculation option.
Short Menus	Removes many of the advanced menu options from Excel's menus. The Short Menus option appears on the Options menu when you are using full menus.

Key	Function
Full Menus	Makes all menus show all the available commands. The Full Menus option appears on the Options menu when you are using short menus.

Formatting the Chart

The Format Menu

The Format options accessed through the Chart menu enable you to change a chart's appearance. You can change the patterns of bars and pie slices, the font of the chart titles and legend entries, and the chart legend and axis scale, for example. Table 1.15 lists the Format menu options.

Table 1.15
Format Menu Options

Key	Function
Patterns	Determines the patterns used for the various chart elements (bars, pie slices, and so on).
Font	Determines the font used for text labels on the chart.
Text	Controls the appearance of the chart's text labels, enabling you to, among other things, specify vertical text and one of six alignment options.
Scale	Determines the chart's axis scale.
Legend	Determines the position of the chart's legend.
Main Chart	Controls various elements of the main chart, including the spacing of bars, stacking, drop shadows, and the angle of a pie chart.

continues

Table 1.15 *(continued)*

Key	Function
Overlay	Controls various elements of the overlay chart.
3-D View	Controls various aspects of 3-D charts, such as the perspective and height-to-width ratio.
Move	Enables you to move an element on the active chart.
Size	Changes the size of an element on the active chart.

The Info Menu

The Info menu gives you control over the Info window, a special window that contains information about the active worksheet cell (see fig. 1.30). The Info menu enables you to display certain information in the Info window. This menu is visible only after you open an Info window by using the Window Show Info command. (This command is available only from the worksheet menus, not the chart menus.) When an Info window is active, Excel adds the Info menu and removes many unusable options from the other menus. Table 1.16 lists the Info menu options.

Getting Help

Excel includes an on-line help feature that contains information about each command and option in the program. The information is cursory but provides the necessary details to get you started with the command in question. You can search for the information you want by choosing the various options in the Help window. You can use Help in three ways, which are described in the following sections.

Table 1.16
Info Menu Options

Key	Function
Cell	Determines whether the address of the active cell appears in the Info window.
Formula	Determines whether the formula of the active cell appears in the Info window.
Value	Determines whether the value of the active cell appears in the Info window.
Format	Determines whether the format of the active cell appears in the Info window.
Protection	Determines whether the protection status of the active cell appears in the Info window.
Names	Determines whether any named ranges containing the active cell appear in the Info window.
Precedents	Determines whether the addresses of cells on which the active cell depends appear in the Info window.
Dependents	Determines whether the addresses of cells that depend on the active cell appear in the Info window.
Note	Determines whether the cell note attached to the active cell (if any) appears in the Info window.

Using Interactive Help

You can activate a command or dialog box and then display the Help window. The Help window automatically displays information about the active command or dialog box. If an Excel message (such as an error message) is in view on-screen, the Help window supplies information on that message. Perform the following steps to activate Help:

1. Bring the message or dialog box into view on-screen. If you want help on a menu option, press the slash (/) key and the letter associated with the menu. Use the down-arrow key to highlight the option you want help on in that menu, but don't press Return; just leave the menu option highlighted.

2. Activate Help by pressing ⌘-? or Shift-Help on the extended keyboard.

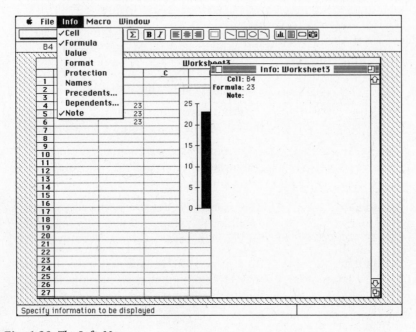

Fig. 1.30. *The Info Menu.*

Using Context-Sensitive Help

You can invoke Help and then specify the topic you want help on by choosing a command or option with the mouse. You activate Help and then point to the menu or command on which you want information. This is the opposite of the first method. Follow these steps:

1. Activate Help by pressing ⌘-?. The pointer appears as a question mark.

2. Select the command you want or click on part of the window. If you choose a command, Excel does not actually perform the command; it gives you a help topic for the command.

Using General Help

You also can open the Help window using the Help command in the
Window menu. The Topics list appears (see fig. 1.31).

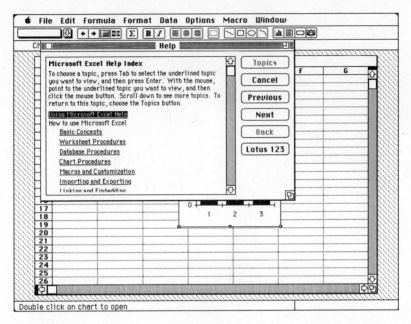

Fig. 1.31. *The Help topics.*

To open the Help window, follow these steps:

1. Select the Help command from the Windows menu.

2. Click on the topic or press Tab to highlight that topic and press
    Return.

3. Use the buttons to browse.

The Help window includes several commands and buttons that help you
navigate through the topics. Following is a description of each:

Topics   Displays a Topics list. You can double-
                          click on any topic from this list to get help
                          information. Each listing leads to a help
                          screen or a screen of more topics.

Jump Terms	Enables you to cross-reference other help topics. Many topics include underlined words in them, which serve as cross-references to other help topics. To view information on a jump term, double-click on the underlined word.
Defined Terms	Enables you to view definitions of terms in topics. These terms are underlined with a dotted line. With the pointer positioned on one of these terms, press and hold the mouse button to view the definition. Release the button and the definition goes away.
Cancel	Returns you to the worksheet.
Previous	Moves you to the preceding topic in the list based on your current position.
Next	Moves to the next topic in the list based on your current position.
Back	Moves backward through the topics you selected. If you used cross-references (jump terms), this may not be the preceding topic in the Topics list, but the previously viewed topic.
Lotus 1-2-3	Shows you information about Lotus 1-2-3 commands and their Excel counterparts. Select this button and enter the 1-2-3 command of your choice. Excel presents a list of related Excel topics from which you can choose.

Summary

This chapter covered some important Excel basics, including the differences among the various Macintosh keyboards, the parts of the Excel worksheet, and the available menu options. Some key points to remember follow:

• The numeric keyboard toggles between number keys and direction keys. Pressing Shift-Clear toggles between these two modes.

- The Command and Option keys work with other keys on the keyboard to provide special actions.

- Each worksheet file you create and save in Excel is stored on disk and is identified with the Excel worksheet icon.

- You can enter Excel by double-clicking on a worksheet icon or double-clicking on the Excel program icon.

- The active cell is the cell in which the pointer is currently located.

- The worksheet has more rows and columns than can fit within one screen view. You can use the scroll bars to view other parts of the worksheet.

- You enter all data into cells of the worksheet.

- You can activate Excel's Help feature in three ways. One good way is to press ⌘-? and then select the command or worksheet feature on which you want help.

In Chapter 2, you learn to create an Excel worksheet that tracks expenses.

Creating Worksheets: A Quick Start

This chapter takes you step by step through the creation of a simple example: a worksheet that tracks expenses. You begin by opening a new Excel worksheet and entering the basic elements of a worksheet application, such as titles and column labels. Next you enter numbers and formulas that calculate the proper results. As you build the worksheet, you use several formatting commands to make it more readable. By the end of the chapter, you will have built, saved, and printed a simple worksheet for expense tracking. You also will be prepared for the quick start in Part II, "Charting and Drawing." All quick start chapters in this book are designed for Excel users who have little or no familiarity with the Macintosh, worksheets, or Excel.

If you have not installed Excel on your system, be sure to read Appendix A before beginning this chapter. Also, be sure to read Chapter 1 for a look at spreadsheet technology in general and Excel in particular.

Opening a New Worksheet

The first step in creating the sample application is to start Excel with a new, blank worksheet in view. With your computer on and the Excel program icon in view, double-click on the Excel program icon.

71

Excel starts and presents a new, blank worksheet named WORKSHEET1. The cell pointer should be on cell A1 (see figure 2.1).

> *Note:* The cell pointer is not the same as the mouse pointer. The *mouse pointer* moves when you move the mouse, and is commonly shaped like an arrow. The *cell pointer* is the cell-shaped square that highlights cells as you press the arrow keys or click the mouse pointer in a cell.

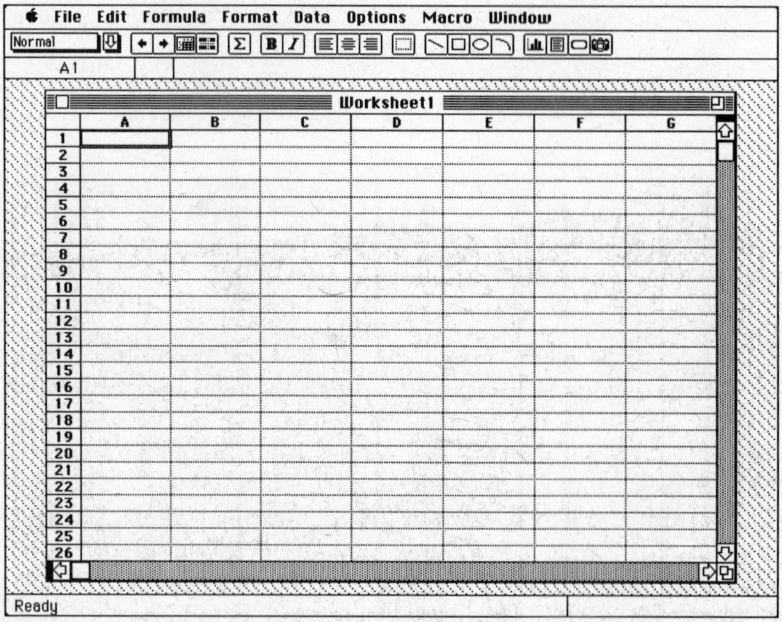

Fig. 2.1. Opening a new worksheet, with the cell pointer on cell A1.

Notice that the worksheet "page" is made up of a series of rows and columns. The rows are numbered, and the columns contain letter names. The intersection of a row and a column is called a *cell*. The name of a cell (also called the *cell address*, or *cell reference*) is the combination of the column letter and row number, such as C5. You can move the cell pointer from cell to cell throughout the worksheet by pressing the movement keys—the most basic of which are the four arrow keys. All movement keys are discussed in Chapter 3.

Saving Your Worksheet

Although you have no work to save yet, saving your worksheet is an important step to learn up front. To save and name the new (blank) worksheet, complete the following steps:

1. Select the Save command from the File menu. The Macintosh Save dialog box appears (see fig. 2.2).

2. Type *expenses* and click on the Save button.

Excel gives you the option of specifying a folder in which to save this file. Open any folder by double-clicking on its name in the list box. You can return to folders opened previously by clicking on the disk na Eject button.

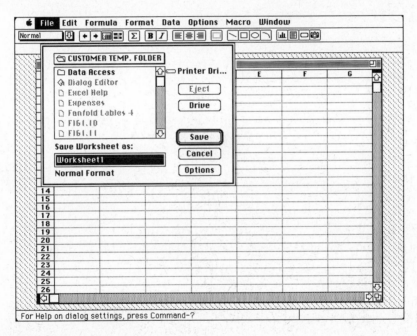

Fig. 2.2. The Save dialog box.

The worksheet now is stored permanently on disk in the specified folder or, if you did not choose a folder, in the same folder that contains the Excel program icon.

Be sure to save the sample worksheet when you reach the end of this chapter (or periodically throughout the chapter). You will use the worksheet in Chapter 10's quick start.

Creating a Worksheet

After the blank worksheet is on-screen, you can begin to enter data. In this section you learn how to enter row labels, column headings, numbers, and formulas. You also see how to change a column width and format data.

Entering Row Labels

The next step in designing the EXPENSES application is to enter the basic labels for the worksheet. These labels will appear in column A. Instead of starting in cell A1, however, you will leave some room at the top of the worksheet for other information. Complete these steps to enter the labels:

1. Press the down-arrow key three times to move the cell pointer to cell A4.

2. Type *Salaries* and press Return.

3. Type *Professional Svcs* and press Return.

4. Continue typing the following labels, pressing the Return key after each:

   Advertising

   Bank

   Freight

   Insurance

   Office Supplies

   Rent/Util/Phone

   Depreciation

   Taxes

The screen now should look like figure 2.3.

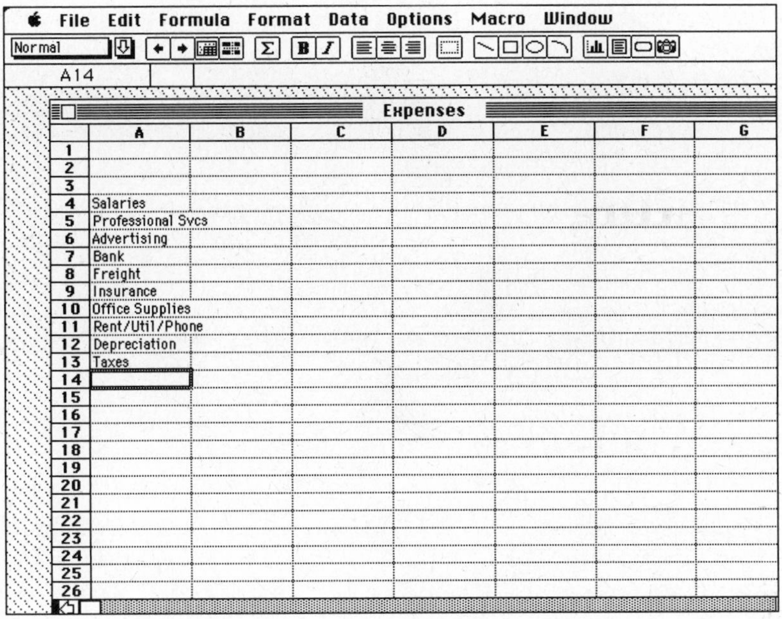

Fig. 2.3. *The expense worksheet, with expense labels entered.*

If you make a mistake while typing the information, simply press the Backspace key to delete the characters to the left of the cursor. If you already pressed Return to move to the next cell, press the up-arrow key to move back to the cell containing the error. When you get to the appropriate cell, simply retype the information. The new information replaces the old information.

Changing the Column Width

Because some of the information in column A spilled into column B, the next step in designing the application is to widen column A. It's not always necessary to widen a column when information spills into the next column; you only need to do this if you anticipate putting information in the column on the right. If you enter information into an adjacent column to the right, Excel displays, in the first column, only the portion of the data that fits in the cell.

Complete the following steps to widen column A so that it displays all the data:

1. Using the mouse, move the cell pointer to the dividing line between columns A and B. When in place, the pointer should change shape, as shown in figure 2.4.

2. Click and drag the mouse to the right to expand the width of column A. Release the mouse button after you expand the column to contain the data (see fig. 2.5).

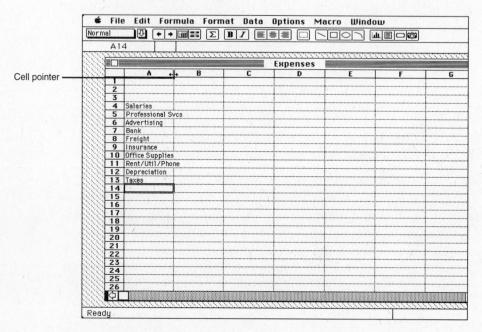

Fig. 2.4. The cell pointer when you move it over the column dividers.

Notice that all the information fits into the new width of column A. You can change the width of any column in this way.

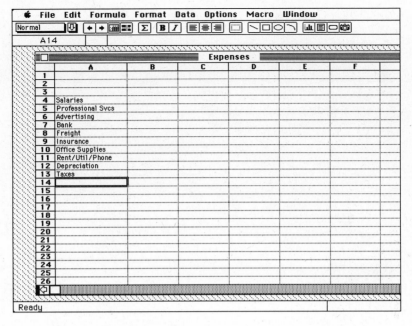

Fig. 2.5. *Column A after the expansion.*

Entering Column Headings

The next step is to enter, across the top of the worksheet, headings that identify the four quarters of the year. To enter these headings, complete the following steps:

1. Click on cell B3 to position the cell pointer; type *First* and then press Tab to accept the entry and move to the next cell. The pointer now should be on cell C3.

2. Type *Second* in cell C3; press Tab to move to cell D3.

3. Type *Third*; press Tab to move to cell E3.

4. Type *Fourth* and press Enter. Your worksheet now should look like figure 2.6.

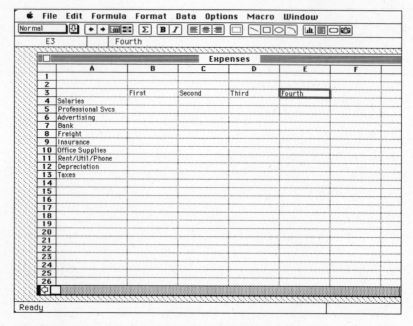

Fig. 2.6. The expense worksheet with column headings entered.

Entering Numbers

To enter numbers into the appropriate columns for each expense category, highlight the block from cell B4 to cell E13 (this block is referred to as *B4:E13*). Highlighting the block makes entering the data easier because the pointer remains inside the block as you fill out each cell and press Return. Complete the following steps to highlight the block and enter the numbers:

1. Move the cell pointer to cell B4, click and drag to cell E13, and then release the mouse button.

2. Type the following entries for row 4 (Salaries), pressing Tab after each entry (pressing Tab moves the cell pointer from left to right and then from top to bottom—that is, across the rows from top to bottom):

   2300

   2300

   3500

   4500

3. For Professional Svcs, type the following entries, pressing Tab after each entry:

   600

   600

   650

   650

4. For Advertising, type the following entries, pressing Tab after each entry:

   9000

   9000

   9000

   9000

5. For Bank, type the following entries, pressing Tab after each entry:

   200

   200

   200

   245

6. For Freight, type the following entries, pressing Tab after each entry:

   5000

   4500

   5690

   7500

7. For Insurance, type the following entries, pressing Tab after each entry:

   3500

   3500

   3500

   3500

8. For Office Supplies, type the following entries, pressing Tab after each entry:

   300

   300

   300

   300

9. For Rent/Util/Phone, type the following entries, pressing Tab after each entry:

   6500

   6500

   6200

   6900

10. For Depreciation, type the following entries, pressing Tab after each entry:

    2200

    2000

    1800

    1600

11. For Taxes, type the following entries, pressing Tab after each entry:

    2500

    4500

    3500

    3500

The worksheet should look like figure 2.7.

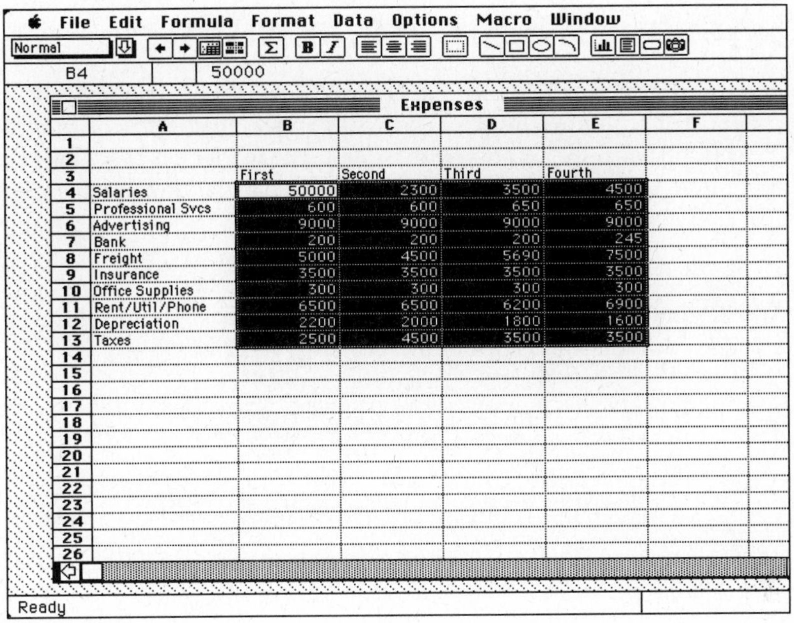

Fig. 2.7. *The expense worksheet showing a highlighted block of cells into which data has been entered.*

If you make a mistake in entering the numbers, just press the Backspace key and retype the information. If you already have completed the entry, press Shift-Tab to move back to the cell and then retype the entire entry. Because the block is highlighted (or selected), the cell pointer moves from cell to cell only within the block.

As mentioned earlier, pressing Tab moves the cell pointer first from left to right and then from top to bottom (across the rows from top to bottom). After you press Return, the cell pointer moves first from top to bottom and then from left to right (down the columns from left to right). Press the arrow keys or click the mouse button to remove the highlight. If you accidentally remove the block highlight, just highlight the block again and press Tab or Return until you reach the last cell you completed.

Performing Simple Formatting

Notice that the quarter headings you entered are not exactly aligned with the numbers in the columns; numbers normally appear flush with the right side of the cell and text appears flush with the left. The worksheet will look better if the numbers are aligned with the headings. To make the text flush right, follow these steps:

1. Select cells B4 to E4 to highlight the headings.

2. Click on the Right Alignment tool in the tool bar. The headings align with the right sides of the cells (see fig. 2.8).

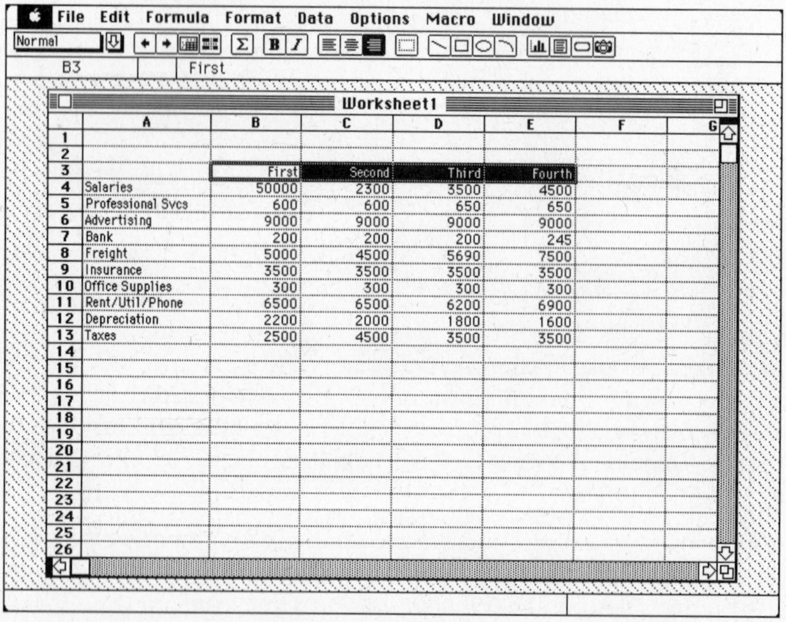

	A	B	C	D	E	F	G
1							
2							
3		First	Second	Third	Fourth		
4	Salaries	50000	2300	3500	4500		
5	Professional Svcs	600	600	650	650		
6	Advertising	9000	9000	9000	9000		
7	Bank	200	200	200	245		
8	Freight	5000	4500	5690	7500		
9	Insurance	3500	3500	3500	3500		
10	Office Supplies	300	300	300	300		
11	Rent/Util/Phone	6500	6500	6200	6900		
12	Depreciation	2200	2000	1800	1600		
13	Taxes	2500	4500	3500	3500		

Fig. 2.8. Using the Right Alignment tool in the tool bar.

3. Make the headings bold by clicking on the Boldface tool in the tool bar (the one containing the letter B).

Now that you're becoming familiar with formatting, try adding a main heading to the worksheet. This heading should be centered over the data and should be large and bold. Complete these steps to insert the heading:

1. Move the pointer to cell C1 and type the heading *Expenses*. Press Enter or click on the enter box at the top of the worksheet after you finish typing.

2. Select the Font command from the format menu. Choose the Times font from the Font dialog box. (If your system does not have the Times font, use any font listed.)

3. With the Font dialog box still on-screen, select the 24-point type size and press Return. (If the font you selected does not have a 24-point size, type *24* in the size box and press Return.) The worksheet should look like figure 2.9. After changing the font and size of the main title, Excel adjusts the height of row 1 to accommodate 24-point type.

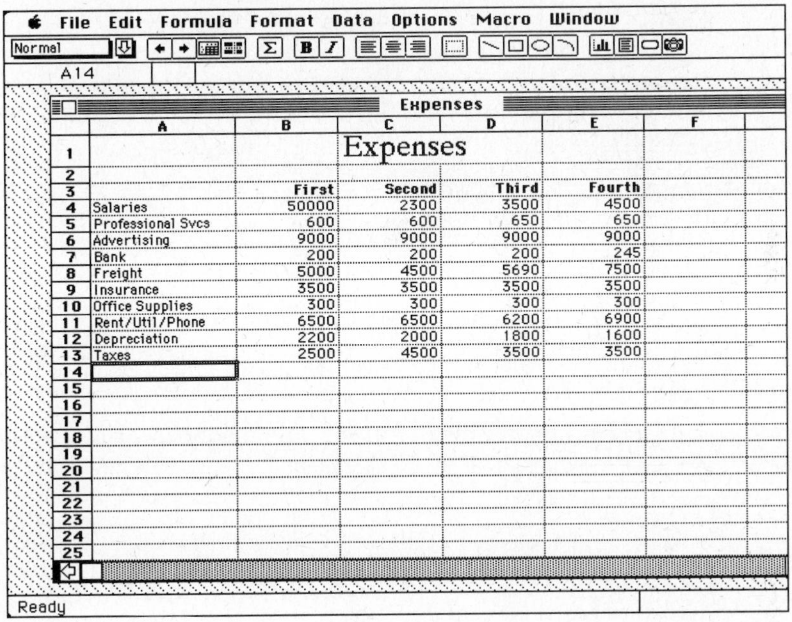

File   Edit   Formula   Format   Data   Options   Macro   Window

	A	B	C	D	E	F
1			Expenses			
2						
3		First	Second	Third	Fourth	
4	Salaries	50000	2300	3500	4500	
5	Professional Svcs	600	600	650	650	
6	Advertising	9000	9000	9000	9000	
7	Bank	200	200	200	245	
8	Freight	5000	4500	5690	7500	
9	Insurance	3500	3500	3500	3500	
10	Office Supplies	300	300	300	300	
11	Rent/Util/Phone	6500	6500	6200	6900	
12	Depreciation	2200	2000	1800	1600	
13	Taxes	2500	4500	3500	3500	

Fig. 2.9. The expense worksheet after you enter a main title.

Entering a Formula

The next step is to enter formulas that total the numbers in each column so that you can show the total expenses for each quarter. In this section, you enter such a formula into cell B15 and another into cell C15. In the following section, you will use the Fill Right worksheet function to copy the formula into cells D15 and E15. Complete the following steps to enter the first two formulas:

1. Use the arrow keys to move the pointer to cell B15.

2. Type the following formula:

   =SUM(B4:B13)

(Be sure to enter a colon character between the cell references.) Press Enter or click on the enter box to place the formula into the cell.

As soon as you press Enter or click on the enter box, the result of the formula appears in the cell. The formula calculates the sum of the range of cells between B4 and B13. You now can change any number in column B, and the formula you entered will recalculate the new result instantly. This capability enables you to play "what-if" with the numbers.

Now try entering the formula using a different method:

1. Highlight the range C4:C15 (click on cell C15 and drag to cell C4). The pointer should be in cell C15 when finished. If it is not, press Return until it is.

2. Click on the Auto Sum tool in the Toolbar (just to the left of the Boldface tool).

The Auto Sum tool automatically enters the SUM function into the active cell in the highlighted range. This makes it easy for you to total rows and columns.

Copying the Formula

To get totals for each of the columns, you can enter the SUM formula three more times (for each of the three remaining columns), or you can use the Auto Sum tool on the other columns. Now try a third method. Copy the formula from cell C15 into the remaining cells. Follow these steps:

1. Click and drag the mouse from cell C15 to cell E15 to highlight the three cells (including cell C15, which contains the formula). Your screen should look like figure 2.10.

2. Select the Fill Right option from the Edit menu and watch the screen. The formula is copied instantly into the selected cells, with the correct result in each.

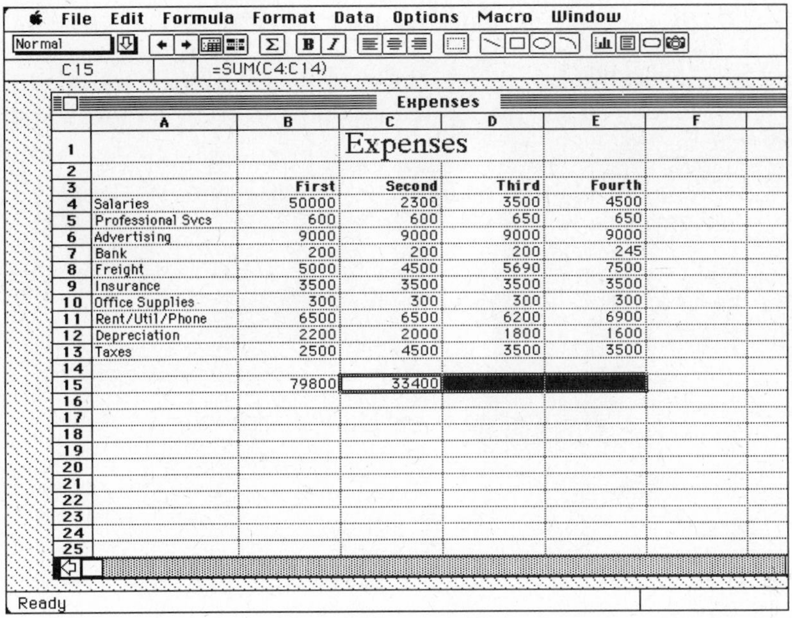

Fig. 2.10. *Selecting the formula and the cells that are to receive the copies.*

Excel copies the original formula, =SUM(C4:C13), to the new cells and changes the copies to =SUM(D4:D13) and =SUM(E4:E13), respectively. The formulas automatically reflect their own columns. If you change some of the numbers in the columns, the formulas will instantly recalculate their values, accounting for the changes.

Formatting the Worksheet

As you become more familiar with Excel, you will find that formatting constitutes much of the work in building worksheets. The worksheet's appearance plays an important part in organizing and displaying information clearly. In the following series of steps, you will remove the worksheet grid (the row and column guides), place lines down the columns and under the headings, and add a gray shade to the totals. Finally, you will format the numbers as dollar amounts.

Removing the Worksheet Grid

Removing the worksheet grid is useful when your worksheet will be seen by others or when you simply find the grid annoying. To remove the grid, complete the following steps:

1. Select the Display option from the Options menu. The Display dialog box appears.

2. With the dialog box in view, click on the Gridlines box to remove the check mark. Then press Return. Your screen should look like figure 2.11.

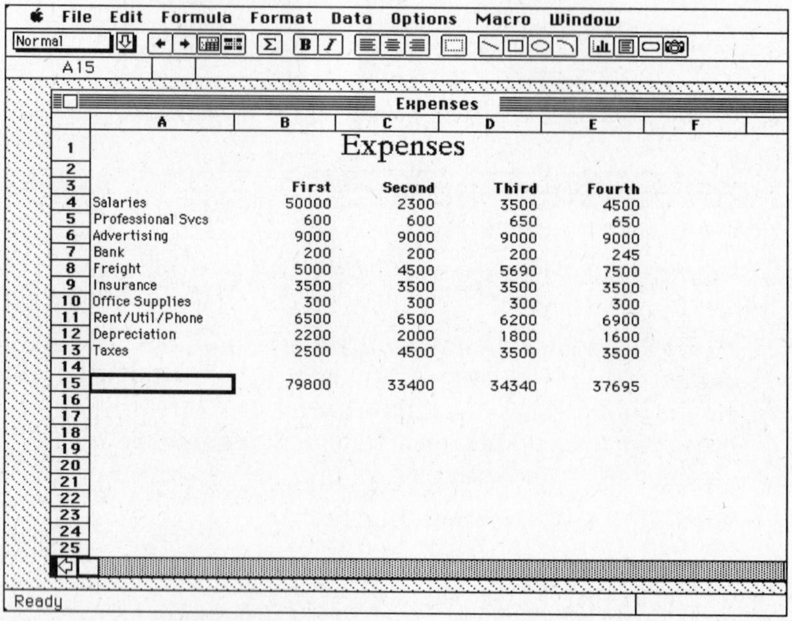

Fig. 2.11. Removing grid lines.

Adding Borders and Shading

The worksheet no longer displays the grid but is instead a clean slate showing the numbers. Now follow the next steps to add borders to the data:

1. Highlight the block C3:E15 by clicking on cell C3 and dragging to cell E15.

2. Select the Border command from the Format menu.

3. Click on the Left option; doing so places a line next to the Left option in the Border dialog box. Press Return.

4. Highlight the range B3:E3.

5. Select the Border command from the Format menu and click on the Bottom option.

6. Click on the thick border style and press Return (see fig. 2.12).

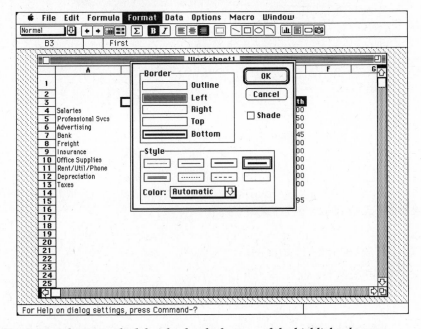

Fig. 2.12. *Selecting a thick border for the bottom of the highlighted range.*

Now add a gray shade to the totals row:

1. Highlight the range B15:E15.

2. Choose the Border command from the Format menu.

3. Click on the Shade box to enter a check mark in it; then press Return.

Figure 2.13 shows the result of these changes.

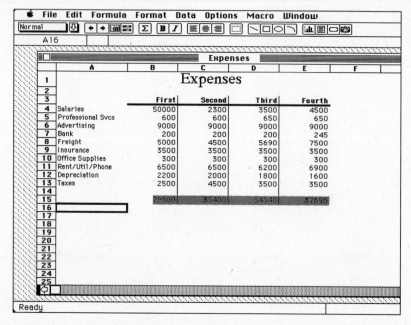

Fig. 2.13. The worksheet after more formatting.

Formatting Numbers

Now add dollar signs, two decimal places, and commas to the totals in row 15. Complete these steps:

1. Highlight the range B15:E15.

2. Select the Number option from the Format menu. The Format Number dialog box appears (see fig. 2.14).

3. Click on the sixth format option: $#,##0_);($#,##0). Then press Return.

The number format you chose displays the totals with dollar signs and commas. The worksheet now should look like figure 2.15.

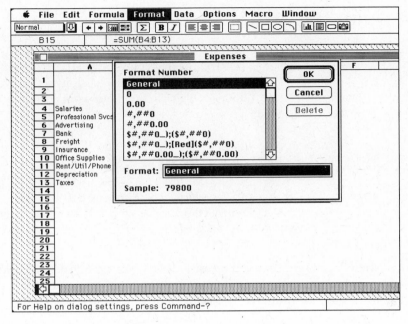

Fig. 2.14. *The Format Number dialog box.*

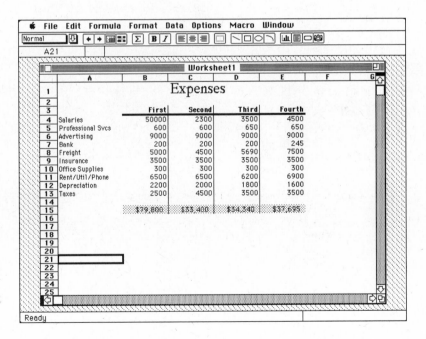

Fig. 2.15. *The completed worksheet.*

Saving the Worksheet Again

Save your work by selecting the Save option from the File menu. Because you saved the work earlier, Excel saves the new changes over the old version. (If you had not saved the work before, you would see a dialog box that you use to name the worksheet.) It's a good idea to save your work periodically.

Editing the Worksheet

Now you can make changes to the worksheet. Suppose that you want to update the values in the columns. This is fairly simple; just move the cell pointer to the value you want to change and retype it. After you press Enter, the new value replaces the old value.

Retyping values is not always the easiest way, however. Suppose that you want to change the heading from "Expenses" to "1991 Expenses." You can add the new information to the existing information. Follow these steps:

1. Click on cell C1.

2. Press ⌘-U. This places the cursor in the formula bar with the data currently in cell C1.

3. Press the left-arrow key to move to the beginning of the entry and add *1991* to the heading; then press Enter.

Now suppose that you want to make a more substantial change to the worksheet, such as removing a row. Try removing row 14:

1. Click on the number 14 in the row numbers on the left side of the worksheet to highlight the entire row (see fig. 2.16).

2. Select the Delete command from the Edit menu.

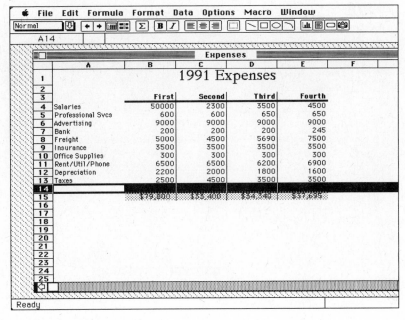

Fig. 2.16. *Highlighting row 14.*

Most worksheet edits are that simple. For a complete discussion of editing worksheets, turn to Chapter 4.

Printing the Worksheet

Because this quick start worksheet is small—taking up only one screen—printing it is easy. When you build large worksheets that take more than one page to print, you will need to use some of the printing commands and techniques described in Chapter 9.

To print the quick start worksheet, follow these steps:

1. Select the Print option from the File menu.

   The Print Options dialog box appears. This dialog box varies, depending on which printer you use. If you have a LaserWriter, the dialog box looks like figure 2.17. Be sure that your printer is hooked up properly and that you have selected it with the Chooser.

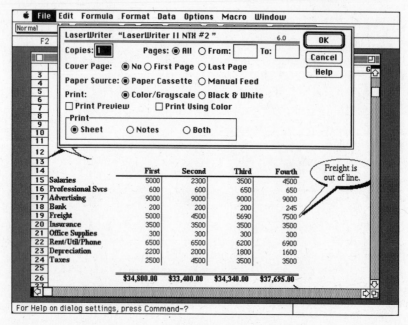

Fig. 2.17. The Print Options dialog box for the LaserWriter.

To use the Chooser, select the Chooser accessory from the Apple menu (at the far left of the menu bar). In the dialog box that appears, click on the icon representing your printer. Then press Return. This is the standard way of selecting an output device for most Macintosh applications.

Depending on which printer you select, the File Print dialog box presents a number of options. These print options are discussed in detail in Chapter 9.

2. Select any print options.

3. Click on the OK button to begin printing.

Quitting Excel

To quit Excel, select the Quit command from the File menu. If you have not made any changes to the worksheet since you last saved, Excel returns to the Macintosh desktop (or start-up screen). Otherwise, Excel gives you the opportunity to save your changes. Figure 2.18 shows the message you see when you quit.

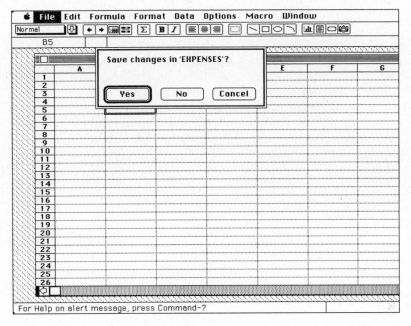

Fig 2.18. *Saving your changes in EXPENSES.*

Click on Yes to save the changes, click on No to reject the changes, or click on Cancel to stop the Quit process.

Summary

In this quick start, you set up a basic worksheet to total the quarterly expenses of an imaginary company. You learned the basics of entering information and formatting cells, as well as how to enter a formula and copy it to other cells. To become proficient in Excel, learn more about formulas and special functions by reading Chapters 3, "Creating Worksheets," and 5, "Formatting Worksheets." Be sure to save this worksheet so that you can build on it in Chapter 10's quick start.

Creating Worksheets

I n this chapter, you learn the basics of creating and using an Excel worksheet. Although worksheets are used for a variety of tasks, most people use them for business tasks, such as budgets, projections, inventory tracking, expense tracking, and sales statistics. This chapter gets you off to a good start in creating and evaluating these types of numeric information.

The chapter begins with instructions for opening files and saving them for future use. You then learn about the four types of information that you can enter into worksheet cells: text, numbers, dates, and formulas. This chapter also includes details about such subjects as moving around the worksheet, selecting information, and applying names to groups (or ranges) of data. By the end of this chapter, you will be able to create a worksheet for almost any basic task, and you will be comfortable with many of Excel's menu commands and options. After covering these basics, you will be ready for Chapter 4's details about editing existing worksheets.

Opening and Saving Worksheets

If you started Excel by clicking on the program icon, you have a new, blank worksheet in view. The rest of this chapter shows you how to turn this blank worksheet into a meaningful file. As you proceed through the chapter, you need to know how to save and retrieve your files. Commands for saving and opening files are located in the File menu.

Opening a File

To open an existing file from within Excel, follow these steps:

1. Select the Open option from the File menu.

2. Locate the file you want in the Password dialog box that appears.

   You can click on folders inside the list or select a previously opened folder from the folders list (above the list box). This takes you back through the folders the way you came.

3. When you locate the file in the list box, double click on its name.

To open a new worksheet, follow these steps:

1. Select the New option from the File menu.

2. Select the Worksheet option.

To close a worksheet after you save it, simply click on the Close box of the worksheet's window. Alternatively, you can use the Close option in the File menu. If you made changes since last saving the worksheet, Excel asks whether you want to save the file before closing (see the following section for information on how to save a file).

> **Tip: Using DIF, Text, and Other File Formats**
> Excel can save and retrieve files in a number of formats other than Excel worksheet files. You can exchange files with a number of applications. A complete discussion appears in Chapter 7.

Saving a File

To save a file, follow these steps:

1. Select the Save option from the File menu.

   If your file does not already have a name, Excel will ask you to name the file before saving it. You can enter any name and specify the folder in which Excel will store the document.

   If the file already has a name, Excel saves the file under the same name, replacing the previous copy on disk with the new copy.

2. If the file is new, enter a name into the Save As box that appears (see fig. 3.1). The file will be saved into the folder that appears at the top of the list box. The files and other folders inside this folder are shown in the list box.

3. To change the folder, click on the current drive name (above the Eject button). Then click on any folder to determine where the new worksheet will be saved. Alternatively, move the mouse pointer to the current folder name, press the mouse button, and then select a higher level of folder or the root directory.

To save a file under a different name, select the Save As option from the File menu. The Save As dialog box appears (see fig. 3.1). Use this box to determine where you want to save the file. The Save As command is useful when you want to keep two versions of a worksheet. The new version, saved with the Save As command, will not replace the older version because you have used a different name.

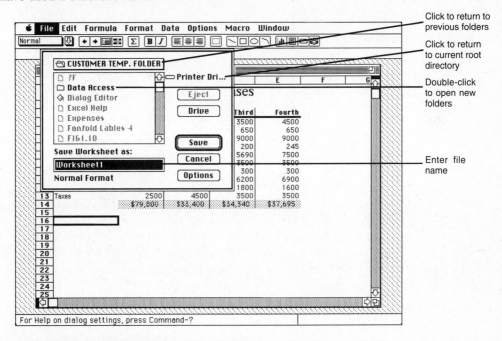

Fig. 3.1. The Save As dialog box.

Protecting Your Files with Passwords

When you save your worksheets, you can protect them by giving them passwords. Without the password, the file cannot be opened.

To password-protect a file, follow these steps:

1. Select the Save As option from the File menu.

2. Click on the Options button in the Save As dialog box.

3. Select from the File Sharing options provided. You may enter passwords for the two password options and/or select the Read-Only Recommended option. You can combine any of these options. As you type the password, Excel displays asterisks (*) so that no one can read the word on-screen.

4. Click on OK to accept your password entry. Excel then asks you to reenter the password. Retype the password and click on OK to return to the Save As dialog box.

5. Enter a name for the worksheet and click on OK to save it with your password-protection options activated.

You can select from three worksheet-protection options; you can combine any of these options. Following is an explanation of each option:

- *Protection Password:* Tells Excel to require the password before it enables anyone to open the file. Enter the password in this box.

- *Write Reservation Password:* Prohibits users from saving the worksheet over the original copy on disk and replacing the existing worksheet. Type the password in this box. Only users who know the password can replace the existing worksheet file with a new one. Users who do not know the password can open the file and save it under a new name (creating an entirely new file on disk), but they cannot replace the existing file. After users open the worksheet, Excel tells them to enter the password or select the Read-Only option before continuing.

- *Read-Only Recommended:* Presents a message when the worksheet is opened, recommending that the worksheet be opened as a read-only file. The user then can select the Read-Only option. Read-Only Recommended is a less strict variety of the Write Reservation Password option.

When you try to open a password-protected file, Excel presents the Password dialog box shown in figure 3.2. (The Read-Only option also appears in this box, when applicable.) Enter the password in the space provided and press Return. If the password is correct, the file opens and all Excel commands and options are available. If the password is incorrect, Excel does not open the file. Be sure to enter the password in its original capitalization. If the password is Open Sesame, for example, you cannot gain access by typing *open sesame*. As a measure of security, Excel does not display the password as you type it.

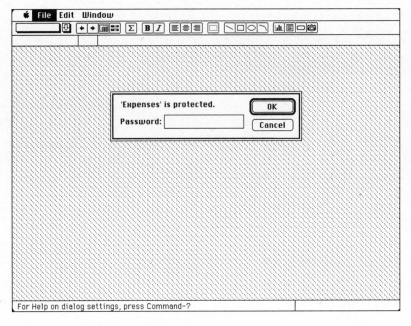

Fig. 3.2. The Password dialog box.

> ***Caution:*** If you forget the password, there is no way to recover it. This problem can be serious if you need to change information that is protected. Be sure to write the password down and store it in a safe place or to keep a duplicate, unprotected copy of the file in a safe place.

> ***Tip: Removing Password Protection***
> To remove password protection, choose Save As from the File menu and erase the passwords that appear in the Options dialog box. Of course, you must use the passwords to do this. After removing the passwords, resave the worksheet.

Making Backup Copies of Worksheets

You can make a backup of your worksheet files by choosing Save As from the File menu. Select the Options button and then choose the Create Backup File option. Click on OK, enter a name for the worksheet, and press Return.

Excel creates a backup copy of the file as it saves the original. Excel places the copy in the same folder as the original and names it COPY OF *file*.

Another way to make a backup is simply to save the file under a new name by choosing the Save As command from the File menu. Do this after you use the File Save command to save the original. Excel stores the file on disk under the new name. Of course, the original file still exists under the original name. Be sure to double-check which file you are using at any given time by looking in the title bar of the worksheet window.

Another way to back up your worksheet files is to use Excel's automatic backup feature. This feature creates a backup copy of the file each time you save it. Follow these steps:

1. Choose the File Save As option from the File menu.

2. Click on the Options button in the Save As dialog box.

3. Check the box marked Create Backup File and press Return.

Excel creates (or updates) the backup file each time you save the worksheet. The backup file is called BACKUP OF [*file name*] and contains a copy of the most recently saved version of the file.

Entering Data

One of the first things to know about creating worksheets is how to enter information. You enter information into an Excel worksheet by moving the pointer to a cell and typing what you want the cell to contain. When you press Tab, Return, or Enter, the information is accepted by the worksheet and appears in the cell.

You can enter four types of information into Excel: labels, numbers, formulas, and dates. As this section describes, each type of information has special qualifications; you must enter data in specific ways.

> *Note:* You can use the numeric keypad to toggle between directional keys and numeric keys. See Chapter 1 for a complete discussion of the Macintosh keyboard.

As you enter data into a cell (but before you accept the data), you can change the entry by using the Backspace key to erase characters to the left of the cursor. After you accept the data, however, you must retype the entire contents of the cell or use the editing commands described in Chapter 4 to change the entry. If you return to a cell that contains information and enter new information, the new data replaces the old as soon as you accept it.

To accept an entry, you can use these keys:

> Enter Box
>
> Tab
>
> Shift-Tab
>
> ↑, ↓, ←, → (text entries only)
>
> Return
>
> Enter
>
> Shift-Return

To reject an entry, use the following:

> Cancel Box
>
> ⌘-.

Entering Text

Text consists of worksheet labels, such as column headings, titles, and descriptions. A text label can consist of up to 255 characters (the maximum allowed by the formula bar). Enter the text you want, and use one of the "accept entry" commands listed in the preceding section. A label too large to fit into one cell spills into the next cell if that cell does not already contain information (see fig. 3.3). This effect is merely visual: the text is contained entirely in the original cell. If the adjacent cell contains information, the cell containing the label shows only what will fit in the current cell width (see fig. 3.4).

Any information you type into a cell that does not begin with a number, minus (–) sign, plus (+) sign, decimal point (.), or equal (=) sign is a label. Also, if you begin by typing a number and then include text, the information is recognized by Excel as a label. The following are examples of labels:

> First Quarter
>
> January 1989
>
> 45 Green
>
> The quick brown fox jumps over the lazy dog

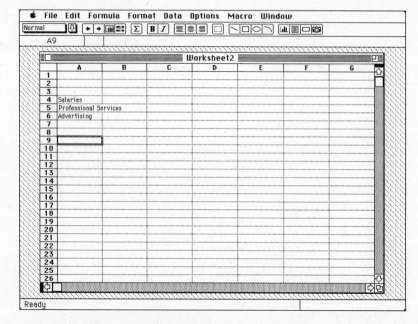

Fig. 3.3. *Text spilling over to the next cell.*

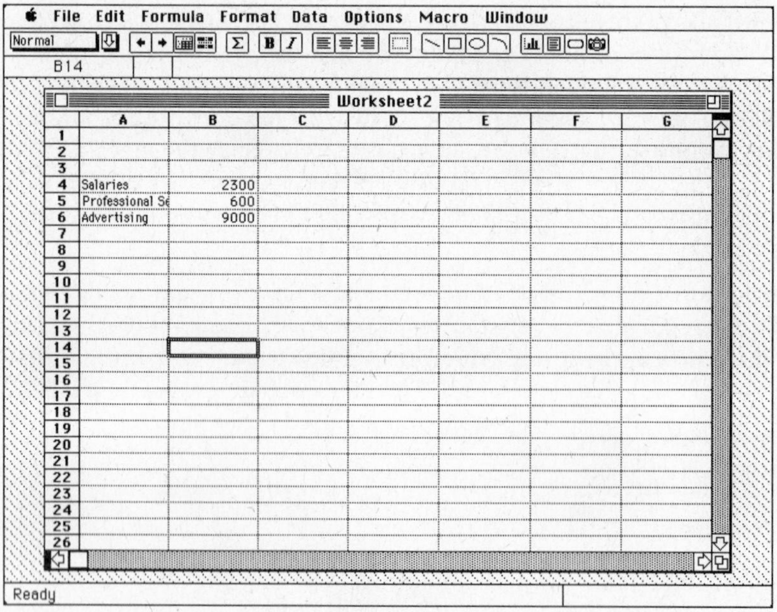

Fig. 3.4. *Text cut off by the contents of the next cell.*

Occasionally you may want to type numeric information but have it appear as a label. Code numbers or years commonly fall into this category. To enter a number as a label, type an equal sign and then surround the text with quotation marks. To enter 1989 as a label instead of a number, for example, type:

="1989"

Excel aligns labels with the left side of the cell and numbers with the right side. You know that a cell's contents are a label if they appear on the left side of the cell. (You can change the alignment of information by using the special formatting commands described in Chapter 5.)

> **Tip: *Changing the Column Width***
> If text spills into an adjacent column or is cut off by it, you can increase the width of the column containing the text. To increase or decrease the width of a column, position the pointer on any cell in the column that you want to change. Next, select the Column Width option from the Format menu. In the space marked Column Width, enter the number of characters you want the column to display; then press Return. Alternatively, just choose the Best Fit option and press Return. (The actual width that corresponds to this number varies, depending on the active font.) For more information on column width changes, see Chapter 5.

> ***Note:*** Another way to make text fit within a column is to wrap the text onto several lines within the cell. This is explained in detail in Chapter 5.

Entering Numbers

The second type of information you can enter into a cell is numbers. Numbers can begin with any numeral or the following characters:

– $ + . (

Numbers also can contain these characters:

) % /

(These characters cannot be the first character in the cell, however.) Including any other character anywhere in the entry turns the number into a label. Table 3.1 lists some acceptable number entries and their results:

Table 3.1
Typical Number Entries Excel Displays

Entry	Excel displays
–349	–349
(349)	–349
35	35
23,200	23200
$40.231	$40.23
12%	12%*
5 1/4	5 1/4*

* The actual value stored for percentages and fractions are the decimal equivalents—in this case, .12 for the percentage and 5.25 for the fraction.

When entering fractions, you must have an integer value preceding the fractional value. Enter a space between the integer and the fraction. If your fraction requires no integer (for example, 3/5), then use a zero (0 3/5). If you leave out the integer, Excel may interpret your entry as a date.

If entered properly, a number can be calculated with any number in the worksheet. This capability is the primary value of a worksheet. See Chapter 5 for more information about adding special symbols (such as $ and %) to numbers and setting decimal places.

> **Note:** Excel uses up to 14 digits when calculating numbers. The ROUND function, described in Chapter 6, enables you to control the number of digits used in calculations.

Entering Dates and Times

In Excel, dates are real numbers displayed in date formats. These real numbers represent the number of days elapsed since January 1, 1904. The date January 2, 1904, for example, is really just the number 1 shown as a date. Excel "thinks" that a cell containing the entry January 2, 1904, holds the value 1. Any number can be formatted as a date—even if it's not meant to be a date—because any number can represent days elapsed since 01/01/04. Of course, these date numbers (also called *serial numbers*) can be formatted as numbers instead of dates. In short, formatting a number as a date is for your benefit; Excel considers dates numbers no matter how they are formatted. If you intend to enter a date, however, choose one of the formats that Excel recognizes (shown in Table 3.2). Because dates are just numbers, you can perform calculations with them (such as subtracting one date from another to determine the number of days elapsed).

Entering Dates

Excel tries to act intelligently when you enter dates. If you enter what Excel considers a date, the program interprets what you typed and chooses an appropriate format for the information. The format makes the date appear as a date rather than a label or a number. Table 3.2 lists examples of acceptable ways to enter dates in Excel:

Table 3.2
Entering Dates in Excel

Entry	Excel Displays
1/23/91	1/23/91
1-91	Jan-91
23 January 91	23-Jan-91
Jan-91	Jan-91
January-91	Jan-91

The cell containing one of these dates has an actual value of 33261—even though the entry appears as a date. This value is the serial number for the date January 23, 1991.

These formats are not the only date formats available; they are merely the ones that Excel recognizes as dates without you using the Format option to format the date manually. You can get the same result by entering the number 33261 into a cell, for example, and then formatting the cell with one of the date formats offered. (Date formats are discussed in Chapter 4.) Because you probably will not know a date by its serial number, however, the preceding list of entries is more useful.

One final way to enter a date into the worksheet is to use the special key combination ⌘- – (hyphen). Doing so enters the current date into the cell. The current date comes from the Macintosh's internal clock. Refer to your Macintosh Users Guide for details on setting the internal clock.

Entering Times

Time entries, like dates, are recognized by Excel and formatted appropriately. You can enter time entries as listed in Table 3.3.

Table 3.3
Entering Time Entries in Excel

Entry	Excel Displays
16:35	16:35
4:35*	4:35
4:35:15	4:35:15
16:35:15	16:35:15
4:35 pm	4:35 PM
4:35 am	4:35 AM

* If you enter a time value that is less than 12, but you do not specify a.m. or p.m., Excel assumes a.m., according to the 24-hour format.

If you use the 12-hour format, it's best to include the a.m. or p.m. designation (which Excel displays in capital letters without periods). You can include seconds in the time entry. Like dates, times are numeric values. The actual time value is the number of 1/100,000-second increments passed since midnight. The time 12:00:01, therefore, is the value 0.00001.

Any decimal number can be formatted as a time entry, but you're better off using the formats recognized by Excel as times. If you enter the number .12542, for example, and then format the decimal as a time, you will get the result 3:00:36 AM.

Another method of entering a time into the worksheet is to press ⌘-; (semicolon). Doing so enters the current time into the cell. This time comes from the Macintosh's internal clock.

> **Note:** You can enter a date and time into a single cell. Just enter any two formats shown in the previous tables. Be sure to enter the date first, followed by a space, and then the time. The serial number consists of a date serial number with a decimal time serial number attached. The entry 23-Jan-89 3:00:36AM, for example, is 31069.12542.

Entering Formulas

The real power of a worksheet is its capability to use formulas that calculate values. When designing a worksheet, you use a combination of labels, numbers, and formulas. Because formulas generally refer not to information in the worksheet but to cell locations where the information can be found, you can alter the information in the locations that are referenced. The formulas automatically recalculate the results, using your changes.

Formulas can be simple or complex, but their purpose is to enable you to make changes to the information in the worksheet. The simplest kind of formula reference is a single cell location, as in the following:

    =A5

This formula means *Make the value of this cell equal to that of cell A5.* The formula can appear in any cell other than A5, and that other cell will hold the same value as cell A5, whether A5 contains a number, a label, or another formula.

The formula begins with an equal sign, which designates the information as a formula. All formulas must begin with an equal sign. If you enter the A5 without the sign, Excel assumes that you are typing a label.

> **Note:** The value of a cell is the number or text that appears in the cell. If a cell contains a formula, the value is the result of the formula.

A variation of the formula =A5 is this:

    =A5+10

This formula means *Make the value of this cell equal to the sum of cell A5 and 10.* If A5 contains the number 25, the result is 35. The cell reference A5 is called a *variable* because its value can vary, and the formula adjusts accordingly. The number 10 in this example is called a *constant* because it is part of the formula and remains the same. You can add constant numbers directly into a cell. You can type the following formula into a cell, for example:

=25+10

This formula provides the same result of 35, but it is not based on variable information in cell A5. Such a formula defeats the purpose of the worksheet. With the reference to cell A5, you can enter any number into A5, and the result changes.

You cannot mix text and numbers in a formula (unless you use special functions discussed in Chapter 6); you would get the error message #Value if cell A5 in the formula =A5+10 contained text. As you saw earlier, however, you can refer to a cell that contains text by using a simple cell reference. The formula =A5, for example, returns whatever is in cell A5, even if the cell contains text.

Entering Cell References

You can enter cell references within formulas in one of two ways: by typing the references or by using the pointer. To type the entire formula, including cell references, you enter every keystroke needed. To enter the formula =A5, for example, you move to a cell, type =A5, and then press Return to accept the entry.

Another method to enter cell references within formulas is to press the equal sign, click on cell A5, and then press Return. The value of using this method is that if you don't know which cell you need to refer to, you can use the mouse to scroll to the cell you want and then click on it.

Suppose that you want the formula in cell A5 of a sample worksheet to read =B1+B2+B3+B4, as in figure 3.5. Rather than type the formula directly into the cell, you can use the pointing method. Begin with the pointer on cell B5 and press the equal sign. Now use the mouse to click on each of the four cells B1, B2, B3, and B4 in sequence. Press Return. Notice that Excel assumes that you are adding the cells and places the plus signs into the formula.

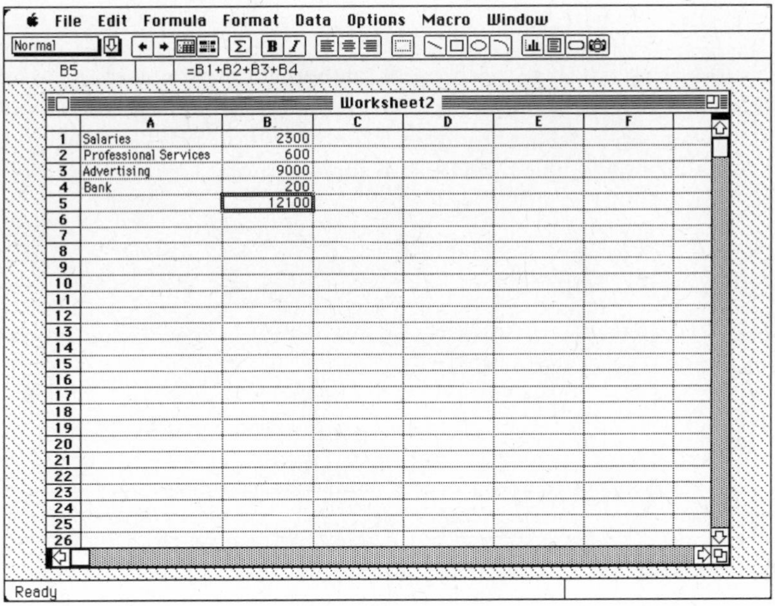

Fig. 3.5. *A formula that adds the numbers in a column.*

You can control the use of operators by entering one from the keyboard before you select the cell that should follow the operator. (*Operators*, discussed in more detail in the following section, are instructions—such as a plus sign or minus sign—that appear in formulas.) For example, you can enter the equal sign to begin, click on cell A1, type the operator you want (a minus sign, perhaps), click on cell A2, and so on. Excel enters a plus sign when you have not entered another operator.

Another way to point to cells is to use the arrow keys on the keyboard instead of using the mouse. When you use the arrow keys, you must enter the operator between each reference, even for addition. You can enter the formula =A1+A2, for example, by typing the equal sign and then using the arrow keys to move the pointer to cell A1 and then typing a plus sign. Then, use arrows to move to cell A2 and press Return.

> **Tip: Navigating Quickly through Formula References**
> Excel provides a useful tool for navigating through formulas on a worksheet. You can double-click on any cell containing a formula and Excel will highlight any cells referenced in those formulas. If cell A5 contains the formula =A1, for example, double-clicking on cell A5 causes cell A1 to be highlighted.

Using Operators

Operators are symbols that represent mathematical processes. A plus sign stands for addition, a minus sign for subtraction, and so on. Formulas depend on operators in order to work, and Excel provides several types of operators: arithmetic, text, relational, and reference.

Arithmetic Operators

Arithmetic operators perform basic mathematical tasks with numbers. Table 3.4 lists Excel's arithmetic operators.

Table 3.4
Excel's Arithmetic Operators

Operator	Example	Result
+ (addition)	=4+3	7
– (subtraction)	=4–3	1
– (negation)	–8	–8
/ (division)	=9/3	3
* (multiplication)	=2*2	4
^ (exponentiation)	=3^2	9
% (percentage)	12%	.12

The equal signs are needed only when two operands are used. This turns the expression into a formula.

You can use these operators with constant numbers, special functions, or cell references, as in the following examples (the functions are explained in Chapter 6):

    =–A1
    =25/10
    =25*A1
    =A5–A1
    =A5+SUM(A1:A4) =SUM(A1:A4)+SUM(B1:B4)

The Text Operator

Excel provides only one text operator: the ampersand (&). This operator joins one piece of text (a label) to another. The process of adding labels is known as *concatenation*.

Like most operators, the ampersand can work between specific pieces of text, cell references, or special functions, as in the following examples:

="Red"&"Wine"

="Red"&A5

=A5&B5

=A5&LEFT(B5,4) (LEFT is explained in Chapter 6.)

When entering text directly into a formula, you must surround the text with quotation marks. You can concatenate numbers with text, or numbers with other numbers, as in the following examples:

="Rams"&17   produces Rams17

=19&A5   produces 1989 (where A5 contains 89)

When using concatenation, keep an eye on spacing requirements. To include a space between words, you must include that space as part of the concatenated text or as a separate piece of text concatenated with the rest. Consider these examples:

="Red"&"Wine"   produces RedWine

="Red "&"Wine"   produces Red Wine

="Red"&" "&"Wine"   produces Red Wine

="Red"&" Wine"   produces Red Wine

The second Red Wine example includes an extra space after the word *Red*. The third example includes an extra space within a set of quotation marks between the two words *Red* and *Wine*. The fourth example includes a space in front of the word *Wine*.

Relational Operators

Relational operators test the relationship between two pieces of information (numbers, text, or formulas) and return an answer of TRUE or FALSE, using the results of the test as a basis. For example, the formula

=A5>B5

uses the greater than operator and means *Is the value of cell A5 greater than the value of cell B5?* Depending on the values, the result will be FALSE (no) or TRUE (yes). Table 3.5 lists Excel's relational operators.

Table 3.5
Excel's Relational Operators

Operator	Example	Result
= (equal to)	=5=3	FALSE
> (greater than)	=5>3	TRUE
< (less than)	=5<3	FALSE
>= (greater than or equal to)	=5>=3	TRUE
<= (less than or equal to)	=5<=3	FALSE
<> (not equal to)	=5<>3	TRUE

These operators can work between text, numbers, cell references, functions, or any combination. When comparing text with something, Excel uses the text's ASCII value, which is also the alphabetical value (in order from A to Z). ASCII always gives text a lower value than numbers, so a comparison of text to numbers always shows the text as less than the number. You will have few occasions to compare text with numbers.

Reference Operators

Excel uses three other operators that relate to the specification of ranges. You use these operators to combine references, creating a new reference from the combination. The exact uses for these operators will become clear as you progress through this book. Table 3.6 lists Excel's reference operators.

Table 3.6
Excel's Reference Operators

Operator	You Enter	Refers To
: (range)	A1:A5	A1:A5
, (union)	A1:A5,C1:C5	A1:A5,C1:C5
Space (intersection)	A1:A5 A4:G4	A4

The *range operator* creates a range from two cell references. The *union operator* combines references into a single, multiple-area range. This process is like highlighting several ranges at one time. In the example, the two ranges A1:A5 and C1:C5 cannot be highlighted as a single range. Using the union operator, you can use this range in formulas, such as =SUM(A1:A5,C1:C5). The *intersection operator* specifies only those cells that are common to the two (or more) referenced ranges. In the example, only cell A4 is common to the ranges A1:A5 and A4:G4.

Understanding the Order of Operations

When you combine various operators in worksheet formulas, you may need to specify the order of operations. An incorrectly specified order can result in incorrect values. First, keep in mind that operations have a natural order as prescribed by algebraic logic. That order is as follows (from highest to lowest priority):

1. Range (:)

2. Intersection (Space)

3. Union (,)

4. Negative and Positive (–,+)

5. Percentage (%)

6. Exponentiation (^)

7. Multiplication and division (*,/)

8. Addition and subtraction (+, –)

9. Concatenation (&)

10. Relations (=, >, <, <>, <=, >=)

When two operations of the same priority occur in the same formula, Excel evaluates them from left to right. Consider this formula:

=A5*2–B25/A5+3

If A5 contains 3 and B25 contains 6, the formula means the following:

3*2–6/3+3

Because multiplication and division are performed before subtraction and addition, the formula evaluates to this:

(3*2)–(6/3)+3 or 6–2+3

Performing the subtraction and addition operations from left to right, Excel provides this result:

(6–2)+3 or 4+3 or 7

You can use parentheses in the initial formula to change the natural order of operations. Suppose that you change the formula

A5*2–B25/A5+3

to the following (where A5 contains 3 and B25 contains 6):

A5*((2–B25)/A5)+3

The new formula evaluates to this:

3*((2–6)/3)+3 or 3*(–4/3)+3 or 3*–1.3333+3 or –4+3 or –1

Entering Worksheet Functions

By combining various operators and cell references, you can design formulas for many tasks. You can add the numbers in a column, for example, with a formula like this:

=A5+A6+A7+A8+A9

Creating such a formula can be tedious, however. Adding a dozen or more cells in a range requires a lot of typing or pointing. This is where Excel's worksheet functions come into action. A worksheet function is a special command you put into a formula to handle common mathematical operations, such as adding numbers in a column or getting the average of a series of numbers. The worksheet functions serve two purposes: they simplify the work involved in complex formulas, and they provide new types of logic that are not available through the basic arithmetic, comparison, or text operators. You can express the formula that adds five cells in a column, for example, like this:

=SUM(A5:A9)

Besides offering a host of mathematical functions, such as SUM, Excel provides functions for business calculations, database functions, date-time functions, decision-making functions, and so on. There is no trick to using worksheet functions, and you probably don't need to learn all of them. But a good knowledge of functions takes you a long way in Excel. See Chapter 6 for a complete explanation and listing of the Excel worksheet functions.

Using the Auto Sum Tool

Excel offers a special tool on the Toolbar that calculates the sum of a range of values. Usually, this range will be in a row or column, but it also can be a block of cells. Instead of entering a formula like +A1+A2+A3+A4+A5, or a function like =SUM(A5:A9), you can highlight the range you want and click on the Auto Sum tool. When you highlight the range, include all cells in the calculation, plus a blank cell below or to the right of the values (see fig. 3.6).

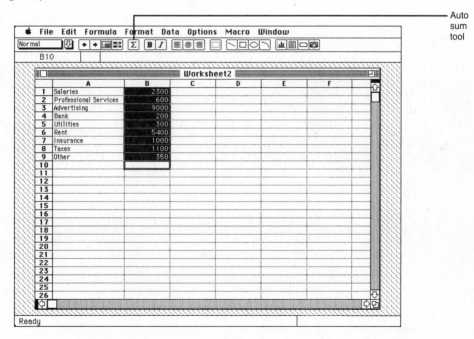

Auto sum tool

Fig. 3.6. Highlight the values you want to include and an extra cell below them before using the Auto Sum tool.

The active cell must be the empty cell of the range when you click on the Auto Sum tool. You know this by looking at the indicator at the top of the screen and because the active cell is shown in reverse. If you begin highlighting the range with the blank cell, it remains highlighted for the Auto Sum tool. In the example, you would click on cell A6 and drag to cell A1. If the empty cell is not the active cell of the highlighted range, press Tab or Return until it is. Click on the Auto Sum tool and Excel enters the formula =SUM(A1:A5) into the active cell. Press Return to accept the formula.

> *Note:* If you click on the Auto Sum tool when no range is high-lighted, Excel guesses at the appropriate range for the calculation. This range will be the block of cells to the left of or above the active cell. This method can provide a shortcut to summing with the Auto Sum tool.

If you highlight a block of cells (multiple columns and rows), the result will be the sum of all cells in the block—not individual column totals.

Working with Complex Formulas

You have seen how formulas can become rather complex through the inclusion of various operators and cell references. In addition to using operators and cell references, you can nest formulas inside one another, using parentheses to order the operations. You can increase the performance of your worksheets by learning the basics of nesting and combining formulas.

The simple cell reference gets information from another cell. Cell references often are used in formulas, as in this formula entered into cell C7:

=C5−C6

This formula means *Subtract the value in cell C6 from the value in cell C5*. If cell C5 contains the value 125 and cell C6 contains the value 100, the result is 25.

What if C5 and C6 contain formulas that produce the values 125 and 100, respectively? Suppose that cells C5 and C6 contain these formulas:

C5: =A5*B5

C6: =A6*B6

In a certain way, cell C7 would be combining two formulas. You can enter either of these formulas into C7 and get the same result:

C7: =C5−C6

C7: =(A5*B5)−(A6*B6)

The second example combines the two formulas from C5 and C6 and makes the formulas in those cells unnecessary. The formula uses parentheses to specify the intended order of operations, although the natural order of operation produces the correct answer in this case. The following example is even more complex. Suppose that cells A5 and A6 have these contents:

A5: =G5<A6

A6: =(R5*S5)−(R6-S6)

The relational formula in A5 contains a reference to cell A6. You can substitute cell A5's reference to cell A6 with the formula actually in that cell, as in the following:

=G5<(R5*S5)−(R6-S6)

Why go to this trouble when both methods produce the same result? Generally, the fewer formulas in a worksheet, the easier the worksheet is to read and use. Also, you do not need to have cells that display various subcalculations within a larger calculation. If these complex formulas are confusing and undocumented, they can cause more problems than they solve. One way to document your formulas is to use cell notes that explain what is going on in the cell. (See Chapter 20 for more information.)

Another way to document your formulas is to use named cells and named ranges in place of standard cell addresses and ranges. Naming cells and ranges is described later in this chapter.

Tip: Matching Parentheses

To make complex formulas easier to decipher, Excel includes a special feature that matches left and right parentheses for you. When your formulas contain several sets of parentheses, you can lose track of which right parenthesis goes with which left parenthesis. As you type the right parenthesis in your formula, however, Excel highlights it and its matching left parenthesis for about two seconds. This gives you a chance to see how your operations are ordered. You can use this feature after you enter a formula by moving to the cell containing the formula and pressing ⌘-U to edit it. Then, use the left-arrow key to move through the formula. Excel highlights the sets of parentheses as you move past them.

Understanding Error Messages

Occasionally Excel presents an error message when you attempt to accept information you have entered into a cell. Typically, error messages are due to unacceptable syntax in formulas and functions or to typing errors.

Excel does not enable you to enter incorrect entries in cells and does not enable you to move on until the entry is corrected or erased. Often, the error message explains the problem and even positions the cursor at the location of the problem. Figure 3.7 shows an Excel error message.

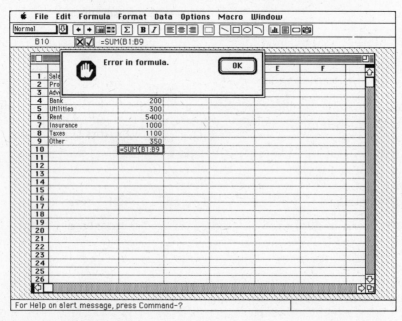

***Fig. 3.7.** An error message.*

Excel also may display a message in the cell itself.

> **Tip: Incomplete Formulas**
>
> Accurately designing large, complex formulas takes time. Your
> initial attempts may produce errors instead of the result you want.
> If Excel does not accept your formula, but you want to keep it for
> future reference, try removing the equal sign that makes the entry a
> formula; save the entry as a label. Put the equal sign back when you
> make further attempts.

Circular logic is a particular kind of error involving more than one formula.
A formula that includes a cell reference depends on the referenced cell for
its own value. When two or more cells reference each other in such a way
that they depend on one another for their calculation, you have a circular
reference. Suppose that you have two cells with these values:

    A1: =C1

    C1: =A1

These two cells reference each other. It is impossible for either to calculate
its value until the other calculates its value: hence a circular reference.
Circular references can be hidden within a complex maze of formulas and
can be difficult to detect. Fortunately, Excel detects errors of circular logic
when you enter them and displays the message shown in figure 3.8.

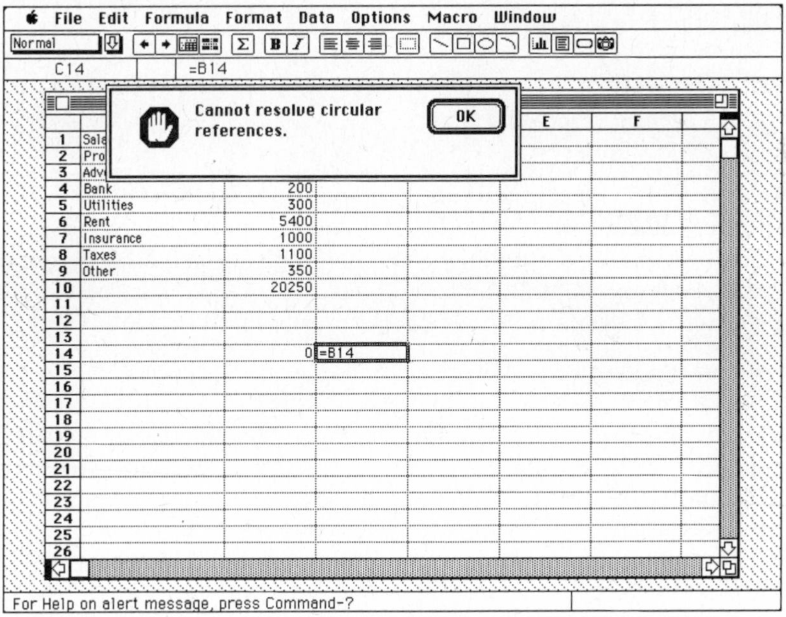

Fig. 3.8. *A circular-reference error message.*

Take a closer look at the references in all cells involved. If you still have trouble finding the circular reference, try using the debugging tools described in Chapter 20.

> *Note:* Circular logic is not always an error. Some advanced formulas actually can use circular references as part of their logic. Excel informs you of circular references, but you can use them anyway. If you continue to use a circular reference, Excel displays the message Circular at the bottom of the screen, but the worksheet is otherwise normal.

Moving around the Worksheet

Now that you know how to enter all kinds of information into the worksheet, you need to move around to various parts of the worksheet. Because you have more than four million cells at your disposal, it's important to be able to locate any one of them at any time. Excel uses four main tools for locating cells on the worksheet: scroll bars, keyboard commands, the Goto command, and the Find command. This section explains these tools and concludes with a discussion of wild cards, which you can use in specifying search criteria.

Using the Scroll Bars

As in most Macintosh applications, Excel provides scroll bars that you can use to view various parts of the file. The vertical bar scrolls the worksheet up and down relative to the entire worksheet. The horizontal bar scrolls the worksheet left and right. By combining the two movements, you can view any segment of the entire worksheet page.

Scroll bars consist of three main parts, as shown in figure 3.9: the scroll arrows, the bars, and the scroll boxes. Clicking on an arrow scrolls the worksheet slowly in the direction of the arrow. When you click on the bar, the worksheet scrolls more quickly (about one screen at a time); the direction of the movement depends on the location of the scroll box relative to where you click on the bar. Click to the left of the box (on the horizontal bar), for example, and the screen moves to the left. Click above the box (on the vertical bar), and the screen moves up.

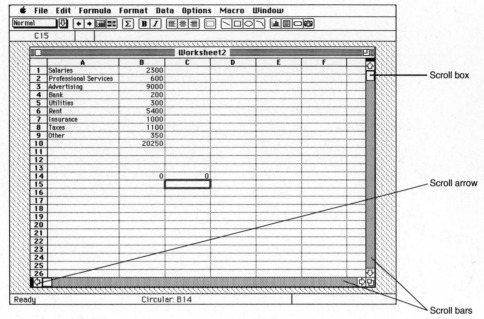

Fig. 3.9. *The scroll bars.*

You also can drag the scroll box to various locations on the bar; by doing so, you can move around the worksheet in large jumps. Click on the box and drag it to the new location on the bar; then release the mouse button. The length of the scroll bar represents the entire size of the worksheet, and the position of the scroll box represents the relative position of the screen on the worksheet. As you scroll across or down the worksheet, the screen shows other cells. The scroll bars control the position of the screen view.

Using Keyboard Commands

Excel offers a number of keyboard commands for moving the pointer. The most common are the four arrow keys. Pressing an arrow key moves the pointer throughout the worksheet, one cell at a time, in the direction of the arrow. Of course, using arrow keys is not a recommended mode of travel if you need to cover a large distance. These keys are ideal for moving across the screen, however, when you enter or edit information. Excel provides the keys listed in table 3.7 for movement.

Table 3.7
Movement Keys

Command	Moves Pointer
Tab	Right one cell
Shift-Tab	Left one cell
Return	Down one cell*
Shift-Return	Up one cell*
↑	Up one cell
⌘-↑	To preceding block
↓	Down one cell
⌘-↓	To next block
←	Left one cell
⌘-←	To preceding block
→	Right one cell
⌘-→	To next block
Home	To first nonblank cell in current row (first cell in row containing information)
⌘-Home	To cell A1
End	To last nonblank cell in current row (last cell in row containing information)
⌘-End	To high cell
PgUp	Up one screen
⌘-PgUp	Left one screen
PgDn	Down one screen
⌘-PgDn	Right one screen

You can modify the Return key so that it does not move the pointer at all but simply accepts information. To do so, select the Options command from the Workspace menu and then click on the Move Selection after Return box to remove the check mark. Click on OK when finished.

Note: If you are not using the extended keyboard, you can press Shift-Clear to toggle between the number keys and the movement keys.

The current row or column is the row or column in which the pointer is located—that is, the row or column containing the active cell. When you combine the Command key with one of the four arrow keys, Excel jumps between blocks of data. (A *block* is a group of cells containing data.) The pointer moves to the end of the current block or the beginning of the next block, depending on the position of the pointer. Figure 3.10 illustrates this movement.

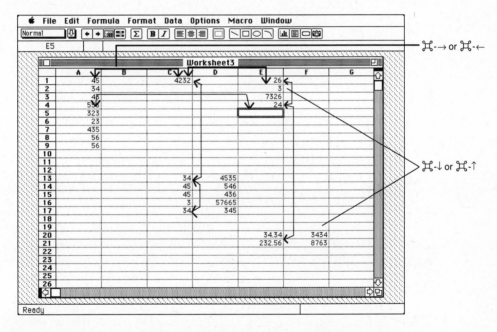

Fig. 3.10. *Using the Command key with the arrow keys. The arrows in the figure indicate possible pointer movements.*

The *high cell* is the intersection of the last row and column containing information. The high cell does not necessarily contain information; it represents the bottom corner of the used portion of the worksheet (see fig. 3.11).

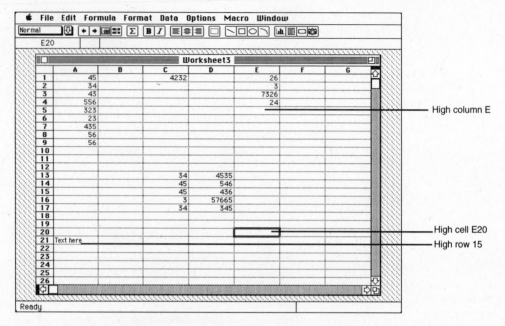

Fig. 3.11. The high cell is the intersection of the high row and column.

Using Scroll Lock

So far, all these ways of moving around the worksheet use the position of the cell pointer as the current position of the screen. In other words, to move around the worksheet, you must move the cell pointer. However, you may want to move the screen without changing the location of the pointer. You can do this by pressing the Scroll Lock key. Next, use any of the movement keystrokes described in table 3.7 to move the screen without moving the pointer. If you move the screen far enough, the pointer moves out of view.

Because the cell pointer can be out of sight, Excel offers a special command for returning the screen to the position of the pointer. Select the Show Active Cell option from the Formula menu to reconnect the screen and pointer.

Using the Goto Command

The Goto command is another way to travel over the worksheet. Goto moves the cell pointer to any cell you specify. If you have the extended keyboard, press F5 instead of choosing Goto from the Formula menu. The procedure is simple:

1. Choose the Goto option from the Formula menu, press F5 on the extended keyboard, or press ⌘-G for Goto. The dialog box shown in figure 3.12 appears.

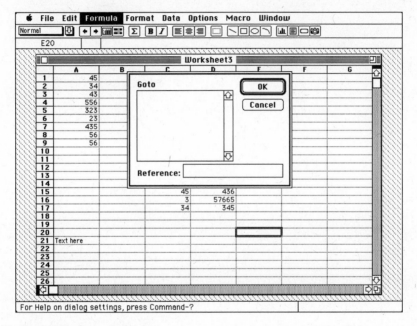

Fig. 3.12. *The Goto dialog box.*

2. Enter the cell address you want.

3. Press Return or click on the OK button.

Excel selects the specified cell. Later you will learn how to name specific cells or groups of cells. When cells have names, you can use the Goto command to locate cells or groups of cells by name. See "Naming Cells and Ranges," later in this chapter, for more details.

Using the Find Command

Another way to move around the worksheet is to use the Find command, available from the Formula menu. The Find command differs from the Goto command because it locates specific information in the worksheet. Instead of locating cells, Find locates information that you have entered into cells. After you select the Find command from the Formula menu, the Find dialog box appears (see fig. 3.13).

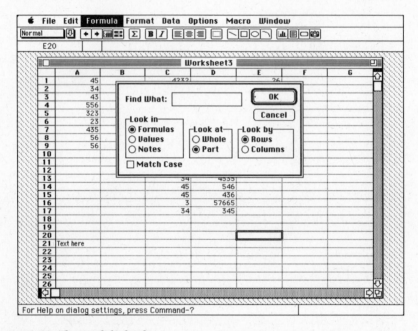

Fig. 3.13. The Find dialog box.

To use the Find feature, follow these steps:

1. Position the pointer on cell A1 or at the appropriate location in the worksheet.

> **Note:** To search a specific block of information, highlight the block before selecting the Find command. Excel will not search outside the highlighted block.

2. Select Find from the Formula menu.

3. Type the information after the Find What prompt that you want Excel to find. This information is called the *criteria*. You can enter any text string, number, or combination. You also can enter function names and cell addresses for Excel to find within formulas.

4. Choose the options in the Look in, Look at, and Look by boxes. (See the next section, "Specifying Search Options.")

5. Press Return or click on the OK button to begin the search.

After you specify the search information and select from the three special options, Excel begins searching from the current position of the pointer. Cells above and to the left of the pointer are searched last. Excel thus finds the first occurrence of the specified text following the current row or column. If the pointer is in column G and you search by columns, for example, Excel begins searching in column H and returns to A when it reaches the end of the worksheet (that is, the last column).

If Excel finds an occurrence of the specified information, the program moves the pointer to the cell containing the matching information.

You can use command keys to repeat the Find process to locate more occurrences. After the first five steps, use the following keys:

⌘-H   Finds next occurrence

⌘-Shift-H   Finds previous occurrence

If you have an extended keyboard, you can use the following keys:

Shift-F5   Invokes the Find command

F7   Finds the next occurrence of
                            the information specified in the
                            Find command

Shift-F7   Finds the previous occurrence of the
                            information

Specifying Search Options

When you use the Find option from the Formula menu, you can select three options from the Look in, Look at, and Look by boxes.

The Look in option box on the Find dialog box enables you to tell Excel whether to search for the specified information as part of a formula, value, or note. Normally, you want to search for a value—the information that appears in the cells of the worksheet, even if that information is the result of a formula. At times, however, you may need to find information that appears in formulas. In such a case, specify the Formulas option.

Suppose that you want to find all references to cell B4 within formulas because, in some cases, you need to change this reference. Using the Find command, you can select the Look in Formulas option and enter B4 as the information to find. Excel searches only formulas for the specified information, not the values of cells or the results of formulas.

The Look at option box on the Find dialog box determines whether Excel finds the specified information only if it appears as a whole word or if it is part of another word. If you type *Com* and select Look at Whole, for example, Excel finds only the word *Com*—not *Computer*, *Communicate*, or any other word containing *Com*. If you select Look at Part, Excel locates all occurrences of *Com*—whether it appears as a whole word or as a partial word.

The Look by option box simply determines the direction in which Excel searches: by rows or by columns. If the information is close to the top of the worksheet, you may want to look by rows to speed up the search. Excel finds the information in either direction.

Using Wild Cards

The Find command can be quite powerful when you use wild cards in your search criteria. A *wild card* is a special character that represents other information. You can use the following two wild cards in search criteria:

- **:* Represents any number of characters appearing at the position of the * within the criterion. For example, *the criterion Com** finds *Communicate*, *Computer*, and *Com*.

   If you use the asterisk (*) at the end of a string, Excel searches for entries that begin with the specified string. If you place the asterisk at the beginning of a string, Excel searches for entries that end with the specified string.

- *?:* Represents any single character appearing at the position of the ? within the criterion. For example, the criterion *Th??* finds *Them*, *This*, and *That* but not *The* or *Th*.

> **Note:** To find the characters * and ? in a text string, you precede them with the tilde (~). To find "*STARS*", for example, type ~*STARS~*.

Selecting Information

Selecting information (groups of cells) is an important part of worksheet manipulation because most commands apply to selected data. Often, you must select data before entering a command. Knowing how to select data efficiently saves you a great deal of time. The following sections discuss the various ways you can select information in Excel.

Selecting Ranges

A *range* is a group of cells in a row, column, or both. At times, formulas and functions require you to specify a range of cells. Almost all formatting commands (such as boldface) require you to select a range of cells. Also, highlighting a range sometimes is useful when you enter information into the worksheet.

Using the Mouse

To select a range by using the mouse, first click the mouse button on the cell that marks one corner of the range; then drag the mouse until the entire range is highlighted. Release the mouse button when finished. You can highlight ranges of any size this way. If you move the mouse beyond the edge of the screen, Excel scrolls over to include more cells.

You also can highlight a range by clicking on the first cell (that is, one corner) and pressing the Shift key while you click on the corner diagonally across from it. If you overshoot the range that you want to highlight, you can move the mouse backward while still pressing the button; the highlighted cells will become unselected as you move the mouse back.

Using the Keyboard

If you have an extended keyboard, you can select a range by using a keyboard alternative to the mouse. Position the pointer on the first cell of the range and then press Shift while using any of the movement keys listed in table 3.8 to create the selection.

Table 3.8
Selecting a Range with Movement Keys

Movement Key	Extends Selection
→,←, ↑, ↓	By one cell in the direction of the arrow
Home	To the beginning of the current row (the first cell containing information in the current row)
End	To the end of the current row (the last cell containing information in the current row)
⌘- Home	To the first cell in the worksheet
⌘- End	To the last cell in the worksheet (high cell)
PgUp	By one screen upward
PgDn	By one screen downward
⌘- PgUp	By one screen to the left
⌘- PgDn	By one screen to the right

As you may have noticed, these are the same key commands used for moving the pointer. When combined with the Shift key, these commands become range-selection keys. Here's another keyboard method to select a range:

1. Position the pointer on the first cell of the range you want (in the upper left corner).

2. Press F8.

3. Move to the last cell in the range by using the mouse, the arrow keys, or any directional key listed earlier.

Using this technique, you press F8 rather than Shift. Pressing and releasing F8 once is like pressing Shift while you select.

Using the Goto Command

A third way to select a range is to use the Goto command. The advantage of using this command is that you can cover a large area in a short time. Follow these steps:

1. Position the pointer on the first cell of the range you want (in the upper left corner).

2. Select the Goto command from the Formula menu.

3. Enter the reference of the last cell of the range you want to select.

4. While pressing Shift, press Return (or click on the OK button in the Goto dialog box).

You also can select a range of cells with the Goto command by choosing—from any cell location—the Goto command from the Formula menu. Then, in the space provided, enter the name of the range you want to select. This name should be the references of the upper left corner and lower right corner, separated by a colon. Type *A1:D10* in the dialog box, for example, to highlight the corresponding range (see fig. 3.14). You also can use a range name in this dialog box. For more information about naming ranges, see "Naming Cells and Ranges," later in this chapter.

Be sure to include a colon between the cell references. After entering the range, press Return; Excel highlights the block you specified.

Selecting More than One Range

You can highlight more than one range at a time. This capability is useful when you need to format worksheet information or apply certain commands to noncontiguous blocks of information. You can choose from several methods to highlight multiple ranges. After highlighting one range, for example, you can add a second and subsequent ranges by selecting another range while pressing the Command key. To use this method, complete the following steps:

1. Highlight the first range, using any method described in table 3.8.

2. Press the Command key.

3. While still pressing Command, click on the first cell of the next range; then drag to the last cell in that range.

4. Release the mouse button and the Command key.

To highlight multiple ranges by using the keyboard, follow these steps:

1. Highlight the first range, using any method described in table 3.8.

2. Press Shift-F8.

3. Highlight the second range.

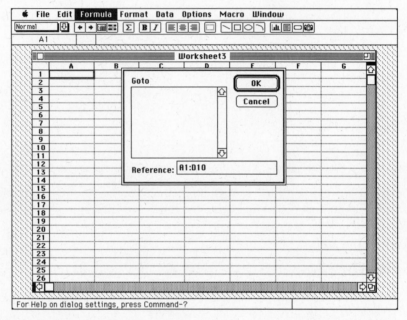

Fig. 3.14. The range reference A1:D10.

To highlight multiple ranges by using the Goto command, follow these steps:

1. Select the Goto command from the Formula menu.

2. Enter two or more ranges into the space provided. Separate each range with a comma. To highlight the ranges A1:A10 and G5:H6 at the same time, for example, type the following in the Goto dialog box:

    A1:A10,G5:H6

3. Press Return.

Finally, you can use the following shortcut to highlight multiple ranges:

1. Click on the first cell of the first range.

2. Hold down the Shift key while clicking on the last cell of the first range. This action highlights one range. Release the mouse button and the Shift key.

3. Hold down the Command key while clicking on the first cell of the second range. Doing so moves the pointer without extending or removing the existing range.

4. Hold down the Shift key while clicking on the last cell of the second range. Doing so highlights another range while leaving the first intact. Release the mouse button and the Shift key.

When more than one range is active, you can use the movement keys (Tab, Shift-Tab, Return, Shift-Return, and so on) to move the pointer from cell to cell within a range, and then from range to range. Figure 3.15 shows multiple active ranges.

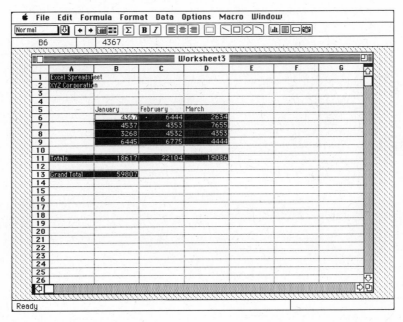

Fig. 3.15. *Multiple active ranges.*

Selecting Rows and Columns

You can select entire rows and columns by clicking on the row or column heading at the left or top of the screen. To select a series of adjacent rows or columns, click on the first row or column and drag the mouse to highlight as many rows or columns as you like. Release the mouse button. Figure 3.16 illustrates the results of this process.

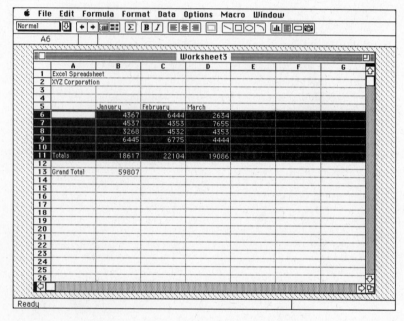

Fig. 3.16. Selecting a series of rows.

To select multiple rows or columns that are not adjacent, hold down the Command key while clicking on the various row or column headings. Figure 3.17 shows multiple selected rows and columns.

Table 3.9 lists keyboard commands that help you select rows or columns.

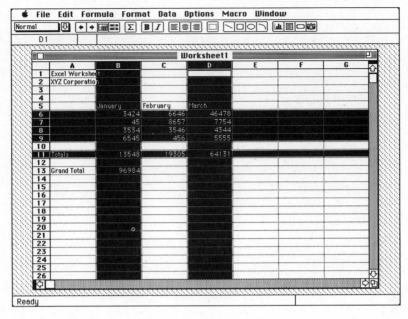

Fig. 3.17. Multiple selected rows and columns.

Table 3.9
Keyboard Commands for Selecting Rows or Columns

Command	Function
Shift-space bar	Selects the current row
⌘-space bar	Selects the current column
F8	Extends the selection
Shift-↑, Shift-↓, Shift-←, Shift-→ (numeric keypad)	Extends the selection in direction of the arrow
⌘-F8	Adds to the selection

Complete these steps to use the keyboard commands to select rows or columns:

1. Position the pointer on the row or column you want to select.

2. Press Shift-space bar to highlight the current row; press ⌘-space bar to highlight the current column.

3. To extend the selection, press F8; then use the arrow keys to highlight adjacent rows or columns. Alternatively, you can extend the selection by holding down the Shift key while pressing one of the arrow keys (the up or down arrow for rows; the left or right arrow for columns).

   You can complete the remaining steps to highlight a second (nonadjacent) row or column, leaving the first one highlighted.

4. To select a second row or column, press ⌘-F8.

5. Move the pointer to the row or column you want to select.

6. Press Shift-space bar or ⌘-space bar to select the current row or column.

7. Extend the selection as described in step 3.

Selecting the Entire Worksheet

Selecting the entire worksheet can be useful for making global changes to data. You can select the entire worksheet by clicking on the intersection of the row and column headings, at the upper left corner of the worksheet (see fig. 3.18).

The keyboard alternative to this mouse command is Shift-⌘-space bar.

Automatically Entering a Series

Excel provides a special feature that automatically enters a series of numbers, months, days, or years into a worksheet. Using a single entry that you type, Excel can finish a series of entries—in a row or a column. You can do this in three ways:

- *Date:* Creates a chronological series that increases or decreases by a specified amount: days, weekdays, months, or years. The increase or decrease amount is the *step value*, which can be positive or negative. The series stops when it reaches the end of your highlighted range or the stop value, whichever comes first. The *stop value* is the maximum value for the series, which you specify.

- *Linear:* Creates a linear series of values that increases or decreases by a specified amount. You can start with the value 0, for example, and increase by 5 each time: 0, 5, 10, 15, 20, and so on. The growth amount is specified by the step value you enter. The series continues until it reaches the end of the highlighted range or the stop value, whichever is first.

- *Growth:* Creates a series that grows factorially by a specified amount. A factor of 5, for example, causes the value 1 to grow into the series 1, 5, 25, 125, and so on. The factor for growth is the *step value*. The series continues until it reaches the end of the highlighted range or the *stop value*.

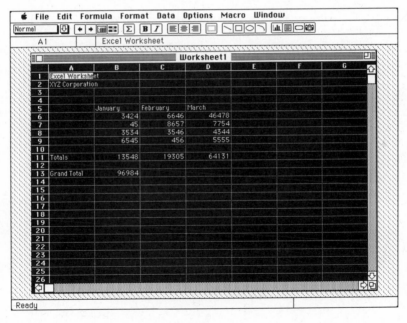

Fig. 3.18. *Selecting the entire worksheet.*

To enter a series, follow these steps:

1. Enter the first value of your series. If this is a date, format the date using any date format.

2. Highlight the entry and any adjacent cells in a row or column.

3. Select the Series option from the Data menu. The Series dialog box appears (see fig. 3.19).

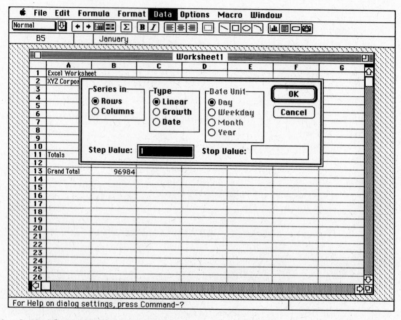

Fig. 3.19. The Series dialog box.

4. Specify whether the series will be entered into a row or column (if Excel has not already indicated the correct button).

5. Select the series type: Linear, Growth, or Date.

If you choose a date, select the date unit also: Day, Weekday, Month, or Year. This selection does not specify the increment of growth; it specifies only the type of date unit being used. If you select Month and enter a step value of 2, for example, the series will grow by two-month intervals.

6. Enter the step and stop values. The stop value is optional.

    The *step value* is the amount of increase as described for each of the three types of series. The *stop value* is the value at which the series should stop—assuming that you have highlighted enough cells to reach this value. If not, Excel stops the series at the end of the highlighted range.

7. Click on OK.

For some examples of series combinations, see figure 3.20.

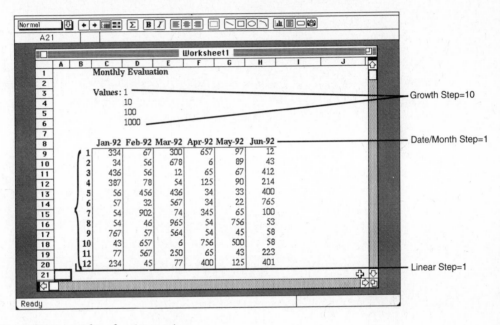

Fig. 3.20. *Examples of series entries.*

Tip: Using Date Formats in Series
Use the Format Number command to format your starting value before using the Series command. Excel duplicates the format for each of the calculated values in the series.

Automatically Duplicating a Value

The Series command is useful for sequential entries, but Excel also provides a useful command for filling a range with the same number, label, or formula automatically. Follow these steps:

1. Highlight the range (or ranges) you want, using any method described in table 3.8.

2. Type the label, number, or formula into one of the cells (while the range is still selected).

3. Press Option-Return.

When you press Option-Return after making the first entry, Excel copies the entry into all highlighted cells. If the information you entered is a number or label, each cell in the range will contain exactly the same number or label.

This feature is useful for entering information throughout a worksheet at one time. If the information you entered is a formula, Excel copies the formula into the remaining cells in the range—making them relative to their new locations. For more information about copying formulas, see Chapters 4 and 8.

Naming Cells and Ranges

To use Excel effectively, you almost certainly have to make references to ranges of cells. A *range* is a group of cells (one or more cells) in a rectangular block. A single cell can be a range of one, but your ranges most likely will contain several cells. Often, a portion of a row or column is used as a range; sometimes a block of several rows and columns is needed.

Ranges are required by certain formulas and functions that process information over one or more cells. The function SUM, for example, adds the values in a range. To specify a range within a function such as SUM, enter the cell addresses of two opposite corners, separated by a colon. The range shown in figure 3.21, for example, can be defined as any of the following:

A1:D5

D5:A1 A5:D1

D1:A5

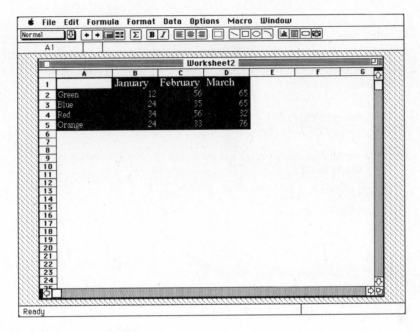

Fig. 3.21. *A range of cells.*

Rather than define a range by using two corner cells, you can name ranges and use the names instead. Rather than typing a function as =SUM(A1:D5), for example, you can type =SUM(SALES). Using names for ranges makes them easier to identify—especially when they are used frequently in the worksheet. Range names also serve to document your worksheets if you use names that help identify the information in the ranges.

Range names can consist of several words but must begin with a letter. After the initial letter, you can include numbers, periods, or the underscore (_) character. You cannot use spaces and special symbols. The following are some acceptable range names (upper- and lowercase letters are acceptable):

SALES

PRODUCT.TABLE

TABLE25

SINGLE_WEEKLY_STATE_TAX

Although you can specify range names that look like cell addresses (such as B34), avoid doing so. Such names can cause problems in formulas. When using a range name in a formula, simply enter the name where the standard range reference would appear:

=SUM(SALES)

Using range names in formulas is explained in "Using Names in Formulas and Functions," later in this chapter. To create a range name, first highlight the range you want; then select the Define Name option from the Formula menu. (The range can include data, or it can be blank.) The Define Name dialog box appears (see fig. 3.22).

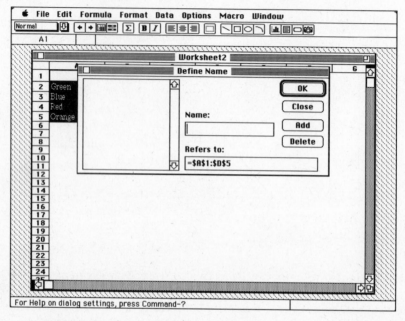

Fig. 3.22. The Define Name dialog box.

After the Name field, enter the name of the range, following the rules for range names. The name can consist of up to 255 characters, but a practical limit is about 21. The cell addresses defining the range are listed in the Refers To field of the dialog box. Excel uses absolute cell references in the range definition, as indicated by the dollar signs ($) in the cell addresses. (See Chapter 4 for more information about relative and absolute cell addresses.)

> *Note:* If a label appears in the first cell of the range, Excel suggests the label as the name for the range. If you don't want this label as the range name, type over the suggestion.

When you finish specifying the range name, press Return or click on the OK button. You also can click on the Add button to add the name to the current list and remain in the dialog box so that you can define other names. All previously defined range names appear in the left-hand portion of the dialog box so that you can avoid using the same name twice. If you enter a name that already has been used for a range, Excel applies the name to the new range and removes the old range. In other words, the name applies to the new range only. Excel does not warn you of this, so be careful.

Although applying one name to two ranges is not acceptable, it is acceptable to apply two names to one range. Having two names for the same range can be useful, because different formulas can use the same range for different reasons. Each name can imply the purpose of the range. Not only can one range have two different names, but cells that are part of one range can appear in another.

Finally, you can highlight a range consisting of multiple blocks and give it a single name. As described in "Selecting More than One Range," earlier in this chapter, you highlight multiple-block ranges by highlighting the first range and then holding down the Command key while highlighting a second range.

If you use the Formula Define Name command while several ranges are highlighted, the name you specify applies to all the highlighted cells as if they were one range.

Automatically Defining Range Names

Because range names are so handy for worksheet references, you may want to use them whenever possible. A typical worksheet, showing a block of information in rows and columns, may use several names. Suppose that you create the worksheet shown in figure 3.23.

> **Tip: Using Range Names for Data Entry**
> You can make data entry easier by applying a range name to your entry area and then highlighting the range when you need to enter data. First, select the Define Name command from the Formula menu. Next, type *Enter* in the Name box and press Tab to move to the Refers To box. Erase the existing reference by pressing the Backspace key, and then click and drag on the worksheet to highlight the range you want. If you require a multiple-range reference, highlight the first range, press the comma key, and highlight the second range. Press the comma key between each block of the multiple-range reference. Finally, press Return to accept this range name. When you want to perform data entry, use the Goto command to highlight the Enter range before typing your data.

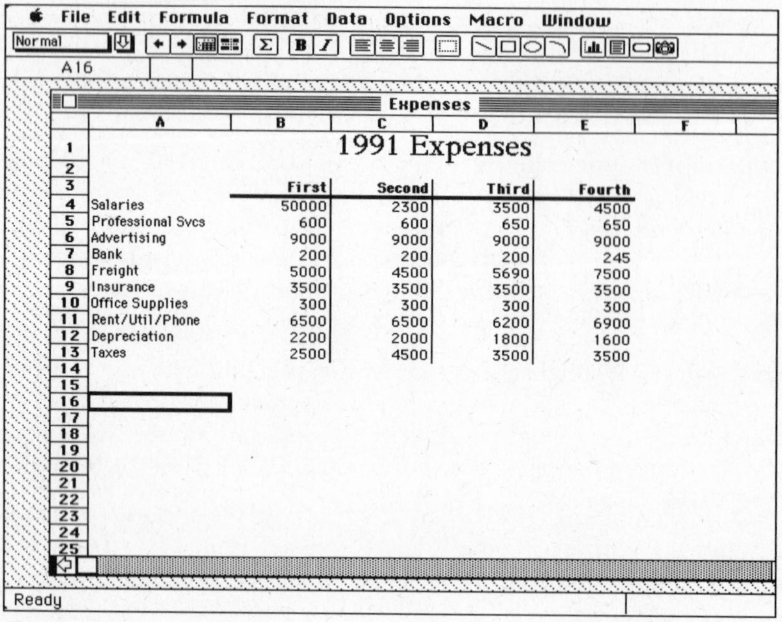

Fig. 3.23. A sample worksheet.

You may want range names for each of the four quarters of information (the four columns) as well as for each of the expense lines (that is, the 10 rows), for a total of 14 named ranges. The best names for the ranges are probably the very titles contained in the worksheet. The range B5:B14 may be called First, for example, the range B5:E5 may be called Salaries, and so on.

Rather than use the Define Name command 14 times, you can use the Create Names option on the Formula menu to create all 14 names in one step. First, highlight the entire block A4:E13; then select the Create Names command. The Create Names In dialog box appears (see fig. 3.24).

You select the Top Row option to create names for each of the columns; Excel uses the labels contained in the top row (row four in the example). You select the Left Column option to create names for each of the rows; Excel uses the labels in column A. If you don't have labels in the specified row or column of the range, Excel does not name the ranges. The block shown in figure 3.25, for example, will not provide Left Column range names because there are no label cells highlighted on the left column of the block.

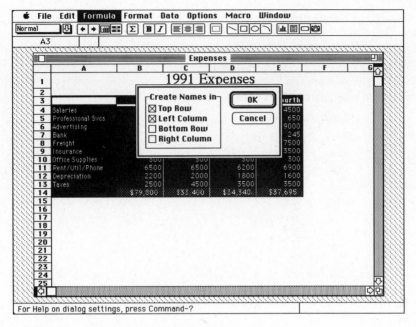

Fig. 3.24. *The Create Names In dialog box.*

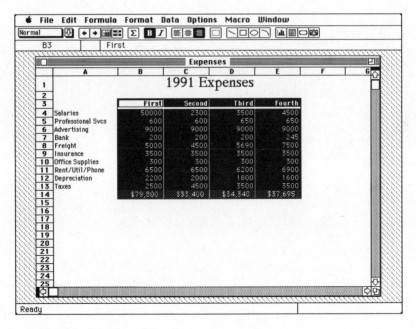

Fig. 3.25. *A block without left column range names.*

If a label appears in the corner of a range when you select both Top Row and Left Column names, Excel applies the name to the combination of columns and rows. In other words, the name refers to the entire range. In the example, you enter a name into cell A4 and then highlight the range A4:E13 to apply the names. The name in A4 applies to the entire range, while each individual row and column gets its own name as well.

You can include a cell in several named ranges. Similarly, you can include an entire range that has its own name in a larger range. Keep in mind that restrictions apply to the characters you can use in range names and that Excel does not enable you to enter invalid names when you use the Create Names command. If you use invalid names, Excel presents an error message to point out the problem. Sometimes Excel will convert your invalid name into a valid one by changing some characters. Excel turns spaces into underlines, for example.

Although Excel normally does not enable you to enter spaces in range names, Excel does not display this error message if your names have spaces. Instead, Excel converts spaces to underscore characters and then uses the name. Similarly, Excel converts dates to text labels and then uses them as names. The text label will have the same format as the date entry.

> ### Tip: Creating a Multitude of Names
> By using the Command key to highlight multiple blocks at the same time (as described in the section "Selecting Information," earlier in this chapter), you can name these multiple-block ranges by using the Create Name command. No matter how many blocks are highlighted, if labels exist in the top row of a block, they will constitute range names when you use the Top Row option. If labels exist in the far left column of the range, they will constitute range names when you use the Left Column option.

Removing Range Names

Although there is no limit to the number of ranges you can name in a worksheet, you may need to remove a name. You don't have to highlight a range or even know where it is to remove its name. Simply select Define Name from the Formula menu, click on the name you want to remove (shown in the window), and then click on the Delete button. The range name (not the information in the range) will be removed. If the range name is being used in a worksheet formula, Excel enters the value #NAME?

into the formula to indicate that a range name is needed. At this point, you can change the range name in the formula to the standard range reference or define a new range with the required name. Remember that you can have two names for the same range, if necessary.

Changing Range Names and References

You can edit any part of a range name specification, including the name itself and the range it references. One way to change a name or range reference is to delete the name, as described earlier, and then redefine the range by using the Define Name command. Excel provides a shortcut, however. To change the name of a range or change the range referenced by a name, follow these steps:

1. Select the Define Name command from the Formula menu and select the range name you want to change from the list provided.

2. To change the name, click to place the cursor in the Name key; then use standard editing commands to change the name.

   To change the range reference, click to place the cursor in the Refers To box; then use standard editing commands to change the range reference. Be sure to include dollar signs to make the reference absolute.

3. Press Return.

For a summary of the standard editing commands, see Chapter 4.

Finding Range Names

When you apply names throughout a worksheet, you can forget which range is which—even if you use descriptive names. By using the Goto command in the Formula menu, you can jump to any range by specifying its name. This feature is handy for moving quickly to specific locations throughout the worksheet. Choose the Goto command and then click on the name shown in the list. Alternatively, you can type the name in the space provided. Excel highlights the specified range.

Using Names in Formulas and Functions

As mentioned earlier, range names can help make cell references easier to use and remember. Wherever you would insert a range of cells into a formula, you can use a name. Rather than enter =SUM(A1:A5), for example, you may enter =SUM(SALES), where SALES defines the range A1:A5. As you can see, range names are more descriptive than range references. Because ranges usually apply to a block of cells, they are most commonly used with the Excel functions that require a block designation. A name can represent a single cell, however, and Excel is smart enough to know whether a name is attached to a single cell or a block. You usually can use range names, therefore, when Excel expects a single cell reference. Table 3.10 shows the various types of formulas and how you can use range names.

CELL indicates a range name attached to a single cell. RANGE indicates a range name attached to a block.

The first column in table 3.10 shows how you can use range names in formulas; the second column shows the same formula with cell or range references instead of range names. Excel understands the different uses of range names, even when the name applies to a single cell reference.

Table 3.10
Using Range Names in Formulas

Formula Example with Names	Formula Example with Cell References
=SUM(RANGE)	=SUM(A3:A9)
=SUM(CELL)	=SUM(A1)
=SUM(CELL:CELL)	=SUM(A2:A9)
=IF(CELL=0,1,2)	=IF(A2=0,1,2)
=CELL	=A2
=RANGE*	=A2:A5
=CELL+CELL	=A2+A6

* Returns first cell in range

> **Tip: Getting a List of Range Names**
> You can create a list of all defined range names and include it in your worksheet for later reference. Position the pointer in a blank area and then select the Paste Name option from the Formula menu. After the Paste Name dialog box appears, select the Paste List button. Each name appears in a separate cell; the references appear in adjacent cells.

Naming Formulas and Values

In addition to being useful for naming cells and ranges, the Define Name command is useful for naming formulas and values that you use throughout a worksheet. You can assign a name to any formula or constant value and then use it by name in a cell or in another formula. This feature comes in handy with frequently used formulas and with values that have representative meaning. You can define the formula =A4*(3/B4), for example, with the name RATE. Whenever you need that formula in a cell, type =RATE. As another example, suppose the figure 75,565.59 is the amount of an investment and is used over and over throughout the worksheet. Rather than type this number each time it comes up, assign it a name and use the name. You may name the figure AMOUNT and then use that name in formulas or functions that require the number.

You can use cell addresses, or even other range names, in your formula. The only rule is to include an equal sign in front of the value or formula you are naming. Complete these steps to name a formula or value:

1. Select the Define Name command from the Formula menu.

2. Enter the name into the Name box.

3. Press Tab to highlight the Refers To box.

4. Type the formula or value in the Refers To box. Be sure to include the equal sign at the beginning. Also, make sure that your entry completely removes the existing information.

5. Click on Add to add the name to the worksheet and clear the dialog box for another entry. Press Return to return to the worksheet.

Naming a formula or value is very much like naming a cell that contains the formula or value. The difference is that the formula or value does not have to appear on the worksheet. Instead, you can define the formula or value with a name. Otherwise, this procedure is identical to naming a cell.

> **Tip: Changing Existing Formulas for New References**
> If you use a range reference in a formula and later name that same
> range, Excel does not replace the range reference with the range
> name. Suppose that your worksheet contains the formula
> =SUM(A1:A10). Now you highlight the range A1:A10 and name it
> SALES. Excel does not automatically replace the range reference in
> this formula with the name =SUM(SALES). Use the Apply Names
> option in the Formula menu to replace all appropriate range
> references with a selected name. Using this option saves you
> some time.

If you forget a range name while entering a formula, select the Paste Name
option from the Formula menu. The Paste Name dialog box appears, listing
all available names for use in the formula (see fig. 3.26). After you select a
name from the list, Excel enters the name into the formula at the position
of the cursor.

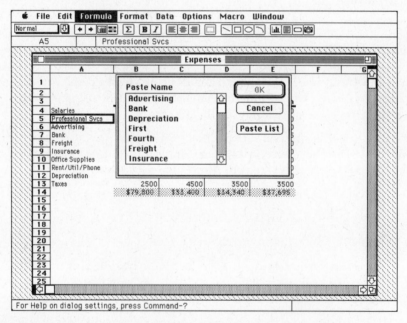

Fig. 3.26. *The Paste Name dialog box, showing sample range names.*

To select the name you want from the list, double-click on the name.
Alternatively, click on the name and then click on OK.

Protecting Information

At the beginning of this chapter, you saw how Excel enables you to assign passwords to your worksheets to protect them from being viewed by unauthorized persons. Excel also offers another kind of protection called cell protection. *Cell protection* prevents a cell from being changed. You can use cell protection in addition to file protection to prohibit unwanted changes to the worksheet. Cell protection often is considered an unnecessary detail for applications. Its primary value is for worksheets that are used by someone other than the worksheet's designer.

Cell protection not only protects your worksheets from being tampered with; it also protects you from unknowingly entering the wrong kind of information in the wrong place.

When a cell is protected, it is "locked" from use. You cannot change the information in it, and you cannot add information if the cell is blank. If you try to enter anything into a protected cell, you get the message shown in figure 3.27.

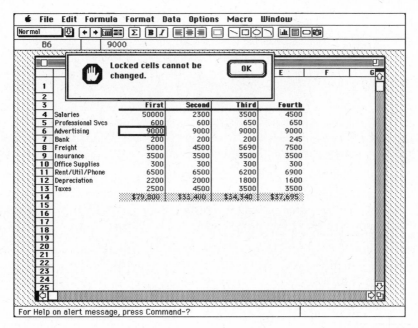

Fig. 3.27. *An error message indicating a locked cell.*

To protect cells, select the cells you want and use the Cell Protection option from the Format menu. The Cell Protection dialog box in figure 3.28 appears.

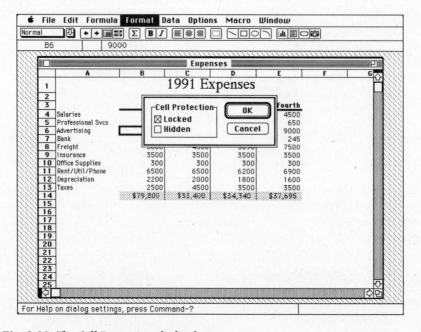

Fig. 3.28. *The Cell Protection dialog box.*

Excel offers two options for cell protection: Locked and Hidden. Use the mouse to click on the box next to the option you want. When the check mark is present, the option is on. To turn the option off, select the cells again and then click on the box to remove the check.

The Locked option locks a cell so that it cannot be tampered with. If you highlight a cell or range and then check the Locked option, you cannot change information or enter anything in the highlighted cells.

The Hidden option hides from view the information in the formula bar. That is, the information in the cell does not appear in the formula bar when you move the pointer to the cell. This option is most useful for hiding involved formulas. The values of the hidden cells still appear in the cell. For information on hiding completely a cell from view, see Chapter 5.

Note: It's common to overlook the fact that worksheet cells always start out protected—not unprotected. You can enter data into them because cell protection is turned off at the source. You can turn protection on by choosing Protect Document from the Options menu as described later. This activates the protection applied to all your worksheet cells—except those you have changed specifically to unprotected status.

When working on a worksheet with many protected cells, you may find it inconvenient to continually switch cells to an unprotected mode so that you can edit the worksheet, only to have to protect those cells again. To avoid this inconvenience, Excel provides a *master switch* that turns cell protection on and off for the entire worksheet. When this master switch is off, all cells that have been protected are temporarily unprotected so that you can make changes. Turn the master switch back on, and the cells are protected again. Turning on protection also deselects many of the Excel menu commands. Commands that can be used to change the worksheet are not available. Excel automatically applies protection to all worksheet cells, but leaves the switch off so that you can enter data into the worksheet. Most likely, you will be switching cells to unprotected status throughout your worksheets.

You can access this master switch by choosing Protect Document from the Options menu. The dialog box shown in figure 3.29 appears.

The Protect Document options follow:

- *Password:* Prevents anyone who does not know the password from turning cell protection off.

  If you enter a password into the space provided, Excel requires you to enter the password whenever you use the Options Protect Document command. If the password is entered correctly, you can turn cell protection on and off with this command. Otherwise, you cannot use the Options Protect Document command at all. If you do not enter a password into the space provided, Excel will not require one when you use this command. Therefore, anyone can use this command to turn protection on and off for the worksheet. In short, entering a password actually protects the Options Protect Document command.

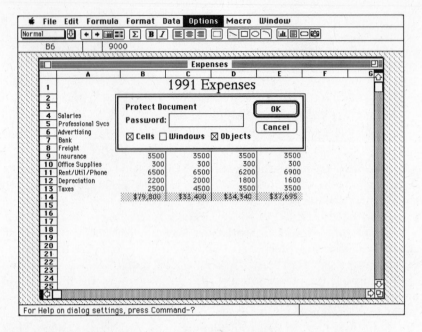

Fig. 3.29. *The Protect Document dialog box.*

> *Caution:* If you forget the password that you entered, there is no
> way to recover it. This problem can be serious if you need to
> change information that is protected. Be sure to write down the
> password and store it in a safe place.

- *Cells:* Protects all cells that have been locked with the Format Cell
  Protection command. In other words, checking this option turns
  on the master switch. Click on the box again to uncheck the option,
  turning off the master switch. When the master switch is off, locked
  cells can be changed.

- *Windows:* Freezes worksheet windows. When you use several
  windows for one worksheet, you may want to freeze them to
  prevent these windows from being moved or resized. This command prevents all windows associated with the document from
  being changed. The windows remain in place each time you open
  the document. See Chapter 7 for more information about using
  multiple windows in Excel.

- *Objects:* Freezes objects on the worksheet that have been protected with the Format Object Protection command. This prevents the objects from being moved, sized, or even selected. For more information about objects, see Chapter 13.

> **Tip: Using Quick Protection**
> If you select the Protect Document command from the Options menu and immediately press Return, you will be turning on protection without password protecting the Protect Document command. To turn off protection, select Protect Document again and deselect the Cells, Windows, and/or Objects buttons.

Summary

This chapter discussed the basics of creating Excel worksheets. You now know how to create, save, and reuse a worksheet. In addition, this chapter provided some details about entering text, numbers, and formulas into the worksheet. You also learned the basics of how to move around the worksheet and select various cells and ranges—important tasks that you will use in working with many worksheet features. The following is a list of key points covered in this chapter:

- Number entries must begin with numerals or the following characters:

    – + $. (

    Number entries also can contain the following characters (although they cannot begin with them):

    % /)

- Text entries (or labels) can begin with numbers or letters but must contain letters somewhere in the entry.

- Dates and times are really just "serial numbers" formatted to look like dates and times.

- All formulas must begin with equal signs.

- Formulas use operators to perform calculations.

- By using cell references within a formula, one cell can calculate a value based on the values in other cells.

- The Auto Sum tool sums the values in a range and places the total into the active cell of the highlighted range.

- You can move the pointer to various locations on the worksheet by using the arrow keys, the scroll bars, the keyboard commands, the Goto command, or the Find command.

- In addition to moving the pointer to a specific cell, the Find command also locates information in the worksheet.

- You can select a row or column by clicking the mouse on the row or column heading.

- By choosing Define Name from the Formula menu, you can name cells and ranges to make them easier to reference.

- Excel stores all defined names and presents them to you on request. To see a list of defined names, select Define Name from the Formula menu.

- You can prevent a cell from being changed by protecting it.

Chapter 4 explains how you can change the contents of a worksheet by using Excel's editing features.

4

Editing Worksheets

Now that you know how to create a worksheet, you must learn how to edit one. Using the features described in this chapter, you can edit information in cells, erase information from the worksheet, and insert and delete rows and columns. You also can discover how to use several commands to duplicate information in the worksheet.

Be sure to have a sample worksheet on which to practice some of these commands. If you use the quick start sample worksheet, keep one copy in its current state for the next quick start lesson.

Editing Cell Contents

Chapter 3 shows that typing information into a cell removes whatever information that cell contains. One of the most common needs you encounter when creating worksheets, however, is the need to edit cell contents without retyping the entire entry. Excel enables you to modify cells easily. Follow these steps:

1. Place the pointer on the cell you want to edit.

   The cell's contents appear in the formula bar. By changing the information in the formula bar, you change the information in the cell. Excel offers familiar Macintosh editing procedures for changing information in the formula bar.

157

2. Position the cursor by clicking on the appropriate location in the formula bar.

   You can select a section of text by clicking and dragging the mouse. Alternatively, you can select text by clicking at the beginning of the text, holding down the Shift key, and then clicking at the end of the text. You can select a single word by double-clicking on the word.

3. Press Backspace to remove the highlighted text. Alternatively, you can begin typing to replace the text with new information.

In addition to offering these standard Macintosh editing commands, Excel provides a host of special keyboard commands for editing text and formulas in the formula bar.

First, click to place the cursor in the text shown in the formula bar. Then use the editing commands in the following list to make your changes:

Command/Action	Effect
Double-click	Selects a word.
←, →, ↑, ↓*	Moves the cursor one character in the direction of the arrow. The left and right arrows most commonly are used; the up and down arrows are useful when the entry is very long.
Shift-←, Shift-→**	Selects one character at a time in the direction of the arrow.
Shift-↑, Shift-↓**	Moves cursor from its original position to the same position on the preceding or next line.
⌘-←, ⌘- → ⌘-↑, ⌘-↓***	Moves one word in the direction of the arrow (left, right, up, and down).
⌘-Shift-←, ⌘-Shift-→, ⌘-Shift-↑, ⌘-Shift-↓***	Selects one word in the direction of the arrow (left, right, up, and down).
Home*	Moves to the beginning of the current line. (Used for multiline entries.)

Command/Action	Effect
Shift-Home*	Selects from the cursor position to the beginning of the current line.
⌘-Home*	Moves to the beginning of the entry.
⌘-Shift-Home*	Selects from the cursor position to the beginning of the entry.
End*	Moves to the end of the current line. (Used for multiline entries.)
Shift-End*	Selects from the cursor position to the end of the line.
⌘-End*	Moves to the end of the entry.
⌘-Shift-End*	Selects from the cursor position to the end of the entry.

* Macintosh Plus keyboards require that you also press the Option key for this effect.

** You must use the numeric keypad arrows. On the Macintosh Plus keyboard, you also must press the Option key to get this effect.

*** Command not available on Macintosh Plus keyboard.

You may notice that you can use each of the three basic keys (Home, End, or any of the cursor-movement keys) with the Command key for a different effect. Also, if you add the Shift key to any of the movement keys, Excel highlights as the cursor moves.

Keep in mind that the cursor should be flashing somewhere in the text shown in the formula bar in order for you to perform these functions. If the cursor is not in the formula bar, these commands will perform standard worksheet movement actions (see Chapter 3).

As an example of editing using the standard commands and the special keyboard commands, suppose that you have the following label in cell A2 of the worksheet:

Net Salles for North Company Products

You want to correct the spelling of the word *Sales,* remove the word *Products,* and change the word *Company* to *Corp.* Follow these steps to make the corrections, using the mouse:

1. Using the mouse or the Goto command from the Formula menu, select cell A2. The contents of the label appear in the formula bar, as shown in figure 4.1.

Formula bar ———

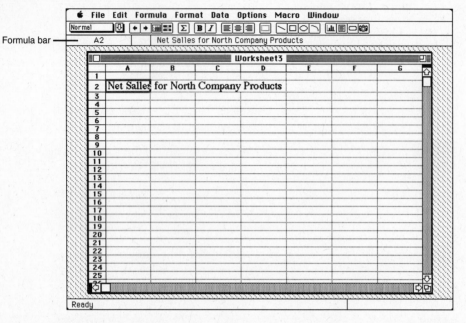

Fig. 4.1. *Editing cell contents.*

2. Move the mouse pointer to the formula bar. Notice that the pointer shape changes to the I-beam, which is used for entering and editing text.

3. Click between the two *l* characters in *Salles*.

4. Press the Backspace key.

5. Move the mouse pointer to the *C* in *Company*; click and drag to the end of the entry.

6. Type *Corp.* and press Return.

You can make the same edits with keyboard commands. Follow these steps:

1. Select cell A2.

2. Press ⌘-U to begin editing.

3. Press ⌘-Home to move the cursor to the beginning of the entry. (Remember that the Home key is the 9 on the numeric keypad, with Num Lock off.)

4. Press ⌘-→ to move one word to the right.

5. Press the right-arrow key until the cursor is between the two *l* characters in the word *Salles* (see fig. 4.2).

Note: If pressing arrow keys moves the pointer to the next cell, try pressing the Option key with the arrows. Your keyboard may require this step.

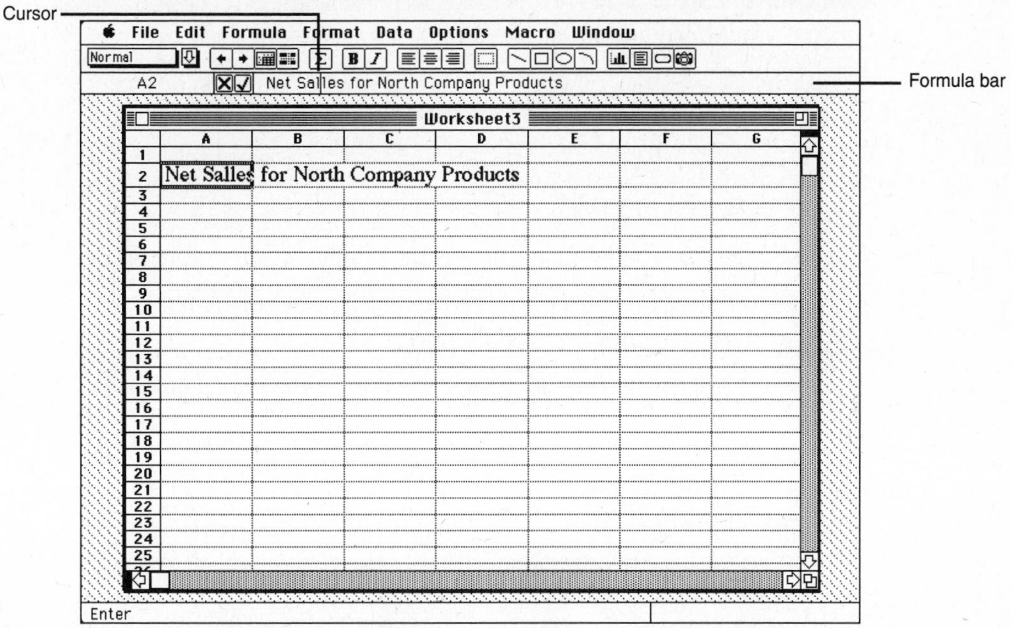

Fig. 4.2. Positioning the cursor in the formula bar.

6. Press the Backspace key once to remove the first *l*.

7. Press ⌘-→ three times to position the cursor at the beginning of the word *Company*. Select the word by pressing ⌘-Shift-→.

8. Type *Corp*. As you begin typing, the new word replaces the highlighted word.

9. Double-click on *Products* to highlight the word. Because you must remove this entire word, press the Backspace key once to erase the word. Then press Return.

With these editing features, you can completely change a cell's contents. By dragging the mouse, you can select larger portions of information for editing. If you change a cell's contents and decide that you don't want to keep the changes, click on the Cancel box at the top of the screen. Excel replaces the original information in the cell and does not make your changes.

Searching and Replacing

You also can change a cell's information by using Excel's Replace command from the Formula menu. Similar to the Find command, Replace locates any information in your worksheet and replaces the information (or portions of the data) with information that you specify.

Replace is most useful when you need to edit labels, numbers, or formulas that appear in more than one cell. You may want to change a particular cell reference used in formulas throughout the worksheet, for example. Rather than edit each formula individually, you can use the Replace command to change the formulas all at once.

To use the Replace command and its options, follow these steps:

1. Select the range of cells you want (or select only one cell if you want to use the entire worksheet).

2. Select the Replace command from the Formula menu. The dialog box shown in figure 4.3 appears.

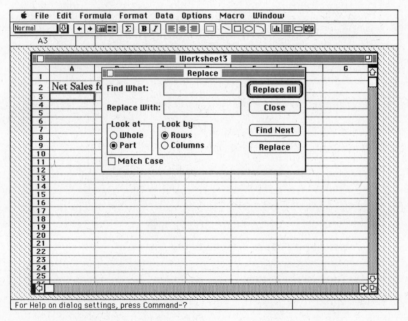

Fig. 4.3. The Replace dialog box.

3. In the Find What box, enter the data you want to find.

   This information can be any character, cell reference, word, or phrase.

4. Enter the replacement data in the Replace With box.

   Suppose that a cell reference has changed from A1 to C5; enter A1 in the Find What box and C5 in the Replace With box.

5. Select Whole or Part from the Look At options.

   The Look At option determines whether Excel finds your entry only when it appears as a whole word or when it appears as parts of other words. When replacing parts of formulas, be sure to use the Part option. The Whole option can be useful when you replace portions of labels.

6. Select Rows or Columns from the Look By options.

   The Look By selection determines whether Excel searches by rows or by columns. This selection has no bearing on whether Excel finds matching information, but on how quickly Excel finds the matching information. Search by rows if you think that most occurrences appear toward the top of the worksheet. Search by columns if you think the occurrences appear toward the left side of the worksheet.

7. Click on Replace All if you want to replace all matching occurrences. (If you choose this option, steps 8 and 9 do not apply.)

   Alternatively, click on the Find Next button to begin searching.

> *Caution:* Be careful when using the Replace All option. If you use the option mistakenly or inappropriately, restoring the original cell contents may be difficult.

8. Click on Replace to replace the current occurrence.

   Alternatively, click on the Find Next button to skip the current occurrence and find the next one.

9. Continue to click on Find Next and repeat step 8 until you finish with all occurrences, or click on Cancel to exit from the Replace dialog box.

If you highlight a range of cells before using the Replace command, Excel searches for matching information only in the highlighted range. This technique is a good way of limiting the search to a specific area to avoid mistakes. To use the entire worksheet, don't highlight any range—that is, highlight just one cell.

Replacing Range References with Range Names

As you learn in Chapter 3, you can apply names to ranges of cells (or individual cells) throughout the worksheet. The range A1:A5, for example, may be named SALES. In formulas, you can use the name SALES instead of the typical range reference.

Most likely, you start naming ranges after you begin the worksheet. You even may use the standard range reference in many formulas before you name the range. Do not use the Replace command to change all occurrences of the range reference because using the command can be dangerous. Suppose that you want to change the range A1:A5 to the name SALES. Because you're changing a formula, you must use Replace's Part option in the Look At box. Doing so, however, causes Excel to consider the following ranges as matches:

A1:A5:

A1:A5

A1:A51

A1:A55

A1:A500

Using the Find Next feature, however, to examine each potential change is tedious. Excel instead provides a special command for replacing range references with their respective names. Select the Apply Names command from the Formula menu. The dialog box shown in figure 4.4 appears.

Select the appropriate name from the list provided; then press Return. (Alternatively, double-click on the name you want.) You already should have created the range name; you now should be ready to apply the name to formulas throughout the worksheet. The range name is used instead of the range reference to which the name applies. You can apply several range names at once by holding down the Shift key while selecting multiple names from the list in the Apply Names dialog box. Finally, you can apply range names in specific areas of the worksheet by highlighting the appropriate area before selecting the Apply Names command. More information on applying range names appears in Chapter 3.

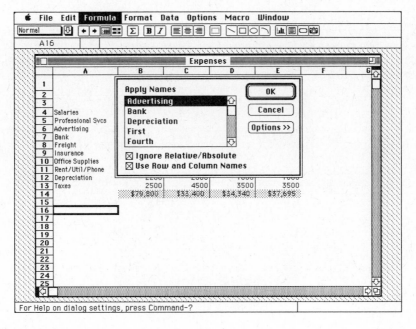

Fig. 4.4. *The Apply Names dialog box.*

Deleting Information

You probably will want to delete information from a cell occasionally. Using the Delete key when the cursor is inside the formula bar is great for erasing portions of a cell's contents, but what if you want to remove everything from a cell? Excel provides an easier way.

First, select the cell containing the information you want to remove; then press the Backspace key. To erase several cells at once, highlight the appropriate range and press ⌘-B. All information is removed, and the cell remains as though it had never been used. Alternatively, you can highlight the cells you want, and then select the Clear option from the Edit menu. Selecting this option brings up the dialog box shown in figure 4.5. The Clear dialog box provides the following options:

Option	Effect
All	Removes everything in the cells.
Formulas	Erases cells that contain formulas.

Option	Effect
Formats	Erases special character formats (such as boldface) and returns the information to normal.
Notes	Erases notes attached to the cells.

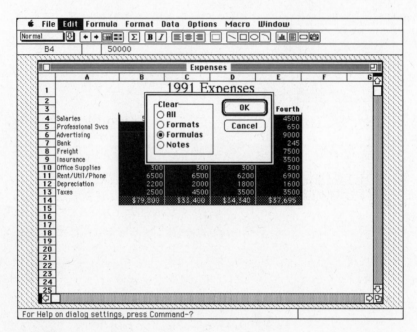

Fig. 4.5. The Clear dialog box.

See Chapter 5 for more information about character formats.

Another way to clear cells is to highlight them and press ⌘-B, which clears all information except formatting.

In addition to clearing the contents of a cell or range, you can clear information in an entire row or column, multiple rows or columns, or the entire worksheet by selecting the appropriate ranges before using the Clear command. To select a row or column, click on the row or column title and select Clear from the Edit menu (see Chapter 3).

> ***Caution:*** Because clearing information does not store a copy of the removed information on the clipboard, you have only one opportunity to change your mind. To cancel the Clear command, you must select the Undo command from the Edit menu (or press F1) immediately after you clear the information. Otherwise, the information is removed permanently.

Deleting Cells

When you use the Clear command from the Edit menu to delete information from a worksheet, the cells containing the information are emptied but remain in place on the worksheet. You also can delete information by removing the entire cell and its contents. This process causes cells to the right of the deleted cell to move left and assume the empty space. If you delete cell C5, for example, all cells from D5 to the end of the worksheet move left one cell. Cell D5 becomes the new C5, cell E5 becomes D5, and so on. You can choose whether cells move to the left to fill the space or whether cells move up from below. These options appear in the dialog box shown in figure 4.6 (which appears after you choose Delete from the Edit menu).

> ***Caution:*** The Delete command from the Edit menu removes the selected cells and all their contents. If you make a mistake, immediately choose Undo from the Edit menu. Otherwise, your information will be removed permanently.

You often delete and insert cells for aesthetic purposes—to reformat the layout of information. If a formula references a cell that has been relocated because of the Delete command, the reference adjusts to show the new cell location. If, for example, cell C5 is removed so that cell D5 becomes the new C5, any references to cell D5 adjust to the new name of the cell. References to the removed cell (C5), however, cannot be adjusted, and result in errors.

The worksheet in figure 4.7 shows an example of this situation. Cell F6 contains the formula =C5; cell F7 contains the formula =D5. After you delete cell C5, cell F6 contains #REF! and cell F7 contains =C5. (Excel inserts the #REF! message if the cell that you originally referred to has been deleted.) Figure 4.8 shows the worksheet before you delete cell C5.

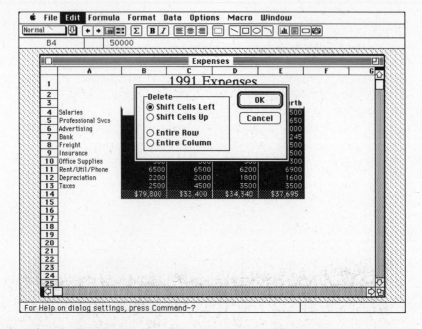

Fig. 4.6. The Delete dialog box.

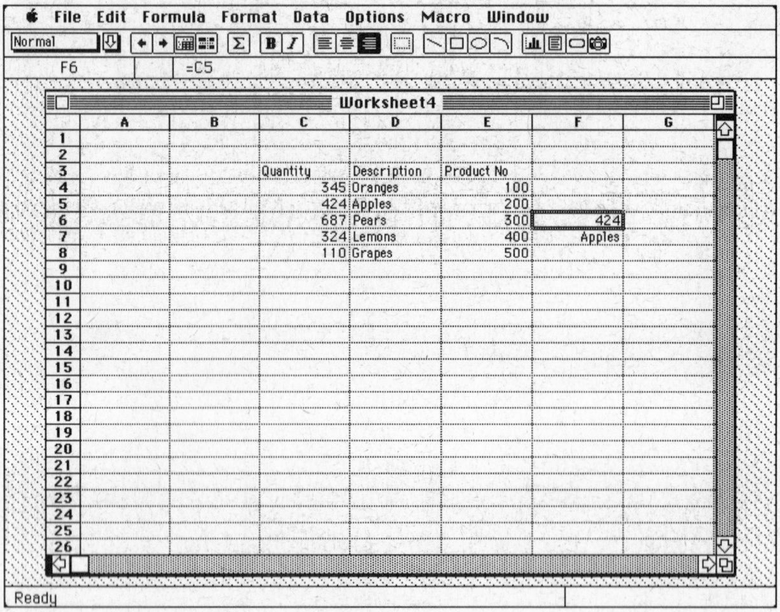

🍎	File	Edit	Formula	Format	Data	Options	Macro	Window

| Normal |
| F6 | =C5 |

Worksheet4

	A	B	C	D	E	F	G
1							
2							
3			Quantity	Description	Product No		
4			345	Oranges	100		
5			424	Apples	200		
6			687	Pears	300	424	
7			324	Lemons	400	Apples	
8			110	Grapes	500		
9							
10							

Ready

Fig. 4.7. Cell references before deleting a cell.

To delete a cell, select the cell and choose the Delete command from the Edit menu. You can delete a block, an entire row, or an entire column of cells by selecting the cells and using the Delete command.

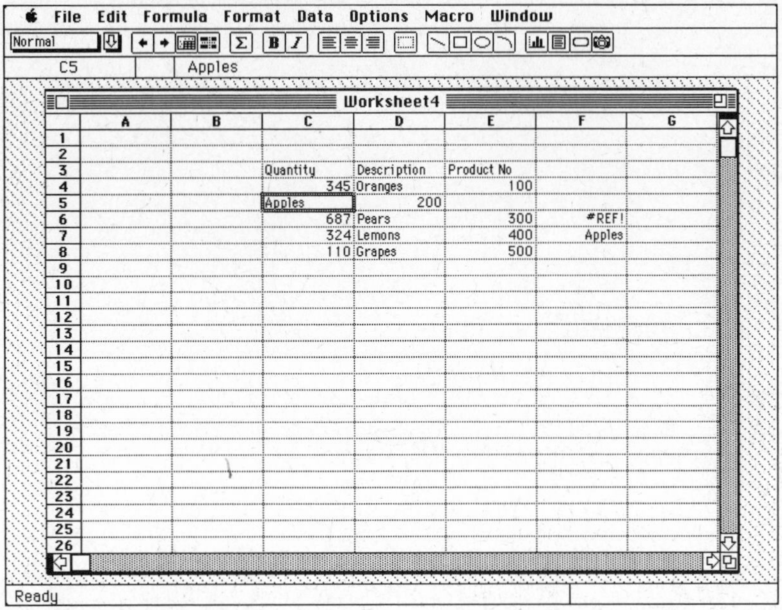

Fig. 4.8. *After deleting cell C5.*

Caution: If you change your mind about deleting information, you can choose Undo from the Edit menu *immediately* after deleting to replace the information. Also, the Delete command places a copy of the information on the clipboard; you can paste that copy back on the worksheet. If you alter the clipboard's contents by deleting or copying something else, however, you cannot retrieve the original data.

Inserting Cells

Suppose that you have entered information on your worksheet but want to add information at the top left side of the page. Perhaps instead you want to move information to a location that already contains some information.

One solution is to insert blank cells where you need them.

When you insert a blank cell, block, or column, existing information moves to the right or down, and cell addresses adjust accordingly. When you insert a blank row, existing information moves down. To insert a cell or block of cells, move the cursor to the area where you want to place the new cells and highlight the number of cells you want to insert.

Next, choose the Insert command from the Edit menu. Existing information moves to accommodate the new cells. Figures 4.9 and 4.10 show how this procedure works.

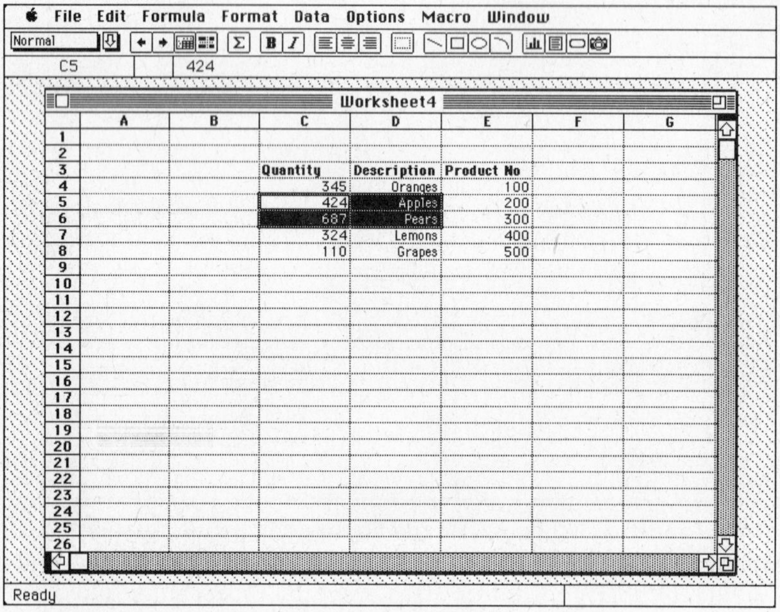

Fig. 4.9. Specifying the size and location of the block to insert.

In figure 4.9, the range C5:D6 is highlighted. After you use the Insert command from the Edit menu, columns C and D from rows 5 and 6 become columns E and F from rows 5 and 6. Rows 7 and 8 are unaffected.

To insert an entire row or column at once, select the row or column that moves down or to the right, and then select the Insert command from the Edit menu (see figs. 4.11 and 4.12).

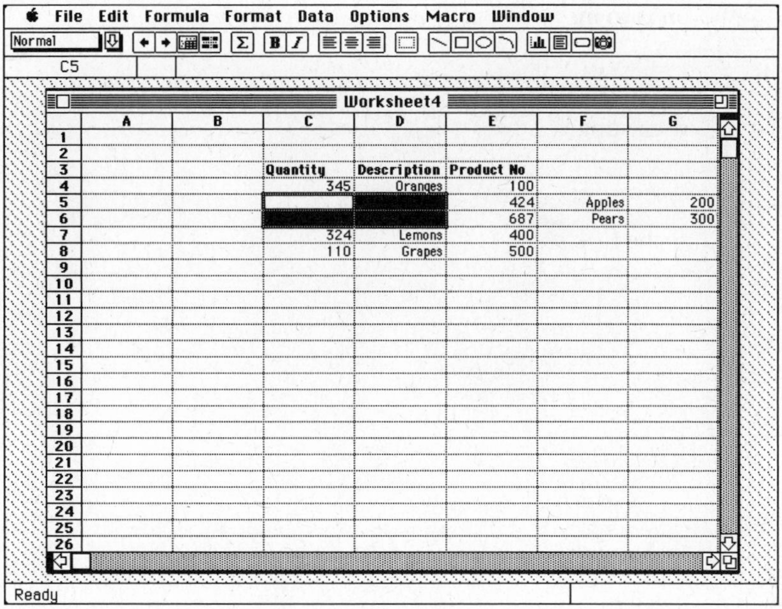

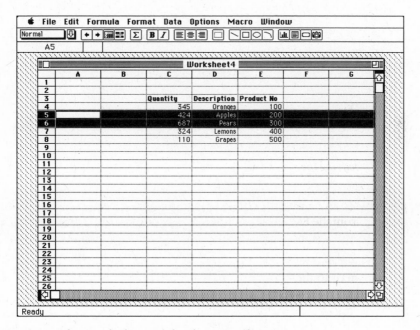

Fig. 4.10. *The worksheet after inserting the block.*

Fig. 4.11. *Selecting the location for the inserted row.*

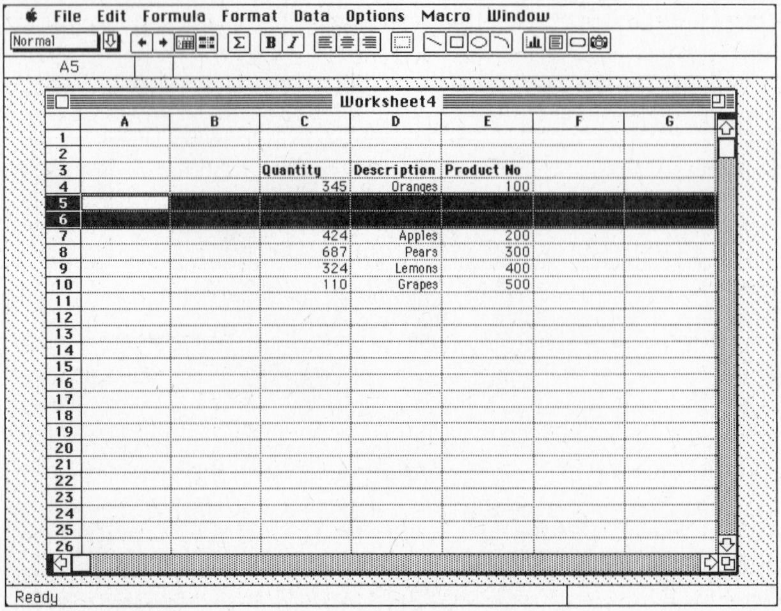

Fig. 4.12. *The worksheet after inserting the row.*

Note: When you highlight an entire row or column for inserting, Excel does not offer its delete options.

Moving Information

The process of moving information from one location to another is an extension of the Cut command. To move information, first choose Cut from the Edit menu to remove the data from its original location. Next, place the pointer at the new location and select the Paste command from the Edit menu. You also can invoke Paste by pressing ⌘-V. The information appears at the new location. If you cut a range of cells, you can paste the entire range into the new location. Position the pointer where you want the upper left corner of the range to appear and press ⌘-V.

Before pasting, you can highlight a block of cells to designate the exact range for the pasted information. If the destination range is smaller or larger than the range that you cut, Excel does not fill the designated range and presents a message explaining this.

A better way to paste information is to not highlight a destination block at all; instead, click on the cell that defines the upper left corner of the destination and then paste.

If the area where you move the data already contains information, Excel replaces the existing information with the data being pasted. To avoid replacing existing information, you can insert new cells to make room for the pasted data. To insert cells when pasting, select the Insert Paste command from the Edit menu instead of the Paste command (or press ⌘-V).

> *Caution:* Excel does not warn you before it replaces existing data with the Paste command. If you make a mistake, immediately choose the Undo command from the Edit menu.

Note that if the information you move contains references to other cells, the references remain the same when moved to the new location. Suppose that cell A5 contains the formula =A1+A2+A3 and that you want to move this information to cell C12. First, place the pointer on cell A5 and press ⌘-X to delete the cell. Next, move to cell C12 and press ⌘-V. Cell C12 now contains the same formula: =A1+A2+A3. (If you want the formulas to adjust to their new location so that they become relative references, use the Copy command from the Edit menu instead of Cut.)

If information already exists at the location where you are moving the data, that information is replaced with the data you paste in. If you do not want to replace this information, insert space for the new information before deleting the new data from its original location.

For more information about moving and copying, see "Using Advanced Copying and Pasting Procedures," later in this chapter. Information about inserting cells appears in the preceding section, "Inserting Cells."

Copying Information

Copying is similar to moving, except that copying leaves the original data in its original location while placing a copy in your paste location. To copy data, highlight the original data and select the Copy command from the Edit menu (or press ⌘-C). Move the pointer to the destination cell (the cell marking the upper left corner of the range) and select the Paste command from the Edit menu (or press ⌘-V).

Like moving data, copying replaces any data now in the paste range. To avoid this mistake, you can insert cells to accommodate the copied data by using the Insert Paste command instead of the Paste command. Follow these steps:

1. Highlight the cells you want to copy.

2. Select the Copy command from the Edit menu or press ⌘-C.

3. Highlight the range into which the data is to be pasted. This range must match the original range. Alternatively, you can move the pointer to the upper left corner of the new range.

4. Select the Paste command from the Edit menu or press ⌘-V. If you want to insert cells while pasting (to avoid removing existing data), use the Insert Paste command and choose whether you want to move the existing data down or to the right.

> **Tip: Pasting Data Repeatedly**
> You can paste the same copied data repeatedly, without recopying the data. Just highlight the destination cell and choose the Paste command. Then, highlight another destination cell and choose Paste again.

Copying worksheet information involves some special concerns. Besides duplicating data, copying involves the use of worksheet cell references. When you copy formulas containing cell references to other locations, this question comes up: Do the cell references remain exactly as the originals, or do they change to apply to the new position?

Earlier in the chapter, you saw how to use the Cut and Paste commands to move information. When you move information, cell references remain exactly as the original cells (that is, they reference the same cells). This arrangement is fine for labels and numbers, but formulas often must be relative to their new location. The Copy command keeps references relative when they are copied. (Of course, the Copy command also leaves the original intact, whereas the Cut command removes the original.)

> **Tip: Using Copy Instead of Cut**
> If you must move information, but must also make the information relative to its new location, use the Copy command and then erase the original piece of data. This method is an alternative to using the Cut and Paste procedure.

Suppose that your worksheet has a column of numbers indicating the costs of store merchandise. In an adjacent column, your worksheet calculates the price after incorporating a markup of 40 percent. You begin with the first formula, shown in the formula bar in figure 4.13.

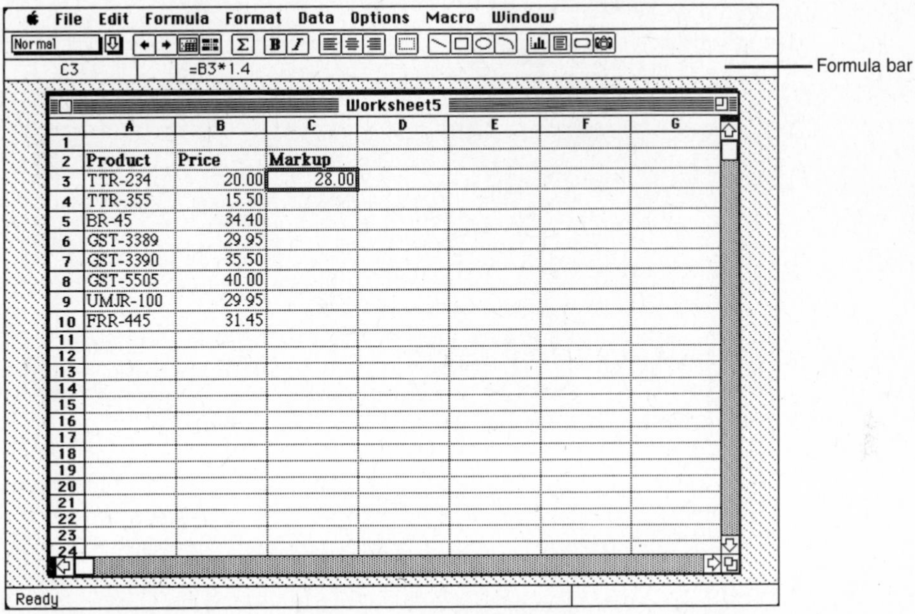

Fig. 4.13. A worksheet with a formula ready to be copied.

Next, you copy the formula into the remaining cells of column C. After you copy the formula, the cell references adjust so that they are relative to the formula's location. Cell C6 references cell B6, cell C7 references B7, and so on. To copy the formula, select cell C3 and select the Copy command from the Edit menu. (You also can use the shortcut ⌘-C.) Next, highlight the remaining cells C4:C10 and choose Paste from the Edit menu. The formula is entered into the highlighted block with cell references relative to the cells' new locations. Figure 4.14 shows the result.

In this example, you also can use the Fill Down command from the Edit menu to copy this information because the targeted cells are in consecutive cells. Fill Down is exactly like the Copy command, except that Fill Down is faster and easier to use in situations such as when the destination cells are next to (in this case, beneath) the original cell. With Fill Down, you must highlight the entire range, with the original cell at the top of that range (in the example, the range C3:C10), and then select the Fill Down command from the Edit menu. The effect is identical to copying, but the Fill Down procedure takes fewer steps. Similarly, if you copy data across several adjacent columns, you can use the Fill Right command instead of the Copy command. Just highlight the original cell and all the adjacent cells to receive copies and select Fill Right.

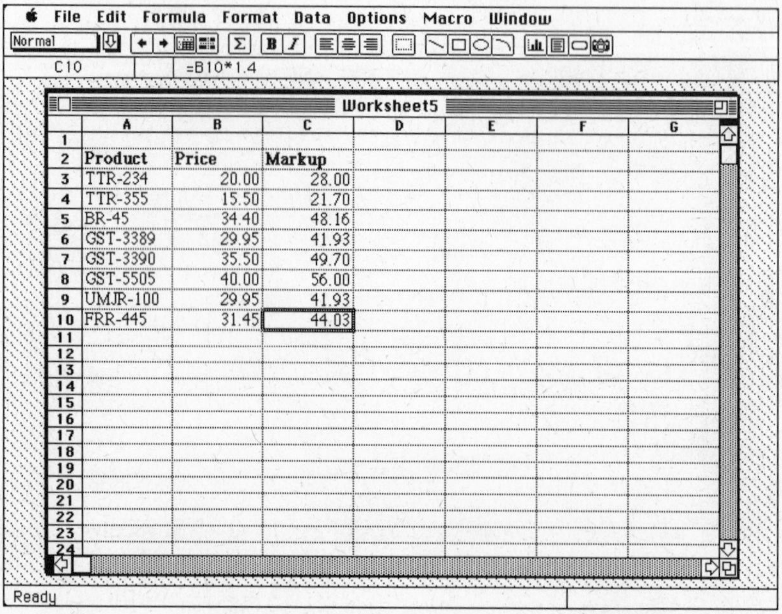

Fig. 4.14. *A formula copied into other cells, making references relative.*

When you press the Shift key while selecting the Edit menu, the Fill Down and Fill Right commands change to Fill Up and Fill Left. Use these commands when you copy in the direction the commands indicate.

Unlike the Fill Down and Fill Right commands, the Copy command can copy into nonadjacent cells. Suppose that the sample worksheet contains an additional column of products next to the first column. Now you must copy the formula into both columns, as shown in figure 4.15.

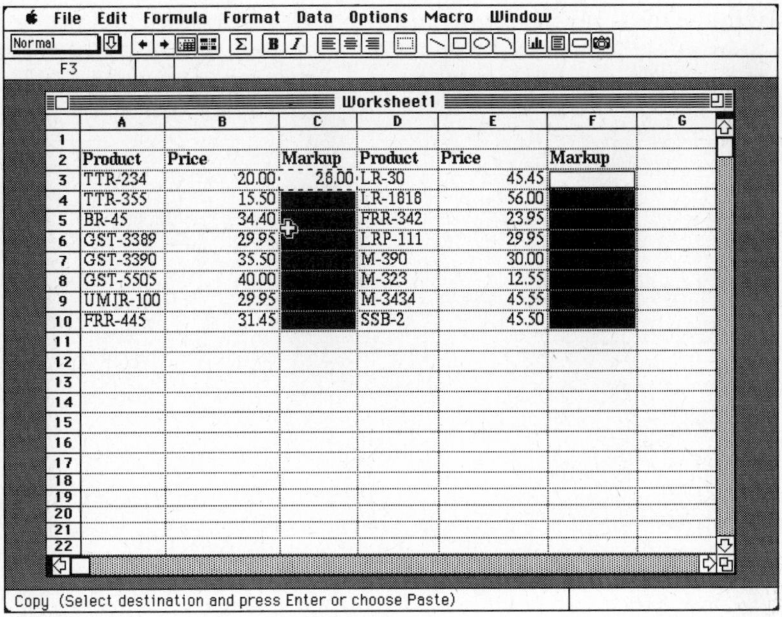

Fig. 4.15. *Copying into nonadjacent cells.*

The difference here is that you must highlight all cells that receive copies of the formula, as shown figure 4.15. When you use the Copy and Paste commands, all highlighted cells receive copies relative to the cells' locations.

Excel copies formulas in a relative fashion unless you specifically prevent Excel from doing so. Preventing this type of copying requires that you use absolute references in formulas, which is the topic of the next section.

Understanding Cell References

At times you may need to copy formulas without making some cell references relative. Perhaps a formula contains two cell references, but one reference should remain the same after copying. A reference that remains the same, no matter what its location, is called an *absolute cell reference*. Look at the price list from figure 4.14, for example. In this case, the formula changes so that the markup amount can be entered into a worksheet cell (C1).

This arrangement enables the operator to experiment with different markup amounts to see how the markups affect the prices. Figure 4.16 shows the new worksheet.

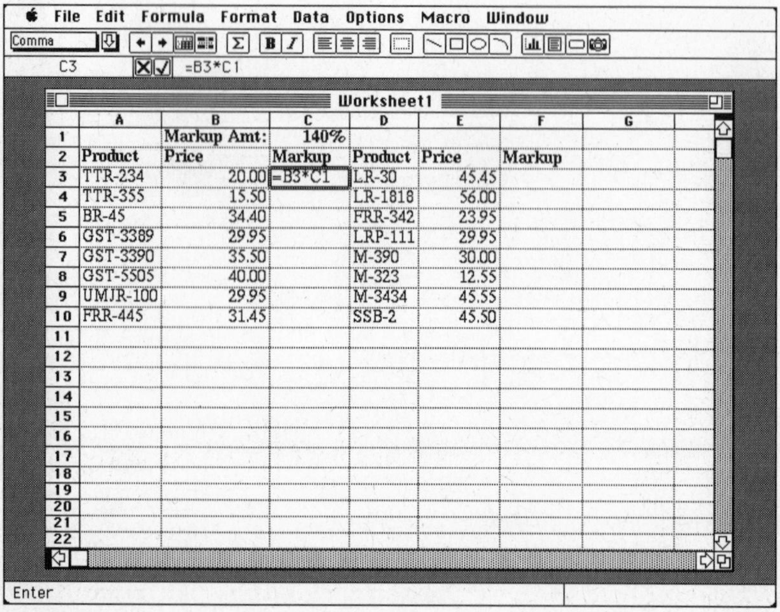

Fig. 4.16. *A worksheet requiring an absolute cell reference.*

The formula in cell C3 now is =B3*C1. Cell C1 contains the markup amount. When you copy this formula into the remaining cells, the first cell reference (B3) should be adjusted for each copy, but the reference to cell C1 should remain the same for every copy. A few of the formulas should look like the following:

    C4: =B4*C1

    C5: =B5*C1

    C6: =B6*C1

If you copied the formula as shown, however, the resulting copies look like the following, where both cell references are adjusted:

    C4: =B4*C2

    C5: =B5*C3

    C6: =B6*C4

To make cell C1 an absolute reference in the formula in cell B3, add dollar signs before the column letter and row number, as follows:

=B3*$C$1

Now when you copy the formula, the reference to C1 remains absolute. Figure 4.17 shows the formulas contained in the cells after the absolute reference is copied.

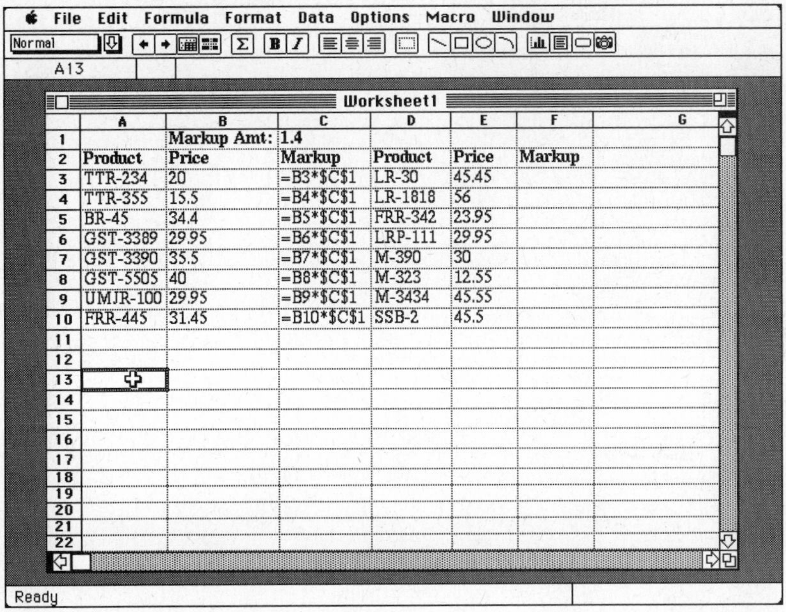

	A	B	C	D	E	F	G
1		Markup Amt:	1.4				
2	Product	Price	Markup	Product	Price	Markup	
3	TTR-234	20	=B3*$C$1	LR-30	45.45		
4	TTR-355	15.5	=B4*$C$1	LR-1818	56		
5	BR-45	34.4	=B5*$C$1	FRR-342	23.95		
6	GST-3389	29.95	=B6*$C$1	LRP-111	29.95		
7	GST-3390	35.5	=B7*$C$1	M-390	30		
8	GST-5505	40	=B8*$C$1	M-323	12.55		
9	UMJR-100	29.95	=B9*$C$1	M-3434	45.55		
10	FRR-445	31.45	=B10*$C$1	SSB-2	45.5		

Fig. 4.17. Copying absolute references.

As a final example, suppose that the worksheet uses two different cell references for the markups—each column with its own reference, as shown in figure 4.18.

In this example, only the reference to row 1 is absolute in the original formula. The original formula in cell C3 is =B3*C$1. This setup causes the formulas to use the appropriate cell from row 1.

When you copy this formula, each column uses the respective mark-up amount relative to the column, as the formulas in figure 4.18 show. Notice that the dollar sign appears before the row reference only. The row therefore stays absolute, whereas the rest of the formula is relative.

You also can make a range reference absolute by including the dollar signs as part of the range. In the example, you may enter this formula into cell C12:

=SUM($C$3:$C$10)

Using dollar signs makes the range C3:C10 absolute. When you copy this formula to another cell, the range remains constant—it does not adjust to the new location. Often you want the range to adjust, such as when you duplicate formulas across a row or column. In the example, you may copy this formula from cell C12 to cell F12. In this case, you want the range reference to be relative.

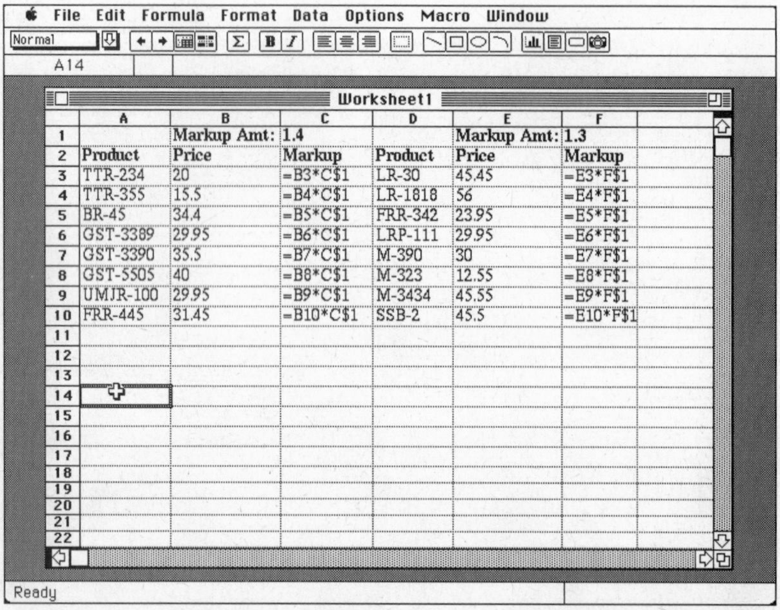

Fig. 4.18. *A worksheet with two mark-up references, or one for each column.*

Note: Using dollar signs for absolute references affects the Fill Down and Fill Right commands, also. These commands will copy formulas with relative and absolute references intact.

Tip: Making References Absolute
Excel offers a quick, easy way to convert cell references from relative to absolute. Press ⌘-U to edit the formula and then highlight the cell reference you want. Then press the F4 key to cycle through the absolute options. Press Return when you finish.

Using Absolute References with Range Names

When you define a range name, Excel assumes that you want the range reference to be absolute and includes the needed dollar signs in the Refers To field of the Define Name dialog box. If you highlight the range A3:C3, for example, and then select the Define Name command from the Formula menu to give this range a name, Excel displays the dialog box shown in figure 4.19.

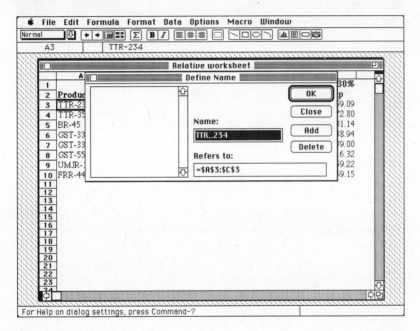

Fig. 4.19. *Range names assume absolute references in the Define Name dialog box.*

As you can see, the range reference contains dollar signs to make the reference absolute. Therefore, when you copy a formula that contains this range name, the range remains constant. Perhaps Excel makes these references absolute because named ranges are more likely to become unique blocks of data on the worksheet. In any event, you can remove the dollar signs from the reference if you want the range to be relative.

You probably do not want to remove all dollar signs from range name references. More likely, you may remove only the row or column dollar signs. This way, the range name can adjust when you copy it across or down the worksheet (see fig. 4.20).

```
 File  Edit  Formula  Format  Data  Options  Macro  Window
Normal │⊡│ ← → │▦▦│ Σ │B│I│ ≡≡≡ □ ╲□○╮ ▦▤□▦
  F12    │        =SUM(prices)
```

	A	B	C	D	E	F	G
1		Markup Amt:	140%		Markup Amt:	130%	
2	Product	Price	Markup	Product	Price	Markup	
3	TTR-234	20.00	28.00	LR-30	45.45	59.09	
4	TTR-355	15.50	21.70	LR-1818	56.00	72.80	
5	BR-45	34.40	48.16	FRR-342	23.95	31.14	
6	GST-3389	29.95	41.93	LRP-111	29.95	38.94	
7	GST-3390	35.50	49.70	M-390	30.00	39.00	
8	GST-5505	40.00	56.00	M-323	12.55	16.32	
9	UMJR-100	29.95	41.93	M-3434	45.55	59.22	
10	FRR-445	31.45	44.03	SSB-2	45.50	59.15	
11							
12			331.95			375.635	
13							
14							
15							
16							
17							
18							
19							
20							
21							
22							

```
Ready
```

Fig. 4.20. Copying a range name (PRICES) that specifies a relative range reference (C$3:C$10).

The range name PRICES refers to the range reference C$3:C$10—a result of selecting range C3:C10, choosing the Define Name command from the Formula menu, and removing the dollar signs from the column C references. The name PRICES is given to the resulting range reference. The formula =SUM(PRICES) is entered into cell C12 and copied to cell F12. Because of the relative nature of the range reference, the range PRICES refers to two different ranges in the two formulas—each one relative to its column.

Caution: Be careful when you use relative range names; you later may need to use the range in a different situation that requires an absolute reference. If you forget that the range name is relative, you may end up with the wrong result. For this reason, you may consider naming the range a second time with a completely absolute reference. Of course, you should use a different name.

Switching Range References

When you choose the Apply Names command from the Formula menu to switch range references with their respective range names, Excel offers several options relating to the references. You can choose the options in the Apply Names dialog box or click on the Options button to view more options (see fig. 4.21). The following sections discuss each option.

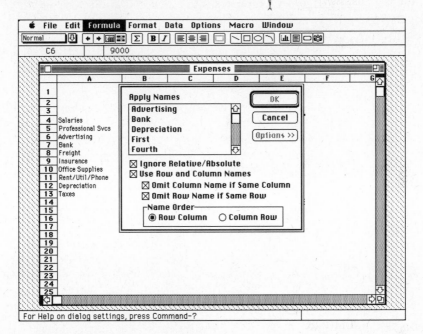

Fig. 4.21. *The Apply Names dialog box.*

These options help you save time when you must apply many names or relative ranges throughout the worksheet. Use these options with care; they can be tricky.

Ignore Relative/Absolute

When you check this box, Excel replaces all ranges that match the range name reference, regardless of relative and absolute status. If the range name PRICES applies to the range $C$3:$C$10, for example, applying the name PRICES with the Ignore Relative/Absolute option replaces the references

$C$3:$C$10

C3:C10

$C3:$C10

$C3:C10

and so on, with the range name PRICES. Note that when the name PRICES appears instead of these references, the name still applies to the range $C$3:$C$10. Therefore, you may be converting some references. Doing so does not change the results of those formulas, but may affect the way those formulas can be copied for future needs. To replace references that match the range name exactly, remove the check mark from the Ignore Relative/Absolute box before applying the name.

You generally use the Ignore Relative/Absolute option if you have referred to a particular range several times, when each time requires a different type of relativity because of its position and the way you copied the range. By applying a range name with the Ignore Relative/Absolute option checked, you can return all these variations to a single norm.

Use Row and Column Names

Figure 4.20 shows why you may need a relative range reference in a formula. Basically, you want a relative range reference (or a name that applies to a relative reference) if you need to copy the formula and adjust the range reference to correspond to each copy.

That method is great if you remember to create the range name before copying the formula, as in figure 4.20. What if you already copied a formula, however, but want to change the range references to range names (see fig. 4.22)?

This figure shows a typical row of totals created by copying one formula across the row using the Fill Right command. Now suppose that you want to change the range reference in each of these cells to the name PRICES. How do you apply this name in one step when each range reference varies? First, define the range B$3:B$10 as the name PRICES, using the Define Name command from the Formula menu. (Note the removal of the columnar dollar signs.) Next, choose Apply Names from the Formula menu and select the name PRICES from the list. Before clicking on the Apply button, remove the check mark from the Use Row and Column Names box.

When you apply this column-relative range name to a series of column-relative formulas without the Use Row and Column Names box checked,

Excel applies the name to each of the respective formulas and keeps the range references column-relative. Although each formula simply refers to the range PRICES, that range is different for each of the formulas.

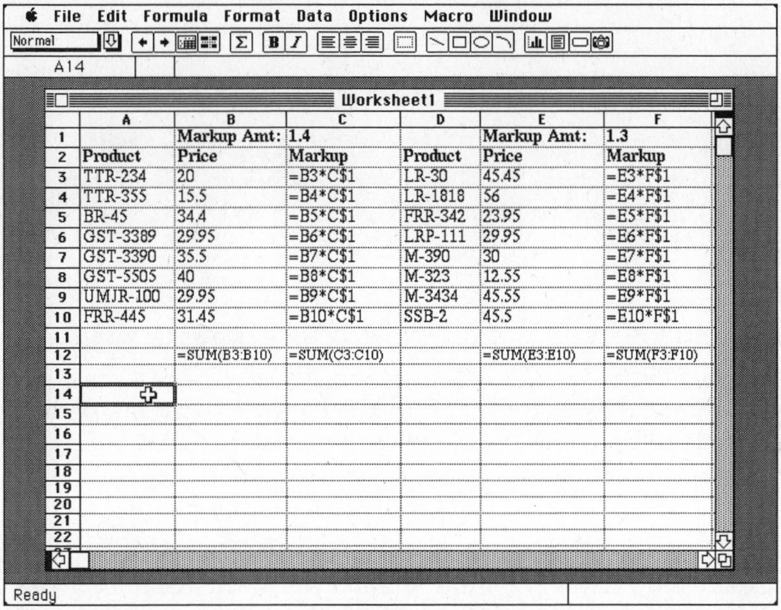

	A	B	C	D	E	F
1		Markup Amt:	1.4		Markup Amt:	1.3
2	Product	Price	Markup	Product	Price	Markup
3	TTR-234	20	=B3*C$1	LR-30	45.45	=E3*F$1
4	TTR-355	15.5	=B4*C$1	LR-1818	56	=E4*F$1
5	BR-45	34.4	=B5*C$1	FRR-342	23.95	=E5*F$1
6	GST-3389	29.95	=B6*C$1	LRP-111	29.95	=E6*F$1
7	GST-3390	35.5	=B7*C$1	M-390	30	=E7*F$1
8	GST-5505	40	=B8*C$1	M-323	12.55	=E8*F$1
9	UMJR-100	29.95	=B9*C$1	M-3434	45.55	=E9*F$1
10	FRR-445	31.45	=B10*C$1	SSB-2	45.5	=E10*F$1
11						
12		=SUM(B3:B10)	=SUM(C3:C10)		=SUM(E3:E10)	=SUM(F3:F10)

Fig. 4.22. *A worksheet with totals copied across the bottoms of columns.*

Omit Column Name if Same Column

When this box is checked (the default setting), Excel ignores the row reference if the reference contains the same column but a different row as the name reference.

This option is intended to save time when you apply names to complex worksheets that have several versions of the range reference. You may find that leaving this option checked and repeating the Apply Names command, if necessary, is easier.

Omit Row Name if Same Row

When this box is checked (the default setting), Excel ignores the column reference if the reference contains the same row but a different column as the name reference.

This option is intended to save time when you apply names to complex worksheets that have several versions of the range reference. You may find that leaving this option checked and repeating the Apply Names command, if necessary, is easier.

Name Order

The Name Order buttons determine whether the row or column name reference appears first when you apply names to a new range. The name order should make little difference.

Using the Ditto Commands

Another way to copy information into a worksheet is to use one of the ditto commands, which, as the name suggests, duplicate information from above. Just as you may use a ditto mark on a piece of paper to indicate "same as above," you can use the ditto marks in a worksheet for the same purpose.

Excel provides two ditto commands. The first is ⌘-' (single quotation mark or apostrophe), which inserts the *formula* contained in the cell above the active cell. This command is similar to Fill Down but is intended to speed up data entry. If the pointer is in a cell that you want to contain the same information as the cell above, just press ⌘-'. This command duplicates formulas as though they were absolute references.

The second ditto command, ⌘-" (double quotation mark), duplicates the *value* from the cell above. If the cell above contains a formula, only its value is duplicated. Suppose that cell A1 contains the formula =B5+25 and its result is 35. Using the command ⌘-" in cell A2 places the value 35 into cell A2.

Using Undo

When you change a worksheet using such methods as copying and moving, you can use the Undo command if you change your mind about an action. If you choose the Undo command from the Edit menu immediately after performing an action, Excel pretends the action never happened and restores the worksheet to the way it was before you performed the last action. You must use the command immediately after the action you want to undo, however, because this command works only on the most recent action you perform. Note that Excel may not be able to Undo every action. The command says `Can't Undo` in these cases.

You also can undo an action that you just undid. If, for example, you move a block of cells and decide that you didn't want to do that, you can immediately select Undo to put those cells back in their original position. Then, if you decide that you *did* want to perform that action after all, you can select Undo again to move the cells once again. You can undo an Undo action as long as you select Undo *immediately* after you select Undo the first time.

Using Advanced Copying and Pasting Procedures

Excel provides a special set of options for copying and pasting information available through the Paste Special command on the Edit menu (or by pressing ⌘-Shift-V). Use this command to paste various types of information into the worksheet while performing mathematical operations on that information. You can paste information into existing data, for example, and add the two values to get the sum. You can consolidate data on worksheets in this way.

After you copy or cut information, you can paste the data into a worksheet by using the Paste command or the Paste Special command from the Edit menu. If you choose the Paste Special command, the dialog box in figure 4.23 appears, displaying your options.

The Paste options on the left side of the box paste one of four parts of the copied cell or cells: the formula or data entered into the cell; the value produced by any formula (that is, the displayed result in the cell); the format of the cell (such as boldface type or special fonts); or the note attached to the cell. The Operation options perform calculations when you paste information on top of existing information. (These operations don't apply if you choose Formats or Notes from the Paste options, since the operation does not apply when no numeric data exists.) The following sections discuss the benefits of each option in the Paste Special dialog box.

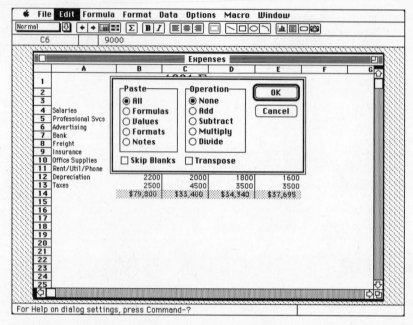

Fig. 4.23. *The Paste Special dialog box.*

> *Note:* If you choose the Paste option All and the Operation option None, the Paste Special command acts exactly like the standard Paste command.

Converting Formulas to Values

You may need to copy information without using the formulas that produce the values. In other words, you may want to copy only the numbers produced by the formulas—not the formulas themselves. You can copy information, stripping away the formulas, by pasting with the Paste Special command and choosing the Values option from the dialog box. The result is the value of the original cell—not the formula that produced the value.

You can convert a formula to its value without using the Paste Special command: first position the pointer on the cell containing the formula, and then highlight the entire formula in the formula bar by dragging the mouse over the formula (see fig. 4.24).

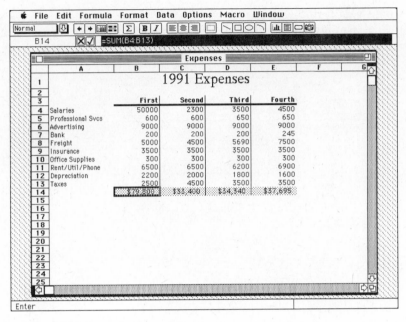

Fig. 4.24. *Highlighting the formula in a cell.*

Now select the Calculate command from the Formula menu or press ⌘-= (equal sign) to calculate the formula. Excel calculates the highlighted formula and replaces the formula with its value. Press Return to enter this value into the cell.

An advantage of using this technique is that you can convert any portion of a formula to its value by highlighting the portion that you want to convert. Figure 4.25 shows an example of converting a segment of a formula. To convert the segment A1+100 to its value, for example, highlight the segment and press ⌘-=.

The advantage of using the Paste Special command to convert values is that the command can convert several cells at once. Also, you can paste the values to cells other than those containing the formulas themselves.

Copying Cell Formats

When you apply several formatting options to worksheet data, you may want to copy those formats to other areas of the worksheet, rather than reselect each option repeatedly. You can apply all Format options to unformatted data by copying them from other cells. First, copy the cell containing the formats you want, using the Copy command from the Edit menu. Next, move to the destination cell(s) and paste the information, using the Paste Special command. Select the Formats option from the dialog box.

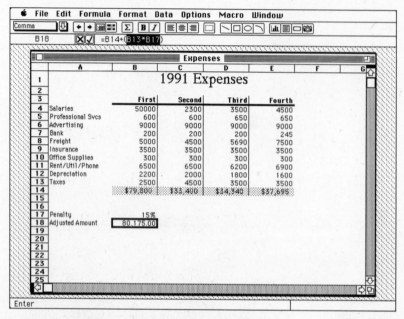

Fig. 4.25. *Converting a segment of a formula.*

Only the format of the copied information applies to the destination cell. If the destination cell already contains information, that information is formatted accordingly.

You can copy the information from one cell to another and ignore all formatting by selecting the Formulas option from the Paste Special dialog box. This option copies only the formula of a cell (or the value of a cell, if no formula exists).

If you copy a range of cells containing one or more formatted blank cells, Excel normally pastes the blank cell with the other cells. You can tell Excel to eliminate the formats used in the blank cells, however, by checking the Skip Blanks option in the Paste Special dialog box. Cell formats are discussed in Chapter 5, including other methods for duplication formats.

Copying Notes

You can attach a note or message to any cell in the worksheet by choosing the Note command from the Formula menu. To copy that note from one cell to another, use the Paste Special command with the Notes option. Only the note attached to the cell is copied to the destination cell. If the destination cell already contains a note, that note is replaced by the copied note.

For more information about creating notes, see Chapter 8.

Combining Values when Pasting

On occasion, you may want to copy information from one location and paste the information into an area that already contains data. Instead of replacing the information in the destination range, you may want to add the two values. Suppose that your worksheet contains a list of merchandise prices that you entered as constant values. This worksheet may look like figure 4.26.

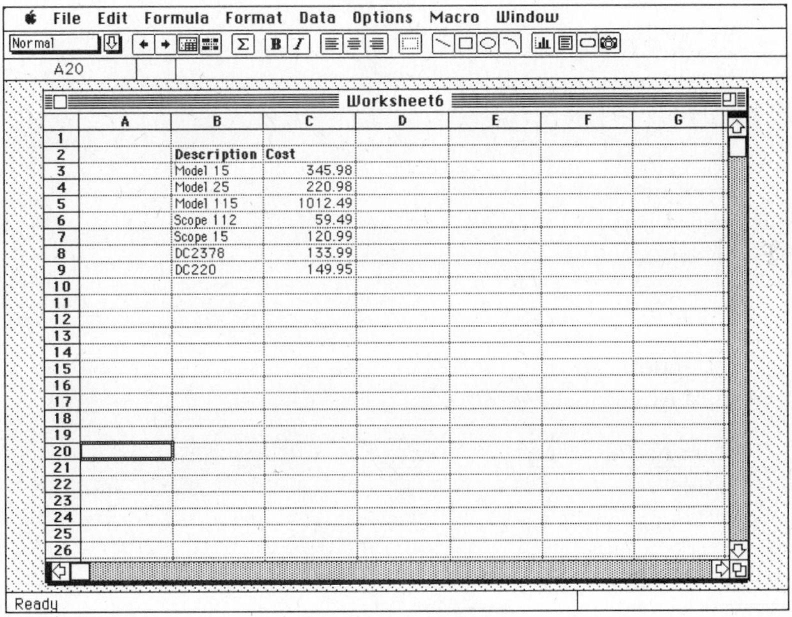

Fig. 4.26. *A worksheet showing merchandise prices.*

Now suppose that you want to adjust the cost of each item to reflect the added three-percent cost of acquiring the merchandise, thus raising the cost of each item. Because the values are typed into the worksheet, you normally must retype each item with the extra three percent added. If you have many items, however, that procedure can be time-consuming. Instead, you can enter 1.03 into an empty cell on the worksheet.

In this case, the value 1.03 is entered in the anticipation of multiplying it with the cost figures, resulting in a three percent increase. You type *103%* (including the percent symbol) to get the same value in the cell.

Next, copy the new figure using the Copy command from the Edit menu. Highlight the destination cells (the column of cost figures); paste the information using the Paste Special command from the Edit menu. Then choose the Multiply option from the Paste Special dialog box and press Return. This procedure multiplies the existing value of the cells by 1.03. Figure 4.27 shows the result.

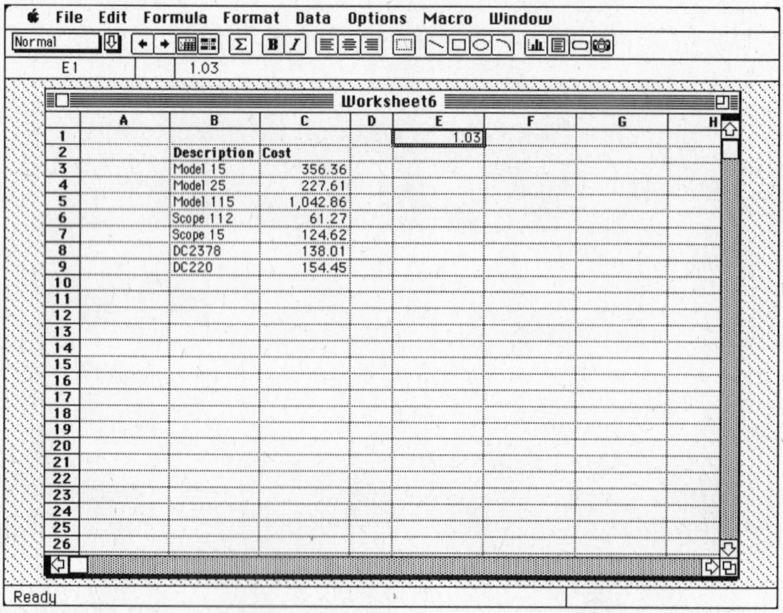

Fig. 4.27. *Using the Multiply option in the Paste Special dialog box.*

Of course, you can add, subtract, multiply, or divide information when pasting. This feature is especially useful for consolidating several similar worksheets into one master worksheet. Suppose that each of five salespeople in an organization uses a specially designed worksheet for tracking sales figures. At the end of each month, the sales manager can copy totals from each of the worksheets and paste them into the master worksheet. He or she can then find the grand total of the worksheets by using the Add option from the Paste Special dialog box. Often, consolidating worksheets in this fashion eliminates the need for worksheet linking. See Chapter 8 for more information on consolidating worksheets.

Skipping Blank Cells

When you copy a range that contains blank cells, Excel pastes those blanks with the other cells when you use the Paste Special command from the Edit menu. When you use the mathematical operations to consolidate information, blank cells may be treated as values of zero—causing unwanted calculations.

You can check the Skip Blanks option to make Excel skip those cells when pasting. A blank placeholder is copied in the same cell position, but Excel does not apply the Paste Special options to it.

Transposing Ranges

The final option in the Paste Special dialog box is Transpose, which changes the row and column order of the original data. Suppose that you copy a range of cells four columns wide by two rows high. If you paste the range by using the Transpose option, two columns wide by four rows high results—the rows and columns are transposed. Figure 4.28 shows an example of a transposed range.

Note: The Transpose option works with any of the other options in the dialog box. You can transpose the cells, for example, while pasting only the formats of cells.

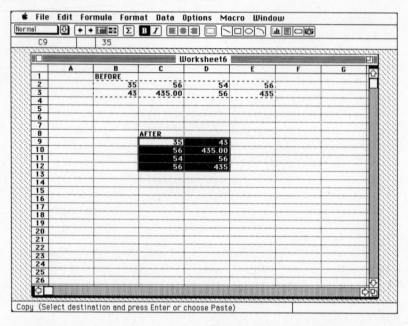

Fig. 4.28. *Using the Transpose option in the Paste Special dialog box.*

Summary

This chapter covered everything you need to know about editing information in a worksheet. Basic editing involves changing information in cells, but you also can use Excel's special tools to change data, formulas, and references throughout the worksheet. The following is a list of points to remember:

- To edit information in a cell, select the cell and use the mouse to change information in the formula bar.

- You can accept your changes by pressing Return; you can reject them by clicking in the Cancel box.

- Choose the Replace command from the Formula menu to change formulas or text throughout the worksheet.

- Use the Clear command from the Edit menu to remove information from cells.

- Use the Delete command from the Edit menu to remove cells, rows, or columns from the worksheet.

- Use the Insert command from the Edit menu to add cells, rows, or columns to the worksheet.

- Use the Cut command from the Edit menu to move data from one location to another.

- You can make a cell reference absolute by adding dollar signs to its row and column specifications, as in $C$1.

- Use the Paste Special command from the Edit menu to copy certain parts of a cell, such as the format or value (without the formula). You also can use Paste Special to consolidate information.

Chapter 5 shows you how to format the information in your worksheets. This formatting includes using fonts, numeric formats, type styles, and more.

Formatting Worksheets

This chapter shows you how to use Excel's formatting commands to improve the appearance of a worksheet. After learning how to change the widths of columns, the heights of rows, and other display aspects of the worksheet, you learn how to use fonts, type styles, and color (the use of color applies only to color systems). Finally, the chapter explains the various numeric formats and attributes available in the Format menu. Format menu options include those for setting the number of decimal places in numerals, showing dollar signs, and displaying negative numbers in parentheses.

With a few exceptions, formatting features apply to information that has been selected. In other words, to format information, you first must select the information and then select the formatting command. The data-selecting methods introduced in Chapter 3 will be useful in this chapter and throughout the book.

Aligning Information within a Cell

Whether a cell contains text, numbers, or dates, you can align the data horizontally within the cell's boundaries. Information can be left-aligned, right-aligned, or centered in the cell (see fig. 5.1).

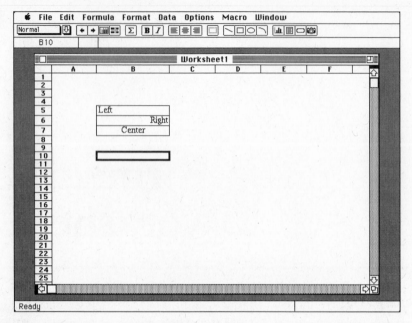

Fig. 5.1. *The three types of alignment.*

Normally, numbers and dates are right-aligned; text is left-aligned. You can change the default alignment, however. To do so, first select the cells you want to change; then click on one of the three alignment buttons in the Toolbar. You can change alignment at any time.

For more alignment options, you can use an alternative method. First, highlight the cells you want to align and then select the Alignment option from the Format menu. The dialog box shown in figure 5.2 appears.

Choose the alignment option you want and press Return. A description of each option follows:

General	Aligns numbers with the right side and text with the left side. This is the default alignment for the worksheet.
Left	Aligns data with the left side of the cell.
Right	Aligns data with the right side of the cell.
Center	Centers data in the cell.
Fill	Fills each cell with the information already in it. In other words, the information in the cell is repeated until the cell is full. This option can be useful for creating visual effects with special fonts and symbols.

Wrap Text   Splits long text entries onto two or more lines within a cell. The cell's height is adjusted to accommodate the extra lines. You may want to adjust the cell's width. You also can align this wrapped text with the Left, Right, or Center options. When you are typing an entry into a wrapped cell, press Option-Return to wrap the text onto the next line. You can use ⌘- Return when editing a wrapped entry to control where Excel wraps the lines.

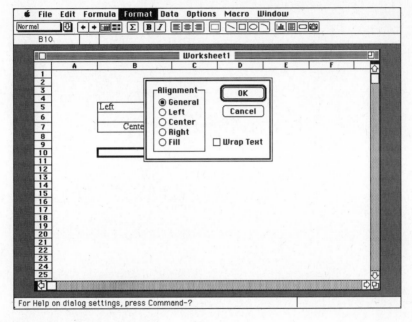

Fig. 5.2. The Alignment options.

Figure 5.3 shows some examples of these alignment options. Notice that you can wrap numeric entries also. These were created by pressing Option-Return between each number and applying right alignment to the cells.

Creating Columns of Text

Although Excel is not a word processor, it has a special feature for creating columns of text. You can use this feature to add explanatory information to a worksheet or chart. Using the font capabilities described later, you can make this column of information an attractive addition to the worksheet. Excel takes rows of text entered into the worksheet and merges them into a specified portion of the original area, making the width of each row uniform. This specified portion includes the far left column of the text plus any additional columns.

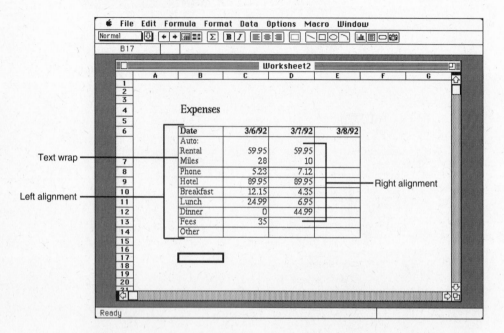

Fig. 5.3. *Examples of alignment in a worksheet, including wrapped text.*

To use the column-creating feature, move to the area of the worksheet where you want the column and follow these steps:

1. Type each line of each paragraph in a separate row, pressing the down arrow or Return between the lines. For now it's okay if the information spills into several columns. Just make sure that you begin each line in the column that you will use for the final information. Leave a blank row to separate paragraphs. The result will look like figure 5.4.

2. Select a range of cells containing the first column of the text entered in step 1, plus as many rows or columns as you want to fill with the text. If you're unsure of how many rows to select, select as many as possible that do not interfere with other information. You can select more than one column to achieve the width you want; just make sure that you select the first column. Figure 5.5 shows a selected range.

   Notice that the selected area includes the first column of the entered text plus one more column for extra width.

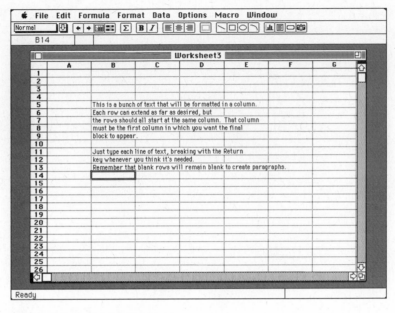

Fig. 5.4. *Preparing a column of text.*

3. Select the Justify command from the Format menu. The text will fit into the selected range, as shown in figure 5.6.

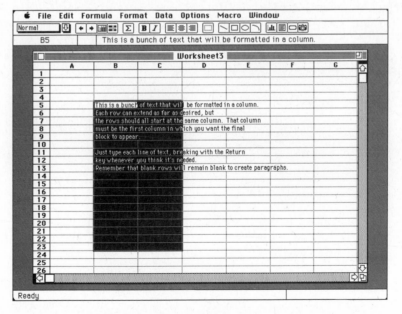

Fig. 5.5. *The selected area to be filled by columnar text.*

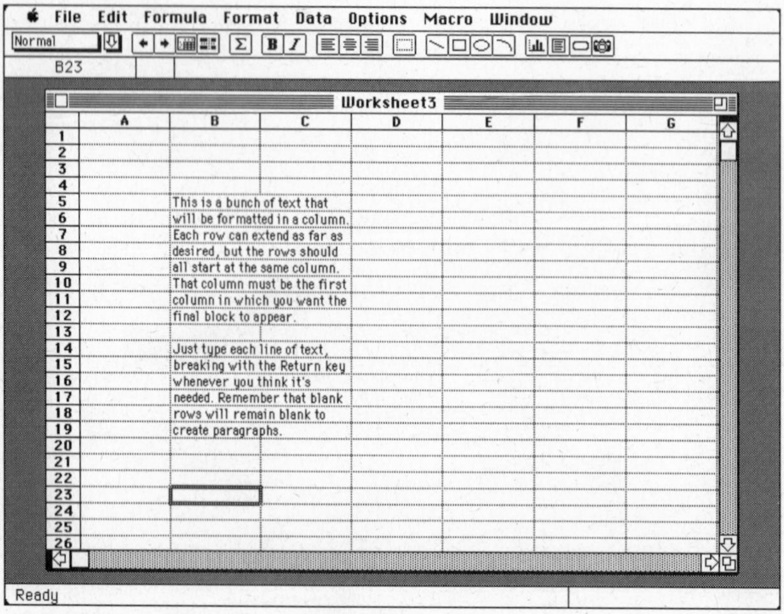

Fig. 5.6. The finished column of text.

Excel merges the lines of text and fits them into the specified range. Blank rows are used to separate paragraphs. If there is too much text to fit into the selected range, Excel presents a dialog box asking whether it can go beyond the range you selected. Click on OK if you want Excel to proceed. Note, however, that clicking on OK can cause information beyond the selected range to be overwritten. If you do not click on OK, Excel truncates the text at the bottom of the range.

> *Note:* Another way to add columns of text to a worksheet is to use a text box. Chapter 11 describes text boxes and worksheet graphics in detail.

Formatting with Boldface and Italic

Excel gives you several type styles for your worksheet data, but you can apply two styles quickly and easily by using the Toolbar. Just select the cell or range that you want to format and click on the Boldface (B) and/or Italic (I) tool in the Toolbar. The data is formatted immediately.

When you move the pointer to a cell that has been formatted with boldface or italics, the tools on the Toolbar are highlighted to indicate that the format is active in that cell (see fig. 5.7)

To remove boldface from your data, highlight the cell or range and click on the boldface tool again to remove the format. You can do the same with italics.

> ***Note:*** Boldface and italics are just two of many type styles available in Excel. They are included as tools on the Toolbar because they are used so commonly. Other formats appear in the Font list that appears when you select the Format Font command.

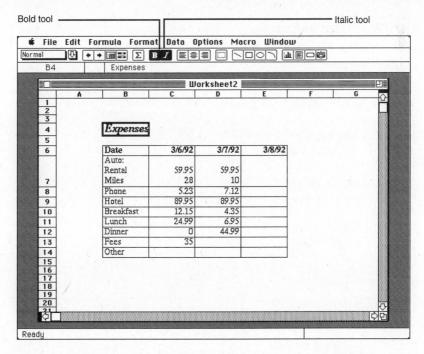

Fig. 5.7. *Move the pointer to a boldface or italic cell and the tools become highlighted in the Toolbar to reflect the format.*

Formatting with Fonts, Sizes, Styles, and Colors

One of the most dramatic things you can do to control the appearance of information is to employ fonts, sizes, styles, and colors. Like many Macintosh applications, Excel accesses fonts installed in your system file. The type and number of fonts available on your system depends on the way you set up the system. Excel supports PostScript fonts as well as bit-mapped (or screen) fonts. For more information on using fonts with your Macintosh, refer to your computer's documentation.

You can change the fonts used in individual cells throughout the worksheet by selecting the cells to be changed and then choosing the Font option from the Format menu. Available fonts and their sizes are shown in the Font dialog box that appears (see figure 5.8).

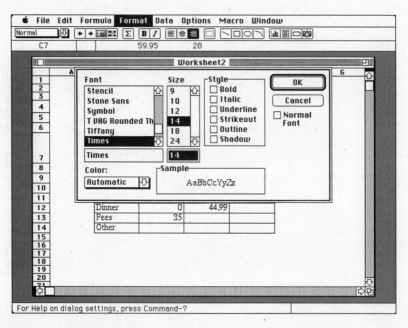

Fig. 5.8. *The Font dialog box.*

From the lists, select the font and size you want. If you check the Normal Font box, Excel applies the standard font to your selected cells. This feature is useful for removing font changes from cells and returning them to the current standard. Unless you change it, the standard font is 10-point Helvetica.

You can specify a point size that is not listed; just enter the custom size (up to size 409) in the box directly under the list of available sizes, as shown in figure 5.9. (Normally, the box shows the size selected in the list.)

Press Tab until you select the entry box for the point size; then type the size you want. In addition to changing fonts and sizes, you can select one or more of the character styles shown in the Style box. Examples of these styles follow:

Bold

Italic

Underline

~~Strikeout~~

Outline

Shadow

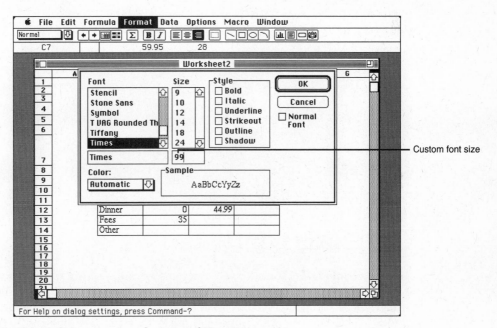

Fig. 5.9. *Defining a custom font size of 99 points.*

You also can choose a color for the selected data. Just click on the color list and choose from the available colors. You have 16 colors from which to choose. Chapter 11 tells you how to change these to any 13 colors you want by using the color palette. You can choose the Automatic option to tell Excel to select the font's color.

> ### Tip: Applying Colors Conditionally
> Excel enables you to specify the color of data based on the value of that data. You can make all values over 100 appear in blue, for example, and all other values in red. This is done by using custom number formats, described in "Designing Custom Number Formats," later in this chapter.

Excel automatically adjusts the heights and widths of cells to accommodate your font and size selection. This automatic adjustment, however, applies only to rows and columns that have not been adjusted individually or that have been set to the standard width. If Excel does not adjust a column's width or a row's height to accommodate the selected font, you already have set a width or height for the column or row. You can change the width and height as described in "Changing Column Widths" and "Changing Row Heights," later in this chapter.

The font change you make with the Format Font command applies only to selected cells. Refer to Chapter 3 for information about selecting rows, columns, or the entire worksheet to help you make font changes.

> ### Tip: Preformatting Blank Cells
> You can select a range consisting of blank cells and then set the font, size, and style for that range. When you enter information into those cells, it appears in the format specified. This arrangement can save you some time. The ability to preformat blank cells is especially useful for formatting a row or column that will contain headings, for example.

Copying Formats

A useful technique is to format cells containing formulas before you copy the formulas to other cells. If the formula is formatted when you copy it, the formatting gets copied also. In other words, the Copy and Paste commands duplicate everything about a cell, including its format. Taking advantage of this feature can save you much time when you design worksheets.

You may want to copy only a formula, however, and not the formatting applied to it. Or you may want to copy only the formatting you have applied to a cell so that you don't have to repeat the formatting process. In these cases, copy the original cell by using the Copy command; then use the Paste Special command from the Edit menu. The Paste Special dialog box appears (see fig. 5.10).

The default settings in the Paste Special dialog box paste all information from the original cell. The All option includes the formula (if any), its value, the cell's format, and any notes attached to the cell (cell notes are explained in Chapter 8). You can control what Excel pastes into the new cell by choosing one of the Paste options from this dialog box (other than All). Select the Formulas option to avoid getting the format of the original cell. Select the Formats option to paste only the format of the original—not the data itself. You can format existing data by copying a cell containing the format you want and then pasting the cell to the range of cells that are unformatted. Use the Formats option when pasting. The Values option converts formulas to their values when you paste, and the Notes option pastes cell notes from the copied cell. Selecting one of the Operation options enables you to perform mathematical computations when pasting copied data. For details, see Chapter 8.

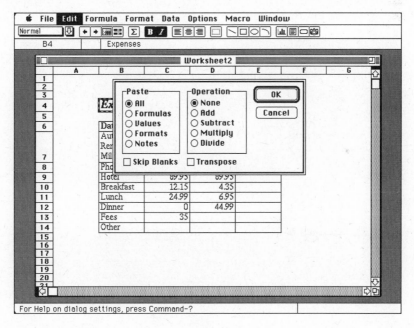

***Fig. 5.10.** The Paste Special dialog box.*

Changing Column Widths

When a label or value does not fit into a cell, you probably will want to expand the width of the cell so that the information fits. To change the width of a cell, you must change the entire column in which the cell appears. First, place the pointer on the line between the column you are changing and the column to the right. Find this line within the column title area at the top of the worksheet. After you place the pointer on the line, the pointer shape changes (see figure 5.11).

Now click and drag the mouse to the right or left to increase or decrease the width of the column. If you double-click on the column line, Excel adjusts the column width to best fit the data in the column. You can expand a column's width to the full size of the worksheet window.

Another way to adjust column widths is to enter a width value by choosing the Column Width command from the Format menu. The Column Width dialog box appears (see fig. 5.12).

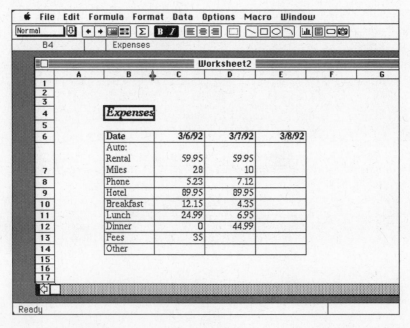

Fig. 5.11. Expanding column widths. The pointer shape changes when it passes over the column divider.

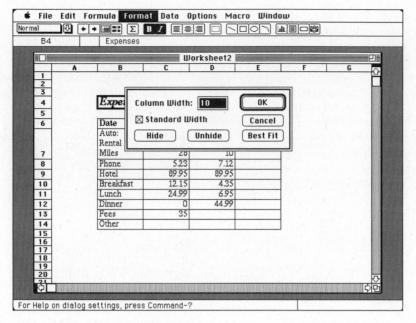

Fig. 5.12. *The Column Width dialog box.*

Enter the number of characters for the column and press Return. The actual width of the column varies depending on the active font. That is, 10 characters in Times may be smaller than 10 characters in Helvetica. Excel uses the width of the numeral 8 to measure columns.

You can return a column to the worksheet's standard width by checking the Standard Width option on the Column Width dialog box and pressing Return. Unless you have changed it, the standard width is the original width of all worksheet cells.

> **Tip: Changing the Widths of Several Columns at Once**
> You can change the widths of several columns at one time by select-ing all the columns before selecting the Column Width command. To change all the columns in a worksheet, select the entire worksheet. See Chapter 3 for information on selecting columns.

Hiding and Unhiding Columns

Other options in the Column Width dialog box include the Hide and Unhide buttons. Clicking the Hide button is the same as entering a width of 0; it makes the column too narrow to be seen. Although the information in the column still is used in the worksheet (that is, formulas remain intact), the column will be invisible, and you may notice a skip in the sequence of column letters at the top of the screen. Hidden columns can be useful in worksheets that contain sensitive data, such as payroll amounts, markup amounts, commission rates, and so on.

To expand a column that has been hidden, select the column to the left of the hidden column; then drag across to the column to the right of the hidden column. If column C is hidden, for example, drag across columns B and D. Next, choose the Column Width command from the Format menu and click the Unhide button.

Using the Best Fit Option

The Best Fit button from the Column Width box tells Excel to choose a column width that best fits the data in the column. If you have selected a block of cells, Excel adjusts the column widths to best fit the data in that block. Instead, you may want to select an entire column and then choose the Best Fit option. This ensures that all entries in the column are taken into account. A quick way to apply the Best Fit option is to double-click on the line to the right of the column heading.

Changing Row Heights

You can change the height of a row the same way that you alter the width of a column. This ability can be useful when you design forms and tables in Excel. Just select the rows you want and then choose the Row Height command from the Format menu; the dialog box shown in figure 5.13 appears.

You can specify a row height by entering a specific point size. The Row Height Hide and Unhide buttons work identically to the Column Width Hide and Unhide buttons. Refer to "Changing Column Widths," earlier in this chapter, for details.

As with column widths, you can adjust row heights by moving the mouse to the row headings on the left side of the screen and dragging the separation line between the row you want to change and the row below it. If you double-click on the separation line, Excel adjusts the row height to fit the tallest font in the row.

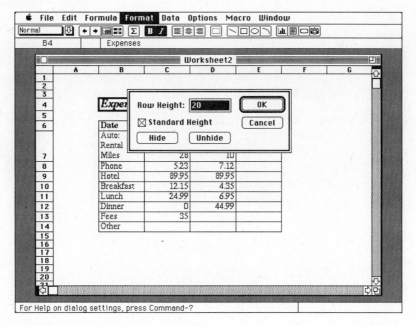

Fig. 5.13. *The Row Height dialog box.*

Adding Borders, Boxes, and Shading

The Border command on the Format menu enables you to add borders and boxes to the worksheet and to shade areas of the worksheet for emphasis. Excel can draw lines around any cell or range to create a box or add single lines along the top, bottom, or sides of information. You can draw a line on any of the four sides of a cell. You can create a grid pattern by adding lines to all four sides of several cells. Figure 5.14 shows various lines added to the sides of worksheet cells, as well as the shading pattern.

You don't have to draw these line segments one cell at a time. You can create lines for an entire range at once. Just select the range you want; then use the Format Border command. In addition, Excel provides an option for creating a box around a specified range, so you don't have to draw lines on the top, bottom, left, and right sides individually.

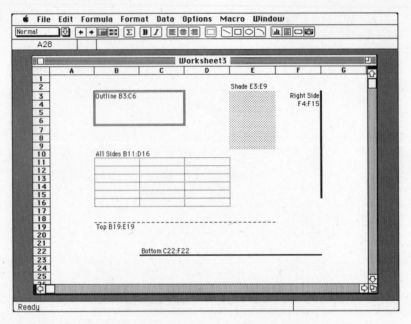

Fig. 5.14. *Using the Border command to draw lines and boxes.*

To use the Border command, follow these steps:

1. Select the cell or range to which you want to add a line (or lines).

2. Choose the Border command from the Format menu.

    The Border dialog box appears (see fig. 5.15).

3. Select Left, Right, Top, or Bottom to draw a line on the respective side of each selected cell. (Simply click on the word or the box beside it.) Select Outline to draw a box around the range. Select Shade to fill in the range with a gray pattern. Excel displays the line style inside the selected border options.

    Choosing the Outline option differs from selecting all four sides (left, right, top, and bottom). Selecting all four sides with a range of cells produces a grid pattern in which all cells in the range contain borders. The Outline option produces an outline around the range without outlining each cell.

4. Click on the line style you want immediately after choosing the border position for the line. You can select a line type for each position. Remember that you must select the position first, and then the style will apply to it. Click on the line position again to remove the line from that position.

5. Click on OK to close the box and apply the changes.

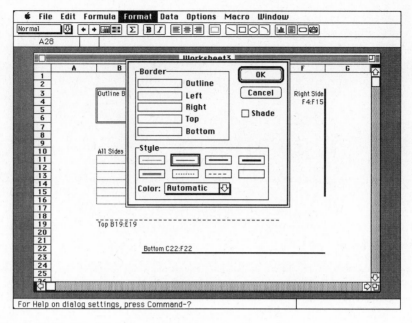

Fig. 5.15. *The Border command options.*

In addition to offering locations for the borders, the Border dialog box offers many types of lines. You can mix and match these types on a single cell or range.

Note: The shade option applies a standard gray shade to the worksheet. Your data will be readable on this shaded area—especially if it is formatted in boldface. You also can apply shades to cells using the method described in the next section, "Applying Patterns."

Tip: Using a Quick Outline Command
Because Outline is the most common of the border commands, Excel provides a keyboard shortcut to outline a range. Just select the range and then press ⌘-Option-O to add the outline. You can change the dimensions of a box by manipulating row heights and column widths.

Normally, placing a line on the bottom of one cell produces the same result as placing a line on the top of the cell below that first cell. Moving to cell A1 and using the Bottom option, for example, is the same as moving to cell A2 and using the Top option. Page breaks, however, may affect the appearance of these lines on the printed page. If a line appears on the bottom edge of a cell and a page break occurs just after that cell, the first page will display the line and the second page will not. Alternatively, if a line appears on the top edge of a cell and that cell marks the top of a new page, the new page will contain the line and the preceding page will not.

Applying Patterns

The Shade option in the Border dialog box applies a standard gray shade to your worksheet. This shade is useful for highlighting information. If you print your worksheet in high resolution, you will be able to read your worksheet data on top of this light gray shade—even if the information is hardly readable on-screen.

Excel provides many more shades for your worksheet cells. By using the Format Patterns command, you can apply numerous patterns to your worksheet, including up to 16 colors. You also can mix colors and patterns for more effects. Figure 5.16 shows some examples.

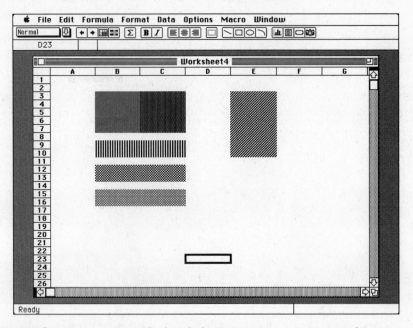

Fig. 5.16. Some patterns applied with the Format Patterns command.

Following are the steps for applying these special patterns to your worksheet:

1. Highlight the cell or range you want on the worksheet.

2. Select the Patterns command from the Format menu. The Cell Shading dialog box appears (see fig. 5.17).

3. Select the pattern you want, as well as its foreground and background colors from the lists provided. Click on OK when finished.

On a color system, the Foreground option controls the color of the pattern lines; the Background option controls the color on which those lines are shown. Sometimes a simple reversal of foreground and background colors can produce dramatically different effects. You also can choose the Solid Pattern option (first pattern in the list), which gives you a solid version of the foreground color you selected. You can click the None button to display only the background color with no pattern at all. Both methods are useful for applying a color with no pattern.

Some of these color and pattern choices can overshadow the data that appears in the cells. After you apply a pattern and color to the cell, you can use the Format Font command to change the color of the data in the cell. Sometimes a light text color on a dark cell pattern gives an attractive reversal effect.

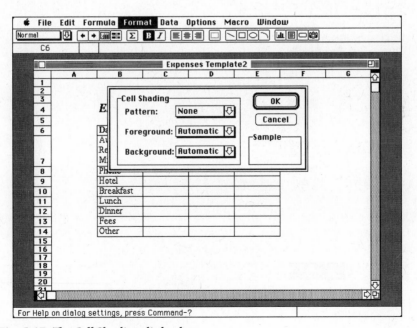

Fig. 5.17. *The Cell Shading dialog box.*

Tip: Getting More Colors

Excel enables you to replace the 16 colors in the foreground and background lists with 16 of your own creations. You can create custom colors by mixing primary colors. You can create up to 16 million different colors this way. Use the Color Palette command in the Options menu to mix your own colors and substitute them for the existing 16 colors. Details about mixing colors appear in Chapter 10.

Tip: Using Black-and-White Systems

If you are using a black-and-white system, the only really useful colors in the background and foreground lists are black and white. Some of the color choices give you gray patterns; however, most of these colors have no effect. If you use a black foreground color with the solid pattern, the result will cover up any data in the cells. Therefore, you should make the data white by using the Format Font command. This provides a reversal effect for your worksheet data.

Tip: Adjusting Line Thickness

To apply bold, thick lines to your worksheet, use the Format Border Shade command or the Format Patterns command to apply a shade to a row of cells (or portion of a row). Change the row height to control the thickness of the line. You can use the Format Border Shade command with color shading to apply colored lines to your worksheet.

Changing the Display

One of the easiest ways to make a worksheet more readable is to change the way it is displayed on-screen. Besides enabling you to add your own display elements (such as borders), Excel enables you to remove or alter some of the built-in display elements (such as the worksheet grid lines). By manipulating these built-in display features, you can make your worksheets more readable on-screen.

Options to control the built-in display elements of a worksheet appear in two places: the Options Display command (figure 5.18) and the Options Workspace command (figure 5.19). Note that the Options Display choices affect only the current worksheet and are saved with the worksheet. The Options Workspace choices are global settings for Excel and affect all worksheets equally.

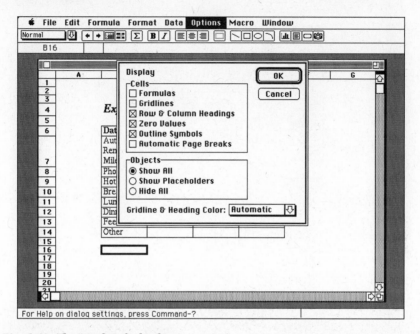

Fig. 5.18. *The Display dialog box.*

The options in the Display Options dialog box follow:

- *Formulas:* Controls whether cells display the results of formulas or the formulas themselves. Displaying the formulas can be useful when you create complex worksheets. If you display formulas by checking the Formula option, printouts from those worksheets will show formulas rather than results. On macro sheets, this option is set to display formulas.

- *Gridlines:* Displays or removes the gridlines that appear on the worksheet. Gridlines help you visualize the different rows and columns, but you may find them distracting. Removing the gridlines can make it easier to see your colors, shades, and borders.

- *Row & Column Headings:* Displays or removes the column and row headings from the worksheet. Although these are useful when you need to reference cells, you may want the extra worksheet space. Removing row and column headings also can be useful for custom worksheet applications.

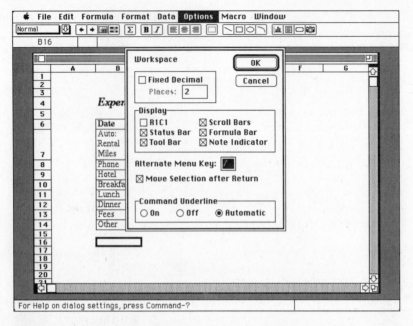

Fig. 5.19. The Workspace dialog box.

Note: The Gridlines and Row & Column Headings options affect only the screen view. Printouts may still display the grid lines and headings. To remove these elements from printouts, use the Page Setup options from the File menu (see Chapter 9).

- *Zero Values:* Causes values of zero to be displayed or hidden. Worksheets can look neater when values of zero are suppressed. Eliminating zeros is useful especially in forms. To blank out values of zero, uncheck the Zero Values option in the Display Options dialog box. This option affects the entire worksheet and ignores your selected range. To hide zero values in specific cells or portions of the worksheet, use a custom number format, as described in "Custom Number Formats," later in this chapter. Custom number formats give you even more control over values of zero, such as enabling you to display them in red. If you use a custom number format to control the display of zeros, the Zero Values option will not affect cells that use the custom format.

- *Outline Symbols:* Displays or removes the outline symbols that appear when you apply outlining to your worksheets. For details about outlining and this option, see Chapter 8.

- *Automatic Page Breaks:* Shows or hides Excel's automatic page break markers. You may want to view these markers when you use Excel's automatic page breaks. For information on page breaks—automatic and custom—see Chapter 9.

- *Show All:* Displays all objects as you create them.

- *Show Placeholders:* Displays objects without detail. Showing placeholders can save memory while basically showing you where objects are located.

- *Hide All:* Hides all objects.

- *Gridline & Heading Color:* Changes the color of the worksheet gridline and headings. Select one of the 16 colors in the list. The Automatic option tells Excel to choose a color.

The options in the Workspace Options dialog box follow:

- *Fixed Decimal Places:* Sets the number of decimal places for all worksheet numbers. This is useful for accounting and financial applications to make the 10-key pad automatically add decimal places. Cells formatted individually with conflicting number formats are not affected by this setting.

- *R1C1:* Activates the R1C1-style headings when checked or the A1-style headings when unchecked.

- *Status Bar:* Displays or removes the status bar from the screen. This does not give you extra space for your worksheet, but merely "blanks out" the status bar so that you cannot see its messages. This option is useful for custom applications.

- *Toolbar:* Displays or removes the Toolbar.

- *Scroll Bars:* Displays or removes the scroll bars. If you remove the scroll bars, you must use keyboard actions to move around the worksheet.

- *Formula Bar:* Displays or removes the formula bar. If you remove the formula bar, you cannot edit the information in the worksheet cells.

- *Note Indicator:* Displays or removes the note indicators that appear in the corners of cells that contain notes. For more information about notes, see Chapter 8.

- *Alternate Menu Key:* Determines the Alternate Menu Activation key. You can use this key instead of the Alt key for activating the menus.

- *Move Selection after Return:* Changes the effect of the Return key. If you check this option, pressing Return moves the pointer down one cell. If you do not check this option, pressing Return leaves the pointer in place.

- *Command Underline:* Displays (On) or hides (Off) the underlined characters that appear for each menu, option, and dialog box option. These are keyboard-action keys. You can choose Automatic to make the underlined characters appear only when you activate a menu or dialog box using the keyboard.

Tip: Hiding Multiple Elements at Once

You may find that you prefer working with several worksheet elements hidden. But constantly returning to the Options menu and selecting the appropriate commands can be tedious. This procedure is especially annoying when you hide the same elements for many worksheets. Try using a macro to show or hide a preset combination of elements. One macro can show the elements, and another can hide them. See Chapter 19 on macros.

Figures 5.20 and 5.21 show a worksheet before and after applying some of these options.

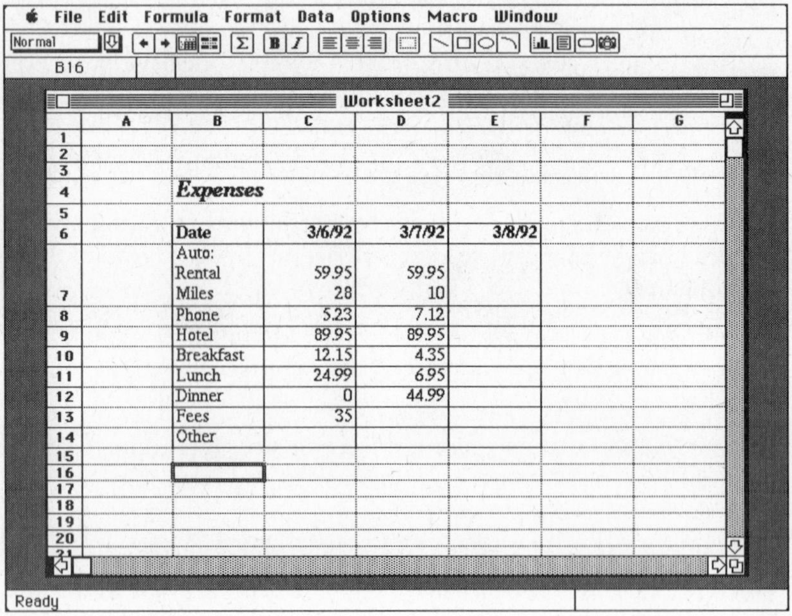

Fig. 5.20. A worksheet before applying some options in the Display Options and Workspace Options dialog boxes.

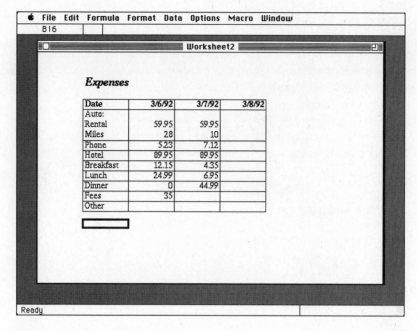

Fig. 5.21. *A worksheet after applying some options in the Display Options and Workspace Options dialog boxes.*

Using Number Formats

Number formats affect the way numbers appear on the worksheet. A number that normally appears as

3984.3

can be displayed in many ways, based on the particular format used. Here are some of the ways the number can appear in Excel:

3984

3984.30

3,984.30

$3984.30

398400%

Number formats control special symbols that apply to numbers, the display of negatives, and the display of zeros. Excel provides several formats for numbers, but also enables you to design custom formats.

Built-In Number Formats

To select one of the predesigned formats, first select the cell or range you want to format; then choose the Number option from the Format menu. The dialog box shown in figure 5.22 appears.

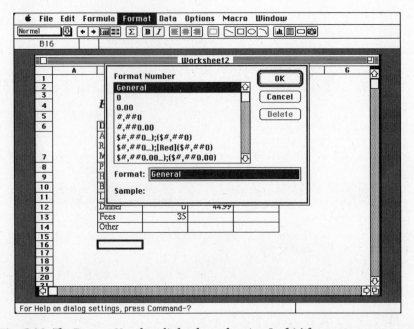

Fig. 5.22. The Format Number dialog box, showing 8 of 14 formats.

The dialog box lists all predesigned number, date, and time formats. Use the scroll bar to see more formats. Table 5.1 shows the effect of each built-in number format on a positive number, a negative number, and the number zero.

Table 5.1
Built-In Number Formats

Format	Positive	Negative	Zero
General	3595.5	–3595.5	0
0	3596	–3596	0
0.00	3595.50	–3595.50	0.00
#,##0	3,596	–3,596	0

Format	Positive	Negative	Zero
#.##0.00	3,595.50	–3,595.50	0.00
$#,##0 ;($#,##0)	$3,596	($3,596)	$0
$#,##0 ;[RED] ($#,##0)	$3,596	($3,596)*	$0
$#,##0.00 ;($#,##0.00)	$3,595.50	($3,595.50)	$0.00
$#,##0.00 ;[RED] ($#,##0.00)	$3,595.50	($3,595.50)	*$0.00
0%	359550%	–359550%	0%
0.00%	359550.00%	–359550.00%	0.00%
0.00E+00	3.60E+03	–3.60E+03	0.00E+00
# ?/?	3595 1/2	–3595 1/2	0
# ??/??	3595 1/2	–3595 1/2	0**

Displays in red.

** *Uses different alignment than the # ?/? format.*

You can access some of these formats by using the preexisting cell styles in the Toolbar Styles list. Click on the Toolbar Styles list on the far right side of the Toolbar to reveal the following existing styles:

Currency	$#,##0; ($#,##0)
Comma	#,##0
Normal	General
Percent	0%

Just highlight the range you want and select one of these cell styles. The data is formatted quickly and easily. Excel also provides keyboard shortcuts for some of these built-in formats. Just select the cell or range you want and then use one of the following commands:

Command	Format
⌘-Option-~	General
⌘-Option-!	0.00
⌘-Option-$	$#,##0; ($#,##0)
⌘-Option-%	0%
⌘-Option-^	0.00E+00

> **Tip: Formatting with Data Entry**
> In Chapter 3 you learned that you can apply certain number formats just by the way you enter values. If you include a dollar sign, you apply the Currency format. If you include a percent sign, you apply the Percent format. See Chapter 3 for more details.

> **Tip: Formatting the Entire Worksheet**
> Remember that formatting applies to selected ranges. You can select rows, columns, or the entire worksheet. The format you select applies to all selected cells. You may want to format an entire worksheet if most cells use the format that you specify.

You may have noticed that some of the formats round numbers. This rounding effect is for display purposes only. Excel remembers the full value in the cell and uses the full value for all calculations. You can change the true number to the rounded version, however, by using the ROUND function. Such a change affects all calculations based on the number. See Chapter 6 for more information on the ROUND function.

You can convert all numbers to their displayed formats. Excel's Options Calculation Precision as Displayed command converts numbers from their true values (values entered) to their formatted values (displayed values). Be careful when using this command; Excel permanently changes the values. Of course, because the values match the display, you no longer need the number formats. Therefore, Excel applies the format 0.00 to all worksheet numbers after you convert them.

Custom Number Formats

Although the built-in number formats are useful, you may need to create a custom format at times. Using a custom number format enables you to deal with positive and negative numbers in many ways. In addition, you can add any text or symbol to a number format (such as *lbs* or £). Custom formats also give you control over colors used for positive numbers, negative numbers, zeros, and symbols. Finally, Excel stores custom formats with your worksheet, so they become a permanent part of your application.

To create a custom number format, select the cell or range that you want to format. Then select the Number option from the Format menu and enter your custom format into the Format field. If this field already contains a format (that is, the one selected in the list), just erase the entry and begin a new format. When entering your format, follow these rules:

- *Rule 1: Use the number-formatting symbols discussed later in this section to specify the format.* Number formats use these symbols to indicate the various elements of a number. The symbols include # to represent a number, 0.00 to represent the treatment of zeros, and [RED] to indicate color. You have seen these and other symbols used in the built-in formats, but Excel provides many more symbols to use in custom formats.

- *Rule 2: Combine the symbols into three groups, separated by semicolons.* Each group represents a different element of a number. The first group controls positive numbers; the second group controls negative numbers; the third group controls zeros. Using these three groups, you can format all types of numbers. You can display positive numbers in blue; negative numbers in red, surrounded by the brackets < and >; and zeros in green. The custom format may appear as follows:

  [BLUE]#;[RED]"<"#">";[GREEN]#

Notice that the three groups of symbols are separated by semicolons. If you leave any of the three groups blank, the appropriate type of number will be hidden. To make values of zero blank (hidden) in the above example, use this variation:

  [BLUE]#;[RED]"<"#">";

Notice that the third group (after the second semicolon) is empty. Be sure to specify three separate groups by including two semicolons—even if a group is blank. (If you're wondering why all the built-in formats do not use three groups, see rule 3.)

- *Rule 3: You can break Rule 2, in some cases.* To save time when creating certain formats, you can include only one or two groups of symbols. If you include only one group of symbols (no semicolons will be present), then the format applies to positive numbers, negative numbers, and zeros in the same way. If you use two groups (one semicolon), then the first group applies to positive numbers and zeros and the second group applies to negative numbers. This practice is not the same as leaving groups blank by including the semicolon with no symbols after it. The following is an illustration of the various groupings:

  format if positive; format if negative; format if zero

  format if positive or zero; format if negative

  format for all numbers

The following is a list of the symbols you can use in each group of your number format. You can combine any of these symbols for various effects:

- *0 (Zero):* Indicates any numeric digit. If 0 appears on the left side of a decimal point (or with no decimal point), you do not need to repeat the symbol to indicate the number of digits allowed. In other words, if the number entered is larger (more digits), Excel displays it anyway. If the number you enter has fewer digits than the number of repeated 0 symbols, however, Excel displays the extra zeros. Suppose that you enter the following as the number format:

  00000

  If you type the number *1*, Excel displays 00001. If you type the number *8398727*, Excel displays 8398727.

  If the symbol 0 appears on the right side of a decimal point, Excel rounds the number if it exceeds the indicated length. If the number you enter has fewer digits than the indicated length, however, Excel includes extra zeros to match the indicated length. Suppose that you enter the following as the number format:

  .000

  If you type the number *.55*, Excel displays .550. If you type *.4568*, Excel displays .457.

- *# (Number Sign):* Indicates any numeric digit. This symbol is similar to the 0 symbol, but numbers that have fewer digits than specified with this symbol appear as you enter them. Consider the following format:

  ##.##

  If you enter 150.629, Excel displays 150.63 (as if you had used the 0 symbol). If you enter 3.5, however, Excel displays 3.5 (inserting no extra zeros to fill the spaces).

  It's a good idea to include at least one zero to the left of the decimal point, as in the following:

  #0.##

  If you entered .3, for example, it now would appear as 0.3, showing the leading zero.

- *.(Period):* Indicates a decimal point. The placement of this symbol among the # and 0 symbols determines the number of digits displayed on either side of the decimal point. Be sure that at least one zero appears on the left side of the decimal point.

- **?** *(Question Mark):* Indicates any numeric digit. This symbol is similar to the 0 symbol, but it substitutes spaces for insignificant zeros. The 0 placeholder displays zeros. The question mark displays numbers without trailing zeros while maintaining decimal alignment. The format ?.?? results in these entries:

You Type	Excel Displays
5.67	5.67
345.40	345.4
459.00	459.
9.90	9.9
120.330	120.33

- **%** *(Percent Sign):* Indicates a percentage. Excel converts the entry to a percentage by multiplying by 100 and adding the percent character. You should combine this symbol with the # or 0 symbol to specify digits, as in the following example:

  0%

  The format 0% is one of Excel's built-in formats. If you enter *.016*, Excel displays 2%.

- **,** *(Comma):* Indicates separation of thousands. Inserting a comma between # or 0 symbols causes Excel to include commas in all appropriate places of a number. The format

  #,##0

  is a standard comma format. If you type *3892*, for example, Excel displays 3,892. If you type *3892782*, Excel displays 3,892,782.

Note: As explained in Chapter 2, you cannot enter commas when you type numeric values. Doing so converts them to labels.

- **E– E+ e– e+:** Displays numbers in scientific notation. Excel converts all zeros that follow these symbols into scientific notation. The E+ and e+ symbols use a plus sign for positive and negative exponents. Here are some examples:

Number	Format = 0.0e+00	Format = 0.0e–00
78678	7.9e+04	7.9e04
–78678	–7.9e+04	–7.9e04

- *$ – + ( ) / : (space):* Appear as part of the number format. Their position in the number is relative to their position among the # and 0 characters. For example, the format

    $(#0.00)

displays numbers in parentheses and with a dollar sign preceding the number, as in $(123.00). You can use the format ###–#### for phone numbers or (###) ###–#### to handle area codes. Try ###–##–#### for Social Security numbers. Use a standard space character to insert a space in the format. To use other characters in your number formats, read the following discussion of the backslash and "Text" parameters.

- *\ (Backslash) and "Text":* These parameters produce similar results. The backslash symbol enters any single character into a format at the location of the backslash. The actual character to insert into the format must appear immediately after the backslash:

    #0.00\¢

This format includes the ¢ character after all numbers. If you type *12.45*, for example, Excel displays 12.45¢. The backslash does not print.

The "Text" parameter enters any text into the format. Just enclose in quotation marks the text you want to insert:

    #0.00 "units";(##0.00);0.00

This format prints the word *units* after all positive numbers but not after negatives or zeros. If you enter *34*, for example, Excel displays

    34.00 units

Notice the space that appears in front of the text *units* in the custom format. As you can see, this space appears in the final formatted number.

- ** (Asterisk):* Causes the character that follows it to repeat until the cell is full. The repeated character will not replace other numbers or symbols used in the format.

Consider this example:

    #0.00* (space)

A space character appearing just after the asterisk causes the number to be left-justified in the cell. In this case, you can use an alignment option with better results. The asterisk is useful for many tasks, however. It often is used to align currency symbols with the left edge of the cell while leaving the numbers right-justified, as in this example:

$* #0.00

Notice the space character between the asterisk and the # symbol. If you type *45.95* in a cell formatted this way, Excel displays `$ 45.95`.

Be sure to include an asterisk in each group if you use more than one group.

- *_ (Underscore):* Creates predictable amounts of space in your formats. Enter this symbol followed by a character representing the amount of space you want to allow—that is, the character with the width you want to use. (Note that character widths vary depending on the active font.) The formatted cell will use this much space at the location of the symbol. You can use the format 0.00_%, for example, to add the width of one percent (%) character after the two decimal places. This format is used to align the number 34.24 in the following example:

   5%

   34.24

Normally, these values would align like this:

   5%

   34.24

- *[BLACK], [BLUE], [CYAN], [GREEN], [YELLOW], [MAGENTA], [RED], [WHITE], [COLOR n];* Indicates the respective color. Use one of these symbols to change the color of the number. You can use a different color in each group of the format. To display negative numbers in red, for example, enter this:

   #0.#;[RED]#0.#

[RED] does not have to be in uppercase letters. *[COLOR n]* indicates a color from the Options Color Palette list where *n* is the number of the color on the list (from 1 to 16). You can use this command to access your customized colors while still keeping the standard colors available. This gives you 32 possible colors for your worksheet data.

- *[< n], [> n], [= n], [<= n], [>= n], [<> n]:* Specifies a condition for custom formats. Use these symbols to apply custom formats under specified conditions. The conditions are as follows, where *n* is any value:

Symbol	*Condition*
[< *n*]	Less than *n*
[> *n*]	Greater than *n*
[= *n*]	Equal to *n*
[>= *n*]	Greater than or equal to *n*
[<= *n*]	Less than or equal to *n*
[<> *n*]	Does not equal *n*

You can create the following format, for example, which prints numbers greater than 100 in red, the number 100 in green, and numbers less than 100 in black:

[>100][RED]0.00;[=100][GREEN]0.00;[<100][BLACK]0.00

If you omit a condition in any section, Excel assumes the default conditions, which are

[>0];[=0];[<0]

Using Text Formats

Text formats enable you to display text in any color or add any character or phrase to the text you have entered. You can make any text entry (label) appear in blue, for example. Text formats are really just an extension of number formats. The text format is added as a fourth group of symbols to a number format.

If you add a third semicolon to a number format and then use one or more of the symbols after the semicolon (that is, if you create a fourth group), Excel uses the fourth group as the format for the cell if the entry is text. The following illustrates this setup:

format if positive; format if negative; format if zero; format if text

Most likely, if you expect a number to be entered into a particular cell, the text format is meaningless. You can use the text-format group, however, to display a message in case someone enters text into a cell intended for numbers:

#0.00;(#0.00);;[GREEN]"Please Enter a Number"

In this format, the third group (controlling the format of a zero value) is blank; zeros do not appear. The fourth section prints the message

```
Please Enter a Number
```

in green if someone makes a text entry. Because there is no text placeholder (discussed in the next section) in the format, the user's text entry does not appear. This result is what you want for cells in which the user is to enter only a number.

At times, however, you may want to accept a text entry and format it with a color or message. In this case, you need to use a text placeholder. The *text placeholder* is to text what the *#* and *0* symbols are to numbers. The following are descriptions of the text placeholder and other symbols available for the text-format group:

- @ *(At Sign):* Indicates text. You do not need to repeat this character to specify the length of the text entry. Whenever this character appears in the text-format group, any text entry is accepted. For example, the format

    ;;;[BLUE]@

    displays all numbers as blank but displays text in blue. If you enter "Hello", Excel displays Hello in blue. Notice that the number-formatting groups are blank. This arrangement is common when you expect the entry to be text. You can, however, format all four groups at once.

- *[BLACK], [BLUE], [CYAN], [GREEN], [YELLOW], [MAGENTA], [RED], [WHITE], [COLOR n]:* Indicates the respective color. Use one of these symbols to change the color of the text.

Using Date Formats

You can apply date formats to any number. Usually, however, you use date formats to alter the format that Excel automatically applies to a date. You can enter the date January 23, 1991, for example, in any of the following ways:

1/23/91

23 Jan 91

23 January 1991

January 91

23 January

23 Jan

1/23

1-23

Depending on how you entered the date, Excel formats your entry in one of four ways. These four date formats are the built-in formats shown when you select the Number command from the Format menu. Instead of using these four built-in formats, you also can design custom date formats.

Remember that these formats simply are displaying numbers as dates. The numbers represent the number of days elapsed since January 1, 1904. See Chapter 3 for details about dates and date serial numbers.

Built-In Date Formats

The four date formats appear directly under the number formats when you select the Number command from the Format menu. The date formats follow:

Format	Date Displayed
m/d/yy	1/23/91
d-mmm-yy	23-Jan-91
d-mmm	23-Jan
mmm-yy	Jan-91

When you enter a date that Excel recognizes as a date, Excel applies one of these formats. You can specify a particular format from this list. To select a format, choose the Number option from the Format menu and select one of the four date formats. You also can press ⌘-Option-$ to format a date in the d-mmm-yy style.

Custom Date Formats

Unlike number formats, date formats have no groupings. Just enter a single format for all dates, using the symbols in the list that follows. After you custom format a cell or range, if you enter a date that Excel recognizes as a date, Excel displays the entry in the specified format.

The following are the symbols available for dates:

Format	Effect
m	Indicates a single-digit numeral for the month name. If the month can be represented by a single digit (January through September), its number is displayed as a single digit. January, for example, appears as month 1 as opposed to month 01.
mm	Indicates a two-digit numeral for the month name. A single-digit month is displayed with a leading zero. January, for example, is displayed as month 01.
mmm	Indicates a three-letter abbreviation for the month name. January, for example, is displayed as Jan.
mmmm	Indicates a full-name month. January, for example, is displayed as January.
d	Indicates a single-digit numeral for the day. If the day can be represented by a single digit (days 1 through 9), it is displayed with only one digit (for example, 1 instead of 01).
dd	Indicates a two-digit numeral for the day. A single-digit day is displayed with a leading zero. The fifth of August, for example, is displayed as day 05.
ddd	Indicates a three-letter abbreviation for the day name. Sat, for example, is displayed for a day that falls on Saturday.
dddd	Indicates a full-name day. Saturday, for example, is displayed for a day that falls on Saturday.

You can combine these symbols in the date format in any way you want. Feel free to use two different day symbols to include both the day name and the number. Consider the following example:

    dddd,mmm d

If you enter 1/25/91, this format displays Friday, Jan 25. Notice that the format also includes a comma after the day-name symbol. You can include any of the formatting symbols listed for number formats, including color specifications. The format

    [Red] dddd,mmm d

for example, displays the date Friday, Jan 25 in red.

Using Time Formats

Excel formats numbers to represent time in much the same way that it formats numbers into dates. Time values represent the amount of time elapsed since midnight. You can apply time math, like date math, to values. To enter a valid time, you must enter the amount of time elapsed since midnight. The number .2967, for example, produces a valid time (7:07:14) when you format the number with one of the time formats. Instead of figuring the elapsed time value, however, just enter the time in one of the recognized ways. The following are various ways to enter the time 4:35:

16:35

4:35

4:35:15

16:35:15

4:35 pm

4:35 am

If you enter time values in one of these ways, Excel uses one of the built-in time formats to display your entry. Excel stores the time, however, as a value representing time elapsed. You also can specify a custom time format by using the special time-formatting symbols.

Built-In Time Formats

The built-in time formats, listed under the date formats in the Number command of the Format menu, are the following:

Format	Example
h:mm AM/PM	9:35 PM
h:mm:ss AM/PM	9:35:15 PM
h:mm	21:35
h:mm:ss	21:35:15
m/d/yy h:mm	1/23/91 21:35

Highlight the cell or range that you want to format and select the Number command from the Format menu. Then select one of the time formats listed. Notice that the last format includes the date and time. You also can press ⌘-Option-@ to format a time in the h:mm format.

Custom Time Formats

Custom time formats work much like custom date formats. You need enter only one group of symbols for all time values. The following are descriptions of the available symbols.

Format	Effect
h	Displays the hour as a numeral. If the hour has only one digit to the left of the colon, Excel displays only one digit before the colon (as in 1:00). If you don't specify an AM or PM symbol, the symbol h uses the 24-hour format.
hh	Displays the hour as a numeral. If the hour has only one digit to the left of the colon (as in 1:00), Excel adds a leading zero (01:00). If you don't specify an AM or PM symbol, the symbol hh uses the 24-hour format.
m	Displays the minutes as a numeral. If the minutes portion contains only one digit (as in 1:05), Excel displays only one digit (1:5).
mm	Displays the minutes as a numeral. If the minutes portion has only one digit (as in 1:05), Excel adds a leading zero (1:05).
s	Displays seconds as a numeral. If the seconds portion contains only one digit (as in 1:25:05), Excel displays only one digit (1:25:5).
ss	Displays seconds as a numeral. If the seconds portion has only one digit (as in 1:25:05), Excel adds a leading zero (1:25:05).
AM/PM or am/pm	When added to the time symbols listed earlier, the AM or PM symbol (or its lowercase equivalent) specifies the 12-hour format for time values. Times are labeled AM or am if before noon; times are labeled PM or pm if after noon.

Format	Effect
A/P or a/p	These symbols are the same as the AM/PM and am/pm symbols listed in the preceding section, except that only A, a, P, or p is displayed.

Managing Formats

After you create formats, you need a way to manage them; you need to be able to save, edit, delete, and clear your formats. This section discusses these topics.

Saving Formats

Excel saves custom number, date, and time formats with the worksheet. These custom formats appear in the dialog box list with all other formats (at the bottom of the list). To reuse a custom format, simply choose the Number command from the Format menu and select the custom format from the list.

To copy a custom number format to another worksheet, follow these steps:

1. From the original worksheet, select the Number command from the Format menu.

2. Click on the format you want. Its symbols should be highlighted in the Format box.

3. Press ⌘-C to copy the format.

4. Click on the Cancel button to close the dialog box.

5. Open the new or existing worksheet into which you want to copy this format.

6. Select the Number command from the Format menu.

7. Press ⌘-V to paste the format into the Format box.

8. Press Return.

Editing Formats

To save time when creating custom formats, try editing an existing format. Just use the standard editing commands in the Format box after clicking on the format that you want from the list (see Chapter 4 for more information). When you save the format, it does not replace the original format. In fact, there is no way to remove the built-in formats—you cannot even delete them.

Deleting Formats

To delete a custom format, select it from the Format Number dialog box. Then click on the Delete button. If information in the worksheet currently is formatted under the deleted format, Excel returns that information to the General format.

Clearing Formats

When you use the Cut or Delete commands in the Edit menu to remove information, Excel also removes the format from the original cells. Using the Clear command, however, gives you the option of what you want to clear. By selecting the Formats option available through the Clear command, you can remove only the formatting applied to a range—not the information. If you select the Formulas option, Excel leaves the formats intact but removes the information.

Using Format Styles

In "Using Number Formats," earlier in this chapter, you saw how Excel includes four common number formats in the Styles list located on the left side of the Toolbar. When you need one of these existing formats, you can select it easily from the Styles list. The real benefit of the Styles list, however, is to hold customized style sets that you can apply over and over by selecting the set (by name) from the list.

Excel saves custom styles with your worksheets; you can create as many custom styles as you want. If you have a group of formatting options that you apply over and over in your worksheet, add it to the Styles list. This makes it easy to repeat. Formatting options that are included in style sets include fonts, character styles, number formats, borders, and patterns.

To create a custom style, follow these steps:

1. Apply the font, style, border, number format, and pattern you want to any worksheet cell.

2. Place the pointer on the formatted cell and select the Format Style command.

3. Enter a name for the style in the space provided and click OK.

This procedure adds the style set to the Styles list in the Toolbar. You now can apply this style to other worksheet cells by choosing its name from the list or by selecting the Format Style command and choosing the style name from the list provided.

Another way to create a custom style is to choose the Format Style option and click on the Define button in the Style dialog box. Next, click to activate or deactivate the formatting choices for that style. (When an option is checked, it is active.) Enter a name for the style and click on OK. This does not actually apply the formatting to the worksheet—it just creates the style.

Editing Styles

To change an existing style, select the Format Style command and click on the Define button. Next, choose the style you want in the list provided and then edit the check-box items for that style.

Another way to change an existing style is to use the style on a cell, change the cell's formatting, and then reapply the style to the cell again. Follow these steps:

1. Apply the style to any worksheet cell by moving to the cell and formatting it with the style you want from the Styles list.

2. Change the formats in the cell by using menu options.

3. Move the pointer to the cell and apply the same style to the cell again (by selecting it from the Styles list). Because you changed the cell's format, Excel asks if you want to use it to update the style. Click on Yes to update the style or click on No to apply the old style back to the cell.

Defining the Normal Style

The Normal style is one of the existing sets. This style is special, however, because it controls the way the worksheet "normally" looks. In other words, it contains the default font, size, style, number format, border, and pattern selections for all worksheet cells that are not formatted manually.

You can change the Normal style as you change any other style, but doing so changes all the worksheet cells formatted with that style, which is all the worksheet cells not otherwise formatted. You can use this to alter the defaults for the worksheet.

> ### Tip: Normal Style Not Affecting all Cells?
> If the Normal style you establish does not affect all cells in the worksheet, you already have formatted some cells manually. To reapply the Normal style to all cells in the worksheet, select the entire worksheet by pressing ⌘- Shift-space bar or ⌘- A and choose the Normal style from the Styles list on the Toolbar.

Copying Styles

An easy way to copy styles from one worksheet to another is to copy an example of the style (that is, a formatted cell) to the new worksheet. Use that cell to create a new style in the new worksheet.

You also can merge all the styles from one worksheet into another at once. To do this, follow these steps:

1. Open the worksheet containing the styles and the worksheet to which you want these styles copied. Activate the destination worksheet.

2. In the destination worksheet, select the Format Style command.

3. Click on the Define button in the Format Style dialog box. Excel presents the Define options.

4. Click on the Merge button. Excel presents a list of open worksheets.

5. Double-click on the name of the worksheet containing the styles you want.

6. Click on Close to return to the worksheet.

Excel copies the styles to the active worksheet. If the active worksheet contains styles with conflicting names (that is, the same names as those being copied), Excel presents a warning before copying.

Using Worksheet Templates

Custom styles are useful tools for repeating formatting choices throughout a worksheet. You also may find the need to reuse all the formatting in an entire worksheet again. This formatting may include not only fonts, styles, borders, and patterns, but also headings, range names, column widths, and worksheet display changes. You may need to create monthly expense reports that contain the same basic formatting, for example. Each month you can erase the data in your previous report to start a new one, or you can create a template to serve as the starting point for each new worksheet. (All formatting options are saved with the template.) This template may look like figure 5.23.

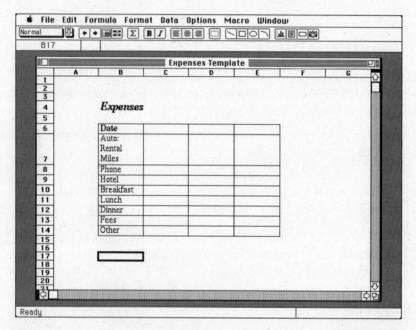

Fig. 5.23. *A template containing headings, styles, and other formatting choices.*

Here are some advantages to using templates:

- You cannot accidentally replace a template with a completed worksheet. Templates are distinctly different from the worksheets created from them. When you open a template, Excel presents a worksheet based on the template design. When you save this worksheet, you will not be replacing the template—even if you use the same name.

- When you create a worksheet based on a template, Excel considers this a new document even though it already may contain some data. When you save this worksheet for the first time, Excel asks you to name it.

- Templates make your work consistent. Worksheets created from templates will have many of the same attributes.

- If you save a template in the Excel start-up folder (located in the System folder), its name appears after you select the File New command. File New enables you to open a blank worksheet, a new chart, a new macro sheet, or a new copy of a template.

> ### Tip: Excel's Predesigned Templates
> Excel 3.0 comes with several predesigned templates ready for use. Check for these after you install the program. You can move these templates into the Excel start-up folder inside the System folder to make them available when you choose the New command from the File menu.

Creating Templates

You can create templates from existing worksheets or from scratch. The trick is in saving the worksheet. If you think that you will need to use the same basic worksheet structure over and over again, save the worksheet as a template. Remember that all formatting and data in the worksheet will become the template—so include only the information that you need for each copy of the worksheet.

To create a template, follow these steps:

1. Create a worksheet that contains only the elements you want to use over and over. You can start from an existing worksheet and remove its data—leaving only the framework.

2. Select the File Save As command.

3. Enter a name for the template in the space provided. Also, choose the folder in which you want to save the template. If possible, make this the Excel start-up folder inside the System folder.

4. Click on the Options button in the Save As dialog box.

5. Select the Template option from the File Formats list and click on OK.

Excel saves the template in the specified folder (preferably the Excel start-up folder). You now can use the template as a starting point for future worksheets. To use the template, select the New command from the File menu. The template's name appears in the File New dialog box where you can open it. If the template's name does not appear, then you did not save it in the Excel start-up folder. Use the File Open command to open the template worksheet as you would open any worksheet.

Editing Templates

When you create and save worksheets created from the template, Excel does not change the original template. To change the template itself, follow these steps:

1. Select the File Open command and locate the template in the list of files that appears in the dialog box.

2. Highlight the template's name and press ⌘-Return to open it.

3. Make any changes to the template and then choose File Save to resave it under the same name.

Summary

Formatting your worksheets is an important step in processing data: it helps you organize the information and present it properly. This chapter discussed ways you can format data in Excel, including specifying alignment, number formats, and column widths. The following are some important points covered in this chapter:

- You can align information by using the Format Alignment command or the alignment tools in the Toolbar.

- You can format each cell in a worksheet with a different font selected from the Format Font menu.

- To remove the formatting from a cell, choose the Clear command from the Edit menu.

- You can add borders to cells or ranges by choosing the Border command from the Format menu.

- You can choose the Workspace command from the Options menu to remove the scroll bars, status line, and formula bar from a worksheet.

- You can control the appearance of a number by choosing the Number command from the Format menu.

- You can save and name sets of formats so that you can use them over and over. Just apply the formats to a cell and then choose the Style command from the Format menu to name the set.

- The Normal style controls the defaults for the worksheet. Changing the Normal style set changes the entire worksheet.

Turn to Chapter 6, "Using Worksheet Functions," for a discussion of how to use the worksheet functions available in Excel.

6

Using Worksheet Functions

*F*unctions are self-contained routines that calculate values or perform operations. By referencing a function's name inside a formula, you can achieve its specific result. Some functions take the place of complex calculations; others perform special tasks that cannot be accomplished without the function.

Functions are the key to powerful worksheets. After the first spreadsheet products appeared, developers added function after function to provide more powerful calculation capabilities. You can divide Excel's worksheet functions into 11 categories: database, date/time, financial, information, logical, lookup, mathematical, matrix, statistical, text, and trigonometric. Each category contains many functions that enable you to manipulate data.

This chapter is a guide to all worksheet functions available in Excel. It can help you learn basic functions and then serve as a reference to functions you seldom use. You probably don't need to know all the Excel functions; most worksheets require only a few—often the same few functions.

The following list gives the functions in each category in the order in which they are discussed:

- Database

  DAVERAGE, DCOUNT, DCOUNTA, DGET, DMAX, DMIN, DPRODUCT, DSTDEV, DSTDEVP, DSUM, DVAR, DVARP

- Date/Time

  DATE, DATEVALUE, DAY, DAYS360, HOUR, MINUTE, MONTH, NOW, SECOND, TIME, TIMEVALUE, TODAY, WEEKDAY, YEAR

- Financial

  DDB, FV, IPMT, IRR, MIRR, NPER, NPV, PMT, PPMT, PV, RATE, SLN, SYD, VDB

- Information

  ADDRESS, AREAS, CELL, COLUMN, COLUMNS, INDIRECT, INFO, N, NA, OFFSET, ROW, ROWS, T, TYPE

- Logical

  AND, FALSE, IF, ISBLANK, ISERR, ISERROR, ISLOGICAL, ISNA, ISNONTEXT, ISNUMBER, ISREF, ISTEXT, NOT, OR, TRUE

- Lookup

  CHOOSE, HLOOKUP, INDEX, LOOKUP, MATCH, VLOOKUP

- Mathematical

  ABS, EXP, FACT, INT, LN, LOG, LOG10, MOD, PI, PRODUCT, RAND, ROUND, SIGN, SQRT, SUM, TRUNC

- Matrix

  MDTERM, MINVERSE, MMULT, SUMPRODUCT, TRANSPOSE

- Statistical

  AVERAGE, COUNT, COUNTA, GROWTH, LINEST, LOGEST, MAX, MEDIAN, MIN, STDEV, STDEVP, TREND, VAR, VARP

- Text

  CHAR, CLEAN, CODE, DOLLAR, EXACT, FIND, FIXED, LEFT, LEN, LOWER, MID, PROPER, REPLACE, REPT, RIGHT, SEARCH, SUBSTITUTE, TEXT, TRIM, UPPER, VALUE

- Trigonometric

  ACOS, ACOSH, ASIN, ASINH, ATAN, ATAN2, ATANH, COS, COSH, SIN, SINH, TAN, TANH

Displaying a List of Functions

You can display a list of Excel's functions at any time with the Paste Function command from the Formula menu. In fact, if you select a function from the list and click OK, Excel enters the function at the cursor position. To select a function, you can type the first letter of the function you want; Excel goes directly to the function beginning with that letter. To include the names of the arguments, check the Paste Arguments box. For an explanation of arguments, see "Understanding How Functions Work," later in this chapter.

Note: If custom functions are active, they appear in the Paste Function dialog box. See Chapter 19 for information about creating custom functions.

Learning Function Basics

Because worksheets are often similar, requiring similar types of calculations, a handful of functions may prove to be the most useful for you. The following functions are good to start with:

Function	Effect
AVERAGE	Calculates the average of a series of values
CHOOSE	Finds a value in an established set based on input
COUNT	Counts the number of entries in a series
DGET	Retrieves information from a database
HLOOKUP	Searches a horizontal table based on input
IF	Tests a condition and then branches based on the result
ISERR	Detects an error in the worksheet
ISNA	Detects an unavailable value
MAX	Finds the maximum value in a series
MIN	Finds the minimum value in a series
NOW	Calculates the current time using the internal clock
ROUND	Rounds a number
SUM	Calculates the sum of a series of values
TODAY	Calculates the current date using the internal clock
VLOOKUP	Searches a vertical table based on input

A working knowledge of these functions can take you a long way into worksheet construction. If you want, you can turn directly to the explanations of these functions and then examine some of the other functions available in Excel.

Understanding How Functions Work

To use functions properly, you must follow the syntax and cell-entry requirements for each function. Functions are composed of three basic parts: the function name, parentheses, and arguments, as in the function SUM(A1:A5,5).

You must enter all three parts of functions into cells or formulas. The parentheses are the same for all functions; they hold the *arguments*—the values on which the function operates—and come directly after the function name. Arguments differ greatly from function to function. The following sections describe some of the arguments you encounter in these functions.

> *Note:* Throughout this chapter, the arguments in the functions are given names to remind you of the kind of value required by the function. Often, a simple name such as *list*, *range*, or *value* is given, but sometimes a function has a more descriptive argument name, such as *lookup_range*. When an argument name consists of two words, the underline character (_) separates the two words to remind you that the name applies to a single argument. **Do not enter the underline when you use the function in your worksheets.** The following function, for example, contains two arguments, as the comma between them indicates:
>
> LOOKUP(*value,lookup_range*)

Using Range Arguments

A *range argument* can be any valid range of cells. This type of argument includes a range reference (such as A1:A5), a range name (such as SALES), or any other valid form of range reference, such as references constructed from formulas. You also can specify a multiple range as a range reference (A1:A5,C1:C5, for example) that contains the *union operator* (the comma). Because the range union operator also separates arguments in functions, however, you must enter multiple range references in a separate set of parentheses. Otherwise, Excel may think you have entered too many arguments. Consider these examples:

ROUND(A1:A5,G12,G15)

ROUND((A1:A5,G12),G15)

The ROUND function requires exactly two arguments, but the first function contains three. The second function contains only two arguments: the first argument includes the multiple range reference in the inner parentheses (A1:A5,G12); the second argument is G15. You also must use parentheses for *intersection operators* (ranges combined with the space operator). See Chapter 3 for more information about these operations.

You often can mix range references with values and range names. Whenever you include more than one argument or mix arguments, you must separate the arguments with commas, as the following example shows:

SUM(A5:A9,B5:B9,SALES,G5)

If you include range names in your functions, you must place single quotation marks around names containing spaces:

SUM('NET SALES')

> ### Tip: Entering Range References
> Chapter 3 showed you how to create formulas by pointing to cells instead of typing cell references. You can do the same for range references in functions. The SUM function, for example, adds the numbers in a range of cells. You can enter a range reference into a function in two ways: by typing the entire function and its range argument by hand, or by typing
>
> > SUM(
>
> and using the mouse to click the first cell in the range. Then, click and drag the pointer to the last cell in the range and press the close parenthesis key [)] to finish the function (or enter a comma to precede the next argument). Alternatively, you can click the first cell, enter a colon, and then click the last cell in the range.
>
> You also can use the cursor-movement keys to specify the range. You can indicate an entire column or row as a range reference by using the form A:A. (A:A indicates the entire column A; thus, the designation for row 5 would be 5:5.)

Using Value Arguments

A *value argument* may be a numeric value, a numeric expression, or a cell reference that contains a numeric value. In other words, anything that results in a number can serve as a value argument. A *numeric expression* is any formula or calculation resulting in a number, as in the following:

    SQRT(A5–40+(C5*3))

The expression A5–40+(C5*3) results in a single value that serves as the argument for the SQRT function. The SQRT function operates on the result of this expression; Excel calculates this result before acting on the function. A value also can be a range name applied to a single cell, as Chapter 3 describes.

Using List Arguments

A *list* is similar to a range argument, but it lists each cell reference or constant value, separated by commas. You often can use lists when you need a range reference, but you usually cannot substitute range references when a function requires a list. Each item in a list must be a numeric value or expression as described in the preceding section. Look at this example:

    SUM(A3,B3,B5,C24-10,45)

Notice that the fourth item is a numeric expression. You also can include a range as one of the items in a list. In a way, using a range by itself (as in SUM(A3:A10)) is simply specifying a list with only one item.

Using Text Arguments

Text is any label, text string, text expression, or cell reference containing a label or text expression. If you enter text directly into a function, you must surround it by quotation marks, as follows:

    LEN("Hello")

If you don't include the quotation marks, Excel assumes that you are entering a range name and looks for such a range. This situation usually results in an error.

The rule for using quotation marks applies even when text is part of a text expression:

> LEN("Hello"&"there")

You can enter a cell reference in a text argument, provided that the cell contains text or a text expression:

> LEN(A5)

Notice that the reference contains no quotation marks. Cell A5 must contain text or a text expression.

Converting Data for Functions

Functions require arguments in various forms. Your information or references must be in the proper form for the function you are using; therefore, you may have to convert data from one form to another. The function WEEKDAY(*date*), for example, tells you the day of the week for any given date. You must enter the *date* argument as a valid date serial number. Using a reference as the argument requires that the referenced cell contains the correct type of data:

> WEEKDAY(B5)

In this case, cell B5 must contain a valid date serial number. Thus, if the date in cell B5 is a text string, you must convert the text to a valid date before using it in the WEEKDAY function. You can use the DATEVALUE function to convert the text date to a date serial number.

The following is a list of the functions Excel provides for converting values to and from various forms:

Function	Converts
DATEVALUE	Text to a date
DOLLAR	Numbers to text in the currency format
TEXT	Numbers to text
TIMEVALUE	Text to a time
VALUE	Text to a value

To convert information, these functions must be able to decipher the original data. Converting text to a valid date serial number, for example, requires that the text look like a date.

In addition to converting values with these functions, you can include functions in formulas to create a desired result. You can create valid R1C1-style range references, for example, by concatenating column and row numbers with the letters R and C, as follows:

    +"R"&1&"C"&1

The values of 1 can be calculated with numeric expressions or cell references. Following are some useful functions for constructing arguments:

Function	Specifies
ADDRESS	Address of a reference
CELL	Information about a cell or its value
COLUMN	Column number of a cell
DATE	Date
DAY, MONTH, YEAR	Portions of a date
HOUR, MINUTE, SECOND	Portions of a time
OFFSET	Cell reference offset by another cell
ROW	Row number of a cell
TIME	Time
TYPE	Type of information in a cell

In addition to requiring arguments in specific forms, functions also return values in specific forms. Some functions return their results as numeric values; other functions return results as text strings. Therefore, sometimes you must stack several conversion functions together to get information into the form you want. The forms in which functions return their results are described throughout this chapter.

> **Note:** Macros also can be useful for converting values. See the macros listing in Appendix B for more information.

Using Functions in Formulas

You have seen how some functions can have formulas (expressions) as arguments. You also can include functions within other formulas and functions. The simplest is a function that is a formula by itself:

=SUM(A1:A5)

This function includes an equal sign, making it a valid formula for a cell. You also can include a function in a more complex formula:

=A4*SUM(A1:A5)

Similarly, you can use a function whenever a value is expected in another function. Just be sure the function returns an appropriate value for the function in which you are using it. The following is an example:

=SQRT(A4–SUM(A1:A5))

Inserting and Deleting within Ranges

A useful feature of range references is their capability to expand and contract to accommodate changes in the worksheet. Suppose that you enter the function =SUM(A1:A8) in cell A10 to add the range A1:A8. Later, you decide to insert a row above row 4, expanding the range to A1:A9. Excel automatically changes the range reference in the formula to read =SUM(A1:A9). Likewise, when you delete, copy, or move information, Excel adjusts the cell or range references.

Remember that the range adjusts only when the inserted or deleted cells are part of the range. If you are using the same function, =SUM(A1:A8), and you insert a row at row 1, the function changes to =SUM(A2:A9), indicating that the original range has moved down without changing in size.

Listing Excel Functions

The following sections describe Excel functions and provide examples of their uses.

Database Functions

Database functions apply to information found in a database. A *database* is a table of information in which the rows correspond to records and columns correspond to fields. The structure of an Excel database is discussed in Part III of this book (Chapters 14 through 16). The following sections do not provide details about how to set up an Excel database or the rules that apply to databases. Before you use these functions, you should have a general understanding of Excel databases.

The primary reason for setting up a database is to find or extract information according to specific criteria. When you establish *search criteria* for a database, the matching records that have the criteria in common become a subset of the entire database. The database functions enable you to perform statistical analyses of these database subsets. You can establish search criteria to find the subset and then make calculations on the results of the search. When dealing with a large block of information, using a database function is the only way to perform statistical analyses on particular groups.

The function of an Excel database, in a nutshell, is as follows. You normally set up a database by selecting the database block and designating it as the *database range*. Another range, called the *criteria range*, contains the criteria used to search the database range. When Excel performs a search, it highlights matching records or extracts them into an *extract range*.

Surprisingly, you don't need to set up a database range or criteria range in order to use these database functions. The arguments within the functions themselves specify the database range, criteria range, and information to return for the calculation. Because database functions are mirror images of statistical functions, this section does not include examples for each database function. Rather, it explains how to use these database functions properly.

The first function, DAVERAGE, includes a full explanation and example that applies to all the functions. For more information about the calculations being performed, refer to the statistical functions described earlier in this chapter.

DAVERAGE

The DAVERAGE function calculates the average of particular fields over a database subset determined by search criteria. The field used for the average is determined by an offset value; the database itself is determined by the database range. The syntax for DAVERAGE follows:

DAVERAGE(*range, field_offset, criteria*)

Range is the range of cells containing the database information; it should adhere to the guidelines for databases described in Chapter 14. The database range must include field names (column labels) over each column. You do not, however, have to establish this range as the database range with the Set Database command from the Data menu. In other words, the range can be any block of data that represents a database. If you do use a database that has been set with the Data Set Database command, you can simply enter the range name *database*, which Excel interprets as the currently set database range.

Field_offset is the field that serves as the operand for the DAVERAGE function; in this case, it is the field to be averaged across the database subset. This variable should be any number from 1 to the number of fields in the database, where 1 represents the first field, 2 represents the second, and so on.

Criteria is the range of cells containing the search criteria for the database. This reference should adhere to the rules for criteria ranges described in Chapter 14. Namely, the criteria range should contain required field names and search formulas beneath those names. This range does not have to be the criteria range currently set with the Set Criteria command from the Data menu. If you plan to use the current criteria range, however, you can enter the range name criteria as the criteria argument; Excel assumes the currently set criteria range.

Figure 6.1 shows an example of a database and the DAVERAGE function used to calculate the average of a subset of data.

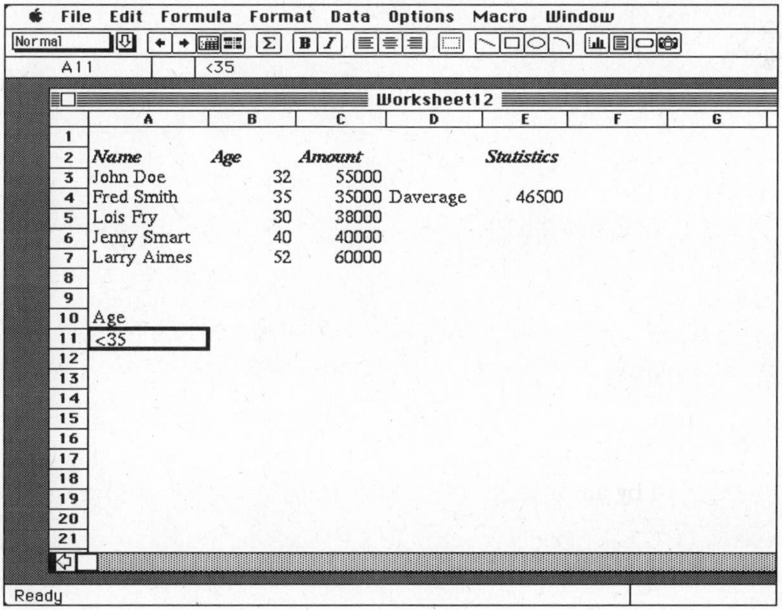

Fig. 6.1. *Using the DAVERAGE function.*

In the example, the database contained in the range A2:C7 holds the names, ages, and salary amounts of a small group of workers. The criteria range A10:A11 contains the formula <35, which establishes a subset of all workers under the age of 35. The DAVERAGE function is set up to calculate the average income of all workers under 35 when you specify the database range, the criteria range, and the offset value.

The offset value should point to the third column in the database, which contains the income figures. The third column's offset is 3. Therefore, the formula for the DAVERAGE function is as follows:

DAVERAGE(A2:C7,3,A10:A11)

Unless the database range or criteria range changes, you need not alter this formula to calculate other salary averages; simply enter new criteria for the search. You can, for example, find the average income of all workers who are 35 and over by changing the criteria formula to >=35. The DAVERAGE formula recalculates its value according to the new criteria.

> ### Tip: Naming Criteria Formulas
> If you commonly switch among several criteria formulas in the database criteria range, try naming each criteria formula with the Define Name command from the Formula menu. Then you can enter the appropriate criteria by typing the formula name in the correct cell of the criteria range (with an equal sign). The name may be easier to remember and enter than the criteria formula. In the example in figure 6.1, one formula may be "Income_Over_34" and the other "Income_Under_35".

DCOUNT, DCOUNTA

The DCOUNT function counts the number of records that match the criteria established for a database search. Only records containing numbers are counted. The DCOUNTA function counts database records and all matching records that are not blank. The syntax is the following:

DCOUNT(*range, field_offset, criteria*)

DCOUNTA(*range, field_offset, criteria*)

Range is the range of cells containing the database information; it should adhere to the rules for databases described in Chapter 14.

Field_offset is the field that serves as the operand for this function; in this case, the offset is insignificant because the function is counting the number of records that match the criteria, with no regard to any particular field. In fact, you can leave this argument out of the function. If you specify a field offset and some records do not have information in that field, those records are not counted.

Criteria is the range of cells containing the search criteria for the database. This reference should adhere to the rules for criteria ranges described in Chapter 14.

Figure 6.2 shows the same sample worksheet given in figure 6.1, with the DCOUNT function added.

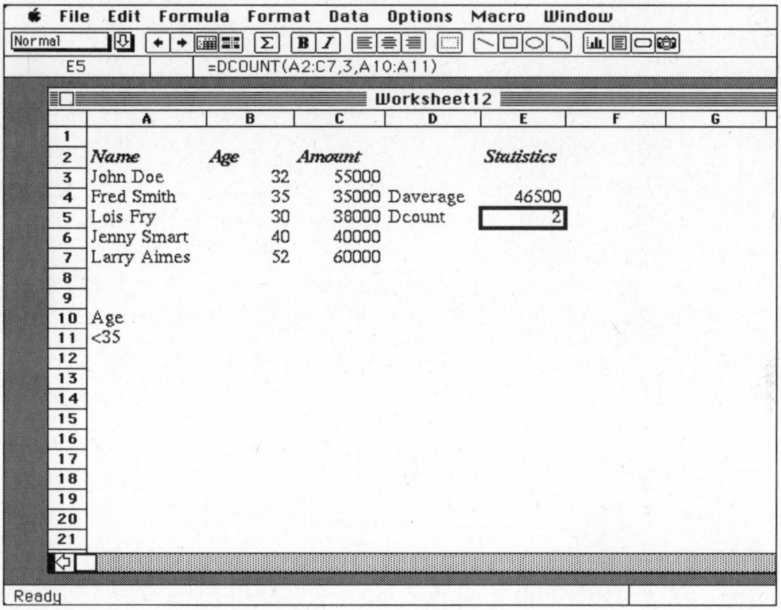

Fig. 6.2. Using the DCOUNT function.

The formula used for the DCOUNT function appears in the formula bar of figure 6.2. This function uses the same database and criteria ranges as the DAVERAGE function. Database functions, when used together in this way, perform different calculations on the same data. Note that you can substitute *database* as the argument for the database range and *criteria* as the argument for the criteria range. When you make these substitutions, Excel uses the database and criteria ranges currently set.

DGET

The DGET function extracts a field from a database range according to criteria you establish. You can string several DGET functions together to extract an entire record or just a few fields. The syntax is as follows:

DGET(*range,field,criteria*)

The *range* argument specifies the database range on the worksheet. This range reference should indicate a block of data that adheres to the basic rules for databases. That is, it must contain unique column headings and have no empty rows. This range does not have to be established as the active database with the Set Database command from the Data menu. If it is the active database, however, you can simply enter the text *"database"* as the range argument. Chapter 16 provides more details about database setup.

The *field* argument indicates the column heading of the field to be extracted from the database. Enter the text of the column heading (for example, *"Name"*) or the number of the field in the database. Fields are numbered from left to right starting with 1.

The *criteria* argument specifies the range of cells containing the criteria for the search. This range should contain data set up as a valid criteria range, but it need not be defined with the Set Criteria command from the Data menu. If it is defined as the active criteria range, however, you can enter the text *"criteria"* for this argument to indicate the active criteria range.

If the database contains no matching records, the DGET function returns the error #VALUE!. If the database contains more than one matching record, DGET returns the error #NUM!.

DMAX, DMIN

The DMAX and DMIN functions find the maximum and minimum values in a database subset. The functions require offset values to determine the field used for the search. The syntax follows:

> DMAX(*range, field_offset, criteria*)

> DMIN(*range, field_offset, criteria*)

Range is the range of cells containing the database information. *Field_offset* is the field that serves as the operand for this function; in this case, the offset is the field through which the function searches for the maximum value. *Criteria* is the range of cells containing the search criteria for the database.

Figure 6.3 adds the DMAX function to the worksheet that illustrated the DAVERAGE and DCOUNT functions in the preceding sections.

The formula used for the DMAX function appears in the formula bar in the figure. This function uses the same database and criteria ranges as the previous functions and establishes the offset of 3 to return the maximum salary within the selected subgroup. An offset of 2 returns the maximum age.

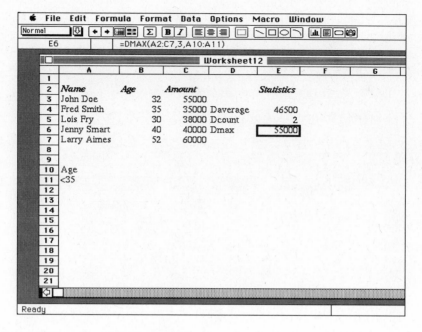

Fig. 6.3. *Using the DMAX function.*

DPRODUCT

The DPRODUCT function works in the same way as its counterpart PRODUCT, multiplying each value in the database group by each preceding value in a running total. The syntax for DPRODUCT is

DPRODUCT(*range, field_offset, criteria*)

Range is the database range. *Field_offset* is the field for which the product is being calculated (on every record that matches the criteria). *Criteria* is the range containing the lookup criteria for the database group.

Figure 6.4 shows the sample worksheet with the DPRODUCT function added.

DSTDEV, DSTDEVP

The DSTDEV and DSTDEVP functions find the standard deviation among the subset of records selected with the criteria range. DSTDEVP assumes that the subset is an entire population; this situation almost never occurs because a subset is a sample of the whole. The DSTDEV function therefore is more likely to be used in database statistics. The DSTDEV function uses sample statistics to determine the standard deviation. The syntax for the two functions follows:

DSTDEV(*range, field_offset, criteria*)

DSTDEVP(*range, field_offset, criteria*)

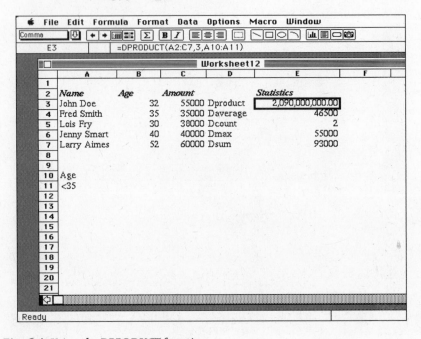

Fig. 6.4. *Using the DPRODUCT function.*

Range is the range of cells containing the database information. *Field_offset* is the field that serves as the operand for the function; in this case, it is the field for which the deviation is determined. *Criteria* is the range of cells containing the search criteria for the database.

DSUM

The DSUM function commonly is used to calculate the total of a particular field in a database subset. The syntax follows:

DSUM(*range, field_offset, criteria*)

Range is the range of cells containing the database information. *Field_offset* is the field that serves as the operand for this function; in this case, it is the numeric field for which the sum is calculated. *Criteria* is the range of cells containing the search criteria for the database.

Figure 6.5 shows the sample database with the DSUM function added.

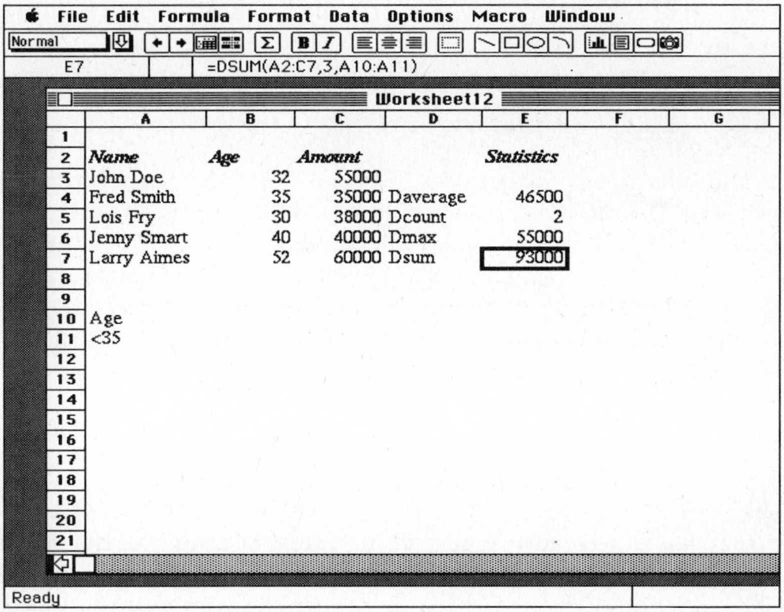

	File Edit Formula Format Data Options Macro Window						
Normal							
E7	=DSUM(A2:C7,3,A10:A11)						

Worksheet12

	A	B	C	D	E	F	G
1							
2	*Name*	*Age*	*Amount*		*Statistics*		
3	John Doe	32	55000				
4	Fred Smith	35	35000	Daverage	46500		
5	Lois Fry	30	38000	Dcount	2		
6	Jenny Smart	40	40000	Dmax	55000		
7	Larry Aimes	52	60000	Dsum	93000		
8							
9							
10	Age						
11	<35						
12							
13							
14							
15							
16							
17							
18							
19							
20							
21							

Ready

Fig. 6.5. *Using the DSUM function.*

The formula for the DSUM function appears in the formula bar of the figure. The arguments for this function are the same as for the other database functions. This function therefore returns the total salaries earned by workers under the age of 35.

DVAR, DVARP

Similar to DSTDEV and DSTDEVP, the functions DVAR and DVARP show the amount of variance over a database group. In this case, the group is the subset of data that matches the criteria. DVAR uses sample statistics to calculate the variance. DVARP calculates the variance over the entire population. The syntax for these functions follows:

DVAR(*range, field_offset, criteria*)

DVARP(*range, field_offset, criteria*)

Range is the range of cells containing the database information. *Field_offset* is the field that serves as the operand for this function—in this case, the field for which the variance is calculated. *Criteria* is the range of cells containing the search criteria for the database.

Date/Time Functions

Date and time functions perform date and time math calculations and conversions. Date and time math includes calculating elapsed time, adding time to a given date or time, and calculating the difference between two dates or times. This type of math is useful for creating payment schedules or determining payment delinquency. The following sections discuss the functions used for these purposes. (For more information about date math, see Chapter 8.)

DATE

The DATE function creates a date from individual values for the day, month, and year. This function is used primarily in macros when a date specification must be variable; it enables you to enter variables as the arguments for the date. The syntax follows:

DATE(*year, month, day*)

Year can be any value from 1904 to 2040, *month* can be any value from 1 to 12, and *day* can be any value from 1 to 31. If any of the variables is invalid, the function returns an error. Otherwise, the function returns a number corresponding to the number of days elapsed since January 1, 1904. You can format this number into a date by using the Number option from the Format menu.

DATEVALUE

The DATEVALUE function converts a text string into a valid date. It has the following syntax:

DATEVALUE(*text*)

The text string must contain data that is recognizable as a date. The function recognizes text entered in any of the date formats available through the Number command on the Format menu. You can specify any date from January 1, 1904, to February 6, 2040. Consider the following example:

=DATEVALUE(B5)

If cell B5 contains the text string "1/25/91", this function returns 31801—the number of days between 1/1/04 and 1/25/91. You can format this date value by using any of the date formats available through the Number command on the Format menu.

DAY, MONTH, YEAR

The DAY, MONTH, and YEAR functions return the respective day, month, or year that corresponds to a specified date, breaking a date into separate portions. The syntax follows:

DAY(*date*)

MONTH(*date*)

YEAR(*date*)

Date can be any valid date entered as the number of days elapsed since January 1, 1904. It also can be a reference to a cell containing a valid date or any date expression resulting in a valid date. Consider the following examples, in which cell B2 contains the date 2/24/90:

Formula	*Returns*
DAY(B2)	24
MONTH(B2)	2
YEAR(B2)	1990

You can combine these functions with IF to test the value of a date. You can determine whether a person is within a certain age limit, for example, by checking whether the birth date entered falls before a minimum date, as in the following formula:

=IF(YEAR(B2)<=1970,"OK","Must be 21 or older")

This formula tests whether the year portion of the date in cell B2 falls before 1970.

DAYS360

The DAYS360 function calculates the number of days elapsed between two dates, based on a 360-day year (12 months of 30 days each). Accounting applications that follow a 360-day year may find this function useful. The syntax follows:

DAYS360(*start_date,end_date*)

Enter the *start_date* and *end_date* as two valid date serial numbers or references to cells containing valid dates. The *end_date* must be later than the *start_date*.

HOUR, MINUTE, SECOND

The HOUR, MINUTE, and SECOND functions return the respective hour, minute, or second that corresponds to a specified time. The syntax follows:

HOUR(*time*)

MINUTE(*time*)

SECOND(*time*)

The time variable can be any valid time or cell reference containing a valid time. If cell B2 contains the time 3:30:25 AM, these functions return the following values:

Function	Returns
HOURS(B2)	03
MINUTES(B2)	30
SECONDS(B2)	25

Chapter 8 provides details about time math.

NOW

The NOW function pulls the current date and time from the Macintosh internal clock, returning the value as a number with a decimal, as in 2245.2025. The integer portion of this number represents the date (in days-elapsed format) and the fractional part represents the time (in time-elapsed format).

The syntax for NOW has no argument:

NOW()

You can format the value into a date or time using any of the date or time formats from the Number command on the Format menu. You also can separate the two portions with the TRUNC function, as in the following line:

=TRUNC(NOW())

This formula strips off the decimal portion of the date/time serial number, converting it to a date. You then can format this date or use the DAY, MONTH, and YEAR functions to split the value even further.

Excel extracts the time from the internal clock so fast that even if you have hundreds of NOW functions throughout the worksheet, the variance in time is less than one-millionth of a second.

Tip: Entering the Current Date and Time
A quick way to enter the current date into a worksheet cell is to press ⌘-— (the Command key and the hyphen key). To enter the current time, press ⌘-;.

Tip: Stopping the NOW Calculation
Each time the worksheet recalculates its values, the NOW function updates the current date and time. If you want to stop the date and time or archive the date and time with a worksheet, convert the NOW function to its value.

First, move the pointer to the cell containing the NOW function. Copy the contents of the cell by pressing ⌘-C. Then move to a blank cell and choose the Paste Special command from the Edit menu. Select the Values option and press Return. The value of the NOW function is pasted into the cell, but it is not recalculated. Alternatively, you can highlight the =NOW() function in the formula bar and press ⌘-= to convert it. Either method should be done immediately after you enter the =NOW() function.

Tip: Formatting Dates and Times Together
If you retrieve the current date and time with the NOW function and you want to format the entire value (without splitting off the date or time), use a custom number format that includes both date- and time-format symbols, as in *dddd, mmm dd, yyyy hh:mm:ss* AM. This format converts the value into the format Sunday, May 25, 1991 5:35:15 PM.

TIME

The TIME function converts individual numeric values for hours, minutes, and seconds into a valid time. The syntax follows:

TIME(*hour,minute,second*)

The TIME function is most useful in macros when a time must be variable. The three arguments represent the elements of the time and can range from 0 to 59. Excel creates a valid time from these specifications and returns that time in time-elapsed format. You then can format this value by choosing the Number command from the Format menu. Be sure to enter the time in 24-hour format. For example, the function

=TIME(23,30,05)

returns the time 0.97922454, which can be formatted as 11:30:05 PM.

TIMEVALUE

The TIMEVALUE function converts a text string to a valid time. The text string must be recognizable as a time entry. This requirement should be no problem if the text string resembles any of the time formats in the Number command from the Format menu. The result is displayed in time-elapsed format, which you can format with the Format Number command. The syntax for TIMEVALUE follows:

TIMEVALUE(*text*)

Enter times as text strings by typing them in two or three parts (for example, 12:30 or 12:30:15) or by including the AM or PM (for example, 12:30:00 AM). The following is an example:

=TIMEVALUE(B4)

If cell B4 contains the text string "11:35:15 PM", this function returns 0.9828125, which can be formatted as the valid time 11:35:15 PM.

TODAY

The TODAY function returns the date serial number of the current date. You then can format this value with a date format. The TODAY function contains no arguments:

TODAY()

Each time you calculate or open the worksheet, the TODAY function recalculates its value. Do not use the TODAY function when you want the date to remain as the date you entered.

WEEKDAY

The WEEKDAY function returns a value from 1 to 7 to indicate the day of the week of any valid date. The value 1 equals Sunday, 2 equals Monday, and so on. The syntax is as follows:

> WEEKDAY(*date*)

To format the returned value as the appropriate day name, use the Number command from the Format menu and specify the custom date format *dddd*. For example, the function

> =WEEKDAY(1/1/91)

returns 6, which you can format as the name Thursday by using the *dddd* format. See Chapter 5 for more information on date formats.

Financial Functions

Financial functions are used for such calculations as interest rates, loan terms, present values, and future values. Financial functions are essential for performing detailed financial analyses for purchases, investments, and cash flows.

DDB, SLN, SYD

The DDB, SLN, and SYD functions calculate depreciation using three methods. The DDB function uses the double-declining balance method, which allows for an accelerated rate of depreciation for the initial period; it also can accelerate depreciation by a specified rate. The SLN function uses the straight-line method and the SYD function uses the sum-of-the-years digits method. With each function, when the book value depreciates to the salvage value, depreciation stops. The syntax for these functions follows:

> DDB(*cost,salvage,life,period,factor*)
>
> SLN(*cost,salvage,life*)
>
> SYD(*cost,salvage,life,period*)

You provide the initial cost, the *salvage value* (value after the life), the life of the asset, and the period for which depreciation is calculated. The *life* and *period* arguments should be given in the same terms; that is, they should indicate years, months, days, or whatever period you choose. Optionally, you can enter a factor for the rate of depreciation (DDB only). If you do not enter a factor, the function assumes a standard DDB factor of 2 (double-declining).

The *period* argument determines the period in the asset's life for which depreciation is being calculated. To see depreciation for all periods requires multiple copies of the function—one for each period. *Period* should be equal to or smaller than *life*, and both variables must be integers. *Cost* and *salvage* can be any numbers. Figure 6.6 shows a worksheet that uses the three depreciation methods.

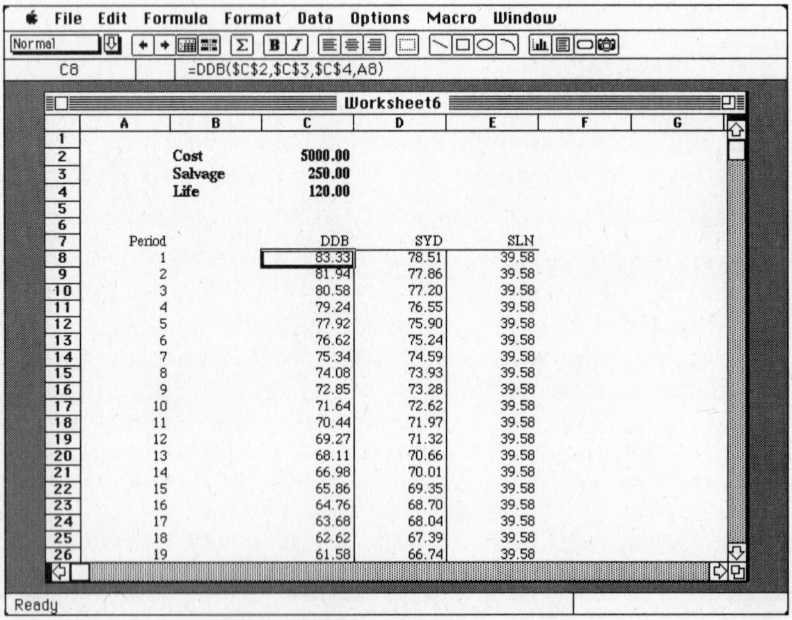

	A	B	C	D	E
1					
2		Cost	5000.00		
3		Salvage	250.00		
4		Life	120.00		
5					
6					
7	Period		DDB	SYD	SLN
8	1		83.33	78.51	39.58
9	2		81.94	77.86	39.58
10	3		80.58	77.20	39.58
11	4		79.24	76.55	39.58
12	5		77.92	75.90	39.58
13	6		76.62	75.24	39.58
14	7		75.34	74.59	39.58
15	8		74.08	73.93	39.58
16	9		72.85	73.28	39.58
17	10		71.64	72.62	39.58
18	11		70.44	71.97	39.58
19	12		69.27	71.32	39.58
20	13		68.11	70.66	39.58
21	14		66.98	70.01	39.58
22	15		65.86	69.35	39.58
23	16		64.76	68.70	39.58
24	17		63.68	68.04	39.58
25	18		62.62	67.39	39.58
26	19		61.58	66.74	39.58

***Fig. 6.6.** The results of three depreciation methods.*

The variables for each method are taken from the appropriate values entered into the worksheet range C2:C4. The formula for the DDB depreciation in cell C8 follows:

=DDB($C$2,$C$3,$C$4,A8)

Notice that the formula contains no *factor* argument, so the function calculates depreciation at a factor of 2. The *period* argument is taken from the numbers in column A, which represent months. Obviously, the method of depreciation has an effect on the amount of depreciation you can claim.

Determining the best method for a particular asset and company can be a challenge, because many variables must be analyzed together. A CPA or financial analyst can use these functions for a detailed study of a company's finances.

FV

The FV function calculates the *future value* of an investment—the value after payments have been made at a specified rate over a period of time. This function can determine the amount of money you will have after the term of an investment is over. FV uses a regular payment amount over a period of time, the interest rate, and the number of payment periods. The syntax follows:

FV(*interest_rate,periods,payment_amount,present_value,type*)

Interest_rate is the rate per period; you specify it as any numeric value. You should specify *periods* in the same units used for the *interest_rate* (months, years, and so on) because FV figures interest earned per period. Both arguments must be integers.

Payment_amount is the income from the loan or outflow from the investment. *Present_value* is the starting value of the investment.

Remember that cash paid out must be shown as a negative number, and interest or cash received must be shown as a positive number. If you are calculating the future value of an investment such as a savings account, therefore, the *present value* (amount deposited) and the *payment amount* (monthly deposits) are negative numbers because they are paid out to the investment. If no starting value exists, you can enter 0 as the *present_value* argument or omit the argument.

The *type* argument can be 1 or 0. If you enter 1, Excel assumes that payments occur at the beginning of the period; if you enter 0, Excel assumes that they occur at the end of the period. If you omit this argument, 0 is the default. Figure 6.7 shows a worksheet that uses the FV function.

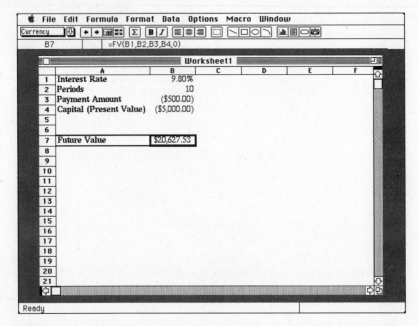

Fig. 6.7. *Calculating the future value of a loan.*

This example calculates the future value of a standard loan. The formula in cell B7 is =FV(B1,B2,B3,B4,0). Each value except *type* is contained in the worksheet. Notice that the payment and investment amounts are negative, calculating the future value in terms of the investor, not the lender. The example shows that with an investment of $5,000 and deposits of $500, you will have $20,627.53 in 10 years. Notice that the periods and rate arguments are given in years.

You can use this worksheet to calculate the future value of a *lump sum investment* (an investment with no payments). Just enter the total lump sum investment in cell B4 and enter 0 in cell B3.

IPMT

The IPMT function calculates the interest paid for a particular payment, given the interest rate, the number of periods in the term, and the present value. The syntax is as follows:

IPMT(*rate,period,periods,present_value,future_value,type*)

Specify the period for which you want to determine the interest paid by entering the period value as the *period* argument. *Type* determines whether payments are made at the beginning of the period (1) or at the end (0). If you omit the *type* argument, Excel assumes that 0 is correct. Figure 6.8 shows the IPMT function that determines the interest paid in month 20.

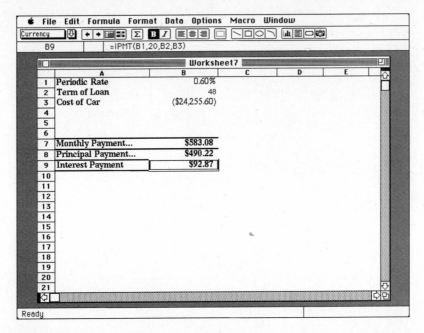

Fig. 6.8. *Calculating the interest paid in a given period.*

Note that the *future_value* and *type* arguments are omitted. The *future_value* argument is omitted to leave it at zero because this is a standard loan and not an annuity. The *type* argument is omitted to use the default of 0.

IRR

The IRR function calculates the internal rate of return (IRR) on an investment, basing the calculations on the initial cash outlay and the expected payments. This function tells you the rate earned on your investment when the payments (income) equal the cash outlay. To begin, you can estimate that rate; Excel then makes 20 calculations to find the IRR, based on the estimate. The syntax for IRR follows:

IRR(*range,guess*)

The *guess* argument represents your expected interest rate; *range* is the range of values representing payments out (on the investment) and in (return from the investment). Range also is known as the *range of cash flows*.

Suppose that you buy a video arcade game for your hotel lobby. You buy the equipment for $2,000 and estimate that it will earn you $200 a month. Beginning with your initial cash outlay, the cash-flow worksheet may look like figure 6.9.

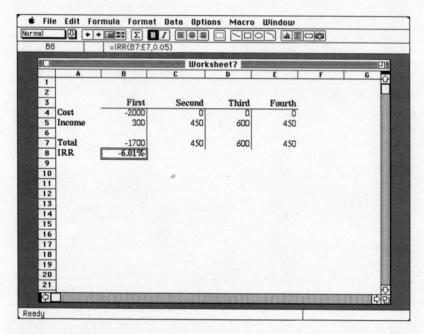

Fig. 6.9. Cash flows for IRR investment function.

The IRR function is entered into cell B8 as follows:

IRR(B7:E7,0.05)

The resulting rate of return for the first four quarters is –6.01 percent, indicating that your investment will not pay off this year. If you spread the cost of the equipment over four quarters, however, the rate of return increases dramatically.

The rate of return is influenced by relative inflow and outflow over time. In this case, paying more for the equipment in order to spread the payments out would be worthwhile.

MIRR

The MIRR function provides a modified form of the internal rate of return on an investment and accounts for the reinvestment rate of the positive cash flows—similar to combining two IRR functions in one. The syntax for MIRR follows:

MIRR(*range, finance_rate, reinvest_rate*)

Range is the worksheet range containing the investment's positive and negative cash flows. *Finance_rate* is the rate paid on those investment payments. *Reinvest_rate* is the rate at which you can reinvest the return on this investment. This formula primarily provides more information for an investor; thus, payments made to the investment should be negative, and income received from the investment should be positive. That income then can be invested at the *reinvest_rate*, making your total rate of return higher.

Figure 6.10 shows the same worksheet from figure 6.9 with the MIRR function added. Although the MIRR function returns a much better rate than IRR, the investment is still not a good one.

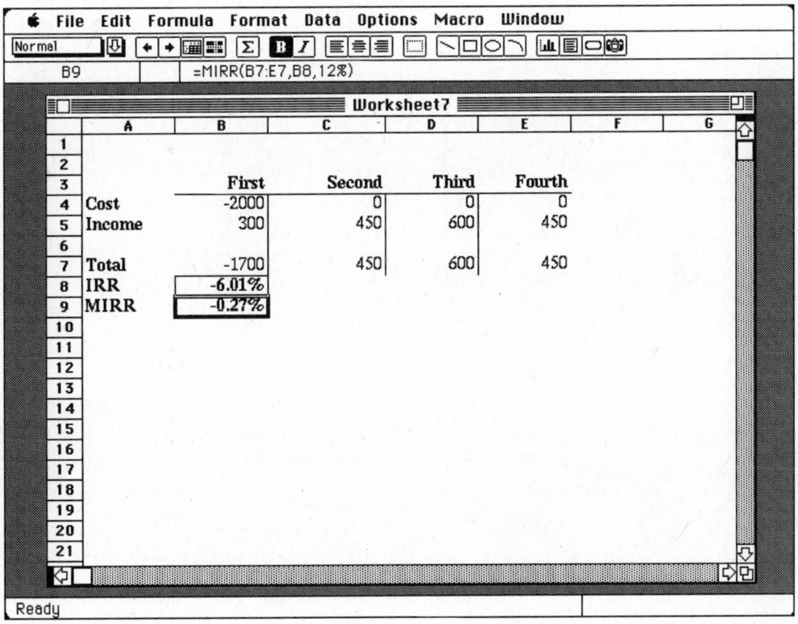

Fig. 6.10. *Comparing MIRR with IRR.*

NPER

The NPER function determines the amount of time (number of payment periods) required for a payment amount to equal an investment, given a specific interest rate. Alternatively, you can calculate the number of periods required for a payment amount to build to a specified future value, based on a present value and an interest rate. This function is useful for playing "what if" with interest rates to see how they affect the term of an investment. The syntax for NPER follows:

NPER(*rate,payment,present_value,future_value,type*)

Rate is the periodic rate of interest; you can calculate *rate* by dividing the annual interest rate by the number of periods. (Dividing the annual rate by 12 calculates monthly interest, for example). This value should be consistent with the *payment* argument, which is the periodic payment amount. (If you enter a monthly payment amount for the *payment* variable, for example, *rate* should be the monthly interest rate.)

Present_value is the original investment without interest, otherwise known as the principal. *Future_value* is the amount of the investment after interest; if you omit this argument, Excel calculates the number of payments required for the payment to equal the principal. *Type* can be 1 (payments occur at the beginning of the period), or 0 (payments occur at the end of the period). If you omit this argument, Excel assumes that 0 is correct.

Figure 6.11 shows a worksheet that uses the NPER function in two ways. The two formulas are NPER(B1,B2,B3,B4) in B7 and NPER(B1,B2,B3,0) in B8. Notice the difference when the future value is 0.

NPV

The NPV function returns the net present value of an investment and has the following syntax:

NPV(*rate,range*)

The net present value (NPV) is the present value of an investment's cash flow less the initial cash outlay. The interest rate used to compute the NPV is called the *discount rate*—the return that you can earn on investments of equivalent risk.

The *rate* argument is the interest rate of the loan and can be any value or expression. *Range* is the range of cells containing the monthly payments and can be any valid worksheet range.

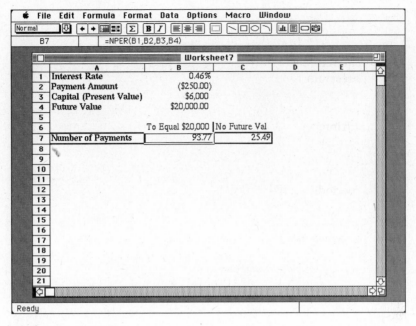

Fig. 6.11. *The NPER function.*

The concept of present value is based on the premise that $1 today is worth more than $1 a year from now because you can invest it. (If you invest $1 today at 10 percent annual interest, for example, you will have $1.10 in a year.) The present value of a dollar paid to you in a year can be said to be worth approximately 90 cents at a prevailing 10 percent interest rate.

NPV enables you to consider the future value of your money and helps you determine whether an investment is worthwhile. To calculate the NPV of an investment, you need a list of the payments to be made to you for the use of your investment as well as the current interest rate that you can earn on investments of equivalent risk.

Suppose that a friend wants to borrow $1,000 from you and agrees to pay you $100 a month for 12 months, for a total of $1,200 in one year. Suppose also that your bank will pay you 12 percent interest, compounded monthly, for the same $1,000. The NPV function can help you determine whether it is more profitable to loan the $1,000 to your friend or deposit it in the bank.

To use the NPV function, first enter the 12 loan payments of $100 into the worksheet. Next, enter the NPV function into another cell. In this case, you enter .01 as the interest rate (the monthly equivalent to a yearly rate of 12 percent) and A1:A12 as the range. The function returns the present value of the money you receive back (see fig. 6.12).

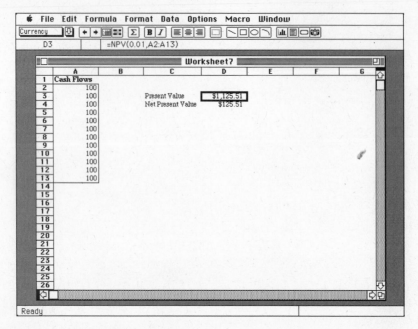

Fig. 6.12. *Using the NPV function.*

Generally, if the result of the NPV function is a positive value, the investment is a good one. In this case, loaning the money to your friend is more profitable because that act results in a $125 difference in your favor over the bank.

Because the function returns the present value, you have to calculate the net present value by using the formula shown in figure 6.12. This function simply subtracts the original investment from the present value. Note that the values of the payments do not have to be the same. Remember that cash out is represented as negative and cash in is represented as positive.

PMT

The PMT function calculates the payment amount required to pay off an investment, given a specific term and interest rate. This function is useful for playing "what if" with the term or interest rate of an investment to see how a change affects the amount of the payment. The syntax follows:

PMT(*rate,periods,present_value,future_value,type*)

You enter *rate* as the periodic interest rate, matching the period desired for the payment result. If you want to calculate a weekly payment amount, for example, *rate* should be a weekly rate (the annual rate divided by 52). *Periods* is the number of periods desired for the term of the investment. *Present_value* is the principal amount of the investment. If you want to determine the amount of the payment for the investment to equal a specified future value (after interest), enter that value as the *future_value* argument. Excel would use this value for annuities and cash flows, but the value would otherwise be zero.

If you omit this argument, Excel calculates the payment amount, based on its equaling the present value. *Type* can be 1 (payments occur at the beginning of the period), or 0 (payments occur at the end of the period). If you omit this argument, Excel assumes that 0 is correct.

Figure 6.13 shows a worksheet using the PMT function. The PMT function calculates the payment amount from the principal amount of the investment, the term, and the interest rate. In this example, the *future_value* argument is not required because of the type of investment involved—it is not an annuity.

Fig. 6.13. *Using the PMT function.*

PPMT

The PPMT function is similar to the PMT function. However, PMT returns the payment amount required for a given investment over a given time at a given rate, whereas PPMT returns the amount of principal paid in any given period under the same conditions. The syntax for PPMT follows:

PPMT(*rate,period,periods,present_value,future_value,type*)

Figure 6.14 shows a worksheet that illustrates the PMT function, with the PPMT amount shown for payment 20. The formula is =PPMT(B1,20,B2,B3). If the normal payment amount is $583.08, the principal paid in month 20 is $490.22.

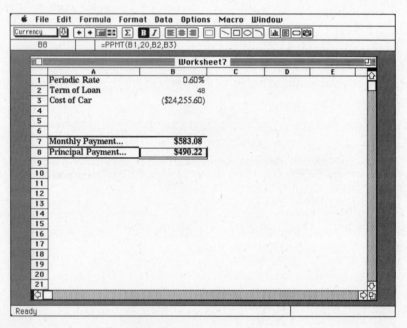

Fig. 6.14. *Comparing the PMT and PPMT functions.*

Note that the *future_value* and *type* arguments are omitted. The *future_value* argument is omitted to leave it at zero because this is a standard loan and not an annuity. The *type* argument is omitted to use the default of 0.

PV

The PV function calculates the present value (principal) of an investment, given the payment amount, interest rate, and number of payment periods.

You can supply the argument *future_value* to base the present value on a specific future value. The syntax follows:

PV(*rate,periods,payment,future_value,type*)

These arguments can be any valid numbers or expressions. *Periods* should be an integer value; *rate* is the periodic interest rate. *Type* can be 1, (payments occur at the beginning of the period), or 0 (payments occur at the end of the period). If you omit this argument, Excel assumes that 0 is correct.

RATE

The RATE function calculates the interest rate required for a present value to become a future value, given a particular number of periods. The syntax follows:

RATE(*periods,payment,present_value, future_value,type,guess*)

The variables can be any numbers or expressions. *Periods* should be an integer.

The RATE function can help you determine the interest rate you are paying on a loan. When you are quoted a price and a monthly payment amount, you can figure the periodic interest rate by using the RATE function. Then, when you know the interest rate, you can calculate the total interest you are paying with the IPMT function.

Excel calculates the interest rate using an estimate entered into the formula. Start by leaving the *guess* argument blank so that Excel tries the calculation on its own. If Excel fails to calculate a correct interest rate (indicated by the #NUM statement in the cell), enter an estimate of the interest rate as the *guess* argument. Enter the payment amount as a negative number if you are the investor; enter the present and future values as negative values if you are the lender. Figure 6.15 shows an example of the RATE function.

Note that the *future_value* and *type* arguments are omitted. The *future_value* argument is omitted to leave it at zero because this is a standard loan and not an annuity. The *type* argument is omitted to use the default of 0.

Auto dealers often play with the payment amount to make the payments "fit your budget." Using RATE, you can determine what you really are paying in interest for that low monthly payment. In the example, multiply the result by 12 for the annual interest rate.

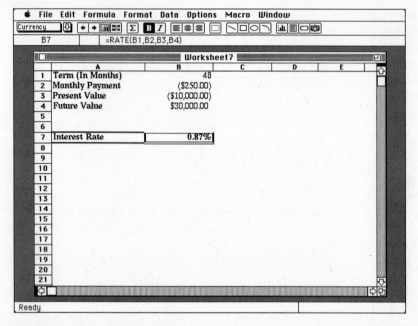

Fig. 6.15. *Using the RATE function.*

VDB

The main purpose of the VDB function is to calculate declining balance depreciation for any combination of periods within the life of the asset and to enable you to alter the depreciation rate (from double-declining to another rate) for this calculation. The VDB function can replace the DDB function, however, enabling you to calculate depreciation for partial periods. The syntax follows:

VDB(*cost,salvage,life,start_period,end_period,factor,switch*)

The *cost*, *salvage*, and *life* arguments are identical to the other depreciation functions. Instead of asking for the period, however, the VDB function requires a starting and ending period. Depreciation is calculated for all periods from start to end, inclusive. *Factor* is assumed to be 2 (double-declining) unless you specify another rate. The *switch* argument tells Excel to follow straight-line depreciation when the depreciation is greater than the declining balance. Change this argument to TRUE if you do not want Excel to apply straight-line depreciation in these cases. Normally, you omit the *factor* and *switch* settings so that Excel uses its defaults.

For example, you can enter the following into the example in figure 6.6:

=VDB($C$2,$C$3,$C$4,0,1)

=VDB($C$2,$C$3,$C$4,2,5)

The first example is identical to the function DDB($C$2,$C$3,$C$4,1). The second calculates depreciation for periods 3, 4, and 5 and presents the total.

Information Functions

Special functions serve various purposes that do not fit into the other categories. Many of these functions are designed primarily for macros. Uses for many of these functions appear in the sample macros provided later in this book.

ADDRESS

The ADDRESS command creates a valid cell address from row and column values. It can convert variable information into a valid reference for use in other functions or in macros. The syntax follows:

ADDRESS(*row,column,abs,A1,sheet*)

The *row* and *column* arguments can be any positive integers; they represent the row and column numbers for the reference. (You can produce these values with the ROW and COLUMN functions.) The *abs* argument determines the absolute status of the resulting cell reference. Enter any of the following values for this argument:

Value	Description
1	Totally absolute ($A$1)
2	Absolute row with relative column (A$1)
3	Absolute column with relative row ($A1)
4	Totally relative (A1)

If you omit this argument, Excel assumes the value 1. The A1 argument, if set to FALSE, returns the reference in the R1C1 style. If TRUE or omitted, the default A1-style reference is used. (Remember that the R1C1-style reference also can be relative or absolute.)

Finally, the *sheet* argument adds a worksheet name to the reference. This argument is useful when you use the ADDRESS function in macros that require sheet names. Enter any name in quotation marks, or use a function that returns the desired name, such as the CELL function. Following are some examples of the ADDRESS function:

Enter	*Excel Returns*
ADDRESS(3,4,2)	D$3
ADDRESS(3,4,2,,"Worksheet1")	Worksheet1!D$3
ADDRESS(ROW( ),COLUMN( ),4)	Address of the active cell

AREAS

The AREAS function tells you how many individual ranges make up the specified range reference; it is most helpful when used with range names or in macros when a range reference is variable and selectable. The syntax follows:

AREAS(*range*)

The following is a simple example:

=AREAS(A1:A5,B5)

This function returns 2, indicating that the reference contains two range areas.

> **Tip: Determining Areas in the Currently Selected Range**
> You can determine the number of areas currently selected by using a macro. After you select a range, the macro can use the Define Name command from the Formula menu to assign a temporary name to the selected range—CURRENT, for example. Then you can issue the AREAS function =AREAS(CURRENT) to return the number of areas in this range. When the macro is run, the cell containing this AREAS function returns the number of areas in the current selection. The macro appears as follows:
>
> ```
> macro
> =DEFINE.NAME("current")
> =AREAS(!current)
> =ALERT("You've selected "&A3&" areas.",1)
> =RETURN
> ```

CELL

CELL is a multipurpose function that can tell you virtually everything about a cell—its format, location, contents, alignment, and so on. The syntax for CELL follows:

CELL(*type,cell*)

The *type* argument, which must be enclosed in quotation marks, specifies which type of information you want for *cell*. You can get only one type of information. If *cell* is a range, Excel uses the first cell in the range. If you omit *cell*, Excel uses the highlighted cell or range. The CELL function can be useful in macros when you want the reference to be variable or selectable. Table 6.1 lists the *type* arguments allowed.

Table 6.1
Types for the CELL Function

Type Argument	Information Returned
"address"	Cell's address. The address is returned as a text string but can be used where any cell address is expected in a formula.
"col"	Cell's column number. Similar to COLUMN.
"color"	Cell's color status. If zero values are formatted with color, Excel returns 1. Otherwise, Excel returns 0.
"contents"	Cell's contents.
"filename"	File name (including the full path) of the file containing the referenced cell. Excel returns the file name as a text string. If the file has not been saved, the null string ("") is returned.
"format"	The number format of the data (if the data is numeric). This value is returned as a text string.
"parentheses"	The status of parentheses used in the cell. Excel returns 1 if positive numbers are formatted with parentheses. Otherwise, it returns 0.
"prefix"	The cell's alignment. One of the following characters may be returned as a text string to indicate the alignment:

continues

Table 6.1 *(continued)*

Type Argument	*Information Returned*	
	"	Cell is right-aligned.
	'	Cell is left-aligned.
	^	Cell is centered (this type returns no value if any other alignment is used).
	/	Cell is formatted with the Fill option.
	null ("")	Cell has another format.
"protect"	Cell's protection status. If the cell is protected, Excel returns 1. If the cell is not protected, Excel returns 0.	
"row"	Cell's row number. Similar to ROW.	
"type"	Type of data in the cell. One of the following characters may be returned as a text string to indicate the type of data:	
	b	Cell is blank.
	l	Cell contains a label.
	v	Cell contains a numeric value.
"width"	Cell's width. Excel estimates the width of a font by using the width of a numeral character.	

Table 6.2 provides a list of symbols returned for each format.

Table 6.2
Formats Returned When Type Is *"format"*

Symbol	*Format*
G	General or # ?/? or # ??/??
F0	0
,0	#,##0
F2	0.00
,2	#,##0.00
C0	$#,##0 ;($#,##0)

Symbol	Format
C0-	$#,##0 ;[RED]($#,##0)
C2	$#,##0.00 ;($#,##0.00)
C2-	$#,##0.00 ;[RED]($#, ##0.00)
P0	0%
P2	0.00%
S2	0.00E+00
D1	*d-mmm-yy*
D2	*d-mmm*
D3	*mmm-yy*
D4	*m/d/yy* or *m/d/yy h:mm*
D6	*h:mm:ss* AM/PM
D7	*h:mm* AM/PM
D8	*h:mm:ss*
D9	*h:mm*

Note: Remember that the symbol is returned as a text string indicating the format.

If the reference is to a cell that has a custom format, Excel tries to identify the format by using many of the codes listed in table 6.2. The first digit can be one of the following:

Digit	Format
G	General
,	Comma
C	Currency
F	Fixed
P	Percent
D	Date
H	Hidden
S	Scientific

The next digit may reflect the number of decimal places as 0, 1, 2, 3, and so on. A minus sign (–) indicates that negatives are displayed in color.

> *Note:* When you change the format of a cell, you may need to recalculate the worksheet before the CELL function reflects the change. Press ⌘-= to recalculate.

> *Tip: When NOT to use the CELL Function*
> The CELL function, when combined with the logic of the IF function, can duplicate the effects of certain other functions. You can test for a blank cell, for example, by using either of these two functions:
>
> =IF(CELL("type",B5)="b",TRUE(),FALSE())
>
> =ISBLANK(B5)
>
> Obviously, the ISBLANK function is simpler. The CELL function also duplicates the ISNONTEXT, ISNUM, and ISTEXT functions but is usually more difficult to use.

COLUMN, ROW

The COLUMN function returns the column number of the cell reference; ROW returns the row number. The syntax follows:

COLUMN(*cell*)

ROW(*cell*)

Simply enter any cell address as the argument; the functions return the corresponding column or row number. Consider the following example:

=COLUMN(G5)

This function returns 7 because column G is also column 7. If you omit the argument, the function assumes the address of the cell containing the formula. Because you are not likely to need to know the column or row number of a range you have specified, this command is intended for use with range names, as in the following:

=COLUMN(SALES)

If SALES is the name of a cell, the function returns the column number of that cell. If SALES is the name of a range, the function returns the column number of the leftmost cell in the range.

Note: The COLUMN and ROW functions also are useful in macros for finding the position of the pointer. Omitting the arguments (that is, specifying COLUMN() and ROW()) serves this purpose.

COLUMNS, ROWS

The COLUMNS and ROWS functions return the number of columns or rows in a specified range of cells. The syntax is the following:

COLUMNS(*range*)

ROWS(*range*)

The range can be any valid worksheet range. Entering =COLUMNS(A1:D1), for example, returns the value 4, indicating that the range has 4 columns.

INDIRECT

The INDIRECT function returns the value of any cell specified with a text string. This function is useful when you need the value of a variable cell reference. INDIRECT converts the text string into a cell reference and then returns the value of that cell reference. The text must contain characters that can be interpreted as a cell reference in the R1C1 or A1 style. The syntax follows:

INDIRECT(*text*)

Consider the following example:

=INDIRECT(B5)

If cell B5 contains the text string "A24" and cell A24 contains 100, the function returns 100. This function is intended to be a parameter for other functions or formulas, as in the following:

=SQRT(INDIRECT(B5))

If cell B5 contains "A24" and cell A24 contains 9, this function returns 3 (the square root of 9). If the text reference is in the R1C1 style, add the parameter FALSE to the end of the function:

=INDIRECT(B5,FALSE)

If B5 contains "R5C6" and cell E5 contains 100, the function returns 100. Omitting the second argument or making it TRUE indicates the A1-reference style.

INFO

The INFO function is similar to CELL, but it returns information about the current Excel workspace environment, including the current directory, recalculation status, and available memory. The syntax follows:

INFO(*type*)

Enter *type* as any of the following text strings, making sure you include the quotation marks:

Text String	Information Returned
"directory"	The current folder (including the entire directory path). The folder is returned as a text string.
"memavail"	The amount of memory available.
"memused"	Total memory in use.
"numfile"	The number of worksheets currently active.
"osversion"	Operating system version, returned as a text string.
"recalc"	The Recalculation mode. Returns "Automatic" or "Manual" as text.
"release"	The version of Excel in use, returned as text.
"system"	The operating environment. Returns Mac for Macintosh, PCOS2 for the OS/2 environment on the PC, or PCDOS for Windows under DOS.
"totmem"	Total available memory, including memory in use.

N

The N function returns the value of a cell if the cell contains a numeric value, numeric expression, or cell reference resulting in a numeric value. The syntax follows:

N(*value*)

If the reference is formatted as a date or time, this function returns the numeric value (serial number) of the date or time. If the reference contains the logical value TRUE, Excel returns 1. If the reference contains the logical value FALSE, Excel returns 0. If the reference contains text, Excel returns 0. Figure 6.16 shows several N functions in column B and the cells they reference in column A.

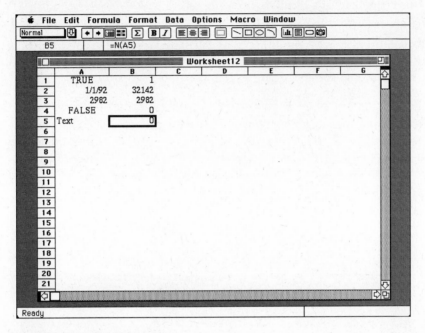

Fig. 6.16. *Using the N function.*

NA

The NA function has the syntax

    NA()

and returns #N/A to a cell, indicating that the information needed to produce a result is not yet available. Excel does not know when information is not available; you must program that logic into your worksheets with the NA function.

As you can see, this function has no arguments. If a cell produces the value #N/A, all calculations that access that cell produce the value #N/A. Later, you can convert the #N/A value to a meaningful message with an IF statement.

Suppose that the formula in cell B2 calculates its value based on the number you enter into cell B1. In cell B2, you may want to use the NA function in a formula to test whether anything has been entered into B1, as in the following:

> =IF(ISBLANK(B1)=TRUE,NA( ),B1*2)

This formula means *If cell B1 is blank, return #N/A; otherwise, calculate B1*2.* (See the ISBLANK function for more information about its syntax.)

Now suppose that a formula in cell B3 calculates its value based on the value of cell B2. You can have the formula test whether the value of B2 is #N/A before making its calculation:

> =IF(ISNA(B2)=TRUE,"Amount not entered in cell B1",B2+100)

This formula means *If the value of B2 is #N/A, print the message 'Amount not entered in cell B1'; otherwise, calculate B2+100.* The formula converts the #N/A value into something more useful to the operator. (See ISNA for more information about testing for the #N/A value.)

Figure 6.17 shows the result of the formula before a value is entered into cell B1.

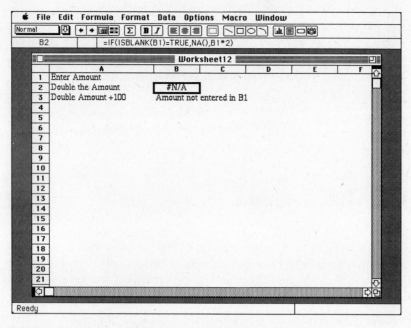

Fig. 6.17. *Testing for a blank cell in B1 and then for #N/A in B2.*

OFFSET

The OFFSET function creates a cell or range reference (as a text string) that is offset from (or distanced from) a given cell or range. You can use OFFSET in macros when you need to locate or select a range that is offset from the current position of the pointer by a specific (or variable) amount. Although this function returns only the address, you can combine it with the SELECT macro function to highlight the resulting reference. The syntax of the OFFSET function follows:

OFFSET(*reference,rows,cols,height,width*)

The *reference* argument is the starting reference from which the function calculates an offset reference. You can use the CELL or ADDRESS functions for this argument to achieve different results. The *rows* and *cols* arguments, which can be any positive or negative integer, determine the number of rows and columns to offset the result from the reference. The *height* and *width* arguments, which can be any positive integer value, determine the size of the offset range; *height* determines the number of rows and *width* determines the number of columns.

T

The T function returns the value of a cell if the cell contains text, a text expression, or a cell reference containing text. The syntax follows:

T(*value*)

If *value* is text, this function returns the value as a text string. If *value* is not text, this function returns a null string (""). This function can be useful in translating worksheets created by other programs.

TYPE

The TYPE function tells you the type of information a cell contains. The syntax follows:

TYPE(*cell*)

Cell can be a range or a constant value. If *cell* is a range, the function returns the type of information contained in the first cell of the range. The following is a list of values that this function returns; the values correspond with the type of information in the cell.

Values Returned	Cell Contents
1	Numeric value
2	Text
4	Logical value (TRUE or FALSE)
16	Error
64	Array

The formula =TYPE(B5) returns 2 if cell B5 contains "January". This formula returns 16 if B5 contains the error #VALUE!.

Logical Functions

Logical functions create logical tests that enable a formula to account for more data. A test may determine, for example, whether a particular value is greater than 25. The formula carrying out the test then performs one function if the value is true and another if the value is false. In short, logical functions enable formulas to branch according to particular values. The most common logical function is IF, which enables you to develop several kinds of tests based on the operators used in the test statement. IF is combined often with other logical functions for more variety.

AND, OR

You have learned that you can nest IF functions to make multiple tests in one formula. Excel also provides two important logical functions for this purpose. You can add more power to the IF function by adding the logical functions AND and OR. When added to an IF function, AND adds a second test to the condition. The syntax follows:

AND(*condition1,condition2*)

If both conditions are true, the IF statement proves true. If one or both are false, the IF statement proves false. An example may appear as follows:

=IF(AND(A1=A2,A1=A6), "Right","Wrong")

This function adds a second test to the condition; it means *If cell A1 equals the value of A2 and if cell A1 equals the value of A6, print 'Right'; otherwise, print 'Wrong'*. Notice that two conditional tests appear before the first comma in the IF function. Both tests fall in the parentheses of the AND function, so that the AND function and its two tests replace the single test used before.

The OR function also adds a second test to the IF function. If one or both conditions are true, the IF statement proves true. If both conditions are false, the IF statement proves false. The syntax for OR follows:

OR(*condition1,condition2*)

Consider the following example:

=IF(OR(A1=5,B1=25),"Right","Wrong")

This function is similar to the preceding example, but it means *If the value of A1 equals 5 and/or if the value of B1 equals 25, print 'Right'; otherwise, print 'Wrong'*. Note that the OR function serves as an and/or condition, meaning that both conditions can be true in order for the statement to prove TRUE. You can stack several tests into one AND or OR statement, as in the following:

=IF(AND(A1=5,B1=25,G5=G6),"Right","Wrong")

This statement is true if all three conditions are true.

Tip: Exclusive OR

Remember that the OR logical operator means *and/or*. That is, one or both of the operands must be true for the statement to be true. Some applications call for an exclusive OR statement, in which only one of the operands can be true if the statement is true; if both operands are true, the statement is false.

Excel does not provide an exclusive OR logical operator (often listed as XOR), but you can achieve the same result with nested IF functions. The statement can apply to any information in the worksheet and appears as follows:

=IF(A1=5,(IF(B1=5,FALSE(),TRUE()),IF(B1=5,TRUE(),FALSE())))

In this example, if cell A1 equals 5 and B1 does not, or if B1 equals 5 and A1 does not, Excel returns TRUE. Otherwise, Excel returns FALSE.

IF

The IF function is probably the most powerful of all worksheet functions, providing most of the logic you need for evaluating information. The IF function tests whether a condition is true or false. If the condition is true, one value is returned; if the condition is false, another value is returned. The syntax for IF is the following:

IF(*condition,value_if_true,value_if_false*)

Proving a condition true or false requires a comparison operator. Excel offers several operators:

Operator	Definition
>	Greater than
<	Less than
=	Equal to
>=	Greater than or equal to
<=	Less than or equal to
<>	Not equal to

In the following examples, you can substitute any of these operators for the ones given. Consider this example:

IF(A1=A2,"Right","Wrong")

This formula means *If the value of A1 is equal to that of A2, then return 'Right'; otherwise, return 'Wrong'. Value_if_true* and *value_if_false* can be any constant value, cell reference, or formula resulting in a numeric value or text.

Suppose that you are creating a worksheet for sign-ups on a group vacation. Two packages are available, and you have numbered them 1 and 2. Package 1 costs $1,500; package 2 costs $2,000. The worksheet is designed to hold the names and addresses of the participants in columns A through C. Column D holds the number of the trip package—1 or 2—that a participant wants. Finally, column E automatically enters the cost of the package specified in column D. Figure 6.18 shows the worksheet.

The formulas in column E use the IF function to calculate the price of the package. For example, cell E3 contains

=IF(D3=1,1500,2000)

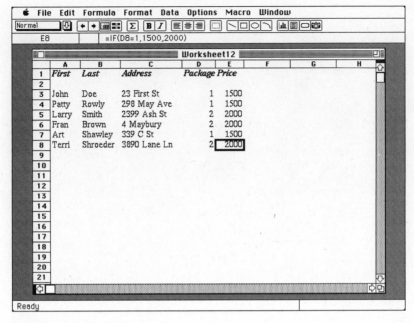

Fig. 6.18. *Using the IF function.*

This formula means *If cell D3 contains 1, enter 1500; otherwise, enter 2000*. Because only two options are available, this formula does not need to test for 2 in cell D3. If cell D3 does not contain 1, it should contain 2. If you enter 3 into cell D3, you get 2000 in column E by default because cell D3 does not contain 1.

Many users like to ensure a correct answer by adding another level to the formula. The preceding example tested for only one condition and entered 2000 if it was not met; however, the following formula tests for two conditions and enters 0 if neither condition is met:

=IF(D3=1,1500,IF(D3=2,2000,0))

This formula contains two nested IF statements. The second IF statement is entered as the "else" of the first statement. If D3 does not contain 1 or 2, 0 appears in cell E3.

> **Tip: Creating a Not To Exceed Formula**
>
> A simple IF formula provides not-to-exceed protection for your worksheet. If the value in question exceeds your limit, the formula returns Too Large in place of the value. The formula follows:
>
>   =IF(A1<100,A1,"Too Large")
>
> This formula ensures that the number in cell A1 does not exceed 100. If the number is smaller than 100, the formula returns that number in A1; if the number is 100 or larger, the formula returns Too Large. The not-less-than formula works in reverse:
>
>   =IF(A1<100,"Too Small",A1)
>
> This formula ensures that the number in cell A1 is no smaller than 100. If the number is smaller than 100, Too Small is returned.

ISBLANK

The ISBLANK function tests for a blank cell. Its syntax follows:

    ISBLANK(*cell*)

If the specified cell is blank, the function returns TRUE; otherwise, the function returns FALSE. The referenced cell can be any valid cell in the worksheet. The function commonly is used with the IF function to test for a blank cell and then perform some action based on the outcome. You can combine ISBLANK with IF, for example, to print a message next to cells that need to be filled in; you can remove the message after the data is entered.

Consider the following example:

    =IF(ISBLANK(B5)=FALSE," ","Enter your ID number in cell B5")

The IF function tests whether the result of the ISBLANK test is 0. If so, the blank string is returned. Otherwise, the message appears.

The ISBLANK function also can determine whether a value has been entered before you use the cell reference in a formula. For example, the formula

    =IF(ISBLANK(B5)=FALSE,NA( ),B5*B6)

means *If B5 is blank, return #N/A; otherwise, multiply it by B6 and return the result*. The formula suspends calculation until the number is entered.

ISERR, ISERROR

These functions test whether a specified cell contains an error. If so, the function returns TRUE; otherwise, the function returns FALSE. The syntax follows:

ISERR(*cell*)

ISERROR(*cell*)

The ISERR function ignores the #N/A error, but the ISERROR function picks it up. These functions commonly are used with the IF function to trap errors in the worksheet and enable the operator to control the errors.

Normally, any calculation that references a cell containing an error calculates to #VALUE! or some other error, but ISERR enables you to pinpoint the error. Consider the following example:

=IF(ISERR(B5)=TRUE,"Invalid entry in cell B5",B5*B6)

This formula tests whether the value of B5 is an error. If so, the function returns "Invalid entry in cell B5". Otherwise, the calculation is performed.

ISLOGICAL

The ISLOGICAL function tests whether a cell contains the logical value TRUE or FALSE. The syntax follows:

ISLOGICAL(*cell*)

If *cell* contains TRUE or FALSE as produced by a logical test, the function returns TRUE. Otherwise, it returns FALSE. The uses for this function are rather esoteric because it does not distinguish between TRUE and FALSE.

ISNA

The ISNA function tests whether a cell contains #N/A. The syntax follows:

ISNA(*cell*)

The value #N/A may appear because a function is unable to find data or because a formula has specifically returned it. #N/A implies that information the function needs in order to continue is not available. You can convert #N/A into a more meaningful statement through a formula containing ISNA:

=IF(ISNA(B5)=FALSE,B5*B6,"Unable to complete this calculation")

This formula returns the phrase

```
Unable to complete this calculation
```

if #N/A is discovered in cell B5.

ISNONTEXT, ISNUMBER, ISTEXT

The functions ISNUMBER, ISTEST, and ISNONTEXT have the following syntax:

ISNUMBER(*cell*)

ISTEXT(*cell*)

ISNONTEXT(*cell*)

The functions test whether a cell's value is a number or a text string. Such a test can help you determine whether a cell contains a number before you reference it in a formula. Blank cells are considered text. You really don't need all three functions; if you use ISNUMBER to determine that a cell does not contain a number, you already know that the cell must contain a text string. The only reason for using ISNONTEXT is to distinguish between text and blank cells.

These functions often are used with the IF statement to act on the result of the test. You can differentiate among text, numbers, and blank cells by using a formula such as the following:

=IF(ISBLANK(B1)=TRUE,"BLANK",IF(ISNUMBER(B1)=TRUE, "NUMBER","TEXT"))

Because the function tests for a blank cell first, the ISTEXT function is not needed and therefore does not evaluate a blank cell as text. To determine whether a cell is text but not blank, use the ISNONTEXT function, as follows:

=IF(ISNONTEXT(B1)=TRUE,FALSE(),TRUE())

This formula returns TRUE if the cell B1 contains text and FALSE if the cell does not contain text. You can blank a cell by choosing the Clear command from the Edit menu.

ISREF

The ISREF function tests whether a cell contains a cell reference. It has the following syntax:

ISREF(*cell*)

If a cell contains a cell reference, Excel returns TRUE; otherwise, Excel returns FALSE. Combine this function with IF to act on the result of the test, as follows:

=IF(ISREF(B5)=TRUE,"Reference","Not a Reference")

This function returns the message Reference if cell B5 contains a reference to another cell. Otherwise, the function returns the message Not a Reference.

NOT

The NOT function causes the function to return TRUE if a condition does not match your criterion. The syntax follows:

NOT(*condition*)

The example

=NOT(A5>B5)

asks *Is A5 not greater than B5?* The answer is TRUE if A5 is not greater than B5 (rather like saying *Yes, it is not true*). You can use the NOT function with any of the comparison operators listed earlier, as in the following example:

=IF(OR(C5=25,NOT(A5=B5)),TRUE(),FALSE())

TRUE, FALSE

The TRUE and FALSE functions carry out logical tests that return the value TRUE or FALSE, depending on the result of the test. You can achieve the same result by using the text strings "TRUE" and "FALSE", but you can use the TRUE and FALSE functions when text strings are not accepted. The syntax follows:

TRUE()

FALSE()

As you can see, the functions have no arguments.

The following functions serve the same purpose. The first uses the TRUE and FALSE functions; the other uses the "TRUE" and "FALSE" text strings.

=IF(A1=25,TRUE(),FALSE())

=IF(A1=25,"TRUE","FALSE")

Lookup Functions

Lookup functions search for values within tables or lists. Each lookup function follows a different method for searching and returning values. You will find that each method is suited for a particular task. Whenever your worksheet places values in tables (such as tax tables or price tables), you can employ a lookup function for added power in the application.

CHOOSE

The CHOOSE function uses a value to look up another value in a specified set. The syntax follows:

CHOOSE(*value,list*)

Value can be any number, formula, or cell reference that results in a value; it designates which item from *list* is to be returned. *List* is a series of values to be returned. If the value is 1, the first item in the list is returned; if the value is 2, the second value is returned, and so on. Suppose that you enter the formula as follows:

=CHOOSE(A1,"primero","second","trio")

If the value of cell A1 is 3, the formula returns trio because it is the third item in the list. In this example, the list contains text references; however, numbers, cell references, formulas, or any combination also is acceptable. You must supply the values as a list, however; a range reference is not acceptable. If *value* is a blank cell or text, Excel assumes that the argument is 0.

You probably already can see some limitations to this function. What *value* is 141? Must you have 142 values in the list? The answer is yes. Keep in mind, however, that the CHOOSE function is meant to be used when the first value is sequential (as in 141, 142, 143, 144, and so on), not variable. Because the possible values are sequential, not variable, you can convert them to 0, 1, 2, 3, 4, and so on, by using the following formula:

=CHOOSE(A1-140,"primero","second","trio")

Notice that the first value consists of the formula A1-140, which converts the values to a more manageable range for the function—the values 1, 2, 3, and 4.

The CHOOSE function is very much like the HLOOKUP and VLOOKUP functions, which are described next. One major advantage of the CHOOSE function is that it can choose its parameters randomly, whereas HLOOKUP and VLOOKUP require parameters to be in a range of cells. For example, CHOOSE may appear as follows:

CHOOSE(A5,C4,G25,H2,B33,F2)

The listed items are not adjacent cell references. If the value in the CHOOSE function is larger than the greatest item in the list, the function returns `#VALUE!`

HLOOKUP, VLOOKUP

The HLOOKUP and VLOOKUP functions search for values in tables, basing the search on a specified lookup value. A *lookup value* is a value you are trying to match in the table. In a tax table containing tax rates based on income, for example, *income* is the lookup value. VLOOKUP searches vertically in a column of values and returns a corresponding value from the table. HLOOKUP searches horizontally in a row of values and returns a corresponding value from the table. The syntax of the two functions follows:

HLOOKUP(*value,range,row_offset*)

VLOOKUP(*value,range,column_offset*)

Value is any valid number, text string, or expression resulting in a valid number or string, including formulas and cell references. *Range* is the worksheet range containing the table. *Row_offset* and *column_offset* determine the value to be returned.

The VLOOKUP function takes the search variable and looks down the first column of the table for a match. When a match is found, the function maintains the row position of the matched value but moves across the table to return one of the columns, determined by the offset value specified.

Suppose that your worksheet contains the table of values shown in figure 6.19.

In the figure, cell B16 contains the formula

=VLOOKUP(A1,$A$6:$D$13,2)

and cell B17 contains the formula

=VLOOKUP(A1,$A6:$D13,3)

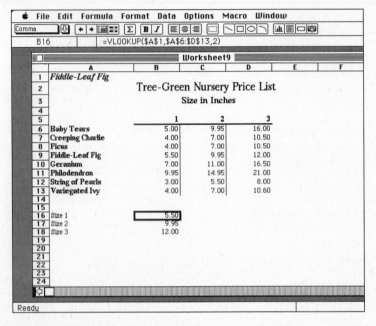

Fig. 6.19. *Using the VLOOKUP function.*

Note: You can ignore the dollar signs ($) in these formulas. They make the references absolute (or partially absolute) for copying purposes. Refer to Chapter 4 for details about relative and absolute references.

The first formula (in cell B16) takes the value in cell A1 and tries to match it in the first column of the range A6:D13, column A6:A13. This column is called the *lookup column*; in a VLOOKUP statement, it is always the first column in the specified range. (In an HLOOKUP statement, the *lookup row* is always the first row.)

When a match is found, the function returns the corresponding value from the table column specified by *column_offset*. (The lookup column offset value is 1.) Because the offset value in the formula is 2, the corresponding value in the first column to the right of the lookup column (column 2)—5.50—is returned. The second formula (cell B17) performs the same operation but returns the value from the third column of the table.

Note: You cannot specify negative values for the offset.

Figure 6.20 shows an example of an HLOOKUP function. HLOOKUP follows the same rules as VLOOKUP but searches horizontally across the first row of the specified range and returns the corresponding value from rows below the lookup row.

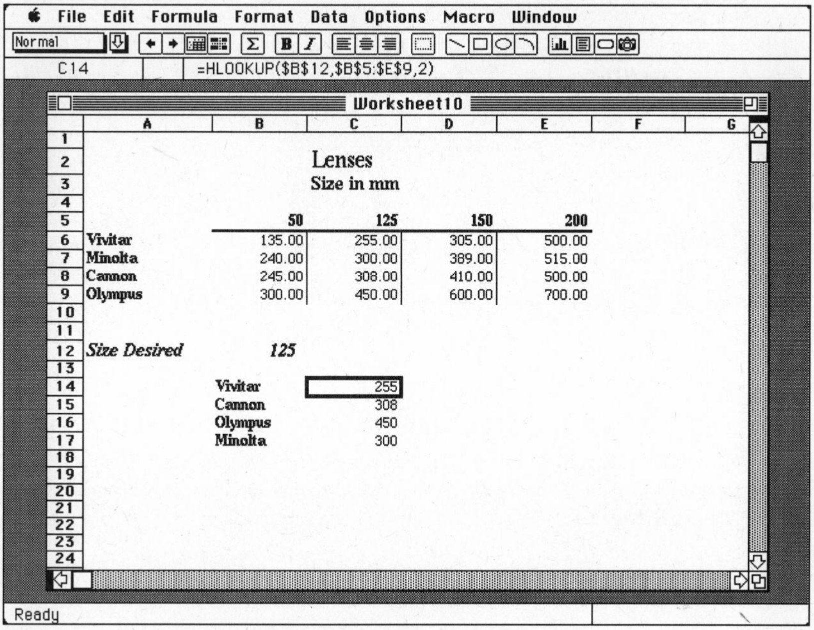

Fig. 6.20. *Using the HLOOKUP function.*

In this example, the HLOOKUP function in cell C14 searches across row 5 for the size entered into cell B12. Row 5 is the lookup row for the table in the range B5:E9. Remember that this row is also the first offset row; an offset value of 1 returns a value from row 5. Hence, the formula in cell C14 uses an offset of 2 to return the row corresponding to Vivitar.

Making the Offset Variable

The preceding VLOOKUP example uses a separate lookup function for each possible column in the table. Because the table has only three columns, this arrangement is not prohibitive. Based on the search value, each function (in cells B15, B16, and B17) returns a value from one of the three columns in the table. However, if you want to make the offset selectable instead of using a different formula for each possible offset, you can reduce the three formulas to one, with the offset selected according to other input. Figure 6.21 shows how the new worksheet would look.

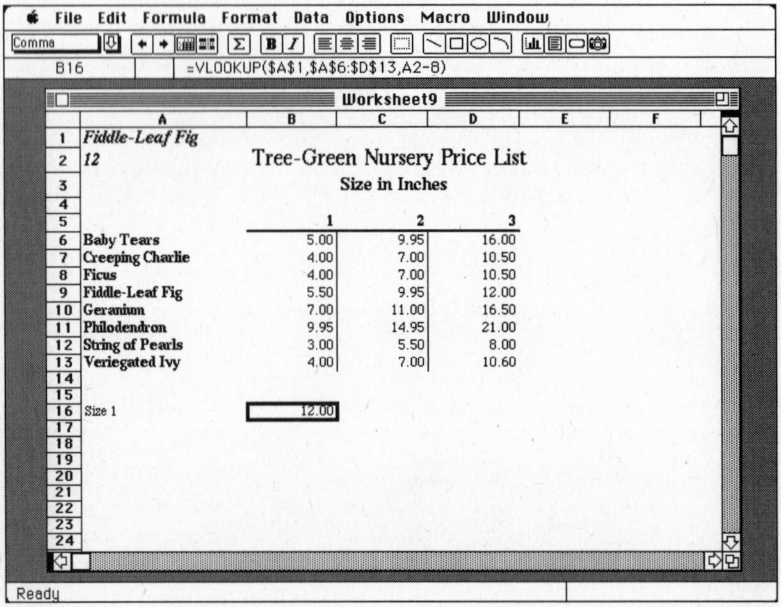

Fig. 6.21. Making the VLOOKUP offset variable.

The formula in cell B16 follows:

=VLOOKUP(A1,A5:D12,A2–8)

Excel uses the value in cell A2 to calculate the appropriate offset value. Because the offset value must be a number ranging from 1 to the number of columns in the lookup table, the calculation A2–8 converts the value to a usable form. This formula works only when the values are sequential and an equal amount apart; otherwise, a double-variable table is required. (Chapter 8 explains double-variable tables in detail.)

Understanding Lookup Table Rules

Several rules apply to performing lookups with HLOOKUP and VLOOKUP. First, if the search variable is numeric, the values in the lookup column (or row) should be numeric. Moreover, these values should be in ascending order, as in figure 6.21. If the lookup column is not in ascending order, the functions may return incorrect values. Excel searches the lookup column until it finds a match; if Excel cannot find a match, it uses the value closest to—but smaller than—the search variable. If a lookup value is greater than all values in the table, therefore, the last value in the table is used because it is the largest.

If the lookup value is smaller than all values in the table, the function returns the error #VALUE!. Remember that if a match is not made, Excel returns the first value smaller than the search variable.

If the lookup range within the specified table range contains text strings, the search variable also must be a text string. In such cases, the lookup function must be able to find a match for the specified information, including upper- and lowercase letters. If no match is found, the function returns the error #VALUE!. The data in the table (that is, the value to be returned) can be numeric or text.

INDEX

The INDEX function returns a value from a table according to the row and column offsets specified. Instead of matching a value in the table, INDEX goes directly to the row and column offset values you specify and returns the contents of the intersection. The syntax follows:

INDEX(*range, row_offset, column_offset*)

Row_offset and *column_offset* must be equal to or less than the number of rows (or columns) in *range*. If either argument is too large, the function returns the error #REF!. If either is 0, the function returns the error #VALUE!.

Figure 6.22 shows an example of the INDEX function as used in the same worksheet given in figure 6.21. The function in cell B12 is =INDEX(A5:E9,3,3). The result is 300, the value at the intersection of row 3 and column 3 of the range.

If a range entry includes two or more ranges, the INDEX function requires an additional argument, placed after the others, to indicate which range to use. The ranges are numbered sequentially from top to bottom and from left to right.

Thus, the function

=INDEX(A5:D12,H24:K30,3,3,2)

returns the value in cell J26, the intersection address of row 3 and column 3 of the second range in the reference.

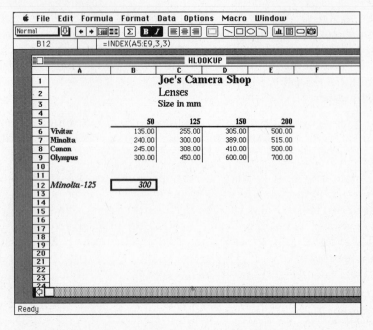

Fig. 6.22. *Using the INDEX function.*

LOOKUP

The LOOKUP function follows the same principle as HLOOKUP and VLOOKUP: it searches a horizontal or vertical range (that is, a row or column) for a specified value and returns a corresponding value. With HLOOKUP and VLOOKUP, Excel determines the position of the resulting value according to the position of the lookup range. With LOOKUP, however, you must specify both ranges as arguments, as the following syntax indicates:

LOOKUP(*value,lookup_range,result_range*)

Thus, the result range can be anywhere on the worksheet. In fact, it can be vertical (a column) when the lookup range is horizontal (a row) and vice versa. The only restriction is that the number of cells in the lookup range and the result range must match. Figure 6.23 shows an example.

In this example, the lookup range is C3:F3, and the result range is B5:B8. Notice that the two ranges have the same number of cells. When you enter the search value into cell B1, cell B2 displays the result of the lookup using the following function:

=LOOKUP(B1,C3:F3,B5:B8)

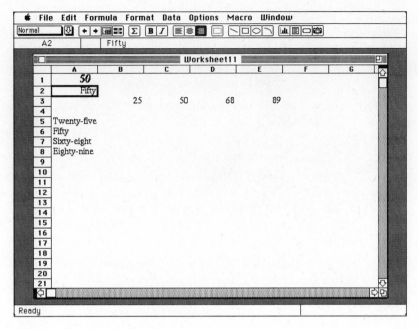

Fig. 6.23. *Using the LOOKUP function.*

Another form of the LOOKUP function follows:

LOOKUP(*value,lookup_range*)

Using this syntax, the function searches for the value in the specified lookup range and returns a corresponding value. However, the corresponding value is always taken from the last column or row in the lookup range—as if you had used an offset value pointing to the last column. This form of the LOOKUP function can be easier to use with two-column tables than HLOOKUP or VLOOKUP.

MATCH

The MATCH function is the opposite of the CHOOSE function. Whereas CHOOSE uses a sequential value to select items from a list, MATCH finds a value in a list and returns its sequential value (that is, its placement in the list). The syntax for MATCH follows:

MATCH(*value,range,type*)

Value is the number or text that you want to find in the table. *Range* is the row or column range containing the table; the items in this table should be in ascending order and can be numbers or text. If *value* matches the first item in *range*, the function returns a 1; if *value* matches the second item in *range*, the function returns a 2, and so on.

Type determines the type of search made on the range. The following are the *type* entries you can make:

Type	Tells Excel to Find
1	The value closest to (but smaller than) *value* if a match cannot be made. If a smaller value cannot be found, Excel returns an error. If *value* is larger than all values in the table, Excel returns the last value in the table (that is, the largest).
–1	The value closest to (but larger than) *value* if a match cannot be made. If a larger value cannot be found, Excel returns an error. If *value* is smaller than all values in the table, Excel returns the first value in the table (that is, the smallest). When using this type, make sure the values appear in descending, not ascending order.
0	Only the value that matches *value*. If Excel cannot find a match, it returns an error.

If you enter 0 for *type*, and *value* is a text string, then you can include wild cards in the string. As mentioned previously, the ? wild card represents any single character; the * wild card represents any number of characters. (For more information about wild cards, see Chapter 3.)

Figure 6.24 shows an example of the MATCH function. The range B3:F3 contains the table of values. The functions in cells B5, B6, and B7 follow:

=MATCH(24,B3:F3,-1)

=MATCH(80,B3:F3,1)

=MATCH(25,B3:F3,0)

As you can see, the three types of MATCH values produce different results. The first formula returns #N/A because the values are listed in ascending order.

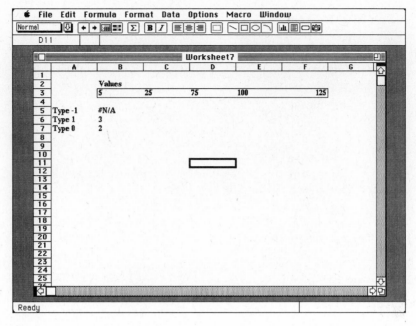

Fig. 6.24. Using the MATCH function.

Mathematical Functions

Mathematical functions apply to general mathematical needs, such as finding the absolute value of a number or rounding a number; they also include some logarithmic functions. The following sections describe Excel's mathematical functions:

ABS

The ABS function returns the absolute value of a number or cell reference. The *absolute value* of a number is that number without positive or negative status. (The absolute value of –34, for example, is 34.) The function's syntax follows:

ABS(*value*)

Value can be a number, formula, or cell reference. In other words, it can be any expression resulting in a value, as in the following examples:

ABS(–354)

ABS(A5)

ABS(TOTAL)

ABS(TOTAL–(A5*4))

EXP

The EXP function computes the value of *e* raised to a specific power (*e* is the base of the natural logarithm). The syntax is

EXP(*value*)

where *value* is any number or cell reference. The constant *e* equals approximately 2.7182818.

FACT

The FACT function computes the factorial of a number and has the following syntax:

FACT(*value*)

The factorial is equal to the following calculation:

(*value*) * (*value* – 1) * (*value* – 2) * (*value* – 3)
...(value – (*value* – 1)) *[or 1]*

Value must be a positive integer. The factorial of 4, for example, is calculated as follows:

4 * 3 * 2 * 1 = 24

Thus, the function =FACT(4) returns 24.

INT

The INT function rounds a number down to the nearest integer, resulting in a positive or negative number without decimal values. The INT value of 829.98, for example, is 829; the INT value of –829.98 is –830. This function, commonly used in financial worksheets, has the following syntax:

INT(*value*)

Insert a number, formula, or cell reference as the *value* argument, as follows:

=INT(B5)

If cell B5 contains 45.55, for example, the function returns 45.

LN, LOG, LOG10

The LN, LOG, and LOG10 functions calculate the logarithm of a number. The syntax of each follows:

LN(*value*)

LOG(*value,base*)

LOG10(*value*)

LN calculates the logarithm at base *e*; LOG calculates the logarithm for a specified base, and LOG10 calculates the logarithm at base 10. The value and base can be any number greater than 0. Consider this example:

=LOG(100,3)

This function calculates the value 100 at base 3, which is 4.191807.

MOD

The MOD function returns the remainder, or *modulus*, of two numbers: a *divisor* and a *dividend*. For example, 3 (the divisor) goes into 10 (the dividend) 3 times, with 1 remaining. The modulus of 10 and 3, therefore, is 1. The MOD function is useful in business worksheets for calculating averages or remaining inventory. It has the following syntax:

MOD(*dividend,divisor*)

The *dividend* and *divisor* can be any number or expression resulting in a number, except that the divisor cannot be 0. Figure 6.25 shows a worksheet that includes the INT and MOD functions.

Notice that the formula at the bottom checks the results by multiplying the divisor by the dividend and adding the remainder. The result should match the original number.

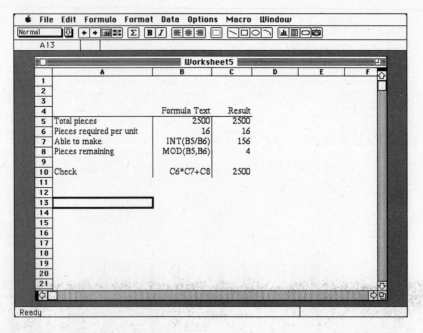

Fig. 6.25. *The INT and MOD functions.*

PI

You can use the PI function wherever the value pi (π) is required. Excel calculates pi to 14 decimal places and keeps track of all 14 places. The syntax follows:

    PI()

Be sure to include the empty parentheses even though the function has no argument. To calculate the area of a circle, for example, you can enter the following:

    =PI()*B5_2

Cell B5 contains the radius of the circle. If B5 contains 35, for example, the resulting area is 3848.45.

PRODUCT

The PRODUCT function calculates the product of the specified values and has the following syntax:

PRODUCT(*list*)

The product is based on the following calculation:

*value * value * value **

Excel ignores references to blank cells or cells containing text. You can list the values in the function or enter a range reference to specify the values. The following are some examples:

Function	Excel Returns
=PRODUCT(5,3,7,8)	840
=PRODUCT(A1:D1)	840 (if the range contains 5, 3, 7, and 8)
=PRODUCT(SALES)	840 (if SALES is the name of the range A1:D1)

RAND

The RAND function produces a random number between 0 and 1. Each time you calculate the worksheet, this function produces a new random number. Although the function requires no arguments, parentheses must follow the function name, as the syntax indicates:

RAND()

To calculate a random number between any two numbers, use this syntax:

=START+RAND()*(END–START)

Substitute the starting number for START and the ending number for END. To calculate random numbers between 4 and 24, for example, enter =4+RAND()*(24-4). Note that this formula produces the decimal values between two numbers. You may want to remove the decimals. Doing so, however, can distort the beginning and ending values. Often, you end up with numbers equal to or greater than the starting value but less than the ending value. To remove the decimal values, try the following formula, which produces numbers from the START to the END values, inclusive:

=START+INT(RAND()*(END–START)+.5)

To choose a random number from a list of numbers, try the formula

=CHOOSE(1+RAND()*5,33,35,39,45,60)

where the 5 in the random-number calculation indicates the number of items in the list.

ROUND

The ROUND function rounds a value to a specified number of places. The difference between using this function and formatting the cell to display a specified number of places (using the Number command from the Format menu) is that the ROUND function permanently changes the number to the rounded version. Any subsequent calculations based on this number are made with the rounded number. A number rounded with the Number command from the Format menu merely displays a number in a certain format; it does not change the number. Calculations including the number use the original number, not the formatted version.

The syntax of the ROUND function follows:

ROUND(*value,precision*)

Value is the number to be rounded; *precision* is the number of places to which it is rounded. If the value 5.2573 appears in cell A1, for example, you can round it to two decimal places with the following formula:

=ROUND(A1,2)

The result of this formula is 5.26.

The standard for rounding monetary values is to two decimal places. This procedure also can be termed *rounding to the nearest penny*. You can round an amount to the nearest dime by entering 1 in place of 2 in the formula, as in the following:

=ROUND(A1,1)

When 0 is the precision argument, the formula rounds to the nearest dollar. When –1 is the argument, the formula rounds to the nearest 10 dollars, and when –2 is the argument, the formula rounds to the nearest 100 dollars.

> **Tip: Rounding to the Nickel**
>
> Although the ROUND function is useful for most rounding needs, it doesn't round to the nearest nickel. Rounding to the nearest nickel requires using the following formula:
>
> =IF(C3*10-INT(C3*10)<0.25,INT(C3*10)/10,
>
> IF(C3*10-INT(C3*10)<0.75,(INT(C3*10)+0.5)/10,
>
> (INT(C3*10)+1)/10))
>
> This formula rounds any number in cell C3 to the nearest nickel.

SIGN

The SIGN function performs a query to test whether the sign of a number is positive or negative. If the sign of the value is positive, the function returns 1. If the sign is negative, the function returns –1. If the number is 0, the function returns 0.

The syntax follows:

SIGN(*value*)

Consider this example:

=SIGN(C5)

If cell C5 contains –35, this function returns –1. If C5 contains the formula 24=4, the function returns 1.

SQRT

The SQRT function calculates the square root of a number, using the following syntax:

SQRT(*value*)

Value is the number whose square root you want to find. This value can be any nonnegative number, cell reference, or formula, provided that the formula does not calculate to a negative value. Consider this example:

SQRT(C5)

If C5 contains 9, this function returns 3.

> **Tip: Calculating the nth Root**
> You easily can determine the square root of a number with Excel's SQRT function. But how do you find, for example, the fifth root of a number? Enter the following formula into cell A3 with the desired root in cell A1 and the number in cell A2:
>
> =A2 ^ (1/A1)
>
> To find the fifth root of 259, for example, enter 5 into cell A1 and 259 into cell A2. The formula returns 3.0385.

SUM

SUM, the simplest of functions, is an easy way to add values. Its syntax follows:

SUM(*range*)

Range can be a row or column (or portions thereof) or a block of cells. If you want to add values not in a row or a column, enter a list. Suppose that you have the following values in your worksheet:

C1: 5
C2: 25
C3: 14
C4: 102
C5: 68

You can enter the following formula into cell C6 to add the column:

=SUM(C1:C5)

The sum of the five cells, 214, appears in cell C6.

You also can add the numbers in a block of cells by entering the entire range as the argument for the SUM function. The formula =SUM(C1:D5) adds the numbers in a two-by-five block of cells. You can specify any valid range in the SUM function.

TRUNC

TRUNC is similar to the INT function but does not round a number down to the nearest integer. Instead, TRUNC truncates the decimal value of a number, leaving the integer portion. Hence, the TRUNC value of –35.89 is –35. The function's syntax follows:

TRUNC(*value*)

The TRUNC function is a natural way to calculate the decimal value associated with a number. (The decimal portion of 829.98, for example, is .98.) Suppose that you want to find the decimal portion of a number in cell C5. The formula follows:

C10: =C5–(TRUNC(C5))

The formula in cell C10 takes the integer portion of the value in C5 and subtracts it from the original value in C5, resulting in the decimal portion.

Matrix Functions

Matrix functions perform calculations on matrices of values. A *matrix* is simply a range of values in rows and columns. Often, the matrix must represent a square range consisting of the same number of rows and columns.

This section describes Excel's matrix functions, but does not attempt to explain their purposes or teach matrix math. This section is written with the assumption that readers know why they want to use a matrix function.

MDETERM

The MDETERM function calculates the determinant value of a matrix. This value is derived from a special calculation of the values in the matrix. Its syntax follows:

MDETERM(*range*)

Range can be any valid range reference, provided that the range has the same number of rows and columns (that is, the range is square). If any cell in the range is blank or contains text, however, the function returns an error. The function also returns an error if the range is not square. The following is an example of an MDETERM function:

=MDETERM(A1:C3)

This function performs the calculation

$$A1*(B2*C3–B3*C2)+A2*(B3*C1–B1*C3)+A3*(B1*C2–B2*C1)$$

which is the determinant of the range A1:C3.

MINVERSE

The MINVERSE function calculates the inverse of a matrix of values. The matrix can be any valid worksheet range that is square, with the same number of rows and columns. The syntax follows:

MINVERSE(*range*)

When *range* is any square range of cells, this function calculates the inverse matrix of the specified range. To use this function, highlight a range of cells of the same proportions as the range specified in the argument; then enter the function using the syntax shown. Next, press ⌘-Return to create an array range as the result. The range reference must not contain text or blank cells.

MMULT

The MMULT function multiplies the values in two ranges, returning the matrix product of the ranges. The syntax follows:

MMULT(*range_1,range_2*)

The number of columns in *range_1* must be equal to the number of rows in *range_2*. To enter the formula, highlight a square range of cells (a third range). The number of rows and columns in this highlighted range must match the number of columns in *range_1* and the number of rows in *range_2*. Next, enter the function, identifying the two ranges, and press ⌘-Return to enter the function as an array into the highlighted range.

SUMPRODUCT

The SUMPRODUCT function calculates the sum of the products of 2 to 14 ranges of values. The first cell in each range is multiplied by the others, as are the second, third, and remaining cells in the ranges. Excel then adds these results for the sum of the products. The syntax follows:

SUMPRODUCT(*range1,range2,range3...*)

You can include up to 14 ranges. Note that all ranges must have the same number of cells and the same dimensions, or this function returns the #VALUE! error.

TRANSPOSE

The TRANSPOSE function transposes the values in a range of cells. You can convert the range A1:A5, for example, to the range A6:E6. The second range has the rows and columns from the first range transposed. A one-by-five range becomes a five-by-one range with the same values. The syntax is

TRANSPOSE(*range*)

where *range* is any valid worksheet range. First, highlight a range of cells that is the transposition of the range reference. Then enter this function as an array calculation by pressing ⌘-Return. If you have the values 1, 2, 3, 4, and 5 in cells A1:A5, for example, highlight any range containing five columns and one row (the transposition of A1:A5). Next, enter the function =TRANSPOSE(A1:A5) into the first cell of the highlighted range and press ⌘-Return to complete the transposition. The result appears in figure 6.26.

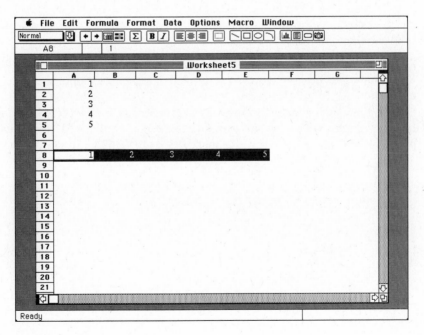

Fig. 6.26. Transposing a range.

Statistical Functions

Statistical functions work on groups of numbers. Common statistical tasks include calculating the average of a group, finding the minimum and maximum value of a group, and adding the numbers in a group. Statistical functions also include much more advanced functions, such as standard deviation and sample statistics calculations.

AVERAGE

The AVERAGE function calculates the average of a group of numbers. Typically, the numbers being averaged fall in a row or a column, but AVERAGE also can average randomly plotted values. The syntax follows:

> AVERAGE(*range*)
>
> or
>
> AVERAGE(*list*)

The first syntax line accommodates a range of cells in a row, column, or block; the second accommodates a group of cells placed at various spots in the worksheet. As with most formulas, you can substitute constant values, cell references, or other functions as the arguments.

Keep in mind that unwanted values of 0 destroy the accuracy of an average when the values being averaged are derived from IF statements or contain text. When used with a range reference, the AVERAGE function skips blank cells and interprets text as having a value of 0. When used with individual cell references, the function interprets text and blank cells as having values of 0. This interpretation can cause inaccuracies in AVERAGE calculations.

One way to avoid unwanted values of 0 in your AVERAGE functions is to enter formulas that "manually" calculate the average. Suppose that you have the following values in the range A1:A8:

> 36
> 66
> 18
> 99
> Text
> 33
> 0
> 0

To avoid any cell containing 0 or text, add the following formulas to the range B1:B8:

    =IF(AND(A1<>0,ISTEXT(A1)<>TRUE),1,0)

    =IF(AND(A2<>0,ISTEXT(A2)<>TRUE),1,0)

    =IF(AND(A3<>0,ISTEXT(A3)<>TRUE),1,0)

    =IF(AND(A4<>0,ISTEXT(A4)<>TRUE),1,0)

    =IF(AND(A5<>0,ISTEXT(A5)<>TRUE),1,0)

    =IF(AND(A6<>0,ISTEXT(A6)<>TRUE),1,0)

    =IF(AND(A7<>0,ISTEXT(A7)<>TRUE),1,0)

    =IF(AND(A8<>0,ISTEXT(A8)<>TRUE),1,0)

This basic formula means *If the value in column A is not 0 and is not text, place 1 here; otherwise, place 0 here*. This function produces a column of 1s and 0s. Now add column B in cell B10; for this example, column B produces a sum of 5. Next, add column A in cell A10; for this example, column A produces a sum of 252. Finally, divide cell A10 by cell B10 (using the formula =A10/B10) to obtain the average, 50.4.

COUNT, COUNTA

COUNT and COUNTA count the number of cells in a range or list of references. The COUNT function counts only numeric values; the COUNTA function counts all cells that are not blank. The syntax follows:

    COUNT(*range*)

    COUNTA(*range*)

Suppose that the range A1:A7 contains the following values:

    A1: 1

    A2: 0

    A3: Text

    A4: 983

    A5:

    A6: 298

    A7: 2

The COUNT and COUNTA functions produce the following results when you enter this range:

Function	Returns
COUNT(A1:A7)	5
COUNTA(A1:A7)	6

GROWTH, LOGEST

GROWTH and LOGEST are similar to the LINEST and TREND functions; however, they calculate the values for a regression line (the values m and b) as an exponential curve using the regression formula y=b*mx. The result is a curve that best fits the sample data expressed as *known_ys*. The syntax follows:

GROWTH(*known_ys,known_xs,new_xs,const*)

LOGEST(*known_ys,known_xs,const,stats*)

If the *known_xs* argument is omitted, the function assumes the values 1, 2, 3, 4, and so on to match, one for one, the *known_ys*. If you enter a range for *known_xs*, it should be the same size and shape as *known_ys*. If the *const* argument is set to FALSE, the constant value (b) is set to 1. If this argument is TRUE or omitted, Excel calculates the constant.

The result of the GROWTH function is an array of values that matches the *known_xs* based on the regression formula. Highlight a range of cells equivalent in size and shape to the *known_xs* range; then enter this formula as an array by pressing ⌘-Return to accept it.

The result of LOGEST is returned as an array range of two elements. You therefore should highlight a one-by-two range, enter the function, and press ⌘-Return to calculate the constant and coefficient values that fit the sample data. You then can use these values to calculate the *new_xs*.

LINEST, TREND

LINEST and TREND calculate the linear trend associated with known values, expressed as *known_xs* and *known_ys*. They have the following syntax:

LINEST(*known_ys,known_xs,const,stats*)

TREND(*known_ys,known_xs,new_xs,const*)

These functions calculate regression statistics and return the values that form a regression line that best fits your data. Given a set of *known_xs* values and *known_ys* values, the TREND function calculates the regression line as a series of new y values that correspond to the x values using the regression y=mx+b, where the following is true:

Value	Represents
y	Dependent value
x	Independent value
b	Constant value
m	Coefficient(s)

The *known_ys* value is called a *dependent value* because it is plotted based on the *known_xs* value; it is dependent on the x values. The TREND function calculates a new set of *y* values that also are dependent on the x values through the calculation y=mx+b. These new y values can be plotted on a chart to show the line. (If *known_xs* is omitted, the function assumes the values 1, 2, 3, 4, and so on to match, one for one, the *known_ys*.)

The steps for using the TREND function follow:

1. Enter two sets of values in adjacent ranges that contain the same number of cells.

2. Highlight a third range to contain the new y values. This range should be blank and should have the same number of cells as the other ranges.

3. Enter the TREND function into the first cell of the highlighted range. Reference the other ranges as the *known_ys* and *known_xs* values (see fig. 6.27).

4. Press ⌘-Return to calculate *new_ys* as an array range.

5. You may plot these values on a chart (see Chapter 11).

The LINEST function is similar to the TREND function, but it does not calculate the resulting *new_ys*. Instead, it calculates the constant and x coefficient values that produce the new y values using the formula y=mx+b. This calculation can be helpful for viewing the constant and coefficient values.

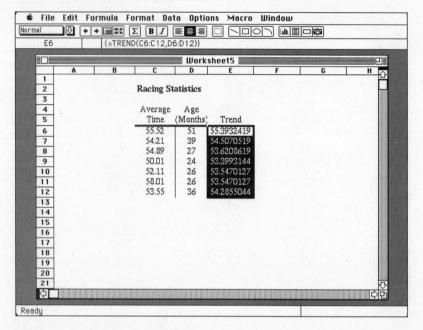

Fig. 6.27. *Entering the TREND function.*

This function can produce other regression statistics as well. If you enter the *const* argument as FALSE, Excel sets the constant value to 0 rather than calculating it. (Set *const* to TRUE or omit it to use the function normally.) If you enter the *stats* argument as TRUE, Excel provides extra stats for the regression.

To use the LINEST function, follow these steps:

1. Enter two sets of values in adjacent ranges that contain the same number of cells.

2. Highlight two blank cells in a row (a 1 x 2 array).

    If you plan to set *stats* to TRUE, highlight a block of cells five rows by five columns plus enough additional columns to match the number of values in your *known_xs* range. If *known_xs* contains 5 cells, then the range should be 5 rows by 10 columns.

3. Enter the LINEST function in the first of the two highlighted cells. Refer to the appropriate x and y values from step 1.

4. Press ⌘-Return to enter the function as an array. The first cell contains the coefficient value and the second cell contains the constant. Figure 6.28 shows the result.

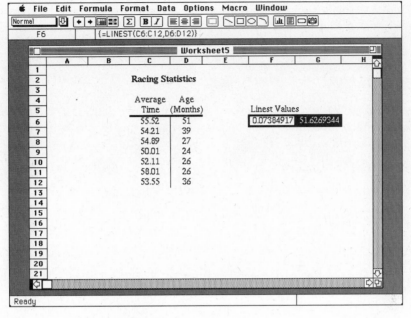

Fig. 6.28. *Calculating the LINEST function.*

5. To calculate the regression line values, enter the formula y=mx+b in cells adjacent to the *known_xs* and *known_ys* arguments.

Chapter 11 provides details about plotting regression lines on an xy chart.

MAX

The MAX function returns the maximum value in a group of cells. The syntax follows:

MAX(*range*)

Range can be a range of cells, random cell references, a formula, direct entries, or some combination of these, as in the following examples:

MAX(A1:A5)

MAX(A1,25,C23*3,"green")

If the range A1:A5 contains the values 1, 25, 3, 6, and 13, the first function returns 25. If cell C23 contains 100, the second function returns 300.

The MAX function ignores text cells and references to blank cells. If it cannot find a maximum value, the function returns 0.

MEDIAN

MEDIAN calculates the *median* of a group of values, defined as the middle value among the values. You can enter a range or include up to 14 values in a list. The syntax follows:

MEDIAN(*range*)

The median of the values 1, 2, 3, 4, and 5, for example, is 3.

MIN

The MIN function returns the minimum value in a group of cells. The syntax follows:

MIN(*range*)

Range can be a range of cells, random cell references, a formula, direct entries, or some combination of these, as in the following examples:

MIN(A1:A5)

MIN(A1,25,C23*3,"green")

The MIN function ignores text cells and references to blank cells.

Tip: Calculating the Span of Numbers
When evaluating a column of numbers, you may need to determine the span between the smallest and largest numbers. Suppose that you have the list 25, 49, 33, 120, 101, and 40. The span is 95 because the difference between the smallest number (25) and largest number (120) is 95. The following formula calculates this value:

=MAX(*range*)–MIN(*range*)

For both functions, enter the range containing the numbers.

STDEV

The STDEV function uses sample statistics to calculate its value. The syntax follows:

STDEV(*range*)

You can specify a range or list with this function. References to blank cells or text result in errors. The standard deviation of a population is different from the standard deviation of a partial (or sample) population.

STDEVP

The STDEVP function returns the standard deviation of a complete *population*, or group of numbers. (Because standard deviation is an advanced statistical function, the assumption in this chapter is that you know why you want to calculate it.) The syntax follows:

STDEVP(*range*)

Range can be any combination of two or more cell references, values, or expressions resulting in values. You also can enter a list of up to 14 arguments. References to blank cells or text result in errors. Figure 6.29 shows an example of the STDEVP function.

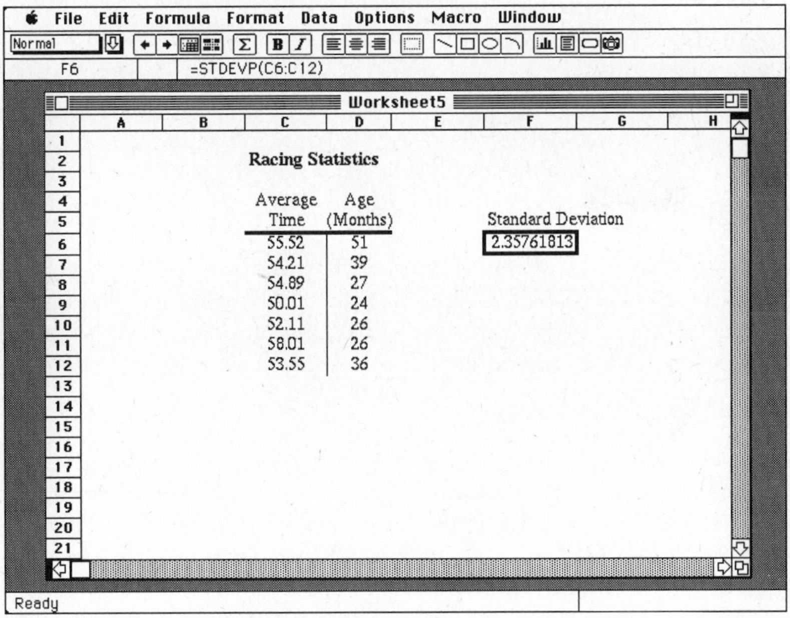

** File Edit Formula Format Data Options Macro Window**

F6   =STDEVP(C6:C12)

Worksheet5

	A	B	C	D	E	F	G	H
1								
2			Racing Statistics					
3								
4			Average	Age				
5			Time	(Months)		Standard Deviation		
6			55.52	51		2.35761813		
7			54.21	39				
8			54.89	27				
9			50.01	24				
10			52.11	26				
11			58.01	26				
12			53.55	36				

Ready

Fig. 6.29. Finding the standard deviation of a population.

The formula bar in figure 6.29 displays the formula used in the worksheet. Experiment with entering different numbers into the range. The more the numbers vary, the higher the STDEVP value.

VAR, VARP

Variance, which is similar to standard deviation, shows the amount of variance from an average that occurs over a population. The VAR function computes variance for a sample population, and the VARP function computes it for an entire population. (Because these are advanced statistical functions, the assumption in this chapter is that you know why you want to calculate them.) The syntax follows:

VAR(*range*)

VARP(*range*)

References to blank cells or 0 result in errors.

Text Functions

Text functions enable you to manipulate text strings. Besides simple concatenation, text manipulation involves dividing strings, extracting text from strings, determining the length of a string, changing upper- and lowercase status, and converting strings to values and back. Text functions are useful when you create forms or manipulate database information.

CHAR

The CHAR function sends a character to the worksheet (and consequently to the printer) when you enter the character's decimal value. This function is most useful for sending control codes to printers and for achieving special results such as color print or special characters. The syntax follows:

CHAR(*decimal_value*)

ANSI code charts, given in your printer or computer manual, show the character value (ASCII or ANSI) and decimal value of all keyboard characters. The CHAR function accommodates decimal values ranging from 1 to 255. Sending a printer control code by this method may require you to stack CHAR functions, as in the following:

CHAR(27) CHAR(88)

This combination, when sent to an ImageWriter printer, sets the line spacing at 8 lines per inch by sending the ANSI characters Escape and X. Remember that this function does not send the decimal value to the worksheet; it converts the value to the character equivalent and sends the ANSI character.

CLEAN

The seldom used CLEAN function removes nonprintable characters from a text string. The primary use for CLEAN is to convert data from another system that uses Excel. Characters that cannot be printed on-screen are removed. The syntax follows:

CLEAN(*text*)

CODE

The CODE function complements CHAR. Instead of returning a character based on a decimal value, CODE returns the decimal value based on a character. Using this function, you can produce your own ASCII chart by converting every keyboard character. The syntax for CHAR follows:

CODE(*character*)

Character can be any single character or reference to a cell containing a character or it can be a full text string or reference to a string. If a string is used, only the first character in the string is converted to the decimal value.

DOLLAR

The DOLLAR function converts a number to a *label*, or text string. After converting the number to a label, the function adds a dollar sign and two decimal places. The syntax follows:

DOLLAR(*value,decimal_places*)

Value can be any number or numeric expression. *Decimal_places* is the number of places you want to apply to the converted number. If you omit this argument, Excel assumes 2 places. The following is an example:

=DOLLAR(B5)

If cell B5 contains the numeric value 54.5, DOLLAR returns the text value $54.50. This function is useful when a text function requires you to convert a number to text before it accepts the value.

EXACT

The EXACT function compares two text strings to determine whether they match. The syntax follows:

EXACT(*text1,text2*)

If *text1* and *text2* match, upper- and lowercase included, the function returns the value TRUE; otherwise, it returns FALSE. Consider this example:

=EXACT(A1,A2)

If A1 contains *Elaine Smith* and A2 contains *Elaine smith*, this function returns FALSE. To circumvent Excel's consideration of upper- and lowercase, combine EXACT with the LOWER function, as in the following example:

=EXACT(LOWER(A1),LOWER(A2))

This variation converts both strings to lowercase letters before comparing them. The conversion does not appear on the worksheet; it is used only within this formula. The EXACT function often is combined with the IF function to act on the result of the test:

=IF(EXACT(LOWER(A1),LOWER(A2))=TRUE,"Match","No Match")

This formula returns Match if the two cells match and No Match if they don't match. For more details, see the descriptions of the IF and LOWER functions later in this chapter.

FIND

The FIND function searches for a text string within another text string and enables you to begin looking at a specified position. The function then returns a number representing the character position of the matched string. The syntax follows:

FIND(*text1,text2,position*)

If you omit the *position* argument, the function returns the first position of the matching text, relative to the leftmost character. The following is an example:

=FIND("a","Atlas")

This function returns 4, the position of the matching character relative to the left of the string. Notice that the function considers the case of the characters you specify. In this example, the formula did not return the position of the uppercase A. If you include a starting position for the FIND function, the result is the same, except that Excel begins searching at the specified character:

=FIND("a","atlas",3)

This function returns 4, showing that the first *a* was skipped because of the starting position. To ignore case, combine this function with the LOWER function to convert the text to lowercase letters before searching:

=FIND("a",LOWER(B5))

If B5 contains *"Atlas"*, this function returns 1, indicating that the first A was found.

If Excel cannot find the specified string, it returns #VALUE! to the cell. This message can be interpreted as an error.

> ### Tip: Use Quotation Marks in Constant Text Values
> Remember to use quotation marks when you enter a text string directly into a function or formula. Otherwise, Excel assumes that you have entered a range name.

FIXED

The FIXED function converts any number to a text string with a fixed number of decimal places. The syntax follows:

FIXED(*value,decimal_places*)

Value is the number being converted; *decimal_places* is the number of places to which the number is rounded, much like the DOLLAR format without the dollar signs. Note that the value is rounded to the number of places specified. Consider this example:

=FIXED(23.558,2)

This function returns the text string 23.56. If you omit the *decimal_places* argument, Excel assumes 2.

LEFT, MID, RIGHT

The LEFT, MID, and RIGHT functions return a specified portion of a text string. They have the following syntax:

LEFT(*text,position*)

MID(*text,position,length*)

RIGHT(*text,position*)

The function LEFT returns the leftmost portion of a text string, beginning at the first character and ending at the specified position. RIGHT returns the rightmost portion, beginning at the specified location and ending at the last character in the string. MID returns a specified portion from the middle of the string, beginning at the specified character and ending at the specified length.

The *text* argument is any text string in quotation marks, a reference to a cell containing a text string, or any text expression resulting in a text string. *Position* is the character position for the function; it can be any integer value less than the total number of characters in the string. You enter the starting character for the MID and RIGHT functions and the ending character for the LEFT function. The *length* variable is the number of characters to return from the middle of the string.

These functions are useful for concatenating or separating text. Suppose that you are converting an address database from another computer system. When you read the information into Excel, you notice that the city, state, and ZIP code are merged into one field (see fig. 6.30). You want to separate the ZIP code from the city and state so that you can manipulate the ZIP Code field independently. The RIGHT function can help you separate the ZIP Code field.

The formulas in column E use the RIGHT function to extract the last five characters in the address. If an address contains a ZIP+4 code, however, you must include the MID and RIGHT functions in a more complex formula in order to extract the ZIP+4 and standard codes as needed. The formula for extracting either code, to be entered in cell E2, follows:

=IF(ISERR(FIND("-",D2))<>TRUE,MID(D2,FIND("-",D2)
–5,10),RIGHT(D2,5))

Copy this formula down column E to extract all the ZIP codes. The result appears in figure 6.31.

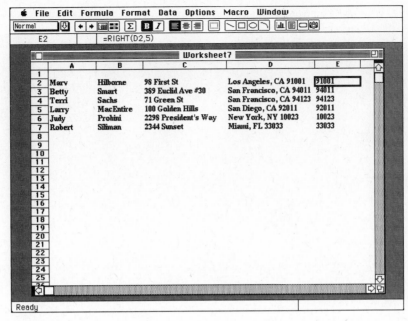

Fig. 6.30. *City, state, and ZIP code data in one field.*

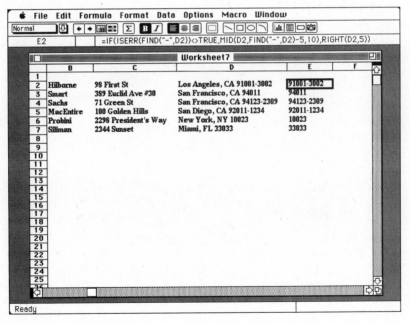

Fig. 6.31. *Extracting ZIP codes from a field.*

For more information about this formula, refer to the descriptions of the FIND, IF, and ISERROR functions elsewhere in this chapter.

> *Note:* You also can use the Parse command from the Data menu to separate imported data into individual cells. Refer to Chapter 8 for more information.

LEN

The LEN function returns the number of characters in a text string. It can be useful with the LEFT, MID, and RIGHT functions. The syntax follows:

> LEN(*text*)

You can specify any text string, text expression, or cell reference as the *text* argument. All spaces and special characters are counted. For example, the function

> =LEN("This is the string")

returns 18.

LOWER, UPPER

The LOWER function converts text from uppercase to lowercase; UPPER converts text from lowercase to uppercase. The syntax follows:

> LOWER(*text*)

> UPPER(*text*)

These functions convert the entire string specified. You can change only certain parts of the string by combining these functions with the LEFT, MID, and RIGHT functions. You can convert the first character of a string to an uppercase character, for example, with the following formula:

> =UPPER(LEFT(B4,1))&MID(B4,2,100)

This formula combines the UPPER and LEFT functions to make the first character of the string in cell B4 uppercase. Then the formula uses the MID function to concatenate this uppercase character with the rest of the string. Notice that the MID function uses the value 100, indicating that the function can return up to 100 characters in case the string is long.

PROPER

The PROPER function converts the first character of a text string to upper-case, exactly like the example in the preceding section, but PROPER does everything for you so you don't need the LEFT and MID functions. The syntax follows:

> PROPER(*text*)

The function

> =PROPER(john doe)

returns `John Doe`. Notice that the first character in both words is capitalized. If the first character in any word already was capitalized, no harm has been done.

REPLACE

The REPLACE function works much like the MID function. Instead of extracting a particular portion of a text string, however, REPLACE replaces it with a specified replacement string. As with the MID function, you specify the text string, the starting character within the string, and the number of characters to replace. Then you specify the replacement text. The syntax for REPLACE follows:

> REPLACE(*text,position,length,replacement_text*)

Text is the text or cell reference containing the text you want to modify. *Position* is the starting position in the text. The first character is at position 1, the second is at position 2, and so on. *Length* determines the number of characters after the starting position to be replaced. *Replacement_text* can be any text, text expression, or cell reference containing text. It replaces the text data starting at and including the character specified in *position*.

The replacement string does not have to have the same number of characters as the text being replaced. You can, for example, replace the word *white* with *very bright and shiny*, as in the following formula:

> =REPLACE(B5,16,5,"very bright and shiny")

If cell B5 contains *The object was white*, the new string reads *The object was very bright and shiny*.

REPT

The REPT function repeats a text string across a cell or cells. You determine the character or string you want to repeat and the number of times you want to repeat it, using the following syntax:

REPT(*text,value*)

Text is the character or string that you want to repeat; *value* is the number of times you want it repeated. REPT's primary purpose is to enhance the appearance of a worksheet by creating borders and divisions in a worksheet. The formula bar of figure 6.32 demonstrates the most common use of the REPT function, creating a line across the page.

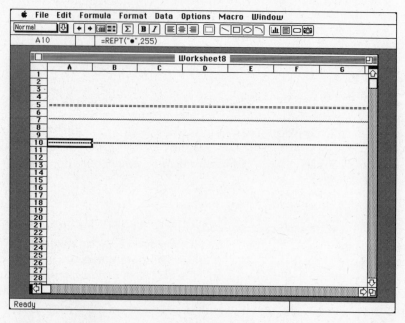

Fig. 6.32. Using REPT to create a line across the page.

SEARCH

The SEARCH function is identical to the FIND function, except that SEARCH ignores the case of the characters in the text and allows wild cards as part of the *text1* variable. The syntax follows:

SEARCH(*text1,text2,position*)

Excel searches for *text1* within *text2*, beginning its search at the location specified by *position*. You can include either of the following wild cards in the search string:

Wild Card	Represents
*	Any number of characters appearing at the position of the * within the criteria
?	Any single character appearing at the position of the ? within the criteria

SUBSTITUTE

The SUBSTITUTE function, which is similar to REPLACE, searches for a specified text string within another string and then replaces that text with new text. Unlike REPLACE, which replaces at a specified location, SUBSTITUTE searches for specified text within the specified string and replaces it. The syntax follows:

SUBSTITUTE(*text,search_text,replace_text,occurrence*)

Text is the string in which you are replacing information. *Search_text* is the information in *text* that you want to replace; *replace_text* is the new information replacing *search_text*. (The replacement text does not have to be the same length as the original text.) Finally, *occurrence* determines which occurrence of the search text is replaced (assuming that the text occurs more than once). If you omit this argument, Excel assumes that you want to replace the text only at the first occurrence.

Examples of the SUBSTITUTE function follow:

Formula	Returns
=SUBSTITUTE("Adam","a","o")	Adom
=SUBSTITUTE("one on one","one","two",2)	one on two

TEXT

The TEXT function is the same as the DOLLAR function except that it enables you to choose any number format for the resulting text string. The syntax follows:

TEXT(*value, format*)

Value can be any number or reference to a cell containing a number. *Format* is any format specification entered as a text string. (Chapter 5 provides a list of formats.) If you reference other cells, Excel ignores the original format of the data.

TEXT functions are most useful in macros when you want to place numeric information where text is more appropriate, such as in the text column of a custom-dialog-box control. The following is an example:

=TEXT(B5,"$#,##0 ;($#.##0)")

If cell B5 contains –5445.5, this function returns the text string ($5,445.50). You also can enter date and time formats in this function.

TRIM

The TRIM function removes unnecessary spaces from a string—spaces in front of the string, spaces after the string, and extra spaces between words. When splitting text strings or searching strings for specific information, unwanted spaces may confuse the process; you can issue the TRIM command to remove these spaces. The syntax follows:

TRIM(*text*)

Consider this example:

=TRIM(B4)

If cell B4 contains "Now is the time   for all   ", the function returns *Now is the time for all*.

VALUE

The VALUE function converts text strings into numeric values, as long as the string contains only characters that can be interpreted as values. The function recognizes numeric symbols as parts of numeric values, including the following symbols:

$, . ( ) %

The syntax follows:

VALUE(*text*)

For example, the formula

=VALUE(A1)

returns 2 if cell A1 contains the text ="2". If cell A1 contains the text string
="$(2,443.00)," the function returns the numeric value –2443.

Trigonometric Functions

Trigonometric functions perform trigonometric calculations, such as finding the degrees of an angle and figuring sine, cosine, and tangent values. Some of the following explanations give examples of how to use the functions; these explanations, however, do not offer complete lessons in trigonometry. The assumption in this book is that you know how to apply these functions.

The functions and their examples follow a basic trigonometric model. The right triangle in figure 6.33 shows a quadrant in which the angle POX is identified as z.

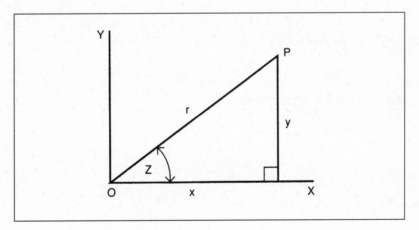

Fig. 6.33. *Basic trigonometric model.*

Given that the lines OP and OY increase in a positive direction, the following formulas apply:

$\cos z° = x/r$

$\sin z° = y/r$

$\tan z° = y/z$ (where x is not 0)

$\tan z° = \sin z°/\cos z°$

Working with the values you know (that is, the given values in the problem), you can use the functions in this section to calculate unknown values and angles. Remember that angles are always expressed in radians.

ACOS

ACOS calculates the arccosine of a value. The syntax follows:

ACOS(*value*)

Value must be in the range –1 to 1. The resulting value is in the range from 0 to pi. If the value you supply is not acceptable, Excel returns an error.

Suppose that you are flying a plane at 140 mph from point A to point B and the wind is traveling at 5 mph perpendicular to your direction (see fig. 6.34). You can use the angle ACB to calculate your flight. This example calculates the angle with the ACOS function, but you can use the ASIN function to determine the angle CAB.

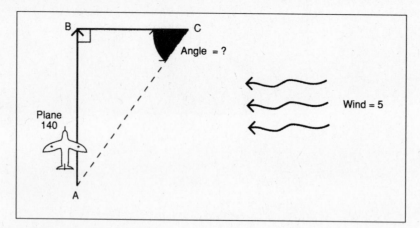

Fig. 6.34. Calculating your flight.

The formula for this calculation is =ACOS(5/140). Dividing 5 by 140 produces the cosine of the angle ACB. The result is 1.54—the radian value of the angle ACB. To display this value in degrees, use the following formula:

=ACOS(5/140)*180/PI()

The result of this calculation is 87.95 degrees, which is the angle ACB.

ACOSH, ASINH, ATANH, COSH, SINH, TANH

These functions return inverse hyperbolic values for the cosine, sine, tangent, arccosine, arcsine, and arctangent, respectively. They work in the same way as their counterparts described in the preceding sections. Their syntax follows:

ACOSH(*value*)

ASINH(*value*)

ATANH(value)

COSH(*value*)

$$\text{calculates} \quad \frac{e \char`^ value + e \char`^ -value}{2}$$

SINH(*value*)

$$\text{calculates} \quad \frac{e \char`^ value - e \char`^ -value}{2}$$

TANH(*value*)

$$\text{calculates} \quad \frac{\text{SINH(value)}}{\text{COSH(value)}}$$

ASIN

The ASIN function calculates the arcsine of a value and has the following syntax:

ASIN(*value*)

Value must be between -1 and 1; the value returned is between the values -π/2 and π/2.

The following example illustrates an application of the ASIN function. Suppose that you are driving up a 5-mile hill that is 1,000 feet above sea level, and you started your drive 100 feet above sea level. The ASIN function calculates the angle at which you are driving uphill, as shown in figure 6.35.

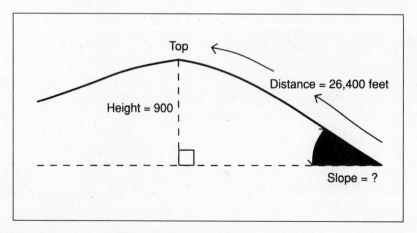

Fig. 6.35. *Using the ASIN function.*

Note that the height of the hill is the difference between the two elevation levels, because the desired height is relative to the current elevation of the car. The ASIN function calculates the angle (in radians) by using the sine of the angle. You calculate the sine by dividing elevation by distance:

=ASIN(1000–100/(5280*5))*180/PI()

The following is a breakdown of this function's calculations:

1000-100	Calculates the height of the hill relative to the current location of the car.
(5280*5)	Converts the 5 miles to feet.
(1000–100/(5280*5))	Calculates the sine (in radians) of the desired angle. This expression is required as the argument for the ASIN function.
*180/PI()	Converts the resulting angle (expressed in radians) to degrees.

This function displays the angle in degrees. The result is 1.95 degrees.

ATAN

The arctangent is calculated by the ATAN function, which uses the angle (in radians) of a tangent. The result also is expressed in radians. The syntax of the ATAN function follows:

ATAN(*value*)

where *value* is the tangent value. The result is in the range $-\pi/2$ to $\pi/2$. This function is similar to ASIN, but instead of knowing the hypotenuse of the triangle, you know the two sides.

Continuing with the example from the ASIN function, suppose that you don't know the distance of the road, but you know that the aeronautical distance between points A and B is 26,500 feet. Now the calculation is

=ATAN(900/26500)*180/PI( )

This function determines the slope of the hill in degrees—1.945.

ATAN2

The ATAN2 function calculates the four-quadrant tangent of the tangent values *x_value* and *y_value*. It has the following syntax:

ATAN2(*x_value,y_value*)

The result is displayed in radians (unless converted to degrees). The two values cannot both be 0; if they are, Excel returns an error. The function

=ATAN2(140,25)

returns the value 0.18.

Note that the ATAN2 function acts on the two tangent values used to produce the tangent angle for the ATAN function. In other words, using the function ATAN2(x,y) is identical to using ATAN(y/x), as shown with the ATAN function.

COS, SIN, TAN

The COS, SIN, and TAN functions calculate the cosine, sine, and tangent of angles expressed in radians. The result is a value between –1 and 1. The syntax for these functions follows:

COS(*radians*)

SIN(*radians*)

TAN(*radians*)

You can use the SIN function, for example, to determine the height of a triangle for which you know the hypotenuse and an angle in degrees (see fig. 6.36).

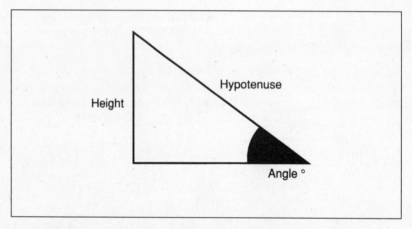

Fig. 6.36. *Calculating the sine.*

The formula for calculating the height of the triangle is

=hypotenuse*SIN(angle*2*PI()/360)

Summary

This chapter provided details about Excel worksheet functions. Worksheet functions perform special calculations that you can enter in your formulas. Many of these functions are useful for financial calculations. When entering a function, remember that Excel expects you to follow the syntax for that function. Although the syntax varies for the different functions, all functions have three basic parts: the function name, parentheses, and arguments. Some additional points to remember follow:

- Arguments come in many different types, including ranges, values, text, and cell references.

- You usually can enter an argument that requires a numeric value as a number, a numeric expression, or a reference to a cell containing a number or numeric expression.

- You usually can enter an argument that requires a text value as a text string in quotation marks, as a text expression, or as a reference to a cell containing text or a text expression.

- When you use the ROUND function to round a number up or down, the value of the number changes for subsequent calculations.

- The trigonometric functions return values that represent angles. These angles usually are expressed in radians, not degrees. You can convert the values to degrees if you want.

- Many financial functions enable you to assume either side of a transaction—the lender's side or the borrower's. Negative values (cash out) for the lender are positive values (cash in) for the borrower. Negative and positive values determine which side of the transaction you are on.

- The HLOOKUP and VLOOKUP functions are useful for finding a value in a table.

- The IF function is one of the most powerful functions available. It enables your worksheet formulas to make decisions based on values throughout the sheet.

- Date and time functions are useful for performing date and time math calculations.

Chapter 7, "Using Multiple Worksheets and Linking Worksheets," explains how you can work with more than one Excel worksheet and window at a time.

7

Using Multiple Worksheets and Linking Worksheets

As your worksheets grow larger and more complex, you may need to view more than one part of the worksheet or more than one worksheet at the same time. Suppose that you have a worksheet containing a complex table of values used in a look-up procedure and an area for data input. Because both areas cannot fit in a single screen, how do you view both areas at the same time?

Now suppose that you want to view a single worksheet in two ways at the same time—one screen showing the formulas used throughout the worksheet and another screen showing the results of those formulas. (This procedure can be useful in editing and debugging worksheets.) To view a worksheet in two ways at the same time, you can use several methods, all of which are explained in this chapter.

You sometimes may need to break up tasks into individual worksheets. Because the data in each worksheet is related, however, you may want to link them so that worksheets reference one another's information. When you change the information in one worksheet, all other worksheets that reference the information change accordingly.

In this chapter, you learn how to link worksheets. First, you learn how to split a single worksheet into multiple areas, or *panes*—a method that is useful especially for creating permanent worksheet titles. Next, you learn how to view several worksheet windows at one time and how to display one

347

worksheet in several windows. Other topics discussed in this chapter include linking worksheets by using external references, using Dynamic Data Exchange (DDE) and edition files to link worksheets with files from other applications, and converting files among various formats. (DDE is a standard for linking data between different programs and may or may not be used with your other programs.)

Manipulating Windows

When you have a large worksheet, viewing all the information on-screen at the same time is difficult. Excel provides different methods to help you view the worksheet. You can split the screen, and you can freeze the split-screen panes. This section discusses both methods.

Displaying Titles and Splitting the Screen

Often, worksheets are designed to display permanent titles (such as month names) in the first few rows at the top. The first one or two columns on the left side also may be used for displaying permanent titles. As you scroll down and across the worksheet, you may want to keep these titles from scrolling out of view.

Suppose that you have a 12-month-projection worksheet in which all month names appear across the top, and expense categories appear in the first column. This worksheet may look something like figure 7.1.

Because all 12 months do not fit into one screen view, you have to scroll left and right to see the various months. When you scroll left and right, however, the expense categories in the left column scroll out of view, making the job of identifying categories difficult. Likewise, when you scroll up and down past the bottom of the screen, the month names disappear from the top.

Excel's split-screen feature can solve this problem. You can designate a portion of the worksheet (at the top and/or side) as a title area by splitting the screen at the appropriate location. Each pane operates independently, which enables you to keep one pane in view as you scroll through another pane. This feature is useful especially for keeping headings in a fixed position above or to the side of your data.

	A	B	C			K	L	M	N
1									
2									
3		January	February			October	November	December	
4	Salaries	5000	2300			3000	3500	4500	
5	Professional Svcs	600	600			600	650	650	
6	Advertising	9000	9000			9000	9000	9000	
7	Bank	200	200			230	200	245	
8	Freight	5000	4500			5500	5690	7500	
9	Insurance	3500	3500			3500	3500	3500	
10	Office Supplies	300	300			300	300	300	
11	Rent/Util/Phone	6500	6500			6400	6200	6900	
12	Depreciation	2200	2000			1500	1800	1600	
13	Taxes	2500	4500			3500	3500	3500	
14		34800	33400			33530	34340	37695	
15									
16									
17									
18									
19									
20									
21									
22									
23									
24									
25									

Fig. 7.1. *A large worksheet.*

To split the screen at the top of the worksheet, click on the vertical split-screen marker, as shown in figure 7.2. The cursor changes shape as it passes over this marker.

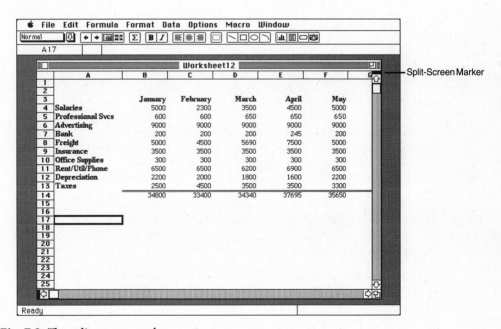

Fig. 7.2. *The split-screen marker.*

Click and drag the pointer downward to move the marker to the position you want. Figure 7.3 shows the marker in a new position.

		January	February	March	April	May
4 Salaries		5000	2300	3500	4500	5000
5 Professional Svcs		600	600	650	650	650
6 Advertising		9000	9000	9000	9000	9000
7 Bank		200	200	200	245	200
8 Freight		5000	4500	5690	7500	5000
9 Insurance		3500	3500	3500	3500	3500
10 Office Supplies		300	300	300	300	300
11 Rent/Util/Phone		6500	6500	6200	6900	6500
12 Depreciation		2200	2000	1800	1600	2200
13 Taxes		2500	4500	3500	3500	3300
14		34800	33400	34340	37695	35650

— Split-Screen Marker

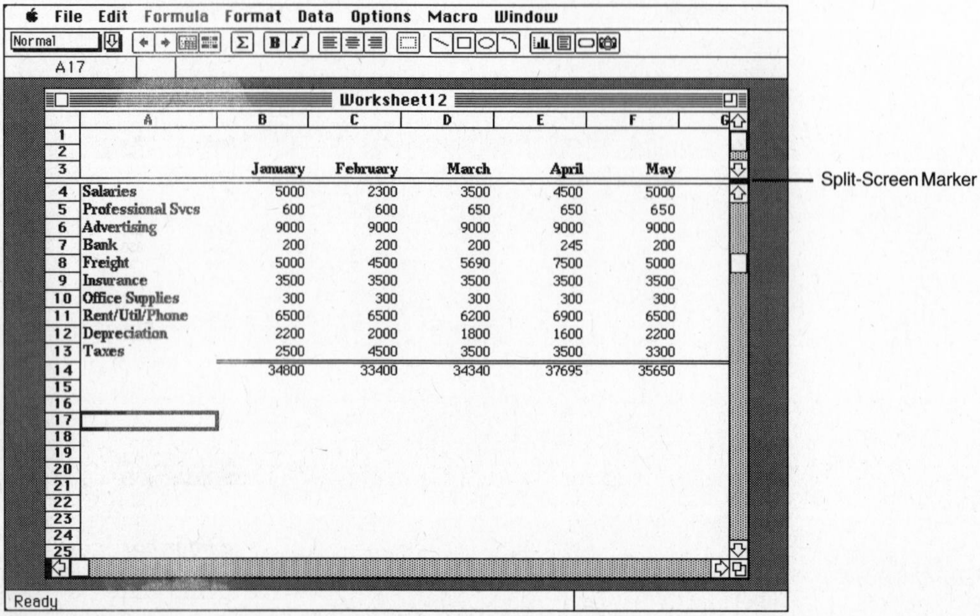

Fig. 7.3. The split-screen marker in a new position.

After you move the marker into place, Excel splits the screen into two panes. Each pane acts independently of the other with respect to vertical movement, such as vertical scrolling. In fact, each pane has its own vertical scroll bar (see fig. 7.3). Because both panes reflect the same worksheet, you can display the same information in both areas by moving both vertical scroll bars to their topmost positions (see fig. 7.4).

When you split the screen horizontally, as shown in figure 7.4, vertical movement is independent. Horizontal movement—that is, horizontal scrolling—is synchronized. In other words, when you scroll left and right, both panes move simultaneously.

You also can split the worksheet vertically. When you split the screen vertically using the horizontal split-screen marker, the two panes of the worksheet appear side by side, as shown in figure 7.5. In this case, each pane has its own horizontal scroll bar and moves independently of the other horizontally. When you use the vertical scroll bar, both sides move simultaneously.

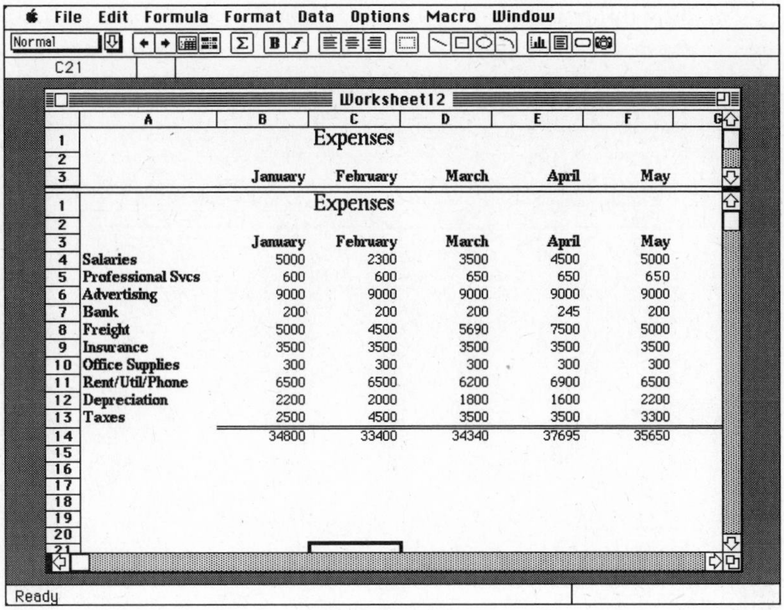

Fig. 7.4. *Both panes of the split screen showing the same information.*

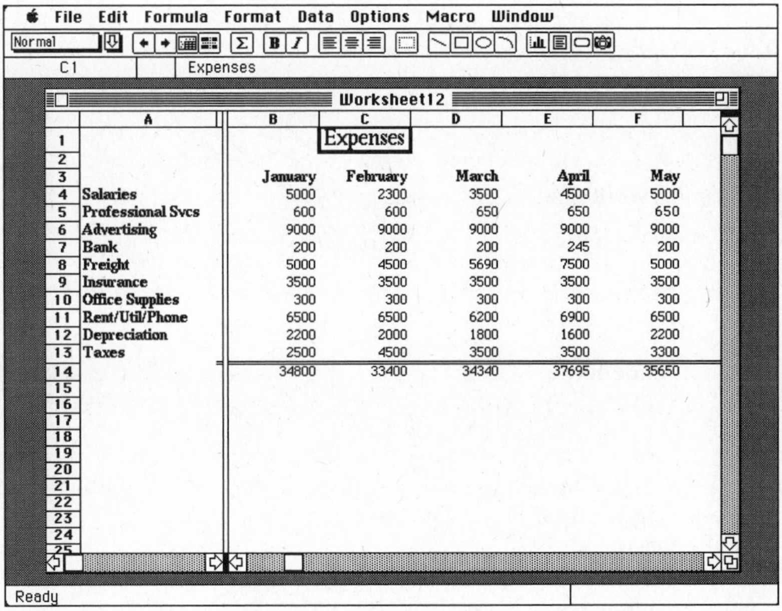

Fig. 7.5. *Setting the vertical split-screen display.*

As you may have guessed, you can set both the vertical and horizontal split-screen markers to create four panes, as shown in figure 7.6.

	File Edit Formula Format Data Options Macro Window

	Worksheet12					
	A	**B**	**C**	**D**	**E**	**F**
1			Expenses			
2						
3		January	February	March	April	May
4	Salaries	5000	2300	3500	4500	5000
5	Professional Svcs	600	600	650	650	650
6	Advertising	9000	9000	9000	9000	9000
7	Bank	200	200	200	245	200
8	Freight	5000	4500	5690	7500	5000
9	Insurance	3500	3500	3500	3500	3500
10	Office Supplies	300	300	300	300	300
11	Rent/Util/Phone	6500	6500	6200	6900	6500
12	Depreciation	2200	2000	1800	1600	2200
13	Taxes	2500	4500	3500	3500	3300
14		34800	33400	34340	37695	35650

Fig. 7.6. Setting both vertical and horizontal split-screen markers.

To move among the various panes of the split-screen display, click on any cell in the pane you want to move to, or use the following keys on the extended keyboard:

Key Combination	*Effect*
F6	Moves the pointer to the next pane of the split-screen display
Shift-F6	Moves the pointer to the preceding pane of the split-screen display

Because you are looking at one worksheet, changes made in one pane appear in all other panes. To return to the normal display, move the split-screen markers to their original positions.

> *Note:* If you do not see a separate scroll bar on each side of the split screen, you have not allowed enough room for a scroll bar on each side. If the information you want to see is showing, however, you may not need to make adjustments by moving the markers.

Freezing Split-Screen Panes

In addition to using the split-screen feature to show any two parts of a worksheet at any time, you can split the screen to display titles at the top or side. Each pane does not need to have its own scroll bar for independent movement; in fact, you may want to freeze the information in place at the top or side of the screen.

Suppose that you split the screen to display month names at the top. When you scroll the bottom pane vertically, the month names remain in place. You do not care about scrolling the top pane at all. You can prevent vertical scrolling in the top pane and horizontal scrolling in the left pane, thus keeping the title information in place.

To freeze the panes, move the split-screen markers into place and then choose the Freeze Panes command from the Options menu. When you freeze the panes, the individual scroll bars disappear (see fig. 7.7).

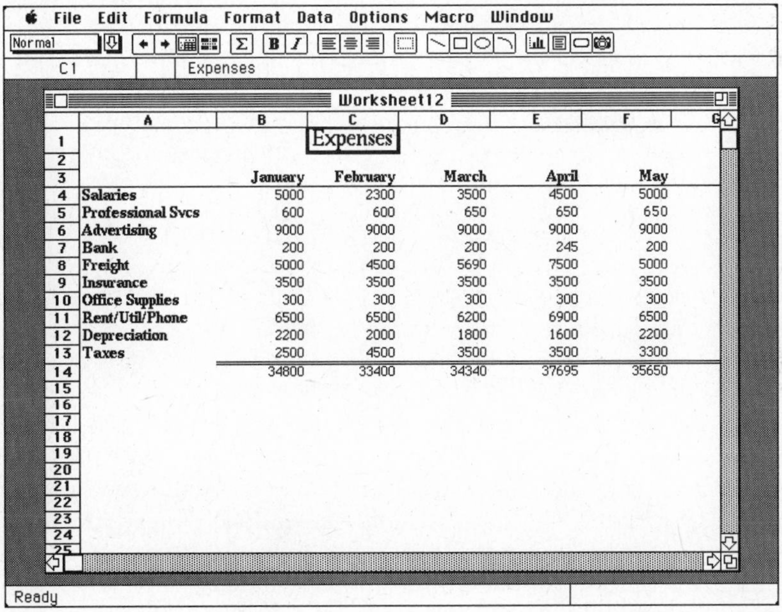

Fig. *7.7. Freezing the panes and removing the individual scroll bars.*

You can move the pointer to any area of the screen, including the frozen panes. To prevent the titles from being changed, combine the split-screen features with the cell-protection features described in Chapter 3.

After you freeze the panes in a worksheet, the Freeze Panes command on the Options menu changes to the Unfreeze Panes command. Use the Unfreeze Panes command to return the worksheet to normal. You cannot use the Freeze Panes command to freeze one pane and not the other pane; the command applies to the top and left panes at the same time.

Using Multiple Windows

The split-screen feature is handy for keeping some information in view as you scroll through other parts of the worksheet. This feature can help extend the limited view of the worksheet imposed by the screen. You may, however, find the split-screen technique insufficient for displaying exactly what you want, because not all information fits neatly into rows at the top of the screen or into columns on the left side. The split screen really is meant for headings.

You may have a large block of information, such as a table or chart, that you want to keep in view. The best solution is to open a new window in the worksheet and display various parts of the worksheet in the various windows. Unlike split screens, you can have numerous windows for the same worksheet. The windows also can show various sizes and shapes of the worksheet. You can move among windows, resize them, and close them at any time.

Creating several windows in a worksheet can be useful in many ways. You can enter tables, lists, and other reference data in a remote area of the worksheet and use a separate window to display that area for data-entry reference. (This procedure is a good way to display notes or help screens designed for your worksheet.) You also can display formulas in one window and the results of those formulas in another window. To display formulas, select the Display command from the Options menu, and then check Formulas in the dialog box. (This procedure is useful for debugging worksheets.) Finally, you can use multiple windows instead of using the scroll bar or the Goto command to simply move from section to section within a worksheet. Just keep the various sections of the worksheet in various windows and switch between them.

Opening New Windows

To create a new window in a worksheet, select the New Window command from the Window menu. The New Window command duplicates the current window, providing two identical views. The next time you pull down the Window menu, Excel displays the names of the two windows at the bottom of the menu. The new window has the same name as the original window, but Excel adds :1 to the original name and :2 to the new name, indicating that two versions of the same worksheet exist (see fig. 7.8).

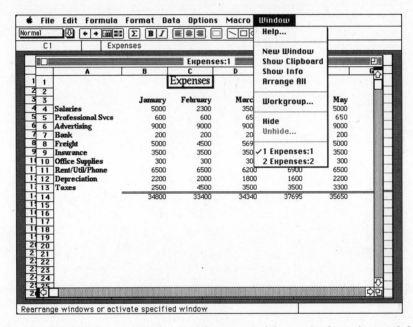

Fig. 7.8. *The Window menu, showing the names of the original window and the new window.*

When you create a new window, its dimensions are the same as those of the original, and the two windows probably will overlap. For the sake of convenience, you may want to change the sizes of the two windows.

To close a window, click on the Close box. If other windows to the same worksheet are open, Excel will not close the worksheet until all the windows are closed.

Sizing and Arranging Windows

The best aspect of the window feature is that you can use the Size box to shrink the windows so that you can see all windows simultaneously. You then can use each window's scroll bars to display the information you want. Figure 7.9 shows an example of resized windows.

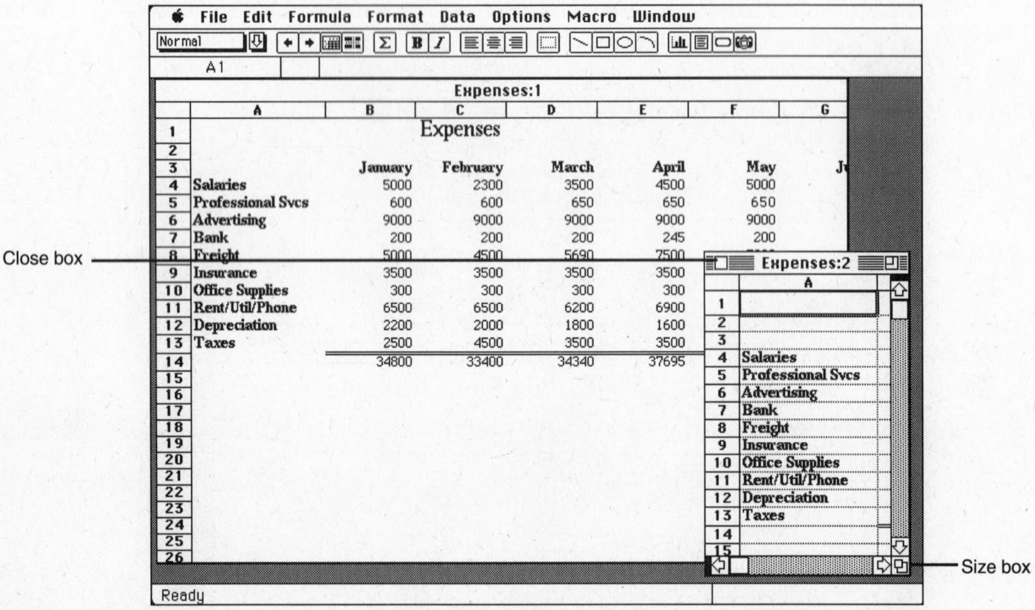

Fig. 7.9. Two windows, resized so that both are in view at one time.

Using standard Macintosh techniques, you can move the windows to any location, shape them, overlap them, expand them, and so on. These "windowing" techniques are common to most Macintosh programs (see your Macintosh user's guide for details). In addition, Excel provides a special command that enables you to arrange multiple windows quickly. When more than one window is open, select the Arrange Windows command from the Window menu; Excel arranges all open windows side by side in an orderly fashion (see fig. 7.10).

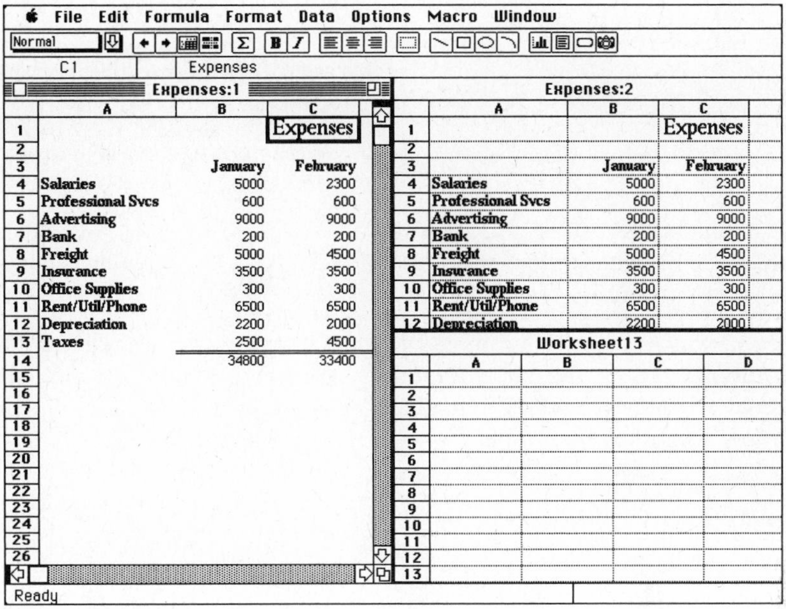

Fig. 7.10. *Using the Arrange Windows command.*

Activating Windows

When you click on the Window menu, the bottom of the menu displays the names of all open windows. Notice that beside one of the names is a check mark, indicating that the window is selected and in view; the other windows are beneath the selected window. The current window (the one on top) is the one that you can work in. To work in another window, bring that window to the top. One way to activate a window is to select its name from the Window menu. (You always can tell which window is selected by comparing title bars. The entire title bar of the active window is displayed.)

If you have used the Arrange Windows command or shrunk the windows by using the Size box, you may be able to see more than one window at a time. In this case, the active (or current) window is not necessarily on top of the others; the active window may be beside the others. You still can select a window name from the Windows menu; however, if several windows are in view, you may find it easier to click on the window you want.

In addition to using the Window menu or mouse to activate a window, you can use the following combinations on the extended keyboard:

Key Combination	Effect
⌘-F6	Moves the pointer to the next window and activates that window
Shift-⌘-F6	Moves the pointer to the preceding window and activates that window

The extended keyboard also provides keys for closing and maximizing windows, a process also called *zooming out*. To close the current window, press ⌘-F4. To maximize the current window, press ⌘-F10.

You can add as many windows as you want (within the limit of available memory) by using the New Window command. Remember that each window displays the same worksheet; when you make changes in one window, those changes appear in all other windows. Likewise, when you save the worksheet, only one file appears on the disk.

Freezing Windows

Suppose that you add a second window to your worksheet so that you can view two areas at the same time. Scrolling the information you want into view may take some time, and you do not want the window to be changed. Because you do not plan to use the scroll bars to display different data, you may decide to protect, or freeze, the worksheet window arrangement so that the arrangement cannot be changed. When you *freeze* windows, you prevent them from being moved, sized, or closed independently of the others.

To freeze your window arrangement, select the Protect Document command from the Options menu and check the Windows box. When the check mark is present, all open windows in the active worksheet are frozen. Remember to save the worksheet to make these changes permanent. If you have other worksheet windows open, you must activate them before you can freeze them.

Frozen windows contain no Close boxes. You still can activate any window by clicking on it or selecting the window's name from the Window menu. You can remove scroll bars by using the Options Workspace command with the Scroll Bars option.

To close the worksheet, select the Close command from the File menu. The Close command closes all windows associated with the worksheet. See Chapter 3 for more information about the Options Protect command and the use of passwords.

Saving Worksheets with Multiple Windows

When you save a worksheet that has more than one window, Excel saves one copy of the worksheet and "remembers" how many windows were open, as well as their positions. When you open the worksheet again, all windows will be intact. If you used the Protect command from the Options menu to freeze the windows, Excel remembers that also. The windows will appear just as they were when you saved the worksheet.

To save a file without its various windows, first close the windows by clicking on their Close boxes; then save the worksheet. Remember that this procedure applies to multiple windows in the same worksheet created with the New Window command from the Window menu—not to different worksheets.

Using Multiple Worksheets

Excel enables you to open simultaneously several worksheets, each in a separate window. To perform this procedure, select the Open option from the File menu (even though another worksheet already is open and in view). Because each worksheet also creates a new window, the worksheets' names are displayed in the Window menu.

Opening multiple worksheets at one time is an important part of linking worksheets. This procedure is explained in more detail under "Linking Worksheets" later in this chapter.

Because all new windows look roughly the same, opening multiple windows in a worksheet and multiple worksheets at the same time can be confusing. Some windows will apply to different worksheets; other windows will apply to the same worksheet.

If you open several windows simultaneously, the Window menu may not be capable of displaying all the names at the same time. In this case, the More Windows option appears in the menu (see fig. 7.11). After you select the More Windows command, Excel presents a dialog box containing the names of the other open windows. Be careful, however, when you open many windows at one time—you easily can run out of memory.

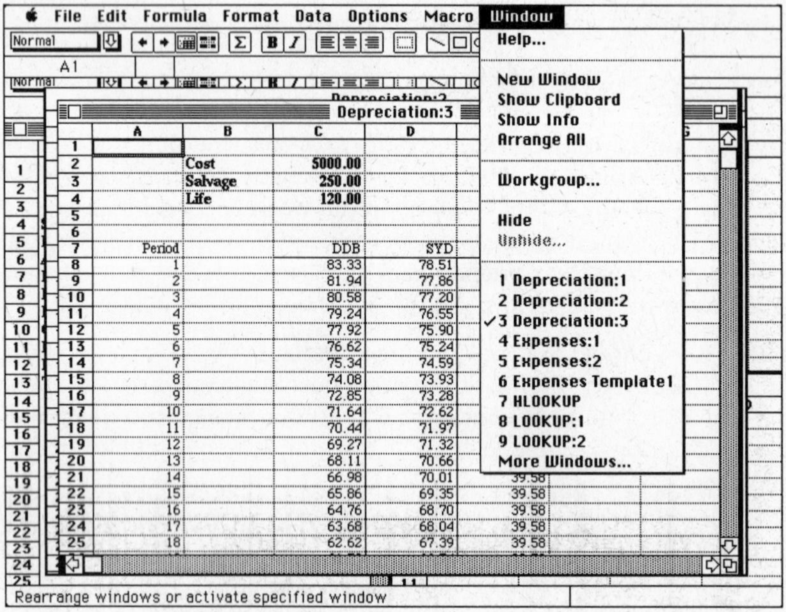

Fig. 7.11. The More Windows option.

Hiding Windows

When you have multiple files open—such as those linked with complex external references—you may want to hide one or more of the open windows to clean up the desktop and protect the hidden worksheets from tampering. The hidden worksheets still are open and available to other worksheets.

To hide a window, activate the window by clicking on it or by selecting its name from the Window menu. Next, choose the Hide command from the Window menu. The window disappears, and its name no longer appears in the Window menu. The worksheet appears to be closed, but it actually still is open, and any complex external references to the worksheet function normally. The Hide command also is useful for hiding macro sheets.

When you hide a window, the Hide Command in the Window menu changes to the Unhide command. Select Unhide to return hidden windows to normal. If you hide all the windows on the desktop, Excel places the Unhide command in the File menu.

Saving Arrangements of Worksheets

If you spend a lot of time arranging windows, hiding them, and generally setting up the workspace, you may decide to save the arrangement for future use. Suppose that you have several linked worksheets open and in view. To clean up the desktop, you decide to hide one of the windows. You arrange the other two windows for maximum efficiency and even protect one window by using the Protect command from the Options menu. Although each worksheet's window arrangement and protection status is saved when you use the Save command from the File menu, this command cannot recreate the group of worksheets. You must open each worksheet to get them all into view again.

Excel has a special command for saving the arrangement of several worksheets that are open at the same time. You can save the arrangement of several worksheets with the Save Workspace command from the File menu, which saves the following information:

- Size and position of all on-screen windows

- Current Display and Workspace settings from the Options menu

- Current preferred chart type (see Chapter 12)

- Current calculation settings

- Current Info window settings

This information is saved in a special file called a *workspace file*, which appears on disk with a special icon. When you enter Excel by double-clicking on this icon, all files are opened in the arrangements that you saved—so you don't have to open the files individually. You also can use the Open command from the File menu to open a workspace file. First open the files you want and arrange their windows; then use the Save Workspace command from the File menu to save the arrangement. The Save Workspace dialog box shown in figure 7.12 appears.

Enter a name for this workspace. Do not use the name of an existing worksheet. This procedure saves the arrangement on disk as a workspace file and also saves the individual files.

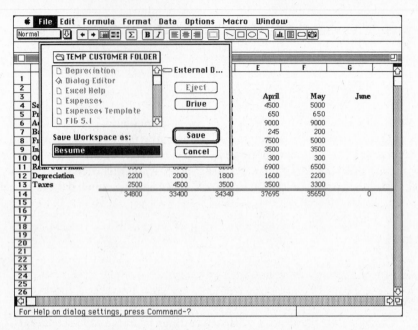

Fig. 7.12. *The Save Workspace dialog box.*

> ***Caution:*** Remember that a workspace is not a worksheet; do not delete worksheet files because you have saved them in a workspace file. The workspace file contains only the window arrangement of the worksheets—not the worksheets themselves. Saving the workspace saves the worksheets, but each in its original file under its original name. Copies of the worksheets are not saved with the workspace. You therefore can open the files individually by using the Open command from the File menu and then choosing the worksheet name—not the workspace name.

Avoid moving the individual worksheets to different folders when they are part of a workspace. Excel may not be able to locate the file when you open the workspace. Also, if you rename the worksheets, you have to recreate the workspace.

Saving Time with Workgroups

Excel enables you to edit worksheets in groups called *workgroups*. The worksheets in a workgroup all are affected simultaneously when you make formatting changes, apply display options, and enter or edit data. When you need to modify several worksheets that all have the same basic design and structure, you can save time by defining them as a workgroup.

Workgroups work hand in hand with worksheet templates (described in Chapter 5). A *template* enables you to create several worksheets that all have the same structure and design—even some of the same data, such as headings and important formulas. Saving a worksheet as a template enables you to create similar worksheets without starting from scratch. This feature is useful for worksheets that you change monthly, such as budgets or financial reports.

Excel's workgroup feature enables you to make changes simultaneously to several similar worksheets—such as those created with the same template. Suppose that you used a template to create six monthly reports, and you need to go back and add a formula to all the worksheets. Turn the six worksheets into a workgroup, and you can perform the entire operation in one shot. When you add data, the data appears in the same range on all the worksheets. When you edit data, all worksheets reflect the edit. When you format cells, the same cells on all the worksheets are affected.

Creating Workgroups

To set up a workgroup, follow these steps:

1. Open all the worksheets you want to include in the workgroup.

   These worksheets do not need to have been created from a template (but that situation is likely). You can have other worksheets (worksheets not to be included in the group) open at the same time. Hidden worksheets cannot be used in a workgroup.

2. Activate one of the worksheets in the group. You will enter the changes into this worksheet.

3. Select the Workgroup command from the Window menu. Excel displays a list of all open (unhidden) worksheets.

4. Excel automatically highlights all the names in the list, assuming that you want all open worksheets in the workgroup. You can

select names from this list individually by holding down the Command key and clicking on each worksheet name that you want to include in the workgroup.

5. Press Return or click OK when finished. (To remove a worksheet that you have selected, click on the worksheet name again.)

The active worksheet is now the entry sheet for all other worksheets in the group. When you make any changes in this worksheet, Excel applies the changes to all other worksheets in the workgroup. Figure 7.13 shows several worksheets in a workgroup. The Window Arrange Workgroup command was used to show all worksheets at the same time, while keeping the current worksheet active.

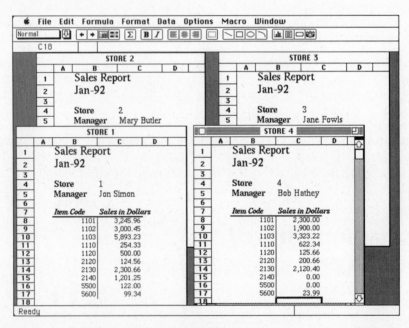

Fig. 7.13. Worksheets displayed as a workgroup.

Tip: Viewing All Worksheets in a Workgroup
When the active worksheet is part of a workgroup and you select the Arrange Workgroup command from the Window menu, Excel arranges the worksheets in the group so that you can see them all. This feature is similar to the Window Arrange All command but applies only to the worksheets in the current group.

Note: Only one workgroup can be active at one time.

Tip: Using Workgroups Instead of Templates
You can use the workgroup feature instead of saving a template. This feature can be useful when you want to create several copies of a document but don't plan to create more copies later. Just open several new blank worksheets and define them as a workgroup. When you create one worksheet, all the worksheets will be created.

Removing Workgroups

To remove the workgroup designation from the worksheets, simply activate any worksheet other than the current workgroup master sheet. This process breaks the group and returns the workspace to normal. Use this process when you want to work on files individually.

Tip: Saving Workgroup Settings in the Workspace
When you use the Save Workspace command from the File menu to save the current window arrangement, Excel saves the workgroup designation. This feature can be useful for returning to a set of worksheets that you always handle as a group.

Consolidating Worksheet Data

When you use templates or workgroups to manipulate several similar worksheets, you may require a consolidated report that summarizes all the worksheets. If, for example, you have sales reports from four stores, you may want to create a report that shows the totals for all four stores (see fig. 7.14).

You may remember from Chapter 4 that the Paste Special command on the Edit menu offers one way of consolidating worksheets. You can copy the data you want from each of the original worksheets (called the *source worksheets*) and paste the data into the destination worksheet. Simply select the Paste Special command from the Edit menu and then use the Add option. Perform this procedure four times—each time adding the new data to the existing sum in the destination worksheet.

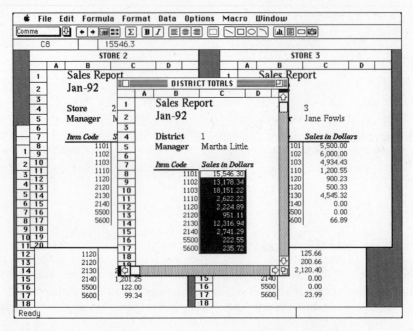

Fig. 7.14. *Consolidating four worksheets into one summary worksheet.*

This process can be useful for consolidating data within a single worksheet (or between two worksheets) but can become tiresome when you have to repeat the procedure for three or more worksheets. Fortunately, Excel provides an easier method. You can perform this task by using the Consolidate command from the Data menu. Follow these steps:

1. Open all source worksheets and the destination worksheet. Activate the destination worksheet.

2. Highlight the range in the destination worksheet that will contain the final consolidated values. (This is range C8:C17 in the example.)

   This range should be the same size as the source ranges. Do not include headings in this range. (You also can highlight a single cell, row, or column for various effects. See the next section, "Noting Some Consolidation Guidelines," for details.)

3. Select the Consolidate command from the Data menu. The dialog box shown in figure 7.15 appears.

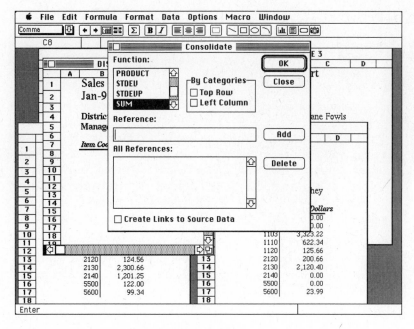

Fig. 7.15. *The Data Consolidate dialog box.*

4. Click on the Source Range box to position the cursor there.

5. Click on the first source worksheet and select the range of cells by highlighting it. You can move the Consolidate dialog box out of the way, if necessary, by dragging on its title bar (it will remain in view on the screen, however). The range you highlight will appear as an external reference in the dialog box. Click on the Add button to add this reference to the list.

6. Repeat Step 5 for all other source worksheets.

7. Select the function you want by clicking on it in the Function listing in the Consolidate dialog box. This feature determines the mathematical operation performed across the data.

8. After you specify all source worksheet ranges and select the appropriate function, click on the OK button in the Consolidate dialog box. Excel consolidates the data across all references.

Noting Some Consolidation Guidelines

When you are consolidating data, remember the following points:

- The source worksheets do not have to be open when you perform consolidation. Source worksheets must be saved on disk, however. If the source worksheets are not open, you must type the source ranges you want as external references rather than click on them. External references specify the drive and folders in which the worksheet is stored, and the cell or range in that worksheet. (An example is 'STORE 4'!$C$8:$C$17.) External references are explained later in this chapter in "Linking Worksheets."

- If the highlighted destination range is smaller than the source ranges, Excel fills as much as possible. If the destination range is larger than the source ranges, Excel skips extra cells. Excel presents a message explaining these facts.

- The source ranges do not have to be located in the same positions in the worksheet. As long as you highlight the ranges you want, consolidation takes place.

- The source ranges do not have to be the same size or shape. Excel consolidates the information that overlaps within the source ranges. If you consolidate the ranges A1:A10 and C5:E5, for example, the result is the sum of cells A1 and C5. These two cells are the only overlapping cells in the two ranges. The other values in these two ranges will appear unchanged in the destination worksheet.

- Excel does not replace formulas or formatting in the destination range. Number formats, however, are copied from the source ranges.

- If you highlight a single row as the destination, Excel expands the range downward to accommodate the number of rows being consolidated. Excel consolidates only as many columns as you highlight, however—even if the source ranges contain more columns. If the source ranges each contain four columns and 10 rows, for example, and you highlight three cells in a row for the source, Excel fills three columns and 10 rows in the destination. Similarly, if you highlight a single column, Excel expands the destination to the right to accommodate the number of columns being consolidated.

- If you highlight a single cell for the destination range, Excel automatically makes the destination range match the size of the consolidated data.

- You can choose from 11 worksheet functions for consolidation. These functions include AVERAGE, COUNT, COUNTA, MAX, MIN, PRODUCT, STDEV, STDEVP, SUM, VAR, and VARP. Normally, you use the SUM function to add all the source data together.

- You can create automatic links (*external references*) between the source data and the destination range. This procedure makes the relationship between the worksheets more permanent. When you change data in a source worksheet, the destination changes accordingly. To establish links, select the Consolidate command from the Data menu, and then check the Create Links to Source Data box. For more information on linking, see "Linking Worksheets," later in this chapter.

- Within source ranges, you can consolidate specific information—rather than all the data. This process is described in the following section, "Consolidating Selected Entries."

Consolidating Selected Entries

You may not always want to point to the exact range of cells containing the source data for consolidation. You may want to consolidate selected items from within a large range found on each source worksheet. Then only the items (or categories) that you specify will be consolidated across the worksheets. Suppose that you calculate the monthly loan payments for three loans. The loan calculation worksheets list each payment date and the corresponding principal and interest payments. The dates are calculated to increase by one month from the loan's starting date. Figure 7.16 shows three such worksheets. These worksheets simply are different versions of the same basic worksheet template.

Now suppose that you want to consolidate values in these three worksheets. You want to determine the total interest payment you owe for any particular quarter. Because each loan worksheet begins with a different date, however, the quarter you want to consolidate does not appear in the same rows on each worksheet. To accomplish the consolidation, follow these steps:

1. Enter the dates (category names) into the destination worksheet. These dates must match the source categories exactly. Figure 7.17 shows the destination worksheet for the loan worksheets in figure 7.16.

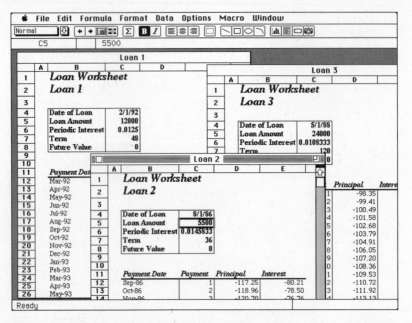

Fig. 7.16. *Three loan worksheets ready for consolidation.*

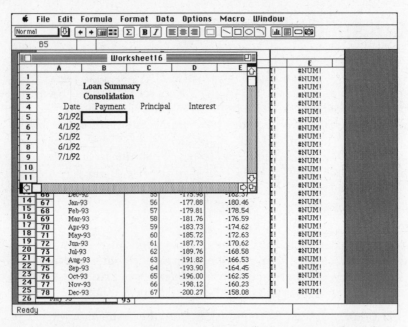

Fig. 7.17. *Starting your destination worksheet with the categories from the source worksheets.*

2. Highlight the cells you created in step 1. These are called the category names.

3. Select the Consolidate command from the Data menu and specify the first source range by highlighting it in the worksheet or (if the worksheet is not open) by entering the reference into the Reference box in the Consolidate dialog box. Include the entire range of data on the source worksheets—not just the categories in the destination range. Excel will locate the chosen categories from within the range. Also, include the headings in these ranges. Figure 7.18 shows the first source range in the example.

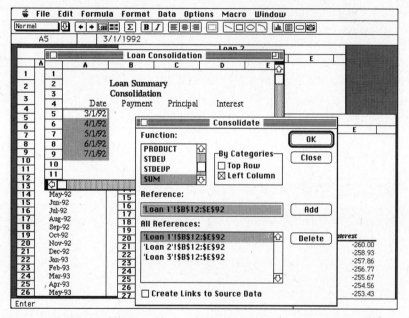

Fig. 7.18. *Highlighting the source data ranges, including all category names from the source worksheets.*

4. Click on the Add button to add the source range to the list. Then repeat Steps 3 and 4 for the remaining source worksheets.

5. Click on the Top Row or Left Column check box to specify where the categories are contained. In this example, check the Left Column box.

6. Click on the OK button to begin the consolidation.

The advantage of this method is that you can change the categories in the destination range to consolidate a new set of categories. Just enter new headings in the destination range, highlight the destination range, select the Consolidate command from the Data menu, and press Return. The previous settings still are active and apply to the new headings. This technique also can be accomplished with the DSUM function but is much easier to use.

Copying Data between Worksheets

You can copy data from one worksheet to another without using a workgroup or template. Often, the easiest way to duplicate information is to copy it from one worksheet and paste the information into another worksheet.

Excel makes copying or moving data from one worksheet to another easy. Just use the Copy or Cut command from the Edit menu in the following manner:

1. Open both worksheets.

2. Activate the source worksheet (the worksheet containing the original data).

3. Highlight the cell or range that you want to copy or move. Select Copy or Cut from the Edit menu to copy or move the data.

4. Activate the destination worksheet by selecting its name from the Windows menu.

5. Move the pointer to the upper left corner of the destination range and select Paste from the Edit menu (or ⌘-V) Excel pastes the data into the worksheet and returns to the source worksheet.

The copying and cutting features use the Clipboard to store data temporarily. This data remains on the Clipboard after being pasted into the destination worksheet. You therefore can paste the data again and again, as long as the data remains on the Clipboard. Data will remain on the clipboard until you copy or cut again.

Use this procedure to copy information between Excel and another program. If you are copying from a different program—such as a graphics program—you must use that program's method of copying data. Switch to Excel and use the Paste command from the Edit menu. If you are copying from Excel to another program, you must choose Copy from the Edit menu in Excel and then switch to the other program and use its paste procedure.

Linking Worksheets

Linking is the procedure by which a worksheet accesses information in a different worksheet through special formulas called *external references*. Very much like standard cell references, external references draw information from other cells by using the cell's address.

Unlike standard references, external references also include the name of the worksheet in which the information appears. The worksheet containing the formula (in which the linked information will appear) is called the *dependent worksheet* because it depends on the other worksheet for its values. The worksheet containing the original data is called the *supporting worksheet*.

You are not limited to linking one worksheet to one other worksheet only; you can link a worksheet with many others or design complex links among several independent worksheets. This procedure can take the form of an interoffice accounting or job-tracking system, for example.

Linking enables you to design large worksheets by using separate worksheets, or *modules*, each of which interacts with the others, making creating and updating the application easier. Because linking enables you to open only those modules that you need at any given time, the application takes less memory and therefore runs faster.

Another advantage of using several linked worksheets rather than one large worksheet is that you may be able to use some of the modules over again in different systems.

When several people in an organization need to use different parts of a system, linking may be the only efficient way to handle the task. The sales department, for example, may use an order entry system for tracking orders, while the accounting department consolidates that data into financial reports (see fig. 7.19).

Entering Linking Formulas

To link worksheets, you enter a linking formula into a cell of the dependent worksheet. The formula must contain the name of the supporting worksheet and the cell that you want to extract.

Consider this simple external reference formula:

    =Payroll!B5

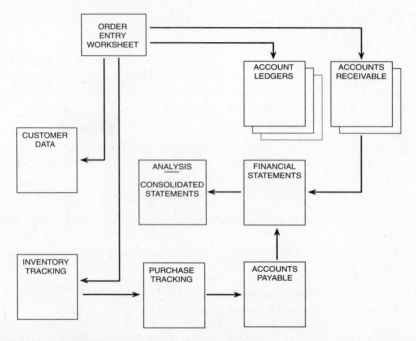

Fig. 7.19. *A large system of worksheets that interact.*

This external reference formula begins with the equal sign, includes the name of a worksheet (PAYROLL), and is followed by an exclamation point. The worksheet name and exclamation point tell Excel that this formula is an external reference. The particular cell being referenced in the Payroll worksheet is B5. The two worksheets involved in this link may look like those in figure 7.20.

> *Note:* If the name of the supporting worksheet contains spaces—as in Payroll 1991—the external reference must include the name in single quotation marks, as in ='Payroll 1991'!B5. Notice that the exclamation point falls outside the quotation marks. To avoid this requirement, use a period or underscore instead of a space.

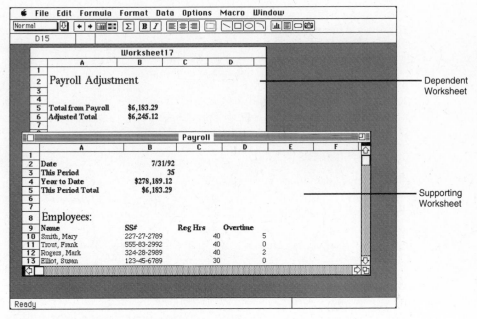

Fig. 7.20. *A dependent and supporting worksheet.*

Tip: Entering Linking Formulas By Pointing

You also can use the pointing method to enter an external reference. First, open the supporting and dependent worksheets. Next, move to the appropriate cell in the dependent worksheet and press the equal sign. Then activate the supporting worksheet by clicking on it or selecting its name from the Windows menu. Click on the cell that will be linked to the dependent worksheet (or use the keyboard-movement commands to highlight the cell you want). To complete the formula, press Return. The dependent worksheet moves back to the top of the screen, and the external-reference formula is complete.

If the supporting worksheet is closed when you enter the formula, you must include the disk name and any folder names in which the supporting worksheet is located, as in the following example:

='Disk_name:Folder:Worksheet'!$B$5

Notice that the name is entered in single quotation marks. The disk and folder names are separated by a colon. Also, the cell reference is entered as an absolute reference. This procedure prevents reference errors that can occur when the supporting worksheet is closed.

Obviously, creating an external reference is easier when the supporting worksheet is open, because you may not know the names of folders as you type the formula. Because opening the supporting worksheets first may not always be possible, this technique is available.

You can reference an external cell by using a defined name instead of a cell address. If, for example, the supporting worksheet contains the name SALES_TOTAL for cell B5, you can enter the external reference formula as follows (assuming that the supporting worksheet is open):

    =Payroll!SALES_TOTAL

Using names instead of cell references is good practice when you link worksheets. This procedure eliminates many problems when a supporting worksheet is changed, because Excel does not automatically update external references when a supporting worksheet is altered. Suppose that the dependent worksheet refers to cell B5 in the source worksheet.

If you inserted a row above row 5, cell B5 becomes B6. Excel adjusts references when you insert or delete such information, but Excel does not update external references and continues to reference cell B5, causing an error. If, however, you apply a name to cell B5 and then use the name in the external-reference formula, this problem does not occur.

Using Ranges in Links

Often, a dependent worksheet contains a range of cells that comes from a similar range in a supporting worksheet. In other words, the entire range is extracted from the supporting worksheet. In such a case, entering all the external reference formulas independently can be tedious. Instead, you can enter the first external reference formula containing the appropriate relative and absolute references to the supporting worksheet and then use the Copy or Fill command to copy the formula to the rest of the range. If you use the pointer method of creating an external reference, Excel assumes that you want the absolute cell reference and enters the dollar signs accordingly, as in the following example:

    =Payroll!$B$5

To remove the dollar signs, use the editing techniques described in Chapter 4. Then use the Copy, Fill Down, or Fill Right commands from the Formula menu to copy this formula into the remaining cells.

Another way to reference a range of cells in an external worksheet is to use the Paste Link command from the Edit menu. Follow these steps:

1. Open the dependent and supporting worksheets.

2. Copy the range of cells you want from the supporting worksheet by choosing the Copy command from the Edit menu.

3. Return to the dependent worksheet and position the pointer on the first cell in the range that will contain the external references (the upper left corner).

4. Select the Paste Link command from the Edit menu.

The result of these steps is a range of cells in the dependent worksheet that contains external references to the range you copied from the supporting worksheet. Important to note, however, is that these references are array references, as indicated by the braces surrounding the formulas in the following example:

> {=Payroll!$B$5}

Array references have special qualities and must be treated differently from standard references; most important, array references cannot be edited individually. (For details on array references, see Chapter 8.)

Using Functions and Formulas in Links

So far, this chapter has discussed only simple external references. You can make an external reference part of a formula, however, as in the following example:

> =Payroll!B5*A6

This formula takes the value of cell B5 in the supporting worksheet (PAYROLL) and multiplies it by the value in cell A6 of the current worksheet. Instead of using an external reference as part of a calculation, you always can use simple external references to bring the raw information to the dependent worksheet and then make calculations in other cells of the dependent worksheet. Adding calculations to your external references can save time and memory, however. If, for example, you want to reference the sum of a range of cells contained in an external worksheet, you can use a formula similar to the following:

> =SUM(Payroll!B5:B10)

This formula brings only the total value to the dependent worksheet. Likewise, external references can be useful when data is kept separate from other calculations. A database function, for example, can refer to a database range contained on a different worksheet, as in the following example:

=DSUM(Payroll!B5:E10,2,criteria)

This function searches an external database and totals the values in column 2 of that database. The result is placed in the dependent worksheet. If you apply a name to an external reference within the dependent worksheet (regardless of whether the reference has a name in its own worksheet), you easily can use the name in commands like Data Set Database to specify the external range. This database example is shown in figure 7.21.

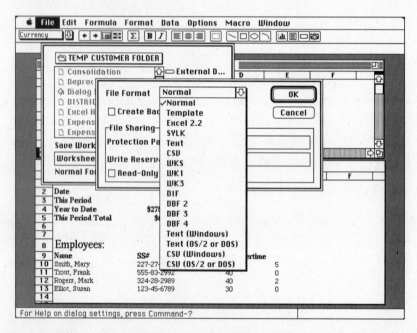

Fig. 7.21. *Using external references in database functions to access data on a separate worksheet.*

When you must enter a range as an external reference, you can "point" to the range by starting the formula and then highlighting the range on the external worksheet. You can type =*SUM(*, for example, and then point to the range you want on the external worksheet. Press Return to complete the reference and return to the starting worksheet.

Opening Linked Worksheets

If you open a dependent worksheet when its supporting worksheet already is open, Excel automatically updates the external references. Likewise, if you change data in the supporting worksheet while the dependent worksheet is open, the dependent worksheet reflects your changes immediately.

If, however, you open a dependent worksheet and its supporting worksheet is closed, Excel updates the dependent worksheet only after asking whether you want to update the worksheet. If you answer Yes, Excel uses the most current information in supporting worksheets as the dependent worksheet is opened. If Excel cannot find the supporting worksheet because it was moved, erased, or renamed, the system asks you to locate the file on disk. When the file is located, Excel stores the location for the next time.

When a dependent worksheet is open but its supporting worksheet is not, Excel displays the external reference formula differently: the reference includes the entire path name of the supporting worksheet rather than just the file name. If you use the reference

=Payroll!B5

in a dependent worksheet, however, and then close the Payroll worksheet, Excel displays the following reference:

```
='Disk_name:Folder:Payroll'!:B5
```

where *folder* represents the folder in which the Payroll worksheet is located. If more than one folder is required, Excel simply stacks up the references and separates them with colons. Excel produces these names automatically—you should not alter them. If you open the supporting worksheet, Excel returns the reference to its original state without the folder names. When you enter the linking formula, the supporting worksheet does not have to be open.

Viewing Linked Worksheets

If you double-click on any linking formula or linked picture, Excel activates the supporting worksheet connected to that data. If the supporting worksheet is not open, Excel opens it and highlights the formula or range that is linked to the data you double-clicked. This procedure provides an excellent way to check links and modify the original data. When you modify the original data, the linked data changes.

When you activate a supporting worksheet in this manner, Excel stores your starting location in the Goto dialog box so that you easily can return to your starting point by pressing F5 (or by selecting the Goto command) and pressing Return.

> *Note:* This navigation feature also applies to data linked to other programs through Direct Data Exchange (DDE). For more information, see "Linking and Exchanging Data with Other Programs," later in this chapter.

Repairing Damaged Links

When an external link is damaged, an error message appears in the dependent worksheet when Excel attempts to calculate the dependent worksheet's values. The following actions can damage links:

- Changing the name of a supporting worksheet on the desktop.

- Moving a supporting worksheet into a different folder.

- Changing the name of a supporting worksheet from within Excel when the dependent worksheet is not open.

- Inserting or deleting cells, rows, or columns in a supporting worksheet, causing the referenced cell to change position. (This change occurs when the dependent worksheet uses the cell address in the external reference.)

- Changing the name of a cell that is being referenced by its name.

- Entering the linking formula without absolute references (possible when both worksheets are open) and then opening the dependent worksheet without its supporting worksheet.

When an error occurs, you can fix the damaged links by using the Links command from the File menu. Follow these steps:

1. Open the dependent worksheet.

2. Select the Links option from the File menu.

3. Choose the name of the supporting file that contains the damaged links. You can select more than one file by holding down the Shift key as you click on the names. Excel displays the dialog box shown in figure 7.22.

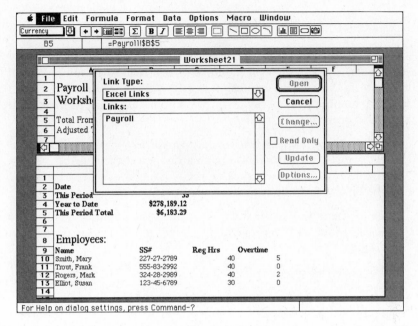

Fig. 7.22. *Updating external references with the File Links command.*

4. In the dialog box provided, enter the name of the supporting worksheet. Type the entire path name, including any folders in which the file is located.

    Use colons between folder references as follows:

    Disk_name:*Folder*:*Filename*

    Do not type the exclamation point or cell reference; this procedure only updates the location of the supporting file. Press Return when you are finished.

5. If you selected more than one supporting file in step 3, repeat step 4 for each file you selected.

If this procedure does not solve the problem, you need to remove the old external reference formulas and link the documents again. Be sure to open all supporting files before linking them.

Turning Links Off

You may want to stop (or deactivate) linking formulas within dependent worksheets. You can turn off the links in two ways. You can convert the linking formulas to their values, or you can deactivate remote requests (ignore incoming data). To convert the linking formulas to their values, follow this procedure:

1. If the linking formula has produced an array, highlight all cells in the array. If the formula is not an array, select the cell you want. If the link is to a picture, click on the picture to select it. In all cases, the linking formula appears in the formula bar.

2. Using the mouse, click and drag in the formula bar to highlight the entire formula. This procedure is an editing technique described in Chapter 4.

3. Press ⌘-= to calculate the highlighted formula and turn the formula into a value.

The following steps leave the linking formulas intact but cause Excel to ignore incoming data from the supporting worksheet:

1. Select the Calculate command from the Options menu.

2. Click the Update Remote Requests box to remove the check mark and press Return.

If you turn off remote requests, you always can turn them on again later. This procedure therefore gives you more freedom than converting linking formulas to their values. This is useful when you want to work on the source worksheet without your changes affecting the linked worksheet.

Linking Data via Pictures

Excel offers a special way to link data from one worksheet to another—or even between applications. This method involves creating a *picture* of the data that you want to reference. The picture is placed into the dependent worksheet and refers to data in a supporting worksheet. Several characteristics make this picture different than a normal external reference. First, the picture is an object that resides on the worksheet's object layer. You can move, size, copy, and overlap the picture like any other object. (For this reason, you may want to refer to Chapter 13 before continuing with this section.)

In addition, the picture refers to an *area* in the supporting worksheet—not to individual cells. This subtle distinction has many ramifications. In particular, objects that appear in this area become part of the picture. Finally, all formatting applied to the original data becomes part of the picture, and you cannot format the picture independently.

You may wonder why you would use a picture instead of direct linking formulas. The following list offers several reasons:

- Pictures enable you to link formatting as well as data. When you alter the formats or values in the supporting worksheet, the picture changes.

- Pictures enable you to link any objects that reside in the original area on the supporting worksheet. If you move an object into the linked area on the supporting worksheet, that object appears in the picture. This is useful for linking forms or completing reports.

- You can move, size, group, and manipulate pictures as you can any object. If you change the size of a picture, you can achieve interesting effects.

- You cannot alter the data inside a picture (including objects that appear in the picture) by changing the data in the dependent worksheet—only by changing the data in the original supporting worksheet. Because the linked values are placed in an object, the linked values do not occupy cells that you can edit. This feature can be useful for protecting data.

Figure 7.23 shows an example of a linked picture and its various qualities.

Notice that the picture in figure 7.23 has been resized and that the original range contains an object, which appears in the picture. To link data with a picture, follow these steps:

1. Open the supporting and dependent worksheets.

2. Highlight the data in the supporting worksheet that you want to copy (and link) to the dependent worksheet.

3. Click on the Picture tool in the Toolbar.

4. Activate the dependent worksheet using the Window menu.

5. Click anywhere on the dependent worksheet to place the picture. You can move and edit the picture after the picture is in place.

Alternatively, you can copy data with the Copy command from the Edit menu and then press Shift while pulling down the Edit menu and selecting the Paste Picture command to paste the data as a picture.

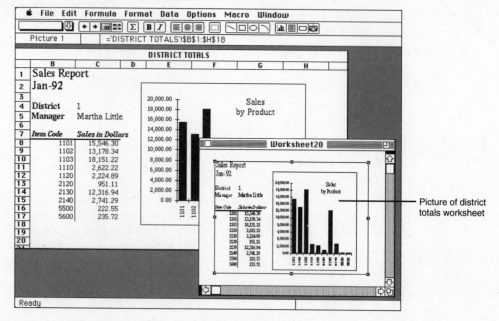

Fig. 7.23. *Using a picture to link data between worksheets.*

Linking and Exchanging Data with Other Programs

You can access information contained in other programs and bring that information into Excel. Likewise, you can use Excel data as supporting data for another program, such as a word processing document. You can use two methods to exchange data between Excel and other programs: linking data and data exchange.

Linking Data

You can link data between an Excel worksheet and data in another application in two ways. One method, commonly called Publish/Subscribe or "edition management," was devised by Apple for System 7. The other method, called Dynamic Data Exchange (DDE), was devised by Microsoft. Both methods require that you have System 7 running on your Macintosh and that the external application supports DDE or Publish/Subscribe, depending on which you decide to use.

If the external program does not support DDE or Publish/Subscribe procedures, you will be unable to create direct links between the program and Excel 3.0. Instead, consider using the data-exchange techniques described in the section "Exchanging Data."

Using Publish/Subscribe

Applications that support the new Publish/Subscribe features of System 7 can link data and graphics to other applications by using an *edition file*. An application can store data into an edition file and any other application can access that file and the data in the file.

This procedure is different than simple copying and pasting between applications. Linking to an edition file gives you a "live link" to the original document that created the file. If you change the original document, the edition file changes, and so does the file linked to the edition file. Creating an edition file from your data is called *publishing*. Linking to an edition file to access the data is called *subscribing*. Advantages to the Publish/Subscribe feature follow:

- Several different applications can link to (subscribe to) a single edition file.

- The edition file is stored on disk for permanent reference.

- Many Macintosh applications support Publish/Subscribe.

To create an edition file from data in your Excel worksheet, select a range of cells (or a graph) and then choose the Edit Create Publisher command. The options in the Create Publisher dialog box enable you to select a name and location for the file.

To subscribe to an existing edition file from within Excel, use the Edit Subscribe To command. Use the Subscribe To dialog box options to locate and select the edition file. The information is brought into Excel at the location of the active cell.

Using Dynamic Data Exchange (DDE)

You may want to use Microsoft's DDE linking instead of the Publish/Subscribe features of System 7. Some advantages to DDE linking between applications follow:

- DDE linking between applications is similar to simple worksheet linking between two Excel worksheets.

- Many Microsoft products support DDE, including the PC versions of their products. DDE also can be used between Macintosh computers and PCs.

- DDE requires no extra file to be stored on the disk. Links are direct references to data in other applications.

- DDE is gaining support from several software publishers—on the Macintosh and PC computers.

To use DDE linking, you must create links between your Excel worksheet and the external document.

Creating direct links between programs is like creating links between Excel worksheets. To create direct links, follow one of these four procedures:

- Enter in the dependent worksheet a linking formula that contains an external reference to the other program and its document. This formula requires the following syntax:

  =*application*|*document*!*reference*

  where *application* is the name of the program to which you are linking, and *document* is the particular file name. *Reference* is the cell, field, or reference point in the document to which you are linking. Each program has its own standards within DDE to follow.

- Enter a linking formula by pointing to the information in the external program and file.

- Copy data from the supporting file and paste the data into the dependent file by using the program's Paste Link feature. If the program does not have a Paste Link feature, it does not support DDE.

- Copy the data from the supporting file and paste the data into the dependent file using the Paste Picture feature.

Each of these methods follows the basic rules outlined in this chapter for linking between Excel worksheets.

Exchanging Data

If you cannot link data directly between programs, you may be able to exchange data using the Clipboard. This process is a simple matter of using the Copy and Paste procedure between the different programs and their files. Almost all Macintosh programs support Clipboard Copy and Paste procedures. The resulting data is not linked to its original document but merely is transferred to the new document.

You also can transfer entire files to and from Excel. Opening a file created by another program is as simple as choosing the Open command from the File menu and selecting the file you want. You can convert the following formats into Excel:

Format name	Description
CSV	Comma Separated Values
DBF 2	dBASE II
DBF 3	dBASE III
DBF 4	dBASE IV
DIF	Data Interchange Format
Excel 2.x	Excel Versions 2.0 through 3.0
Normal	Microsoft Excel Standard
Text	Text, ASCII, or ANSI
SYLK	Symbolic Link
WK1	Lotus 1-2-3 Release 2
WKS	Lotus 1-2-3 Release 1, Lotus Symphony
WK3	Lotus 1-2-3 Release 3

When opening a text file, use the following steps:

1. Select the Open command from the File menu.

2. Use the dialog box options to locate the text file you want.

3. Click on the text file's name.

4. Click on the Text button. Figure 7.24 shows the screen at this point.

5. Indicate whether the text file uses comma or tab delimiters by selecting the appropriate option. Then press Return to continue.

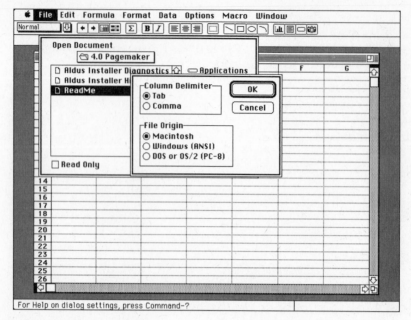

Fig. 7.24. *Opening a text file.*

To save an Excel worksheet in one of these formats, use the Save As command, specify the file name you want, and click on the Options button.

Click on the button next to the file type you want to specify. The following list presents brief explanations of the file types supported by Excel for opening and saving files:

- *Normal:* Normal is the standard Excel 3.0 file type. You do not have to select this option unless you have saved the file as a different type; the Normal option is the default.

- *DIF:* DIF (data-interchange format) is a long-time standard format for spreadsheet documents. DIF retains the row and column structure of data so that a file translated from DIF to another format will have data in the correct cells. Unfortunately, DIF files do not retain any worksheet formulas or formats. (Bringing a DIF file into Excel never creates a calculation problem because there are no formulas to translate.) Use DIF files only if no better format in which to save the data is available.

- *Text:* ASCII, or text, files are similar to DIF files but do not always contain the row and column structure. ASCII most often is used for word processor documents that do not contain rows and columns.

Macintosh ASCII files (called *text files*), however, use a tab-delimited format. Tab-delimited ASCII files have tab characters between the columns of data, and carriage-return characters between the rows. The result is very similar to DIF files. The advantage of using ASCII over DIF is that you can save files other than worksheets in this manner. You can save a database file in tab-delimited ASCII format, for example, and read it into Excel. The result is an Excel worksheet in which rows of information equate to the records in the database and in which columns contain the fields. Likewise, an Excel file saved as text can be read by nonspreadsheet programs (such as databases) with reasonable success.

The standard Macintosh Cut and Paste commands preserve the tab-delimited nature of data. If you create a table in Microsoft Word by pressing Tab between each column and Return between each row, for example, you can copy the information and paste it directly into Excel.

• *CSV:* CSV stands for *comma-separated values*. The CSV format is identical to the text format except that Excel uses commas to separate the columns of information. CSV (also called *comma-delimited format*) has been a standard data-translation format for years.

When you use the CSV format, data coming from another program or computer should use commas to separate individual items or fields and carriage returns to separate rows or records. When you open a file that uses this format, Excel removes the commas and places each piece of information into a separate cell.

• *SYLK:* SYLK files are similar to DIF files in that both types apply specifically to worksheets. SYLK files, however, include enough information for Excel to re-create the formulas from the original worksheet. The translated result is a fully operational worksheet. Different spreadsheet programs, however, contain different sets of commands.

Excel 3.0 has many commands that are not available in other spreadsheets (including earlier versions of Excel), and some spreadsheets have commands not supported in Excel. When Excel tries to translate an unsupported formula from a SYLK file, Excel turns the formula into a text string. Often, you can translate these formulas yourself. Use the SYLK format when your file will be used by another spreadsheet.

- *WK?*: Excel recognizes Lotus 1-2-3 files and translates formulas directly into Excel equivalents. The 1-2-3 formats WK1, WK3, and WKS are available. Some formulas do not have direct equivalents and appear as text cells. 1-2-3 macros also appear as text cells—unless you use the macro translator that comes with Excel. Getting a 1-2-3 file from a PC to a Macintosh disk requires a translation program such as the Apple File Exchange and a Macintosh disk drive capable of reading PC disks, such as the Apple Super Drive. (This drive comes standard with some Macintosh configurations.) After translating the file into a Macintosh file, Excel reads the file and converts it to an Excel worksheet file. You also can save Excel files as 1-2-3 files and translate them into 1-2-3.

> *Note:* Excel includes other Lotus 1-2-3 support, such as custom help screens for translating 1-2-3 commands.

- *dBASE*: Excel can write to a dBASE format by using the DBF 2, DBF 3, or DBF 4 option.

Understanding the Guidelines for Linking

The following list summarizes the guidelines for creating simple external references and includes information about saving linked worksheets:

- If the supporting and dependent worksheets are open together, create a link by typing the name of the supporting worksheet, followed by an exclamation point and the external cell reference.

  This formula constitutes the external reference formula. Be sure to include an equal sign at the beginning of the formula.

- Use absolute references in your linking formulas. This guideline is necessary especially if the dependent worksheet is opened without the supporting worksheet. If the two worksheets always will be open at the same time, then you can avoid the absolute references.

- If the supporting worksheet is closed when you create a linking formula, include the entire path name to the worksheet in the following form:

  =*'disk_name:folder:worksheet'*!$B$5

  where $B$5 can be any absolute cell reference. Note the use of the single quotation marks.

- Use names instead of cell addresses whenever possible. The cell reference in the external reference formula can be a name applied to a single cell of the supporting worksheet. Simply name the cell first, and then use the name in the external reference. This practice eliminates problems in linked worksheets.

- If the name of the supporting worksheet contains spaces or special characters, enter its name in single quotation marks. This rule does not apply to names that contain periods or underscore characters. Remember that the exclamation point should go outside the single quotation marks.

- If the external references are entered properly, you do not have to open the supporting worksheet for the dependent worksheet to update its link. Excel remembers the location of the supporting worksheet.

- Whenever possible, save linked worksheets in the same folder. Saving linked worksheets together is not necessary but is considered good practice. If linked worksheets must be in different folders, you must save the supporting worksheets by using the File Save As command, not the File Save command. Open the appropriate folders and enter the worksheet name in the Save As dialog box; then click on the OK button to save the worksheet. Do this step before you save the dependent worksheet.

- Do not use the same name for two supporting worksheets referred to in the same dependent worksheet. Excel cannot access information from two different worksheets that have the same name. (Although this rule may seem obvious, worksheets saved in different folders may have the same name; you may make this error inadvertently.)

- You can link data as a picture by using the Picture tool in the Toolbar or by pasting copied data with the Shift Edit Paste Picture command (press Shift while opening the Edit menu, and then choose Paste Picture). The picture links to the original data in ways that linking formulas do not.

Linking is an important part of building custom applications in Excel. With these guidelines, you should be able to complete any linking operations required. For more information about building applications, see Chapter 21.

Summary

Using multiple worksheets and windows is a natural part of using Excel. With Excel, you easily can view your worksheet in different ways by adding more windows. You also can link two different worksheets together so that one worksheet references data contained in the other worksheet. The key to this arrangement is the external reference formula. The following points are important to remember:

- You can split a worksheet into as many as four panes. This feature is useful for keeping titles in place along the top and left side of the worksheet.

- To move between panes, simply click on a cell in the pane you want to move to.

- Use the New Window command from the Window menu to create a second window for the active worksheet. This step enables you to view two parts of the worksheet at one time.

- Although you can have several windows to the same worksheet, Excel stores only one copy of the worksheet itself.

- To activate a window, click on the window (if possible) or select its name from the Window menu.

- Prevent a window from being closed or moved by using the Protect Document command from the Options menu.

- To reference data contained in an external worksheet (that is, a different worksheet), use an external reference formula, which consists of the worksheet name and the cell name.

- The easiest way to create an external reference is to open both worksheets and use the pointing method to create the formula.

- The Save Workspace command from the File menu saves the arrangement of all open windows (including hidden ones) so that you can return to the arrangement later. The arrangement is stored as a worksheet file on disk.

- Workgroups can save time when you need to make the same changes to several worksheets. You can turn the worksheets into a workgroup and make the changes once; Excel applies the changes to the entire group.

- Use the Consolidate command from the Data menu to summarize the data across several worksheets in a single report.

Chapter 8, "Building Advanced Worksheets," covers such worksheet operations as advanced copying and pasting, working with tables, using arrays, and trapping errors.

Using Advanced Worksheet Features

O nce you have a general understanding of the worksheet and how to enter text, numbers, and formulas, you are ready for information that is more advanced. This chapter describes some special techniques that you can use in your worksheets. In particular, this chapter covers the following:

- Using date math

- Using tables (including double-variable tables)

- Using arrays

- Using the Solver utility to solve complex scenarios

- Selecting calculation methods

- Analyzing your worksheet data using outlines, data-selection tools, and Info sheets

Using Date Math

Date math is the process by which you can make calculations based on dates. You can find the number of days elapsed between two dates, for example, add a number of days or months to a date, or determine what a particular date will be using a given number of days and a starting date as a basis. You can use date math in many business-worksheet applications, such as determining the delinquency of payments and calculating due dates based on worksheet variables. The following sections discuss the various date-math operations that you can perform using many of the date and time functions discussed in Chapter 6. Be sure to read about those functions before you continue with this section.

Calculating the Difference between Two Dates

Calculating the difference between two dates is fairly easy, especially if you want the result displayed in days or weeks. The task is simply a matter of subtracting the earlier date from the later one. Suppose that you have the dates Jan-1-89 and Mar-4-91 in cells A2 and A3, as shown in figure 8.1.

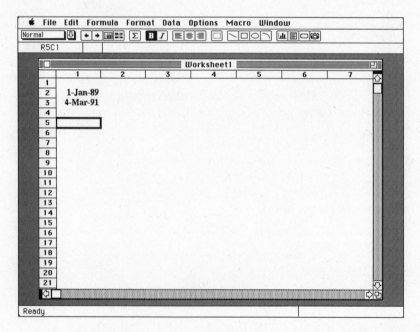

Fig. 8.1. *Two dates ready for date calculation.*

The formula =A3–A2 produces the number of days between the two dates. Because Excel tracks dates by the number of days elapsed since January 1, 1904, a result showing the difference in days will always be accurate. To calculate weeks, you can use the formula =(A3-A2)/7, which divides the number of days between the dates by 7. Because there are always seven days in a week, this figure will always be accurate, no matter what year you use. This calculation, however, often will produce fractional values for the number of weeks. You may want to display the number of weeks as whole weeks and the remainder as days. Figure 8.2 shows such a calculation.

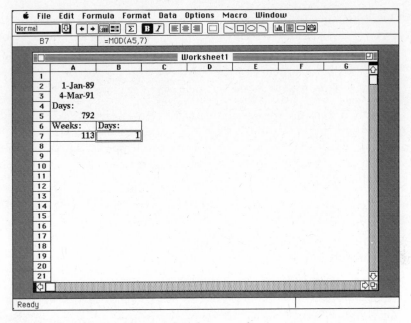

Fig. 8.2. *Calculating weeks and days between dates.*

The formulas look like this:

    A5: =A3-A2

    A7: =INT(A5/7)

    B7: =MOD(A5,7)

The formula in A5 calculates the number of days elapsed between the dates. The formula in A7 calculates the number of elapsed weeks and displays only the integer portion, showing only whole weeks. The formula in B7 shows the days left after the number of days is divided by 7.

Adding Days, Weeks, and Months to a Date

Because Excel dates are represented in units of days, adding a number of days to a date is a simple calculation. To add 30 days to the date in cell B5, use the formula =B5+30. The result is the serial number of the date 30 days after the original. Because Excel knows how many days occur in each month of each year, the resulting serial number represents the correct date. To add a number of weeks to a date, first convert the weeks to days by multiplying them by 7.

Adding a number of months to a date is more complicated because the number of days in a month varies and leap years add a day to February. You can use the DATE function to construct a date that is a certain number of months greater (or less) than a starting date:

=DATE(DAY(DATE),MONTH(DATE)+1),YEAR(DATE))

This formula steps up the month by exactly one—provided that you start near the beginning of the month. To add two months to a date, change the 1 in this formula to a 2. To subtract three months, change the value to –3. The range name DATE applies to the cell containing the original date; this could be a simple cell reference.

Another date calculation you may want to make is to determine whether a particular year is a leap year:

=IF(OR(AND(MOD(YEAR(B4),4)=0,MOD
(YEAR(B4)100)<>0),MOD(YEAR(B4),400)=0),"Leap", "No Leap")

If cell B4 contains a date, this formula determines whether the date falls in a leap year. A leap year occurs every four years, except in centennial years (1800, 1900, 2000, and so on), in which case, leaps occur every 400 years. The preceding formula takes all this information into account.

Date math that accounts for leap years can be very complex. If possible, use days as a unit of measure for elapsed time.

Working with Tables

Table lookups are an important part of many worksheet applications. To find a value in a table, you must search horizontally, vertically, or both ways to match values.

Single-Variable Tables

To find a value in a tax table, you must match the salary range vertically, and then find the number of withholdings horizontally. The cross section of the salary and withholdings ranges is the value that will be returned. A sample tax table is shown in figure 8.3.

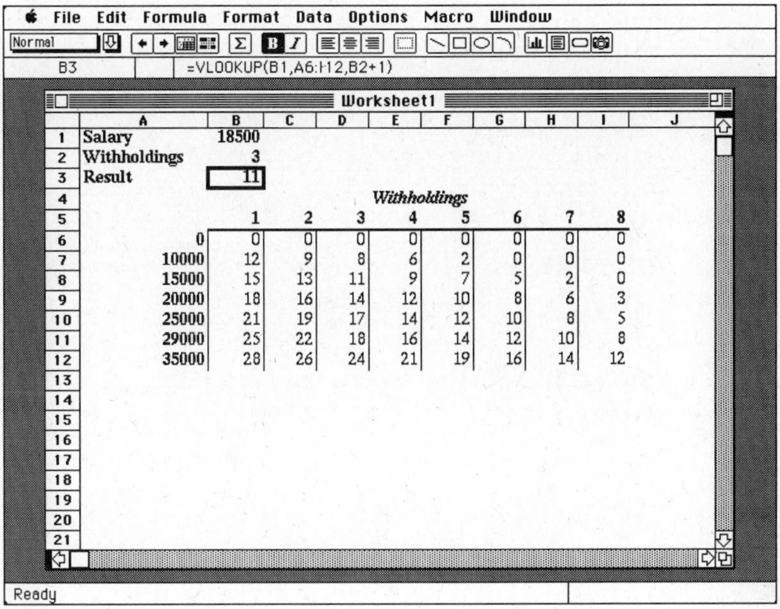

Fig. 8.3. *A sample tax table.*

Notice that the values across the top (horizontal lookup values) are sequential; therefore, this table is actually a single-variable table because the horizontal variable is the same as the column number. The lookup function for this table searches vertically for the salary range, and then returns the column corresponding to the number of withholdings. The actual formula is shown in the formula bar of figure 8.3:

=VLOOKUP(B1,A6:I12,B2+1)

The formula looks up the value from cell B1 in the table range A6:I12; it then returns the amount corresponding to the value in cell B2, plus 1 (to account for the first column). For more information about single-variable tables, see the VLOOKUP and HLOOKUP functions in Chapter 6. This chapter discusses the more complex double-variable tables. You should be familiar with the discussion of simple tables in Chapter 6 before you continue with this material.

Double-Variable Tables

A double-variable table is required when the vertical and horizontal lookup values are variable and nonsequential. The tax table shown in figure 8.3

would require a double-variable table if the withholding amounts were random. Figure 8.4 shows an example of a double-variable table. (Notice that the text labels in the column are arranged in alphabetical order, which Excel requires in order to perform text lookups.)

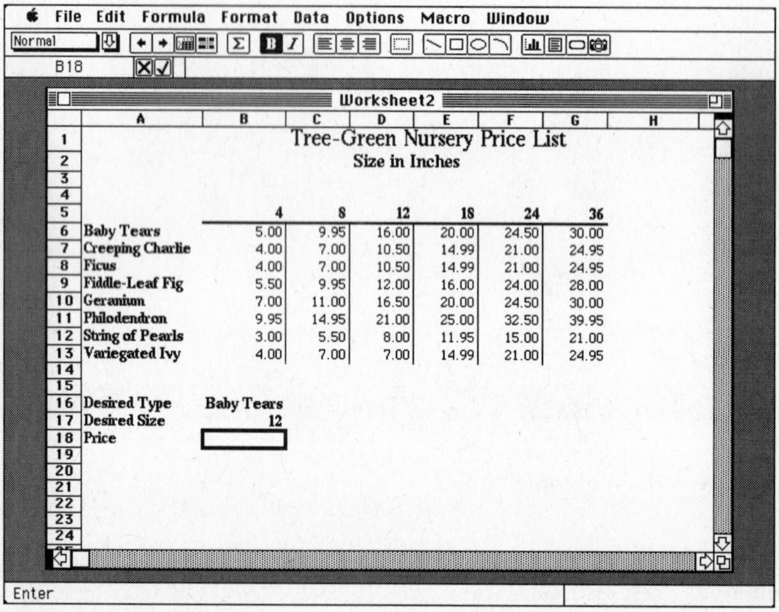

Fig. 8.4. *A double-variable table.*

The top row and the left column are variable. Ideally, you want to look up the price of a plant by using its name and size as input. But what do you use if the column values do not correspond to the offset value? You can perform table lookups for double-variable tables in several ways. The following sections discuss two techniques, each of which has advantages and disadvantages. Choose the method that works best for your applications.

Numbering Columns

One way to find a value in a double-variable table is to number the columns in the table. The lookup function uses the column number as the offset for the vertical lookup. Figure 8.5 shows a worksheet in which this technique is used.

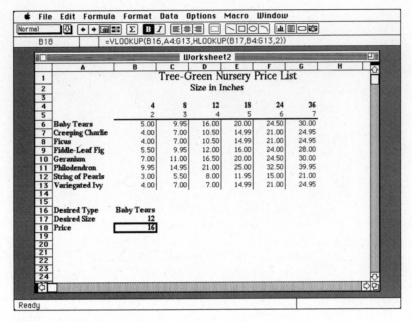

Fig. 8.5. *A double-variable table with the lookup function in place.*

The lookup function is entered into cell B18 and looks like this:

=VLOOKUP(B16,A4:G13,HLOOKUP(B17,B4:G13,2))

Notice that a row of sequential values is inserted—as column numbers—below the horizontal lookup values. The HLOOKUP function returns the number corresponding to the column of the table by means of the following portion of the function:

HLOOKUP(B17,B4:G13,2)

Excel uses the result as the offset value of the VLOOKUP function. The VLOOKUP function therefore knows where to find the correct value, horizontally, in the table. You also can use this technique with numbered rows instead of numbered columns.

The advantage of this technique is that it is easy to perform. Inserting a row of numbers above the columns is a simple procedure. The disadvantage is that you must separate the headings from the columns by inserting a row. This may not always be possible.

> **Tip: Hiding the Extra Row of Numbers**
>
> If you don't like the extra row of numbers required for this technique, try hiding those cells by selecting them and then entering the number format ;;; in the Format Number command. You also can reduce the row height of the extra row by choosing the Row Height command from the Format menu.

Extracting Rows

Another way to perform this lookup function is a two-step method. Rather than number the columns, use a lookup function to return a particular value from each column. To do this, add a row at the bottom of the table. In each cell of this new row, use a VLOOKUP function that returns a value from the column based on the vertical match. This extra row, in other words, contains one full row extracted from the table. Figure 8.6 shows what this type of lookup might look like.

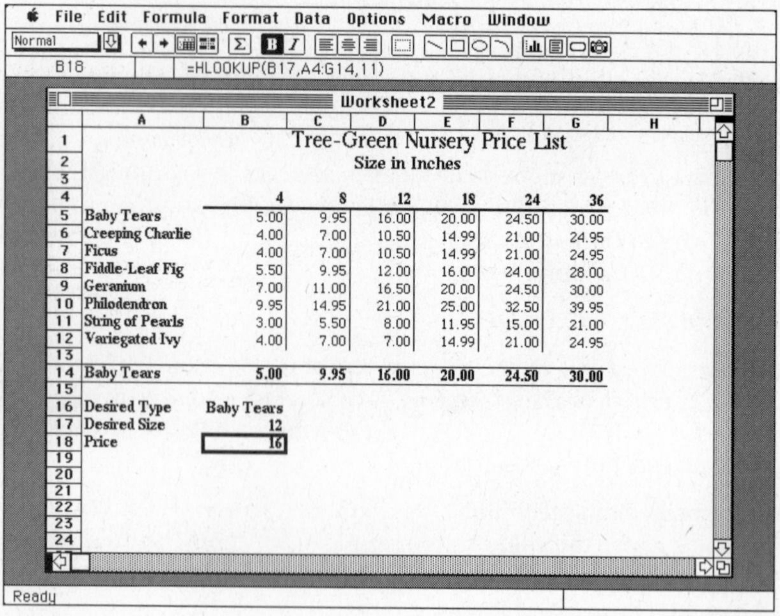

	A	B	C	D	E	F	G	H
1			Tree-Green Nursery Price List					
2			Size in Inches					
3								
4		4	8	12	18	24	36	
5	Baby Tears	5.00	9.95	16.00	20.00	24.50	30.00	
6	Creeping Charlie	4.00	7.00	10.50	14.99	21.00	24.95	
7	Ficus	4.00	7.00	10.50	14.99	21.00	24.95	
8	Fiddle-Leaf Fig	5.50	9.95	12.00	16.00	24.00	28.00	
9	Geranium	7.00	11.00	16.50	20.00	24.50	30.00	
10	Philodendron	9.95	14.95	21.00	25.00	32.50	39.95	
11	String of Pearls	3.00	5.50	8.00	11.95	15.00	21.00	
12	Variegated Ivy	4.00	7.00	7.00	14.99	21.00	24.95	
13								
14	Baby Tears	5.00	9.95	16.00	20.00	24.50	30.00	
15								
16	Desired Type	Baby Tears						
17	Desired Size	12						
18	Price	16						

B18   =HLOOKUP(B17,A4:G14,11)

Fig. 8.6. A double-variable table lookup, using an extracted row for the horizontal lookup.

The formulas in this row (row 14) follow:

A14: VLOOKUP(B16,A5:G12,1)

B14: VLOOKUP(B16,A5:G12,2)

C14: VLOOKUP(B16,A5:G12,3)

D14: VLOOKUP(B16,A5:G12,4)

E14: VLOOKUP(B16,A5:G12,5)

F14: VLOOKUP(B16,A5:G12,6)

G14: VLOOKUP(B16,A5:G12,7)

Together, these formulas extract one of the rows from the table based on the matching VLOOKUP. After the VLOOKUP function finds its match, Excel places the entire row at the bottom of the table. Next, Excel performs a simple HLOOKUP function within this extracted row. Because one of the values on the row is the desired value, the HLOOKUP function matches its value with the top row and then returns the corresponding column from the extracted row. In the example, the offset value for this HLOOKUP function is 11:

=HLOOKUP(B17,B4:G14,11)

The advantage to this technique is that you can place the extracted values anywhere on the worksheet. You also may find it useful to see the entire row of values extracted from the table. This technique, however, requires more formulas than the preceding method.

Performing a What-If Analysis

One of the most useful features of a worksheet is that it enables you to perform what-if tests based on variable information. By changing the values referenced in formulas, you can view different results. You may use a formula to calculate the future value of a series of deposits over time, for example. Then, by substituting various monthly deposit amounts, you can determine how your savings will add up as you deposit more or less of your monthly income.

At times, you may want to compare several what-if tests, but it can be tiresome to substitute values for those tests repeatedly. You also may want to view the resulting values side by side. This type of what-if testing calls for a *data table*—a table (or matrix) of values that Excel creates from a series of variables.

To perform a data-table calculation, follow these steps:

1. Create a single example of the calculation that you want to use in the table. Make sure that the variables used in the calculation appear in the worksheet. One of these variables will be the *input cell* (the cell containing the value that will be tested over and over).

2. List the variables that you want to use for the what-if tests. List these variables in a column, leaving a blank column at the right for the answers. You can use as many variables as you want, and these columns can appear anywhere in the worksheet.

3. Enter the formula that uses the variables specified in step 1 into the cell above the empty column of the table range. You can think of this as a heading for the column that will contain the results. Be sure that this formula references the input cell specified in step 1. This cell should calculate the first resulting value.

4. Highlight the column of test variables and the adjacent column. Be sure to include the row containing the formula that you entered in step 3. The first cell in the first column will be blank; the first cell in the second column will contain the first formula.

5. Select the Data Table command and enter the input cell into the dialog box. If the table is columnar, as described in these steps, enter the input cell in the space marked Column Input Cell.

Suppose that you want to examine the result of saving part of your income each month for five years at 9.6 percent interest. You want to see how much you will save after five years, specifying different monthly deposit amounts. The Future Value (FV) function performs the basic calculation, as shown in figure 8.7. For more information on the FV function, see Chapter 6.

In figure 8.7, the FV formula in cell D3 calculates the future value of the deposits using the rate, period, and payment information from row 3. (Note that the rate is entered as the monthly interest rate: =9.6%/12.) Notice also that rows 5 through 12 contain additional tests for the payment amount. The plan is to show the future value, using each of the payment amounts in the column (substituted for –100). The original payment amount, in cell C3, is the variable for the data table and is called the *input cell*.

The first step in creating this automatic data table is identifying the table range—the area that contains the test variables plus an extra column for the results. This range should include an extra row above these two columns. In figure 8.8, the table range is C4:D12. In cell D4, enter the formula that calculates the future value for the first set of variables. Because this formula already exists in cell D3, the formula in cell D4 would be =D3. Now highlight the entire table range, as shown in figure 8.8.

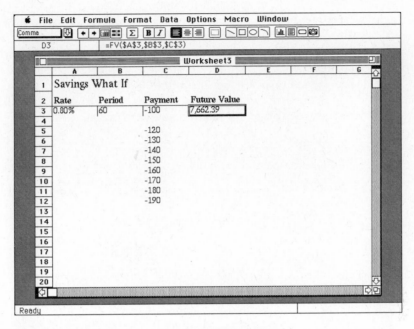

Fig. 8.7. *Using what-if tests to examine different monthly savings amounts.*

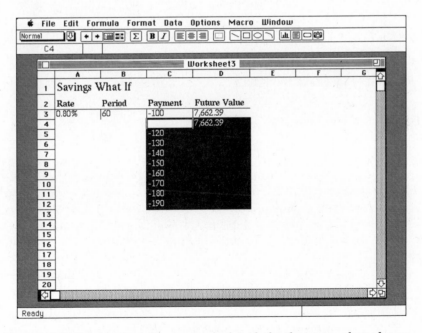

Fig. 8.8. *Highlighting the table range, which includes the input values plus an extra row above them and an extra column for the results.*

Next, select the Data Table command. The dialog box in figure 8.9 appears. Excel asks you for the row or column input cell. Cell C3 is already identified as the input cell. But is it row or column input? Because the data table will appear in a column, it is the column input cell, so type *$C$3* in the space provided and press Return. Use an absolute reference for this entry (see Chapter 4 for details). Excel calculates the formula using each of the variables listed and then places the result beside each variable (see fig. 8.10).

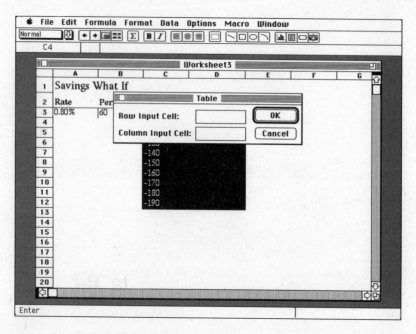

Fig. 8.9. The Data Table dialog box.

The input cell can appear anywhere in the worksheet; it does not have to appear on top of the other input variables. The formula that uses the variable information, however (the FV formula, in this example), must appear at the top of the second column in the table range (the column that will contain the results). Correct placement of this formula is very important because Excel uses the formula to calculate the values of the table. In the example, you could remove the formula in cell D3 and place it in cell D4. You do not need to duplicate this formula; it can appear only in the second column of the data table.

You can set up the input table with rows instead of columns. In this case, you must enter the input cell into the space marked Row Input Cell in the Data Table dialog box. The first row of the worksheet should contain the input variables, and the second row should be blank.

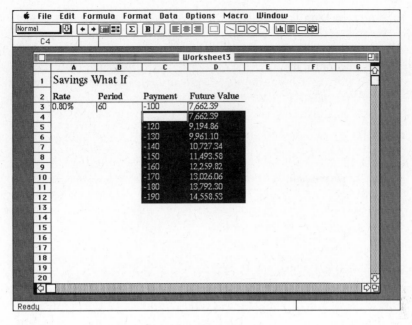

Fig. 8.10. *The result of a data-table calculation.*

Working with Complex Data Tables

The data table described in the preceding section is not the most complicated table you can use; you also can perform what-if tests on a second variable. The result will be a matrix of values that corresponds to combinations of the two variables. In order to add a second variable to the data table, you must enter test values across the top of the table range and down the first column.

To create a data table with two test variables, follow these steps:

1. Enter the series of values for the first test variable into a column.

2. Enter the series of values for the second test variable into a row. The first cell in this row should be one cell above and to the right of the first cell in the column created in step 1. This procedure forms an empty table with entries at the top and along the left side.

3. Enter another test value for each of the two variables outside the table range. These values can duplicate two of the values in the table.

4. Enter the formula that uses the two variables. Be sure that this formula includes references to the input cells *outside* the table range—not to cells *inside* the range. Enter this formula into the cell, marking the upper left corner of the table range (the intersection of the row and column). This formula can use more variables than the two used in the table, but it must include at least those two.

5. Highlight the entire table and select the Data Table command.

6. Find the cell outside the table range that corresponds to the values in the column of the table. Enter this cell address as the column input cell. Find the cell outside the table range that corresponds to the values in the row of the table. Enter this cell address as the row input cell.

7. Press Return to complete the calculation.

Using the same what-if example, suppose that you want to test the future value of your savings based on various monthly deposits and various periods of time (terms). You want to find out what a deposit of $100 per month will earn over 60 months, over 72 months, and so on. You want to find out the same thing for deposits of $120 per month, $130 per month, and so on. Figure 8.11 shows how this table is set up.

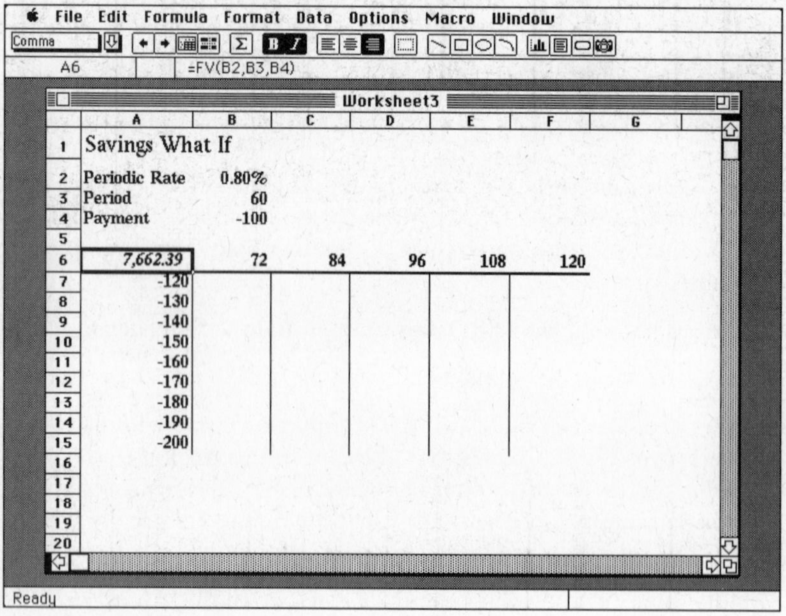

Fig. 8.11. *A data table in which two variables are used.*

Note: The worksheet in figure 8.11 has been rearranged slightly so that the values appear in column B rather than row 3, as in the preceding example. This change helps keep the entire table and all related values in view at one time.

As in the preceding example, the values for the first test variable are listed in a column. The values for the second text variable are listed in a row across the top of the table. The column shows the various monthly payment amounts, and the row shows the various terms. In figure 8.11, the table range is A6:F15.

Next, enter a formula to calculate one iteration of the test. Enter this formula into the corner cell of the table range. The variables used in this formula should not be in the table. In figure 8.11, the formula is entered into cell A6 and uses the values in cells B2, B3, and B4:

=FV(B2,B3,B4)

Notice that the worksheet uses three variables. The interest rate in B2 remains constant for the entire table. Also note that this formula uses variables outside the table range, and the table continues the tests.

The final step is to highlight the entire table and select the Data Table command. Enter the row and column input cells into the Data Table dialog box and press Return. In this example, you enter the row input as $B$3 because the row of variables in the table is used instead of cell B3. The column input cell is $B$4. Figure 8.12 shows the result of this data-table calculation.

The formula in the upper left corner of the table does not have to be the original calculation of the variables; you can simply reference a formula from another cell in the worksheet. Cell A6 may contain the formula =B5, for example, if cell B5 contains the formula =FV(B2,B3,B4).

Using data tables is not as complicated as you may think. You may even be using the Copy command to create such tables from your worksheet formulas. You will find data tables useful in many worksheet situations—for example, in creating a table of what-if values.

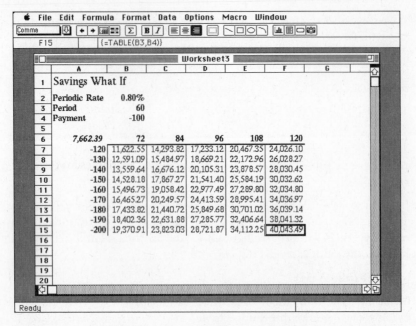

Fig. 8.12. *The result of a data table in which two test variables are used.*

Recalculating and Editing Data Tables

You can change any of the row or column input values in a data table, and the table will recalculate, using the new values as a basis. In the preceding example, you can change the values in row 6 and column A to calculate a new table. You also can change other values used in the formula in cell A6. Changing the value of cell B2, for example, changes the calculation for the entire table.

You cannot edit individual results of a data table—only the table's formula as a whole. For more information on editing arrays, see "Editing Arrays," later in this chapter.

Cycling through What-If Variables

The what-if data tables discussed earlier in this chapter are useful for comparing a series of values that are calculated from inputs. The inputs are the what-if part of the model—they enable you to see various scenarios for your calculation.

You probably perform what-if tests on your worksheets without using data tables, however. Just adjusting different values in a worksheet constitutes what-if testing. Anytime you change a value on which other values depend, you are testing a new scenario.

Obviously, you don't have to structure your worksheets into tables in order to perform what-if tests. Although using data tables is handy for comparing (side by side) the changes caused by one or two variables, they do have some disadvantages.

Data tables enable you to change a maximum of two variables in your model. Your worksheet may require more than this. Also, you may not always want to use the tabular format for your worksheets. You may not be able to place your variables into adjacent rows and columns.

The What-If Add-In

Excel 3.0 provides a useful new tool that enables you to perform what-if tests without using tables. By using this tool, you don't have to adjust individual cells by hand. You can use this tool to cycle through several input values for an existing worksheet model—just as if you were typing the values by hand. Excel gives you the tool as a worksheet add-in. This means that you must open (or activate) the add-in to add its features to Excel. To activate the what-if add-in, follow these steps:

1. Select the Open command from the File menu.

2. Locate the Excel worksheet called What If. This worksheet should be in the same folder as the Excel program or possibly in a folder called Macro Library.

3. Double-click on the what-if add-in to open it.

> **Tip: Locating the What-if Add-in**
> If you cannot find the what-if add-in—or any other add-ins for that matter—you may have opted not to install them onto your hard drive. When you install Excel, you are given the option of installing the Macro Library. This library includes several add-ins, including What If. You can run the installation program again and install only the Excel Library to add these files to your drive without reinstalling Excel. See Appendix A for installation instructions.

Using the What If Command from the Formula Menu

After you open the what-if add-in, the What If command appears in the Formula menu. This command does two things:

- It stores the what-if information about the current worksheet. This includes the cells that will be adjusted (called the *variable cells*) and the values to cycle through these cells. The What If command stores this information in a normal worksheet so that you can save it for repeated use. Although this is a normal worksheet in every respect, this book refers to it as a *data sheet*.

- It enables you to select from existing data sheets that you created previously. These sheets must be open already for the What If command to list them.

Here are the steps for creating a new data sheet:

1. Open the worksheet that will be used for the what-if tests. This is called the model.

2. Activate the what-if add-in as described earlier in this section.

3. With the worksheet in view, select the What If command from the Formula menu. If this command does not appear in the menu, you have not properly opened the what-if add-in. The dialog box shown in figure 8.13 appears.

4. Click on the New button from the dialog box. Excel presents the message

   ```
   Reference of variable #1
   ```

5. Enter the address of the first variable cell in the model and click on OK. Do not use dollar signs to make this reference absolute.

6. Excel now asks for the first value to cycle through variable #1. Enter the value and click on OK.

7. Enter the second value for variable #1 and click on OK. Continue this procedure to list all values for variable #1. When finished, click on Done.

8. Excel displays the following prompt:

   ```
   Reference of variable #2.
   ```

   Repeat steps 5, 6, and 7 for the second and subsequent variable cells.

9. When finished, click on Done. Click on Done again to return to the worksheet.

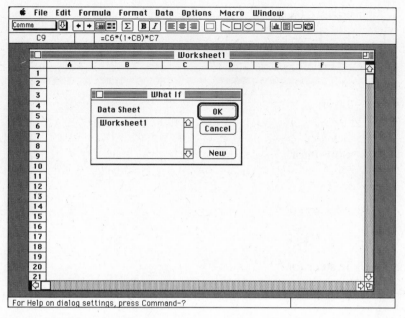

Fig. 8.13. The What If dialog box.

When you finish specifying all the variable cells and the values to cycle through each of them, the What If command enters your information onto a new worksheet. You can view this worksheet by selecting its name from the Worksheet menu. It looks something like figure 8.14.

If you save this worksheet, you can use it again to repeat the same tests.

> **Tip: Editing an Existing Data Sheet**
> Because the data sheet is a normal worksheet of values, you can edit its information to change your tests. The variable cells are listed in row 1 and under each is its values. Make changes to these and then resave the worksheet. If you add or remove a variable call, be sure to update the number in cell A1, which reflects the number of input cells in the data sheet.

To select an existing data sheet, follow these steps:

1. Open any data sheets you have saved previously.

2. Open your model worksheet and bring it into view.

3. Activate the what-if add-in as described earlier in this section.

4. Select the What If command from the Formula menu. The list of open worksheets appears in the What If dialog box.

5. Choose the data sheet from the list by double-clicking on its name.

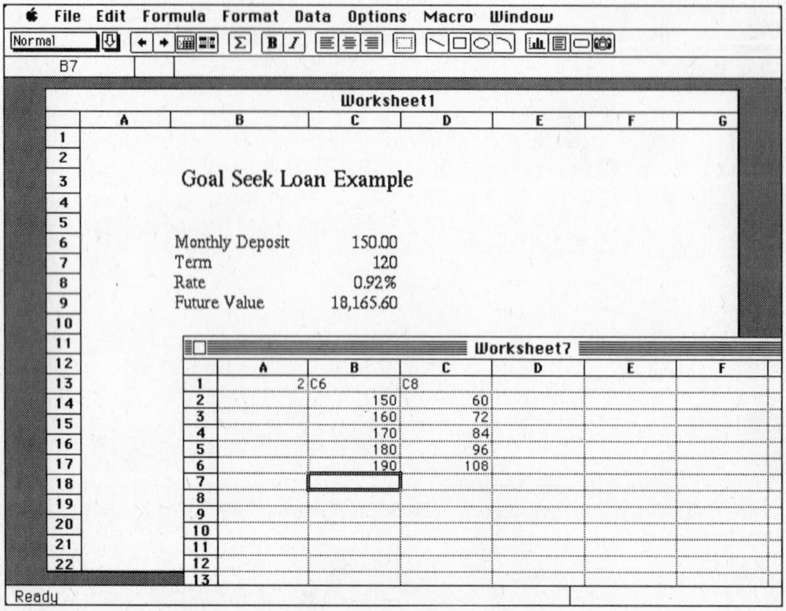

Fig. 8.14. *A data sheet created by the What If command.*

Cycling through the Values

After you create a data sheet (or select an existing data sheet), you are ready to cycle through the values. First, move the cell pointer to any of the variable cells you specified for the model worksheet, and then use one of the following commands:

⌘-Option-A — Each time you press this combination of keys, Excel inserts a new value into the model. The cell pointer jumps among the input cells to change their values and eventually presents all the inputs.

⌘-Option-Shift-A — Each time you press this combination of keys, Excel inserts a new value into the active cell. You eventually cycle through all the values for this cell. You then can move the pointer to a different cell and cycle through its values. Each cell is handled separately.

Tip: Activating the What If Command Each Time You Use Excel
You may want the What If command to appear each time you start
Excel so that you don't have to activate it each time. You can do this
by returning to the Macintosh start-up screen (desktop) and locating
the What If add-in icon. This probably will be in the Macro Library
folder. Next, drag this icon into the Excel Start-up folder located
inside the System folder. (If you are running System 7.0, the Excel
Start-up folder is located inside the Preferences folder, which is
inside the System folder.)

*Tip: Removing the What If Command by
Switching to Short Menus*
If you use the Short Menus command from the Options menu, the
What If command is removed from the Formula menu (along with
several other commands). If you return to full menus by choosing
the Full Menus command from the Options menu, the What If
command does not return to the Formula menu and you must
reactivate the add-in.

Tip: Applying Data Sheets to Any Model
You can use your data sheets on any model worksheet—not just the
one for which it was created originally. This capability can be useful
for repeating the same what-if tests on different worksheets created
from the same template.

Seeking Goals

You may find yourself using what-if data tables to find a particular goal rather
than a table of possible goals. In fact, you may be interested in only one value
from the table—the one closest to your goal. Rather than using a table, you
simply may adjust the variables in an equation until you reach your goal. You
may want to know how much you should deposit monthly, for example, to
accumulate $25,000 in 10 years at 11 percent annual interest. The goal is
$25,000 and you are seeking the monthly deposit amount. (You also can
achieve the same thing with the PMT function, as described in Chapter 6.
You can achieve most loan-related examples with functions.)

To use goal seeking, follow these steps:

1. Enter a full example of the formula into the worksheet. This formula does not have to come close to your goal. Figure 8.15 shows the investment example with the formula showing in the formula bar. In this example, you want to know what the value of cell C6 should be to make the formula in C9 produce 25,000.

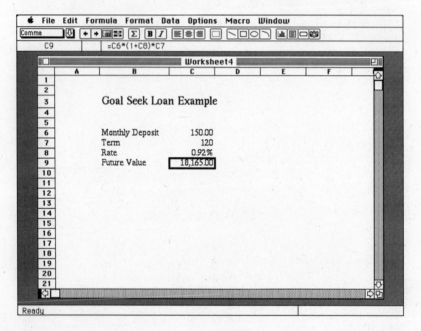

Fig. 8.15. *An investment example of goal-seeking.*

2. Move the pointer to the cell containing the formula (cell C9 in figure 8.15) and select the Formula Goal Seek command. The Goal Seek dialog box appears.

3. Enter the cell reference containing the formula in the Set Cell field of the Goal Seek dialog box. Excel may already have entered this for you.

4. Enter the goal value in the To Value field.

5. Enter the variable cell in the By Changing Cells field. Figure 8.16 shows the entries for the sample worksheet.

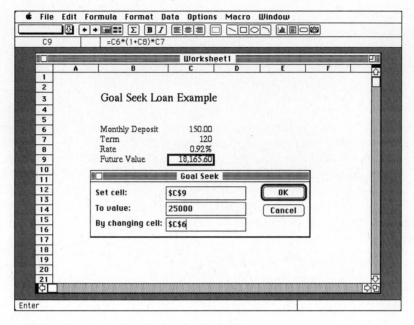

Fig. 8.16. *The Goal Seek dialog box with sample entries.*

6. Click on OK. Excel calculates the value of your variable cell and presents a message informing you of its success. Click on OK to place the value into the cell. Excel places its value into cell C6, and cell C9 calculates the goal you want.

Most financial needs can be solved with Excel's financial functions rather than with the Formula Goal Seek command. This command is useful when you can change one variable in a formula to achieve a goal. More complex goal-seeking may require you to manipulate several variables to get a particular result. You can solve these larger models by using Excel's Solver program, described in the next section.

Seeking Goals with the Solver

The Solver is a special utility that can solve your worksheet's formulas backward in order to locate the variables required to reach a certain result. Often, your worksheets produce results by calculating values contained in several cells. By changing these values, you can view different results. This is known as *what-if analysis*; it enables you to use the spreadsheet to ask questions such as *What if sales were five percent higher than last year?* or *What if I invest 10 percent more every month?*

Changing certain cells gives you a completely new result.

Rather than entering what-if values into the cells of your worksheet, however, you can use the Solver to adjust those values to reach a specified result. In this way, the Solver solves formulas backward. You may wonder *How much must I increase sales to reach 100,000 in profits?*, for example. In this case, you set the result of your calculation, the profit, to a particular value; your goal is to find the inputs needed to reach that value. You could enter various sales figures until you get $100,000 in profit. This may take several guesses, however—especially if the relationship between sales and profit is affected by several other inputs as well. The Solver can do this for you in seconds.

Suppose that you want to purchase inventory for your camera store. You stock six types of cameras, and you have $30,000 to spend. Each camera has a unique discount rate, cost, and markup amount. You want to know which combinations you can purchase without exceeding your $30,000. This is a job for the Solver. The goal is to reach a purchase price of $30,000 by adjusting the quantities of the cameras. Obviously, there is more than one correct answer to this model. The Solver can show all answers or just the ones that meet certain conditions (known as *constraints*).

Now suppose that you want to purchase $30,000 worth of cameras, but you want 20 percent more Nikons than the other brands because you know that you sell about 20 percent more Nikons. Also, you want to spend at least $2,000 on each brand. This setup eliminates combinations that include all of one brand and none of the others. These constraints can be expressed mathematically like this (later, you will use expressions much like this to add constraints to the Solver model):

Nikon = 120% * Canon

Nikon = 120% * Kodak

Nikon = 120% * Olympus

Nikon = 120% * Agfa

Nikon - 120% * Vivitar

Canon >= 2000

Kodak >= 2000

Olympus >= 2000

Agfa >= 2000

Vivitar >= 2000

Notice that the expression "Nikon >= 2000" is not required because being 120 percent of the others will result in this condition anyway. Excel finds the various quantity combinations that meet these constraints and keeps your budget at $30,000.

The Solver can do even more. It can calculate the maximum result from a combination of values within certain constraints. Suppose that you want to know how many of each type of camera you should purchase to maximize your net sales. This may be more complex than simply purchasing more of the camera type that has the highest markup value. You must account for the fact that you sell 20 percent more Nikons and that each camera's mark-up is different. In this example, the markup values are part of the model and the budget of 30,000 becomes a constraint rather than the goal:

Total Cost <= Budget of 30,000

The goal is now the net sales total from selling these items with the indicated markups. The Solver can tell you how many of each item to purchase (within the given constraints) to maximize your net sales total.

Now that you understand what the Solver can do, read the following sections to examine the Solver's options. Then, in "Creating Solver Examples," you will see how Excel creates and solves the previous examples.

Using the Solver

The Solver is a special utility, called an *add-in*. Like the what-if add-in discussed earlier in this chapter, you must activate the Solver before you can use it. You may have installed the Solver when you installed Excel 3.0, however. In this case, the Solver is activated already and the Solver command should appear in the Formula menu. Check the Formula menu for this command now. If the Solver command does not appear, you must activate the Solver add-in.

To activate the Solver add-in, select the Open command from the File menu and locate the file called Solver. This should be in the Macro Library folder. Open this file by double-clicking on its name. This adds the Solver command to the Formula menu.

Note: If you cannot find the Solver file or the Macro Library folder, you probably did not install the macro library when you installed Excel. You are given the option to bypass the installation of the macro library in order to save disk space. In this case, you must restart the Excel installation program and install only the macro library in order to add it to your system. See Appendix A for details.

You access the Solver by choosing Solver from the Formula menu. You then enter information into the dialog box that appears. Follow these steps to access the Solver:

1. Create the worksheet model so that it calculates a sample result. This can be an existing model or one created specifically for the Solver. The worksheet does not have to meet the desired constraints or produce the desired result at this point.

2. Select Solver from the Formula menu. The Solver Parameters dialog box in figure 8.17 appears.

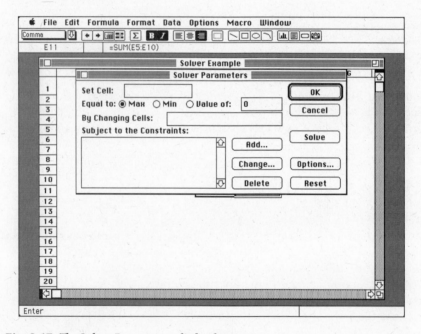

Fig. 8.17. The Solver Parameters dialog box.

3. Enter the cell containing the goal in the Set Cell field. You can click on the cell in the worksheet while the dialog box is in view to establish this setting.

4. Select one of the Equal To options from the dialog box. If you select the Value Of option, enter the value you want into the space provided. This is the goal to be reached in the cell indicated. Maximize and Minimize tell Excel to find the maximum or minimum value possible.

5. Enter the input (or variable) cells into the By Changing Cells field. You can click on the worksheet to enter these cells. These are the values that you want Excel to adjust until it reaches your goal. To specify more than one cell, type a comma between each cell.

6. Enter constraints, if you want them. Click on Add and enter constraint formulas in the Subject to the Constraints list. Examples of constraint formulas appear later.

7. Click on Solve to begin solving the problem.

When you add constraints as described in step 6, enter them as formulas that can be evaluated as TRUE or FALSE by using the options provided. When you complete step 6, the Constraints dialog box appears for you to enter your constraints. Enter a cell reference in the Cell Reference box; select an operator from the list; then enter a value, cell reference, or expression in the Constraint box. To enter C10 > 2000, for example, make these entries:

Cell Reference: C10

Operator List: >

Constraint: 2000

If you require several constraint formulas, click on Add after each formula so that you don't return to the Solver dialog box each time. When finished with all of the constraints, click on OK to return to the Solver dialog box.

If the Solver comes up with a solution, it enters the results into the appropriate cells and informs you of its success. You are given the option to keep the results or replace the original results. If you want to view other solutions to the same problem (assuming that other solutions exist), accept the first solution and repeat the Solver process using the new cell values as the starting values. The Solver begins its calculations using the current cell values. Changing these values can result in different solutions. To find new results, you may even try entering various input values by hand—even if they don't calculate the correct goal.

Creating Solver Examples

Now look at what the previous examples look like in Excel. The initial worksheet is a simple model that contains ordering quantities for six cameras, their descriptions, unit costs, and extended total cost for each item. The worksheet also includes a grand purchase total. Figure 8.18 shows this worksheet.

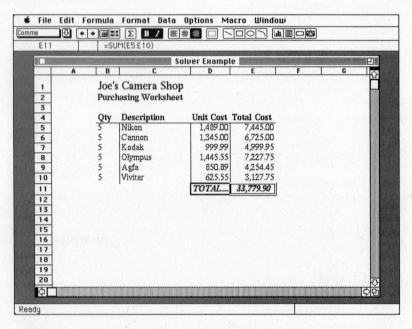

Fig. 8.18. The sample worksheet containing a Solver problem.

The first Solver task is to come up with scenarios for the various quantities, while maintaining a total cost of $30,000. Open the Solver dialog box by selecting the Solver command from the Formula menu and enter the following data:

Set Cell: E11

Equal to Value of: 30000

By Changing Cells: B5,B6,B7,B8,B9,B10

Now click on Solve, and Excel finds the first solution. Remember that the starting values in the cells determine the first result when more than one result is possible. Figure 8.19 shows the result from figure 8.18.

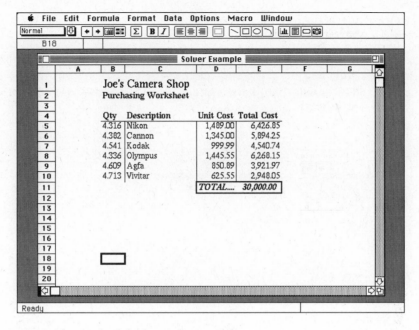

Fig. 8.19. *The result of the first Solver model.*

The next step is to add some constraints. In this case, you want to spend at least \$2,000 on each item and you want 20 percent more Nikons than the other cameras. Enter the following constraints, as described earlier in "Using the Solver."

B5 = 120% * B6

B5 = 120% * B7

B5 = 120% * B8

B5 = 120% * B9

B5 = 120% * B10

E6 >= 2000

E7 >= 2000

E8 >= 2000

E9 >= 2000

E10 >= 2000

The constraints can control any cells used in the worksheet—not just the ones containing the input variables. Of course, there are fewer solutions that meet this model than the first model. After you add the constraints and return to the Solver dialog box, select Solve to get a solution.

The final example is for the Solver to suggest ordering quantities for each item to provide maximum income when you sell the items. For this, you need to add some data to the worksheet. Figure 8.20 shows these additions to the sample worksheet.

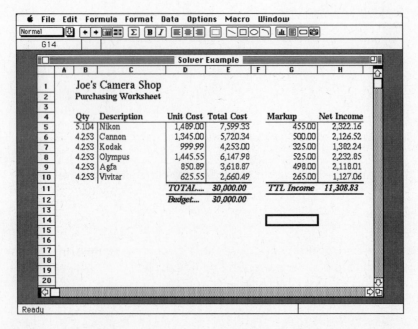

Fig. 8.20. Adding markup and income calculations to the sample worksheet.

The new worksheet includes a markup and net income figure for each camera. Excel calculates this figure by multiplying the markup by the quantity, as in =B5*G5. Excel calculates the grand total of income in cell H11. Finally, Excel enters the budget amount in cell E12, under the Total Purchase Price column. In this case, you want to maximize the value of cell H11 while adhering to the established constraints. You need to add the following constraint:

E11 = E12

This constraint keeps the total of the purchase equal to the budget. Here are your Solver settings:

Set Cell: H11

Equal to: Max

By Changing Cells: B5,B6,B7,B8,B9,B10

The result is the number of each item you should purchase under these conditions to maximize your income.

Working with Arrays and Array Calculations

An *array* is a special type of range, also known as an *array range*. Although an array resembles a normal range of cells that contains formulas or values, it differs in one major respect: The cells in the array range cannot be edited independently but only as a group. You cannot change the formula or value in one of the cells of an array range; you must change the entire array together.

The values in array ranges are also created as a group through a procedure called an *array calculation*. These calculations are required in certain instances, such as when you perform trend analysis with the TREND function. You can use arrays in place of standard ranges, however, to save time and conserve memory in your worksheets.

Although arrays and array calculations may seem complicated now, they actually make worksheets simpler and can save you time in entering formulas.

Making Basic Array Calculations

A basic array calculation takes the place of a series of individual calculations spread over a range. In figure 8.21, the formulas in column C add the corresponding values in columns A and B.

Each cell in column C contains an individual formula, such as =A3+B3. An array formula can take the place of these formulas by calculating the range A3:A10 plus the range B3:B10. The result is a range of answers in cells C3:C10.

You enter the formula used for this calculation into column C as an array; Excel treats the other two ranges as arrays. Enter the formula in this way:

1. Highlight the range—for example, C3:C10.

2. Type the formula—for example, *=A3:A10+B3:B10*.

3. Press ⌘-Enter to accept the formula.

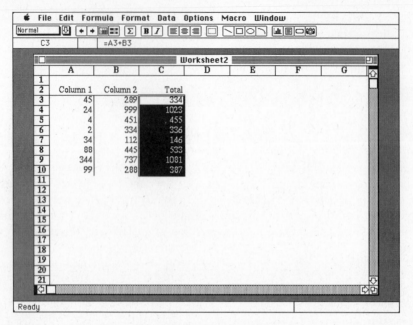

Fig. 8.21. *A sample range of formulas.*

The result is a range of cells (an *array range*) containing the answers to the set of calculations. You cannot alter individual cells in this range; you must treat them as a single unit. Excel uses special array math to calculate these values, all of which are dependent on one another. Each cell in the array contains the formula surrounded by brackets, as the formula bar in figure 8.22 indicates.

You do not have to use two arrays in the formula. Figure 8.23 shows an array produced with the formula =A3:A10+$B$3.

When you use this formula, Excel adds each cell in the range A3:A10 to the cell B3, producing eight values. You can replace the reference to B3 with a constant value, as in =A3:A10+2. You can even enter an array formula that contains no ranges, as in the formula =A3+B3. The result is a range of cells containing the same value, however.

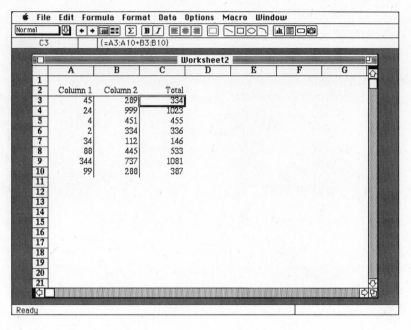

Fig. 8.22. *Each cell in the array contains this formula.*

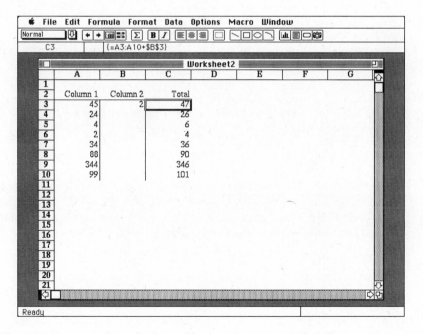

Fig. 8.23. *An array formula that adds one range to a single cell.*

Normally, the *resulting array* (the array containing the results) must be the same size as the largest range referenced in the formula. In the previous examples, the resulting array contains eight cells because the ranges in the formula contain eight cells. If you highlight fewer cells, Excel completes the array calculation for as many cells as you highlight. If you highlight a range that is larger than the largest referenced range, Excel enters an error into the extra cells. If you highlighted 10 cells in the previous examples, for example, the last two would contain errors.

Using Functions in Array Calculations

When you use a function in an array calculation, keep in mind that there are three types of functions: those that have no arguments, those that have values or expressions as arguments, and those that have ranges as arguments. The following are examples of each:

PI( )	No arguments
SQRT(value)	Numeric expression or value argument
SUM(range)	Range argument

Each type of function is handled differently in an array calculation. The simplest function is the one that has no arguments. You can use this function in an array calculation just as you would use any value or single cell reference. You can highlight the range C3:C10, for example, and enter the formula =B3:B10*PI( ), pressing ⌘-Return to create the array. The function is part of the array calculation. The result is a series of values in cells C3:C10, which are the values of B3:B10 multiplied by pi.

When you use a function that requires values as arguments, you must enter the value as a range, thus causing the function to work on an array range rather than a single value. Of course, you should highlight an equal-size range for the results. To calculate the square root of each cell in the range B3:B10, for example, highlight a blank range for the result, enter the formula *=SQRT(B3:B10)*, and press ⌘-Return. You also can use this expression in a larger array calculation, such as the following:

=A3:A10+SQRT(B3:B10)

This formula takes the square root of each cell in the range B3:B10 and adds it to the corresponding cell in the range A3:A10.

The final type of function includes those with ranges as arguments, such as SUM, AVERAGE, and COUNT. Because these functions produce a single value from a standard range, they act like single values in array calculations—like a cell reference, a constant value, or functions like pi. Because formulas use standard ranges for their arguments, however, they can be confusing. The array formula =SUM(A3:A10)*B3:B10, for example, multiplies the sum of the range A3:A10 to each cell in the range B3:B10 and places the eight results in the result array (see fig. 8.24). The sum of the range A3:A10 is 640, which is multiplied by each cell in the range B3:B10 to produce eight values.

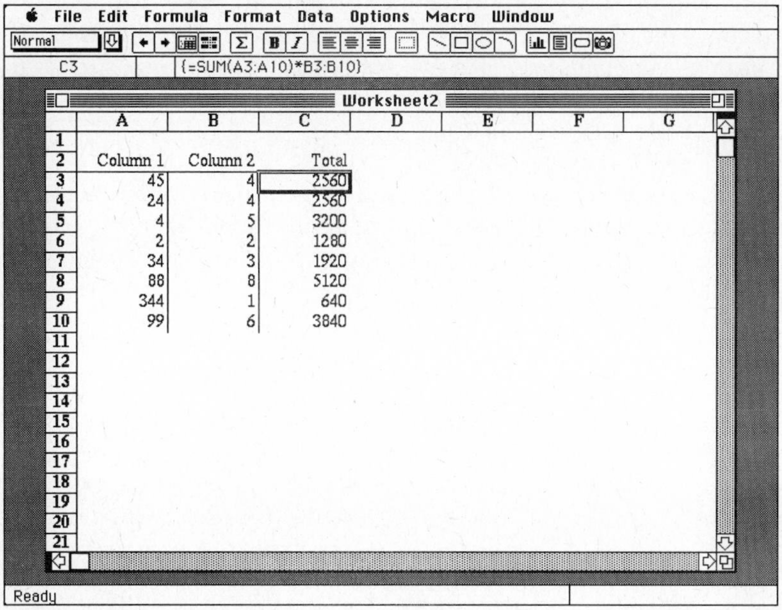

Fig. 8.24. *Using a range function in an array formula.*

Another way to use a range function in an array calculation is to make an array calculation in the argument of the function. Suppose that you have values in the ranges A3:A10 and B3:B10. You can enter an array formula such as =SUM(A3:A10*B3:B10). In this case, the result is a single value, and you should highlight only one cell as the result array. You do this because the SUM function calculates a single value from a range—even an array range. The resulting range (one cell) still will be an array range. In this example, the formula multiplies each cell in the range A3:A10 by its corresponding cell in the range B3:B10 and then totals the values. You can express the formula like this:

(A3*B3)+(A4*B4)+(A5*B5)...(A10*B10)

Using Constant Array References

Normally, Excel constructs arrays from your range references. You also can create an array formula by multiplying a series of individual values to another series of values. This is like specifying each cell in a range, rather than using the range reference. You would do this primarily when you must use an array range in your formula, but you don't want to enter values onto the worksheet where they can be referenced.

Constant array references require that you separate values within a column by using commas and each column by using semicolons. The range A1:B4, for example, contains values in two columns and four rows, such as these values:

> {5,2,4;7,8,9}

Each value on the left side of the semicolon represents a different cell in the first column and those values on the right represent the second column's cells. This is not the range A1:B4, but any two-by-four array range. Here are some other examples:

Constant Array Reference	Rows/ Columns	Similar Range Reference
{1,2,3,4}	1 x 4	A1:D1
{1;3;4;4}	4 x 1	A1:A4
{1,2;1,2;5,6;7,8}	4 x 2	A1:B4

Note that these references must have the same number of values within each column separator. The array range {1,2;3,4;5}, for example, is invalid because it contains only one reference in the third column.

You can use constant array references in formulas—just as you would use an array range. Just highlight the appropriate number of cells for the resulting values and then enter the constant range reference surrounded by the braces ({}) and any other ranges or values for the formula. Press ⌘-Return to calculate the resulting array. Following is an example:

> {45;24;4;2;34;88;344;99}*B3

Highlight a range containing eight rows and one column, such as the range C3:C10, and enter this formula. Press ⌘-Return when finished. The result is a range containing the values 45, 24, 4, 2, 34, 88, 344, and 99—each multiplied by the value in cell B3. In this example, you used constants instead of a worksheet range. The resulting formula looks like this:

> {{45;24;4;2;34;88;344;99}*B3}

The outside braces indicate that the entire formula is part of an array. The inside braces indicate the array range within this formula. You can multiply two ranges using either of the following formulas. The first formula uses one constant array and one worksheet range; the second uses two constant arrays:

{45;24;4;2;34;88;344;99}*B3:B10

{45;24;4;2;34;88;344;99}*{289;999;451;334;112;445;737;288}

You cannot use formulas, expressions, functions, or cell references in your constant array ranges; they must be constant values.

Editing Arrays

You cannot insert new cells, rows, or columns into an array range; Excel presents an error message if you try. Similarly, you cannot change individual cells within the array range. You can change the formula for an entire array at once, however. Just highlight the entire array range and press F2 to edit the formula. When finished, press ⌘-Return to establish the array again.

To convert array results into constant values, highlight the array range and choose the Copy command from the Edit menu to copy the range. Then use the Paste Special command from the Edit menu and choose the Values option to paste the values back to the worksheet. Click on OK to complete the conversion. The values are placed into the cells that originally contained the array.

You also can turn an array range into a series of constant array references. To do this, highlight the entire array and then use the mouse to highlight the entire array formula in the formula bar. Press ⌘-= to convert the references and ⌘-Return to place the new formulas into the range.

Calculating Worksheets

Excel calculates the results of formulas each time you make a change in the worksheet or when you open a worksheet. When you start to create large, complex worksheets, this feature may get in your way by forcing you to wait for calculations. You can control the way Excel calculates worksheets, however, by using the Calculation options in the Options menu. The dialog box shown in figure 8.25 appears.

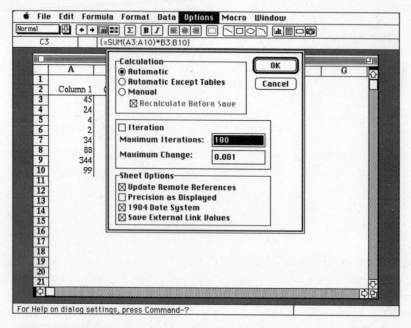

Fig. 8.25. The Options Calculation dialog box.

The options in the Options Calculation dialog box follow:

- *Automatic.* Sets the normal mode of calculation. Excel calculates the worksheet after every change. Automatic calculates the entire worksheet (except data tables) at each change.

- *Manual.* Calculates the worksheet only when you select the Options Calculate Now command.

- *Iteration.* Enables or disables the iteration feature, causing the worksheet to calculate a certain number of times based on changes in worksheet data.

- *Maximum Iterations.* Sets the maximum number of calculations performed during each calculation (for example, repeated calculations).

- *Maximum Change.* Sets the amount of change that is unacceptable to Excel. If data does not change this much, Excel stops the repeated calculations.

- *Precision as Displayed.* Sets the number of decimal places used in calculations to the number displayed in the cells. Unless the number is rounded off by the ROUND function, Excel normally uses the maximum number of decimal places (15) for each value, even if the decimal places are not displayed. If you check the Precision as Displayed box, Excel uses only the digits displayed in the cells. You therefore do not have to use the ROUND function throughout the worksheet.

- *1904 Date System.* Sets the starting date for all date calculations to 1904 when checked. If you do not check this option, the starting date is 1900. This option is useful for making Excel compatible with PC-based worksheets that use the 1900 date system.

When you perform a manual calculation, the Options Calculate Now command is the only way to calculate the worksheet. (You also can use the keyboard equivalent ⌘-=.) This command enables you to calculate whenever you want.

Analyzing Worksheets

Excel provides some useful worksheet analysis features that can help you locate errors and evaluate complex worksheet references. You probably will not need these features unless your worksheets are fairly large and complex. If you build worksheets that will be used by others, you will find these features quite helpful.

Finding Dependents and Precedents

Because worksheets can contain a tangled network of formulas that refer to one another, finding problems in formulas can be difficult. Excel provides some tools for locating incorrect values and problematic calculations. Although these tools will not help you correct the problems, they can help you find the problems.

A cell that contains a reference to another cell is dependent on that value for its own value. All cells containing references, therefore, are dependent cells. The precise cells they depend on, however, can be difficult to determine.

Suppose that cell A2 contains a reference to cell A1 and cell A3 contains a reference to A2. Cells A2 and A3 are dependent on cell A1. Cell A2 is a *direct dependent*; cell A3 is an *indirect dependent*. Cell A3 is a direct dependent of A2. When Excel asks you for the dependents of cell A1, list A2 and A3. Just as cell A2 is the dependent of A1, cell A1 is the precedent of A2. A *precedent* is a cell that is used (or depended on) by another cell. Precedents also can be direct or indirect. In the example, cell A1 is a direct precedent of cell A2 and an indirect precedent of cell A3.

Using the Select Special Command

Excel can locate any cell's dependents or precedents for you. This capability can be helpful in tracking down worksheet bugs across complex formulas. Follow these steps:

1. Move the pointer to the desired cell.

2. Choose the Select Special command from the Formula menu. The Select Special dialog box appears on-screen (see fig. 8.26).

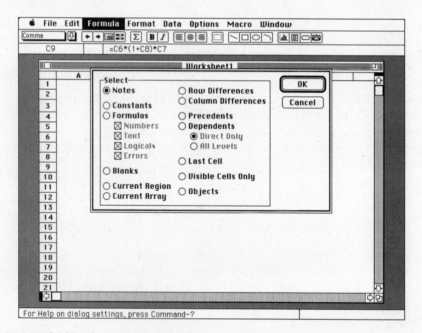

Fig. 8.26. *The Select Special dialog box.*

3. Select the Dependents or Precedents option by clicking on it.

4. Select Direct Only or All Levels by clicking on it.

5. Click on OK. Excel highlights the dependents or precedents of the cell you selected in step 1.

Using Worksheet Navigation

Excel provides another way to locate a cell's direct precedents. This feature, known as *worksheet navigation*, highlights direct precedents of any cell on which you double-click. Just double-click on any cell in the worksheet to view its direct precedents. If the precedents are in an external worksheet, Excel opens the worksheet and highlights the precedent cells.

Using the Info Sheet

A final way to see a cell's dependents or precedents is to use the Info sheet. Here are the steps:

1. Move the cell pointer to the desired cell.

2. Select the Show Info command from the Window menu. This step brings up the Info sheet and adds the Info menu to the menu bar.

3. Select the Dependents command from the Info menu to list the cell's dependent references.

   Excel then asks you to select Direct Only or All Levels. Choose one of these options and click OK. When finished, the Info sheet displays a list of dependents for the cell you selected in step 1.

4. Repeat step 3 using the Precedents command from the Info menu to display the cell's precedents in the Info sheet.

For more information about using the Info sheet, see "Displaying Cell Information," later in this chapter.

Using the Auditor

The worksheet auditor is a useful debugging tool for your worksheets. It provides useful information about a worksheet and its formulas. This information includes a list of potential errors on your worksheet, an overall map of your worksheet for a synopsis of its contents, details about formula dependencies and logic flow, and specialized information about the worksheet.

The worksheet auditor is an add-in macro, which you must invoke as any other add-in. To use the auditor, follow these steps:

1. Choose the Open command from the File menu to open the worksheet called Worksheet Auditor. This worksheet should be located in the Excel Program folder. (You also can start the auditor add-in using any of the methods described earlier for using add-ins.)

2. Make sure your worksheet is open and in view.

3. Choose the Worksheet Auditor command from the Formula menu.

4. Choose from the auditor's basic tools.

Brief descriptions of the worksheet auditor's basic tools follow:

- *Generate Audit Report:* Creates a report of various aspects of the worksheet. A dialog box enables you to choose the various elements you want in this report. These elements include the following lists:

  Cells with errors

  Cells that refer to blank cells

  Cells that refer to text

  All cells involved in a circular reference

  Unused worksheet names

- *Map Worksheet:* Prints a map of the worksheet. This map lists all cells containing formulas, all cells with data, all cells with labels, and so on. This tool can be useful in providing an overall look at the worksheet.

- *Interactive Trace:* Enables you to trace cell dependencies on the fly. The option brings up a control panel that interacts with the worksheet. Highlight any cell on the worksheet and then use the following control panel options:

Option	Function
Find Dependents	Displays all cell dependents.
Find Precedents	Displays all cell precedents.
Reset Active Cell	Changes the active cell in the worksheet.
Move Back	Repeats preceding step.
Move Forward	Moves forward through steps.

Option	Function
Go to Sibling	Moves to the next or preceding cell in a dependency. Use this with the Find Dependents button.
Exit Trace	Exits the interactive trace feature.

- *Worksheet Info:* Prepares a report about your worksheet. Check this report for useful information.

Using Cell Notes

A cell note is an excellent way to provide detailed information about a cell. This information can be for an operator to access or simply to document the formula used in the cell. To enter a cell note, follow these steps:

1. Select the cell you want.

2. Select the Formula Note command.

3. Enter the note in the space provided.

Excel uses the first line of the cell note as a title for the note. Therefore, you may enter a descriptive word or phrase on the first line, and then begin the text of the note on the next line. Press Option-Return to move the cursor to the next line before you reach the end of the current line. Pressing Return accepts the note and returns you to the worksheet. Figure 8.27 shows a sample cell note.

The options in the Cell Note dialog box follow:

- *Cell.* Displays the highlighted cell or the cell corresponding to the note selected in the Notes in Sheet list. You can enter a cell note for any cell, even if it is not highlighted, by entering its address in this box before entering the note.

  When you are finished, click on Add. This option is useful for entering several notes without returning to the sheet.

- *Note.* Displays the text of the note. You can type beyond the bottom of this box; Excel scrolls down to display the text. To view text beyond the edge of this box, click on the box and drag the pointer down.

- *Notes in Sheet.* Lists all notes in the worksheet, using the first line of each. If you click on one of these listings, the note appears in the Note field, and the associated cell address appears in the Cell field.

You can then edit the note without returning to the worksheet and highlighting the cell.

- *OK.* Completes the changes you made with the other options and returns to the worksheet.

- *Close.* Returns to the worksheet without completing your changes.

- *Add.* Adds the note to the cell listed in the Cell field. Clicking on Add is not necessary if the cell listed in the Cell box is also the highlighted cell.

- *Delete.* Removes the note from the cell listed in the Cell box.

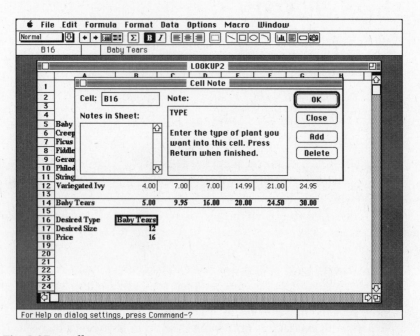

Fig. 8.27. *A cell note.*

To view a note, move the pointer to the appropriate cell and select the Formula Note command, or select the command from any cell. Then choose the note you want from the Notes in Sheet list.

You also can view a cell note by moving the pointer to the cell and selecting the Window Show Info command. The Info window is explained in the next section.

Displaying Cell Information

Another useful debugging tool is the Info sheet—a special pane that displays information about the highlighted worksheet cell. To view this sheet, move the pointer to a cell and select the Window Show Info command.

At first, the Info worksheet displays the cell address, the formula (if any), and any notes attached to the cell. You can add to this information by selecting items from the Info menu. This menu appears whenever you activate an Info worksheet. Figure 8.28 shows an Info window.

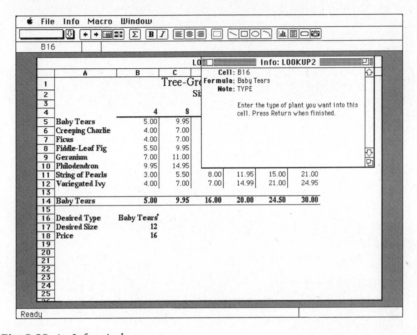

Fig. 8.28. *An Info window.*

> **Tip: Viewing Info on Several Worksheets**
> If you have several worksheets open at the same time and want to view information about different cells in each worksheet, try this: First, select the Show Info command from the Window menu. Next, use the Arrange All command from the Windows menu to organize all the worksheets on-screen—including the Info window. Finally, click on each worksheet and the cell you want to activate it in the Info window. Each time you activate a different worksheet, new information appears in the Info window.

Outlining Worksheets

Most worksheets have a natural progression, or hierarchy, of data. Individual cells are summed with formulas and those sums are summed into grand totals, and so on, giving your worksheet several levels of data. Excel's outlining feature finds these levels in your worksheets and enables you to work with each level independently.

In a worksheet, the lowest level of information is a simple value entered into a cell. All these values are on the same level. Formulas that total these values are on the next level up. Formulas that total the previous formulas are another level up, and so on. Figure 8.29 shows a worksheet with this type of structure. You can see that many worksheets may contain these levels.

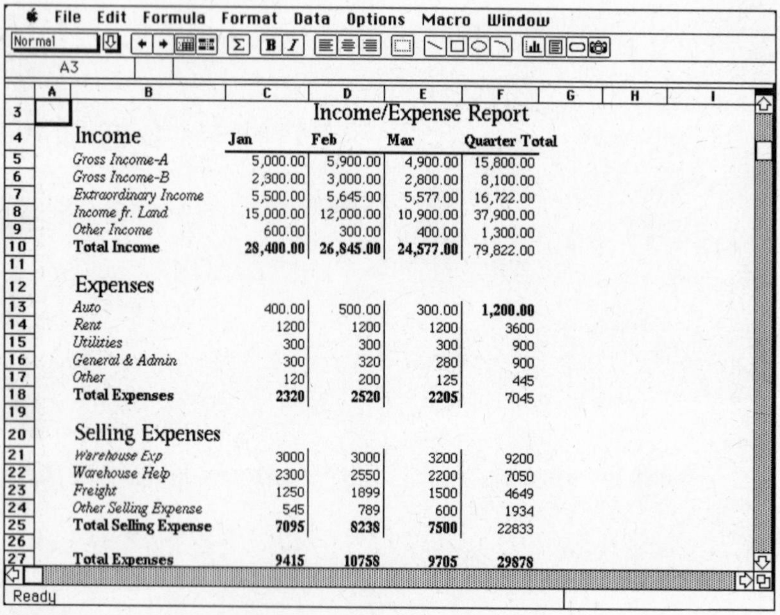

	A	B	C	D	E	F
3				Income/Expense Report		
4		Income	**Jan**	**Feb**	**Mar**	**Quarter Total**
5		*Gross Income-A*	5,000.00	5,900.00	4,900.00	15,800.00
6		*Gross Income-B*	2,300.00	3,000.00	2,800.00	8,100.00
7		*Extraordinary Income*	5,500.00	5,645.00	5,577.00	16,722.00
8		*Income fr. Land*	15,000.00	12,000.00	10,900.00	37,900.00
9		*Other Income*	600.00	300.00	400.00	1,300.00
10		**Total Income**	**28,400.00**	**26,845.00**	**24,577.00**	79,822.00
11						
12		Expenses				
13		*Auto*	400.00	500.00	300.00	**1,200.00**
14		*Rent*	1200	1200	1200	3600
15		*Utilities*	300	300	300	900
16		*General & Admin*	300	320	280	900
17		*Other*	120	200	125	445
18		**Total Expenses**	**2320**	**2520**	**2205**	7045
19						
20		Selling Expenses				
21		*Warehouse Exp*	3000	3000	3200	9200
22		*Warehouse Help*	2300	2550	2200	7050
23		*Freight*	1250	1899	1500	4649
24		*Other Selling Expense*	545	789	600	1934
25		**Total Selling Expense**	**7095**	**8238**	**7500**	22833
26						
27		**Total Expenses**	**9415**	**10758**	**9705**	**29878**

Fig. 8.29. *A worksheet with several levels of data.*

When using such a worksheet, it can be useful to view only certain levels of data—while the other, lower levels are hidden. This is one of the main features of outlining; you can collapse and expand the levels to hide or reveal more detail about the worksheet. Figure 8.30 shows the worksheet with some lower levels collapsed.

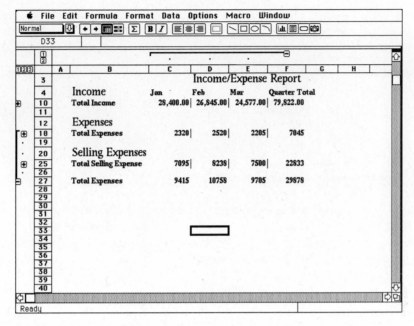

Fig. 8.30. *Using outlining to collapse some levels while keeping others in view.*

Here are some advantages to collapsing lower levels:

- Hiding the detail in a worksheet enables you to print more summarized reports without copying or moving data to fit on a page.

- When detail is hidden, it is easier for you to copy, paste, format, and generally manipulate the remaining totals. This is because the totals are displayed in adjacent cells rather than being spread throughout the worksheet.

- Totals and other higher-level data can be charted more easily.

Creating Outlines

The easiest way to create an outline is to let Excel do the work for you. Usually, Excel can locate the levels in your worksheets and group them for the outline. Follow these steps to create an outline:

1. Highlight the data that you want to outline. To outline the entire worksheet, select only one cell.

2. Select the Formula Outline command and press Return or click the Create button to create the outline.

Excel outlines the worksheet and displays the outlining symbols on the side and top of the worksheet headings. These symbols are explained in the next section.

Note: Outlines can be both row-wise and column-wise if the worksheet contains levels of formulas in both directions.

Using the Outline Symbols and Tools

Excel adds outline symbols to the worksheet after creating the outline. These symbols tell you various things about the worksheet data. The symbols also give you control over which levels you can view at any time. Figure 8.31 shows these symbols and other outlining tools.

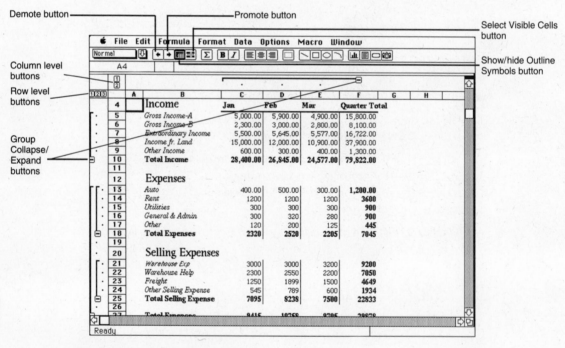

Fig. 8.31. The outlining symbols.

All formulas (or totals) in the outline are given a Group Collapse/Expand button. At first, this appears as a square containing a minus sign. The line attached to this button brackets the data that comprises the total. In figure 8.31, cells C6, C7, and C8 equal the total in cell C9. Therefore, row 9 contains the Group Collapse/Expand button and the attached line brackets rows 6, 7, and 8. All formulas on the same level are grouped together under a Row Level button, which indicates the level. (Column Level buttons apply to column-wise outlines.)

If you click on the Group Collapse/Expand button, Excel hides the data in that group and shows only the group total. The Group Collapse/Expand button beside that total changes to a plus sign to indicate that additional data is available by expanding the outline. Figure 8.32 shows an example.

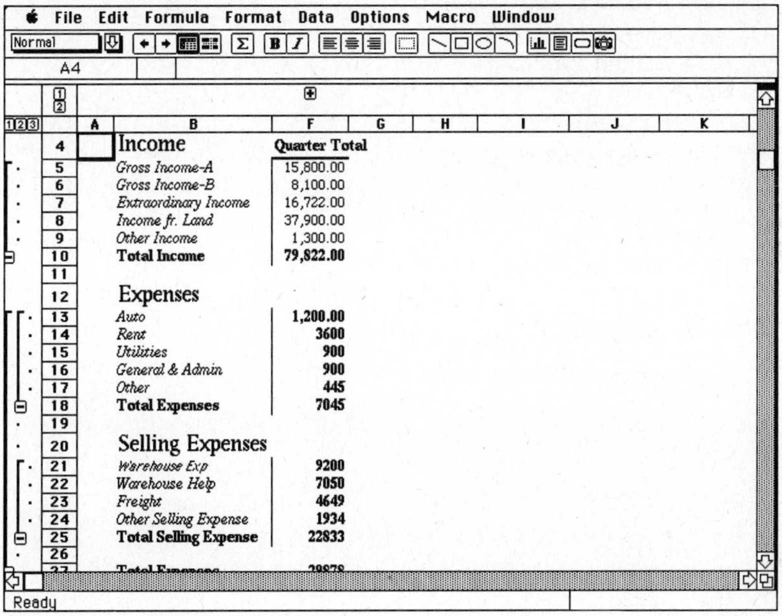

Fig. 8.32. *Collapsing a group so that only the total appears, and the minus sign changes to a plus sign.*

The plus sign indicates that you now can expand the group to reveal the hidden data. In other words, there is more data in that level. To collapse or expand an entire level (all groups on the same level), use the Row Level buttons. Click on the button indicating the highest level you want to show. To collapse level 3 data, for example, click on the level 2 button. To show level 3 data, click on the level 3 button.

Following is a summary of these buttons and the other outlining tools in the Toolbar:

- *Row Level Buttons.* Indicates the level of each group in a row-wise outline. Click on the Row Level button that indicates the highest level of data you want to show.

- *Column Level Buttons.* Indicates the level of each group in a column-wise outline.

- *Group Collapse/Expand Button.* Indicates what data makes up the group and whether it is showing (collapsible) or hidden (expandable). Click on the button to collapse or expand the data in that group.

- *Promote Button.* Increases the level of the selected group. First, select the cell containing the group total and click on the Promote button to increase its level.

  You can use this button if Excel does not properly outline the worksheet and you need to change the level of a particular total. You also can use the Promote button if you change the total so that it actually applies to a different level.

- *Demote Button.* Decreases the level of the selected group. Select the cell containing the group total and click on the Demote button to decrease its level.

  Reasons for this option are similar to those for the Promote button.

- *Show/Hide Outline Symbols Button.* Displays or removes the outline symbols from the screen.

- *Select Visible Cells Button.* Makes your highlighted range apply to only the visible cells in the worksheet. When you collapse levels of the worksheet, the remaining totals appear in adjacent cells.

If you highlight a block of collapsed totals (which apply to collapsed data), you are also highlighting all the hidden data between the totals. This affects many procedures, such as copying, charting, and moving. If collapsing the worksheet causes rows 4 and 10 to be adjacent (because cells between them are hidden), for example, highlighting the cells A4 and A10 actually includes the entire range A4:A10—including the collapsed cells.

If you click on the Select Visible Cells button after you highlight the totals you want, however, Excel uses only the visible cells in the worksheet as the highlighted range—eliminating the hidden data. You then can chart this data or copy it to another area. To chart the data, use the Edit Copy command, open a new chart with the File New command, and paste the data into the new chart with the Edit Paste command. See Chapter 11 for more information on charting.

> **Tip: Using Outlining**
> There is no reason not to create an outline on your worksheets. You may find it useful at some point in the worksheet's development. If you don't like the symbols, remove them with the Show/Hide Outline Symbols button.

Summary

Excel contains many advanced features that your worksheet applications may require. These features include ways of using complex tables, using multiple windows, linking worksheets, using arrays, and analyzing worksheets. This chapter discussed these features and provided some examples of their use. Some important points to remember follow:

- The HLOOKUP and VLOOKUP functions work well by themselves when the lookup tables require only a single variable. When the table requires two lookup variables, you need to employ one of the double-variable table techniques described in this chapter.

- A data table helps you create what-if scenarios by using one or two variables for a formula.

- An array calculation takes the place of a series of normal calculations and saves computer memory.

- Create an array formula by highlighting the destination range, entering the formula, and pressing ⌘-Return to accept it.

- You cannot split, expand, or edit array ranges. Instead, you must reenter the array.

- The Formula Solver command enables you to solve complex models to achieve an optimum value or a specific goal.

- You can turn off automatic worksheet calculations by using the Options Calculation command.

- You can attach a note to any cell on the worksheet by highlighting the cell and using the Formula Note command. You also can view an existing note this way.

- Cell notes also appear in the Info window. Display this window by entering the Windows Show Info command.

- Outlining is a way of hiding certain levels of data on the worksheet so that you can manipulate the higher levels more easily.

Chapter 9, "Printing Worksheets," discusses techniques for formatting and printing reports.

Printing Worksheets

9

This chapter describes how to print a worksheet. Although Excel makes printing an easy task, some special features and complexities may be involved. This chapter begins with the basics of printing and moves on to features such as margin settings, page breaks, headers, and page numbers. Before continuing, make sure that your printer is installed and running properly with your Macintosh systems.

Printer support is not so much a feature of Excel as of the Macintosh itself. Excel supports PostScript printers as well as Macintosh-compatible dot-matrix printers. You also can get printer drivers for many different printers, which are available from your Apple dealer and other sources. For information about printer support and installation, refer to your printer manual or a basic book about the Macintosh. In this book, the assumption is that your printer is installed and is selectable from the Chooser in the Apple menu.

Performing Basic Printing

You can get a no-frills printout by using the automatic setup in Excel. In the automatic setup, Excel gives you standard letter-size pages printed vertically. Excel begins printing at the top left side of the worksheet and continues page by page down the sheet until no more cells are active. Excel then moves one page to the right and begins at the top again, continuing until no more cells are active in the worksheet.

You can change the automatic setup and add special effects to the printout if you want; such changes are discussed throughout this chapter. To begin printing without making changes, choose the Print command from the File

447

menu and then click on the OK button in the File Print dialog box. If you chose the correct printer with the Chooser, Excel begins printing your file.

The *Chooser* is an Apple-menu desk accessory that enables you to select from various printers and output devices. When you installed the Macintosh System file, you were instructed to copy the printer devices to the System folder. This step made the printer drivers available for Apple-brand printers. You can buy other printer drivers for your system from various manufacturers.

Using the Page Setup and Print Options

Excel provides several options for controlling printouts. Like many Macintosh applications, these options appear in the File Page Setup and File Print dialog boxes. When you select the Page Setup command from the File menu, the dialog box in figure 9.1 appears. This figure shows a typical LaserWriter dialog box. Your printer may produce a different set of options.

You can add effects to the printout by using the options in the dialog box. Note that some printers (non-Apple printers) will provide slightly different options.

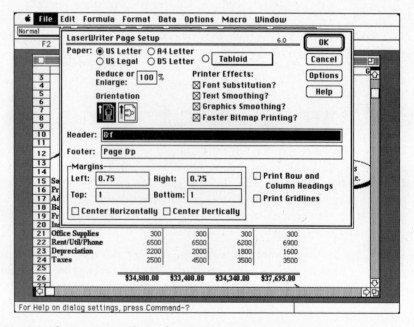

Fig. 9.1. *The Page Setup dialog box for laser printers.*

Page Setup Options

Note that printer options vary, depending on the version of the Macintosh System you are using. Descriptions of the Page Setup options follow:

- *Paper:* Enables you to select the size you want by clicking on the appropriate button. For laser and dot-matrix printers, several paper sizes are available for printing. Your choices include US Letter, US Legal, A4 Letter, B5 Letter, and Tabloid. Selecting a button "unselects" the others.

- *Printer Effects:* Enables you to choose several printer options in the LaserWriter Page Setup dialog box that alter the printout:

Font Substitution?	Provides laser fonts when nonlaser fonts are used in a document.
Text Smoothing?	Takes some of the jagged edges off curved lines in large fonts.
Graphics Smoothing?	Takes the jagged edges off curved lines in graphics.
Faster Bitmap Printing?	Speeds the printing of bit-mapped graphics.

All of these special options usually are left on, which is their default setting. Choose as many of these as you like.

- *Special Effects:* Enables you to choose from several printer options. Click on the options you want to select them. Dot-matrix printers may offer the following options:

50% Reduction	Reduces the image to 50 percent of its normal size.
Tall Adjusted	Makes the dot-matrix printout match the proportions of the screen.
No Gaps between Pages	Prints continuously on tractor-feed paper (useful for printing large worksheets sideways).

- *Orientation:* Enables you to print pages horizontally or vertically. Because the paper feeds through the printer in only one direction, producing horizontal pages is up to the Macintosh. This feature is useful for printing worksheets sideways across many sheets of paper. Click on the orientation you want to highlight it.

- *Reduce or Enlarge:* Enables you to control the size of the final printout. This option is available for laser printers and some other printers. Normally, the size is 100 percent of the original size. To change the size, enter a percentage into this box. To enlarge the printout, enter a figure larger than 100 percent. Experiment for best results.

- *Header:* Adds a header to the top of each page in the printout. You can include any text, as well as special commands, to control the appearance of the header. (See "Working with Report Headers and Footers," later in this chapter, for more details.)

- *Footer:* Adds a footer to the bottom of each page.

- *Margins:* Controls the top, bottom, left, and right margins of the printout. Excel causes information to break to the next page if it does not fit within the specified margins. The Center Horizontally option ignores the Left and Right margin settings and centers the information on the page. Likewise, the Center Vertically option ignores the Top and Bottom margin settings to center the information vertically.

- *Print Row & Column Headings:* Prints your specified row and column headings with the data. The option is useful when you print a worksheet with formula text showing.

- *Print Gridlines:* Prints the cell gridlines on the page with the data. This option can be useful for debugging worksheets.

Besides the options in the initial Page Setup dialog box, Excel offers another set of print options for LaserWriter printouts. If you click on the Options button, another dialog box appears (see fig. 9.2).

The following section describes the options available in this dialog box.

Additional Page Setup Options

The choices in the Page Setup Options dialog box follow:

- *Flip Horizontal:* Creates a mirror image of the print area. When used with text, the option makes the text unreadable. This option can be useful when you are printing graphics or printing onto film to create a reversed image.

- *Flip Vertical:* Creates a vertical mirror image of the print area. In other words, the printout appears to be upside down.

- *Invert Image:* Changes everything that is white to black and every-thing that is black to white. Invert Image can be useful when you are printing to film to create negatives.

- *Precision Bitmap Alignment (4% Reduction):* Makes bit-mapped graphics appear to be more true to scale, producing a four percent reduction.

- *Larger Print Area (Fewer Downloadable Fonts):* Expands the print area available for the page by reducing the margins to a minimum. Because this option uses part of the LaserWriter's memory, you cannot download as many fonts when you select this option.

- *Unlimited Downloadable Fonts in a Document:* Frees memory from the printer by reducing the printable area of the page. As a result, you can get more downloaded fonts in each document. (Most users prefer the larger image area.)

After the special LaserWriter options are set, click on the OK button to return to the Page Setup options. When the Page Setup options are established, click on OK to continue with the printout.

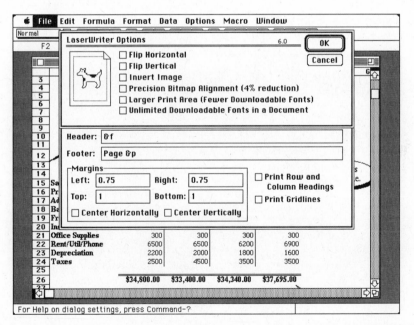

Fig. 9.2. *The LaserWriter Options dialog box, accessed through the LaserWriter Page Setup dialog box.*

Print Options

After clicking on OK in the Page Setup dialog box, you can establish the print options by selecting the Print command from the File menu. The File Print dialog box in figure 9.3 appears, depending on which type of printer you have.

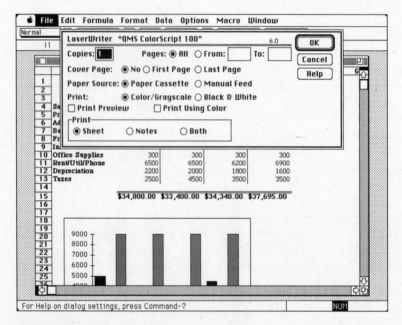

***Fig. 9.3.** The File Print dialog box for laser printers.*

The options available in the File Print dialog box follow:

- *Print Quality:* Enables you to select any of three print qualities (this is a dot-matrix option and does not appear if you are using a laser printer):

Best	Causes the print head to strike the paper twice on each pass across the page.
Faster	Prints in full graphics mode but causes the print head to strike the page only once.
Draft	Prints the data by using the printer's built-in font.

- *Pages:* Enables you to select the page or pages you want to print. You can specify the range or indicate that you want to print all pages.

- *Copies:* Enables you to print multiple copies of each page. Enter the number of copies that you want into the space provided.

- *Cover Page:* Enables you to use the first or last page as a cover sheet for the printout (this is a LaserWriter option). The cover sheet does not contain a header or footer and is not numbered.

- *Paper Source:* Enables you to use tractor-feed paper (Automatic) or individual sheets (Hand Feed) with your ImageWriter. LaserWriters enable you to select the Paper Cassette (Automatic Feed) or the Manual Feed option, which causes the printer to wait for you to insert a page.

- *Page Preview:* Causes the printout to appear on-screen, enabling you to examine the printout before printing. This is identical to choosing the Preview command from the Print menu.

- *Print Using Color:* Prints the worksheet with all colors you established for color output devices.

- *Print:* Enables you to choose from one of three things to print:

Sheet	Prints the worksheet
Notes	Prints the notes attached to the worksheet cells
Both	Prints the worksheet and the notes

When you finally print the worksheet, Excel adheres to the specified page-setup and printer options. If you are not satisfied with the printout at this point, you can use many other features to enhance the final printout.

Previewing the Printout

Excel offers a print-preview feature that enables you to view each page before printing it. To preview the printout, select the Print Preview command from the File menu. You see the first page of the worksheet (in reduced form) on-screen, as shown in figure 9.4.

> **Tip: Another Way To Preview**
> You also can preview worksheets by checking the Print Preview option in the File Print dialog box before printing. This is handy for viewing changes you make in the Print dialog box.

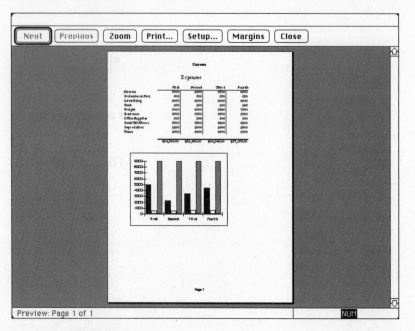

Fig. 9.4. The print-preview feature.

The following buttons appear at the top of the preview screen:

Button	Effect
Next	Moves to the next page of a file with multiple pages.
Previous	Moves to the previous page of a file with multiple pages.
Close	Returns you to the worksheet.
Print	Tells Excel to print directly from the preview screen. This brings up the Print dialog box.

Button	Effect
Zoom	Enlarges the preview to actual size so that you can examine the printout more closely. When viewing the larger preview, click on Zoom to return to the small view.
	Instead of using the Zoom button, you can click on the area of the preview that you want to view more closely. (The pointer changes to a magnifying glass when you do this.) Click on the larger preview page to return to the smaller size.
Margins	Adjusts the page margins and column widths directly from the preview screen. After you press the Margins button, Excel displays the margins and column widths as shown in figure 9.5.

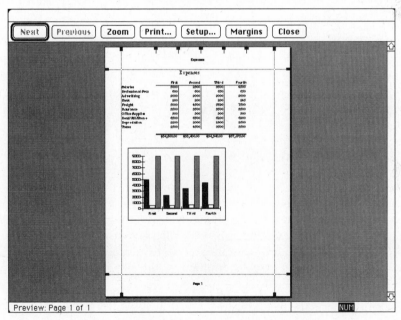

Fig. 9.5. *The current margin settings from the preview screen.*

To adjust the margins or column widths, drag on the margin indicator lines. Excel converts your visual margin settings to actual margin values. Note that you can zoom the preview with the margin lines showing to give you a better view of the margin indicator lines and the data within them.

As indicated in the figure, the lines between the left and right margins indicate the widths of each column in the printout. By adjusting these lines, you change the worksheet's column widths. This procedure is useful for adjusting columns returning to the worksheet.

Printing Sideways

If you have wide worksheets, you may need to print them without breaks between pages so that you get one extra-wide printout of the worksheet.

With Excel you easily can print worksheets sideways on dot matrix printers. To do so, click on the horizontal orientation icon in the Page Setup dialog box. Then check the No Gaps between Pages box (for dot-matrix printers) to eliminate the margin between pages. If you are using a laser printer, you can select the additional Options button and the Larger Print Area option to help reduce the margins, although you will not completely eliminate them. Because laser printers use individual sheets of paper, you cannot print continuously.

Instead of printing the entire worksheet, you may want to print a specific area. See "Printing Specific Areas," later in this chapter.

Inserting and Deleting Page Breaks

When you print the entire worksheet, Excel may have to break the data onto several pages—a procedure known as *breaking the pages*. Normally, Excel begins your printout at the top and left margin settings that you specified. (If you include a report title, the printout will begin just below the title line. See "Printing Report Titles," later in this chapter, for details.) The right side and bottom of the page are determined by the size of the worksheet or range you are printing.

If the worksheet is small enough to fit onto one page, it will simply fall short of the established right and bottom margins. If the worksheet is too wide for one page, however, Excel breaks the page at the nearest column that fits entirely within the right margin. Excel never splits a column between two pages. If your columns are wide, this may result in plenty of empty space on the right edge of the page. Of course, you can adjust column widths and the right margin setting to accommodate more data per page. Similarly, if your printout is too long for one page, Excel splits it at the nearest row that fits within the bottom margin. These are Excel's automatic page breaks.

If the automatic page breaks are not adequate for your worksheet, try setting your own custom page breaks, which give you control of the information on each printed page. Of course, the page you specify should fit into the prescribed page size and setup.

Setting Page Breaks

You can set page breaks in three ways:

- You can establish the rightmost side of each page and let Excel break the pages at the bottom. To do this, keep the pointer in row 1 and move to the first column you want to appear on page 2; then select the Set Page Break command from the Options menu. The page break will occur to the left of the column in which the cursor is located, indicating the end of the preceding page. Unless you specify other columns for the beginning of page 3 and the following pages, Excel automatically breaks the pages.

  Suppose that Excel splits your printout at column J and you wanted to break the page at column H. Move to cell I1 and insert a page break with the Set Page Break command from the Options menu. The result looks like figure 9.6. Any printout that crosses this column splits onto a new page at this point. Excel then measures the next page break starting at this point—or, you can insert another manual break further in the worksheet. Excel determines the right edge of the pages in columns to the right of H. You can, however, also establish breaks for those pages.

  Notice that Excel marks the page break with a thick dotted line, indicating a manual page-break setting.

- You can set the bottom of a page by moving the pointer to the row with which you want to begin the new page. (Be sure to remain in column A.) Then select the Set Page Break command from the Options menu. The page break affects all pages above the selected row. Unless you enter another row break lower on the worksheet, Excel will control the breaks of pages below the inserted break (assuming that you print that much of the sheet).

- You can set both the bottom and right side of a page by selecting the cell below and to the right of the bottom right corner of the page, and then selecting the Set Page Break command from the

Options menu. The cell you select establishes bottom and right-edge breaks for the page. If you use cell G47, for example, the right margin appears at column F, and the bottom is at row 46. This procedure is the same as setting a column break and a row break separately, but it requires only one step (see fig. 9.7).

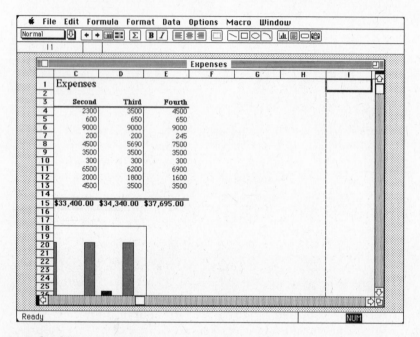

Fig. 9.6. *Adding page breaks.*

Removing Page Breaks

Page breaks remain active until you remove them. Establishing new page breaks does not alter existing breaks. To remove a page break, reselect the column, row, or cell that was used to create the break and select the Remove Page Break command from the Options menu. This command appears only when the pointer is in the correct cell, row, or column.

Remember that manual page breaks show up as darker dotted lines than automatic page breaks. Trying to remove an automatic page break is useless. Instead, try to position manual breaks to make the automatic breaks unnecessary. Also, try turning off the worksheet grid lines to view the page breaks more easily. This procedure helps you distinguish between manual and automatic breaks.

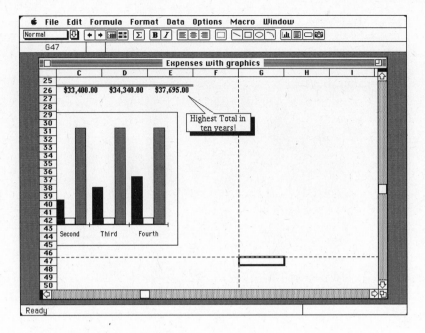

Fig. 9.7. Setting right-side and bottom page breaks.

Printing Specific Areas

You may need to print specific sections of a worksheet, such as a range of cells or a graph. The easiest way is to define the area as the print range, and then print it by itself. Highlight the range you want to print and select the Set Print Area option from the Options menu.

When you select the Print command from the File menu, Excel prints only the established print area. If the area is too large to fit on one page, Excel breaks it into multiple pages. If the print area is larger than one page, you can use manual page breaks to control how it splits between pages.

As another option, try reducing the printout by using the Reduce or Enlarge option in the File Print dialog box. Often, reducing the print range slightly can make everything fit onto a single page. Use the Print Preview feature to test your reduction setting before printing.

If you highlight multiple ranges as the print area, Excel prints each range on a separate page. To highlight multiple ranges, press the Command key when you select the second and subsequent ranges. When all the ranges are highlighted, choose the Set Print Area command from the Options menu. Figure 9.8 shows a worksheet with two print areas established.

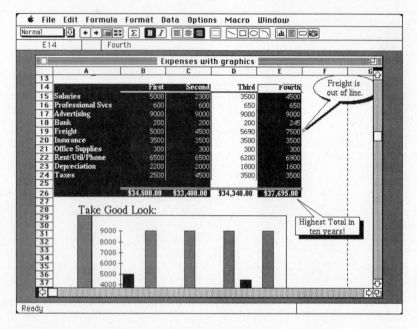

***Fig. 9.8.** Selecting multiple print areas.*

The print areas will print in the order in which you selected them. Remember that print areas remain set until you remove them or establish new print areas. You can reprint the same area over and over without reselecting it as long as you have not removed or changed the area.

Using the Goto Command To Select Print Areas

You may find that you switch among a few frequently used print areas, which may require you to set and reset the same areas over and over. To save time, try defining a range name for each area by choosing the Define Name command from the Formula menu. (You can use names such as Report_1 and Report_2.) To print one of the areas, select the Goto command from the Formula menu and select the print area from the list provided. Then select the Set Print Area command from the Options menu and print.

Using a Macro To Select Print Areas

Perhaps the easiest way to switch among multiple print areas is to use a macro to select and print the range you want. You can, for example, create a custom menu that presents a list of named ranges on the worksheet and then prints the range you select. The macro can include the Goto command to select the range, the Set Print Area command to make the range the current print area, and the Print command to print the area. All these steps would take place automatically. See Chapters 18 and 19 for details on creating macros.

Erasing the Print Area

To remove the established print area, first choose Define Name command from the Formula menu to view all established names. If a print area is set, you will see the name `Print_Area` in the name list. Excel automatically applies this name to the selected print area. Select this name and click on the Delete button; Excel removes the print area setting. You now can establish manual page breaks or set a new print area.

Working with Margins

The left and right margins of your printouts are measured from the edges of the paper. The paper size and margins settings are specified in the File Page Setup dialog box, as described in "Page Setup Options," earlier in this chapter.

The easiest way to adjust the margins is to select the Page Preview command from the File menu to view the printout on-screen. Then, press the Margins buttons and adjust the margins on the preview screen. This shows you the effects of your margin settings as you change them.

Note that the top and bottom margin settings have no effect on the vertical placement of the header and footer. The header and footer are measured from the top and bottom edges of the page. The top margin affects the placement of the automatic report titles, because they appear directly under the top margin.

Working with Report Headers and Footers

Excel includes options for adding headers and footers to your printouts. A *header* is a line of text repeated at the top of each page (except the title page). A *footer* is a line of text repeated at the bottom of each page. Headers and footers can contain any text you want, as well as commands for automatically entering the date, time, and page number. Other commands placed inside the header or footer control the placement and style of text in the header or footer.

Excel automatically prints the header one-half inch from the top of the page. If you define a header, make sure that your top margin is greater than one-half inch so that it does not interfere with the header. Likewise, Excel prints the footer one-half inch from the bottom of the page, and your bottom margin should accommodate this.

To define a header or footer, select the Page Setup command from the File menu, enter the header text and any special codes into the Header space, and then enter the footer text and any special codes into the Footer space. Table 9.1 explains the special codes.

Table 9.1
Special Printer Codes

Code	Effect
Alignment	
&L	Aligns with the left margin the characters that follow
&R	Aligns with the right margin the characters that follow
&C	Centers the characters that follow
Inserting Values	
&P	Prints the page number at the location of this command
&D	Prints the current date in the format 2/24/91 at the location of this command
&T	Prints the current time in the format 1:30:00 PM at the location of this command

Code	Effect
&F	Prints the current file name at the location of this command
Character Attributes	
&B	Prints in boldface the information that follows
&I	Prints in italics the information that follows
&U	Prints in underscore the information that follows
&O	Prints in outline the information that follows
&S	Prints in strikeout the information that follows
&H	Prints in shadow the information that follows
Fonts and Sizes	
&fontname	Prints in the specified font the information that follows
&size	Prints in the specified font size the information that follows
&&	Prints the & character

Aligning Headers and Footers

The commands &L, &R, and &C align information in the header and footer. You can use these codes individually—to align the entire header or footer—or together, to break the header or footer text into sections. Following are some examples:

Header Entry: &RSales Report
Result:

Sales Report

Header Entry: &LSales Report&RJohn Smith
Result:

Sales Report   John Smith

Header Entry: &LSales Report&CJanuary&RJohn Smith
Result:

Sales Report   January   John Smith

Header Entry: &CSales Report&RJohn Smith
Result:

                          Sales Report   John Smith

By using more than one alignment code, you can break the header or footer into three areas. Just be sure that the text in any area does not overlap into other areas. Also, enter the text for each area in order from left to right, as shown in the examples.

Adding Page Numbers and Date/Time Stamps

Excel offers codes for entering the current date, time, and file name into the header or footer. Another code prints page numbers on each page. Enter these commands at the place in the header or footer where you want the information to appear; align the commands with the alignment codes.

You cannot change the format of the date and time entries, and you cannot change the type of numbering system used for page numbering. You can, however, begin numbering the pages at any number you choose. To start numbering at page 15, for example, enter the page-numbering code like this:

&P+15

To start numbering at a page number that is less than the natural page number, use the minus sign (which is the hyphen on your keyboard):

&P-15

This procedure can be useful when you are printing some pages from the middle of a worksheet as a separate report.

Printing Report Titles

At times, you need to print column headings at the top of each page in a report. These headings should match with the columns printed in the report. The headings may be the first row of a table that provides the titles for the numbers below. You may be tempted to use the header as a way of printing column headings on each page, but Excel offers a better way. Highlight the rows in the worksheet that contain the title information (often, the top few rows). Be sure to highlight the entire row by clicking in the row heading area. Next, select the Set Print Titles command from the Options menu to establish the selected rows as the titles.

Excel uses an *intelligent titling system*, printing only the column headings (titles) that correspond to the columns selected for the report. See the column titles shown in figure 9.9.

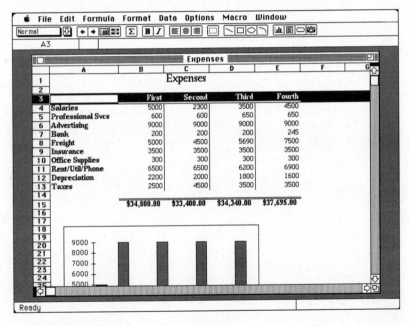

***Fig. 9.9.** Column titles.*

If you print any of the columns A through C, the titles in cells A3 through C3 are used for each page of the table in columns A through C. If you then print from columns D through E, the titles in cells D3 through E3 print. The titles therefore apply only when information from the respective columns is printed.

To remove the print titles you have established, choose the Define Name command from the Formula menu and delete the name Print_Titles from the list of names. Then press Return. The interesting thing is that the headings don't actually have to appear above the data. They can appear in any row of the worksheet. This enables you to use information different from the actual column headings above the columns. You may enter a second set of headings, for example, *below* the data (in the same columns) and use these for the report titles.

> **Tip: Using Report Titles**
> When using report titles, be sure that you don't include the titles in the print range; otherwise, they will print twice on the first page.

When printed, the titles appear below the header and top margin, taking up part of the space allotted for the printout.

Summary

When it comes to printing your worksheets, Excel offers several options for setting up the printout—as well as the standard printer options that reflect the particular printer you are using. The Print Setup and Print commands from the File menu provide most of the options. The following are points to remember:

- Use the Page Setup options from the File menu to control the printout before printing.

- Print Setup options are different for different printers. The ImageWriter, for example, produces different options than the LaserWriter.

- You can add a header and footer to your printouts by using the Print Setup options.

- Entering &P in the header or footer prints the page number on each page.

- You can print the worksheet sideways, without gaps between the pages, by changing the print orientation and by selecting the No Gaps between Pages option from the Print Setup dialog box.

- To print a specific area of the worksheet, highlight the area and select the Set Print Area command from the Options menu.

Chapter 10, "Charting and Drawing: A Quick Start," offers a brief lesson in building a chart.

Part II

Excel Charts

10

Charting and Drawing: A Quick Start

This second quick start is designed to get you up and running with Excel's charting and drawing features. If you have not completed and saved the worksheet from Chapter 2, do so before starting this chapter. The step-by-step guide provided in this chapter builds on that worksheet. Using the worksheet, you will select the data range and create a new chart representing the data. Next, you will customize the chart by changing its typeface and adding titles and other elements. Finally, you will draw simple object-oriented graphics to enhance the chart. By the end of this chapter, you will be ready for more details about Excel's charting and drawing options.

Opening the Worksheet

To open the worksheet that you saved from Chapter 2, click on the worksheet icon (which should be named EXPENSES) from the Macintosh desktop view. If you are already in Excel, choose the Open command from the File menu and select the EXPENSES file from the list provided. The worksheet appears on-screen, as shown in figure 10.1.

471

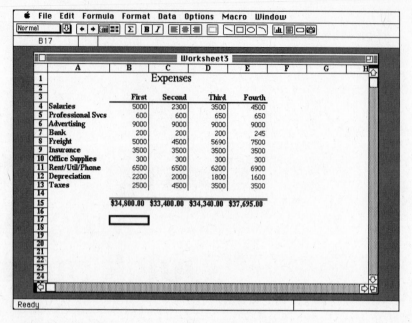

Fig. 10.1. *The worksheet created in Chapter 2.*

Creating the Chart

The goal is to create a chart that best displays the change in total expenses from quarter to quarter. In other words, you want to compare expenses for each of the four quarters.

Selecting Data

The chart will represent all expense items and make it easy to compare changes over the four quarters. The first step is to select the data that will be represented in the chart—the entire data range from cell A3 to cell E13. Click on cell A3 and drag the pointer to cell E13 to select the entire block of data (without the heading or totals).

The worksheet looks like figure 10.2 when all the information is selected.

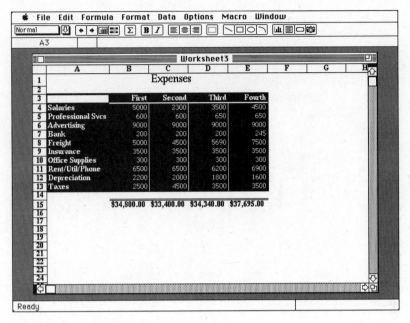

Fig. 10.2. Selected information in the chart.

Drawing the Chart

After you select the chart data (or data range), the next step is to create the chart by drawing it onto the worksheet. To do so, complete the following steps:

1. Click on the Chart tool in the Toolbar. (This tool is fourth from the right in the Toolbar.)

2. Click on the worksheet just below the data and drag the mouse to the right and down to create a box. When you release the button, the box contains a chart. Figure 10.3 shows what this chart looks like.

The basic chart displays the selected data in columns. Unless you specify otherwise, the column chart is the default (or preferred) format for all new charts. You can change this format to meet your needs; Excel provides many commands for this purpose. See the chapters on charting in this book.

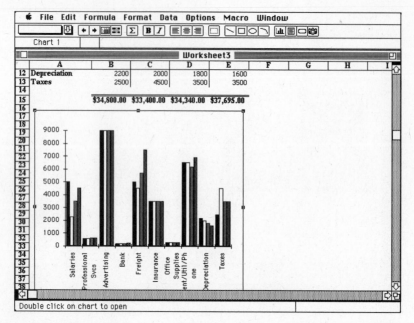

Fig. 10.3. The basic chart.

Moving the Chart

The first thing you may want to do is move the chart. You can position the chart anywhere in the worksheet—even on top of data. To move the chart, follow these steps:

1. Click the mouse inside the chart area and drag. The chart moves as you drag the mouse.

2. Release the mouse button to place the chart.

Shrinking and Enlarging the Chart

You can change the size and shape of a chart after you draw it. This capability enables you to fit the chart into existing worksheet data. At any time, you can modify the chart's size and shape by using these steps:

1. Click once on the chart area to select the chart. The chart is selected when small boxes appear around the edges of the chart area.
Figure 10.4 shows what this looks like.

2. Click and drag the mouse on one of the selection boxes around the
chart—preferably the box in the bottom right corner. As you drag
the mouse, the size and shape of the chart changes.

3. Release the mouse button when your chart reaches the size and
shape that you want (see fig. 10.5).

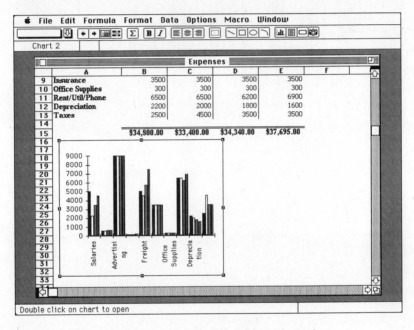

Fig. 10.4. A selected chart has selection boxes around its edges.

Editing the Chart

Excel provides dozens of charting commands and options for modifying
your charts. To view these commands, double-click on the chart in the
worksheet. This activates the chart window (see fig. 10.6).

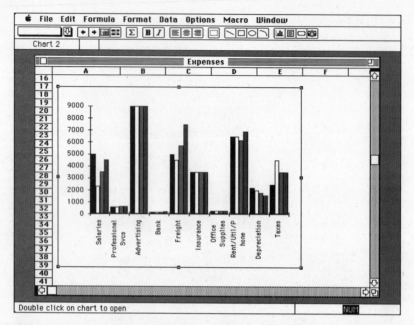

Fig. 10.5. *Change a chart's size and shape by dragging the selection boxes.*

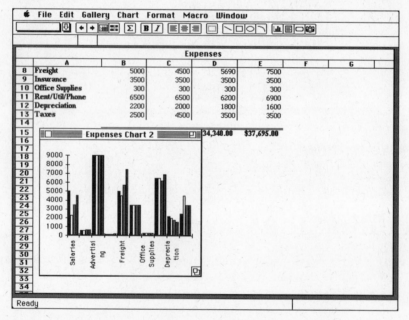

Fig. 10.6. *Activating the chart window and charting commands.*

The chart now appears in a window that has all the typical window features, such as a title bar, zoom box, and scroll bars. You can change the size and shape of this window without affecting the original size and shape of the chart.

Changing the Chart's Orientation

Currently the chart displays the expense items as categories along the horizontal axis (or category axis). The four bars in these categories represent the four quarters. When the data is presented in this way, you easily can compare the quarterly changes, but you cannot get a clear picture of how the expense items compare with one another. The idea for the chart is to compare expense items and totals quarter by quarter; this chart, however, compares the quarters item by item.

In this case, you can flip the orientation of the data so that the categories become quarters and the bars become items. Because Excel determines the orientation of all new charts, you must make any changes to the orientation after you create the basic chart. Follow these steps to change the orientation:

1. Choose the Select Chart command from the Chart menu. Then select the Clear command from the Edit menu. Select All to clear the entire chart. (Remember to activate the Chart menus by double-clicking on the chart.)

2. Select the EXPENSES window from the Windows menu to activate the original worksheet. The chart's data range still should be selected.

3. Press ⌘-C to copy the chart data.

4. Activate the chart window using the Window menu.

5. Select the Paste Special command from the Edit menu. Excel presents the dialog box shown in figure 10.7.

6. Select the Rows option; then press Return. Excel flips the orientation and pastes the chart range back into the chart window. The result is shown in figure 10.8.

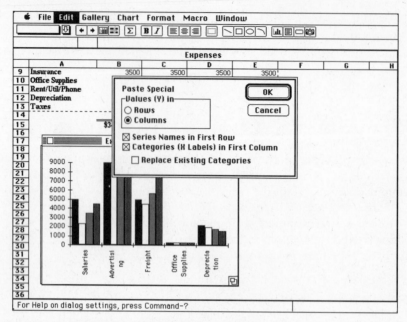

Fig. 10.7. *The Edit Paste Special dialog box for charts.*

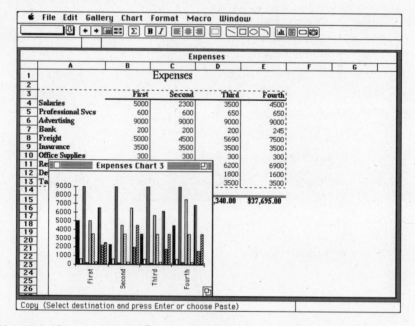

Fig. 10.8. *The new chart with the proper orientation of data.*

Now the chart displays the quarters as categories and the expense items as bars (or data points). This revision makes it easier for you to compare quarters and prepares the chart for the next step.

Changing the Chart Type

Excel can produce many kinds of charts—including bar, column, line, scatter, pie, and area—and several variations of each kind. If none of the variations meet your needs, you can customize the chart that comes closest.

Follow these steps to change the column chart to a stacked-column chart:

1. Activate the chart menus by double-clicking on the chart in the worksheet.

2. Select the Column option from the Gallery menu.

3. Select chart 3 by clicking on the third chart option presented. Then click on the OK button. The chart now looks like the one in figure 10.9.

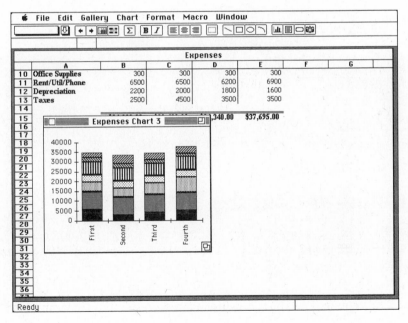

Fig. 10.9. *Changing the chart to a stacked column format.*

Now you easily can compare expenses for each quarter by comparing the heights of the bars, and you can determine the proportion that each expense item represents within each bar. You can close the chart window at this point if you want to see how this modification looks on the worksheet.

Adding and Formatting a Legend

Because this chart has so much data, supplying a legend would be helpful. Excel already knows the titles for the various data series (the titles are part of the data range), so all you have to do is activate the legend. Follow these steps to add a legend:

1. Activate the charting menus by double-clicking on the chart.

2. Select the Add Legend command from the Chart menu.

   The legend appears along the right side of the chart. The chart adjusts to fit the legend in the window. You can move the legend by dragging it to another location in the chart window, but leave the legend on the right side for now.

   The next goal is to format the legend. Excel offers several formatting options; try these steps. Be sure that the chart window still is open and that the charting menus are active.

3. Double-click on the legend box. This action brings up the Patterns dialog box, which controls the interior and border patterns for the legend box.

4. Select the None option under the border section and press Return. The legend no longer has a border (see fig. 10.10).

Adding and Editing a Chart Title

When you create a chart title, Excel centers it above the chart. After creating a title, you can select its font, size, style, and color. You can modify the title at any time. To create and modify a title, follow these steps:

1. Select the Attach Text command from the Chart menu. Excel presents a dialog box showing the various chart elements to which you can attach text.

2. Confirm that Chart Title is selected; then press Return. A title placeholder appears in position above the chart (see fig. 10.11).

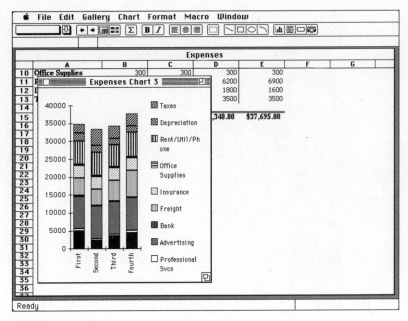

Fig. 10.10. Removing the legend border.

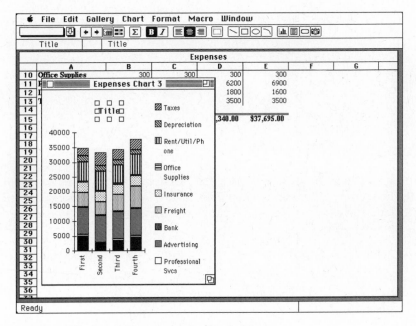

Fig. 10.11. The chart, showing a title placeholder.

3. Type *Expenses* as the title; then press Return. The word *Title* is now replaced by *Expenses*.

4. Select the Font command from the Format menu to choose a font, size, and style for the title. You may want to use a large typeface, such as 18-point Times. To add an underline, press ⌘-Shift-U.

   When the title is selected, a formula bar appears at the top of the screen. You can edit the information in this formula bar to change the title text. Press ⌘-U and use the editing keys to modify the text. See Chapter 4 for details on these keys. In the next steps, you link the chart title to the worksheet.

5. When the chart title is selected, place the cursor in the formula bar by using the mouse or the F2 key.

6. Select the entire title by double-clicking on the word. Next, type an equal sign to replace the existing text with the beginning of a new formula.

   If your title has more than one word, be sure to highlight the entire title before pressing the equal sign.

7. Activate the EXPENSES worksheet from the Window menu.

8. Click on cell C1 and press Return.

Excel activates the chart and completes the linking formula. The chart title now is linked to cell C1 of the EXPENSES worksheet. Whenever this cell changes, the chart title changes. Experiment with entering various titles in this cell.

Adding Other Descriptive Text

You also can add text or labels to the chart as descriptive text. This text is not attached to any particular element of the chart, so you can move it around the chart window. With the chart window active, try the following procedure to add descriptive text to your chart:

1. Type *Exceeds Last Year* and press Return. The text appears in a box on the chart.

2. Click on this text box and drag it into position, as shown in figure 10.12.

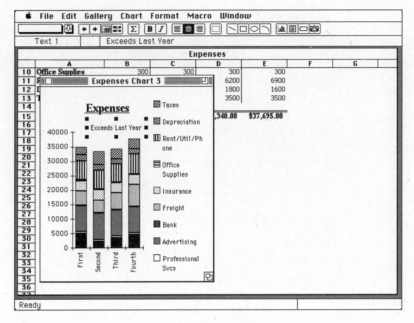

Fig. 10.12. *Moving the descriptive text into position.*

When selected, the descriptive text has black squares around its edges; the chart title and many other elements have white squares around their borders. The black borders indicate that the text is not attached to any element and can be moved around the chart freely. White squares indicate a fixed element.

Adding and Deleting Data Points

After you select a data range and create a new chart, you still can add or remove data. Suppose that you want to add information to the sample chart. Follow these steps:

1. Change the chart back into a standard column chart by selecting the Column command from the Gallery menu and choosing Chart Type 1. You don't need to do this step to remove data points, but for this example, following this step is helpful.

2. Close the chart window to return to the worksheet menus.

3. Select the range A9:E9, which contains the data for the Insurance item.

4. Press ⌘-C to copy this data.

5. Activate the chart window by double-clicking on the chart.

6. Press ⌘-V to paste the data into this chart. Excel creates a new bar for this item and places it at the end of the current data (see fig. 10.13).

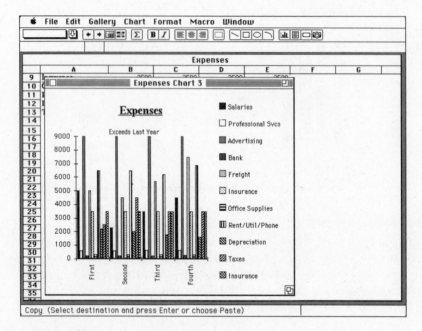

Fig. 10.13. *Adding a data series to the chart.*

Excel adds the new data series after the existing ones, so that the new item appears last in the legend. Although you cannot use this feature to control the placement of the added data, you can use the feature to rearrange the columns. Cutting and pasting is not the best way to rearrange columns, however; a better way is described in "Rearranging the Columns," later in this chapter.

To remove a data series from the chart, follow these steps:

1. Click on one of the bars representing the Insurance data series. The information appears in the formula bar. (Excel uses this information to create the corresponding data points.)

2. Press the Backspace key. The information in the formula bar disappears.

3. Press Return. The chart now reflects fewer expense items.

The proportions of the remaining chart elements change to fill the available space. Likewise, the legend changes, and the patterns adjust to the new set of bars.

Rearranging the Columns

The next step is to change the sequence of the columns in the chart. Suppose that you want to show the Rent/Util/Phone data in front of the other data. Complete these steps:

1. Click on one of the Rent/Util/Phone columns to select the item.

2. Examine the formula displayed in the formula bar. Excel uses this formula to create the selected column. The last number in the formula indicates its position in the series. In this case, the formula indicates that Rent/Util/Phone is in position 2.

3. Change the 2 to a 1 to move the item to the first position. Be careful not to change any other elements in this formula. Then press Return.

After changing the formula, Excel rearranges the columns in the chart. Because Excel renumbers the remaining items, begin with the first item if you plan to make several changes. This way, subsequent changes will not affect your progress.

Drawing Graphic Objects

A chart is a graphic object that appears above the worksheet data. This positioning is why you can move the chart on top of the worksheet data, as well as move and size the chart box. You also can draw other objects onto the worksheet. Excel includes several object tools for this purpose. Generally, these tools are useful for annotating your data and charts. Using drawing tools located in the Toolbar, you can draw lines, boxes, ovals, arcs (semicircles), and text boxes. All of these objects are drawn in the same basic way:

1. Make sure that you closed the chart window to return to the worksheet menus.

2. Click on the rectangle tool in the Toolbar (the seventh tool from the right edge).

3. Click and drag on the worksheet to create a box about the same size as the chart. When you release the mouse, the box appears on the worksheet.

4. Click on the rectangle and drag it on top of the chart, but slightly offset. Figure 10.14 shows what this rectangle looks like.

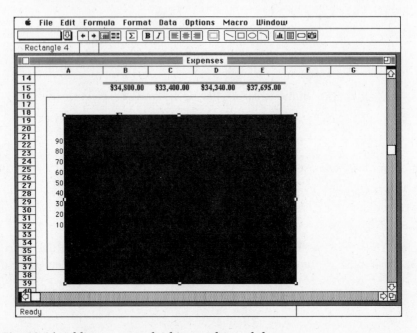

Fig. 10.14. *Adding a rectangle object to the worksheet.*

Objects appear in the order in which you draw them. Objects drawn last overlap those drawn first. You can change this order by following these steps:

1. Click once on the rectangle object to select it.

2. Select the Send to Back command from the Edit menu.

This places the object in back of the chart object, making it appear as a shadow. Figure 10.15 shows the result.

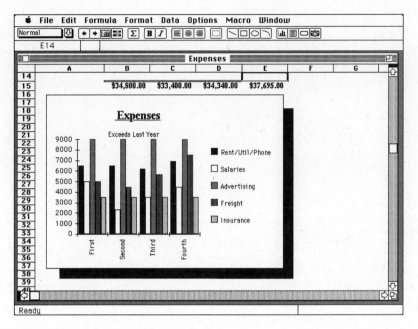

Fig. 10.15. *Changing object overlapping.*

Saving the Chart

When you draw a chart onto the worksheet as in this chapter, Excel saves the chart with the rest of the worksheet whenever you choose the Save command from the File menu. You can save a chart to its own file, however, apart from the worksheet that created it. Excel uses the special Chart icon to identify these files on disk. You then can reopen the chart by clicking on its icon. You also can open a chart by using Excel's Open command from the File menu. Saving a chart in a separate file does not save the worksheet containing the chart. Using this procedure results in two copies of the chart—one on the worksheet and one saved as a file. Try these steps on the sample chart:

1. With the chart window active, select the Save command from the File menu.

2. Type the name *Expense Chart* and press Return.

Charts do not have to be saved in the same folder as the original worksheet; Excel remembers where the original is located. Moving the worksheet may break the link between the chart and the worksheet, and Excel may ask you to reestablish this link. The original worksheet does not have to be open when you open a chart. If you open a chart without the original worksheet, however, Excel asks whether you want to update the chart with the most current worksheet information.

One reason for saving charts separately is when you don't want the chart to appear on the worksheet. Also, saving charts separately reduces the amount of RAM and disk space required for the worksheet.

Summary

This chapter continued with the worksheet you started in the first quick start lesson. You used Excel's charting capabilities to represent the expense data in chart form. You saw how Excel creates a chart with your selected data. You also learned how to customize many aspects of the chart. Customizations include changing the chart type; adding titles, text, and legends; and changing the size and shape of the chart.

From here, you are ready to proceed to the next quick start lesson—Chapter 14, "Using Databases: A Quick Start"—or you can find more details about Excel's charting commands in Chapter 11, "Creating Charts."

11

Creating Charts

I n this chapter you learn how to create and manipulate charts in Excel. Because Excel has extensive charting capabilities, this chapter covers a lot of information. You first learn about the basic elements of a chart. Then you learn about the charting process and the chart menus. The chapter describes how to get started making charts and continues with a discussion of the various kinds of charts you can produce. You also learn how to manipulate the chart window.

Getting an Overview of Charting

The following sections provide some basic information about charting. Figure 11.1 shows a chart with the various elements labeled. Excel offers numerous charting features that can make the charting process appear complicated. Actually, you can create most charts with a minimum of effort; follow the basic procedure for creating charts, and you can start charting data right away.

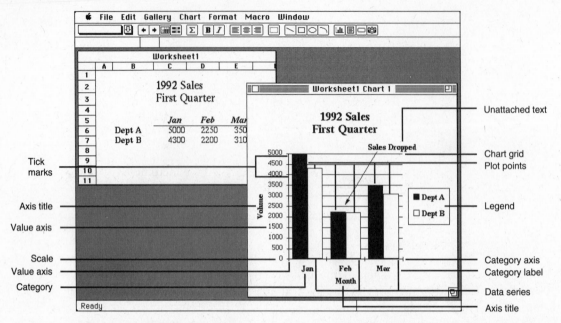

Fig. 11.1. *The elements of a chart.*

Understanding the Parts of a Chart

Figure 11.1 lists the names of a chart's elements. The following paragraphs describe each element in detail. The names of the elements are used throughout this chapter and the rest of the book. These elements follow:

- *Plot points*, or series markers, are the bars of a bar chart, the pie slices of a pie chart, the plot points of a line chart, and so on. Plot points are the essential data elements that make up the chart; they represent the values being charted. Excel assigns colors and patterns to these markers, but you can change them. Figure 11.1 contains six plot points.

- *Data series* are groups of like plot points. When you chart more than one value for a particular item, Excel creates more than one plot point for that item. Each plot point gets the same color and pattern—indicating that it belongs to a certain data series. If you chart the sales of apples over four quarters, for example, you will have four similar bars: one data series consisting of four plot points. Figure 11.1 has two data series—one for department A and one for department B.

- *Categories* consist of different plot points within a single grouping. When you chart more than one value for an item, you get a data series, which is divided into categories. Using an earlier example, if you chart sales of apples over four quarters, you have one data series and four categories; the quarters are the categories. In other words, the number of like plot points within a data series is the number of categories for that series. Figure 11.1 has three categories, labeled First, Second, and Third. Each category contains two plot points.

- A *tick mark* appears on an axis and shows the increments by which a data series increases. You can choose to display or remove tick marks in Excel; you also can change the line thickness of the tick marks.

- Charts contain two types of axes: value (vertical) and category (horizontal). The *value axis* usually shows the scale that measures the various series. The *category axis* displays the various categories. This does not apply to scatter (xy) charts, which have two value axes—one horizontal and one vertical. Also, 3-D charts have a third axis, called the *depth axis*. Each data series is displayed on a different depth of this axis, creating a 3-D effect.

- The *scale* is the numeric measurement of the values on the axes (particularly the value axis). Excel enables you to specify the upper and lower values of the scale.

- The *axis title* describes the scale of the value axis. This label appears vertically along the value axis or horizontally along the category axis. These are `Volume` and `Month` in figure 11.1.

- *Category labels* appear on the category axis and relate to the category groupings. Category labels are not the same as labels appearing in the legend. Normally, worksheet column headings are used as category labels; row headings are used as the legend entries (series marker labels). The category labels in figure 11.1 are Jan, Feb, and Mar.

- The *legend* is the key to the chart. The legend displays the names of the data series and shows their patterns and colors. Normally, the entries in the legend come from the row headings used in the worksheet and Excel creates the legend automatically. For figure 11.1, the legend shows Department A and Department B.

- A *chart grid* is a formatting element that you can add. Grids are useful for showing the height of bars or series relative to the scale. You can control the color, pattern, and thickness of the grid lines.

- The *plot area* is the background for the chart. You can change the color and pattern of this area to give the series more emphasis. The chart grid resides in the plot area.

You can add various chart titles to a chart, including a main heading, horizontal- and vertical-axis titles, and footnotes. Although Excel uses standard default positions, you can position the titles where you want them.

You can add text to a chart and position the text anywhere you want. Text you add is called *unattached text* because you are free to move it around the chart.

Understanding the Charting Process

Version 3.0 of Excel makes charting simple. You can create a chart in two steps and customize the chart in a few more steps. The entire process takes only a few moments. The following is the basic procedure:

1. Select the data you want to chart. You can use the mouse or keyboard to highlight a range consisting of a single row, a single column, or a block. You also can highlight multiple ranges. Details about selecting the data block appear in "Selecting Information for Charting," later in this chapter.

2. Click on the Chart tool in the Toolbar at the top of the screen (the chart tool is fourth from the right end). Now click on the worksheet and drag the mouse to create a box. When you release the mouse, the box contains the chart.

The result is the default column chart (or current *preferred chart*) representing the data you highlighted. You can go beyond these basic steps and customize the chart in some of the following ways:

- Move the chart box to any location on the worksheet.

- Change the size and shape of the chart box.

- Change the type of chart to a line, area, scatter, or other chart type.

- Change the orientation of the charted data. Doing so affects the number of data points within each category.

- Change the fonts used by the chart.

- Add labels to the axes and select the fonts for the labels.

- Move the text labels to any location on the chart.

- Add a legend and change the fonts used in it.

- Change the background color or pattern of the legend.

- Move the legend to another location on the chart.

- Change the vertical-axis scale.

- Change the color and pattern of the plot points.

- Change the background color and pattern of the chart itself.

- Add a main title to the chart and choose its font.

- Change the data being charted.

- Change the viewing angle and perspective of a 3-D chart.

The rest of this chapter discusses these two main steps to creating charts: selecting chart data and creating the chart. Also, you learn how to use the charting menus to make basic changes to the default chart, such as changing its type and saving it. Chapter 12 provides details on all kinds of chart customization options.

Selecting Information for Charting

To create a chart, you first must have data that can be displayed in chart form. Chart data can be any range of cells: a single row or column, or a block of rows and columns. In general, the data range should be *contiguous*; that is, it should contain no blank rows or columns. Blank cells appear to the chart as data points with values of zero.

When you select a data range for charting, you may include headings at the top and left side. These headings will appear on the chart as legend entries and category labels. Figure 11.2 shows an example that includes headings in the top row and left column.

If your chart range contains no headings, or if your chart headings are numeric values, Excel asks whether the first row and/or column should be treated as chart data or chart labels. This query gives you the freedom to choose the data you want to chart, without concern for the headings.

The data you want to chart may not appear in an orderly block; Excel therefore enables you to highlight multiple ranges for charting. As discussed in Chapter 3, you can highlight multiple ranges by pressing the Command key while you select each range with the mouse. Be sure that each range contains the same number of data points and that no blank cells appear within the highlighted ranges. Figure 11.3 shows an example of highlighted multiple ranges.

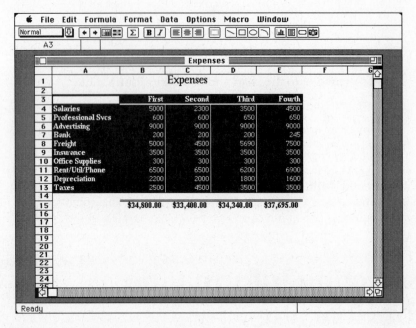

Fig. 11.2. *Selecting a chart range.*

One disadvantage to charting from multiple ranges is that you cannot copy multiple ranges with the Copy command from the Edit menu. This factor eliminates certain procedures that you can perform on the chart, such as changing its orientation.

If you must create a chart from noncontiguous ranges, try using Excel's outlining feature to bring these ranges together as one single block of cells. Then, use the Select Visible Cells tool in the Toolbar after highlighting the block. This procedure enables you to use the Copy command from the Edit menu on the selected cells as if they were a single block. You then can create a chart from this data. Use the following steps for this procedure:

1. Use the Toolbar's Demote button on each row or column that will not be part of the chart (first highlight the row or column, and then click on the Demote button). These rows and columns are between the data you want to chart. (The Demote button is the Right Arrow button in the Toolbar.)

2. After demoting all unwanted rows and columns, select the Row/Column Level buttons that hide the demoted rows and columns. These buttons appear on the left side of the worksheet, near the top of the screen. See Chapter 8 for details. (This will be button level 2 if you have demoted unwanted data only once.) This step condenses the chartable data into a contiguous block.

3. Select the data range for charting. This now should be a single range.

4. Click on the Select Visible Cells button (the fourth button in the Toolbar).

5. Select the Copy command from the Edit menu.

6. Select the New command from the File menu and choose the Chart option from the list provided. When you press Return, a blank chart window appears on-screen.

7. Select the Paste command from the Edit menu. This command enters the chart data into the new chart window and creates a default column chart from the data.

8. You now can customize the chart (see Chapter 12 and the rest of this chapter).

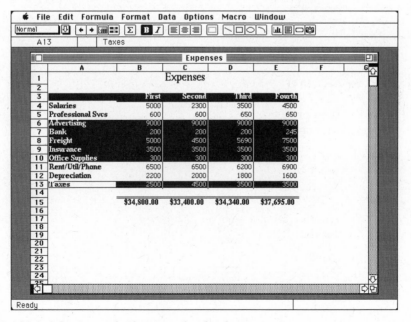

Fig. 11.3. *Selecting multiple ranges for the chart.*

After these steps, the chart is not on the worksheet, but only in the chart window. You can copy the chart onto the worksheet by using the Copy and Paste commands in the Edit menu. See "Saving Charts," later in this chapter, for more information.

Creating a Chart on the Worksheet

After you select the data range, you can create the chart by drawing it onto the worksheet using the Toolbar's Chart tool. Follow these steps:

1. Highlight the chart data as described in the preceding section.

2. Click on the Chart tool in the Toolbar.

3. Click on the worksheet and drag the mouse down and to the right to create a chart box. After you release the mouse button, the box contains the default chart. Figure 11.4 shows a chart drawn onto a worksheet.

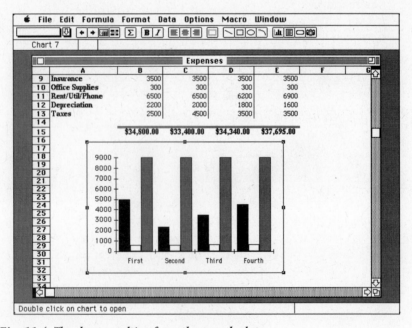

Fig. 11.4. The chart resulting from the sample data.

The category labels come from the rows of the worksheet. Each row creates a data series and each column creates a new category. This orientation is not always the case; sometimes, Excel uses the opposite orientation. Controlling the chart's orientation is explained later in "Changing the Chart's Orientation."

If you press Shift while you draw the chart, Excel makes the chart perfectly square. This is useful for xy (scatter) charts that require a square perspective. Also, if you press the Command key while you draw the chart, Excel makes the chart adhere to the worksheet grid. In other words, it *snaps to* the worksheet grid and fits exactly within a block of cells. This is useful for making the chart align with worksheet information.

You also can draw the chart onto a different worksheet than the one containing the highlighted area. Just activate the worksheet you want after you click on the Chart tool. The chart then is linked (via external references) to the original worksheet so that when both worksheets are open, changes you make in one affect the other.

If you open the worksheet containing the chart without opening the worksheet containing the data, however, changes you may have made in the original worksheet will not have affected the chart—even though the worksheets are linked. To update the chart with the original worksheet, simply open the original or double-click on the chart and then use the Links command from the File menu with the Update option to refresh the links. See Chapter 8 for details about linking worksheets.

Note: If you draw a chart onto an external worksheet, be sure to save this worksheet after you save the original worksheet. This procedure helps keep the links accurate.

Moving the Chart

The first thing you do after drawing the chart is adjust its position on the worksheet. This maneuver is easy to perform. Just click the mouse in the middle of the chart box and drag the box to another location. Excel shows you the position as you drag. When you release the mouse, the chart appears in the indicated position. Be sure to drag from the middle of the chart.

If you press the Command key while you move the chart, Excel makes the upper left corner of the chart snap to the worksheet grid. This feature is useful for aligning the chart with worksheet information.

Changing the Size and Shape of the Chart

Excel enables you to change the chart's size and shape at any time. To resize the chart, click on the middle of the chart and release the mouse to select the chart. When a chart is selected, small boxes appear around its edges. To change the shape of the chart, click on one of the selection boxes on the edge of the chart and drag it to another location. You can use this feature to emphasize certain proportions of the chart, as shown in figure 11.5.

Deleting a Chart

To remove a chart from the worksheet, click on the chart to select it. Next, press the Delete key or choose the Clear command or the Cut command from the Edit menu. Excel removes the chart box.

Note that the Clear and Cut commands from the Edit menu work differently for charts (and other objects) than they do for worksheet data. The Clear command removes the chart without offering the options you would get for clearing worksheet data. The Cut command removes a chart as soon as you use the command—you do not need to use the Paste command at all. On worksheet data, however, the Cut command does not remove information until you paste.

Creating a Chart That Does Not Appear in the Worksheet

You can create a chart in a chart window without ever drawing it onto the worksheet. This procedure can be useful for saving space in your worksheet when the chart is not going to be part of the worksheet presentation. To bypass the worksheet chart, follow these steps for creating the chart:

1. Select the chart data, as described earlier in this chapter.

2. Select the New command from the File menu.

3. Select the Chart option from the list provided. After you press Return, the chart appears in a chart window, but does not appear on the worksheet.

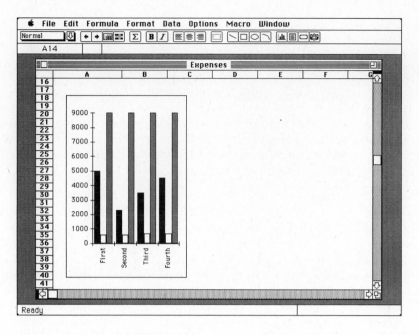

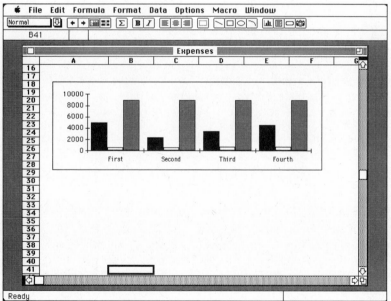

Fig. 11.5. *Creating different effects by resizing the chart box.*

> ***Tip: Using the Shortcut Key to Create Chart Windows***
> You can create a chart by highlighting the data you want to include and then pressing Shift-F2. This step opens a new chart window for you.

If you do not draw the chart onto the worksheet, but use a window instead, you should save the chart window as a separate file by using the Save command from the File menu when the chart window is active. Excel then asks you to name the chart and specify its location.

You can save a chart as a separate file even when it appears on the worksheet by double-clicking on the worksheet chart to get the chart menus. Next, use the Save command from the File menu to save the active chart window. The chart remains on the worksheet, but you also have a copy saved under a separate file, which gives you two independent charts that represent the same data. Saving a chart under a separate file can be useful when you want to transfer an Excel worksheet to another spreadsheet format without including the chart, or when you want to move the chart to another program or computer without the associated worksheet.

Copying a Chart onto the Worksheet

If you create a chart without drawing it onto the worksheet and decide later that you want the chart on the worksheet, you can copy the chart from the chart window into the worksheet. Follow these steps:

1. Activate the chart window.

2. Choose the Select Chart command from the Chart menu.

3. Select the Copy command from the Edit menu.

4. Activate the worksheet window. (This can be an external worksheet.)

5. Select the Paste command from the Edit menu.

Save the worksheet to update it with the new chart in place. You now can modify the chart by double-clicking on the worksheet chart.

You can use this procedure to copy a chart onto an external worksheet (a worksheet other than the one containing the data). Simply activate the worksheet before pasting the chart. Excel links the copied chart to the original worksheet using external references.

Whenever both worksheets are open, changes you make in one affect the other. If you open the external worksheet (the one containing the chart) without the original, however, it will not update to reflect changes you make to the original data. Therefore, you should open the original worksheet to refresh the chart's links.

Alternatively, you can double-click on the chart and then use the Links command from the File menu with the Update option to refresh the chart's links to the original worksheet. See Chapter 8 for details about linking worksheets.

If a chart already appears on the worksheet, you can duplicate it by using the Copy and Paste commands. Simply click on the chart to select it, and then select Copy to copy the chart and Paste to duplicate it onto the worksheet.

You now have two charts that reflect the same data. Do not use this procedure to copy a chart from one worksheet to another because the duplicate will not be linked to the original worksheet. Instead, use the steps listed earlier to copy a chart from one worksheet to another.

> **Tip: Handling Charts as Objects**
> If you have two or more charts on the same worksheet, you may notice that one overlaps the other if you move them close together. This happens because charts behave just like other objects you can create on the worksheet. For details about handling charts and other worksheet objects, refer to Chapter 13.

Opening Chart Files

If you save a chart as a separate file, the chart is stored on the disk in an individual file marked with the Chart icon. You can return to a chart in one of two ways: double-click on the Chart icon from the desktop or open the chart from Excel by using the Open command from the File menu. The worksheet used to create the chart does not have to be open when you open a chart. If the original worksheet is not open, the dialog box shown in figure 11.6 appears when you open the chart.

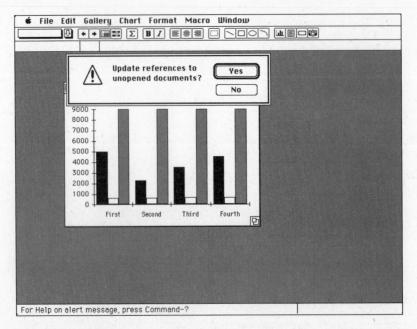

Fig. 11.6. The dialog box that appears when you open a chart without opening the original worksheet.

Excel remembers which charts are linked to which worksheets and offers to update the chart, using the current worksheet data. If you choose Yes, Excel locates the original worksheet on disk and updates the chart accordingly. Excel does not open the worksheet, however. If Excel cannot find the original worksheet (for example, if you have moved, renamed, or deleted it), Excel presents a dialog box so that you can select the file from disk. When you choose the file, Excel updates the chart's link so that Excel can find the worksheet file the next time you open the chart.

If you forget which worksheet is attached to a chart, open the chart and select No from the Update References dialog box. Then select the File Links command. Excel presents the linked file in a dialog box. Select the file's name and choose Open to open the worksheet. If you have moved, renamed, or deleted the worksheet, Excel is unable to find it when you select File Links. Instead, you must find the file manually by using the file-selection dialog box. As soon as you open the worksheet, Excel updates the chart, if necessary.

Note: Charts are not included in workspace files. When you use the Save Workspace command from the File menu to save the window configuration, remember that open chart windows are not included.

Viewing the Chart Menus

Excel provides numerous charting commands and options for customizing the default chart; these are contained in the charting menus. To view the charting menus, double-click on the chart that appears in the worksheet. Excel presents the chart in a window and changes the menus at the top of the screen into the chart menus (see fig. 11.7).

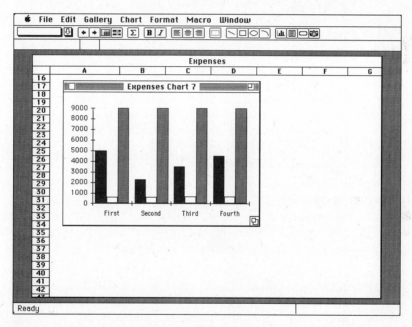

Fig. 11.7. The chart menus and chart window.

Whenever the chart window is active, the chart menus appear on-screen. When you close the window (by clicking on the Close box or using the Close command from the File menu), the menus return to normal.

The chart window is provided for your convenience while customizing the chart. The window is presented with the same size and shape of the chart—and it appears directly over the chart (if possible). You can move and expand the chart window to get a better view of the chart while you are making changes. The size, shape, and position of the chart window have no effect on the chart that appears in the worksheet.

> *Note:* You can use the chart window to save the chart in a separate file. This is explained in "Creating a Chart That Does Not Appear in the Worksheet," earlier in this chapter.

Changing the Chart's Orientation

When the data range for a chart contains more than one row or column, Excel assumes that you are plotting more than one category. Excel must decide whether the columns represent the categories or whether the rows represent the categories. The difference is significant. Figures 11.8 and 11.9 show the same data range plotted according to two different orientations.

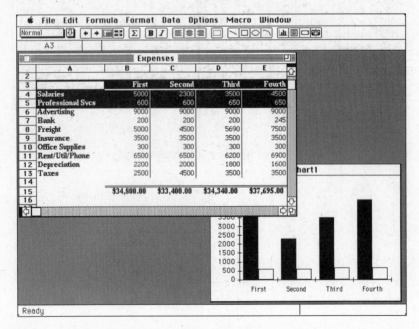

Fig. 11.8. A chart using columns as the categories.

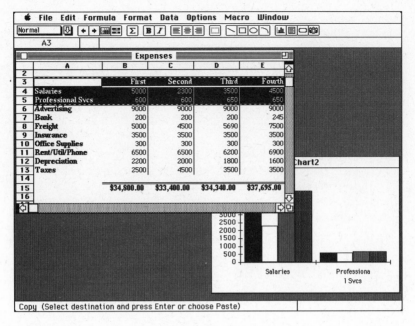

Fig. 11.9. *A chart using rows as the categories.*

In both figures, the chart represents two expense items plotted for four quarters. The chart in figure 11.8 emphasizes the difference between the two expense items during each quarter. The chart in figure 11.9 emphasizes the comparison of quarters.

Because Excel cannot know how you intend to display the data, it makes an assumption: the larger proportion represents the categories. A block of five columns and two rows, for example, produces a chart with five categories, each containing two data series. A block of five rows and two columns produces the same chart.

Excel's default orientation may be confusing because the categories do not consistently correspond to rows or columns.

The default orientation anticipates the most likely organization of the data. If you want to change the orientation, however, follow these steps:

1. Remove the incorrect chart from the worksheet by selecting it and pressing the Delete key.

2. Highlight the chart data you want to use, as described earlier.

3. Select the Copy command from the Edit menu.

4. Open a new chart window with the New command from the File menu. Choose the Chart option from the list.

5. Select the Paste Special command from the Edit menu.

6. Select Rows to use the rows as the categories; select Columns to use the columns as the categories. Because you are changing Excel's default order, the option you want is probably the one not currently selected.

7. Specify the location of the series and category labels and press Return. Depending on the orientation you want, series labels will be in the first row or first column of the copied block. If the labels are in the first row, check the box marked Series Labels in First Row. Similarly, category labels will be in the first row or column.

The chart now reflects the orientation you want. Be sure to change the orientation of your chart before adding any custom formats to the chart. Custom formats are removed during the orientation-swapping process.

Changing the Chart Type

After you create a basic chart (and, if necessary, change its orientation), you can make all kinds of changes to it. One of the most basic changes is to select a different type of chart. Excel offers several types of charts: area, bar, column, line, pie, scatter, combination, and 3-D charts. Within each of these main categories, Excel offers several variations, which are really just short-cuts to formatting a chart from scratch. If you do not like any of these formats, you can customize your chart—beginning with one of the existing charts.

To change the chart type, activate the chart window (double-click on the chart in the worksheet) and select one of the seven chart types from the Gallery menu. Excel displays the built-in chart formats, in picture form, for the selected type. Click on the picture representing the format you want. If you want to view other chart types, click on the Next button to view the next Gallery menu item. Click on the Previous button to view the preceding Gallery menu item. The following sections describe the seven main chart types and the various built-in chart formats.

Note: If the chart has custom formatting, that formatting disappears when you change the chart type.

Note: Some chart types have special data requirements. If your data does not meet these requirements, you may not be able to change your chart to certain types. In particular, xy and high-low charts have data requirements.

Area Charts

Area charts commonly are used to track changes in volume or intensity over time. Instead of comparing one bar to another, these charts compare changes over one or two series. Area charts show continuous divisions of data but stack several series together to show how they relate to the whole. Such charts are useful when you have too many divisions for your stacked bar chart. These charts also can be effective for plotting a single item over time and showing how that item represents volume. Figure 11.10 shows the area-chart formats available through the Area option from the Gallery menu. Figure 11.11 shows an area chart.

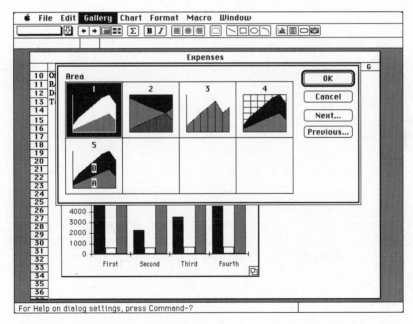

Fig. 11.10. *The area formats available by selecting Area from the Gallery menu.*

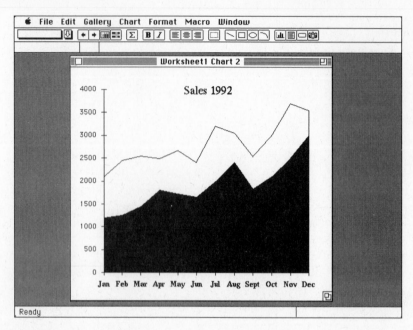

Fig. 11.11. *An area chart.*

The following list describes the area formatting options shown in figure 11.10:

Option	Effect
1	Depicts the basic area chart. Each data series represents a new layer of the area chart.
2	Displays the area chart in percentages, where the combination of the data series is 100 percent and the individual data series represents percentages of the whole.
3	Adds drop lines to the data points in each series and is used best for charting a single data series. Drop lines emphasize the exact placement of plot points on the chart by connecting the plot point to the base of the chart.
4	Adds grid lines to the basic area chart. Grid lines emphasize the values of the plot points by providing a visual scale for reference.
5	Adds series labels to the basic area chart. Series labels help identify the various areas in the chart.

Bar Charts

Bar charts consist of horizontal bars and primarily are used to indicate a distance or goal achieved. The main purpose of bar charts is to show the quantity or quality of items in comparison. Bar charts are not as effective as column charts for comparing one item over time; rather, their purpose is to establish the rank of several different items. The eye is drawn more easily to the length of the bars when the bars are turned sideways. Often, the bars in a bar chart are not shown in different colors or patterns because labels frequently accompany the bars. Use bar charts instead of column charts when the comparison has no connection with changes over time.

Figure 11.12 shows the bar chart formats available through the Bar option from the Gallery menu. Figure 11.13 shows a bar chart.

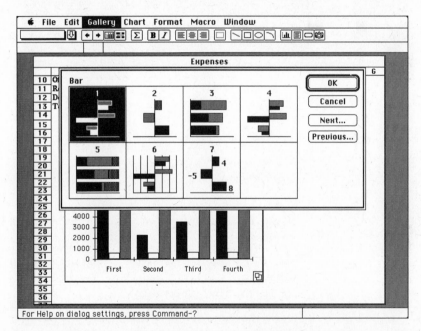

Fig. 11.12. *The bar formats available by choosing the Bar command from the Gallery menu.*

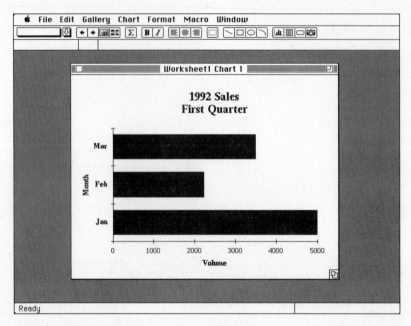

Fig. 11.13. *A bar chart.*

The following list describes the bar formatting options shown in figure 11.12:

Option	Effect
1	Displays data points as bars in a horizontal chart. Negative values appear as bars at the left of the vertical axis.
2	Applies a different pattern to each bar in the series when you plot only one data series. (Normally, each bar has the same pattern.)
3	Stacks the data points within the various series. The chart shows the same number of series, but with only one bar in each series. The bar can contain various patterns. You may want to use this format when you have more than one series—this is a good alternative to pie charts.
4	Overlaps the bars in a bar chart; otherwise, this format is the same as format 1.
5	Displays in stacked-bar chart format each data point as a percentage value. The total of each series is 100 percent.

Option	Effect
6	Adds vertical grid lines to the basic bar chart.
7	Adds value labels to the bars of a basic bar chart to help emphasize the values of the bars.

Column Charts

Column charts are used for standard business applications. Column charts are ideal for directly comparing items over time or over different categories. The immediate ability to compare the heights of the columns helps bring the message home. You can contrast two or more data items in one column chart. This capability is useful for comparing the performance of two related items, such as two products or two expense categories. As with bar charts, you can stack a column chart, overlap the data points, and include various formatting elements.

Figure 11.14 shows the column chart formats available through the Column command on the Gallery menu. Figure 11.15 shows a column chart.

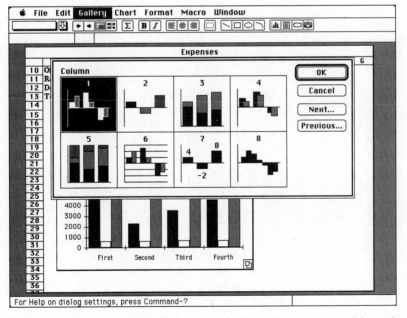

Fig. 11.14. *The formats available by choosing the Column command from the Gallery menu.*

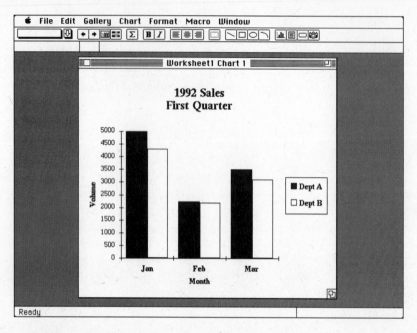

Fig. 11.15. *A column chart.*

The following list describes the column formatting options shown in figure 11.14:

Option	Effect
1	Displays data points as columns (bars) in a vertical chart.
2	Applies a different pattern to each column in the series when you plot only one data series. (Normally, each column has the same pattern.)
3	Stacks the data points within the various series. The chart shows the same number of series, but with only one column in each series. The column can contain various patterns. This format usually is used when you have more than one series, and is a good alternative to pie charts.
4	Overlaps the columns in a column chart; otherwise, this format is the same as format 1.
5	Displays in stacked-column chart format each data point as a percentage value. The total of each series is 100 percent.

Option	Effect
6	Adds horizontal grid lines to the basic column chart.
7	Adds value labels to the columns of a basic column chart.
8	Displays columns without space between columns and uses the same pattern for each data point. You usually use this format to plot only one series; it is similar to an area chart but does not smooth the tops of the plot points.

You often can use stacked-column charts instead of several pie charts. Such column charts present information in much the same way as pie charts, showing how several series of data represent a whole column. You can compare the height of one column to the height of another column. Use stacked column charts when several series and divisions are required at the same time.

Line and High-Low Charts

You use line and high-low charts to show trends and chart numerous plotted points, as in stock analysis. *Line charts* are similar in purpose to column charts. Line charts, however, represent the time factor more dramatically than column charts because the divisions are connected on a continuous line. Line charts can display more divisions than column charts without losing effectiveness. Often, the distinct time intervals are not important—only the change over time (the line's path).

Figure 11.16 shows the line chart formats available by choosing the Line command from the Gallery menu. Figure 11.17 shows a line chart.

The following list describes the line formatting options shown in figure 11.16:

Option	Effect
1	Draws a line for each data series and plots the data points, using a square marker.
2	Identical to format 1 but does not show the markers.
3	Identical to format 1 but does not show the lines.
4	Adds a horizontal grid to the basic line chart.

Option	Effect
5	Adds grid lines to the basic line chart.
6	Uses a logarithmic scale for the vertical axis (this is a basic line chart).
7	Uses markers for the plotted points and lines to connect the markers (this is a high-low chart).
8	Shows three amounts for each data series (this is a high-low chart). The correlation to the stock market is obvious, providing a daily high, low, and closing stock value. You also can use high-low charts to compare bids turned in for a contract—the high bid, the low bid, and the winning bid.

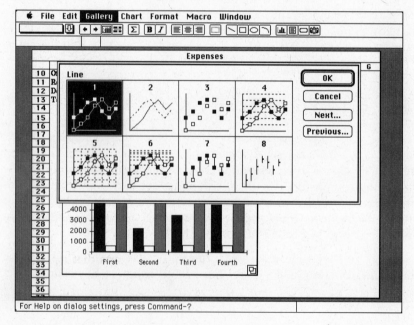

Fig. 11.16. *The formats available by choosing the Line command from the Gallery menu.*

A *high-low chart* is a line chart (any type of line chart) with high-low lines added. High-low lines are vertical lines that connect the plot points of two or more data series. Often only these high-low lines are shown; the series lines are removed, as in Gallery format 7. The two series used in a high-low chart are usually two values for the same item, rather than two different items. A high-low-close chart (Gallery format 8) requires three values to be charted. These values are equivalent to three data series, but they relate to the same item, not three different items.

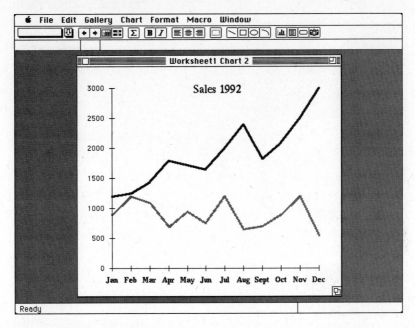

Fig. 11.17. *A line chart.*

Pie Charts

Pie charts are the most graphic representation of parts that make up a whole—where the whole is 100 percent and the slices are proportional values of the whole. A single pie chart shows only one series of data, which is its primary disadvantage when compared with other types of charts.

You should select only one row or column of data for a pie chart. Keep the number of cells in the block to a minimum; too many pie slices can clutter the chart and render its message useless.

Figure 11.18 shows the pie-chart formats available by choosing the Pie command from the Gallery menu. Figure 11.19 shows a pie chart.

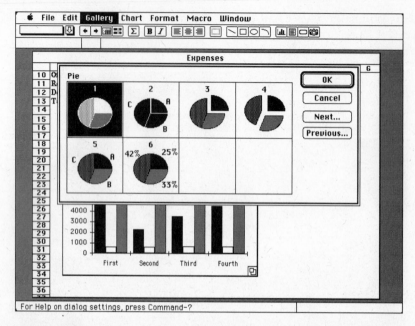

Fig. 11.18. *The formats available by choosing the Pie command from the Gallery menu.*

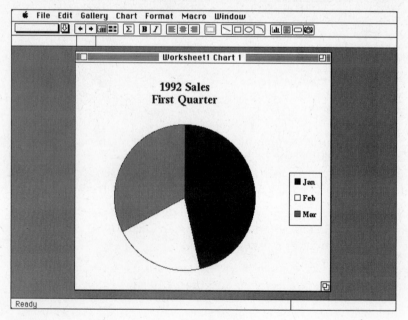

Fig. 11.19. *A pie chart.*

The following list describes the pie formatting options shown in figure 11.18:

Option	Chart Type
1	Basic pie chart with each data point shaded differently.
2	Basic pie chart with each data point shaded the same. This format includes labels for the wedges.
3	Same as format 1, but with one wedge exploded.
4	Same as format 1, but with all wedges exploded.
5	Same as format 1, but with labels for the wedges.
6	Same as format 1, but with wedges labeled as percentages of the whole.

Note: You do not need to use an exploded format (formats 3 and 4) to explode a pie wedge. To determine which wedge of a pie chart is removed from the others, click on the wedge you want to move and drag it to the new location. Pie wedges are independent objects and you can move them at any time. To replace a wedge, move it back past the center of the pie and release the mouse button.

Scatter Charts

Scatter charts compare pairs of numbers that are treated as coordinates for plotting graph points. Each plot point in a scatter chart consists of two values: the first plots the horizontal point, and the second plots the vertical point.

Figure 11.20 shows the scatter chart formats available by choosing the Scatter command from the Gallery menu. Figure 11.21 shows a scatter chart.

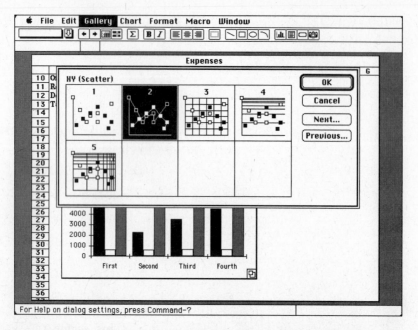

Fig. 11.20. *The formats available by choosing the Scatter command from the Gallery menu.*

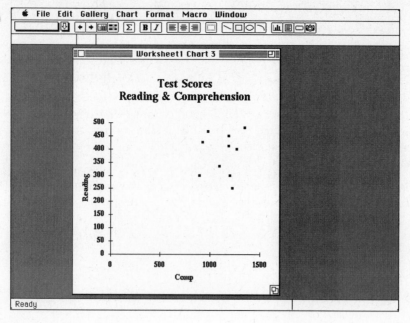

Fig. 11.21. *A scatter chart.*

The following list describes the scatter formatting options:

Option	Chart Type
1	Basic scatter chart with markers representing the data points.
2	Basic scatter chart with markers representing the data points and lines connecting like markers.
3	Scatter chart with vertical and horizontal grid lines.
4	Scatter chart with a logarithmic vertical axis.
5	Scatter chart with logarithmic vertical and horizontal axes.

Creating a scatter chart requires a slightly different procedure than other charts, because each plot point requires two values to appear on the chart. To create an xy chart, follow these steps:

1. Highlight at least two columns (or rows) of data. These can include headings. If you highlight more than two columns, each extra column plots a new series of points on the chart. Excel pairs the values in these columns with the first column to get the two values for each point. (The first column represents the horizontal values.)

2. Click on the Chart tool and press the Shift key as you draw the chart onto the worksheet. This makes the chart box perfectly square, which is important for xy charts. Excel presents the dialog box shown in figure 11.22 asking you what the first column (or row) of values represents.

3. Select the third option in this dialog box, X Values for XY Chart, and click on OK.

Excel sets the scale for each of the chart axes based on the values in your first two columns—the first column creating the x-axis scale and the second creating the y-axis scale. Each additional column creates another set of y-axis values that are paired up with the existing x-axis values. In figure 11.23, for example, three columns were used to create the chart. These three columns created two data series. The first data series was plotted with the values in columns B and C. The second data series was plotted with the values in columns B and D. Excel pairs column B with each column in the graph.

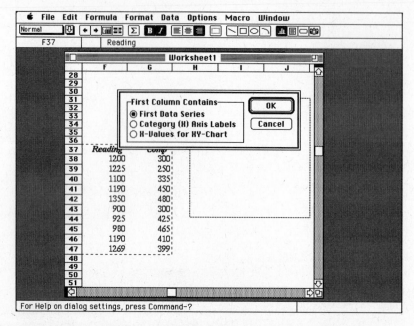

Fig. 11.22. *Viewing Excel's dialog box offering an xy chart option.*

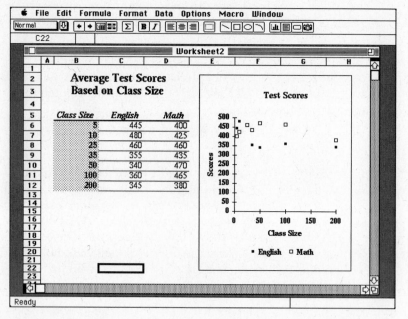

Fig. 11.23. *Using the first column as the x values for all other columns in the data range.*

Many scatter charts include a regression line through the data. To plot a regression line, first create the regression data series as described in Chapter 6 under the functions GROWTH, LINEST, LOGEST, and TREND. This is an additional column for the data range.

When you create the chart, highlight all the columns, including the regression values. These values appear on the chart as a series of points. You can display this data series as a line, contrasting it with the other plot points on the chart. Select the Add Overlay command from the Chart menu. This command turns half of the data series into lines. Use the Overlay command from the Format menu with the First Overlay Series option to control the number of lines that appear on the chart (see Chapter 12 for details).

If you create the xy chart without a regression line and then decide to add one later, use the following method:

1. Create the regression values as described in Chapter 6 under the functions GROWTH, LINEST, LOGEST, and TREND.

2. Highlight two columns of data: the first column of the chart's original data range and the column of regression values. Because these two columns probably will not be adjacent, this most likely will require a multiple-range selection. Press the Command key as you highlight each range.

3. Copy the two columns by using the Copy command from the Edit menu.

4. Double-click on the xy chart to activate the chart menus.

5. Select the Paste Special command from the Edit menu.

6. Click on the Categories (x values) in First Column option in the Paste Special dialog box, and then click on OK.

In these steps, you pair up the existing x values with the regression values to create a new data series. This pairing is necessary when you add a data series to an existing xy chart.

> *Note:* If you use the Copy and Paste commands to add an additional data series to an xy chart after you create it, always highlight two columns (or rows) of data to serve as the x and y values for each plot point.

Highlighting only one column causes Excel to plot the values as y values corresponding to x values of 1, 2, 3, and so on. This probably will not be adequate for your chart, and it definitely will be incorrect for a regression line.

Combination Charts

Combination charts are charts that combine two types of charts into one. You can use these charts to show different data series in different chart types. The emphasis is not so much on the comparison of the data but on the way the two data series fit together.

Figure 11.24 shows the combination-chart formats available by using the Combination command from the Gallery menu. Figure 11.25 shows a combination chart.

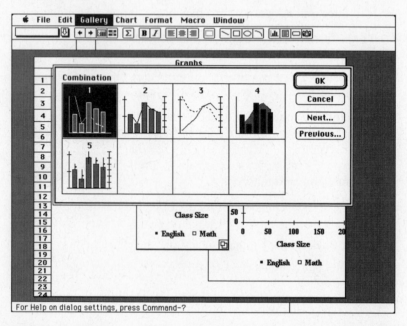

Fig. 11.24. The formats available by choosing the Combination command from the Gallery menu.

The following list describes the format options available by choosing Combination from the Gallery menu:

Option	Chart Type
1	Column chart with a line chart overlay.
2	Column chart with a line chart overlay. The line chart contains its own vertical scale. This chart therefore contains two vertical axes.

Option	Chart Type
3	Line chart with another line chart overlay. The second line chart has its own vertical scale.
4	Area chart with a column chart overlay.
5	Column chart with a high-low-close chart overlay. The high-low-close chart has its own vertical scale.

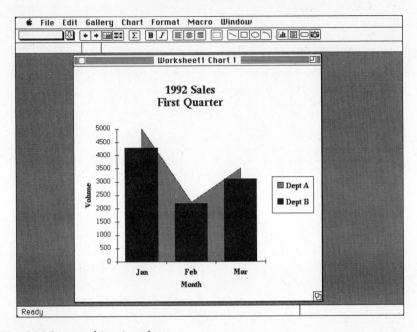

Fig. 11.25. A combination chart.

Combination charts offer some interesting customization options. See Chapter 12 for details on customizing combination charts.

3-D Area Charts

Figure 11.26 shows the area charts available by choosing 3-D Area from the Gallery menu. Figure 11.27 shows a 3-D area chart.

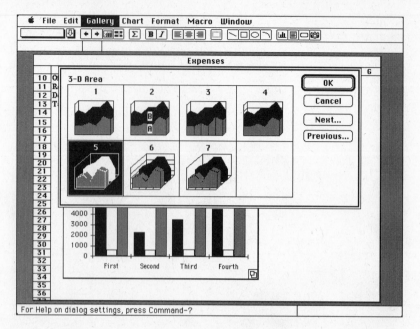

Fig. 11.26. *The formats available by choosing 3-D Area from the Gallery menu.*

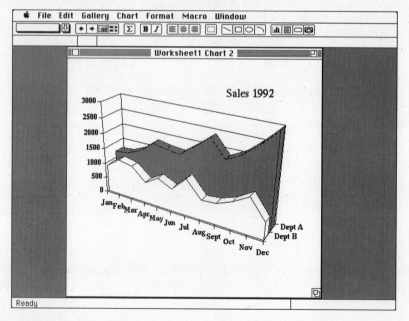

Fig. 11.27. *A 3-D area chart.*

The following describes each 3-D area chart type:

Option	Chart Type
1	Basic stacked 3-D area chart. Each series represents a portion of the total.
2	Same as format 1, but with series labels added.
3	Same as format 1, but with drop lines added.
4	Same as format 1, but with grid lines added.
5	Basic unstacked 3-D area chart. Each series is plotted from the zero line.
6	Same as format 5, but with grid lines added.
7	Same as format 5, but with the depth grid lines added.

In a stacked 3-D area chart, you are concerned primarily with the amount of space in each layer of the chart and the way each layer expands and contracts over time. A stacked chart, however, is not good for comparing the values in each layer (the values in each data series) because, after the bottom layer, each layer is added to the height of the preceding layer; the layers do not all start at zero. For this reason, the top of each layer and its path over time do not show the value of the data.

In contrast, the unstacked 3-D area charts plot each data point from the zero line, enabling you to compare the tops of each data series. These 3-D area charts are not stacked charts at all. In fact, they are more like line charts that have the area beneath the line filled in.

Excel offers seven 3-D area charts: the first four are stacked and the last three are not stacked. These charts represent data in very different ways. First, look at the area charts offered by Excel.

3-D Column Charts

Excel's 3-D column charts are like their 2-D counterparts in that they show the relationships among a series of plot points distributed over time or over specific categories. The difference is that each data series is plotted on a separate depth, which offsets them from one another. This feature makes precise comparisons of the bars' heights more difficult, but makes quick comparisons of numerous data points easier. For this reason, 3-D column charts can be an effective alternative to crowded 2-D column charts. Generally, the series plotted in 3-D column charts should increase in value so that the series plotted behind the others still can be seen. Figures 11.28 and 11.29 demonstrate this principle.

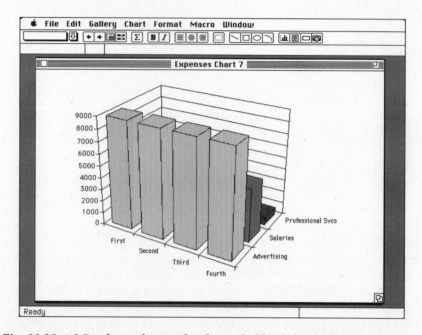

Fig. 11.28. *A 3-D column chart with columns hidden behind others.*

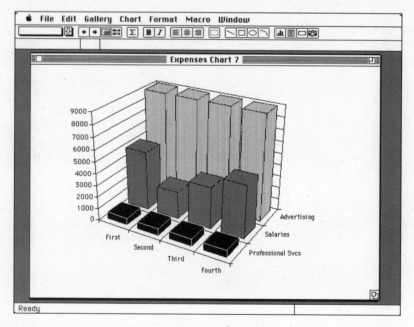

Fig. 11.29. *A 3-D column chart with increasing values.*

You can arrange your data series in ascending order by using Excel's sorting commands, which are discussed in Chapter 15. Arranging your data in ascending order, however, may not be appropriate in your worksheet. Or perhaps your data does not ascend across each category, so that a column is always hidden no matter how you arrange the data. In this case, consider using a 2-D column chart or splitting the data into several charts. You also may consider changing the perspective of the 3-D column chart so that more of each column can be seen. Changing 3-D perspective is discussed in Chapter 12. (The 3-D column formats are similar to their 2-D counterparts and are not listed individually here.)

3-D Line Charts

A 3-D line chart is like a 2-D line chart, except that each data series is plotted on a different depth. This feature makes following each line easier—even when the lines do not have distinct patterns or colors. Making more precise measurements between lines, however, can be more difficult because the 3-D perspective creates an optical illusion. Because each line on the 3-D line chart hovers in space, you have no trouble seeing all the lines. Figure 11.30 shows the 3-D line charts available by choosing the 3-D Line command from the Gallery menu. Because these formats are similar to their 2-D counterparts, they are not listed individually here. Figure 11.31 shows a 3-D line chart.

3-D Pie Charts

3-D pie charts serve the same purpose as 2-D pie charts except that they emphasize the frontmost slices. You can use 3-D pie charts in almost every situation that you can use a 2-D pie chart. Figure 11.32 shows the 3-D pie formats available. Because these formats are similar to their 2-D counterparts, they are not listed individually here. Figure 11.33 shows a 3-D pie chart.

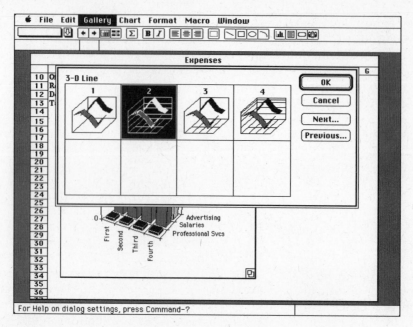

Fig. 11.30. *The formats available by using the 3-D Line command from the Gallery menu.*

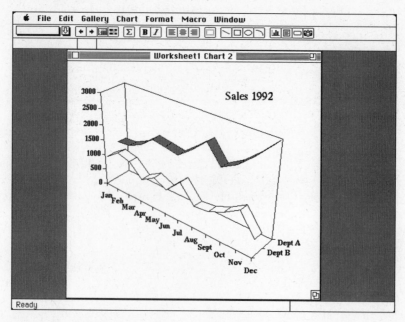

Fig. 11.31. *A 3-D line chart.*

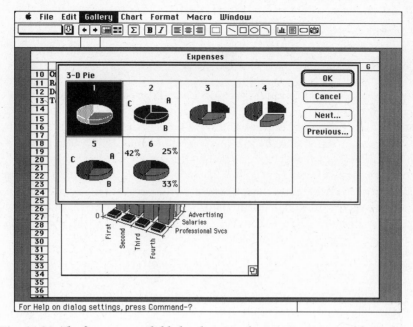

Fig. 11.32. *The formats available by choosing the 3-D Pie command from the Gallery menu.*

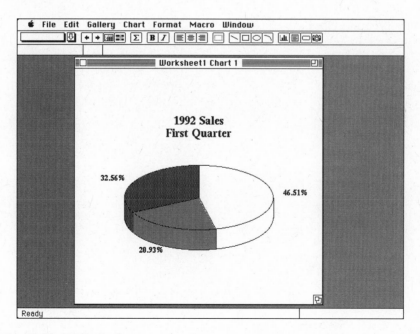

Fig. 11.33. *A 3-D pie chart.*

Changing the Default (Preferred) Chart

When you first create a chart by using a new chart window, Excel draws a standard column chart. This chart is known as the *default*, or *preferred*, chart. You can make the preferred chart any one of the built-in chart formats; you even can change it to a custom-designed format. Being able to specify the default chart is handy when you use the same chart format frequently. To specify the default chart, create a chart that uses the format you want. Then, double-click on the chart to activate the chart menus. Next, select the Set Preferred command from the Gallery menu. The preferred chart is now the same format as the active chart. The next time you create a chart in this worksheet, it appears in the preferred format.

You can change any existing chart to the preferred setting by double-clicking on the chart and then using the Preferred command from the Gallery menu. Making such a change is most useful when the preferred chart is a custom format; otherwise, selecting the built-in format from the Gallery options is as easy as changing the default setting.

Using Picture Charts

A picture chart is a special chart type that does not appear in the Gallery menu. A *picture chart* uses a picture or graphic object to represent the columns of a column chart. Figure 11.34 shows an example.

In this example, the pictures are stretched to represent the proper values. You also can create a picture chart with pictures stacked on each other, as shown in figure 11.35.

You can create a picture chart by starting with a normal column chart and replacing the bars with your selected graphic objects. The graphic objects you use for the picture chart are likely to come from a program other than Excel. After you create the basic column chart, follow these steps:

1. Copy the picture you want from the program that contains it. Use the program's Copy command and place the picture onto the Clipboard.

2. Switch to Excel and bring the appropriate worksheet into view. This worksheet should contain the column chart that will become the picture chart. (If you are not using MultiFinder or System 7, you must quit the graphics program before entering Excel.)

3. Double-click on the column chart to activate it and the chart menus.

4. Click on the data series you want to change into the picture you copied.

5. Select Paste from the Edit menu.

6. Repeat this procedure for the other data series in the chart, using a different object for each.

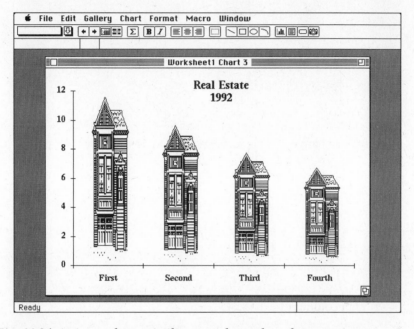

Fig. 11.34. *A picture chart—similar to a column chart that uses pictures instead of bars.*

> ### *Tip: Using Worksheet Objects in Picture Charts*
> You can use any object in an Excel worksheet for a picture chart. Simply copy the object with the Copy command from the Edit menu and paste it into the chart as described in the preceding steps. Try this when you have problems copying pictures between Excel and another program. First, use the Publish/Subscribe features of Excel to get the picture into the worksheet. Then copy the picture from the worksheet into the chart. Refer to Chapter 8 for more information about Publish/Subscribe.

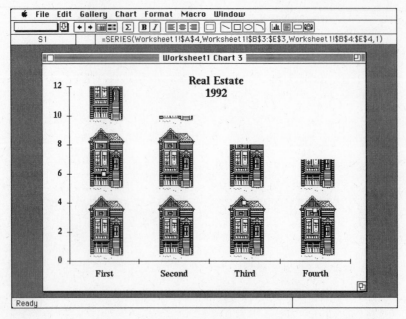

Fig. 11.35. *A picture chart that stacks the pictures on top of each other to represent the bars.*

To stack the pictures instead of stretching them, complete these steps after the six steps listed earlier:

1. Double-click on the data series you want to include in the picture chart. This is the picture you want to change from stretched to stacked.

2. Select the options from the dialog box and click on OK. These options follow:

Option	Effect
Stretch	Stretches the picture to represent the value being plotted.
Stack	Stacks several copies of the picture to represent the value being plotted.
Stack and Scale	Stacks several copies of the picture and makes each one represent a specified amount.

The Stack and Scale option is useful for controlling the size of the stacked pictures so that each one represents a particular amount of the total value.

Summary

Charting is an important feature of Excel. In this chapter you discovered all the necessary steps for creating charts. These steps include selecting the chart data range, drawing the chart on the worksheet, and choosing a chart type from the built-in formats available. You also discovered how to access the chart menus and how to manipulate a chart after the chart is on the worksheet.

Following are some important points to remember:

- Generally, you should select a contiguous block of cells to create a chart. You can select a multiple range, however.

- Draw a chart onto the worksheet using the Chart tool in the Toolbar.

- You can change the size and shape of a chart by dragging on the highlight boxes around the edges of the chart. These boxes appear after you select the chart.

- The chart menus appear when you double-click on a chart. This maneuver also displays the chart in a window, which you can move or resize.

- Normally, Excel saves charts with their worksheets (when you save the worksheet), but you can save a chart in a separate file by using the Save command from the File menu when the chart menus are active.

- The Gallery menu contains many preformatted charts that you can customize.

- When you select a data range for charting, Excel uses rows as data series and columns as categories—unless the range has more rows than columns. If the range has more rows than columns, Excel uses columns as data series and rows as categories.

- You can change a chart's orientation by copying the chart data and then using the Paste Special command to paste the data into a new chart window.

12

Customizing Charts

E xcel's built-in chart formats probably will not provide everything you want in a chart. The next step in charting, therefore, is to learn some basic customization commands. Making even a basic change, such as adding a legend, requires you to customize one of the built-in charts. This chapter explains various ways that you can customize charts by using chart menus. First, the chapter explains how to control individual chart elements, such as axes, labels, and legends. You then learn how to use combination charts and how to control the way those charts display data. Next, the chapter explains how to add and remove data from an existing chart without creating a new data range.

> *Tip: Using the Preferred Chart*
> You can save your customized chart as the preferred chart by choosing the Set Preferred command from the Gallery menu. You then can use the custom chart over and over with the Preferred command from the Gallery menu.

Highlighting Chart Elements

Many of Excel's customization features apply to specific chart elements. Often, you must select, or highlight, the element you want before you can make a change to it. You may find clicking on an element the easiest way to select it. Other selection options exist, however, as described in this section.

You can highlight a chart element by clicking on it with the mouse. If you click in the correct area, the element is surrounded with highlighted squares. These highlighted squares appear as solid black or white squares around the element's edges. Solid squares indicate that you can move the element by dragging it with the mouse. Elements surrounded by white squares cannot be moved freely.

You can use the Select Chart command from the Chart menu to select all chart elements at the same time. You can use the Select Plot Area command from the Chart menu to select the chart's plot area portion.

You also can use the keyboard's arrow keys to highlight various chart elements. If you use the keyboard to highlight chart elements, remember that Excel groups chart elements into classes and items. A *class* is a unique chart element and can consist of several *items*. The data series in a chart, for example, are considered a class, but each plot point is an item within the class. Excel's classes of elements include the following:

- 3-D floor (base)
- 3-D background "walls"
- High-low lines
- Drop lines (area charts only)
- Data series
- Grid lines
- Chart arrows
- Chart text
- Axes
- Legend
- Plot area
- Chart

If you click on a plot point, Excel highlights the entire data series containing that point. To highlight an individual plot point, you must click on the point and then use the right-arrow key to highlight the individual point. (You cannot highlight individual plot points in area or 3-D charts.) You can move between classes with the up- and down-arrow keys and from item to item with the left- and right-arrow keys, as the following information shows:

Key	Moves
↑	Forward through classes
↓	Backward through classes
→	Forward through elements in a class, and then to next class
←	Backward through elements in a class, and then to preceding class

Suppose that a chart arrow is highlighted. Pressing the up-arrow key highlights the first grid line in the chart (if any grid lines exist). After the grid line is highlighted, pressing the right-arrow key selects the next grid line; pressing the up-arrow key highlights the first data series.

Note: The ability to highlight individual items enables you to format each part of a chart. You can change the color and pattern of each plot point in a chart individually, and you can adjust the plot point's height; however, you first have to highlight the point. (This is not available for area and 3-D charts.)

Changing Chart Legends

The *chart legend* is the key to a chart's data series. If a chart contains more than one data series, Excel uses a unique pattern or color for each series. These patterns and colors appear in the legend next to the item's name. Remember that Excel considers the larger number of items (that is, the larger proportion in the data range) to be the categories; Excel considers the smaller number of items to be the data series. The category labels appear on the horizontal axis, and the series labels appear in the legend. If you chart two rows of values over four columns, for example, you get a chart with two data series, as shown in figure 12.1. The legend shows the two series using the row labels as the legend text.

If you change the chart's orientation and display four data series (the four quarters) over two categories, the legend shows four items. If the data series appears in rows of the worksheet, the legend uses the left column for the legend text. If the data series appears in columns, the legend uses the top row (column headings) for the legend text. See Chapter 11 for details on changing a chart's orientation.

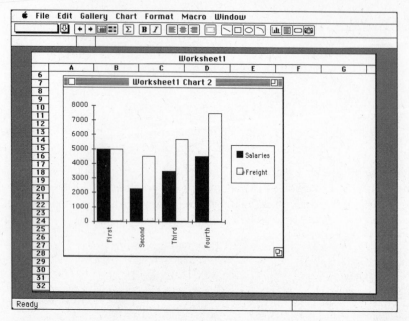

Fig. 12.1. *A legend using the two data series.*

When a chart contains only one data series, the legend does not display the name of the series; instead, the legend duplicates the names of the categories. If you chart only one series from the preceding example, the resulting chart and legend appear as shown in figure 12.2.

Adding and Removing a Legend

To display the chart legend, activate the chart menus and select the Add Legend command from the Chart menu. The legend appears vertically on the chart. Excel redraws the chart so that the legend fits into the window with the chart. If the chart is too small after you add the legend, simply enlarge the window or the chart box on the worksheet.

The legend items should match the labels in the first row or first column of the data range (whichever is not used as the category labels). If the legend does not use these labels, you may not have included the labels when you highlighted the data range. Be sure that no extra blank space appears between the labels and the chart values.

To remove a legend, simply select Delete Legend from the Chart menu.

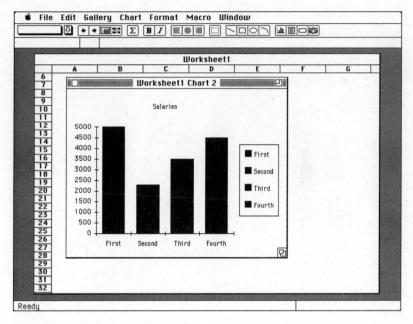

Fig. 12.2. *A legend duplicating the category labels in a chart with only one data series.*

Moving the Legend

After adding a legend to a chart, you may decide to change the legend's position. To move the legend, you can click on the chart's legend box and drag it to another location. If you move the legend as far as possible in any direction (to the chart's edge, for example), Excel adjusts the plot area to make room for the legend's new location. If you don't move the legend as far as possible, the legend overlaps the chart (see fig. 12.3).

You also can move a legend by using the Legend command from the Format menu. Excel presents a set of positions for the legend and changes the proportions of the chart to accommodate the legend's position.

The Top and Bottom options in the Format Legend dialog box are self-explanatory: they place the legend at the top or bottom of the chart, respectively. The Corner option places the legend in the upper right corner of the chart, and the Left and Right options place the legend along the left and right sides of the chart. The Patterns and Font buttons shown in the dialog box take you directly to the Format Patterns and Format Font dialog boxes. These dialog boxes are explained in the next section.

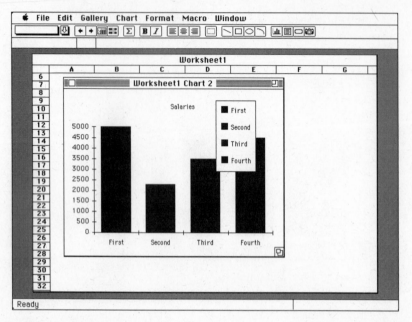

Fig. 12.3. *Moving the legend.*

Formatting the Legend

Using the Format menu options, you can change the fonts used for legend items, change the pattern in the legend box, add a shadow to the box, and much more. Two Format menu commands enable you to format the legend: Patterns and Font. You also can access these commands through the Format Legends dialog box. Figures 12.4 through 12.6 show some of the ways you can format the legend.

To format a legend, first click on the legend box to highlight it. Select the Patterns command from the Format menu to change the border and interior (or area) of the legend box. Figure 12.7 shows the Format Patterns dialog box for legends. To change the fonts of the labels inside the legend box, choose the Format Font option.

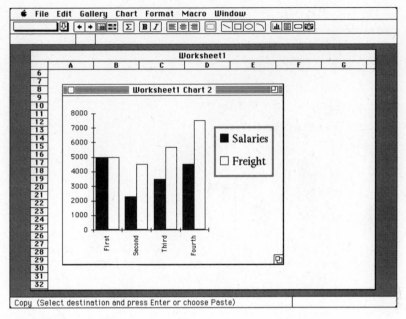

Fig. 12.4. *A legend placed to the right with a patterned border.*

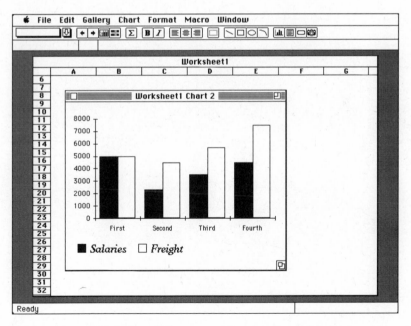

Fig. 12.5. *A legend placed at the bottom with no border and italic font.*

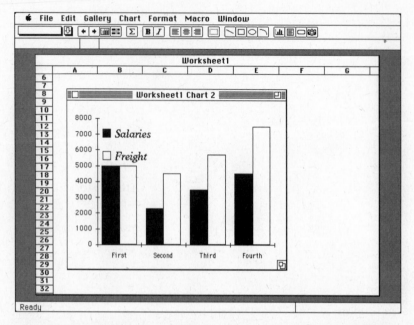

Fig. 12.6. *A legend in a custom location with no border and an italic font.*

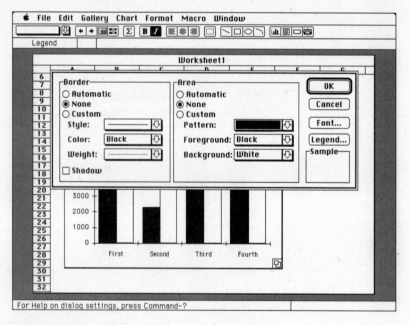

Fig. 12.7. *The Format Patterns dialog box for legends.*

The Border options change the appearance of the legend's border and the Area options change the interior of the legend box. The options you can choose follow:

Option	Effect
Automatic	Enables Excel to choose an appropriate border and/or area.
None	Eliminates the border and/or area. Eliminating the area makes the box transparent.
Custom	Enables you to select from the customization lists to create a custom border and/or area pattern.
Style	Contains border line styles.
Color	Contains color options for the border line.
Weight	Contains line thicknesses for the border line.
Shadow	Creates a drop-shadow effect around the border.
Pattern	Contains patterns for the legend's interior.
Foreground	Contains colors for the pattern's foreground.
Background	Contains colors for the pattern's background.

Note that the sample in the lower right corner of figure 12.7 shows what your selections will look like on the legend. Also, notice that the foreground color you select controls the color of the solid pattern. The background color is the color behind the pattern. In black-and-white systems, you can use the foreground and background options to reverse the patterns (that is, you can specify white on black or black on white).

The Font command from the Format menu provides options for changing the color, font, size, and style of text inside the legend box. The options in the Format Font dialog box are similar to the options for formatting worksheet fonts. See Chapter 5 for details about using the Fonts dialog box.

Changing the Legend Text

You may decide to change the legend labels themselves so that they no longer are linked to the labels in the worksheet; or, perhaps you want to reference a different worksheet range containing legend labels. You can change the legend labels by using the Edit Series command from the Chart menu. Follow these steps:

1. Double-click on the chart you want and select the Edit Series command from the Chart menu.

2. Click on the series name you want in the Series list provided. Excel indicates which cell is being used for this series' legend text by displaying the reference in the Name box to the right.

3. Enter a new cell reference in the Name box by pointing to the worksheet cell containing the legend entry or by typing in the reference, and then press Return. To enter a constant text string as the legend text, simply type the text into the Name box as a text formula. Type *"Item"*, for example, to use the word *Item* as the legend entry for the highlighted series. Figure 12.8 shows an Edit Series dialog box in which an entry has been made.

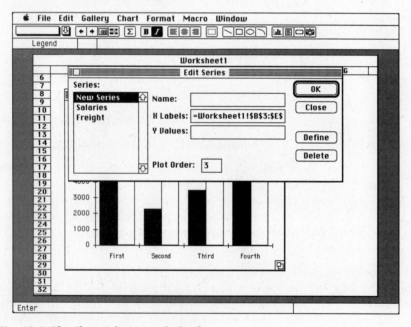

Fig. 12.8. *The Chart Edit Series dialog box.*

Formatting Plot Points

When you create a chart, Excel chooses the patterns and colors of the data series. You can change these settings, however, which include the border around each plot point, its pattern, and its colors. Figure 12.9 shows an example of several formatted plot points within a data series.

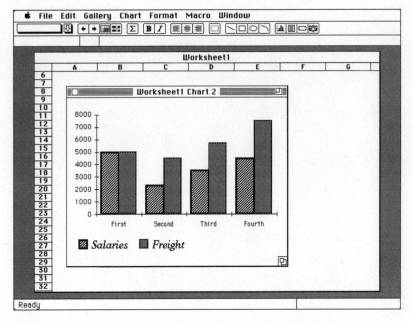

Fig. 12.9. *Changing the patterns and borders of a data series.*

You can change each plot point individually, or you can change an entire data series at one time. Generally, you should change an entire data series rather than individual points. Two different patterns within the same series can create confusion.

To change an entire data series, highlight the series by clicking on it or by using the up- or down-arrow key. In a bar or column chart, just click on one bar; in a pie chart, click on a pie wedge; in a scatter chart, click on a plot-point marker. Next, choose the Patterns command from the Format menu and select from the available area and border options. Remember that when you select the Automatic option, Excel formats the series. When you select the Apply to All option, your settings apply to all data series in the chart.

Note: You can open the Patterns dialog box by double-clicking on the series you want.

To change individual plot points, first highlight the data series by clicking on it. Next, use the right- and left-arrow keys to highlight the point you want within the series. After the individual plot point is highlighted, choose the Patterns command from the Format menu and make your changes.

After you highlight a plot point, you also can change its value. That is, you can change the plot point's height (or position) on the chart. (You cannot make these changes in area and 3-D charts.) Simply drag on the top of the point (a solid square appears on the top of each column in a column chart). Because this change indicates a different value, Excel updates the worksheet value to match the change. You can change the point's value only within the existing y-axis scale. Figures 12.10 and 12.11 illustrate the value change process.

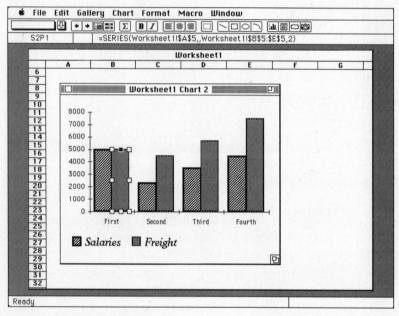

Fig. 12.10. Highlighting a plot point.

Being able to change the value of a data series from the chart rather than from the worksheet is useful for "what if" analysis. You may want to discover which values result in a particular outcome on the graph. Being able to change values also is useful when you want to create a chart without knowing specific values. You can determine the values by adjusting the plot points.

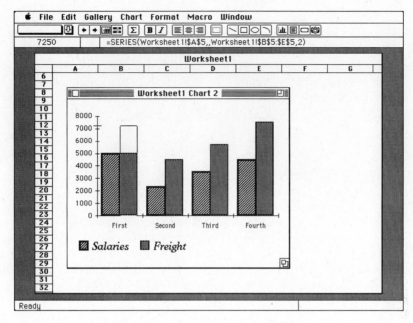

Fig. 12.11. *Dragging on a plot point to increase its value.*

Changing Chart Titles and Labels

Excel applies labels to the category axis and legend, using the worksheet data range as a basis. You can add the axis titles or a main chart title yourself, however. You can type information for the labels on the chart, or you can refer to an original worksheet cell that contains the text you want to use as a chart label.

You can add two types of text to your charts: attached text and unattached text. *Attached text* applies to a particular chart element, such as an axis label. You cannot move attached text freely around the chart. Charts adjust their size and shape to accommodate attached text. *Unattached text*, also called *descriptive text*, does not affect the size or shape of the chart. Unattached text simply sits on top of the chart; you can move it at any time. Solid squares surround unattached text, indicating that you can move the text. Attached text is surrounded by open (or empty) squares, indicating that you cannot move the text.

Unattached text is useful when you want to move text anywhere on the chart. You must find a location for the text that does not obstruct the data, however. Attached text, on the other hand, always fits on the chart because it causes the chart to adjust its size and shape. If you change chart types, edit the data series, or add or remove data from the chart, the attached text remains in its proper place on the chart; unattached text may require adjustments.

Adding Titles and Labels

With the exception of descriptive (or unattached) text, all chart labels are attached to specific chart elements. A value axis title, for example, is attached to the value axis, a category axis title is attached to the category axis, and the chart title is attached to the entire chart area. (Note that axis titles are not the same as axis labels. Excel applies the axis labels from your data; your axis titles describe what these labels represent.)

To attach a label to an element, first click on the element to highlight it. After selecting the element (an axis or the entire chart), choose the Attach Text command from the Chart menu. Excel presents a dialog box listing the various chart elements to which you can attach text. Confirm that the element you want is selected or select the element to which you want to attach text. Then press Return. (If you prefer, you can select the Attach Text command from the Chart menu without highlighting a chart element.) Excel places a small text box on the chart in the appropriate area. Figure 12.12 shows a text box attached to the category axis.

Notice that when the text box is highlighted, the formula bar appears, enabling you to type information. Enter the label for the box and press Return. Remember that pressing ⌘-Return starts a new line in the label. The label appears in the text box.

> ***Tip: Creating Subtitles***
> Subtitles actually are part of the main title. To create a second line of a title (a subtitle), press ⌘-Return when entering the title text.

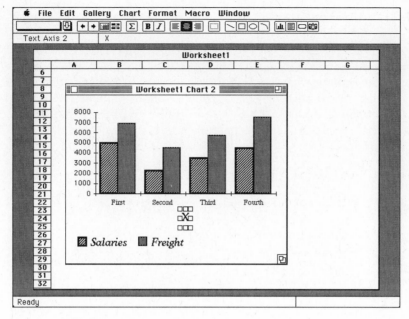

Fig. 12.12. *Adding text to the category axis.*

By using the worksheet linking techniques discussed in Chapter 7, you can link the text in the text box to a cell in the original worksheet or to any other worksheet. Simply enter a simple linking formula, such as =*EXPENSES!$G$5*, into the text box. You can point to the appropriate cell by using the following steps:

1. Attach a text box to the element you want, as described earlier in this section. Click on the text box to make sure that the text box is selected.

2. Press the equal sign key (=).

3. Activate the worksheet containing the cell you want to reference.

4. Click on the cell you want to reference.

5. Press Return.

You now have linked the chart's label to a cell in the worksheet, as indicated by the external reference formula that appears in the formula bar. Whenever the worksheet cell changes, the chart will change accordingly.

Adding Descriptive (Unattached) Text

Descriptive text is not attached to any element; you therefore can move this text around the chart. To add descriptive text to a chart, simply begin typing the text. Press Return, and the text appears on the chart. You then can move the text into place by dragging the text with the mouse. As with attached text, you can reference external worksheet cells for descriptive text. Reference external worksheet cells by editing the text after the text is on the chart, as described in the preceding section.

Moving and Resizing Descriptive Text

You can move descriptive text at any time. To move descriptive text, simply click on the text box and drag the mouse to the new location. The entire text box moves with the mouse.

You can enlarge the text box of unattached text by dragging one of the highlighted squares. By enlarging the text box, you can make room for almost any amount of descriptive information.

You also can use keyboard commands to move and resize an unattached text box. To move unattached text by using the keyboard, follow these steps:

1. Highlight the text box using the mouse or arrow keys.

2. Select the Move command from the Format menu.

3. Use the arrow keys to move the text box.

4. Press Return.

To resize unattached text by using the keyboard, follow these steps:

1. Highlight the text box using the mouse or arrow keys.

2. Select the Size command from the Format menu.

3. Use the arrow keys to change the size of the box.

4. Press Return.

Editing and Deleting Existing Chart Labels

You may need to edit or add to the information in a chart label. To edit or add label information, use the mouse or keyboard to highlight the appropriate text box and insert the cursor in the formula bar containing the text. Click in the formula bar to insert the cursor or press ⌘-U to place the cursor in the formula bar of the highlighted text box. With the pointer in the formula bar, use the editing commands listed in Chapter 4 to change or add to the data. Press Return when you finish editing or adding information. For information about changing the category labels and vertical axis values, see "Changing the Axes," later in this chapter.

To remove a chart label, highlight the label, press the Backspace key, and then press Return.

Formatting Chart Labels

The procedure for formatting a chart label is identical to the procedure for formatting a chart legend. After highlighting the appropriate label, choose the Font or Patterns command from the Format menu. (You also can double-click on the text.) The Format Font command enables you to control the text used in the text box; Format Patterns enables you to specify the interior and border of the text box. For details about these two commands, see "Formatting the Legend," earlier in this chapter.

In addition, you can use the Text command from the Format menu to change the alignment and orientation of the label text. Using the Format Text command, you can rotate the text so that it appears vertically on the chart. This option can be useful for y-axis titles and descriptive text.

You also can format the category axis labels and the values along the vertical axis. To change these labels, highlight the axis (not the text itself) and select the Font or Text command from the Format menu. You can change both axes at the same time by highlighting the chart background and using the Font command from the Format menu. The Patterns command on the Format menu does not apply to these labels. You can find more information about changing axis labels and values in "Changing the Axes," later in this chapter.

Changing the Chart Background and Plot Area

The chart background and plot area are two important elements of a chart. The *background* contains all the chart elements and can be formatted with a unique interior pattern and border. The background also controls the fonts used in the labels applied automatically by Excel. Likewise, the *plot area*, which is the area containing the plot points, can be formatted with a unique pattern and border. Figure 12.13 shows a chart with the background and plot area formatted.

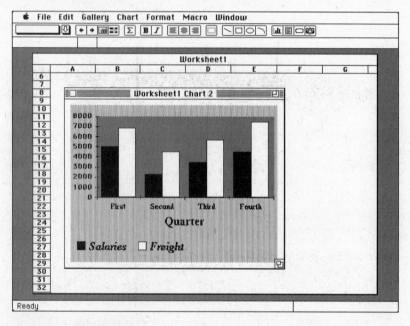

Fig. 12.13. *Formatting the background and plot area.*

To change the background or plot area, use the mouse or the arrow keys to select the background or plot area and then choose the Patterns command from the Format menu. The Format Patterns command controls the border and interior of the highlighted element.

Note that the chart background contains the axis labels. You can change the font used in these labels by highlighting the background and selecting the Font command from the Format menu. You also can change these fonts independently by highlighting the axis and selecting the Format Font command.

Changing the Axes

Excel provides two ways in which you can customize chart axes. You can change the color and thickness of an axis line, and you can change the axis values, making the values fall within the range you specify. The following four commands affect the axes:

Command	Effect
Chart Axes	Specifies the axes displayed on the chart
Format Scale	Changes the scale and tick marks on the axes
Format Patterns	Changes the line type used for the axes
Format Font	Changes the font of the axes labels

The following sections provide details about each of these commands.

Hiding and Displaying Axes

The Axes command from the Chart menu hides or displays the axes. When you choose the Chart Axes command, the dialog box shown in figure 12.14 appears. You then can check the boxes corresponding to the axes you want to display.

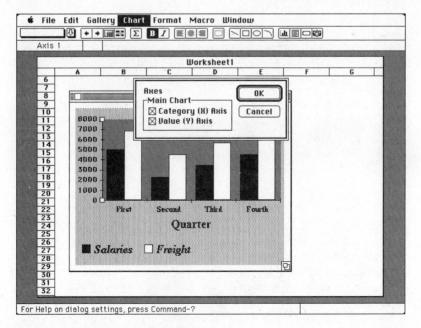

Fig. 12.14. *The Chart Axes dialog box.*

Changing the Axis Scale

The Scale command on the Format menu controls many aspects of the chart axes and offers a different set of options for vertical (value) and horizontal (category) axes (also known as the y-axis and x-axis, respectively). To use the Format Scale command, use the keyboard or mouse to highlight the value or category axis you want to change. Then select the Scale command from the Format menu. If you highlight the value axis, the dialog box shown in figure 12.15 appears.

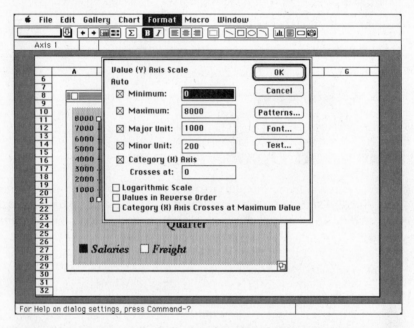

Fig. 12.15. *The Format Scale dialog box for vertical axes.*

Note: On bar charts, the value axis is horizontal and the category axis is vertical—the opposite of most other charts.

Note: Notice that most of the boxes under Auto are checked, which means that Excel controls these values. To customize the axis, enter your own minimum and maximum values in the spaces provided. In the Major Unit field, enter the number of divisions you want along the axis; in the Minor Unit field, enter the number of tick marks between these divisions. Figures 12.16 through 12.18 show some examples of scale option settings.

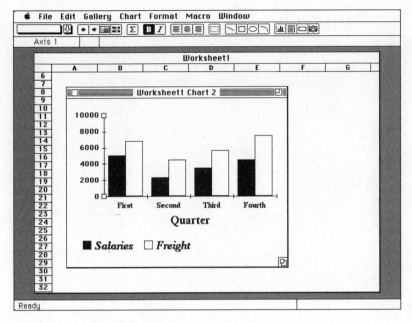

Fig. 12.16. *A value axis with an increased maximum value.*

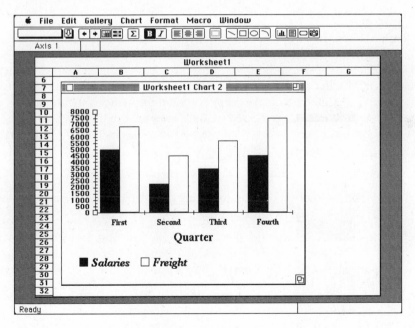

Fig. 12.17. *A value axis with major units set to 500 and minor units set to 250.*

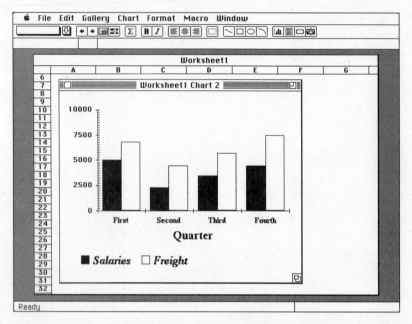

Fig. 12.18. *A value axis with major units set to 2500 and minor units set to 250.*

The Scale command on the Format menu controls the upper and lower limits of the axis values and the number of divisions along the axis. The Format Scale command, however, does not control the format of the tick marks or whether the tick marks appear at all. Use the Patterns command on the Format menu to make formatting determinations for the axis tick marks. See "Formatting the Axis Line," later in this chapter, for more information. The Format Scale options for value axes include the following:

- *Minimum:* Sets the minimum value of the axis scale. Values less than the minimum value are not visible on the chart.

- *Maximum:* Sets the maximum value of the axis scale. Values greater than the maximum value are not visible on the chart.

- *Major Unit:* Sets the number of steps, or divisions, along the axis. Each division is labeled numerically. Enter a number corresponding to the step value you want. Using a value into which the maximum divides evenly is a good idea.

- *Minor Unit:* Sets the number of tick marks between the major units. This number corresponds to the step value of the major-unit entry. Using a number into which the major-unit value divides evenly is best. The tick marks are not labeled.

- *Crosses at:* Determines the horizontal position of the vertical axis; that is, the point along the category axis where this axis starts. Positioning the vertical axis is useful for emphasizing a particular value on the chart. When you use this feature on bar charts, the category and value axes are reversed.

Normally, the category axis crosses the value axis at the bottom— which usually is zero. In this arrangement, negative plot points are drawn as columns extending below the category axis line. By moving the category axis, you can change the way the chart draws negative values. Making the category axis cross at 10 instead of 0, for example, places below the line all plot points that are less than 10. Figure 12.19 shows an example of such a change.

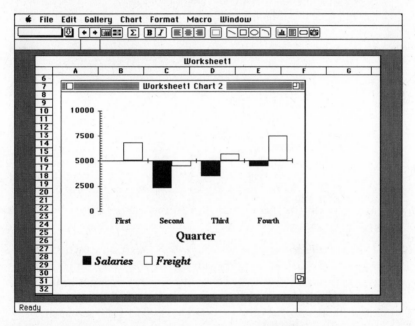

Fig. 12.19. *Making the category axis cross at a value different from zero.*

- *Logarithmic Scale:* Changes the axis to a logarithmic scale.

- *Values in Reverse Order:* Charts the values in reverse order, with the highest value at the bottom and the lowest value at the top.

- *Category Axis Crosses at Maximum Value:* Appears for scatter charts only. This option makes the value axis cross the category axis at the last (maximum) value on the chart.

If you highlight the category axis before choosing the Scale command from the Format menu, the dialog box shown in figure 12.20 appears.

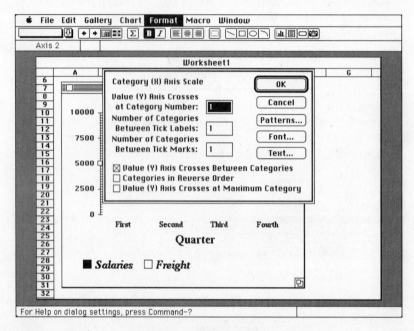

Fig. 12.20. The Format Scale dialog box for category axes.

These options control the display of category axis labels and the axis position. The Format Scale options for category axes include the following:

- *Value Axis Crosses at Category Number:* Determines where on the value axis the category axis begins. Changing the position of the value axis can be useful for showing the current point in time on a graph. Consider the graph in figure 12.21, which places the vertical axis at the beginning of the second category to show that the current quarter is the second—the first quarter is over. Note that the value axis labels have been removed in this example.

  Changing the value axis position may require that you move the value axis labels to the far side of the chart. This is described in "Formatting the Axis Line," later in this chapter.

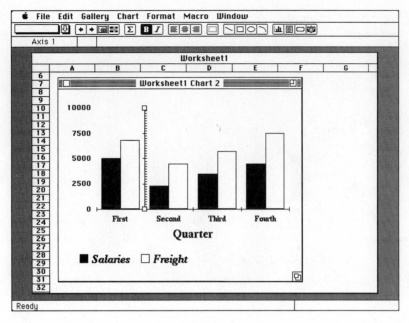

Fig. 12.21. *Changing the position of the value axis.*

- *Number of Categories between Tick Labels:* Determines the number of category axis labels that appear along the axis. By increasing the number of categories plotted between these labels, you effectively decrease the number of labels that can fit on the axis. Increasing this number from one to two, for example, causes every other label to appear along the axis.

- *Number of Categories between Tick Marks:* Determines the number of tick marks that appear along the axis. This option is the same as Number of Categories between Tick Labels but affects the tick marks instead of the labels. Being able to control the tick marks independently from the labels can be useful.

You can use this option with the preceding option to group categories into sets and to label the sets as a unit. Building on the example in figure 12.21, figure 12.22 shows how you can arrange the four quarters (categories) into two groups and label each group as a half-year category. Although four categories still appear in the graph, it appears that only two categories exist because there is only one tick mark between sets. (Note that the number of categories between tick labels is set to two and that the number of categories between tick marks also is set to two. The first and third category labels on the worksheet were changed from First Q and Third Q to First Half and Second Half.)

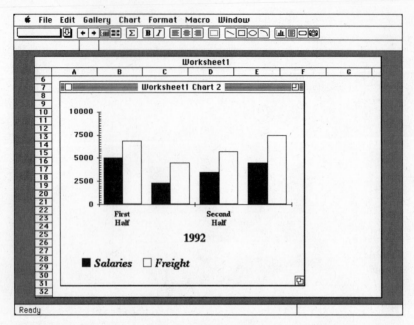

***Fig. 12.22.** Changing the number of tick marks to arrange categories into groups.*

- *Value Axis Crosses between Categories:* Works with the Value Axis Crosses at Category Number option. If you check this box, the value axis crosses the category axis between the category specified in the first option and the next category. If you do not check this box, the value axis crosses the category axis in the middle of the category. This option is useful for area and scatter charts.

- *Categories in Reverse Order:* Plots the axis labels and their respective data series in reverse order.

- *Value Axis Crosses at Maximum Category:* Causes the value axis to cross the category axis at the maximum category.

Formatting the Axis Line

Using the Patterns command from the Format menu, you can change the pattern and thickness of the axis lines. When you highlight the horizontal or vertical axis and select Format Patterns, a dialog box containing various patterns and line thicknesses appears. Choose the appropriate options from this dialog box.

In addition to the standard pattern and line-thickness options, the Format Scale dialog box contains options for formatting the tick marks and tick labels. You can place the major tick marks, minor tick marks, or both types of tick marks inside, outside, or on the axis line. You also can specify that the tick marks be invisible. Options for the labels determine where they appear relative to the axis line. Remember that the Scale command from the Format menu controls the number of tick marks on the axes.

Formatting and Changing the Axis Labels

You can change the font, size, style, and color of labels on an axis. After highlighting the axis to which the labels apply, choose the Font command from the Format menu; the familiar Font dialog box appears from which you can select the font, size, style, and color.

You cannot change vertical axis labels; they are calculated according to the Format Scale settings. You can change the category axis labels, however, by following these steps:

1. Type the new category labels on the worksheet in a block of cells (in an "out-of-the-way" location).

2. Select the range containing the new labels.

3. Select Copy from the Edit menu.

4. Activate the chart menus by double-clicking on the chart within the worksheet.

5. Select the Paste Special command from the Edit menu. Make sure that the Categories in First Row and Replace Existing Categories options are checked. (The Categories in the First Row option changes to the Categories in First Column option if you entered the new labels into a column.)

6. Press Return.

Note that the number of new labels does not need to match the original number of labels. Excel places the labels along the axis from left to right. Another way to change the category labels follows:

1. Enter the new labels on the worksheet in a range of cells.

2. With the chart menus active, select the Edit Series command from the Chart menu.

3. Highlight the data in the X Labels box and press the Backspace key to erase the data.

4. With the cursor still in the X Labels box, click on the worksheet and highlight the range of cells containing the new category labels. The range you specify appears as a reference in the X Labels box.

5. Press Return.

Adding and Moving Chart Arrows

To emphasize a specific message in a chart or to direct a chart label to a specific element, you can use chart arrows. The process of adding and manipulating chart arrows is similar to adding and manipulating descriptive text. You can add as many arrows as you want and place them anywhere on the chart. You also can format chart arrows to achieve different effects.

To add an arrow, activate the chart window and select the Add Arrow command from the Chart menu. An arrow appears in the chart. Use the mouse or the arrow keys to move the arrow into the proper position. Using the mouse, click on the arrow and drag the arrow to a new location. If you use the keyboard, highlight the arrow, select the Move command from the Format menu, use the arrow keys to move the arrow around the chart, and press Return when you are finished.

You can enlarge an arrow by dragging the highlighted squares that surround the arrow object. Alternatively, you can use the keyboard to enlarge the arrow: highlight the arrow, select the Size command from the Format menu, use the cursor-movement keys to change the size of the arrow object, and then press Return.

You can format the arrow with the Patterns command on the Format menu. After you highlight an arrow and select Format Patterns, the dialog box shown in figure 12.23 appears.

Figure 12.24 shows some examples of formatted arrows. Notice that these arrows have different shafts and heads.

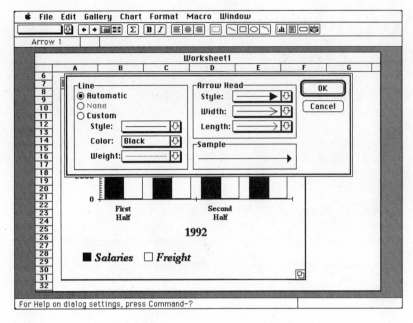

Fig. 12.23. *The Format Patterns dialog box for arrows.*

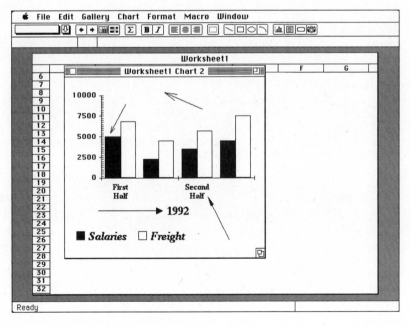

Fig. 12.24. *Several arrow formats.*

Adding and Modifying Grid Lines

Adding grid lines is another way that you can enhance a chart. Excel enables you to add vertical and horizontal grid lines to any chart. In fact, Excel offers two types of vertical grid lines and two types of horizontal grid lines. *Major grid lines* extend from the major axis divisions; *minor grid lines* extend from the minor axis divisions. Figure 12.25 shows an example of grid lines used in a chart.

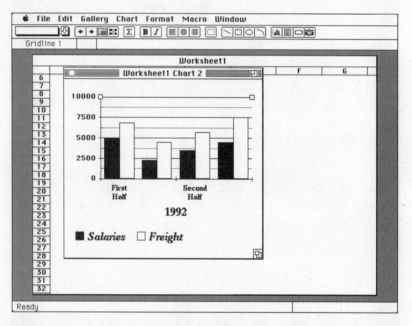

Fig. 12.25. A chart with major and minor grid lines.

To add grid lines, select the Gridlines command from the Chart menu. The dialog box that appears presents major and minor grid lines for both axes. Check the appropriate boxes and press Return to add the lines to your chart.

After you add grid lines, you may want to change their color or pattern. You can format the category axis grid lines independently of the value axis grid lines. First, highlight a category or value grid line. (Using the mouse to highlight grid lines can be tricky. To avoid problems, click on a line in the middle of the grid—as opposed to a line at the edge of the chart—to ensure that you select the grid and not the plot area.) A single vertical or horizontal grid line should be highlighted.

When a grid line is highlighted, select the Patterns command from the Format menu. The dialog box shown in figure 12.26 appears. Select the options to change the pattern, color, and thickness of the lines. When you press Return, Excel applies the format to all the horizontal or vertical lines—depending on your original selection. Major and minor grid lines are changed separately. To change all minor grid line patterns, select a minor grid line; select a major grid line to change all major grid line patterns.

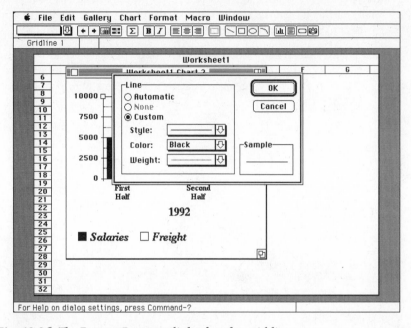

Fig. 12.26. *The Format Patterns dialog box for grid lines.*

Note: Grid lines extend throughout but not beyond the entire plot area.

Tip: Avoiding Beginning with a Plain Chart
Remember that you can select many predesigned or built-in charts from the Gallery menu. You may want to start with one of the built-in charts and then remove or add elements. Working with a built-in chart can be faster than starting with a basic chart and adding the formats.

Changing Overall Chart Formats

The Main Chart command on the Format menu dramatically affects the overall chart format—including stacking, overlapping plot points, changing the chart type, and setting the angle denoting pie wedges. The built-in charts apply many of these options to the basic charts, but you may want to add these formats to a chart without selecting one of the built-in formats.

If you change an existing chart to a built-in format, all custom formatting is erased. If, however, you add formats by using the Main Chart command from the Format menu, existing custom formats remain intact. When you select the Format Main Chart command, the dialog box shown in figure 12.27 appears.

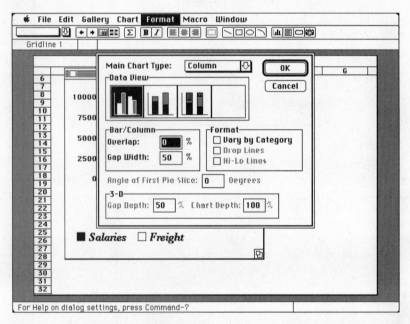

Fig. 12.27. The Main Chart dialog box.

The Main Chart dialog box options include the following:

- *Main Chart Type:* Changes the type of chart without changing any custom formatting already applied. You may have to adjust the position of unattached text after changing the chart type.

- *Data View:* Offers various chart options, including stacked charts, 100% stacked charts, exploded pie charts, and so on. Click on the data view of your choice. Your selected view may change some of the other options in this dialog box. Choosing a stacked data view, for example, enters 100 into the Overlap option.

- *Vary by Categories:* Assigns a different pattern to each plot point when the chart includes only one data series. Usually, similar plot points have the same patterns and colors. When you use this option, you can change the pattern of each plot point individually by selecting the plot point and using the Patterns command from the Format menu.

- *Drop Lines:* Adds a vertical separator line between plot points of area and line charts. This option is useful when points merge together, as in an area chart. Figure 12.28 shows drop lines added to a line chart.

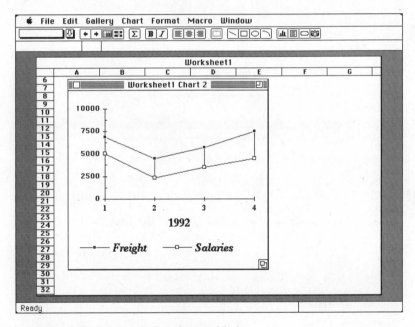

Fig. 12.28. *A line chart with drop lines added.*

- *High-Low Lines:* Adds lines that extend from the highest value to the lowest value in each series. To get vertical lines, you also must enter 100 in the % Overlap option and select Overlapped. The Hi-Lo Lines option is available for line charts only.

- *Overlapped:* Overlaps the plot points within each series. Use this option to adjust the degree of overlap for column and bar charts, as shown in figure 12.29. This example uses 30% overlapping (0% is normal and 100% is completely overlapped and usually is used only on stacked charts).

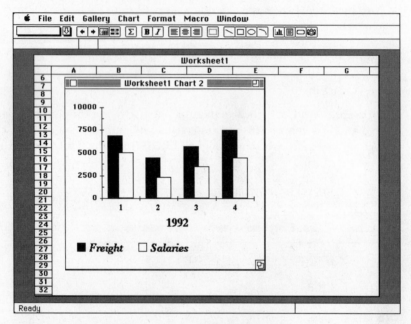

Fig. 12.29. *A standard column chart with 30% overlap.*

- *Gap Width:* Changes the amount of space between the categories.

- *Angle of First Pie Slice:* Sets the angle of the first slice in a pie. An angle of 0 degrees places the first slice vertically at the top of the pie. Angles are measured clockwise from the top of the pie.

- *Gap Depth:* Sets the amount of space between the data series of a 3-D chart. This setting widens or narrows the plot points (for example, bars of a column chart), because a larger gap depth requires a narrower bar to accommodate it. Figure 12.30 shows a 3-D chart with a gap depth of 500.

- *Chart Depth:* Sets the depth of the entire 3-D chart. This setting makes the chart long or short. Combine this with the Gap Depth and Gap Width options for various effects. Figure 12.31 shows a 3-D chart with a gap width of 500 (and a normal gap depth).

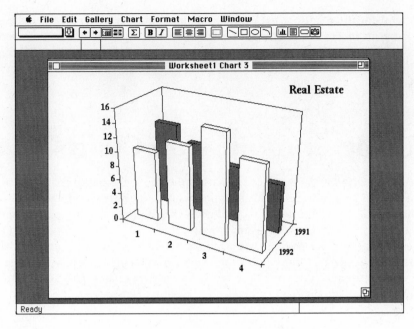

Fig. 12.30. *A 3-D chart with the Gap Depth setting of 500.*

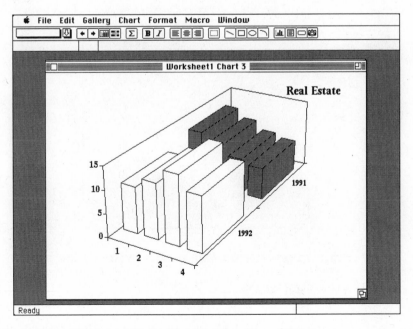

Fig. 12.31. *A 3-D chart with the Chart Depth setting of 500.*

After using these options to customize a chart, you may want to use the chart format again. Set the chart as the preferred format by using the Set Preferred command from the Format menu. You then can reuse the chart by selecting the Preferred command from the Gallery menu (see Chapter 11 for more details).

Using Combination Charts

A *combination chart* is one chart that is split into two types of charts. Some data items are represented by one type of chart and the rest of the data items are represented by another type of chart, but all items relate to the same categories. A combination chart, for example, can show data points in a scatter chart and a line representing the trend or regression among the points. The chart in figure 12.32 shows columns representing actual sales and a line representing projected sales. All the data relates to the same four quarters; in fact, the data comes from the same data range.

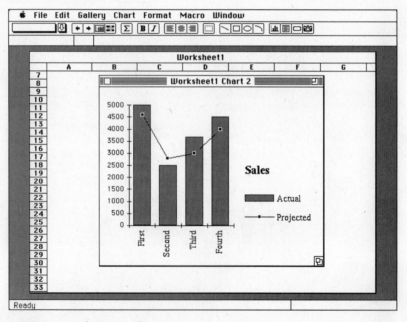

Fig. 12.32. *A combination chart.*

You can create a combination chart in two ways. One method is to choose a preformatted combination chart available through the Combination command on the Gallery menu. (You then can customize the chart.) The other method is to start with any chart type and use the Add Overlay command from the Chart menu to create a combination chart that splits the data items into two groups—one group for each type of chart. When you use the Chart Add Overlay command, Excel creates a line chart as the second (overlay) chart type. You can, however, change the types of charts used in the combination. You also can format both types of charts, as described in the next section.

When you turn a regular chart into a combination chart (by using the Gallery Combination command or the Chart Add Overlay command), Excel splits the data items into two groups. The original chart type (showing the first half of the items) is called the *main chart*, and the new type of chart (showing the second half of the items) is called the *overlay chart*, because it sits "on top of" the main chart. If the chart has an odd number of items, the main chart gets the extra item.

By using the Overlay command from the Format menu after splitting the data, you can determine how many series are displayed in the main chart and how many are in the overlay. The Format Overlay command produces the dialog box shown in figure 12.33. The First Overlay Series option controls where the split occurs. If a chart has 10 items (10 different series), entering the number 6 splits the chart in half (series 6 being the first series in the overlay chart). Entering 10 specifies only the last item in the overlay chart, entering 9 specifies the last two items, and so on.

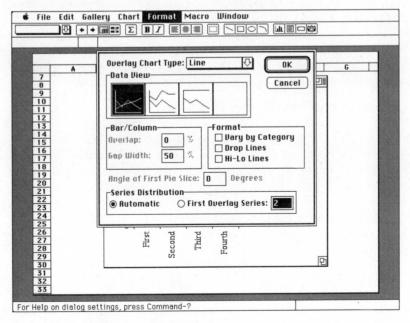

Fig. 12.33. *The Format Overlay dialog box.*

You may want to split the chart randomly—or perhaps you want to use one item from the middle of the chart in the overlay. Although you cannot change the way Excel splits the chart, you can rearrange items so that the desired item is in the overlay. To achieve your goal, you do not have to rearrange the data in the worksheet data range. For details, see "Rearranging Chart Data," later in this chapter.

Changing Combination Chart Types

You can change the main chart and the overlay chart types. Use the Overlay command from the Format menu to change the overlay chart type and the Main command from the Format menu to change the main chart type. Next, select type and format options for the chart. Details about these formatting options are provided earlier in this chapter in "Changing Overall Chart Formats."

Using Stacked Charts in Combination Charts

Be careful when using stacked or 100 percent charts in combination charts, because the resulting plot points may not represent the data accurately. The height of a stacked column chart, for example, represents the total value of items, but if some items are split into an overlay chart, their values still are figured into the stacked chart. This situation distorts the height of the stacked columns and may not accurately represent the data.

Suppose that you want to display quarterly expense items in stacked columns, with the expense totals for each quarter represented by the height of each column. Now suppose that you want to display last year's totals as a line in an overlay chart. Unfortunately, adding a data item with last year's totals changes the heights of the stacked columns and the distribution of data within each stack. The heights of the bars no longer reflect this year's totals but rather this year's totals plus last year's totals, even though last year's data is displayed in the overlay chart.

Formatting Combination Charts

Remember that the overlay chart always is on top of the main chart. Be sure to use an overlay chart that looks appropriate over the main chart. You can choose one of the preformatted combinations with the Combination command from the Gallery menu, or you can select the two chart types individually by using the Chart Type option in the Format Main and Format Overlay dialog boxes. If you use overlapping chart types, such as an area chart with a column chart, format the area chart as the main chart and the column chart as the overlay chart. Figures 12.34 and 12.35 show the contrast.

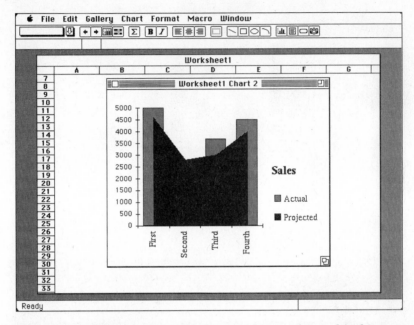

Fig. 12.34. *A combination chart with the area chart as the overlay chart.*

Notice that in figure 12.34 the area chart begins and ends between the columns of the overlay chart. In other words, the area chart does not extend to the edges of the plot area. You may think that the chart would look better if the area or line started at the left edge of the plot area and ended at the right edge, as figure 12.35 illustrates. This is controlled by the area chart's Overlap value in the Format Main dialog box. To change an area chart's Overlap value, temporarily change it to a column chart with the Chart Type option. Change the Overlap value, and then change the chart back to an area chart.

You can create some interesting combinations using only column charts. The chart in figure 12.36 combines two column charts; the overlay chart contains all but one of the data series. Because the main chart has only one data series, the four columns representing that series (the first data series) are expanded to fit comfortably in the chart. The overlay chart was overlapped by 50 percent through the Format Overlay command, which makes the two overlay series overlap each other, as well as the main chart's series.

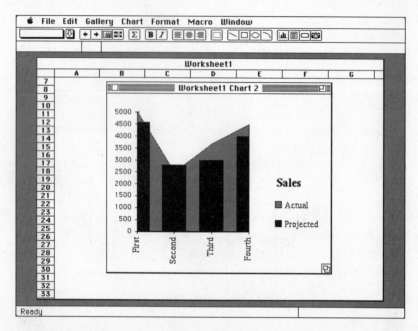

Fig. 12.35. *A combination chart with the column chart as the overlay chart.*

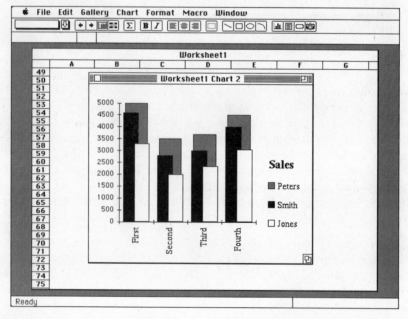

Fig. 12.36. *Using two column charts in a combination.*

Deleting and Adding Data Series

Although a chart is linked to its respective data range in a worksheet file, you can remove or add data without specifying a new data range. If you decide to remove an item from the chart, simply delete the item. If you want to add a new item, simply copy the item. The next two sections provide details.

Deleting Chart Data

Deleting data from a chart is simple. Remember, however, that data points are grouped in series. One item may be represented by several columns or plot points, depending on the number of categories in the chart. When you remove a data item, you remove the entire series. To delete chart data, follow these steps:

1. Click on the data series. (You can click on any data point in the series.)

2. Press the Backspace key to remove the formula in the formula bar.

3. Press Return.

When you select a data item, its formula appears in the formula bar. Excel uses this formula to create the data item in the chart. By removing this formula, you essentially remove the item. (See "Changing a Chart's Data Range," later in this chapter, for more information about the formulas.)

You also can delete all data associated with a chart by selecting the chart and the Clear command from the Edit menu. Excel enables you to clear everything (All), only the format of the chart (Formats), or only the formulas creating the chart (Formulas). Clearing a chart's data can be useful for changing the orientation of the data and for creating blank formatted charts into which you can copy any data. Blank formatted charts are useful as templates for new data. Erasing a chart's data series has no effect on the worksheet data.

Adding Chart Data

You can add a new data series to an existing chart by following these steps:

1. Activate the chart and select the Edit Series command from the Chart menu. The Edit Series dialog box appears.

2. Select the New Series option in the Series list.

3. Press Tab until the cursor is in the Y Values box. The Y Values box should be empty.

4. Click on the worksheet, drag to highlight the range containing the new data series, and press Return.

5. If the series does not contain a label (legend entry), enter a label or cell reference into the Name box for this series. You can find details about changing legend entries in "Changing Chart Legends," earlier in this chapter.

Another way to add a new data series to a chart is to use the Copy command from the Edit menu to copy data from a worksheet. Although the new data range does not need to be adjacent to the original data range, the new data range should contain the same number of categories. After copying the information, activate the chart and use the Paste command from the Edit menu to paste the data into the chart. Excel creates a new data series from the pasted data and adds a column, bar, or other appropriate point to the chart.

If the copied data range contains fewer categories than the original data range, Excel adds the extra series to the first few categories only. If, for example, you copy a block of three data points to a chart that has four categories, Excel adds the extra series (column or bar) to the first three categories. The last category will have fewer bars than the other categories.

When you copy a new series into an existing chart, Excel places the new series after the series already in place. If the existing chart is a combination, the new item appears as the overlay chart. You can use the procedures described in the next section to move the series to another position.

Rearranging Chart Data

Rearranging chart data can be useful for several reasons. You may want to rearrange combination charts to display the desired data series in an overlay chart. You may want to change the order of wedges in a pie chart or the columns in a column chart as well. You do not have to change the order of data in the worksheet data range to accomplish this task; instead, use the Edit Series command from the Chart menu.

To rearrange chart data, select Edit Series from the Chart menu and choose a data series from the Series list. Next, change the Plot Order value for that series. Entering 1 makes the series appear first in the chart. When you change the placement of a data item, Excel rearranges the remaining items so that they remain in order. Therefore, beginning the rearranging process with the first item is a good idea; subsequent changes do not change the order you established.

> *Note:* Another way to rearrange data series in a chart is to edit the series formulas. For more information on this subject, see "Changing a Chart's Data Range".

Note that patterns do not move with the series. In other words, patterns apply to the position and not to the series. You can change the patterns by using the Patterns command from the Format menu.

Changing a Chart's Data Range

Excel uses special formulas, called *series formulas*, to create charts. These formulas consist of the SERIES function and cell references and they appear in the chart window's formula bar when you highlight a data series. Formulas control all aspects of chart values. With a little knowledge of the SERIES function, you can make all kinds of changes to a chart. You can cause a chart to reference data from two worksheets, for example, or you can change the category axis titles used in the chart. You also can change the labels used for the chart's legend so that they reference external worksheets. The series formula uses the following format:

=SERIES(*series_name,category_label_range,data_item_range, placement_in_chart*)

A series formula may look like this:

=SERIES(EXPENSES!$A$2,EXPENSES!$B$1:$E$1,EXPENSES!$B$2:$E$2,1)

This formula indicates the following:

- The name of this data item (used in the legend) is located on the EXPENSES worksheet in cell A2.

- The range containing the category labels (used for the category axis) is B1:E1 on the EXPENSES worksheet.

- The range containing the values of this series is B2:E2 on the EXPENSES worksheet.

- This particular data series is the first in each category.

By changing various elements, you can control the data that the chart uses. You may want to change the external cell and range references to range names, for example. Such a formula may read as follows:

=SERIES(EXPENSES!Salaries_Title,EXPENSES!Headings,EXPENSES!Salaries,1)

Salaries_Title, Headings, and Salaries represent the appropriate ranges in the worksheet. (Of course, you must apply these range names in the original worksheet before you use them in the chart's formulas.) The advantage of using names rather than cell and range references is that changes in the original worksheet do not affect the chart. If you add or remove cells, the range names do not change.

> *Note:* Remember: to view a series formula, highlight a chart's data series and look at the formula bar. The series formula for the selected series appears in the bar.

Summary

This chapter provided everything you need to know about formatting and customizing charts in Excel. You learned how to change the patterns of various chart elements and how to change the font, size, style, and color of all chart text. This chapter also discussed combination charts and how to customize them. The keys to combination charts are the Main and Overlay commands from the Format menu, which control the appearance of the two "combined" charts. This chapter also showed you how to add data elements from a chart by using the Edit Series command from the chart menu. Remember the following important points:

- Use the Add Legend command from the Chart menu to place a legend on the chart. You can move the legend using the mouse.

- Use the Patterns command from the Format menu to change the pattern of most chart elements. First, highlight the element you want to change.

- You can change the font, size, style, and color of chart text by highlighting the text and choosing the Font command from the Format menu. (To change the axis labels, you must highlight the axis, not the labels.)

- You can change the value of any plotted point by highlighting it and then dragging it with the mouse.

- Highlight a plot point by clicking on the data series and using the right-arrow key to highlight individual plot points in that series.

- Combination charts are created out of standard charts. Use the Add Overlay command from the Chart menu to turn a normal chart into a combination chart. Alternatively, select one of the combination charts from the Gallery menu.

- Excel automatically splits the data series evenly between the overlay and main charts in the combination chart. You can change this split by using the First Series in Overlay option in the Format Overlay dialog box.

- You can reposition the series in the chart by editing the Plot Order value in the Chart Edit Series dialog box.

- Add data series to a chart by copying the data from the worksheet and pasting it into the chart.

13

Drawing

Y ou may not think of Excel as a drawing package, but it contains some useful drawing tools. Drawing tools can enhance your worksheet presentations and annotate complex worksheets. This chapter shows how to apply Excel's drawing capabilities to your worksheets. By manipulating basic objects, you can achieve some attractive effects.

Getting an Overview of Drawing

Excel's drawing capabilities can enhance your worksheets in many ways. You will find it easy to annotate your worksheets and charts to enhance your presentations.These annotations include special notes and explanatory information on the worksheets and chart. Figure 13.1 shows an example.

You also may add graphics to your worksheets just for design purposes. You can include logos, special illustrations, or scanned images. Figure 13.2 shows an example.

Graphics also are useful for creating forms. By adding shading, boxes, and other graphic devices, you can create attractive business forms in Excel. Excel is a powerful forms designer. Figure 13.3 shows an example.

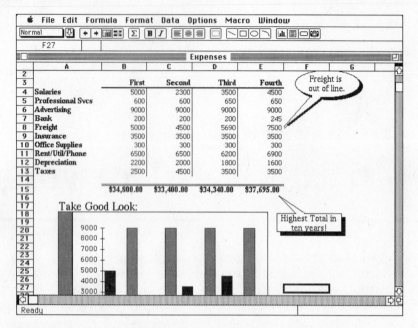

Fig. 13.1. *Using graphics to annotate a worksheet.*

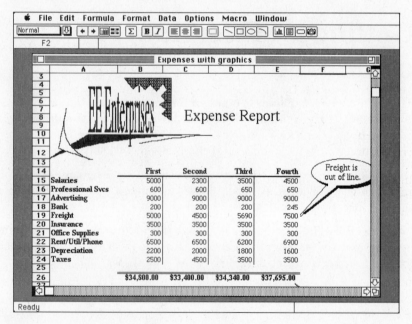

Fig. 13.2. *Using graphics to enhance a presentation.*

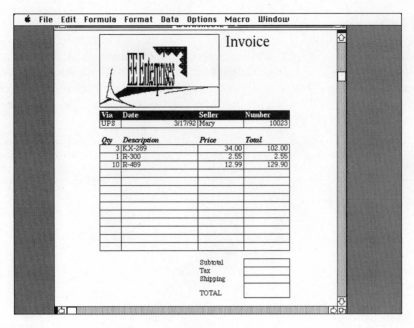

Fig. 13.3. *Using graphics to produce forms.*

Excel enables you to draw on the worksheet with its new drawing tools. Although Excel is no substitute for a drawing or painting program, its tools are sufficient for enhancing worksheets. When you need more than Excel offers, you can bring outside art work into your worksheets by using the Copy and Paste procedures. Alternatively, use the Publish/Subscribe features of System 7 to keep the imported artwork up-to-date. See Chapter 8 for details on this feature.

Excel uses an object-oriented drawing method; it draws rudimentary objects individually. Each object resides on a separate *layer*, which means that objects can overlap each other. All object layers are above (on top of) the worksheet, so all objects cover worksheet data. As you will learn later, however, you can make objects transparent if you want to see through to the worksheet. By overlapping and formatting objects, you can create complex illustrations.

Excel's rudimentary objects consist of ovals, rectangles, curves, and lines. You may be surprised at how much you accomplish with these simple objects. The rest of this chapter shows you how to accomplish these tasks.

Drawing Objects

Excel gives you four basic drawing tools for creating lines, ovals, rectangles, and semicircles (arcs). You also get four tools for creating special objects: text boxes, charts, buttons, and pictures. A final tool enables you to select objects after they appear on the worksheet. All these tools are located on the Toolbar (see fig. 13.4).

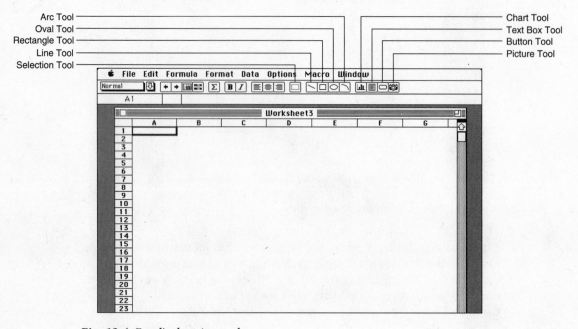

Fig. 13.4. *Excel's drawing tools.*

Descriptions of the drawing tools follow:

- *Selection Tool:* Selects an object or group of objects so that you can move or edit them. Click on the tool and then click to surround the objects you want with the selection box. All objects inside the box will be selected.

- *Line Tool:* Creates lines and arrows. Click on the tool and then click and drag on the worksheet to create the line. Press Shift while drawing to draw only horizontal, vertical, and 45-degree lines.

- *Rectangle Tool:* Creates rectangles and squares. Click on the tool and then click and drag on the worksheet to create the rectangle. Press Shift while drawing to create perfect squares.

- *Oval Tool:* Creates circles and ovals. Click on the tool and then click and drag on the worksheet to create the oval. Press Shift while drawing to create perfect circles.

- *Arc Tool:* Creates arcs or semicircles. Each arc represents one quarter of an oval. The relative distance between your click and release points determines the size and shape of the arc. Click on the tool, and then click and drag on the worksheet to create the arc.

- *Chart Tool:* Creates charts from the highlighted data range. The chart appears in a box, which can be controlled like any object. See Chapter 11 for a discussion of charts.

- *Text Box Tool:* Creates text boxes into which you can type information. Draw this box as you would draw a rectangle. Next, you can type any text into this box and format it with various fonts and styles.

- *Button Tool:* Creates buttons on the worksheet. You can attach any command macro to a button and then run the macro by pushing the button. Buttons are created like rectangles, but have special qualities. See Chapter 18 for a discussion of these qualities.

- *Picture Tool:* Creates a picture of the highlighted worksheet range. The picture is drawn like a rectangle and contains a "live" link to the original range. Pictures and their links are discussed in Chapter 7. Controlling picture objects is discussed in "Inserting Pictures," later in this chapter.

Tip: Drawing Objects with Restriction
If you press Shift while you draw an object, it will be drawn to specific restrictions. Lines are drawn only vertically, horizontally, or at 45-degree angles; ovals are drawn as perfect circles; rectangles are drawn as perfect squares; arcs are drawn as perfect quarter circles.

Tip: Drawing Objects to the Grid
If you press the Command key while you drag the mouse to create an object, the object will be drawn to the worksheet grid. In other words, it will match the size and shape of a block of cells on the worksheet. This procedure can be useful for making your objects line up with worksheet data.

The four basic objects (lines, rectangles, ovals, and arcs) are simple graphic objects that you can draw with the click-and-drag technique. The four special objects (text boxes, buttons, charts, and pictures) require a bit more explaining.

Creating Text Boxes

Text boxes are very similar to rectangles, but they also hold text. After creating the text box, you can begin typing information into it. To create a text box, follow these steps:

1. Click on the Text tool in the Toolbar.

2. Click and drag on the worksheet to create the box. Hold the Shift key while drawing to make a perfect square. Press the Command key while drawing to make the box conform to the worksheet grid.

3. When finished drawing the box, begin typing.

The dimensions of the box control the way text wraps inside the box. You can press Return to wrap a line before it would normally wrap.

After entering text, you can choose the Font command from the Format menu to choose a font, size, style, and color for highlighted text inside the box. You can mix formats within the same text box. You also can choose the Text command from the Format menu to change the orientation and alignment of the text. Figure 13.5 shows a formatted text box.

> **Tip: Using Buttons on Text Box Text**
> You can format the text in a text box by highlighting the text and using the Toolbar tools. You quickly can align text or make it bold and italic by using the tools on the Toolbar. See Chapter 4 for details about highlighting text.

After you click outside the text box on the worksheet, the cursor disappears from the box. You later can edit the text inside a text box by moving the pointer to the box and clicking twice; this places the cursor inside the box. Now you can use standard text-editing commands to make changes (see Chapter 4). If you used the Text command from the Format menu to change the orientation of the text, Excel may change that orientation temporarily so that you can perform your edits. When you finish, the text returns to its assigned orientation.

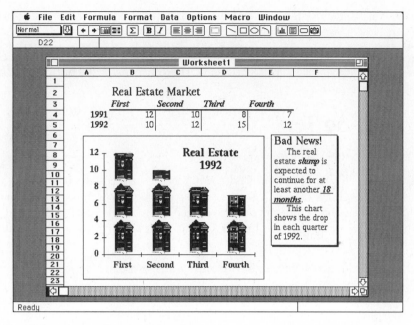

Fig. 13.5. *Formatted text in a text box.*

Creating Buttons

Buttons are like text boxes because they are rectangular and can contain text. You cannot apply as many formatting changes to button text, however, as you can to box text. You use buttons primarily to invoke macros with simple point-and-click movements. Before you create a button, you should have a macro ready to attach to it. To create a button, follow these steps:

1. Click on the Button tool in the Toolbar.

2. Click and drag on the worksheet to create the button.

3. When you release the mouse, Excel asks you to attach a macro to the button. Select from the macros in the list or just press Esc (⌘-.) to skip this step.

Note: When a macro is attached to the button, clicking on it will simply "push" the button. To move or edit the button, press the Command key while clicking on the button.

After you draw the button, Excel asks you to indicate which macro to connect to it. Macros are discussed in Chapter 17.

You may want to use a button instead of a text box. Just click the Cancel button when Excel asks you for a macro. Then click inside the button to edit its text.

Creating Charts

You can create charts with the Chart tool. You can manipulate charts just like any other object you draw. You can overlap charts with other objects, move them, change their sizes and shapes, and so on. Creating and manipulating charts is discussed fully in Chapter 11, but a brief outline of how to create a chart follows:

1. Highlight the data range containing the chart data.

2. Click on the Chart tool in the Toolbar.

3. Click on the worksheet and drag to create the chart box.

4. Double-click on the chart to activate the chart menus, which you can use to customize the default chart.

Remember that charts behave like other objects you can draw. The information in this chapter applies to charts as well as other objects.

Inserting Pictures

The last drawing tool in the Toolbar is the Picture tool. This tool creates pictures of worksheet cells. These pictures are a special kind of copy of the cells and are considered objects by Excel. You can create a picture in any worksheet or any other application that supports OLE (object-linking and embedding). Although pictures are discussed at length in Chapter 8, the following serves as a brief overview:

1. Highlight any block of worksheet cells.

2. Click on the Picture tool.

3. Click on the worksheet to create the picture (you do not need to drag the mouse).

Pictures act like any other objects you can draw; the commands and options discussed in this chapter apply equally to them.

Selecting and Editing Objects

To select an object, simply click anywhere on that object. Selected objects have small squares around their edges called *size boxes*. You can click and drag on these squares to change the object's size and shape (see fig. 13.6).

You also can select an object by using the Selection tool. Click on the tool and then click and drag on the worksheet to surround the object you want to select. When you release the mouse button, the object is selected. You also can use the Selection tool to select several objects at once. Just surround all the objects with the Selection tool as you drag the mouse.

To move an object, simply click and drag it to a new location. If you have trouble moving an object, try clicking and dragging its edges. (Sometimes clicking the middle of an object serves a different purpose.) Avoid clicking on the corners of the object (directly on a size box), because this procedure changes the object's size and shape.

> **Tip: Using Shift-Click to Select Multiple Objects**
> Another way to select several objects is to press Shift while clicking on various objects. All the objects will be selected—provided that you click in the proper places.

Copying, Deleting, and Moving Objects

You can duplicate objects by using the Copy and Paste commands in the Edit menu. Follow these steps:

1. Click on an object to select it.

2. Select the Copy command from the Edit menu (or press ⌘-C).

3. Select the Paste command from the Edit menu (or press ⌘-V).

4. Move the duplicate to the desired position on the worksheet.

This procedure also works between worksheets and between Excel and other applications that support Object Linking and Embedding (OLE). This is not the best procedure, however, for copying graphs or pictures.

To remove an object, you can use the Cut command from the Edit menu. Unlike using this command on worksheet data, you need not follow it with the Paste command. As soon as you use Edit Cut, the object is removed. You also can remove objects by selecting Clear from the Edit menu.

Another way to delete an object is to select it and then press the Backspace key.

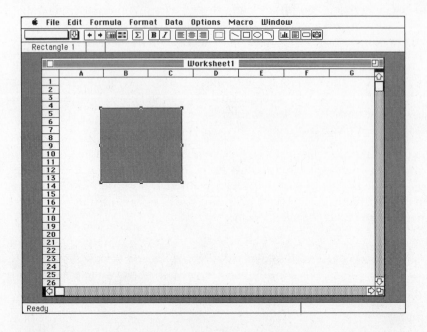

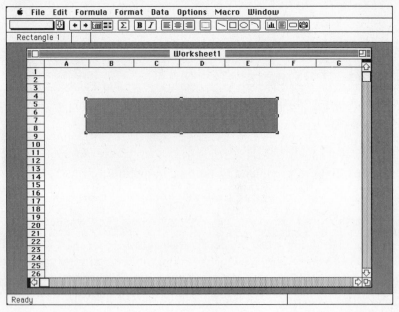

Fig. 13.6. Changing an object's size and shape.

Protecting Objects

Object protection is very much like cell protection. You can lock an object to prevent it from being moved or deleted. Simply select the Object Protection command from the Format menu after you select an object. Then place a check mark in the dialog box to protect the object. You can activate the protection by choosing Protect Document from the Options menu, as described in Chapter 3. Note that all objects start out protected, but the Protect Document command starts out in unprotected mode. All you have to do to protect objects, therefore, is choose Protect Document. (You may want to use the Object Protection command from the Format menu to unprotect individual objects.)

Suppose that you have a worksheet that contains a logo and a graph. Both of these are objects. You may want to prevent the logo from being moved, while being able to move the graph around freely. First, select the graph and choose the Object Protection command. Remove the check mark from the dialog box that appears and press OK. Now turn protection on for the worksheet by choosing the Protect Document command from the Options menu. Only the graph will be moveable.

Overlapping Objects

Objects overlap each other in the order in which they were created. Objects drawn first are covered up by newer objects. This rule can be useful for creating special effects, but you may need to change the overlapping order of objects if you don't draw them in correct sequence.

You can bring any object to the top of the others by selecting it and then choosing the Bring to Front command from the Format menu. The Send to Back command from the Format menu sends the object to the back of the stack. Remember that objects, even when in the back, are always on top of the worksheet data.

Hiding and Displaying Objects

The Display command from the Options menu offers three display options for objects: Show All, Show Placeholders, and Hide All. The Show All option displays all objects normally. You would use Show All after using one of the other two options. The Hide All option temporarily hides all objects (including graphs and buttons) until you use the Show All command. These options can be useful when you are working on the worksheet or in your macros for making objects appear and disappear. The Show Placeholders option is used primarily for graphs and pictures. It shows the position and size of each object using a placeholder, but the object itself does not show. Figure 13.7 shows an example.

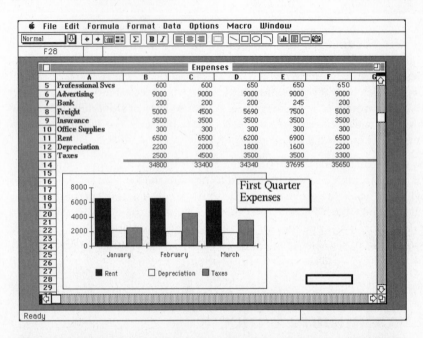

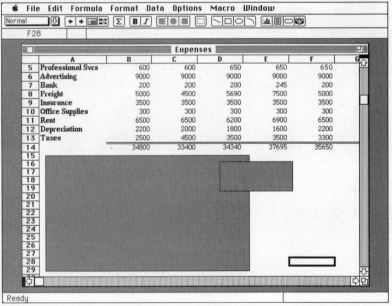

Fig. 13.7. The screen before and after using the Show Placeholders command.

Showing graphs and pictures as placeholders can speed performance of Excel and is useful when you are making numerous changes to a worksheet.

Grouping Objects

Although you can select several objects at the same time and perform operations on them as a group, these objects return to their separate status eventually. You may have difficulty predicting how sizing changes will affect a group of individual objects. Excel therefore enables you to turn several objects into a *grouped object* which it treats as one object. You can group objects by selecting them and then choosing the Group command from the Format menu. To make the objects independent again, highlight the grouped object and select Ungroup from the Format menu.

> **Tip: Using Object Numbers**
> Note that all objects have numbers. When you select an object, its number appears in the active cell indicator box in the top left corner of the worksheet. This number is useful in macros for identifying the object.

> **Tip: Using Grouped Objects in Other Groups**
> You can place grouped objects into other groups. Keep in mind, however, that you will have to perform as many ungroup commands as you did group commands to return the objects to their original condition. Objects are ungrouped in the same order in which they were grouped.

Understanding the Object-Worksheet Relationship

Objects have an interesting relationship with the worksheet. They are not actually part of the worksheet because the objects appear above the worksheet on the object layer. The column widths and cell heights in the worksheet can affect objects, however. Objects can be attached to the worksheet cells that they cover, so when you adjust the column width or row height of cells that appear below an object, the object changes its size and shape to reflect the cell changes.

Similarly, inserting and deleting cells can cause the objects to move with their underlying rows and columns. This feature usually is convenient, because many graphics are drawn on the worksheet to correspond to specific cells. If you want to detach objects from their underlying cells, however, select the object and choose the Object Placement command from the Format menu. You can use the following options:

- *Move and Size with Cells:* Sets the normal attached attributes. Adjustments to rows and columns affect the objects above them. Widening a column, for example, widens the object associated with (above) this column.

- *Move But Don't Size with Cells:* Links the object to its worksheet position but not to the height and width of the cells below it. If you insert or delete cells, therefore, the object moves. If you change cells' heights and widths, however, the object is not affected.

- *Don't Move or Size with Cells:* Detaches the object completely. No cell movement or adjustment affects the object.

You can apply different placement options to different objects on the same worksheet. Figures 13.8 and 13.9 illustrate placement options.

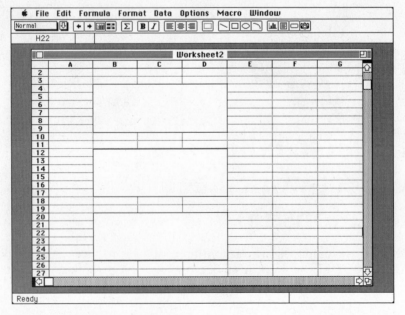

Fig. 13.8. The original worksheet with objects.

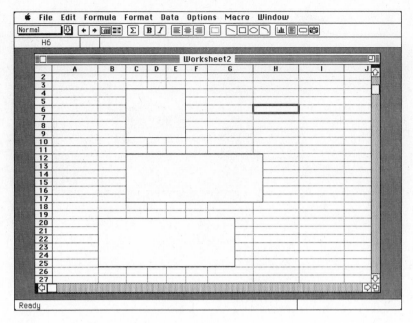

***Fig. 13.9.** The worksheet after adjusting and inserting cells.*

Figure 13.9 shows what happens to each object after inserting a new column (at column B) and making several other columns narrow. Notice that the object that does not move or size with cells did not move over when column B was inserted.

Formatting Objects

The Patterns command from the Format menu enables you to control the pattern that fills an object and the type of line that surrounds an object. Select the object and then choose Patterns from the Format menu. You can use this command on grouped objects also. Alternatively, you can double-click the object you want. The dialog box in figure 13.10 appears.

The dialog box has options for the border and interior of the object. Border options include line styles, colors, and weights (thicknesses). You also can choose None to remove the border. Interior options include patterns and colors. You can select Automatic to have Excel select the interior or None to make the object transparent.

The patterns dialog box is slightly different for lines. Because lines have no interior, you are not offered the interior pattern and color options. Instead, you can choose to add an arrow head to the line, making it into an arrow. Various arrowhead styles are available.

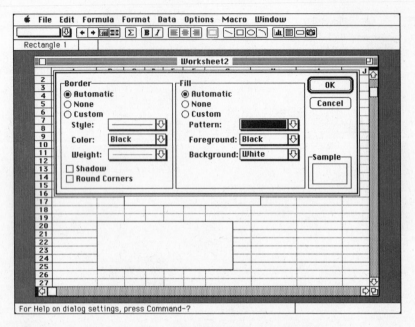

Fig. 13.10. The Format Patterns dialog box for rectangles.

Figure 13.11 shows some objects formatted with these various pattern options.

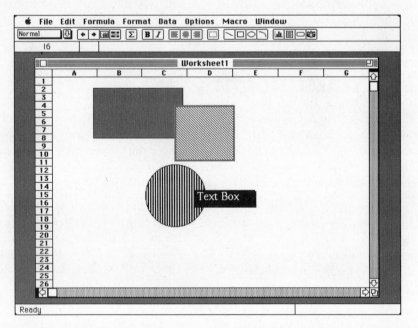

Fig. 13.11. Objects formatted with pattern options.

Customizing Colors

Excel Version 3.0 enables you to customize the 16 colors that appear in the Patterns dialog box. Rather than use the standard 16 colors, you can create 16 of your own for use in the worksheet.

To customize one or more of the 16 colors requires that you select a different "mix" of red, green, and blue. You can customize colors with the Color Palette command from the Options menu. Follow these steps:

1. Select Color Palette from the Options menu.

2. Choose the color you want to change and click on the Edit button.

3. Click and drag in the color wheel to locate the color you want. At the bottom of the dialog box, Excel shows you various elements that comprise the color.

4. After you locate the color you want, click on OK.

5. Click on OK again to return to the worksheet.

You can manually change the aspects of a color to create a color. Simply enter a value for any of the different color aspects. You can choose a color from the color wheel, for example, and then add to its red content by increasing the Red value. Experiment for best results.

Note: When you change one of the 16 colors, all objects or graphs that use the color are updated to the new color.

Tip: Using Custom Colors in Number Formats
You can use your edited colors in Excel's custom number formats by referring to the color number, as in [color 4]. You still can use the normal colors in your custom formats, too.

Tip: Copying Color Schemes between Worksheets
You can copy the colors you create for one worksheet into another. Just open both worksheets, and then activate the destination sheet. Choose the Options Color Palette Edit command and select the source worksheet from the list at the bottom of the dialog box. Click on OK when finished.

Using Outside Art

You can bring illustrations into Excel from other programs, such as MacDraw, Illustrator, or other art packages. Excel uses the Clipboard to transfer images. Follow these steps:

1. Enter the program containing the graphic image and use the program's Copy command to copy the image to the Clipboard.

2. Quit the program and enter Excel or, using MultiFinder, switch applications to enter Excel.

3. Select the Paste command from the Edit menu to insert the image into the worksheet.

> *Note:* Bit-mapped images enter Excel as a single object, but drawn images may remain as individual objects. If the procedure fails, you may have too little memory to keep the image on the Clipboard while you switch programs. Or, the Copy and Paste procedures may not be compatible between Excel and the other program. If this is the case, try using the Publish/Subscribe features of System 7 to exchange graphics between programs (see Chapter 7 for details).

At times, you may want to choose the Edit Paste Picture command (accessed by pressing Shift when you click on the Edit menu) instead of the Paste command from the Edit menu. This procedure pastes the copied data as a picture onto the worksheet; you can use this procedure to convert text to a graphic image. See Chapter 7 for more information about exchanging data between Excel and other programs.

Summary

This chapter discussed Excel's object-oriented drawing capabilities and its ability to import graphics from other programs. Using some simple objects, you can annotate and enhance your worksheets for better presentations. You can draw most objects by using the same basic procedure: click on the appropriate tool and then click and drag on the worksheet. Some objects have unique qualities that determine how you can format and control them, however. Remember the following points:

- To draw an object, click on an object tool and then click and drag on the worksheet.

- Select an object by clicking on it or by using the object selection tool to surround it.

- Graphs, buttons, text boxes, and pictures are objects that you can move, copy, overlap, and group like other objects.

- You can select several objects by pressing Shift while you click on them.

- Click and drag on the selection squares to change an object's size and shape.

- Use the Cut, Copy, and Paste procedures on objects to delete and copy them.

- Choose the Object Protection command from the Format menu to lock and unlock objects from being moved or changed. Use the Protect Document command from the Options menu to enable or disable protection.

- Choose the Patterns command from the Edit menu to control an object's interior and border pattern.

- Choose Bring to Front and Send to Back from the Format menu to change the overlapping order of objects.

- You can group objects by highlighting them and choosing the Group command from the Format menu.

Part III

Excel Databases

Includes

Using Databases: A Quick Start

Creating and Manipulating Databases

Using Advanced Database Techniques

14

Using Databases:
A Quick Start

This chapter takes you on a brief but complete tour of Excel's database features. (A *database* is simply a collection of records, each of which may contain several pieces of information.) Using Excel as a database is really just an extension of using the worksheet. Any worksheet data can be treated as database data; the difference is that database information has been designated as such. This designation increases the number of features you can use on that data: besides being able to use all the standard worksheet commands and options on database data, you can use Excel's database options. These options generally are useful for routinely adding, changing, and locating data within the database.

In this chapter you set up a simple database for an imaginary video rental store. You then discover how to add new records to the database and find records by specifying criteria. Finally, you learn how to extract a list of records from the database. After reading this chapter, you will be ready for the details of database management, which are presented in Chapter 15.

Entering Labels and Data

The first step in creating a database is to plan and enter the data. In Excel, you must set up databases so that records appear in worksheet rows. The data going across the row (that is, in the cells) makes up the record. A collection of rows is a database. To create the quick start sample database, enter the heading for each piece of data that the records will contain and then enter the data. Complete the following steps:

1. Start Excel with a new worksheet by double-clicking on the Excel program icon.

2. Move the pointer to cell A6 and type *Description*; then press Tab.

3. With the pointer in cell B6, type *Inv. No.* and press Tab again. Continue in this manner with the headings *Units Avail*, *Cost/Unit*, *Total Value*, and *Purchased*. The resulting worksheet should look like figure 14.1.

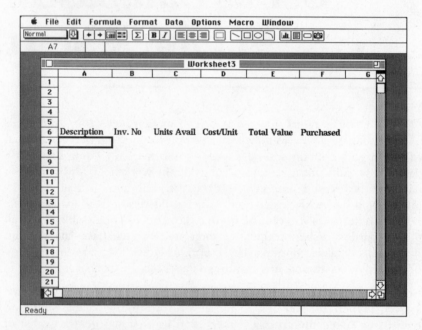

Fig. 14.1. *A database with the column headings entered.*

4. Highlight the range A7:F11.

5. With the pointer in cell A7, enter the following data for row 7, pressing Tab after each entry:

> Casablanca
> 13378
> 2
> 35.5
> C7*D7
> 1/15/85

After completing step 5, you may try skipping the values for column E in steps 6 through 9. If you do, use the Copy Down command from the Edit menu to copy the formula in cell E7 into the remaining cells of column E. See Chapter 3 for details about Copy Down.

6. Enter the following data for row 8, pressing Tab after each entry:

>Batman
>22442
>15
>19.95
>C8*D8
>11/15/89

7. Enter the following data for row 9, pressing Tab after each entry:

>Wall Street
>14554
>5
>19.95
>C9*D9
>5/1/88

8. Enter the following data for row 10, pressing Tab after each entry:

>African Queen
>17459
>1
>45.95
>C10*D10
>1/15/88

9. Enter the following data for row 11, pressing Tab after each entry:

>Star Trek VI
>27789
>9
>24.95
>C11*D11
>3/1/91

The worksheet should look like the worksheet in figure 14.2. Notice that each row represents a different video record.

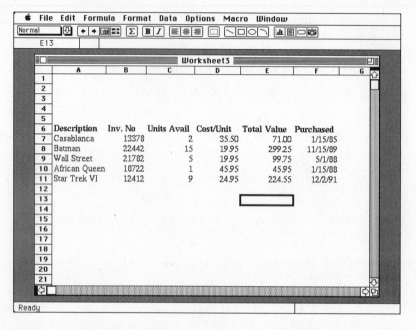

Fig. 14.2. *A database with data entered.*

Defining the Database Range

Now that the data is in place in the appropriate range, the next step is to define that range as the database range. Defining the database range tells Excel where the database exists on the worksheet. After it is aware of the database range, Excel provides several special features that you can use on that data. To define the database range in the sample database, follow these steps:

1. Highlight the range A6:F11, as shown in figure 14.3.

2. Choose the Set Database command from the Data menu. Doing so tells Excel that the selected range is a database.

> **Tip: Adding a Blank Row to the Bottom of the Database Range**
> Including an extra, blank row at the bottom of the database range is good practice. Doing so enables you to add new records at the bottom of the other records, just above the blank row. This procedure will become more clear as you complete the next few sections.

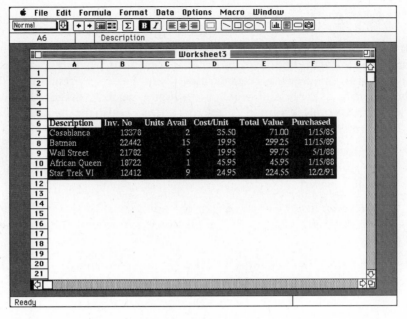

Fig. 14.3. *The selected database range.*

After you set the database range, Excel applies the name DATABASE to the range. This name appears with all other defined range names when you choose the Define Name command from the Formula menu. Because only one range can have the name DATABASE at any given time, you can have only one active database per worksheet. You always can apply the name to some other range, however, and switch from one active database to another. Simply use the Set Database command from the Data menu on the new range.

Adding Records

You can add records to the database any time after your database is established and the range is set. Excel provides two ways to add records to a database. The first method is to insert rows into the middle of the data and then insert new information into the rows. The second method is to use the automatic data form. When you add records through either of these methods, Excel expands the database range to include the new information.

Inserting Rows

If you choose to insert rows into the database range, you can insert them anywhere but at the bottom of the database (that is, anywhere but below the last record). This area may seem the most likely place to insert new records, but inserting at the bottom will not expand the database range to include the new rows (unless you add a blank row as described in the preceding tip). To add records by inserting rows, follow these steps:

1. Highlight a row within the database range. The row can be any database row containing a record. Highlight as many rows as you want to insert.

2. Select the Insert command from the Edit menu. The Insert dialog box appears. Select the Shift Cells Down option from this box; then press Return.

3. Fill in the new rows with the appropriate information.

Using the Data Form

The second way to insert records into the database is to use the *data form*—a special window containing the names of all the fields in the database and spaces for your new information. When you insert a record this way, Excel takes care of inserting it into the database and expanding the database range. Follow these steps to insert records by using a data form:

1. Select the Form command from the Data menu. Excel presents the data form (see fig. 14.4).

2. Click on the New button.

3. Enter the new information for each field of the new record. Press Tab after making each entry on the form. (For the sample database, enter any sample information.)

4. When the form is completely filled out, click on the New button again to insert another record.

5. When you finish entering the last new record, don't click on New to get another new screen. Instead, just click on the Exit button or click in the Close box of the data form window. Doing so returns you to the worksheet and enters the last record.

Notice that the data form inserts new records at the end of the database. Nevertheless, the database range has expanded to account for these new records.

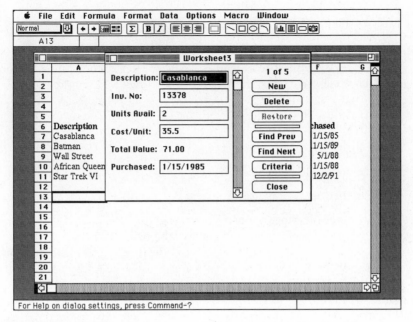

Fig. 14.4. The data form.

Finding Information in the Database

One feature of a database is that it enables you to use complex searches to find records. The more records you accumulate, the more useful this feature becomes. Using search criteria, you can find all records matching specific information, such as all records for Jane Doe. You can use comparison operators to find particular records, such as those with a total less than 125. The more specific the criteria, the fewer records will match. You therefore can find a specific record more quickly by entering as much information as possible about it.

You can find information in a database in two ways. The first method is to establish a criteria range, which contains the search criteria used to locate records in the database. The second method is to use the data form. Because this chapter provides only an overview of database operations, it offers an identical example for each method. In Chapter 15, however, you will discover some advantages and disadvantages to each method.

Using a Criteria Range

The *criteria range* contains a copy of each database heading and criteria specifications beneath those headings. To establish a criteria range for the sample database, first copy the database headings by completing these steps:

1. Highlight the range A6:F6.

2. Select the Copy command from the Edit menu.

3. Move the pointer to cell A1.

4. Select the Paste command from the Edit menu.

A duplicate of the headings appears in the range A1:F1 (see fig. 14.5). In this example, the criteria range is placed above the database range, with a few extra rows to spare. (The dotted line around the headings is from the Copy procedure and can be removed by pressing ⌘-. or the Escape key.) This is a good practice for setting up the two ranges, because it keeps them together. In addition, if the criteria range is below the database range, the criteria range will move down each time you add a record to the database. The criteria range headings can appear anywhere on the worksheet, however.

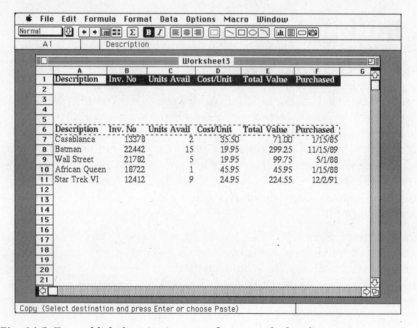

Fig. 14.5. *To establish the criteria range, first copy the headings.*

The next step is to tell Excel where the criteria range is located. Do so by highlighting the range that consists of the headings, plus the row below them. Complete the following steps:

1. Highlight the range A1:F2.

2. Select the Set Criteria command from the Data menu.

Now that the database range and criteria range are defined, you can perform database searches by entering criteria formulas into the bottom row of the criteria range. A database search locates all records that match the criteria. You can locate all video tapes that cost $19.95, for example, or all titles for which you have fewer than 10 copies and that also cost less than $20. Complete these steps to search for all tapes that cost $19.95:

1. Move the cell pointer to cell D2, which is directly under the Cost/Unit heading in the criteria range.

2. Type the search formula *19.95* and press Return or Enter.

3. Select the Find command from the Data menu to find the first matching record (see fig. 14.6). Excel highlights the matching record and enters Find mode, as indicated by the message in the status bar.

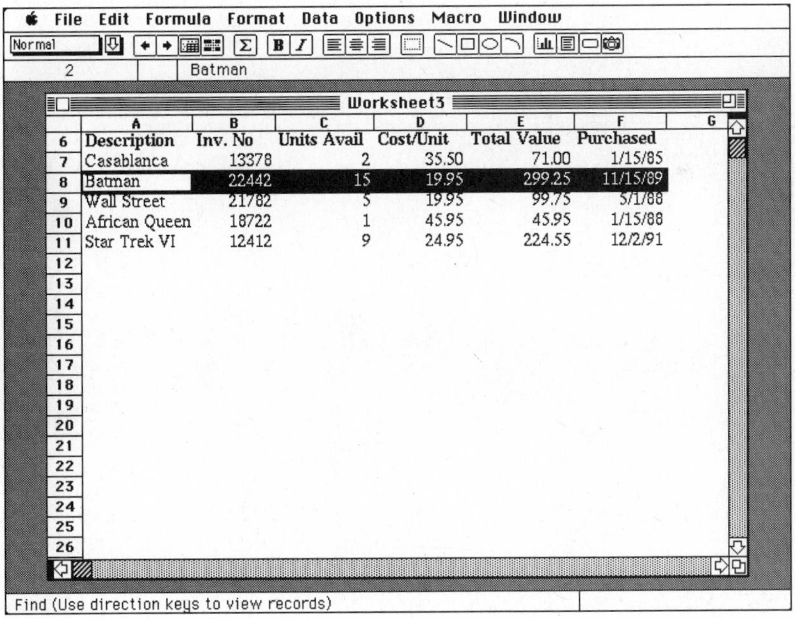

Fig. 14.6. The first matching record: Batman.

4. Press the down-arrow key to view the next matching record or the up-arrow key to find the preceding matching record.

5. Select the Exit Find command from the Data menu.

Be sure to remove the criteria formula before you establish the next criteria formula. Remove the formula by moving the pointer to cell D2 and pressing ⌘-B.

Complete the following steps to search for tapes that cost less than $20 and for which there are fewer than 10 copies:

1. Move the pointer to cell C2, which is directly under the heading Units Avail in the criteria range.

2. Type the search formula <*10*. Press Return or Enter.

3. Move the pointer to cell D2.

4. Type the search formula <*20*. Press Return or Enter.

5. Select the Find command from the Data menu to find a matching record. Excel highlights the record (see fig. 14.7).

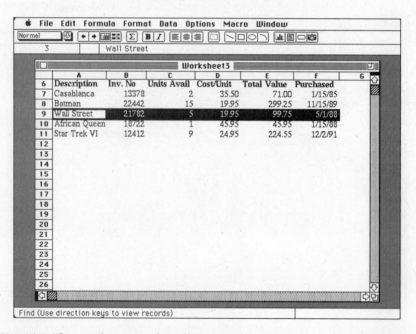

Fig. 14.7. The matching record: Wall Street.

6. Press the down-arrow key to find the next matching record or the up-arrow key to find the preceding matching record. (Only one record matches in this example.)

7. Select the Exit Find command from the Data menu.

You can continue to enter criteria formulas in this manner. Be sure to clear the old formulas before entering new ones. Also, make sure that you enter the formula in the related column of the criteria range.

> *Note:* You will use this criteria again later in the chapter, so avoid erasing it.

Using the Data Form

The data form provides a simple way to find records in the database. If you use the data form, you do not need to establish a criteria range as described earlier. If you have defined a criteria range, however, it will not interfere with the data form search; the two methods are independent of each other. Complete the following steps to use the data form to search for tapes that cost less than $20 and for which there are fewer than 10 copies:

1. Select the Form command from the Data menu. The data form appears.

2. Press Tab until you reach the Units Avail field.

3. Enter the criterion *<10*.

4. Press Tab until you reach the Cost/Unit field.

5. Enter the criterion *<20*.

6. Click on the Find Next button in the data form. This step locates the first record. Click on Find Next again to find the next matching record, or click on Find Prev to find the preceding matching record.

7. Click on the Exit button.

Extracting Records

If you removed the search criteria specified in the last set of steps in "Using a Criteria Range" earlier in this chapter, go back through the procedure to enter the criteria again. In this section, you will use the same criteria for extracting data. Data extraction is very much like searching, but with extraction, matching records are duplicated in an established area of the worksheet. You can use data extraction to print lists of matching records.

Using the sample database, suppose that you want to circulate a list of all tapes that cost less than $20 and for which you have fewer than 10 copies. Follow these steps:

1. Move to cell A16 below the database range and type *Description*. Then move to cell B16 and type *Units Avail*. These two fields represent the data that appears in the extracted list. As you can see, the extracted list does not have to include all the headings.

2. Highlight the extract headings (cells A16 and B16) and then select the Extract command from the Data menu; press Return from the dialog box.

All matching records appear beneath the extract headings. Remember, these records match the criteria you entered into the criteria range. Figure 14.8 shows the results.

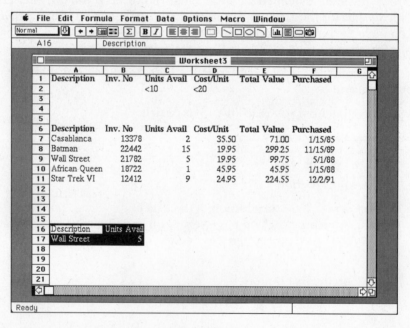

Fig. 14.8. Extracted data from the database range.

Tip: Place the Extract Range in the Proper Location
The extract procedure erases all information below the extracted records. In other words, after the data is extracted and placed in the extract range, all data below the range is removed. Be sure to place the extract range at the bottom of the worksheet.

Sorting the Database

You may find it useful to sort the database from time to time. Not only will sorting the database make the data easier to examine, but extracted data will appear sorted. Complete the following steps to sort the sample database alphabetically by movie title:

1. Highlight the entire database range, excluding the column headings (that is, highlight the range A7:F13).

2. If the pointer is not already in the first column (column A), press Tab until the pointer is in column A. The range still should be highlighted.

3. Select the Sort command from the Data menu. The dialog box shown in figure 14.9 appears.

   Notice that the active cell is entered automatically into the 1st Key box. The first key determines which column will be sorted. You can specify the column by entering the address of any cell contained in the desired column. If you enter C10, for example, Excel sorts the database by Units Avail. In this case, the cell address is already entered for the Description column because it is the active cell.

4. After specifying the sort column that you want, press Return. The data is sorted as shown in figure 14.10.

You can re-sort the data by using other headings. Just use the preceding steps as a guideline.

Saving the Database

Although this database will not be used in the next quick start (Chapter 17, "Using Macros: A Quick Start"), you may want to save it so that you can experiment with database manipulation. As you read through the next chapter, you can use this database to try out the commands and options presented.

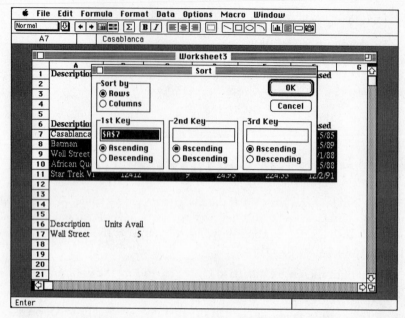

Fig. 14.9. *The Sort dialog box.*

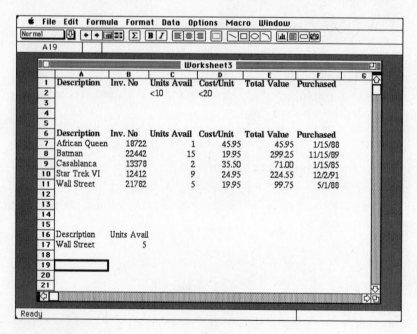

Fig. 14.10. *The database after being sorted by description.*

Save the database by saving the entire worksheet with the Save command from the File menu. Enter an appropriate name for the file for future reference. (See Chapter 2 for details on saving worksheets.)

Summary

This chapter introduced the database features of Excel by providing a step-by-step application. You saw how to set up a worksheet database, including the database range, criteria range, and extract range. The chapter also discussed how to insert and remove records from the database and how to enter search criteria for record location and extraction. Finally, you saw the basic steps for sorting worksheet information, using up to three key fields. For more details on databases, see Chapter 15, "Creating and Manipulating Databases."

15

Creating and Manipulating Databases

You can use the Excel worksheet as a database for data management tasks such as searching, sorting, and reporting information. Database management in Excel is useful in accounting applications and custom business applications, but you also can use database features to create simple address and inventory lists. The Excel database is fast and easy to use, and provides powerful worksheet math capabilities.

An Excel database is really just part of the worksheet; you enter database information into worksheet rows and columns. These rows and columns, however, are specifically dedicated to holding database information. In designating rows and columns as a database, you gain access to features not available to other worksheet data. This chapter explains those features, first discussing database structure and then describing how to set up an Excel database, enter data, sort the database, and find information in the database.

Understanding Database Structure

A *database* stores information in some regular order that makes finding particular pieces of information easy. Consider a filing cabinet that contains information in alphabetical order. To find a particular file or record, you simply search under the appropriate letter in the alphabet.

Some databases, including most computerized databases, are more structured; they include data entry "forms" that ensure that every item of data is located in the same place within each record.

An address file (Rolodex), for example, contains numerous cards (called *records*) that have data arranged in the same manner. Each piece of data on the card is called a *field* and is located in the same spot on each card (record) in the file (database). This way, your eyes do not have to scan the card for the line containing the phone number, or name, or whatever you want (see fig. 15.1).

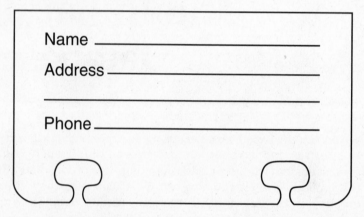

Fig. 15.1. *A typical Rolodex card.*

The address file may not be as flexible as you would like. To find an individual, you search alphabetically through the cards to find the name you want. Because the cards are sorted by last names, this task is easy. However, what if you want to find a particular company's phone number? You would have to search for the company by finding one of its employee's cards in the file. Or, you could create a separate card with just the company name on it and file it alphabetically.

In a computerized version of this address file, you easily could re-sort the records by the company names used in the cards, and then search alphabetically through the cards for the company name. You would need no more than one card per company or individual and you could re-sort the data again by any piece of information on the card. You could sort the cards by cities, for example, creating an alphabetical list of cities and each card within its appropriate city. Then, to find a card, you would search for its city alphabetically.

In short, the way a database is sorted influences how you are able to search for information. It therefore is sensible to sort a database by the information that you are most likely to use for searching. Phone lists are searched by using a person's name, making them so simple that a Rolodex file is usually every bit as good as a computerized phone list. However, some databases are much more complex and really benefit from computerization. A library catalog, for example, is searched by using an author name, a subject, or a book title—requiring three ways of sorting the data. Not surprisingly, standard (uncomputerized) card catalogs are becoming a thing of the past for large libraries.

The Excel database stores information in rows and columns. Each row contains a *record* (the equivalent of a card in a Rolodex). In each cell of the row, or record, is a piece of information called a *field* (the equivalent of each piece of data on the card). The column headings, or *field names*, indicate what type of information each column contains (see fig. 15.2).

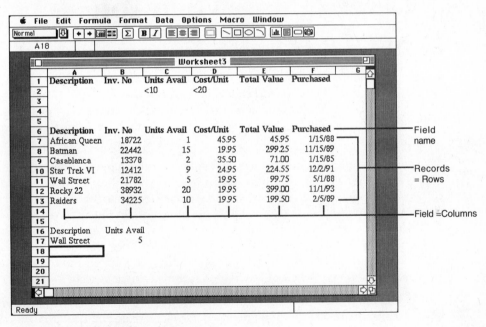

Fig. 15.2. *The Excel database structure.*

A summary of the terms used for databases follows:

- *Field:* An individual piece of information within a record. Each record within a database must have the same fields, but you determine the number and type of fields for the database as a whole.

- *Field name:* The title given to a field within the database. Excel uses field names to perform database functions. To find a record containing the name Smith, for example, you must indicate the field in which you want to search for that name (most likely Last or Last Name).

- *Record:* A database unit containing a set of fields that pertains to a single entry. All records within a database have the same fields, but each field contains information unique to that record. Thus, all records are different. Records are the units that you can sort within a database.

- *Database range:* The range of cells in the worksheet that contains database information.

Determining When You Need a Database

So far, you may be wondering what makes a database so different from a worksheet. You can sort worksheet information even if it is not in a database range, and the Find command from the Formula menu provides some searching capabilities. The row-and-column format is a common structure for data.

By establishing a block of cells as a database, you get an extended range of search criteria for finding information. You also have the capability to make statistical calculations on subsets of the database, to use the automatic data form for manipulating data (adding, deleting, and finding records), and to extract a subset of data from the database using custom criteria. These capabilities are most significant when you consider that databases are changing constantly. Because records are frequently added and changed in databases, the searches and extracted subsets change as well.

If your data does not change much, or if you don't often retrieve data from a group of records, you don't need a database. Nor do you need a database if the Formula Find command provides enough power for your searches or you do not need to extract particular information from a range.

An order-processing system is a good application for a database. The order itself may require specific worksheet calculations. Then, after a purchase order is generated and sent, it must be stored. You can build reports that analyze purchases over time, or you may want to search for orders that have common information, such as all orders to the same manufacturer.

Setting Up a Database

Setting up a database is simply a matter of entering data according to the guidelines of database structure. Make sure that each row contains a separate record and that the column headings represent the fields in the database. The column headings (or field names) must be text labels and may be created from text calculations.

If your field names are numeric values, Excel will be unable to perform search procedures, rendering the database useless. Remember, to enter a number as a text label, use a text formula (="1992", for example).

Because databases expand, you need to leave enough room at the bottom of the database for added records. In fact, you should give the database its own area at the end of the worksheet to provide room for unlimited growth. You also should avoid placing a database to the right or left of other work-sheet data. When you add or remove database records, the change can affect adjacent areas of the worksheet. The only absolute requirements are that you include field names (column headings) for the data and that no blank rows appear below the column headings.

Entering Data

After you establish the database area and field names, you can begin entering data. This process is no different from entering data into a worksheet; you just type the information under each column heading. You may want to highlight the database range before entering data so that the pointer remains in the range as you move from cell to cell (by pressing Tab or Return).

You can insert and delete records simply by inserting rows into or deleting rows from the database range—a process described later in this chapter. You also can use the data form, which is described later in this chapter as well.

Guidelines for creating databases follow:

- Start the database below and to the right of existing worksheet data so the database does not interfere with existing data. (This guide-line is helpful, but not mandatory.)

- Enter column headings in the first row, leaving no blank rows below this row. In other words, the first records should begin immediately below the headings, and no blank records should exist.

- Records do not have to be filled out completely. Although you should avoid completely blank records, you don't have to fill out each column of each record. Sometimes data is not available or pertinent for all records.

- When entering data, highlight a block of cells containing the fields in order to restrict the movement of the pointer. When you reach the end of a record, simply press Tab to move to the beginning of the next record.

- Enter data in the form of text, numbers, or formulas. Any type of worksheet information is acceptable for database data, including worksheet functions and formulas.

- Each field name should be unique. Duplicate field names may result in unpredictable data searches.

Activating the Database

After you enter the field names and one row of data (a record), you can activate the database by telling Excel where your database range is located on the worksheet. When Excel is aware of the database, a number of database features become available. To activate a database, follow these two steps:

1. Highlight the field names and all records beneath them (see fig. 15.3).

2. Select the Set Database command from the Data menu.

No changes are noticeable when you complete these steps; Excel simply records the database range and names it DATABASE. This range name then appears with all other range names when you use the Define Name command from the Formula menu (see fig. 15.4). Because the range is named DATABASE, however, it has special properties found only in databases. You can activate the database anytime you want to, as long as you do so before using the Data Form command.

Like any other range name, the name DATABASE can apply to only one range at a time. A worksheet therefore can have only one active database at a time. You can, however, set up several database ranges on the same worksheet and then activate the one you want by choosing Set Database from the Data menu. Later, you can activate a different one.

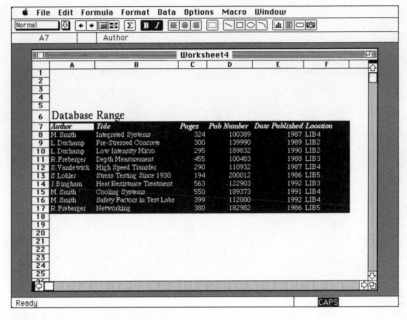

Fig. 15.3. *Highlighting the database range.*

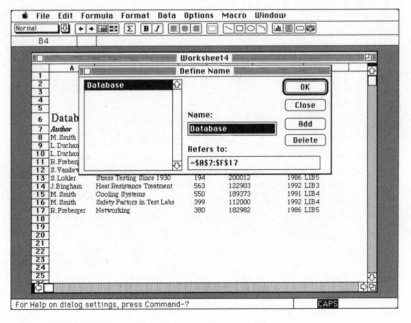

Fig. 15.4. *DATABASE is listed with any other named ranges.*

Tip: Naming a Database Range Manually

To create a valid database range, you also can issue the Define Name command from the Formula menu (instead of the Set Database command from the Data menu) to apply the name DATABASE to a highlighted range. In fact, this technique enables you to establish databases from ranges in external worksheets. Simply enter an external range reference in the Refers To field of the Formula Define Name dialog box and then name the range DATABASE. Chapter 16 provides more information about this technique.

Because the database range name is like any other, you can use the various range name commands on the database. To quickly highlight the database range, issue the Goto command from the Formula menu and select the name DATABASE from the list provided. To remove the database range specification, select Define Name from the Formula menu, select the name DATABASE, and click Delete. Chapter 3 provides more information about using range names.

Tip: Naming the Database Range Again

You should consider using the Define Name command from the Formula menu to name the database range a second time with a name other than DATABASE. If your worksheet has more than one database, give each database a unique name. Then, to select one of the ranges as the database range, issue the Goto command from the Formula menu, followed by the Set Database command from the Data menu.

Basically, you can name any database range with the Define Name command from the Formula menu. Then, when you activate that range with the Set Database command from the Data menu, the range has two names: DATABASE and the unique name you have given it. Adding a second name is useful because you can jump quickly to any range that contains a name. Thus, you can move quickly between databases to activate the database you want. Chapter 16 provides more information on working with multiple databases.

Using the Data Form

One of the most notable features that Excel provides for established databases is the *data form*, a special window that makes inserting, deleting, and finding records easy. As soon as you establish the database range with the Set Database command from the Data menu, you can use the data form. You view the data form by selecting the Form command from the Data menu. Figure 15.5 shows an example of a database and its form.

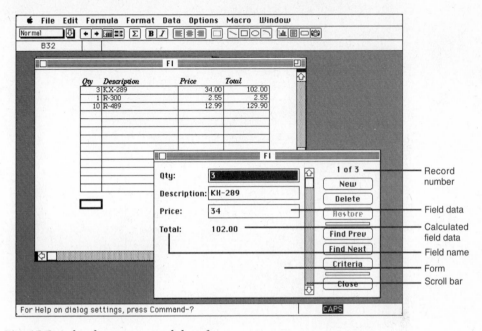

Fig. 15.5. *A database range and data form.*

The data form contains all the fields from the database range and a set of command buttons. Because the form holds all the fields in the database, the data form may not be able to display all the fields on-screen at one time (see fig. 15.6). You can overcome this limitation by customizing the data form following the procedure described in Chapter 16.

Descriptions of each part of the data form (excluding the command buttons) follow:

- *Form:* The area where you enter or edit information. The form represents a single record (or row) from the database range.

- *Field Name:* The name describing the field data. Each field name in the database range appears in the data form. Excel adds the colons (:) and places the field data next to the appropriate name.

- *Field Data:* Data associated with a field name. This data is displayed one record at a time. You can edit the information in these field boxes (unless the information is calculated).

- *Calculated Field Data:* Data determined by a formula. The contents of formula-containing cells in the database are presented in the data form as "uneditable" data.

- *Record Number:* The number of the record in view.

- *Scroll Bar:* A feature that enables you to move through the various records in the database range.

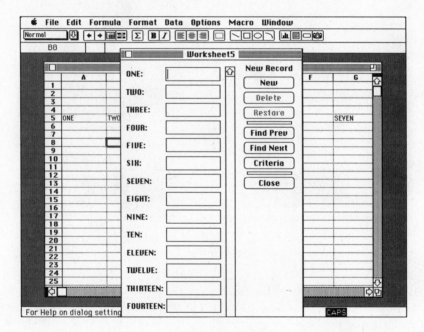

Fig. 15.6. A data form with more fields than the screen can display.

Explanations of the data form's command buttons follow:

- *New:* Adds a new record to the database. After clicking New, you see a blank form into which you can enter the appropriate information. When you move to another record or exit from the form, Excel adds the new record to the end of the database.

- *Delete:* Deletes the record currently displayed in the form from the database.

- *Restore:* Cancels your changes and restores the record to its previous state when you edit or add records.

- *Find Prev:* Locates the preceding record in the database.

- *Find Next:* Locates the next record in the database.

- *Criteria:* Enables you to specify criteria for searching for a record. Click this button and enter the criteria into the form. Then click the Find Next button to start the search.

- *Close:* Returns you to the worksheet.

The following sections describe the tasks you can accomplish with the data form.

Editing a Record

Although you can edit database information in the worksheet with the standard editing commands (see Chapter 4), you may find the data form a handy way to change database records. When you correct the information displayed in the form, Excel updates the database immediately, as if you had edited the cells themselves. Follow these steps to edit a record using the data form:

1. Locate the record you want by clicking the Find Next button or by establishing search criteria.

2. Click the field you want to change and apply standard editing techniques to make changes.

3. Repeat step 2 for all the fields you want to change.

4. Apply the changes to the database by exiting from the form (using the Close button) or by moving to another record (using the scroll bar, the Find Next button, or the Find Prev button).

Excel updates the worksheet as soon as you accept the changes. You cannot edit fields containing calculations (that is, cells in the database that contain formulas) or cells protected with the Format Cell Protection command.

Adding a Record

Adding a record with the data form is easy. Just click on New to get a blank form. Then enter the information you want and accept the new record by exiting from the form or moving to a different record. The only way to cancel the new record before adding it is to select Restore.

When you add a new record through the data form, Excel places that record at the end of the database. If blank records are at the end of the database, the first one is filled with the new information. If the database has no blank records, Excel adds a new record at the end and expands the database range accordingly. If the database has no room to expand (without interfering with existing information), however, Excel does not add the new record and displays a message to that effect.

Remember that you cannot add or edit calculated fields in the database. In other words, if the cells in a database column contain formulas, you cannot type information into the corresponding field in the data form. Instead, Excel duplicates the formula for the new record and adds the data automatically. Likewise, you cannot add or edit protected fields: fields on which you have used the Cell Protection command from the Format menu (see Chapter 13).

Removing a Record

To remove a database record, locate the record you want to delete by clicking on the data form's scroll bar or the Find Next and Find Prev buttons. When the record you want appears in the form, click Delete to remove the record from the database. Excel asks you to confirm your decision and then removes the record. If you change your mind, click on Restore before moving to another record. Otherwise, Excel removes the record from the database and adjusts the database range accordingly.

Finding a Record

Although you can find any record in the database with the data form's scroll bar or the Find Next and Find Prev buttons, this process is too slow for most purposes. To speed up the search, use the Criteria button first to establish search criteria for locating a specific record or group of records. Follow these steps:

1. With the data form in view, click on Criteria. A blank data form appears.

2. Enter the criteria into the fields of the blank data form. Click on Clear or Restore to make changes to your criteria entries.

3. Click on Find Next to find the first matching record in the database.

4. Click on Find Next again to find the next matching record, or click on Find Prev to find the preceding matching record.

5. Click on Form to return to the normal data form.

Entering Criteria

To find a record that contains a specific piece of information, just type that information into the criteria form. To find a record containing the name *Smith* in the Last field, for example, type *Smith* into the appropriate field in the criteria form; then click on Find Next. You can fill as many of the fields as you want with criteria. The more fields you specify, the fewer records are likely to match the criteria. Suppose that five records contain the last name *Smith*, but only one also contains the ZIP code *91006*. To find this record without finding the other four records, type *Smith* into the Last field and *91006* into the ZIP field (see fig. 15.7).

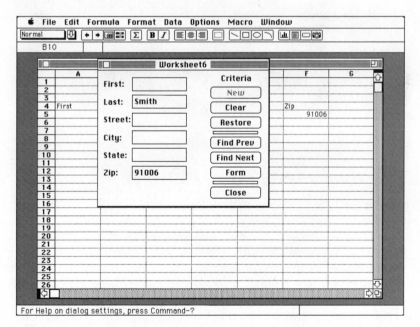

Fig. 15.7. Entering multiple criteria to narrow the search.

Excel looks for direct matches and matches that are parts of a larger word or phrase. If you enter *Rob* as a first-name criterion, for example, Excel matches it with *Rob*, *Robert*, *ROBERTA*, and *Rob and Susan*, ignoring case. In addition, you can include the two standard wild cards in your search criteria. For details about wild cards, see Chapter 4.

Entering a criteria string into the criteria form starts a search for a matching record—that is, a record that is "equal to" the specified criteria. The operator implied is an equal sign. You can, however, specify comparison operators. You can find all records containing an amount of less than 1,500, for example. To specify the comparison, just type one of the following operators in front of the comparison information:

Operator	Meaning
>	Greater than
<	Less than
<=	Less than or equal to
>=	Greater than or equal to
<>	Does not equal
=	Equals (implied when no operator is present)

To specify all amounts less than 1,500, for example, enter the criterion *<1500* into the amount field.

> *Note:* Some Macintosh fonts can produce the characters ≥ and ≤ . You cannot substitute these for the >= and <= entries, however, which require two characters each.

Using the Criteria Form Buttons

When you enter the criteria form, the buttons Clear and Form replace Delete and Criteria, respectively, and the Restore button is activated. Use these buttons to make changes to your criteria entries. The Clear button erases existing criteria entries; Restore restores entries that have been erased. When you find an entry, click on Form to return to the normal data form with that record in view. If you find an entry according to search criteria and then make changes to the entry, Excel automatically returns to the normal data form. In this case, you again must click on the Criteria button to remove or change the criteria.

Sorting the Database

You can sort the information in a database using any field as the key. A Rolodex, for example, may be sorted by last name; that is, all the cards are arranged in alphabetical order by last name, so the Last Name field is the *key field*.

Excel enables you to sort in ascending or descending order and makes a distinction among numbers, text, and dates. Excel sorts numbers numerically, text alphabetically, and dates chronologically. If a column contains a mixture of different types of values, Excel uses the following order:

1. Numbers (negative to positive, including date values)

2. Text (in order of ASCII values)

3. Logical values (FALSE, then TRUE)

4. Error values

5. Blank cells

Start by highlighting the entire database range, excluding the column headings. Next, press Tab to move the pointer into the column by which you want to sort the data. Finally, choose the Sort command from the Data menu. The Data Sort dialog box appears (see fig. 15.8).

> *Caution:* If you include the database's column headings, these will be sorted with the data. If you don't select all the database records, those not selected will remain unsorted and may cause confusion in the worksheet.

The assumption is that you are sorting the rows of the database range so that they are rearranged according to the first key field—the field where the pointer is located. The address of this field appears in the 1st Key box. You can change this entry manually if you want, or press Return to accept these specifications. Excel proceeds to sort the highlighted range by the active column.

Often, sorting by one key field is not enough. Some databases contain duplicate information in the first key field. If you are sorting an address database by the Last Name field, for example, you may find some duplicate last names. Your database may contain six people with the last name *Smith*, for example. In this case, you need a "tie-breaker" to sort the database effectively. After sorting by the Last Name field, therefore, you sort the database by a second key field—First Name—so that *John Smith* appears before *Mary Smith*.

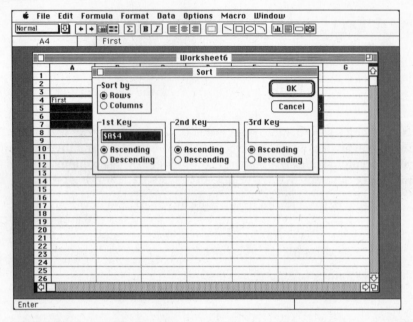

Fig. 15.8. *The Data Sort dialog box.*

> ### Tip: *Sorting Spreadsheet Data*
> You can arrange any worksheet data—not just database data—by sorting. Sorting can be useful before graphing data, for example, in order to arrange it in ascending order. Be careful when sorting data that is referenced by other worksheet formulas; you may disrupt the reference.

Adding a second key field is simple. After highlighting the database and placing the pointer in the 1st Key field (anywhere in the column), select the Sort command from the Data menu. The 1st Key field should be entered for you in the dialog box. Press Tab to position the pointer in the 2nd Key space and click the worksheet cell that marks the 2nd Key field. (You may have to move the Data Sort dialog box out of the way.) When you click on the worksheet cell, Excel enters its address at the cursor location. You now have two key fields for the sort; you can add a third in the same manner if you want.

As an alternative to "pointing" to the second key field, you can simply type its address into the space provided. Likewise, you can change the address of the 1st Key field by using standard editing commands. Note that you can sort each key field in ascending or descending order, independently of the other keys. You can sort last names in ascending order and first names in descending order, for example.

> **Tip: Using Names To Specify Sort Keys**
> You can use range names to specify the sort keys in the Data Sort dialog box. First, highlight the entire database range (including field names), choose the Create Names command from the Formula menu, and choose the Top option to create a name for each database column from the field names. Then enter these field names instead of cell addresses for the 1st Key, 2nd Key, and 3rd Key field specifications.

Sorting Columns

Besides sorting the records of a database, you can rearrange columns in ascending or descending order. To arrange the columns, highlight the entire database range, including the field names. (You can use the Goto command from the Formula menu to specify the range named DATABASE.) With the database range highlighted, issue the Sort command from the Data menu. Next, click on the Columns button. Finally, enter the address of the first key into the 1st Key field; this address should be any cell in the first row of the database (that is, the row containing the field names). Press Return to sort the data.

If you want the columns in an order other than alphabetical, try numbering the columns as you want them to appear; then enter these numbers above each column label (see fig. 15.9).

Include this extra row of numbers when you highlight the database range for the sort, and specify any cell in this row as the first key in the Sort dialog box. After you press Return, the columns are sorted in numerical order (see fig. 15.10).

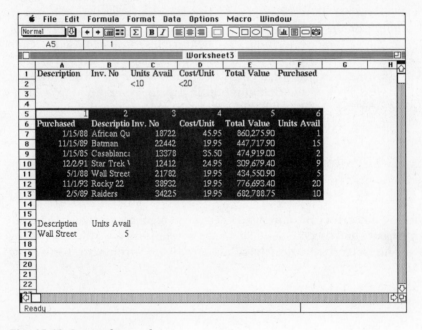

 File Edit Formula Format Data Options Macro Window

	A	B	C	D	E	F	G	H
1	Description	Inv. No	Units Avail	Cost/Unit	Total Value	Purchased		
2			<10	<20				
3								
4								
5	2	3	6	4	5	1		
6	Description	Inv. No	Units Avail	Cost/Unit	Total Value	Purchased		
7	African Queen	18722	1	45.95	45.95	1/15/88		
8	Batman	22442	15	19.95	299.25	11/15/89		
9	Casablanca	13378	2	35.50	71.00	1/15/85		
10	Star Trek VI	12412	9	24.95	224.55	12/2/91		
11	Wall Street	21782	5	19.95	99.75	5/1/88		
12	Rocky 22	38932	20	19.95	399.00	11/1/93		
13	Raiders	34225	10	19.95	199.50	2/5/89		
14								
15								
16	Description	Units Avail						
17	Wall Street	5						
18								

Fig. 15.9. *Numbering columns for a custom sort.*

 File Edit Formula Format Data Options Macro Window

	A	B	C	D	E	F	G	H
1	Description	Inv. No	Units Avail	Cost/Unit	Total Value	Purchased		
2			<10	<20				
3								
4								
5	1	2	3	4	5	6		
6	Purchased	Descriptio	Inv. No	Cost/Unit	Total Value	Units Avail		
7	1/15/88	African Qu	18722	45.95	860,275.90	1		
8	11/15/89	Batman	22442	19.95	447,717.90	15		
9	1/15/85	Casablanc:	13378	35.50	474,919.00	2		
10	12/2/91	Star Trek V	12412	24.95	309,679.40	9		
11	5/1/88	Wall Street	21782	19.95	434,550.90	5		
12	11/1/93	Rocky 22	38932	19.95	776,693.40	20		
13	2/5/89	Raiders	34225	19.95	682,788.75	10		
14								
15								
16	Description	Units Avail						
17	Wall Street	5						

Fig. 15.10. *Sorting by numbers.*

Solving Data-Sorting Problems

If you enter records randomly into the database, you cannot restore the original order of the data after sorting it—unless you include a column of sequential numbers as part of the database. When you number the entries, you can return the database to its original order by sorting the column of numbers. Simply enter the number of the worksheet row into the first column of the database (see fig. 15.11). As a shortcut, you can issue the Fill command from the Data menu to create sequential numbers down the column.

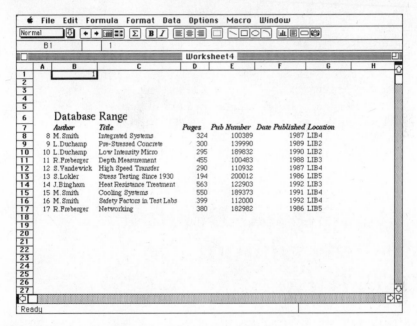

Fig. 15.11. *Copying the row number into the database.*

The problem with this technique is that the record numbers are not entered for each record automatically, so you probably will want to enter a batch of records and then perform this procedure to number them all at once. As an alternative, try adding an extra field to the database that contains a record number. Then, each time you enter a new record, type the next highest record number in this field. Again, this method is not automatic.

> **Tip: Using Formulas To Create Record Numbers**
> In the example in figure 15.11, you may be tempted to use the formula A8+1 in cell A9 and copy this down the column to generate record numbers automatically. This will not work. When you sort the records (including their numbers), the formulas will recalculate their values to produce incorrect numbers. Also, when you delete a record, the formulas will produce errors. Instead, type the number 1 into cell A1, and then enter the formula
>
> =IF($A$1=1,ROW0,A8)
>
> in cell A8 and copy it down the column. This will produce record numbers in the column. Now erase the value in cell A1 before sorting the data (ignore the caution about circular references). As long as cell A1 does not contain the value 1, the formulas will not recalculate their values—thus keeping the record numbers intact. To enter new records, sort the database by the record numbers to restore the original order, and then reenter the value 1 in cell A1. Now add the new records. You may include this column in the data form.

Inserting and Deleting Records without the Data Form

You can insert and delete records from the database without using the data form. To insert a record, just insert a new row into the middle of the database range and fill the row with new information. You can copy any calculated data from other records.

To insert a new record, highlight a row in the middle of the range and then use the Insert command from the Edit menu as described in Chapter 4. When prompted, make sure that you shift cells down to make room for the new information. The highlighted row then is bumped down to make room for the new row. Excel expands the database range to include the extra row.

> *Tip: Highlighting an Entire Row*
> When you highlight an entire row by clicking the row number, Excel moves cells down when you insert a new row. Only when you highlight a partial row does Excel present the option to shift cells down. Be careful when inserting and deleting entire rows because this affects data that may be next to the database data.

When you insert a new record, make sure that you insert it into the middle of the database range—not at the end (that is, not after the last row). If you insert a new record at the end of the existing range, Excel does not expand the database range to include the new data. The record therefore does not become part of the existing database, and you may have to respecify the database range.

For this reason, you should include an extra blank row at the end of the database range. Then, if you insert a new record below the existing records, you are actually still within the database range. Excel thinks you are one record from the end of the database and expands the range to include your new row.

To delete a record, simply delete the row containing the unwanted information. Use the Delete command from the Edit menu, as described in Chapter 4, making sure that you delete the entire record or row.

> *Tip: Changing Recalculation to Manual*
> When inserting database records, you may find that automatic recalculation slows data entry. Try changing recalculation to manual until you finish inserting new data. Then you can recalculate the entire worksheet with the Calculate Now command from the Options menu. Chapter 8 provides more information about automatic and manual recalculation.

Finding Records without the Data Form

Although the data form offers adequate searching capabilities for most databases, you can perform more powerful searches without the form because the data form does not provide OR logic. When you enter criteria into more than one field, the criteria constitutes an implied AND statement.

In other words, if you enter *Smith* into the Last (name) field and 91006 into the ZIP (ZIP code) field, Excel locates only those records that match both criteria. To find records with Last fields containing *Smith* OR with ZIP fields containing *91006*, you must use a special criteria range.

The basic steps for searching without the data form follow:

1. Create the criteria range, which consists of the field names you want, followed by the criteria entries. Make sure that this range appears in an unused portion of the worksheet.

2. Highlight the criteria range (the field names plus the criteria entries) and activate it with the Set Criteria command from the Data menu.

3. Begin the search by selecting the Find command from the Data menu.

4. Use the search options to "flip through" the matching records.

Specifying Criteria

A *criteria range* is a special range of cells in the worksheet that contains search criteria for the database. The criteria range can contain complex and specialized search criteria for finding, deleting, and extracting records.

To create a criteria range, start by copying the database column headings (the field names) to another area of the worksheet. A few rows above the originals is a good place to copy to; just leave a few rows under the copied headings for entering specific criteria. You don't need to duplicate every field name; you only need to copy the ones you intend to use in the search. Duplicating all field names, however, enables you to search all fields.

Figure 15.12 shows a sample database of company documents. Notice that the field names are repeated at the top of the worksheet to create the criteria range and that a few extra rows separate the two ranges.

Under each duplicate heading name, you can enter a criteria formula. If, for example, you want to find all records containing *1989* in the Date Published field, enter *1989* below the Date Published heading in the criteria range (see fig. 15.13).

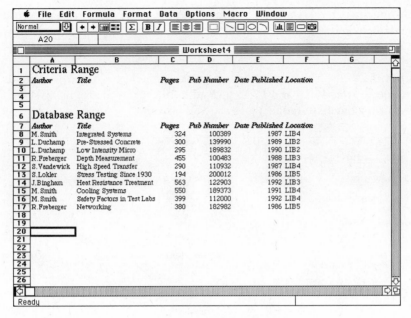

Fig. 15.12. *Copying the field names to the criteria range.*

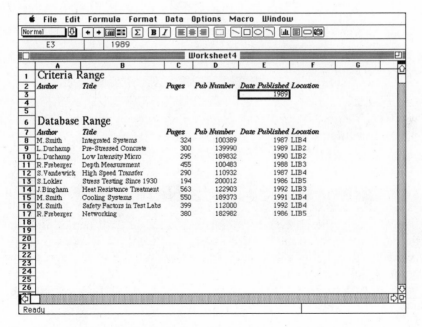

Fig. 15.13. *Specifying criteria in the criteria range.*

Entering the criteria is much like using criteria in the data form. You can use any of the comparison operators

>   >=   <   <=   <>   =

within the cells. The equals operation is implied when no operator is present. Figures 15.14 and 15.15 give additional examples of using search criteria in a database range.

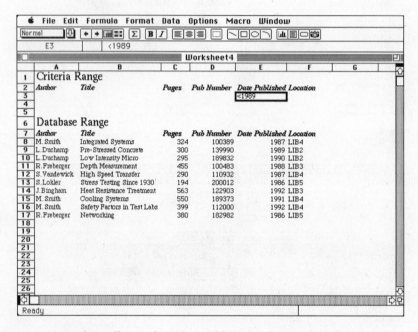

Fig. 15.14. *Finding all records with a publication date earlier than 1989.*

Activating the Criteria Range

After you enter the criteria, highlight the duplicate field names and the criteria; then select the Set Criteria command from the Data menu. Figure 15.16 shows the highlighted range. Issuing the Data Set Criteria command tells Excel where the criteria range is located and activates the range. Even if you change the criteria entries, you need not select this range again unless it moves or expands.

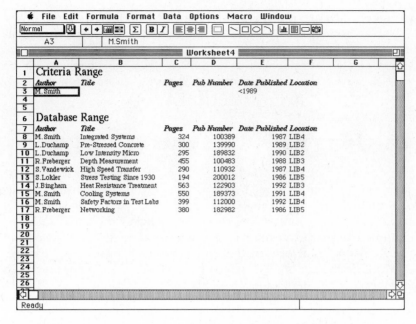

Fig. 15.15. *Finding all records for M. Smith with a publication date earlier than 1989.*

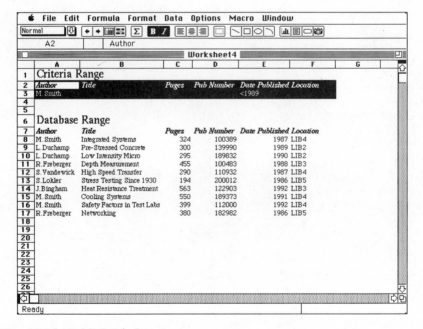

Fig. 15.16. *Highlighting the criteria range.*

Excel stores the criteria range under the name CRITERIA. Like the DATA-BASE range name, CRITERIA is a standard range name and can be used as such. You can highlight the criteria range with the Goto command on the Formula menu, for example, and you can edit the range reference with the Define Name command on the Formula menu.

Searching with the Criteria Range

After you create and activate the criteria range, the final step is to select the Find command from the Data menu to locate the first record that matches the established criteria. When you use the Data Find command, Excel locates the first matching record that appears below the current pointer location. In other words, you can position the pointer in the database and search from that point forward. If the pointer is outside the database range, Excel starts at the top of the database range. Figure 15.17 shows a record located using the criteria range.

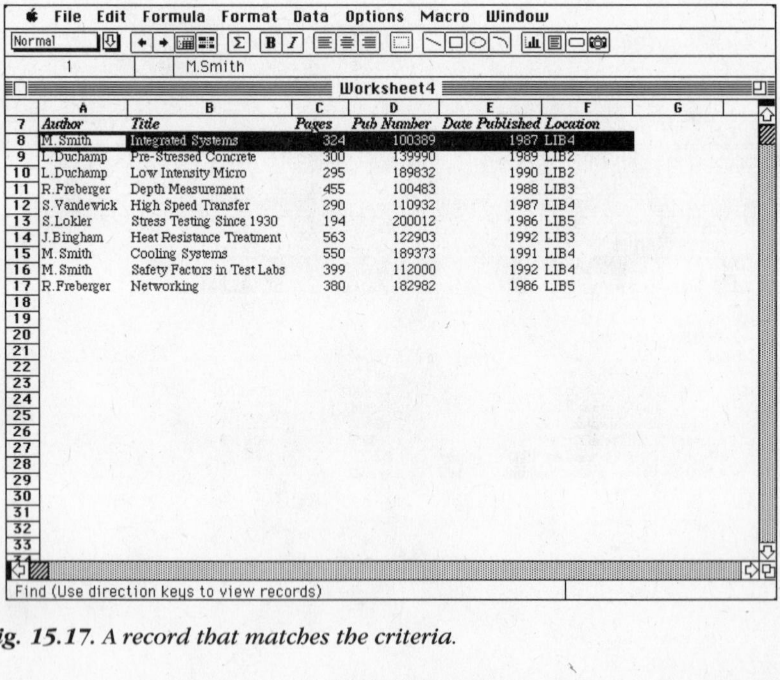

Fig. 15.17. A record that matches the criteria.

Notice the number 1 in the upper left corner of the screen. This number indicates that the highlighted record is the first from the top. This number is updated as you "flip through" the records.

After Excel finds the first matching record, you can use any of the following options to find other matching records. Until you halt the search, all these options apply to matching records:

Option	Moves Highlight and Pointer
↓ or ⌘-F	To the next matching record.
↑ or ⌘-Shift-F	To the preceding matching record.
Scroll arrows	Forward or backward through the matching records, one record at a time.
Scroll box	To a matching record elsewhere in the database. By dragging the scroll box, you can make large jumps within the database and highlight the first matching record at the new position.
PgDn	To the nearest record one screen down from the current record.
PgUp	To the nearest record one screen up from the current record.

When Excel is in the search mode, the scroll boxes change patterns to indicate their changed function. To exit from the database search and return the scroll boxes to normal, select any cell outside the database range. Alternatively, you can select the Exit Find command from the Data menu or press ⌘-. (period).

Using Complex Search Criteria

The Excel database and criteria structure enable you to make many different types of searches. The following sections describe some special techniques and features you can apply in order to conduct more powerful searches. These techniques include combining criteria with AND and OR operators and building advanced formulas for criteria.

Using AND and OR Logic

When you use more than one formula to establish criteria for the search, you can assume an AND operator between them. Entering *>1989* under Date

Published, for example, and *M. Smith* under Author finds all records with a Date Published value greater than 1989 AND an Author value of M. Smith. Although the AND operator does not appear between the two criteria entries, it is assumed because the formulas are on the same row and each entry is under its appropriate heading. Using multiple criteria entries in this way narrows the possible matching records because fewer records are likely to meet both criteria.

You can use OR logic between criteria entries by placing the different entries on different rows. The OR operator extends the possible matching records, because more records are likely to meet one or another criterion; records that meet any of the criteria qualify as matching records. Suppose that you want to search the sample database for all records with a Date Published value greater than 1989 or an Author value of *M. Smith*. The criteria range for this search appears in figure 15.18.

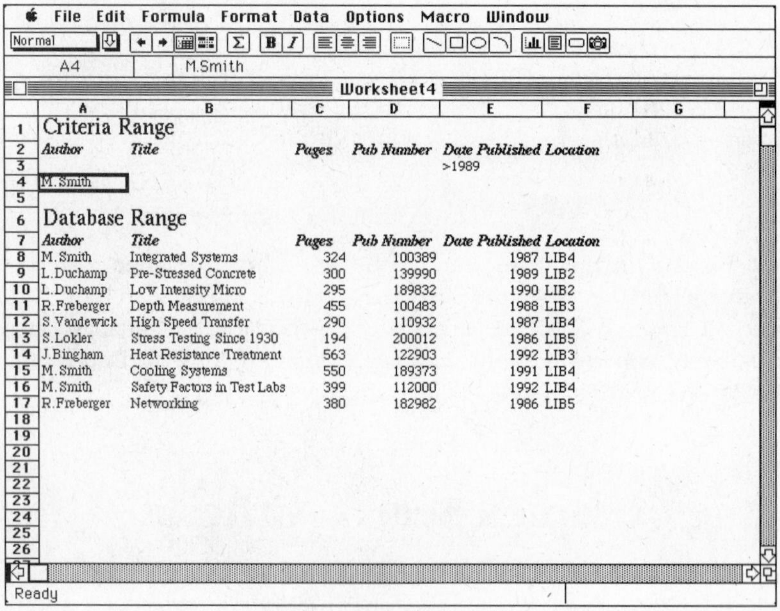

Fig. 15.18. *Using the implied OR operator.*

Notice that the formulas appear on different rows below their corresponding field names. Leaving plenty of space between the duplicate field names and the originals enables you to specify multiple criteria entries with the implied OR operator. When highlighting the criteria range for the search, make sure that you include all rows containing formulas. Formulas on the same row assume the AND operator; formulas on different rows assume the OR operator. This setup enables you to specify intricate search criteria.

Suppose that you want to find all records in the publication log that have a Date Published value of 1989 or a Date Published value greater than 1987 and a Location value of LIB4. The statement may be expressed as follows (although you don't enter the statement this way):

Date Published = 1989 OR (Date Published > 1987 AND
Location = LIB4)

Notice that the parentheses around the second set make it a single criterion. This statement has two separate conditions separated by the OR operator. Figure 15.19 shows how this statement translates to the criteria range. Make sure that you reset the criteria range so that it includes all three rows.

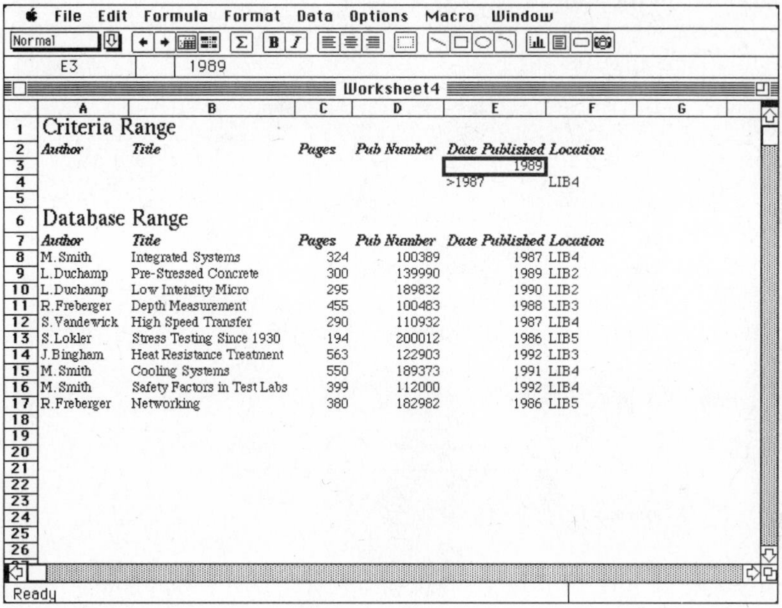

Fig. 15.19. *Specifying more complex criteria.*

Caution: Make sure that all the rows in your criteria range have some data in them. If you are not using some rows, reset the criteria range to only the rows you are using. Blank rows cause Excel to find all the records in your database when you use the Find command from the Data menu, thus making your criteria useless.

Using Computed Criteria

You can use formulas in the criteria range to search for records that match specific calculations or statements. You can search for records containing a particular amount, for example, that, when added to 100, produces a result of less than 150. The formula bar in figure 15.20 shows a formula (criterion) that specifies such a condition.

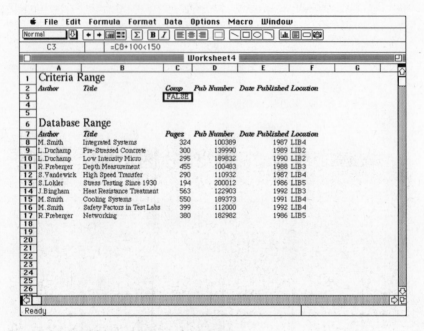

Fig. 15.20. *Specifying a computed criterion.*

Notice that this formula, which searches for all records with fewer than 50 pages, refers to the first cell in the column you are searching (not counting the cell containing the field name). In this case, the reference is to C8, the first cell in the Pages column. This reference causes Excel to repeat the same formula for each record.

> **Note:** When using computed criteria, you must change the headings used in the criteria range so that they no longer match the field names exactly. This step tells Excel that the criteria is computed— not constant.

The sample criterion in figure 15.20 is the computation of a database field plus a constant value. You can use any formula, however, as a search criterion. You can calculate two fields from the database or use references to cells outside the database range. If you use external references, make sure that they are absolute by adding dollar signs. Figures 15.21 and 15.22 show additional examples of computed criteria.

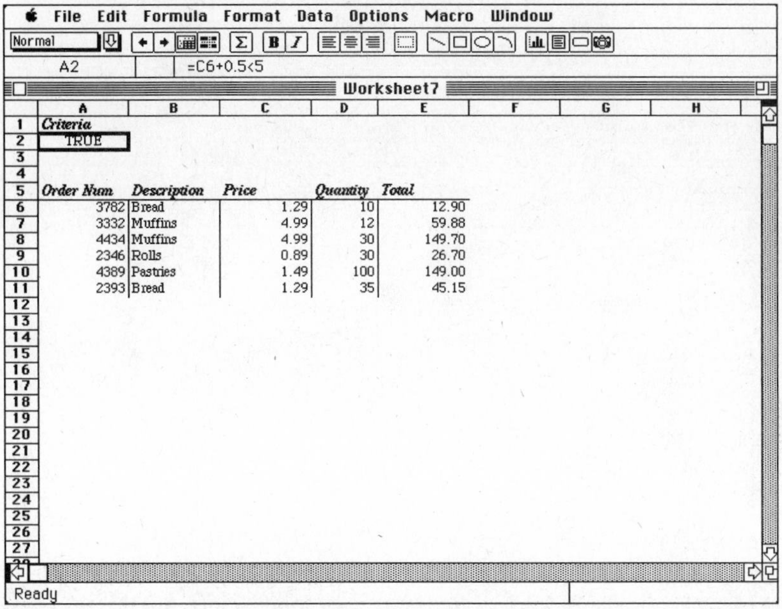

Fig. 15.21. Finding records for which Price plus 50 percent is less than $5.

Notice that you can use logical functions within the computed criteria. The functions ISBLANK, ISERR, ISNUMBER, and ISTEXT can help you find different kinds of values within a database.

Guidelines for using computed criteria follow:

- Change the headings in the criteria range so that they do not match the field names. This step is necessary when you use computed criteria. When you use standard criteria, the labels must match the field names.

- Enter computed criteria as formulas, including the equal sign and any cell references for the calculation. This formula produces an initial result that should relate to the first record in the database but is meaningless for the search operation.

- When entering a computed criterion, refer to the appropriate cell in the first record of the database. Using the first record tells Excel to repeat the formula for each record in the database. Excel then finds all records that match your computed criteria.

- You can use any valid formula in the computed criteria, including special functions, constant values, cell addresses, and linked cells from external worksheets.

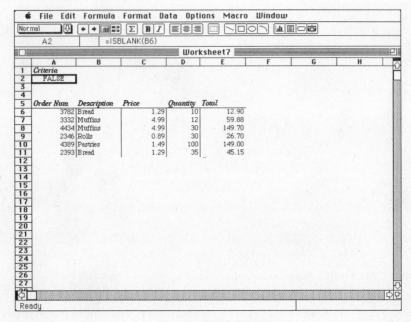

Fig. 15.22. Finding records with a blank Description field.

(Almost) Eliminating the Criteria Range

If you want, you can narrow the criteria range to two cells, a label, and a criteria entry, eliminating the need to duplicate the field names for the criteria range. In other words, you can design a single formula that accomplishes all the matching requirements of several formulas and is sufficient for an Excel criteria range.

The example shown in figure 15.19 uses several cells in the criteria range to find all records in the publication log that have a Date Published value of 1989 or a Date Published value greater than 1987 and a Location value of LIB4. Instead of entering several formulas, you can enter the following formula and use it as the criteria range:

=OR(E8=1989,(AND(E8>1987,F8=LIB4))

Enter this formula into cell B3 and specify B2:B3 as the criteria range. Because this entry is a computed criteria entry, cell B2 must contain a label different from those in the database. The resulting search is the same as the example shown in figure 15.19.

This technique also enables you to specify a range of values for a single field. If you want to find all records with a Date Published value between 1987 and 1989, for example, you can enter the formula as follows:

=AND(E8>1987,E8<1989)

Extracting Records

Extracting records from a database can help you calculate subtotals or print reports based on a subset of the data. If you already know how to find records, learning to extract them is easy, because extracting is an extension of searching. You can extract records from a database range in two ways. You can issue the DGET function, which pulls any field from the database to any other location. Alternatively, you can use an extract range with the Extract command from the Data menu.

Using DGET To Extract a Record

The DGET function enables you to pull any field from a database into any other cell on a worksheet. This function has several useful aspects that make it more useful than an extract range:

- DGET can operate on any range of data, not just the database range defined with the Set Database command from the Data menu. You therefore can use DGET functions to extract data from several databases on the same worksheet.

- DGET updates its information each time the worksheet recalculates. Therefore, changes to the database or criteria immediately affect the result of the DGET function.

- DGET requires only one cell (besides the database and extract ranges); it does not require you to highlight any particular range.

Like all database statistical functions (described in Chapter 6), DGET uses the following syntax:

DGET(*database,field,criteria*)

The *database* argument is the range of cells containing the data. If this range is the active database, you can enter its reference or the range name DATABASE. If the range is not the active database, enter the range reference including the column headings of the database.

The *field* argument is the field within the database that you want to extract. Enter a column number from 1 to the number of the last column in your database, or enter the column heading in quotation marks.

The *criteria* argument is the range of cells containing the criteria for locating the data. This range does not have to be the active criteria range, but if it is, you simply can enter the range name CRITERIA as the reference. Otherwise, the reference must be to a range that contains valid criteria for the database. As soon as you enter criteria into the criteria range, the DGET function extracts the specified data.

The following example of the DGET function extracts data from the fourth column of the active database using the active criteria:

>   DGET(Database,4,Criteria)

This DGET function extracts data from the "Phone" column of the active database using the criteria in the range A4..B5:

>   DGET(Database,"Phone",A4..B5)

Make sure that the criteria narrows the selection to a single record. If several records match the criteria, the DGET function returns the error #NUM!. If no records match the criteria, DGET returns the error #VALUE!.

By stacking up several DGET functions, you can extract an entire database record or just the fields you want. The fields do not have to appear in a row as they do with the extract range procedure; you can extract fields into a form if you want (see fig. 15.23).

Notice the DGET function in the formula bar.

Using an Extract Range

The second method of extracting data is to use an extract range with the Extract command from the Data menu. This method offers some advantages over the DGET function:

- You can extract several records at one time. All records that match the criteria are extracted into a specified area of the worksheet.

- You don't need to enter several formulas to extract complete records; you just type the column headings of the fields you want to extract.

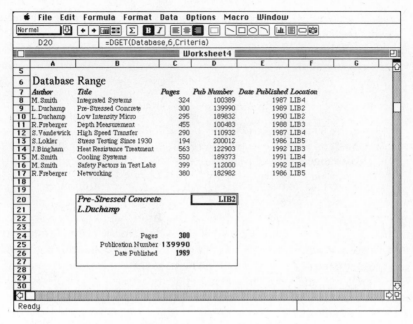

Fig. 15.23. *Using DGET to extract records into a form.*

- You easily can make extract ranges separate databases to use in further data manipulation, such as calculating subtotals.

- The cells containing extracted data contain the actual data from the database (or copies of it) rather than formulas. This makes it easier to copy to other cells.

To extract records from a database, first set up the database range and criteria range as described in this chapter. (You do not use the data form for this procedure.) Next, determine the area, or *extract range*, where you want the extracted records to appear. (Excel does not remove extracted records from the database; it places copies of them in the extract range.)

The extract range should be at the bottom of the worksheet because Excel clears all data below this range when extracting. Excel places every record that matches your criteria into this extract area. Enter the database column headings in the first row of the extract range or copy the headings from the database range.

To extract records with an extract range, follow these steps:

1. Establish the database range and criteria range.

2. Copy the column headings from the database into a range of cells below the database. Make sure there is no data below these headings. (Instead, you can type only the headings you want in the extract range.)

3. Highlight the extract headings and select the Set Extract command from the Data menu. This sets the range for future extract procedures. Alternatively, you can highlight the extract range headings without using the Data Set Extract command. In this case, you must highlight the headings each time you extract data.

4. Select the Extract command from the Data menu.

5. Check the Unique Records Only box and click on OK to extract only one copy of each matching record. Otherwise, just click on OK to complete the extract procedure.

You don't need to extract entire records; you can pull out only the information you want from the records that match the criteria. Suppose that you want to extract records from the publication log database used in a number of examples in this chapter. You have set up the criteria to find all publications with a Date Published value greater than 1987, but you don't want the extracted list to contain all the fields in the records; you need only the Author, Title, and Date Published fields. Enter these three fields at the top of the extract range, which appears in the lower portion of figure 15.24.

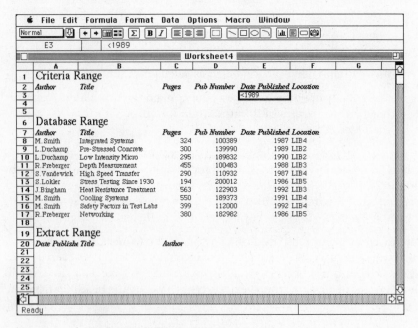

Fig. 15.24. *Specifying fields to be extracted.*

Notice that the three extract fields are not in the same order as in the database. You do not need to use all the fields for the extract, nor do you need to maintain their order. The extract fields also do not have to include the fields used in the search criteria. You can base your search on the Date Published field and extract only the Author information from the matching records. Or, you can extract the entire record.

The next step is to highlight the extract fields you specified and then choose the Set Extract command from the Data menu (see fig. 15.25). Finally, choose the Extract command from the Data menu. Excel copies the information from matching records in the database and fills in the cells below the extract fields (see fig. 15.26).

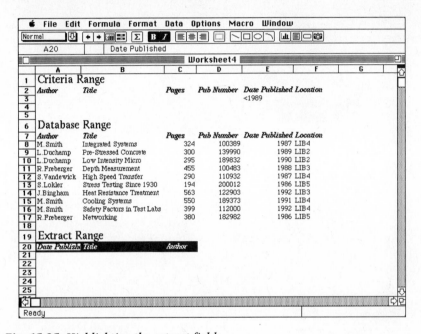

Fig. 15.25. *Highlighting the extract fields.*

The Set Extract command from the Data menu records the extract range you highlighted. You then can repeat the extract procedure later—without having to repeat these steps. You can change the criteria, for example, and select the Extract command from the Data menu to reextract records.

Note: You can extract records without using the Set Extract command from the Data menu. You have to highlight the extract range, however, each time you use the Data Extract command. Actually, this can be useful if your extract range changes position on the worksheet from time to time.

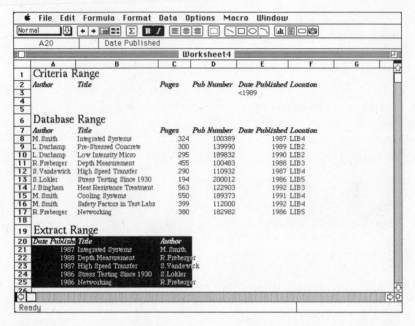

Fig. 15.26. *The extracted data.*

Highlighting the single row as the extract range causes Excel to extract all matching records and fill in the cells below the extract fields. You can limit the number of records displayed by highlighting the extract headings and a block of one or more rows. Excel stops extracting when it fills the highlighted range (see fig. 15.27)

> ***Caution:*** Remember to place the extract range below all other worksheet information. When extracting, Excel erases all information below the extracted data. If data appears below the extract range, that data is deleted from the worksheet.

Extracting Unique Records

When you use the Extract command from the Data menu, Excel presents a dialog box that asks whether you want to extract unique records only (see fig. 15.28). Normally, the box is unchecked, and Excel extracts all matching records from the database, including all identical records. You may, however, have an application requiring that only one of each matching record be extracted. This requirement is common for databases that keep a historical record of activity that may occur several times, creating several identical records. Customer purchases, shipping logs, purchase order records, and other such databases fall into this category.

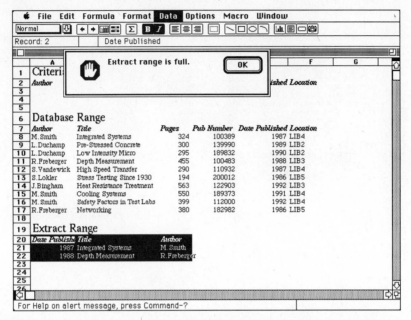

Fig. 15.27. *A message indicating that the extract range is full.*

When extracting, Excel considers two records identical when the *extracted* fields are identical—not when *all* fields are identical. Therefore, customer records that have different dates (but are otherwise identical) still may be considered identical if the Date field is not one of the extracted fields.

Suppose that you have a database of customer purchases and you want to extract a list of all customers who have purchased a particular item so that you can send them a letter. If some customers have purchased this item several times, the database will contain several matching records for each customer. Although the purchase dates will be different, you may not want the date field in the extract range. By checking the Unique Records Only box, you limit the matching records to one for each client. Your resulting extracted list therefore contains only the records you need.

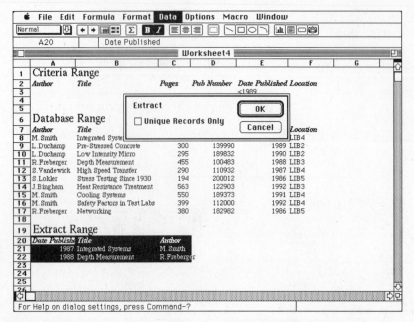

Fig. 15.28. The Data Extract dialog box.

Deleting a Group of Records

Excel enables you to delete batches of database records that share common data. Deleting database records is similar to finding or extracting records, except that after the criteria is established, you choose the Delete command instead of the Find or Extract command from the Data menu. Follow these steps to delete records:

1. Set up the database and criteria ranges as specified in this chapter.

2. Enter the criteria for locating the records you want to delete.

3. Choose the Delete command from the Data menu.

> *Caution:* You cannot replace deleted records after this operation is complete. They are removed permanently from the database.

Summary

This chapter explained the commands used for basic database operations in Excel. These operations include setting up a database, inserting and deleting records, searching for records, and extracting records based on criteria. Chapter 14 gave you a brief tour of these procedures, and this chapter provided all the details. The following are some important points to remember:

- In an Excel database, each row is a record; cells within the rows (that is, the columns) are fields.

- You activate a database by highlighting the entire database range (including the column headings and any records beneath them) and using the Set Database command from the Data menu.

- You can have only one active database at a time in each worksheet—even if the database reference is to an external worksheet.

- After activating a database, you can use the automatic data form to browse through the records, add records, remove records, and find records. Use the Form command from the Data menu to view this form.

- You can conduct powerful searches without the data form by using a criteria range in the worksheet.

- You can use calculations as criteria entries.

- You can sort the database data by highlighting the records (do not include the column titles) and using the Sort command from the Data menu.

- Use the Extract command from the Data menu or the DGET function to extract records.

Chapter 16, "Using Advanced Database Techniques," discusses other techniques you can use in Excel, including using external database ranges.

16

Using Advanced Database Techniques

T his chapter introduces some advanced techniques that you can use for data management. Primarily, the chapter explains how you can build a custom data form by using Excel's Dialog Editor program. Custom data forms enable you to organize information any way you want. Customizing forms also helps you overcome the initial limitation on the size of the data form. In addition, you learn how to manipulate external databases and remove duplicate records from the database.

Customizing the Data Form

The *data form* is a tool for entering and editing database records in Excel. When you define a range of cells as a database, you can then enter, view, and edit its records with the data form. Select the Form command in the Data menu; the data form appears for the active database.

The automatic data form provided by Excel is a useful tool for speeding up the data entry process and the search process. Because the data form presents records in a neat and uniform way, it makes database management easy to understand. The data form has its shortcomings, however. As mentioned in Chapter 15, the form that Excel initially provides cannot display more fields than the screen can hold. By customizing the data form, however, you can overcome this limit by changing the size and shape of the form, as well as the fields used in the form and their positions and sizes.

Customizing the data form is really a matter of rearranging the fields displayed on the form. By changing the field positions, you can gain more working space. Also, you can remove fields and change the titles and text used in the form. You cannot change the buttons or the scroll bar, however; these are added and controlled by Excel.

Excel provides a tool that makes creating a custom data form simple: the Dialog Editor program, which comes with Excel on the program disk. Although you don't have to use the Dialog Editor to customize a data form, you must do tedious extra work if you create a custom data form without using the program. The basic steps for creating a custom data form are as follows:

1. Using MultiFinder or System 7, switch to the Dialog Editor program that comes with Excel. If your system does not support multitasking, quit Excel and enter the Dialog Editor program from the Finder.

2. Using the Item menu in the Dialog Editor, add the desired field boxes and text to the blank data form provided. These should correspond to the database to which the data form applies. That is, you should include a field box for each column in the database and text to describe each field box.

3. Select the first field box and choose the Edit-Info command. This step brings up a dialog box with information about the selected field box.

4. Link the field box to a column in the database by entering the column heading (field name) in the space marked Init/Result in the text box.

5. Repeat steps 3 and 4 for the remaining field boxes in the form.

6. Use the Select Dialog command from the Edit menu, followed by the Copy command from the Edit menu to copy the data form that you have created.

7. Using MultiFinder or System 7, switch back to Excel. If your system does not support task switching, quit the Dialog Editor and reenter Excel from the Finder. Open the worksheet that contains the database.

8. Move the cell pointer to a blank area in the worksheet. This area should have at least eight columns and as many rows as there are items in your custom data form.

9. Use the Paste command from the Edit menu to paste the data form's description table into the worksheet at the current location of the pointer. This table describes the data form that you copied from the text editor.

10. With the data table still highlighted after pasting, select the Define Name command from the Formula menu and enter the name *Data_Form* for the table. Click on OK when you finish.

11. Save the changes that you made to the worksheet.

The next few sections in this chapter describe these steps in more detail. You also will discover a way to create a custom data form without using the Dialog Editor program.

Using the Dialog Editor

The Dialog Editor is a program that helps you design dialog boxes. Technically, the data form is a dialog box. As you see in the next section of this book, you can use the Dialog Editor for other types of custom dialog boxes—specifically, those controlled by macros. For now, this book will concentrate only on those features of the Dialog Editor that apply to data forms.

The Dialog Editor program is a special program that comes with Excel. If your system supports multitasking through MultiFinder or System 7, you can switch between Excel and the Dialog Editor program easily. If necessary, you can switch back and forth to fine-tune your custom data form. Refer to the MultiFinder or System 7 documentation for details about task switching. If your system does not support task switching, exit Excel and start the Dialog Editor program from the desktop by double-clicking on the Dialog Editor program icon (this is in the same folder as the Excel program icon). When you enter the program, the screen looks like figure 16.1. Notice that you begin with a blank data form and a series of menu options.

Changing the Size of the Data Form

The first thing you may want to do is specify the size and position of the data form itself. The Dialog Editor starts with a default size in the middle of the screen. To change the position of the form, follow these steps:

1. Choose the Select Dialog command from the Edit menu.

2. Choose the Info command from the Edit menu. The Info dialog box appears on the screen containing information about the data form.

3. Click on the Auto check boxes next to the items X and Y. These are the first two items in the dialog box. Clicking on these check boxes should remove the check marks and cause numbers to appear in the corresponding entry boxes. Click on OK when you finish.

4. Click the mouse anywhere inside the data form box and drag the form to another location on the screen. You can also move the data form box by using the arrow keys and pressing Return when finished.

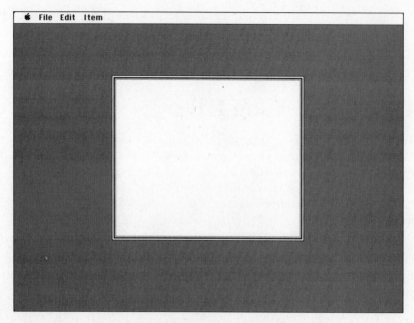

Fig. 16.1. The Dialog Editor screen with a blank data form.

Wherever the data form appears on the screen in the dialog editor is where it will appear when you use it. Excel records the position of the box on-screen.

To change the size and shape of the form, click on any side or corner of the box. The pointer will change shape to indicate that you can click and drag the mouse to change the box. If you click in a corner of the box, you can drag diagonally to change the position of that corner. Using this method changes the overall dimensions of the box. In addition, you can use the keyboard to change the size of the dialog box. Just highlight the box by clicking on it (or using the Select Dialog command from the Edit menu); then press the Shift key with one of the four arrow keys. Figure 16.2 shows a data form with its initial size and shape changed.

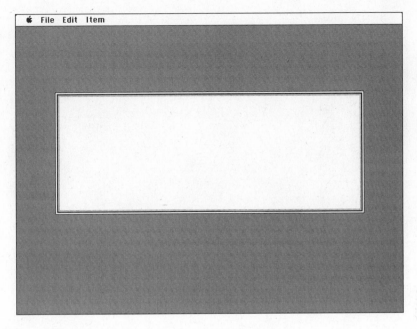

Fig. 16.2. Changing the size and shape of the data form.

Adding Text to the Data Form

Another important part of building a data form is adding text. You can add any text to the data form by using the Item Text command. Initially, this command adds a text box containing the word *Text*. When the box is highlighted, however, you can type any information into the text box. The new information replaces the old. To highlight a text box, click on the box or press Tab. Excel indicates that a text box is highlighted when a dotted border surrounds it (see fig. 16.3).

You can add any text that you want to the form—it merely acts as data labels for the form. Usually, you will want to include descriptive text for each field in the data form, but this is not mandatory. You also can include instructions, titles, or any other text labels in the form.

Add a different text box for each field in the database range (or, at least, for each field that is to appear in the form). These text labels do not have to match those in the database; they can, in fact, be completely different. You will want to use text labels that remind you of the fields in the database. Remember that these text labels simply are descriptive labels on the form and are completely optional.

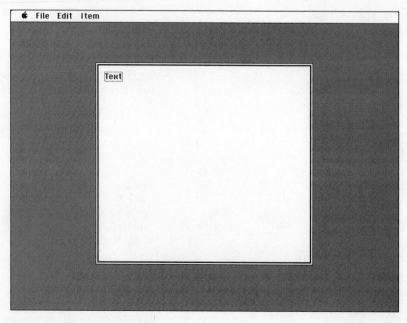

Fig. 16.3. *A highlighted text box.*

To move the text boxes into position, simply click on them and drag them to the new position. Alternatively, you can use the keyboard to move a text box; just highlight the box and use the arrow keys to change its position.

The Dialog Editor automatically makes the text box just large enough to hold all the text that you type. Therefore, you should not need to change the size of a text box. You may consider using text boxes to display fancy characters created with Option-*key* combinations (see fig. 16.4).

The Apple logos were created by pressing Shift-Option-K. Experiment with various keystrokes for fancy characters.

> **Tip: Inserting Multiple Text Boxes**
> After inserting the first text box and changing its text, press Return to add another. Keep pressing Return to enter as many as you like. You can change the text in an existing box by highlighting it and typing new text.

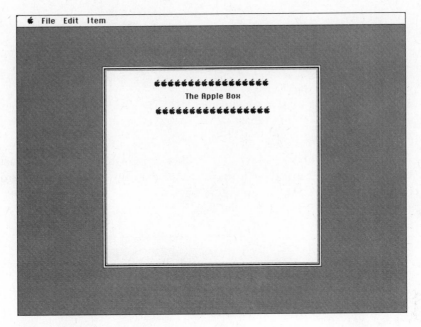

Fig. 16.4. Using special characters in a text box.

Adding Fields to the Data Form

The next step is to add fields to the data form. *Fields* are the boxes that display the data from the database. Because the field boxes relate to the field names, you should line them up with the labels you entered in the preceding section. To create a field box, choose the Edit Box command from the Item menu. A dialog box appears with various edit boxes that you can insert onto the screen. Most of these options do not apply to data forms. In fact, you should select only the Text option for your data forms. The text box that you add will translate to a field box when you use the data form with your database. Add as many field boxes as you want. Usually, these field boxes match up with the fields in the database. Note that Excel places the words Edit Text in the boxes to indicate that they are edit boxes. This phrase does not appear when you use the form.

> ### *Tip: Inserting Multiple Field Boxes*
> After inserting the first field box, press Return to enter a second field box. Keep pressing Return to enter as many fields as you want.

Excel knows which database data to place into the various field boxes because you tell it which database fields are linked to which field boxes. This process is described next.

You can move field boxes as you move other objects in the data form. Just click on the box and drag the mouse. Alternatively, use the keyboard commands to move the boxes. Figure 16.5 shows a completed set of text boxes and field boxes for a custom data form.

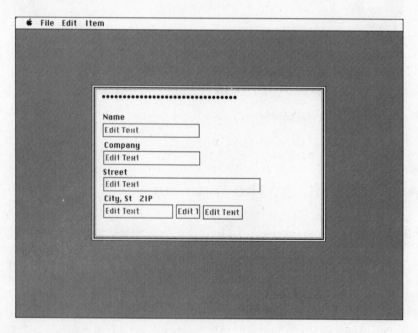

Fig. 16.5. *Field boxes for the data form.*

Entering Special Information about the Data Form

The size and position of the various data form elements are measured and stored by the Dialog Editor. Although you position the elements by using the mouse or keyboard, you can view the coordinates for each data form element—and for the data form itself. Just highlight the item you want to view and select the Info command from the Edit menu. The Dialog Editor presents a dialog box like the one in figure 16.6.

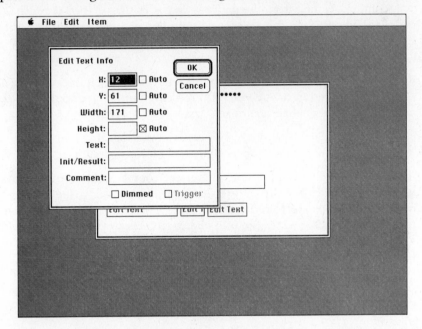

Fig. 16.6. The Edit Text Info dialog box.

The Edit Text Info dialog box contains the following items:

- *X and Y:* Indicate the coordinates for the upper left corner of the highlighted element. In the case of the data form itself, these values indicate the distance (in picas) from the upper left corner of the screen. The x coordinate indicates the horizontal position; the y coordinate indicates the vertical position. In the case of text boxes or field boxes, the x and y coordinates are relative to the upper left corner of the dialog box. Thus, x and y coordinates of 1,1 for a text box place the box in the upper left corner of the data form, regardless of its position on-screen.

- *Width and Height:* Indicates values measured in picas. These values are relative to the upper left corner of the item itself; they are thus constant values. A width of 100 is a specific width, for example, regardless of the item's x and y values.

- *Init/Result:* Specifies the database field that is linked to this field box. A field box is linked to the database field you specify. This value is important only for the field boxes. In fact, do not enter anything into this space for items other than field boxes. Enter the column heading from the database in the Init/Result box for each field box. Be sure to enter the column heading as it appears in the first row of the database. If you forget the headings or make mistakes when entering them, you can make corrections later.

- *Text:* Contains information only for text box items; it indicates the text displayed in the text box. Do not enter anything into this space for items other than text boxes.

- *Comment:* Enables you to enter comments about the item. This information does not appear in the data form.

The main reason for using the Info command from the Edit menu is to link the field boxes with the field names (column headings) used in the database. Click on the desired field box, and then enter its corresponding field name into the Init/Result space in the Info dialog box. Excel will match the field box with the data in the column that you specify. After you link the fields, the final step is to save your work so that you can import it into the desired worksheet.

Saving the Data Form

Because the Dialog Editor is a special tool for customizing the data form, the assumption is that you will be returning to Excel as soon as you finish creating the form. The program thus contains no Save command for permanently storing the form. Instead, you must store the form on the Clipboard and then pass the form into Excel for use with the database for which the form was created.

To store the data form on the Clipboard, choose the Select Dialog command from the Edit menu. Next, choose Copy from the Edit menu to copy the form. The specifications for the form now are on the Clipboard. Another method is to choose Quit from the File menu and answer Yes when asked whether you want to save the form to the Clipboard. After you quit the program, go immediately into Excel with the database worksheet that you want active.

Copying the Data Form into the Excel Spreadsheet

When you finish creating the data form and storing it on the Clipboard, return to Excel with the worksheet you want in view (the worksheet containing the database that relates to the form you created). Next, click the mouse button in an empty area of the worksheet. This area should be a block of at least 8 cells by 20 cells (actually, the number of rows needed corresponds to the number of items contained in the data form). Finally, choose the Paste command from the Edit menu.

When you paste the data form into the empty area of the worksheet, Excel lists the coordinates and other values relating to the data items. In other words, the data form does not appear in the worksheet; what appears is a table of values describing the data form for Excel. Figure 16.7 shows a data form after being pasted into a worksheet.

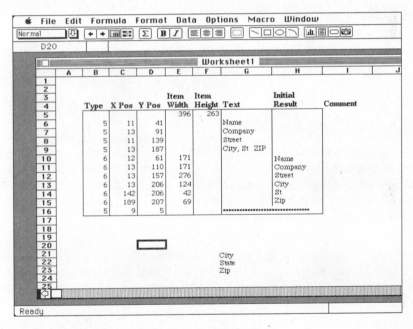

Fig. 16.7. *Pasting the data form into a worksheet.*

In this example, the column headings were added to indicate what data is in each column. Also, the border was added to help separate this data from the rest of the worksheet. (See Chapter 5 for details about creating borders.)

Each row of data represents (or defines) one of the items in the form. Notice that the data in these rows was contained in the Edit Info dialog boxes in the Dialog Editor program. Now that the information is part of the worksheet, you can use the information for the database data form.

The last step is to highlight the range of cells containing this new data (the range should be highlighted when you paste it into the worksheet). Do not include the headings in this range (assuming that you add them as shown in the figure). Next, choose the Define Name command from the Formula menu and enter the name *Data_Form* (include the underscore character) in the space marked Name. Click on OK to complete the naming procedure.

Now when you use the data form for the active database, Excel will read this table of values to create the custom data form. Excel will insert the data into its appropriate field automatically by matching the database's column headings with the Init/Result values in the table. If these values do not match exactly, Excel will be unable to place the data into the form. Double-check that the Init/Result values are identical to the column headings in the database and make corrections to the table if necessary.

> **Tip: Applying a Second Name**
> You might consider applying a second name—besides *Data_Form*— to the data form table. Then you can switch easily between two different databases (and data forms) on the same worksheet.

You can create a data form without the Dialog Editor by setting up a range containing the columns shown in figure 16.7 and then entering the coordinates and other values into the appropriate cells under each column. Each item gets a new row in this range. Note that the specifications for the form itself are contained in the first row (directly under the headings). Descriptions of each column follow:

Column	Specifies
Type	Type of each item. In a data form, you should have only two types: 5 indicates a text box and 6 indicates a field box.
X Pos	Horizontal position of the upper left corner of the item.
Y Pos	Vertical position of the upper left corner of the item.
Item Width	Width of the item.
Item Height	Height of the item.

Column	Specifies
Text	Text (if any) used for the item. Field boxes will not have anything in this column.
Init Result	Name of the field to which the field box is linked. This name must match exactly one of the database field names. Text boxes should not have anything in this column.

Note: If you omit or erase the Item Width and Item Height values, Excel automatically chooses an appropriate width and height for the item. Often, Excel's automatic settings work perfectly in your custom forms.

Comment	Any comments regarding the item.

Be sure to highlight the data table and define its name as Data_Form. You also can edit an existing data form by changing the information in this Table.

Purging Duplicate Records from a Database

The need to remove duplicates is common in database management. Often, record-keeping tasks involve accumulating multiple copies of the same information. In these cases, you may decide to remove duplicates. First, determine which field you want to use as the *determining field* for duplicates. In other words, choose a field in the database that contains information unique to each record, so that if two records contain the same information in this field, they can be considered duplicates. In address lists, for example, the Street field often serves this purpose. At times, you may need two or three determining fields for this procedure. In an address list, for example, it's possible to have two different people living at the same address. You may use both the Name and Address fields in this case.

After settling on the determining field or fields, sort the database by the field (or fields) you have chosen. To do so, follow these steps:

1. Highlight the database records for sorting. Do not include the column headings in this range.

2. Select the Sort command from the Data menu. This brings up the Sort dialog box with three sort key spaces.

3. Press the Tab key to move the cell pointer to the first cell in the column by which you want to sort the database. The address of this cell should be in the space marked 1st Key in the Sort dialog box.

4. If you require more sort fields, use the 2nd Key and 3rd Key spaces to specify the desired columns. (See Chapter 15 for complete details about sorting database records by one or more fields.)

5. Click on OK to complete the sort.

After sorting the database, all duplicate records should be together in adjacent rows. Now you can remove the duplicates by using special criteria in your criteria range. You will need to enter a criteria formula (calculated criteria) for each of the fields used in the sort. Each formula should compare the field in the first record of the database with the same field in the record above it. Figure 16.8 shows an example based on a simple address list.

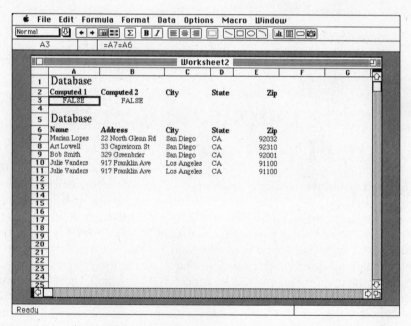

Fig. 16.8. Entering duplication criteria after sorting the database.

In this example, the database has been sorted by two fields: Address and Name. This sorting has placed the duplicates together in the database. In the criteria range above the database, the following formulas were entered:

A3: =A7=A6

B3: =B7=B6

Notice that the criteria entry has been made for each column used to sort the records. Each criteria formula compares the first field in its column with the cell directly above it.

The formula in cell A3 reads =A7=A6. This formula finds all records in which the Name field matches the name above it. It is all right that the first cell (A7) refers to a cell that is not really a record (A6) in this case. The formula performs its function regardless. The formula in cell B3 reads =B7=B6 and adds the address field to the name field for matching records. In short, these formulas find records in which the Address fields and Name fields match the record above.

Finally, use the Delete command from the Data menu to remove the records that match the criteria. As long as the database is sorted properly, this step removes duplicates.

Managing External Databases

You have seen several references to external databases in this chapter and the preceding chapter. An *external database* is simply a database that is not contained on the same worksheet as the reference. Any time you specify a database range, criteria range, or extract range, you can enter it as an external reference—pointing to data contained on a different worksheet.

To enter a database, criteria, or extract range as an external reference requires that you use the Define Name command from the Formula menu instead of the Set Database, Set Criteria, and Set-Extract commands in the Data menu. You can, if desired, have all three ranges on different worksheets. The point is that their ranges must be referenced in the same worksheet using the Define Name command from the Formula menu. Follow these steps:

1. Open the worksheets containing the database data, the extract range, and the criteria range.

2. Open the worksheet in which you want to manipulate the data, such as extracting records. This worksheet can be one of the other worksheets or a completely different one. Activate this worksheet.

3. Select the Define Name command from the Formula menu. The Define Name dialog box appears.

4. Type the name *Database* into the space marked Name and type the external reference to the database in the space marked Refers To. This external reference should take the form *Worksheet!Range*

where *Worksheet* is the name of the worksheet containing the database data and *Range* is the range of cells on that worksheet in which the data is located.

5. Click on the Add button to accept the name that you created.

6. Repeat this process using the names *Criteria* and *Extract* and referring to the criteria data and extract data, respectively. This data can be on separate worksheets.

Suppose that you use a worksheet to track all the transactions you enter into your checking account registers. Because the worksheet tracks several different accounts, you want a separate worksheet to balance and reconcile each account individually. This second worksheet will search through the translations in the first worksheet to extract all rows that apply to a specific account. This worksheet will contain an external database reference to extract specific records from the transaction log. Figures 16.9 and 16.10 show the two worksheets in this example.

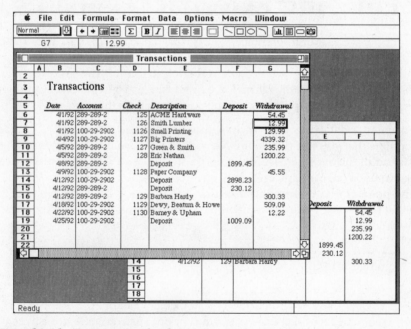

Fig. 16.9. *The Transactions database.*

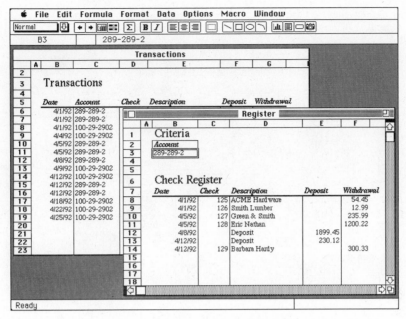

Fig. 16.10. *The check register compiled from the Transactions database.*

The Transactions worksheet is simply a list of checking account transactions for two different checking accounts. This worksheet includes deposits and withdrawals for both accounts. Because this worksheet is a transaction log, the records are not sorted by account number, but are in chronological order—you make entries as they occur.

The second database is the Register. It basically contains records that were extracted from the Transaction database and the criteria range used to extract them. As you can see, the database (Transaction log) is separate from the criteria and extract ranges. Therefore, you must use an external database reference when you establish the active database. The Define Name command from the Formula menu is used in the Register worksheet to create this external reference (see fig. 16.11).

Note that the Set Database command from the Data menu was not used to create this reference. Rather, the Define Name command from the Formula menu was used so an external range could be specified. Notice that the name DATABASE applies to the range named DATA on the Transactions worksheet. The entire external reference is TRANSACTIONS!DATA.

The criteria range is contained on the Transaction worksheet, along with the database reference and the extract range. The Set Criteria command from the Data menu, therefore, was used to establish the criteria range. The Set Extract command from the Data menu was used to reference the extract range.

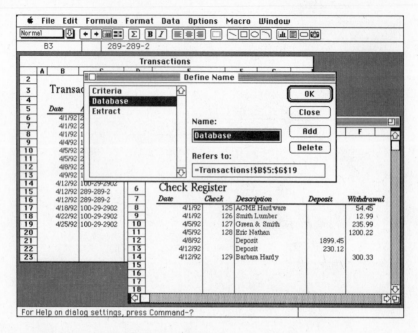

Fig. 16.11. *The external database reference.*

Following is a summary of how you create this example:

1. Name the database range in the Transaction worksheet DATA with the Define Name command from the Formula menu.

2. Create the criteria and extract ranges on the Register worksheet. (Copy field names from the Transaction worksheet to create the extract range.) Activate this worksheet.

3. Highlight the criteria range (B2:B3) and select the Set Criteria command from the Data menu.

4. Highlight the extract range (B7:F7) and select the Set Extract command from the Data menu.

5. Select the Define Name command from the Formula menu and, in the Define Name dialog box, enter the name DATABASE in the space reserved for the name.

6. Press Tab to move to the Refers To space and enter the reference *Transactions!Data* as the external reference to the database range. You also can point to the database range by highlighting it with the mouse. Click on OK when you are finished.

7. Enter the desired account number in cell B3. This is the account that you will be reconciling at this time.

8. Choose the Extract command from the Data menu. All records matching the account number you entered are extracted into the Register worksheet. You now can use the additional formulas to reconcile this information with your bank statement.

When finished, you can change the account number in cell B3 to reconcile the other account. Be sure to save each new Register worksheet you extract.

Although extracting records is an excellent way to draw information from an external database, it is not the only way. You can use database functions with external database references to calculate statistical values from the data. The functions can be entered onto a separate worksheet from the database. Suppose that you want to calculate the total of all deposits that you have made in a particular checking account. Rather than extract all the records for that account and then total the Deposits column, just enter this formula into the Register worksheet (see fig. 16.12):

=DSUM(Transactions!Data,"Deposit",Criteria

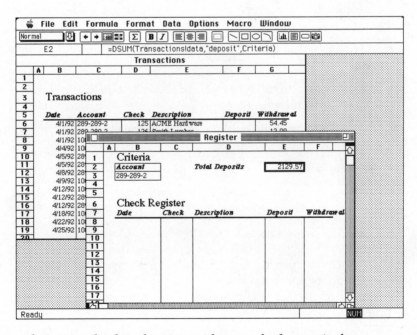

Fig. 16.12. Using database functions with external references in them.

When using database functions like these, it does not matter which database is currently active. This is because these functions can reference any range of cells—not just the active database range.

Summary

This chapter discussed some advanced database tools available for your worksheet databases. In particular, you learned how to create a custom data form. Creating a custom data form enables you to overcome basic limitations of the default form. In the custom form, you can include any fields you want, arrange them in any order, and change the basic size and shape of the form itself. This chapter also included a technique for removing duplicate records from a database and techniques for managing external databases. The following are points to remember:

- Use the Dialog Editor to create a custom data form.

- The size, shape, and position of the data form in the Dialog Editor determine the size, shape, and position of the form when used in Excel.

- Add text to a data form by using the Text command from the Item menu.

- Add field boxes to the data form by using the Edit Box command from the Item menu.

- After you add one field box or text box to the form, press Return to add another.

- Use the mouse to move the boxes into position in the form.

- Use the Info command from the Edit menu to link each field box to a field in the database.

- To use the custom data form in the Excel worksheet, copy the form within the Dialog Editor program, and then enter the Excel worksheet and use the Paste command from the Edit menu to insert the form into a blank area. Finally, name the highlighted data Data_Form, using the Define Name command from the Formula menu.

- External references can appear anywhere you reference a database range, criteria range, or extract range.

Now you are finished with Excel's database features. The rest of this book covers Excel macros. You will find macros helpful in all aspects of your worksheets, including databases.

Turn to Chapter 17, "Using Macros: A Quick Start," to learn how to create macros.

Part IV

Excel Macros

Includes

Using Macros: A Quick Start

Creating Macros

Using Advanced Macro Techniques

Building Custom Applications

17

Using Macros: A Quick Start

Macros are a popular feature of sophisticated programs and make your work easier by automating complex or repetitive tasks. Perhaps you have avoided using macros. Macros may have been advanced and complicated at one time, but today macros are quite easy to use. You don't have to become an advanced macro programmer to benefit from macros.

To get you started with macros, this chapter provides a step-by-step lesson in the basics of creating and running macros. You then will be ready to design your own macros for specific needs.

Working with Macros

A *macro* is a sort of invisible user in the computer that enters commands while you sit back and watch. Whatever action you can perform from the keyboard or mouse, the macro also can do. You just show the action one time, and the macro can repeat the action over and over.

You may be wondering why macros are so great if they simply repeat your commands—commands that you can enter yourself by using the keyboard or mouse. The benefit is that macros don't just repeat your commands: they repeat them instantly. A macro can perform dozens of commands in a second, and the macro never makes mistakes. A macro is like a tape recorder that plays back your commands as you entered them, but much faster. As a

685

matter of fact, you can teach a macro its commands by recording them with other, special commands. Basic steps for recording macro commands follow:

1. Turn on the recorder by choosing the Record command from the Macro menu.

2. Perform any commands or actions that you want to record.

3. Turn the recorder off by choosing the Stop Recorder command from the Macro menu.

4. Run the macro.

Each of these steps is described in this quick start. The sample macro you create in this chapter enters month names into a worksheet automatically. You record and edit the macro and even add a second macro. You will be able to use what you learn to create other macros.

Starting Macros

To create a macro, you must turn on the recorder and choose a name for the macro. Complete these steps to start a sample macro:

1. Start a new worksheet by entering Excel from the desktop or by choosing New from the File menu.

2. Start the recorder by choosing Record from the Macro menu. The dialog box shown in figure 17.1 appears.

   This dialog box asks you to name and select a shortcut key for the macro. The dialog box already contains the name RECORD1 and the shortcut key a. You can replace these entries with your own. (Note that Excel distinguishes between upper- and lowercase letters for the shortcut key, so remember which letter you used.)

   Choose a name that reminds you of the macro's purpose. When you are ready to run the macro later, you can choose it, by name, from a list of available macros. Alternatively, you can press ⌘-Option with the key you specified.

3. Enter the name *MONTHS* into the space provided. If a name is already in that space, replace it with the new name. Press Tab.

4. Press the *m* key to specify a lowercase *m* as the shortcut key for this macro. You will be replacing the default entry of the letter *a*—Excel uses the first available letter of the alphabet as the shortcut key, unless you change it. Press Return.

(Actually, this step is optional because macros do not need shortcut keys. To avoid specifying the shortcut key, remove the entry and press Return.)

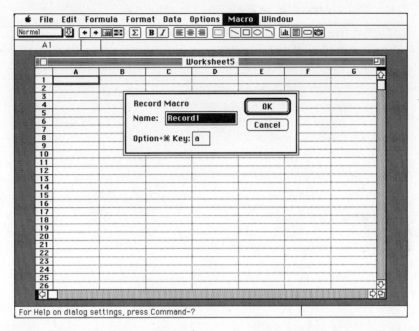

Fig. 17.1. *The Record Macro dialog box.*

You now are ready to record the macro named MONTHS. Everything you do from this point on will become part of the macro until you stop the recorder. The next section continues with this example and lists the steps that you will record in this macro.

Recording Macros

To begin recording the macro, follow these steps:

1. Move the pointer to cell A3.

2. Enter *1/1/91* and press Tab to move to cell B3.

3. Type the formula *=DATE("91",MONTH(A3)+1,"1")* and press Enter.

4. Highlight the range B3:L3.

5. Choose the Fill Right command from the Edit menu.

6. Click the mouse in the horizontal scroll bar to return to the left side of the worksheet. Alternatively, you can drag the scroll box all the way to the left. Now highlight the range A3:L3.

7. Choose the Number command from the Format menu and, at the space provided, type *mmmm* in the Format dialog box to specify a custom format. Press Return.

8. With the range still highlighted, press ⌘-B to *blank* the range (that is, to erase the information). Now select the Undo command from the Edit menu to undo that erasure. These two actions simulate making a mistake and correcting it while you record. You read more about this step later in the chapter in "Editing Macros."

9. Turn the recorder off by choosing the Stop Recorder command from the Macro menu.

You now have completed recording the macro called MONTHS. Steps 1 through 8 enter the month names into a row of the worksheet—a task that is required frequently on new worksheets. You now can accomplish that task at any time by running the macro.

Running Macros

Remember that the macro you just created operates on a new worksheet and enters information into the range A3:L3. To see how this macro works, you first need to erase the current worksheet. Follow these steps to run the macro:

1. Highlight the entire worksheet by clicking in the upper left corner of the sheet (in the intersection of the row and column headings). Then press ⌘-B.

2. Click to place the pointer in any cell.

3. Press ⌘-Option-m (lowercase m).

The macro instantly fills in the month names for the new worksheet. The result should look like figure 17.2.

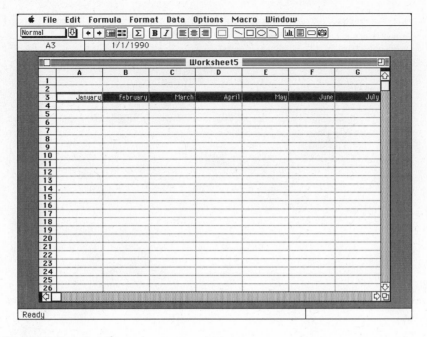

Fig. 17.2. *Running the macro.*

Another way to run the macro is to use the Run command from the Macro menu. This command is useful if you forget the shortcut key or if you don't assign a key to the macro. You also can use this command to view all available macros (by name) at one time. To run a macro with this command, just select Macro Run and then double-click on the appropriate macro name that appears in the dialog box.

Viewing and Saving Macros

When recording your actions as a macro, Excel translates everything you do into codes and places those codes in a macro worksheet. The codes represent the keys you pressed, the mouse movements you made, and the commands you selected. The codes also appear in the order in which you took those actions. These codes, called *macro commands*, are part of a group of codes called the *macro command language*. As you already have seen, you do not need to know what each of these codes means in order to create a macro—but when you take a look at the codes, you see how easy they are to understand. To look at the macro codes for the macro you just created, select the sheet named MACRO1 from the Window menu.

Performing this step activates the macro sheet, which was added and placed behind the current worksheet. The screen should look like figure 17.3.

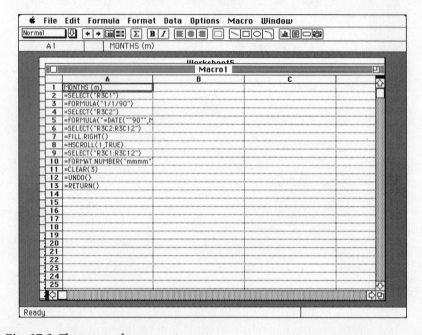

Fig. 17.3. *The macro sheet.*

Excel created the macro sheet when you selected the Record command from the Macro menu in step 2 of the section "Starting the Macro." Excel placed the macro sheet behind the active worksheet, and the macro commands were entered on the sheet "behind the scenes." Notice that the macro sheet contains a column of commands that represent your actions.

At the top of the column is the macro name as you entered it in step 3 of the section "Starting the Macro." Looking over these commands, you get a pretty good impression of what each command does. For complete details about macro commands, however, see Chapter 18 and Appendix B.

You can run the macro in the macro sheet anytime the sheet is open. If a sheet contains several macros, you can run any of them. (Chapter 18 explains how to place more macros on the same sheet. See also "Creating a Second Macro," later in this chapter.) Remember, however, that you must open the macro sheet in order to run a macro contained on the sheet. Although the macro sheet must be open, it does not have to be active (that is, in view); the sheet can be behind the active worksheet, for example.

To save the sample macro for future use, choose the Save command from the File menu, as you would for a typical worksheet. Because Excel saves the macro sheet independently of a worksheet, you can use the macro with any worksheet. The sample macro is useful on new worksheets.

Editing Macros

You can change a macro by editing the codes that appear on the macro sheet. Editing a macro requires a minor amount of knowledge about macro commands. You sometimes may make mistakes while recording a macro. You may select the wrong command, for example, and then undo the action with the Undo command from the Edit menu. The macro records the error and the Undo command and repeats them each time you run the macro. Of course, the result will be what you intended, but the mistake and its correction are unnecessary in the macro.

You can edit mistakes out of a macro or simply change a macro to better suit your needs. To remove the mistake and the Undo operation from the sample macro, do the following:

1. Highlight cells A11 and A12.

2. Select the Delete command from the Edit menu.

3. Choose the Shift Cells Up option.

Now the macro will not repeat the error each time the macro runs. The next thing to notice is the entry in cell A8. This command shows that you scrolled the window to the left by one screen. (Your cell may contain a slightly different entry.) That action was included as a step so that you could highlight the range A3:L3 for the next procedure. The macro does not need to scroll the page in order to highlight a range, however. Do the following to remove cell A8 from the macro:

1. Move the pointer to cell A8 and select the Delete command from the Edit menu.

2. Choose the Shift Cells Up option.

3. Save the edited macro again by choosing the Save command from the File menu.

Changing Cell References

Notice in figure 17.3 that all cell references in the macro were recorded in the R1C1 style. More important is the fact that the cell references are *literal*. Cell A6, for example, contains the range reference R3C2:R3C12, indicating the range B3:L3. This range was designated in preparation for the Fill Right command. Every time you run this macro, the range B3:L3 will be highlighted for the Fill Right command that occurs in the next cell of the macro. In other words, this macro does its work on the same range every time you use the macro.

Suppose that you want this macro to add the month names to any range in the worksheet. You want to be able to position the pointer in a cell, for example, and then have the macro add the month names, beginning in the active cell. Depending on where you begin, the area to be filled with month names could be any 1-by-12 range of cells. Tailoring the macro to meet this requirement really does not change the macro much; you simply must make the range references relative to the active cell.

You can make a macro's cell references relative by selecting the Relative Record command from the Macro menu before starting to record your actions as a macro. For the sample macro, you should select this command after performing step 4 in the section "Starting the Macro" and then finish the recording process. Remember that Excel now records the current location of the pointer and records your movements relative to this position. When you reexamine the macro, the cell addresses look different. For more details, see Chapter 18.

Creating a Second Macro

Creating another macro on the same macro sheet is different from creating the first macro. Because the sheet already exists and contains a macro in cell A1, you must begin the macro in a different cell. Excel makes this easy for you. When you record a second macro, Excel starts the macro in the first empty column of the macro sheet. In this case, Excel starts the second macro at cell B1.

Note: The column to the right of a macro often is used to hold comments about the macro. You therefore may want to place macros at least two columns apart on the macro sheet. In this example, you may want to use column C. If column B contains information, Excel uses column C. If column B is blank, however, you can skip it by using the Set Recorder command from the Macro menu (discussed in Chapter 15).

To create a second macro (this macro removes the worksheet grid lines), follow these steps:

1. Activate the worksheet. If you don't have a worksheet open, create a new one by choosing the New command from the File menu. Make sure that you use the Spreadsheet option when you issue this command, or you may get another macro sheet.

2. Choose Arrange All from the Window menu to arrange the two windows on-screen. This step is not necessary, but it enables you to see the macro record your actions as you perform them.

3. Select the Record command from the Macro menu and type the name *GRIDOFF* when presented with the dialog box. You can use *g* as the shortcut key. Press OK to accept the name and shortcut key and begin recording the macro.

4. Select the Display command from the Options menu and then remove the check mark from the Gridlines option. Click on the OK button.

   This step removes the grid lines from the active worksheet. Notice that your actions are being recorded in the macro sheet, beginning at cell B2.

5. Select the Stop Recorder command from the Macro menu.

You now have recorded a new macro that turns off the grid lines in the current worksheet.

Now the macro is ready to run. Run the macro by pressing ⌘-Option-g. Try the macro on a new worksheet. (Remember to leave the macro sheet open.)

Using Macro Buttons

With Excel Version 3.0, you can add macro buttons to your worksheets. After drawing a button, you can attach a macro to the button. When you press the button, Excel then runs the macro. This is useful for worksheet-specific macros and for creating custom applications in Excel. To add a button to the example, follow these steps:

1. Activate the sample worksheet. The macro sheet still should be open.

2. Click on the Button tool in the Toolbar. This tool is second from the right end of the Toolbar.

3. Click and drag on the worksheet to place the button. When you release the mouse, Excel presents the dialog box shown in figure 17.4. This dialog box contains all the currently active macros.

4. Double-click on the macro you want in this box. For the example, double-click on the Months macro.

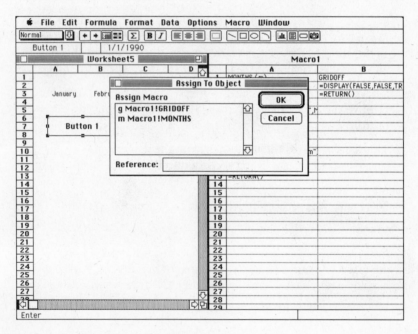

Fig. 17.4. The Attach Macro dialog box.

You now can run the Months macro each time you click on the macro button. Before trying the button, move the cell pointer to an empty row so that you easily can see the results of the macro. See Chapter 13 for details about manipulating button objects on the worksheet.

Summary

This chapter provided a brief step-by-step lesson on creating macros. You learned how to record a macro by using the Record command from the Macro menu, which opens a macro sheet, asks you to name the macro, and begins recording your actions. You also saw how the Stop Recorder command from the Macro menu concludes the recording. Running a macro consists of opening the appropriate macro sheet and entering the ⌘-Option-key combination that you specified for the macro. Finally, you saw how to create a second macro on an existing macro sheet.

With this information, you're ready to discover the details about creating and running macros, which Chapter 18 discusses.

18

Creating Macros

This chapter presents the basics of Excel's macro capabilities. If you have read Chapter 1, you probably are familiar with the purpose of macros. Chapter 17, "Using Macros: A Quick Start," provides step-by-step instructions for building a basic macro. You now are ready to discover how to put macros to powerful uses in your worksheets. Excel's macro language includes dozens of special commands to control the worksheet. You probably will not need or want to learn all the available commands and functions; more importantly, you should understand fully how to create, edit, and run macros.

First, you learn how macros operate, as well as what they are used for. You then learn the guidelines for creating basic macros. You learn how to create two types of macros: command and function. By the end of the chapter, you will be ready to progress in many directions. If you want to begin some macros of your own, you first may want to glance through the macro commands listed in Appendix B. If you want to learn more about creating menus and dialog boxes, as well as building custom applications, read Chapter 20. For details about programming—such as using variables, loops, and special routines—refer to Chapter 19.

Understanding How Macros Work

A *macro* is a special program that controls various operations of Excel. A macro is like an invisible operator that is using Excel from within the computer; it can issue commands just as you would. Besides entering

697

commands and options, macros offer special features. For example, macros enable you to create your own menus that contain options designed for special purposes.

Like programs, macros have a specific language—not unlike programming languages such as Pascal, C, and BASIC. But the macro language can be much easier to use than programming languages, and Excel can do much of the programming work for you. Nevertheless, knowing the macro language and its specific commands is helpful. If you also are familiar with programming concepts such as loops and variables, you are ahead of the game.

Because macros use special commands, these commands must be entered somewhere for Excel to read. Commands therefore are entered on a macro sheet. A *macro sheet* is similar to a worksheet but is a separate window designed to hold macro commands. When commands are typed into this window, the macro sheet can be saved as a separate file. Macros, therefore, are independent of the worksheets to which they apply. In fact, a single macro can be used with several worksheets, although many macros are designed to be used with only one worksheet.

Figure 18.1 shows a macro sheet and a standard worksheet next to it.

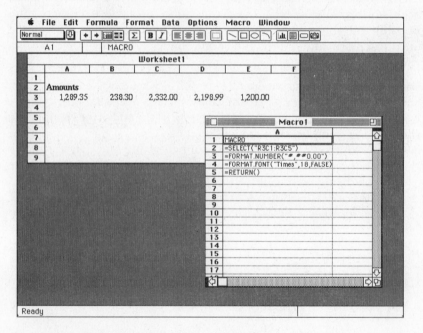

Fig. 18.1. *A typical macro sheet.*

You may be thinking that the macro sheet looks very much like a worksheet. A macro sheet is a worksheet—formatted with wide columns and with cells that display formulas rather than the results of formulas. All of the standard worksheet menus and options are available for your macro sheet.

Why does the macro sheet display formula text rather than the values produced by formulas? Excel perceives macro commands as being formulas. As you will see, these commands are entered with equal signs, and they all produce values. (Many macro commands produce values of TRUE or FALSE, indicating whether the command was used successfully. Some macro commands, however, produce values just as standard worksheet formulas do.) Generally, the values produced by macro commands are not as important to view as are the macro commands themselves, but you always can display the values instead of the formulas by using the Options Display command on the macro sheet.

Notice that the macro in figure 18.1 consists of a series of individual commands, each command in a separate cell in column A (the standard arrangement of a macro). The first cell contains a name; the following cells contain the commands that constitute the actions of the macro. These commands appear in a single column with no blanks. The end of the macro is the special command =RETURN(). Most macros end with this command.

Notice that each command in figure 18.1 (not including the macro name) is entered with an equal sign, like a worksheet formula. All macro commands must include an equal sign because Excel ignores any entry that does not have the equal sign. (Ignored entries can be useful, however, as you will see later.)

Because each macro has a definite beginning (the name) and ending (the =RETURN() command), you can store several different macros on the same macro sheet, each with a unique name. Storing macros in this manner can be useful when the macros are related to one another or to the same worksheet. When you are ready to use one of the macros, you can specify which one.

The final thing to note about macros is that you can run (or invoke) them at any time. You can run a macro in several ways. Remember, however, that you cannot run a macro unless the appropriate macro sheet is open. The sheet that you open should not be the active sheet; instead, you should place the desired worksheet in front of the macro sheet. Macros generally apply to the currently active worksheet.

Macros are fairly simple, but as you can see by now, you must follow certain steps in order to make a macro work properly. The following is a summary of these steps:

1. Open the worksheet to which the macro applies. If you are designing a macro that applies to several worksheets, open any of them.

2. Open a new worksheet with the File New command. Make the worksheet a macro sheet by selecting the Macro Sheet option.

   or

   Select the Macro Record command, and then enter a macro name and shortcut key. Next, perform the actions that you want to record. Excel records everything you do. When you are finished, select the Macro Stop Recorder command. If you use this version of step 2, you can eliminate steps 3 through 6 and proceed directly to step 7.

3. Enter a name for the macro in any cell of the macro sheet.

4. Enter the macro commands under the name you typed. You can do so simply by typing the commands (each command preceded by an equal sign) or by using the automatic macro recorder. Both methods are described in full later in this chapter.

5. Conclude the macro with the =RETURN() command.

6. Activate the macro by moving the pointer to the cell containing the macro name; then use the Formula Define Name command. Click on the ⌘-Option-Command button (hereafter called the Command Key button, for simplicity's sake) in the Define Name dialog box and then enter any character into the corresponding space. Click on OK when you finish.

7. Save the macro sheet if you want to keep the macro.

8. Activate the worksheet in which the macro will be used.

9. Run the macro. You can do so by using the Macro Run command and selecting the appropriate macro name from the list provided, or by pressing the Command key along with the Option key and the "shortcut" key specified in step 6.

Each of these steps is explained in detail in this chapter. After you are familiar with these steps, browse through the macro commands and experiment with macros on sample worksheets. For more advanced information about creating macros, see Chapter 19.

Noting Typical Uses for Macros

Macros are useful for many reasons. Most commonly, they perform repetitive or lengthy tasks when you press a single ⌘-Option-key combination. Anything that you can do by using Excel's menu commands, you can do by using a macro. For this reason, macros often are used to combine sets of menu commands into one simple key command.

Suppose that you prefer to work on worksheets without the grid lines and formula bar showing—and that you frequently use the Options Display command to remove the grid lines and the Options Workspace command to remove the formula bar. Because you have to hide the grid lines and formula bar separately (that is, you have to use two different menu commands), the process can become tedious. You can easily create a macro, however, that hides both in one step. This macro may look like the one in figure 18.2.

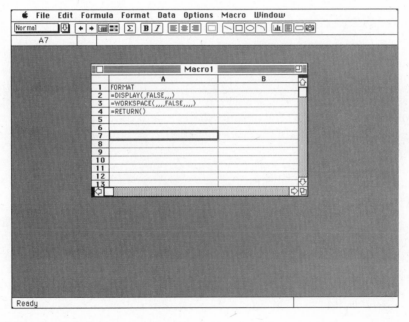

Fig. 18.2. *A simple macro.*

> **Tip: Using Uppercase and Lowercase in Macros**
> You do not need to enter macro commands in uppercase letters.
> This book uses the convention of placing command and function
> names in uppercase and variable information in lowercase.

You also can use macros to provide user interface and worksheet support.
Many businesspeople create worksheets that ultimately will be used by
other people, so the more documentation and support you can build into
a worksheet, the more effectively the worksheet will be used.

Macros are an excellent way to add support; they commonly are used to
control the user's actions in a fashion that prevents errors. Macros also can
be used to display messages as responses to certain actions. By creating
custom menu commands, you almost can eliminate the user's need to know
Excel. Although you would be limiting the user's capabilities and possible
actions, this very limitation would control errors.

Creating Command Macros

You can create macros in two ways, each of which has advantages and
disadvantages. Combining these methods for more control of macros may
be useful. The first method is to enter the macro commands by hand. The
second method is to use the macro recorder to enter macro commands as
you perform them. The latter method is useful especially for beginners
because it does much of the work for you.

Entering Macros Directly

One way to create a macro is to type the commands and functions directly
into the macro window. One disadvantage to this method is that you must
know the proper macro command for each action you want to take. Another
disadvantage is that these macros are subject to typing errors and improper
usage, which can cause the macro to run improperly or not at all. Many
commands and functions are not available through menus, however, and
therefore are not available to the macro recorder. For this reason, the direct-
entry method offers the most control of macros and usually is preferred for
advanced macro programming. The following steps are for entering a macro
by hand:

1. Open a macro worksheet using the File New command and choosing the Macro Sheet option.

2. Type the macro's name in the first cell of the macro sheet.

3. Under the name, enter all macro commands in the proper order. Macro commands are listed in Appendix B and many are discussed in Chapter 19. Be sure to end the macro with the RETURN() command.

4. Highlight the first cell (the cell containing the name) and issue the Formula Define Name command. The name and address of the macro already should be showing in the Define Name dialog box.

5. Click on the Command Key button and then type a shortcut key into the space provided (this can be any letter of the alphabet— either upper- or lowercase). Press Return when finished.

The macro now is ready to run. Ways of running the macro are discussed in "Running Macros," later in this chapter.

Using the Macro Recorder

The second (and easier) way to create a macro is to let Excel create it for you by recording actions that you can play back later. You can create a macro by simply turning the recorder on, issuing the commands, and then turning the recorder off.

The following is a summary of the basic steps for using the macro recorder:

1. Open the worksheet in which you want to use the macro.

2. Select the Macro Record command. The dialog box shown in figure 18.3 appears.

   This command not only starts the recording process but also opens a new macro sheet and begins the macro in cell A1 of that sheet. (Make sure that you are ready to begin recording before you select this command.)

3. Enter a name for the macro, replacing the default name that appears.

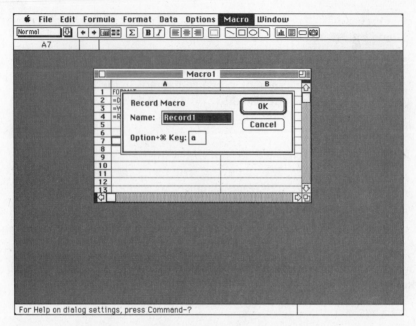

Fig. 18.3. *The Macro Record dialog box.*

4. Specify a character to be used with the Command and Option keys as a shortcut key for the macro. Any alphabet character is acceptable. Excel distinguishes between uppercase and lowercase letters.

5. Press Return to continue.

6. Perform the actions that you want to record. Remember that every move you make is being recorded.

7. When you finish, select the Macro Stop Recorder command.

   You can see the finished macro by activating the new Macro1 window that Excel has opened for you. This window will be behind the worksheet window; you can activate the Macro1 window by selecting its name from the Window menu.

8. Save the new macro sheet (you may decide to change its name before saving). Do this by activating the sheet using the Window menu and then selecting File Save.

These steps complete the macro and make it available for future worksheets. To use the macro, just open the saved macro sheet, activate the desired worksheet, and use the appropriate ⌘-Option-key combination to run the macro. You also can use other methods, which are explained later in this chapter.

Notice that choosing the Macro Stop Recorder command automatically concludes the macro by entering the =RETURN() command. Figure 18.4 shows a completed recording of the following actions (that is, these actions were performed after the recorder was turned on):

1. Select cells A3:E3.

> **Tip: Picking Up Where You Left Off**
>
> After you stop a macro by choosing the Stop Recorder command from the Macro menu, you still can continue with it. Just choose Start Recorder from the Macro menu to pick up where you left off. Excel removes the =RETURN() command that it placed at the end of the macro and begins recording your commands at that point. This capability is useful when you want to perform actions that are not to be recorded. Be careful, though: your unrecorded actions may change the worksheet and affect the way the macro runs.

2. Select the command Format Number.

3. Choose the number format #,##0.00 and press Return.

4. Choose the command Format Font.

5. Select the font Times 18 and press Return.

6. Select the command Macro Stop Recording.

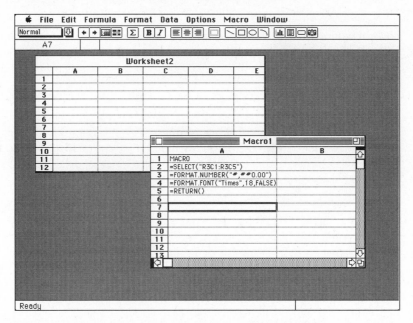

Fig. 18.4. *A sample recording of a few simple menu commands.*

Notice that the macro commands in the figure basically match the actions listed. You often can decipher a macro without really knowing the macro commands in detail.

When you record a macro, Excel shows cell and range references as R1C1-style references entered as text strings (that is, in quotation marks). When you create a macro by hand, you can use this R1C1-style text reference, or you can use an A1-style reference entered as an external reference (not as text). If you do not want to specify a particular external worksheet for the reference, use the exclamation point without the sheet name, as in !A1. For details about how macros use cell references, see Chapter 19.

Recording a Second Macro

The Macro Record command takes care of many steps for you, such as opening a new macro sheet and naming the macro for future use. You don't need to keep each macro on a separate macro sheet. In fact, if you record a second macro while the original macro sheet is still open, Excel automatically places the new macro onto the same sheet, in the first empty column. Just follow the previous steps for recording a macro.

You may not want the new macro to appear in the first empty column of the macro sheet. You may want to control where the second and subsequent macros appear on the sheet. One idea is to place each macro below the previous one. Another idea is to place macros a few columns apart.

To control where a macro will appear on the macro worksheet requires a slightly different procedure, as follows:

1. Make sure that the worksheet and existing macro sheet are open. You may want to arrange the two worksheets using the Window Arrange All command.

2. Enter a name for the second macro in the desired starting cell on the macro sheet. This may be below the first macro or in some out-of-the-way location. After entering the macro's name, press Return to move the pointer down one cell.

3. Select the Macro Set Recorder command, which tells Excel to start entering macro commands at the active cell (the cell below the macro name).

4. Activate the worksheet window by clicking on it or by selecting its name from the Window menu.

5. Position the pointer at the appropriate location; then select the Macro Start Recorder command.

6. Perform the actions that you want to record. Remember that every move you make is being recorded.

7. When you finish, select the Macro Stop Recorder command.

   Excel translates the recorded actions into macro commands and enters them into the open macro sheet at the location you specified with the Macro Set Recorder command. You can repeat this procedure to enter more macros on the same worksheet; remember to set the recorder on a different cell each time, and be sure that Excel has plenty of space under this cell to list the macro commands.

8. Name the macro. All macros must be named before they can be used.

9. Return to the macro sheet, which contains the new macro.

10. Position the pointer on the cell containing the macro's name and then select the Formula Define Name command. The dialog box shown in figure 18.5 appears.

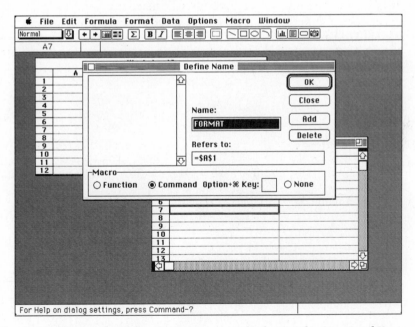

Fig. 18.5. Defining the name of your macro and selecting the Command Key button.

If you position the pointer correctly before choosing the Define Name command, the correct name and reference already will be in place for the macro, saving you some time. (The name used to define the macro does not have to match the name used in the first cell of the macro, but keeping these names the same is good practice; Excel automatically uses the name in the first cell unless you specify otherwise.)

11. Click on the Command Key button, which tells Excel that the name in the box relates to a command macro. This step distinguishes the name from standard named ranges.

12. Enter any alphabetical character in the space marked Command Option+⌘ Key in the dialog box.

> *Note:* Excel distinguishes between uppercase and lowercase letters for shortcut keys, giving you twice as many keys for macros. Pressing ⌘-Option-x can run one macro, for example, and pressing ⌘-Option-X can run a different macro.

Even if you do not assign a shortcut key to the macro, you still must click on the Command Key button, name the macro, and enter the cell address of the first cell in the macro. Be sure to save the macro sheet after you define the macro name (or names). Saving the sheet ensures that the macros will be active the next time you open the macro sheet.

> **Tip: *Editing the Macro Name***
> You can edit the macro name and its cell reference the same way that you edit a range name in a worksheet. Simply activate the appropriate macro sheet and select the Formula Define Name command. Next, select the macro you want from the list provided. Now you can change the name, cell reference, and shortcut key assigned to this macro.

> **Tip: *Using Duplicate Macro Names and Command Keys***
> You may use the same macro name for two different macros as long as they appear in two different macro sheets. Excel associates the macro name with the sheet name. If two macros (regardless of their names) have the same shortcut key, however, pressing ⌘-Option and that key runs only the macro that was defined first. If you define two macros with the same name and they appear in the same macro sheet, the name will apply only to the macro you defined last. The first macro will be undefined and, therefore, unavailable.

Note: Remember that before you can use a macro, you must open its macro sheet by using the File Open command.

Running Macros

You have seen how to create macros using the macro recorder or by typing them into a macro sheet. Next, you explore some ways to run macros in Excel: You can use the Macro Run command, issue the shortcut key with ⌘-Option, invoke the macro from another macro, or use a button.

Using the Shortcut Key

If you assign a shortcut key to a macro when you define its name, you can run the macro whenever the macro sheet is open by pressing ⌘-Option and the specified character. When you run a macro, be sure to activate the worksheet (not the macro sheet) in which the macro will operate. (If the macro sheet is still active when you run the macro, the commands will apply to the macro sheet.)

Remember that Excel distinguishes between upper- and lowercase letters used in macro shortcut keys. Therefore, the shortcut key X must be invoked by pressing ⌘-Option-Shift-X.

Tip: Hiding the Macro Sheet
If you do not like having the macro sheet open at the same time as the worksheet, try making the macro window invisible with the Window Hide command.

Using the Run Command

Besides using the shortcut key to run a macro, you can use the Macro Run command. When you choose this command, Excel displays the dialog box shown in figure 18.6. This dialog box displays the names of all macros that can be run at this time.

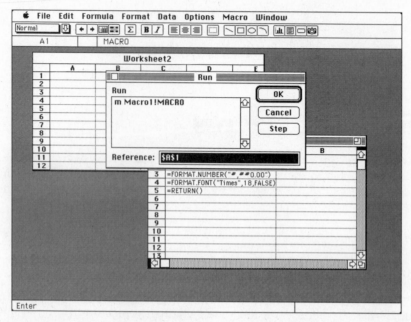

Fig. 18.6. *The Macro Run dialog box.*

All named macros in all open macro sheets appear in this dialog box. If you have opened two or more macro sheets, all their names appear. Notice that the macros are listed as external references to the macro sheets that contain them. If the macros include a shortcut key, this will precede the name. Simply double-click on the macro you want to run.

> *Tip: When a Macro Name Does Not Appear in the Dialog Box*
> If the macro name you want does not appear in the dialog box, you may not have named the macro properly. Place the pointer on the first cell in the macro (its name) and select the Edit Define Name command. Select the Command key button at the bottom of the Define Name dialog box and press Return. When you normally use the Macro Record command, the name already exists and should appear in the Run dialog box.

Using Buttons

One of the most convenient ways to run macros is to attach them to buttons. When you click on the button, Excel invokes the macro attached to it.

Buttons are stored with the worksheets in which they appear. Before you draw the button onto the worksheet, make sure that the desired macro is open (that is, the appropriate macro sheet should be open).

To draw the button onto the worksheet, follow these steps:

1. Click on the Button tool and drag onto the worksheet. (This is described in Chapter 13.)

   After you draw the button, Excel presents a list of active macros and asks you to select one for the button.

2. Double-click on the desired macro in the list.

3. Highlight the button text by selecting it. Then type the new button text. Press ⌘-Return to have more than a single line of button text.

The macro now is attached to the button. When you press the button, the macro will run.

Not all macros are appropriate for buttons. Generally, buttons are useful for macros that can be run over and over on the same worksheet. Also, the macro sheet still must be open for the button's macro to work.

To move or alter a button after a macro is attached to it, you must hold the Command key down while you click on the button. Instead of pressing the button, this selects it. You also can select an "active" button by using the Selection tool in the Toolbar. After the button is selected, you can move it, resize it, or edit its text. You also can attach a different macro to the button by selecting the Macro Assign to Object command and choosing a macro from the list. The new macro will take the place of the old macro.

Using Objects as Buttons

You can attach a macro to any graphic object on a worksheet, turning the object into a button. This includes graphs, rectangles, ovals, pictures and any other graphic object. To turn an object into a button, first click on the object to select it. Next, choose the Macro Assign to Object command and double-click on the desired macro from the list. When you click on the object, the macro will run.

Note: You still can run a macro using its shortcut key or the Macro Run command, even if the macro is attached to a button or graphic object.

Using Macros That Run Automatically

Another way to run a macro is to tell a worksheet to run it automatically. Any worksheet can have two macros defined as the *autoexec macros*, which can be run by the standard methods as well as automatically. Autoexec macros can be any valid macros on any macro sheets. One macro will run as soon as the worksheet is opened; the other will run as soon as the worksheet is closed. Your worksheets can include either or both autoexec macros. Before you can tell a worksheet which macros to use as the autoexec macros, they must be created and defined as described earlier. These macros usually are designed specifically for the worksheet that runs them.

On the other hand, you can use the same autoexec macros repeatedly on several different worksheets. Autoexec macros often are used to create custom menus and to take control of a worksheet by limiting the actions available to an operator.

To designate which macros are to be autoexec macros, open the worksheet that will run the macros (the macro sheets do not have to be open). Next, use the Formula Define Name command. The Define Name dialog box will appear. If a name and reference appear in the dialog box, erase them. Enter *Auto_Open* as the name. In the Refers To box, enter the name of the macro that you would like this worksheet to run whenever the worksheet is opened. Be sure to enter the macro name as an external reference—that is, include the macro-sheet name along with the macro name. For example, if you want to use the macro named FORMAT, which is on the macro sheet named MACRO1, the Define Name dialog box should look like figure 18.7.

Use the name *Auto_Close* to define the macro that will be run when the worksheet is closed. Be sure to save the changes to the worksheet. When you open the worksheet containing the Auto_Open reference, the corresponding macro sheet does not have to be open. Along with running the macro automatically, Excel also opens the macro sheet.

Running Macros from Other Macros

The final way to run a macro is to let another macro run it. Because macros can do anything you can do manually, why not let them run other macros? The purposes for this setup may seem obscure at first, but as you create macros that are more complex, you will discover more and more uses for the feature. The main command used to run a macro within another macro is RUN.

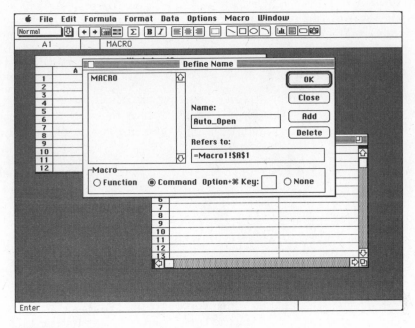

Fig. 18.7. Defining an Auto_Open macro as an external reference.

The following is a simple macro that includes a RUN command. This command locates and runs the specified macro; the macro then finishes its own commands:

=SELECT("R3C1:R3C5")

=FORMAT.NUMBER("#,##0")

=RUN("Macros1!Special")

=FORMAT.FONT("Times",18,FALSE,FALSE,FALSE,FALSE,0,FALSE, FALSE)

=RETURN( )

Notice that the RUN command (located in the middle of the macro) includes the name of the macro sheet and the macro within that sheet. This reference is surrounded by quotation marks. The sheet name is needed only if the reference is external. If the reference is external, the specified sheet should be open and ready to be used. The commands in the referenced macro are executed after the FORMAT.NUMBER command. The macro then continues with the FORMAT.FONT command. For more details on the RUN command, see Appendix B.

Another way to run one macro from another is to simply reference a macro's name inside the second macro. The reference should take the following syntax:

=Worksheet!Macro()

If the macro being referenced is on a different macro sheet, you should use an external reference. This has the same effect as the RUN command. Following is the previous example using a reference instead of the RUN command:

=SELECT("R3C1:R3C5")

=FORMAT.NUMBER("#,##0")

=Macros1!Special()

=FORMAT.FONT("Times",18,FALSE,FALSE,FALSE,FALSE,0,FALSE, FALSE)

=RETURN()

The advantage to this method is that you can pass variables to the macro being referenced. (This would be used only when the macro is designed to require variables, such as with custom functions described later in this chapter.)

You can use a few other commands to run macros from within other macros. A list of these commands follows:

ON.KEY	Runs a macro when a particular key or combination of keys is pressed.
ON.RECALC	Runs a macro when a worksheet is recalculated.
ON.TIME	Runs a macro at a specified time.
ON.WINDOW	Runs a macro when a specified window is activated.

Stopping Macros

You can interrupt a macro while it is running by pressing ⌘-. (period) or by pressing Esc on the extended keyboard. The dialog box shown in figure 18.8 appears.

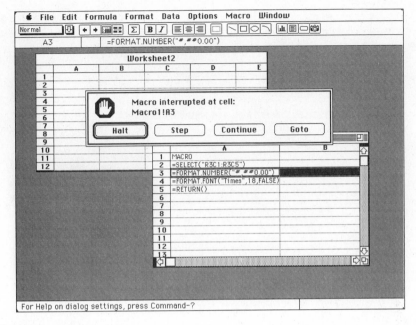

Fig. 18.8. *Stopping a macro.*

Here, you can halt, "step through," or continue the macro. The Step button enables you to run the macro one step at a time by presenting a dialog box that shows each cell in the macro just before the macro is run. This feature is useful for debugging macros. For more information about debugging macros, see Chapter 19.

> ***Tip: Preventing Macro Interruption***
> You can prevent anyone from interrupting your macro by inserting the command =CANCEL.KEY( ) as the first command in the macro. If you place the command elsewhere, the macro may be interrupted up to the point where the CANCEL.KEY command is encountered. See Chapter 20 for more ways to use this command.

Documenting Macros

Documenting your macros as you create them is good practice; providing informative comments throughout the macro will help you correct errors later. Because macros usually are entered in a column of the worksheet, many people enter comments about the macro in an adjacent column. Figure 18.9 shows an example.

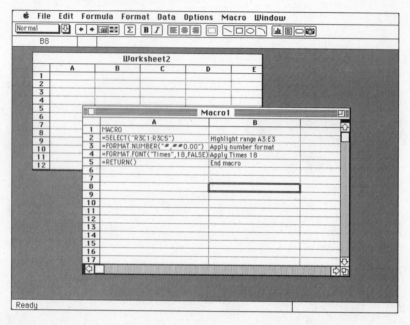

Fig. 18.9. Comments about a macro.

Notice that the comments are placed in cells adjacent to the macro itself. Each important part of the macro has a comment. Also notice that the comment entries have no equal signs. Excel ignores cells that contain no equal signs.

Another handy practice is naming important cells in your macros. In particular, try naming cells that calculate results to be used in the macro. You then can refer to the cell's name whenever you need to make a calculation based on that result. If you create large macros, you also can select these result cells easily by using the Formula Goto command.

Creating Custom Functions

You probably are familiar with worksheet functions; they were discussed in Chapter 6. A *function* is an algorithm or calculation that provides a value. A function often is a shortcut to calculating the value another way. Most important, functions can be entered into cells as formulas, and they can be used in macros for special calculations. The values functions return can be used in other calculations or simply displayed in a cell. One common function is SQRT(*value*). In this function, *value* represents any number for which you want the square root.

Besides providing these built-in functions, Excel enables you to create custom functions for your macros and formulas. *Custom functions*, like the built-in functions, return values that are the results of mathematical calculations or queries. You can use custom functions as you would use any function—by entering it into a formula or macro. Custom functions often require arguments (also specified by you) that are used to produce the value. In short, they are like built-in functions in every way, except that you create them.

To create a custom function, you must enter the following macro commands (in order) into a macro worksheet:

NAME

=RESULT(*value*)

=ARGUMENT(*name_text,data_type,ref*)

=*<calculation here>*

=RETURN(*value*)

Like all macros, this one begins with a name. The next command is RESULT, which specifies the type of result produced by the function. This is followed by one or more ARGUMENT functions, which specify the variables (arguments) used in the function. The calculation is made next, which produces the result. Finally, the RETURN function is used to return the result produced by the calculation.

Suppose that you want to create a function that calculates the cube root of a number. You can calculate the result with a formula, but if you often calculate cube roots, creating a function is much more convenient—and it can be used by anybody. This function requires that you specify the number whose cube root you want to calculate (just like the SQRT function). The function may have the following syntax:

=CUBERT(*value*)

Value is any value or expression for which you want the cube root. The function must process this argument before Excel can calculate the cube root. When you design a custom function, its macro operates on the argument and returns its calculated result. The macro for the CUBERT custom function looks like figure 18.10.

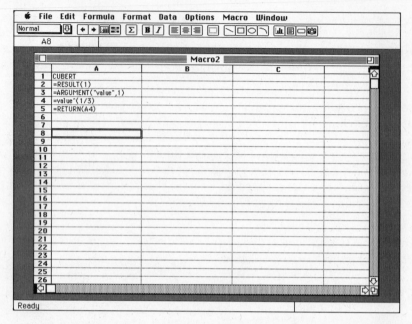

Fig. 18.10. *A function macro designed to calculate the cube root of a number.*

The macro begins with a name, followed by the RESULT command. This specifies that the function will return a value of type 1, which is simply a numeric value. Following are the types available for the RESULT command:

Value	Type
1	Number
2	Text
4	Logical
8	Reference
16	Error
64	Array

Entering any of these numbers restricts the function to returning the corresponding type of result. You can specify a combination of types by adding the values and entering the total. A type of 3, for example, indicates that the function may return numbers or text. Of course, the macro should be able to produce a result that matches the types you specify.

> **Tip: Calculating the Type**
> You can add the various result types within the RESULT command.
> For example, you can enter =RESULT(1+2+4) to indicate the three
> types. Do not add the types 64 or 8 to any other types.

Following the RESULT command, the ARGUMENT command defines the
argument (value) for the macro, thus making it available for calculations
throughout the macro. In fact, you can see that cell A4 uses the *value*
argument as the basis of the cube-root calculation. The ARGUMENT command uses the following syntax:

ARGUMENT(*name_text,data_type*)

In this command, *name_text* is the name of the argument entered as a text
string (in quotation marks). This name can be used in subsequent calculations in this macro; use a name that describes the argument you are defining.
data_type determines what type of value is allowed as the argument. These
are the same as the RESULT types listed above. The *data_type* does not have
to match the RESULT type used earlier. The function may require a value as
its argument, for example, but return text. In this case, the argument type
would be 1 and the result type would be 2.

The macro ends with the RETURN command. The RESULT command
specifies the type of result that is returned when the RETURN command is
used. This type often will be the same as that used in the ARGUMENT
commands, but not always. The RETURN command is needed to conclude
any macro. In a custom function, however, this command also returns the
result of your calculation. Enter the address of the cell containing the final
calculation as the argument for the RETURN command. In the example, this
address is entered as RETURN(A4). Cell A4 is the cell containing the final
cube-root calculation.

Defining Custom Functions

After you create a custom function's macro, you are ready to name the macro
and indicate that it represents a custom function. The procedure is similar
to defining a command macro, as described earlier in this chapter. Follow
these simple steps to name the macro:

1. Highlight the cell containing the macro's name.

2. Select the Define Name command from the Formula menu.

3. Confirm the name and cell address listed in the dialog box, or enter a new name and address.

4. Click on the Function button.

5. Press the Return key.

6. Save the macro sheet.

You now can use the custom function whenever the macro worksheet is open. When you define a macro as a custom function (by clicking on the Function button in the Define Name dialog box as described in step 4) you can use the macro only as a function in the worksheet. Its name will not appear when you use the Run command from the Macro menu and you cannot run the macro in the usual ways. Because custom functions calculate values rather than perform actions, you would not need to "run" them anyway. Custom functions require only the commands RESULT, ARGU-MENT, and RETURN; other macro commands used in the custom function are ignored.

Using Custom Functions

To use a custom function, enter its name into a worksheet formula, along with the required arguments. This name should be an external reference that includes the macro sheet name and the macro name. In the example, to find the cube root of 245, enter the following formula into any worksheet cell:

=MACRO1!CUBERT(245)

The external-reference style is required because the function appears on a different sheet. To make your job easier, Excel lists your custom function at the bottom of the Formula Paste Function dialog box. You can use the function in a worksheet by selecting its name from this box.

The arguments used for the function are passed to the macro as the starting values of the corresponding variables. The order in which the ARGUMENT commands appear in the macro dictates the order in which you should enter the arguments in the function (if there are more than one). In the example, the value 245 becomes the value variable in the function, which is the value used to calculate the cube root.

> ### Tip: Using Add-In Macros for Custom Functions
> Chapter 20 discusses Add-In macros. By making a macro into an add-in, you can eliminate the need for external references when using custom functions. You can just enter the custom function as any other function.

Functions can be more complex than this. You can, for example, use two or three arguments in the function. Suppose that you want to create a function that calculates any root of a number. In this example, the number is a variable and the desired root is a variable (see fig. 18.11).

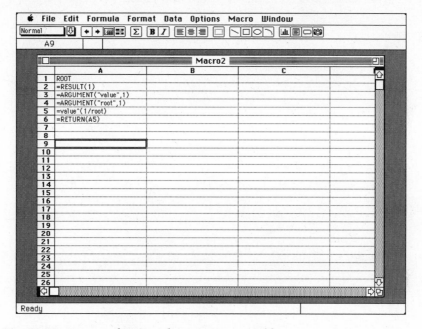

Fig. 18.11. *A custom function that uses two variables.*

The syntax for using this function in a formula is as follows:

=ROOT(*value,root*)

Value is any value or expression for which you want to calculate the root. *Root* is the root to be calculated. The formula =ROOT(25,5) produces the fifth root of 25.

Suppose that your function calls for a range of cells. Because valid worksheet ranges can be passed as variables, this requirement presents no special problem; simply use a variable to represent the desired range. Now suppose that you want to create a function that calculates the span of numbers existing in a range. The span is the difference between the largest and the smallest numbers in the range. The syntax may look like the following:

=SPAN(*range*)

Range is any valid worksheet range. The function that makes this calculation uses the variable *range* to indicate the range entered; its type is 8 (see fig. 18.12).

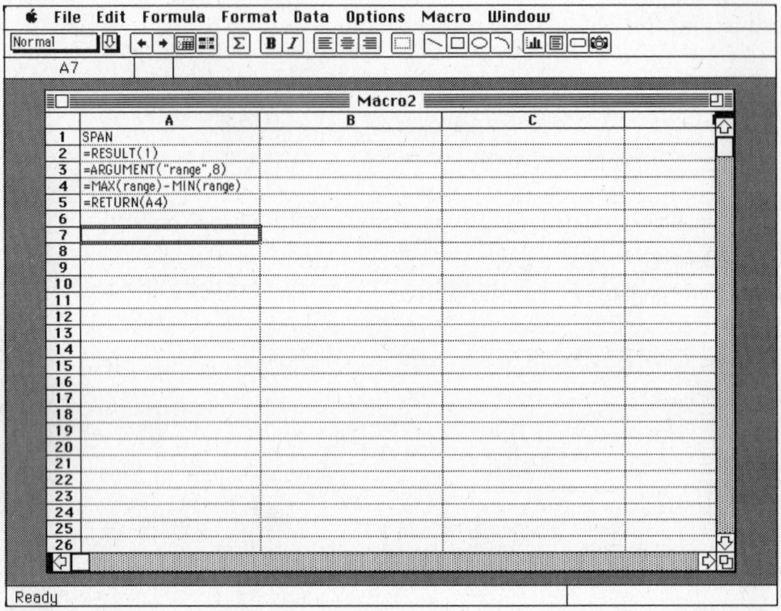

Fig. 18.12. *Using a range as an argument.*

The calculation MAX(range)-MIN(range) subtracts the smallest number in the range from the largest, producing the span of numbers in the range. Excel returns this result to the worksheet.

Noting Guidelines for Custom Functions

The following is a summary of the guidelines for creating custom functions:

- *Begin the macro with a name.* This name will be used as the function name, so use a name that reminds you of the function's purpose. Do not include spaces in the name or use an equal sign in front of the name. Excel does not distinguish between uppercase and lowercase letters.

- *Start with a RESULT command.* This command defines the type of value that will be returned. Be sure that the custom function calculates the correct value indicated by this result. You can specify a combination of results by adding the types. RESULT should be the first command under the macro's name and should begin with an equal sign.

- *Enter the ARGUMENT commands after the RESULT command.* Each argument required for the calculation must have its own ARGU-MENT command, which defines its name and type. The argument types do not necessarily have to be the same as the RESULT type. You may want to create a macro that converts values. The ARGU-MENT commands must begin with equal signs.

- *Enter the required calculations for the function.* Begin with an equal sign and enter the formula or formulas that calculate the results. These formulas should act on the arguments listed in the ARGUMENT commands.

- *Conclude with a RETURN command.* This command should return the value produced by the formulas described in the preceding paragraph. Reference the appropriate cell (the cell that calculates the result) in the RETURN command.

- *Use the Formula Define Name command to define the macro.* Select the Function button.

- *Save the macro sheet for future use.* Many function macros can be used with all worksheets, so you may want to keep those macros on one macro sheet that can be used globally.

- *Open the macro sheet before using a custom function.*

Summary

This chapter has shown you that macros are not really difficult to use and that they can simplify the task of creating worksheets. Your first macros most likely will be designed to simplify repetitive tasks. You have seen two types of macros for this purpose. A command macro duplicates any menu command or action (or combination thereof) and can be run with a single keystroke. A custom function macro mimics Excel's worksheet functions but performs custom mathematical procedures. This type of macro returns results to your worksheets and is useful when you use a calculation over and over in your work. The following are other points to remember:

- You can create a macro by hand or by using the macro recorder.

- A macro entered by hand must be named with the Formula Define Name command. A macro recorded with the Macro Record command is named automatically.

- A macro must begin with a label cell (the macro's name) and end with the =RETURN command.

- You must open a macro sheet before you can run any of its macros.

- To run a macro, use the ⌘-Option-key shortcut you specified when you named the macro. If you did not include a shortcut key, use the Macro Run command and choose the macro's name from the list provided.

- You can cause macros to run automatically whenever a worksheet is opened or closed. These are called *autoexec macros*.

- Custom functions return values to the worksheet and can be used like any worksheet function.

- Custom function macros must begin with a name, followed by the =RESULT() command; each argument in the function must be defined by an =ARGUMENT() command following the =RESULT() command; the function macro should end with the =RETURN() command.

You may not need any additional macro power, but Excel offers more. The next chapter discusses some macro programming techniques you can use for complex macros and shows how to debug macros. When you begin creating worksheets to be used by other people, you will be ready for custom menus and custom dialog boxes, discussed in detail in Chapter 20.

19

Using Advanced Macro Techniques

Creating macros for your worksheets can involve some programming concepts. Although programming in Excel's macro language is not unlike programming in C or Pascal, the macro language is simple and takes much less time to learn. Nevertheless, a few programming concepts will help you create your macros.

This chapter begins with a discussion of macro operation. You learn about using macro variables and different types of macro commands. The discussion then moves to some basic programming concepts, such as loops and subroutines. Finally, the chapter gives some tips for debugging your macros. This chapter will be valuable when your macros begin to grow into large applications.

Understanding How Macros Operate

Macros control the operation of Excel. The macro flows in a linear fashion from the first command to the last, which means the order of your macro commands is critical. As a macro flows from command to command, the macro acts only on formulas that begin with the equal sign. All text entries, blank cells, or numeric values are ignored by the macro (although they may be used by specific commands in the macro). As each command is performed, it returns a value to its cell.

Many macro commands return a value of TRUE or FALSE. (TRUE often indicates that the command was performed successfully.) Other commands return numeric values as the result of their operations. You normally cannot see the values returned by macro commands because macro sheets typically display formulas and not values. You can change this with the Options Display command.

The values that macro commands return to their cells often are useful as variables within the macro. Other commands in the macro can refer back to these cells to use their values. You will see how macro variables work later in this chapter.

Entering Macro Commands

The key to successful macros is an understanding of the commands. Several types of macro commands are available for your macros. Many commands duplicate menu options. Others duplicate actions that you can take with the mouse. Still others offer capabilities that you otherwise cannot get in Excel. The following sections describe these types of commands.

Command-Equivalent Commands

Many macros duplicate Excel's menu commands and options. Most macros created with the recorder use these types of commands. The command =COPY(), for example, is identical to using the Edit Copy command to copy the selected data. Many of these commands require no arguments inside the parentheses. Menu commands that bring up dialog boxes may use arguments in their macro-equivalent commands.

Commands That Use Dialog Boxes

When you duplicate an Excel command that includes a dialog box, you can include the dialog box settings as arguments inside the command. The command Format Number, for example, produces a list of number formats from which to choose. The macro equivalent to that command follows:

=FORMAT.NUMBER(*format_text*)

In this macro command, you can enter the desired number format in the argument *format_text*:

=FORMAT.NUMBER("#,##0.00")

In this way, you include the dialog box choices inside the macro command—including both the command and the dialog box choice.

Instead of including the dialog box options inside these commands by entering them as arguments, you can tell the commands to bring up the normal dialog box so that you can enter choices normally. For example, a variation of the =FORMAT.NUMBER command brings up the list of number formats from within the macro:

=FORMAT.NUMBER?()

This command includes the question mark (?) before its arguments. This question mark tells the command to use the normal dialog box associated with the action. For this reason, the arguments are not required (although you should include the empty parentheses). If you include the arguments anyway, however, they act as default settings in the dialog box that appears.

Action-Equivalent Commands

Some macro commands duplicate mouse or keyboard actions you can perform. These actions include windowing actions, selecting cells and objects, and entering data into the worksheet. An example is the command =FORMULA(*formula_text,reference*), which enters any data into any cell as if you typed the data yourself.

Commands That Control Macros

Several macro commands are used specifically to control macros. These commands are programming constructs and are used for such things as branching and changing program flow. Many of these commands are discussed in this chapter.

Information Commands

Another group of commands provides information about your worksheet data and objects. These commands can tell you the current color of an object or the contents of a cell. You may need to make these queries before you can take certain actions in your macros. Almost anything about a worksheet can be determined from within a macro by using the various information-getting commands. Many of these commands begin with GET, as in GET.OBJECT and GET.WINDOW.

Special Commands

Excel provides several special commands that perform actions which cannot be accomplished normally. The =BEEP command, for example, produces a tone whenever the command is encountered in a macro. Other special commands enable you to create custom menus and dialog boxes, store data files on disk, and present messages on-screen.

Worksheet Functions and Expressions

You can use any normal worksheet function in a macro. Although the function does not control the macro, the function probably provides a needed value that is used in the macro. The =TODAY() function, for example, can be used to provide the current date for a macro. This date can be entered into a cell of the macro. Other macro commands can refer to this cell in their arguments. You also can use functions as arguments in macro commands just as you use them as arguments in other functions. Other mathematical expressions or equations can be used in the same way.

Understanding Macro Arguments

One reason macros are so powerful is that they can use variable information. The variables can be determined by your input, from calculations, or by many other methods. Many macro commands require arguments, and any argument can be turned into a variable. The ROW.HEIGHT command, for example, uses an argument as the height of the row (in points):

=ROW.HEIGHT(18)

You can substitute a variable as the height, letting the macro adjust the row height based on variable information. These variables generally take the form of cell and range references. When a command asks for a value as one of its arguments, you can enter a value or refer to a cell that contains the value. Similarly, when a macro asks for text, you can type the text with quotation marks or refer to a cell that contains text.

Another common argument type is a logical value, which should be entered as TRUE or FALSE or references to cells containing the logical values TRUE or FALSE. Some arguments require you to enter cell or range references.

Any argument can be entered as an expression that produces the desired value. Expressions can produce text, numbers, logical values, cell references, or errors. Expressions can be simple mathematical formulas, or they can include worksheet functions, cell references, and macro commands. Any expression is acceptable, provided the result it produces matches what the function requires for that argument.

Understanding Cell and Range References in Macros

Cell and range references can be entered in various ways for macros. The entry method depends on the requirements of the command you use. You can use cell references anytime a command requires a value. The cell reference must point to a cell that contains an appropriate value. An example of this rule is the ROW.HEIGHT function:

=ROW.HEIGHT(*value*)

The *value* argument can be any constant value, expression, or cell reference. You must use external references if the value you require is not on the macro sheet that contains this command. The following are examples:

=ROW.HEIGHT(B4)   Refers to cell B4 on the macro sheet.

=ROW.HEIGHT(!B4)   Refers to cell B4 on the active worksheet.

If you set Excel to use the R1C1-style references (by using the Options Workspace command), the references then must be entered in R1C1 style. The following are examples in this style:

=ROW.HEIGHT(R[4]C[2])   Refers to cell R4C2 on the macro sheet.

=ROW.HEIGHT(!R[4]C[2])   Refers to cell R4C2 on the active worksheet.

These R1C1-style references are relative. When copied, they are made relative to their new locations. Absolute references can be entered in the A1 style by adding dollar signs and in the R1C1 style by eliminating the brackets. The following is an example of each (see Chapter 4 for details on relative and absolute cell references):

=ROW.HEIGHT($B$4)

=ROW.HEIGHT(R4C2)

In addition to using references in place of values, some macro commands ask for cell or range references in their arguments. An example is the following FORMULA function:

=FORMULA(*formula_text,reference*)

The second argument requires a cell reference. The types of entries you can use in this case are listed in table 19.1. The first six rows of this table are identical to the preceding examples. These examples are simply absolute, relative, and external versions of A1- and R1C1-style references. The R1C1-style references can be used only when the worksheet is set to R1C1 using the Options Workspace command. The relative and absolute versions also affect the way these references act when copied.

Table 19.1
Types of Cell Reference Entries

A1-Style	R1C1-Style	Refers to
B4	R[4]C[2]	Cell B4 on macro sheet (relative)
$B$4	R4C2	Cell B4 on macro sheet (absolute)
!B4	!R[4]C[2]	Cell B4 on active worksheet (relative)
!$B$4	!R4C2	Cell B4 on active worksheet (absolute)
Sheet!B4	Sheet!R[4]C[2]	Cell B4 on specified sheet (relative)
Sheet!$B$4	Sheet!R4C2	Cell B4 on specified sheet (absolute)
"R4C2"	"R4C2"	Cell B4 on active worksheet (text entry)

A1-Style	R1C1-Style	Refers to
"Sheet!R4C2"	"Sheet!R4C2"	Cell B4 on specified worksheet (text entry)
"R[4]C[2]"	"R[4]C[2]"	The cell 4 rows and 2 columns away from the active cell on the active worksheet
"Sheet!	R[4]C[2]"	The cell 4 rows and 2 columns away from the active cell on the specified worksheet

The table also lists several text entries. When a macro command requires a cell reference in an argument, you can enter the reference as text. These entries are always in R1C1 style, even when the worksheet is set to the A1-style references. Text references differ from other references in that they apply new meanings to the terms *relative* and *absolute*. For text references, *absolute* means that the reference always refers to the same range, regardless of the pointer position. A *relative* reference is one that is created relative to the current position of the pointer.

Rather than highlighting the range A3:E3, for example, you may want to highlight a range starting with the current position of the pointer and including the next four cells. If the pointer happens to be on cell A3 when you issue this macro command, you get the range A3:E3. If the pointer is on cell C4, however, you get the range C4:G4. The range reference in this example would read =FORMULA("Text","RC:RC[4]") if it used relative text references. The reference RC is the active cell because it has no row or column positions; the [4] means *add four*. This command therefore means, *Highlight the range starting with the current row and column and ending with the current row and the current column plus four columns*. Consider the examples in table 19.2.

When you record a macro, Excel automatically uses absolute text references. You can use relative references when you record a macro by selecting the Macro Relative Record command before you select the Macro Start Recorder command. When you type macro commands by hand, however, you can enter them in any of the styles listed in table 19.1. (If you need to examine a recorded macro, you may want to convert the worksheet to the R1C1 format by using the Options Workspace command, which makes the worksheet references match the macro references.)

Table 19.2
Examples of R1C1-Style Text References

Text reference	Description
RC	Uses the current location of the pointer.
R[4]C	Moves the pointer down four rows.
RC:R[2]C[2]	Adds two rows and two columns to the current position.
RC:R[−1]C[−4]	Subtracts one row and four columns from the current position. In other words, moves up one row and to the left four columns.
R[4]C[−2]:R[1]C[1]	Moves the pointer four rows down and two columns to the left; then highlights from that position to the current position plus one row and column. If the current position is C5, this action produces the range A9:D6.
"RC"&x	Adds x columns to the current address. This command is useful when you use variables to determine the desired reference. Because variables cannot be entered into the brackets (for example, "R10C[x]"), you must use concatenation to create the reference. x should be a value, range name, or reference. If x is 5, the result is "RC[5]."
"Sales!R1C10"	Uses the reference J1 on the worksheet named SALES. Normally, external references are unnecessary in macros that use the R1C1-style reference. By including a sheet name, however, you can limit the macro's use to only that sheet. If the specified sheet is not active when the macro is run, an error is returned.

> **Tip: Updating Macro Sheet References**
> Inserting and deleting cells from a worksheet updates affected references in that worksheet. However, Excel does not update external references in other worksheets or in the macro sheet. Consequently, making changes in a worksheet does not update the macro sheet. When you program a macro by hand, use range names whenever possible.

Learning Programming Techniques

If your macro needs get complex, you may find some basic programming techniques helpful. The following sections discuss various ways to control and program your macros.

Moving the Pointer and Selecting Cells

Moving the cell pointer in a macro is done primarily with the SELECT function. This function selects any cell you provide as a reference (the same effect as moving the pointer). The function =SELECT(G12) moves the pointer to cell G12. You also can use this function to select a range of cells by providing a range as the reference. For example, =SELECT(B3:D4) selects the range B3:D4.

As discussed earlier, you can provide relative references by using the SELECT function. These references select cells or ranges relative to the current location of the pointer (the location of the pointer just before the macro command is run). The reference "RC" represents the current cell; you can add or subtract rows or columns in that basic reference. The function =SELECT("R[3]C[1]") selects the cell three rows and one column greater than the current position of the pointer. You can use range references this way, too.

Finally, you can use the SELECT function to select existing ranges by their names. As long as the range has been named, you can enter the desired name in place of the cell reference. The function =SELECT(SALES), for example, selects the range named SALES. The range name is not placed in quotation marks.

Inserting Values into the Worksheet

You can use a macro to enter values into a worksheet as if someone had typed them on the keyboard. The FORMULA function is required for this process. The syntax of the FORMULA function follows:

=FORMULA(*formula_text*,*reference*)

Formula_text is the information that you want to enter into the worksheet. Make sure that you enter the formula text as a string, using quotation marks. You also can use a text expression that results in a text string or a reference to a cell containing text. The reference is the cell in which you want the information to appear. If you omit this variable, Excel enters the information in the current cell.

The fact that the formula text must be a text string doesn't mean you cannot enter a formula or value in a cell. Any formula text that can be interpreted as a number is entered as a number. The command =FORMULA("345",!A1), for example, enters the numeric value 345 into cell A1 of the active worksheet. To enter a formula, include the equal sign as part of the formula text variable. For example, =FORMULA("=A1+A2",!A3) enters the formula =A1+A2 in cell A3, and Excel calculates the formula upon entry.

The FORMULA function can enter information into a chart as well. If the active window is a chart when you issue the FORMULA function, Excel enters information into the chart as a text label. To enter the same value in a range of cells, use the function FORMULA.FILL. Entering *=FORMULA.FILL("text",!A1:A5)* enters "text" in the range A1:A5.

Getting User Input

A macro often must ask the operator for a needed value (rather than take the value from the worksheet or macro sheet) via the INPUT function. This function produces a dialog box with a message and entry space. The syntax of the function is as follows:

=INPUT(*prompt_text,type,title,default,x_position,y_position*)

Prompt_text is the message you want to display in the dialog box; it must be a text entry (in quotation marks) or text expression. The *type* variable is the type of entry that the user is expected to provide. Entry types include the following:

Value	Type
0	Formula (returned as text)
1	Number
2	Text
4	Logical
8	Reference
16	Error
64	Array

If you want to use more than one type, add the desired type values and enter the sum as the type value. Using a type value of 3, for example, enables the user to enter numbers or text into the dialog box. You cannot add types 8 or 64, however, to any other dialog boxes.

The value entered by the user is returned to the cell containing the =INPUT command. Consequently, another macro function can refer to this cell to act on the value entered.

> **Tip: Asking for Cell References**
> If your dialog box asks for a cell or range reference, you can move the dialog box window aside and click on the worksheet to make the selection. The appropriate reference appears in the box.

The *title* value represents the title given to the dialog box. You may omit this value to use the word *Input* as the title; otherwise, enter the value as a text string. If you enter a value for the *default* argument (as a text string in quotation marks), this value appears in the input box. The *x_position* and *y_position* values determine the location of the dialog box on-screen. If these values are omitted, the dialog box is centered; otherwise, the values are used as the upper left corner of the box (in picas from the corner of the screen).

The following is an example of an INPUT function. Figure 19.1 shows the dialog box this function creates.

> =INPUT("Type cell address or use the mouse or keyboard commands",8,"Enter Cell","RC",5,5)

The dialog box has a title and a message, indicated by the values in the command. The current cell location becomes the default for the input box because the value "RC" is used as the *default* argument. The box is located five picas from the upper left corner of the screen.

Another way to query the operator for a value is to design your own dialog box that contains text entry areas. This procedure is discussed in more detail in Chapter 20.

Using FOR-NEXT Loops

The For-Next loop repeats an action or series of actions a given number of times. Many macros use the For-Next loop to handle repeated actions. Figure 19.2 shows an example.

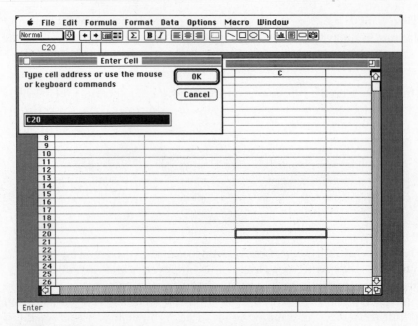

Fig. 19.1. *A dialog box created through the INPUT command.*

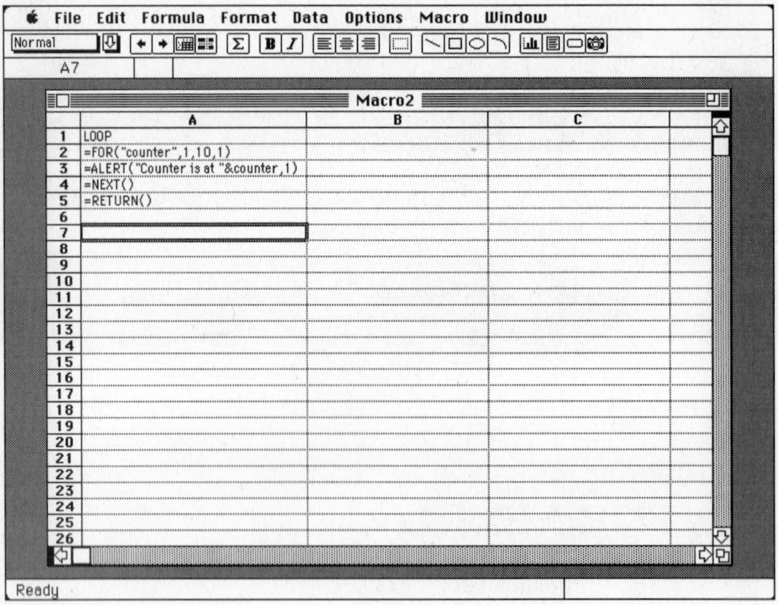

Fig. 19.2. *A FOR-NEXT loop.*

The FOR-NEXT loop contains the FOR function and the NEXT function. The actions to be performed are contained between the FOR and NEXT functions. In this case, a message is printed; the message contains the current value of *counter*. The value of *counter* changes (from 1 to 10) because of the FOR loop. The result of this macro is that a message comes to the screen 10 times, each time with a new value. Try this macro on a sample worksheet. You end up with messages like the one in figure 19.3.

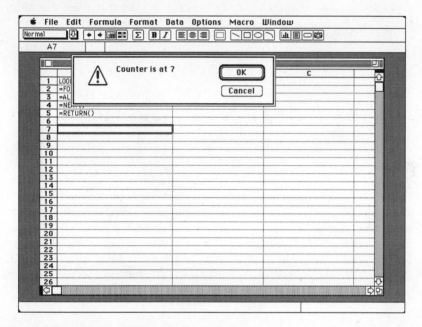

Fig. 19.3. *A message reflecting the loop counter.*

The syntax of the FOR function follows:

FOR(*"counter_text",start_value,end_value,step_value*)

The *"counter_text"* variable is any text string. This text string is a variable that holds the value of the counter; the value increases each time the NEXT function is reached. The name you use for the counter variable does not matter, but the name should not include spaces. If you use more than one FOR loop in the same macro, the loops should have different counter names. The *start_value* and *end_value* arguments determine the minimum and maximum values of the counter; *step_value* determines the increment of increase. If *step_value* is omitted, Excel assumes this value to be 1.

The counter variable often is used only to track the repetitions of the loop; at other times, the counter variable becomes an important value to the macro. In the preceding example, the counter variable actually is used as part of the ALERT message. The message concatenates the string "Counter is at" with the *counter* variable. The following is another example of the counter variable:

FOR("counter",1,10,2)

This formula says *FOR counter equals 1 to 10 step 2* and produces five repetitions having the values 1, 3, 5, 7, and 9. Try the following variation:

FOR("counter",50,40,–2)

The *step_value* is negative, creating a descending counter.

Using FOR.CELL-NEXT Loops

The FOR.CELL-NEXT loop performs an action to all the cells in a specified range, one by one. You can enter the value 34 in all cells of a range, for example, or you can change all the formulas in a range to reference different cells. These examples are simple ones that can be done with the Edit Find command. The FOR.CELL-NEXT loop, however, is intended for more complicated examples, such as when each cell in the range must be changed in a different way, according to a calculation. The tasks accomplished by a FOR.CELL-NEXT loop can be done with a FOR-NEXT loop. The FOR.CELL-NEXT loop, however, makes these tasks easy. The following is the syntax of the FOR.CELL-NEXT loop:

=FOR.CELL(*reference_text,range,skip_blanks*)

=NEXT()

The *reference_text* argument is any name (surrounded by quotation marks) that you want to use. This name applies to the current cell in the range, which changes each time the loop repeats. The purpose for this argument is to identify the address of the current cell so that you can act on the cell during the loop.

The *range* argument is any worksheet range (usually an external reference) to be changed. The *skip_blanks* argument can be TRUE to make the loop skip blank cells in the range or FALSE to include them.

After the FOR.CELL command, enter all the commands required to change one cell in the range. Follow this with the NEXT command. The following example enters the value 34 into the range A5:B8.

=FOR.CELL("current",A5:B8,TRUE)

=FORMULA("34","current")

=NEXT()

=RETURN()

The name "current" is given to the current cell in the loop and is used in the FORMULA function as the reference for the entry.

Using WHILE-NEXT Loops

The FOR-NEXT loop is useful when an action is repeated for a known number of times. The WHILE-NEXT loop is useful when an action is repeated as long as a condition is met, which may be an unknown number of times. For example, you may perform some action as long as a variable is less than 100. If the condition is not met, the macro branches to the NEXT statement and continues operating, skipping all the in-between commands.

WHILE-NEXT loops, which are not very common, usually are used in large macros for internal programming techniques. You often can use IF-THEN-ELSE logic instead of the WHILE-NEXT loop.

Using IF-THEN-ELSE Statements

Perhaps the most powerful programming construct is the decision-making IF function. This function enables you to test for a condition and act on the results of the test. This function is described in Chapter 6 for worksheet formulas but also can be used in macros. IF tests whether a condition is TRUE or FALSE. If the condition is TRUE, the function returns one value; if it is FALSE, the function returns a different value. The syntax follows:

IF(*condition,value_if_true,value_if_false*)

You can use the IF function in a macro in many ways. You can use the IF function to select one of two values, for example, based on a given condition in the worksheet or macro.

Version 3.0 of Excel introduces a new form of the IF statement, especially for macros. The standard IF function assumes the IF-THEN-ELSE logic with its three arguments. But the new IF command uses the IF command with the commands ELSE, ELSE.IF, and END.IF to create programming logic. You can place any commands or functions into the THEN and ELSE sections. The logical process looks like the following:

=IF(test)

<commands if TRUE>

=ELSE

<commands if FALSE>

END.IF( )

The first test argument is a logical test that must prove TRUE or FALSE. If TRUE, the commands directly under the IF statement are performed. These provide the THEN logic. If the test proves false, the commands under the ELSE statement are performed. The END.IF command completes the operation. The primary advantage to this form of the IF command is that it enables you to perform several commands at each stage. You can nest several IF tests by using the ELSE.IF command prior to the END.IF command. This step produces a new condition on which to base the procedure. Figure 19.4 shows an example.

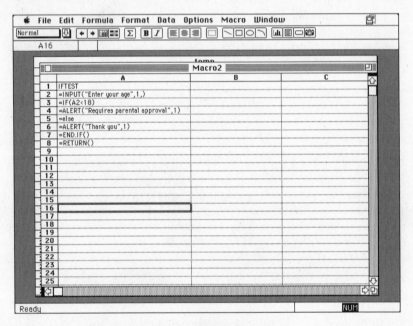

Fig. 19.4. *An example of the new IF statement.*

Working with Branches and Subroutines

Excel processes each function in a macro from top to bottom, beginning with the first cell under the macro's name. A macro should have no blank cells. You can change the normal flow of a macro, however, by using the

GOTO function. When a macro encounters this function, the macro flow branches to the specified location. The syntax follows:

=GOTO(*reference*)

Reference can be any cell or range name to which the macro should jump— a cell within the same macro, or a cell in a different macro. After the macro jumps to the specified cell, the flow continues with the next cell under the new branch. If you branch to a different macro (for example, a subroutine), a RETURN function in that macro returns the flow to the original macro at the previous location. The HALT function often is useful for stopping a macro's flow after a routine is completed and for preventing the macro from returning to an undesirable location.

By using IF with GOTO, you can choose between two sets of functions in the macro. The GOTO function causes the macro to jump to a specific cell and continue from there (see fig. 19.5).

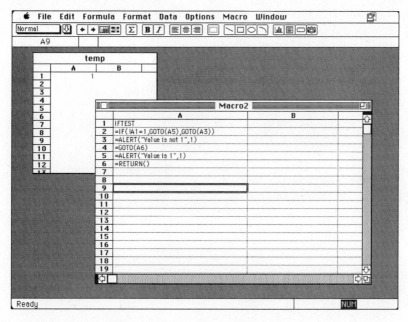

Fig. 19.5. *Using the IF function with GOTO.*

The IF function branches to cell A5 if the value of A1 is 1, producing the message Value is 1. If the value of A1 is not 1, the macro branches to cell A3, producing the message Value is not 1, and then concludes by jumping to the RETURN function. By jumping to the RETURN function, the macro skips the function in cell A5.

You also can branch macros by using the CHOOSE function. Based on the value in a cell, the macro can branch to one of several other macros or subroutines. This process is done by using the GOTO command with CHOOSE, as in the following example:

=CHOOSE(!A5,GOTO(MACRO1),GOTO(MACRO2),GOTO(MACRO3))

The names MACRO1, MACRO2, and MACRO3 refer to macro names already established on the macro sheet. See Chapter 6 for details about the CHOOSE function.

Controlling Objects with Macros

Excel provides several commands for controlling objects on your worksheets. You can create, move, hide, and edit objects from macros. Table 19.3 summarizes the object-manipulation commands.

Table 19.3
Object Manipulation Commands

Command syntax	Description
SELECT(*object_id_text*)	Selects the specified object
COPY()	Copies selected object
CUT()	Cuts selected object (use with PASTE() command)
PASTE()	Pastes object after COPY() or CUT() command
PASTE.PICTURE	Pastes data as a picture
BRING.TO.FRONT	Brings selected object to front
FORMAT.FONT(*name_text, size_num, bold, italic, underline, strike, color, outline, shadow, object_id_text, start_num, char_num*)	Changes font in a text box
GROUP()	Groups selected objects
FORMAT.MOVE(*x_pos, y_pos, reference*)	Moves selected object

Command syntax	Description
PLACEMENT(*value*)	Determines the type of object placement used on selected objects
OBJECT.PROTECTION (*logical*)	Locks or unlocks an object for protection feature
PATTERNS(*bauto,bstyle, bcolor,bwt,shadow,aauto, apattern,afore,aback, rounded*)	Changes object pattern options
SEND.TO.BACK( )	Sends selected object to back
FORMAT.SIZE(*width, height*)	Changes the size of the selected object
FORMAT.TEXT(*x_align, y_align,orient_num, auto_text,auto_size, show_key,show_value*)	Changes the alignment and orientation of text box text
UNGROUP( )	Ungroups the selected group
CREATE.OBJECT(*object_ type,ref_1,x_offset1, y_offset1,ref_2, x_offset2,y_offset2*)	Draws an object onto the worksheet
DUPLICATE( )	Duplicates the selected object
TEXT.BOX(*add_text, object_id_text, start_num,num_chars*)	Changes the text in any text box
GET.OBJECT(*type_num, object_id_text,start_ num,count_num*)	Returns information about an object

Many of these commands require you to specify the *object_id_text* argument. This argument is the name and number of the object you want to control. Excel shows an object's ID in the upper left corner of the screen when you select the object. Be sure to enter this value as text by surrounding the value with quotation marks. You can enter the object name and its number or the number alone. Objects are numbered in the order they are created. If you omit this argument from any of the above functions, Excel assumes the currently selected object. Following are some examples of object arguments:

"Button 1" "Text 4"

"Box 2"

"Oval 5"

"Line 1"

"Arc 8"

"Pict 4"

"Chart 1"

"4"

"6"

If a function does not include this argument, then the function operates on the selected object only. Use the SELECT command to select an object.

Debugging Macros

When your macros get complicated, you may need to apply some debugging techniques to locate and fix problems. The key is to locate the exact command or cell in which the error occurs. Invalid entries or bad formulas can go unnoticed for some time, however, causing problems later in the macro. Excel's macro error message may not point you to the correct location of the problem, but the message gives you a place to start. Several useful techniques exist that can help you pinpoint macro problems. The following sections describe some of these techniques.

Examining Macro Values

Because macro values are often the cause of errors, viewing the values calculated by the macro commands can be useful. The best way to view these values is to use the Window New Window command to duplicate the macro worksheet window. Arrange the windows so that you can see both at the same time. Finally, change the new worksheet display to show the results of formulas by using the Options Display command. When you run the macro, the values produced by its commands can be seen in the new window.

> ### Tip: *Values Returned by Macro Commands*
> Each macro command returns a value to its cell. Some macro com-
> mands return specific values that you need to use throughout the
> macro. The ADD.BAR command, for example, creates a menu bar
> and returns its number to the cell. Other commands may need to
> refer to this number. Other macro commands simply return TRUE
> when they are completed successfully and FALSE when they are not.

Stepping through Macros

Another useful tool is the Step mode. This mode enables you to run a macro
one command at a time to view its progress slowly; you can see exactly where
errors occur. To step through a macro, follow this process:

1. Select the Macro Run command.

2. Highlight the macro you want to run.

3. Select the Step button. This displays a dialog box that shows you
   which cell (command) will be calculated next.

4. Select the Step button to complete the next command. Continue
   to select the Step button for each command you want to complete.
   Select the Halt button to stop the macro or the Continue button to
   resume normal speed.

The Evaluate button calculates each segment of a complex formula. When
you press Evaluate, Excel calculates the next portion of the indicated
command. Continue to press Evaluate to complete each segment of the
command. The Goto button takes you to the cell in the macro sheet that
produces the error.

If you combine this stepping feature with the previous technique of
displaying macro values, you should be able to locate any cell that produces
a macro error. You may find that the error was caused by improper
command syntax. Check the syntax in the cells that give you problems. If the
syntax has not caused the error, then some variable or reference used in the
command may be the problem. You may find the Edit Select Special
command useful for tracking the problem even further. This command
enables you to track the dependents and precedents of formulas. Chapter 8 has details about this command.

> **Tip: Stepping Automatically**
> You can make your macros step through their commands automatically by inserting the STEP command into the macro itself. At the location of this command, the macro presents the Step dialog box.

Using the Debugger

Excel's macro debugger is an add-in utility that helps you find errors in your macros. You can use the debugger to give you feedback on your macros and to stop the macro at specific points. To use the debugger, follow this procedure:

1. Use the File Open command to open the worksheet called Macro Debugger. This worksheet should be located in the Macro Library folder.

   Make sure that your macro sheet and all other needed worksheets are open. The macro sheet should be selected.

2. Choose the Debug command in the Macro menu. This changes the Excel menu bar to the special debug menus.

3. Set trace points in the macro by selecting the desired cell and using the Debug Set Tracepoint command. (Trace points are discussed following the steps.)

4. Set break points in the macro by selecting the desired cell and using the Debug Set Breakpoint command. Then enter any message you want to print when the break point is encountered. (Break points are discussed following the steps.)

5. Choose the Debug Breakpoint Output command to select the variables that will be displayed at the break points. These variables will help you track changes in macro values throughout the macro sheet.

   After selecting this command, a dialog box appears. Enter any cell reference in this dialog box and click the Add button to add the reference to the list. The values of all cells are displayed at each break point.

6. Choose the Debug Run Macro command and select the appropriate macro from the list.

The macro debugger uses trace points and break points to help you locate macro errors. A *trace point* is a point in the macro where the debugger will begin "tracing" each step of the macro. At this point, the debugger causes Excel to enter the Step mode (discussed earlier in this chapter). You can enter Step mode at various points in a macro by marking each location as a trace point. This is similar to using the STEP macro command inside your macros; you can enter the Step mode at several spots in the macro.

A *break point* is a location in the macro where Excel pauses to impart information—most commonly, values used in the macro. If an important value used in your macro is affected by formulas or actions throughout the macro, you may want to check this value at key locations in the macro's flow to see if it has changed appropriately. Set break points at the desired locations (key turning points in the macro, perhaps) by moving to the desired cell and using the Debug Set Breakpoint command. Your break point message should attempt to describe what occurs at this point of the macro, such as `Formula calculates trend here.`

Next, list the cells that contain the values you want to follow. Do this with the Debug Breakpoint Output command. Each time a break point is reached, the debugger lists the values in the cells you specified along with the break point message. If one of the values you are following shows an error or incorrect value, you will know exactly where the error happens in the macro.

Summary

This chapter provides advanced macro concepts. These concepts include programming constructs such as using variables, understanding cell references, loops, and more. In addition, the chapter explains how to use macro debugging techniques to help you find errors in your complex macros. Two add-in utilities make this job easier. Following are some points to remember:

- All macro commands return values to cells. These values can be used in other macro commands to control operation.

- To see the macro values, open a new window to the macro sheet and use the Options Display command to turn the formula text off.

- The FOR-NEXT loop repeats a series of commands for a given number of times.

- The IF command is useful in macros for choosing values or branching the macro's flow. Use IF with ELSE.IF, ELSE, and END.IF.

- The GOTO command is useful for branching the macro's natural flow.

- The FORMULA command inserts information into cells of a worksheet from a macro.

- The INPUT command prompts a user for input.

- The Macro Debugger add-in enables you to step through a macro and locate problem commands.

- The text R1C1-style references are useful when you want to specify a cell or range that is relative to the active cell. The reference "RC" is the active cell; "R[1]C[1]" is one row and column greater than the active cell.

- You can use variables in relative cell references by concatenating them to the end of the text string, as in "R1C"&x.

Turn to Chapter 20 to learn how to use Excel's powerful tools for building *custom applications*—worksheets or templates that other people can use.

20

Building Custom
Applications

E xcel offers powerful tools for building *custom applications,* or worksheets or templates that other people use. These applications can be created on a professional level—even commercially—or just for use within a company. In any case, custom applications can benefit from some of the features discussed in this chapter. First, you learn some techniques for anticipating errors in your worksheets and macros. Next, you discover some useful macro tools for creating custom menus and dialog boxes. You also learn how to make your macros work automatically or as add-ins for Excel.

Defining the Elements of a Custom Application

You do not need to be a professional template programmer to create custom applications. Your custom applications can be used more easily and more productively if you apply some special techniques, such as error-trapping and custom menus. Of course, not all custom applications require all these techniques. Often, however, a little extra time spent on these techniques goes a long way. Some important techniques to use in your custom applications follow.

Buttons

Buttons ease users' access to your macros. You should attach a macro to a button whenever the macro applies to the worksheet specifically. Use buttons for the following purposes:

- Adding and removing custom menus
- Opening and closing linked worksheets or macro sheets
- Changing chart types
- Presenting dialog boxes
- Displaying reports or charts

This chapter provides some button techniques. For details about creating buttons and attaching macros to them, see Chapters 13 and 17.

Custom Menus and Dialog Boxes

Custom menus are an important element of custom applications. The more you can do for the user through custom-menu commands, the easier your application can be used. Custom menus can bring up custom dialog boxes with still more custom choices. This chapter provides techniques for creating and controlling custom menus.

Error-Trapping

Error-trapping essentially is anticipating errors in worksheets and accounting for them with user-friendly messages or specific actions. Errors can occur in many different places but usually are linked to incorrect entries. If you can anticipate possible entry errors, you often can "trap" the error when it occurs and present an informative message to the user. This chapter discusses some error-trapping techniques.

Add-In Support

Add-in macros add commands or functions to Excel itself. Often, these macros do not use a specific worksheet but can be applied to any worksheet in use. Usually, you access add-ins through an Excel menu or a custom menu added to the menu bar. The add-in, when invoked, operates on data in the worksheet that the user inputs. Almost any custom function (discussed in Chapter 18) is a good candidate for an add-in because the function can be applied to any worksheet. Often, an add-in macro provides several custom functions for use in Excel.

This definition of add-in macros, however, is somewhat narrow. Any custom application can be an add-in or a pop-up application from within Excel. Add-in macros are discussed later in this chapter in "Using Add-In Macros."

Start-up Automation

Often you can augment custom menus by making them available as soon as the user opens your worksheet. This way, the user does not have to open your macros, access your custom menus, or even remember what custom features come with the application. You can achieve start-up automation by using the autoexec macros *Auto_Open* and *Auto_Close*, which are explained in Chapter 17.

You also can provide start-up automation by placing certain files in Excel's Startup folder, a method described later in this chapter in "Using Start-Up Automation."

Documentation

Documenting custom applications (worksheets) takes many forms. You can add notes to specific cells or include special text boxes with information for the user. You can document macros in columns on the macro sheet.

These ideas are discussed earlier in this book. (See Chapter 8.) In this chapter, you see some interesting techniques for documenting worksheets, including instructions for creating custom help screens.

Speed and Efficiency

Custom applications must be as fast and efficient as possible. Users should not have to wait longer than necessary for actions to be carried out. Later, this chapter discusses Excel tools to make your macros more efficient. (See "Making Macros Faster and More Efficient," later in this chapter.)

Protection and Invisibility

Protection, a form of error-trapping, prevents the user from changing your work in cells, worksheets, objects, and windows. If you add password protection to the Protect Document command from the Options menu, you can even prohibit advanced users from removing the protection itself. You also may want to prohibit unauthorized users from even opening the file.

To go even further, you may want to make your macro worksheets and other linked worksheets invisible to the user. This way, the user cannot copy and inspect your work. This method is useful especially for commercial applications. Chapters 3 and 7 discuss protection and invisibility.

Design

Worksheets should look good to communicate properly. Well-designed applications can save time and reduce errors. One rule suffices here: keep custom applications simple and uncluttered. Providing too much information at once makes your worksheets confusing and uninviting.

This book does not cover spreadsheet design. You can find useful information in a book about spreadsheet publishing.

Using Buttons

Users rarely should have to run your macros with the Macro Run command; instead, you should provide a liberal number of buttons and custom menu options throughout your worksheet. Chapters 13 and 18 describe buttons, but the next sections describe a few interesting, easy button techniques to apply in your custom applications.

Toggle Buttons

Buttons that toggle between two options commonly are found in Excel and other programs. The data form, for example, has buttons that change after you click on them.

You can create toggle buttons in several ways, and the simplest follows:

1. Open a macro worksheet and enter two macros as follows:

Button1

=SELECT("BUTTON 2")

=BRING.TO.FRONT()

=SELECT()

=RETURN()

Button2

=SELECT("BUTTON 1")

=BRING.TO.FRONT()

=SELECT()

=RETURN()

Be sure to use the Define Name command (with the Command option selected) from the Formula menu to name these macros. Figure 20.1 shows the screen at this point. You can add more macro commands to each button by placing the macro commands before the RETURN() commands. One idea is to branch to another macro, keeping the toggle buttons simple.

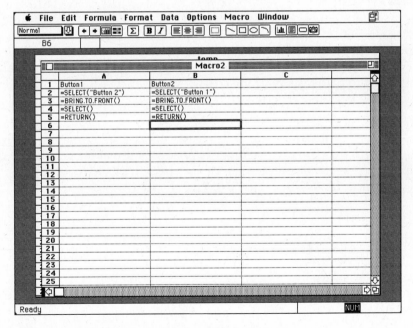

Fig. 20.1. Entering the macros for the toggle buttons.

2. Use the Button tool to create two identical buttons. When asked for macros to attach, assign the macro Button1 to the first button (Button 1) and Button2 to the second button (Button 2). To view a button's number, select the button and look at the upper left corner of the screen for the object number.

> *Note:* If other buttons have been drawn previously, then the button numbers may not be Button 1 and Button 2. Substitute the correct button numbers in these macros.

3. Edit the text inside these buttons to the toggle options you want. You can do this immediately after assigning the macro to a button by simply typing the desired text.

4. Press the Command key while you drag the mouse to move Button 2 directly on top of Button 1. Only one button should be visible.

Now when you click on the top button, the macro switches to the bottom button, resulting in a toggle effect.

Protective Buttons

Because you can attach macros to any graphic object, you can place protective buttons on the worksheet. Protective buttons are large rectangles on top of (covering) all other objects. The rectangle should be formatted with no pattern (transparent) and no border, like a "sheet of glass" above the worksheet and other objects.

The macro attached to this object should present a message informing the user where to click and what to do next. This prevents the user from accidentally clicking in the wrong place. Be sure to place any worksheet buttons above this protective plate. This way, all buttons can be selected, but worksheet cells and other data cannot be changed.

Button Clusters

Consider placing buttons into clusters on your worksheet to make locating important commands easier. Buttons can be organized into "control panels" by overlapping buttons. Figure 20.2 shows an example.

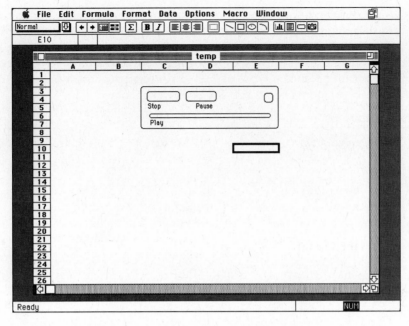

Fig. 20.2. *Creating a control panel using groups of buttons.*

Building Custom Menus

You can use macro commands to add custom menus to your applications. A custom menu contains the options you want, and each option performs the action you specify. Custom menus may appear on the menu bar with regular menus, or you can create an entirely new menu bar to hold your custom menus and then return to the Excel menu bar when you want.

To create custom menus, use a *menu-definition table,* a range of cells containing specific values for the menu, such as option names and the actions the options perform. The menu-definition table can appear on any worksheet or macro sheet and is activated (turned into a menu) by a controlling macro. Often, the menu-definition table appears on the macro sheet that contains the controlling macro.

The controlling macro uses some simple commands to activate a menu-definition table. (These commands are explained in detail later.) A common technique is to make this an autoexec macro so that the macro controls the menus as soon as you open the worksheet.

Each option in a custom menu runs a macro to perform an action. When you specify the names of the menu options, you also specify the macros that link to these options. When the menu option is selected, the appropriate macro runs. Usually, these macros appear together on the same macro sheet, which also can contain the menu-definition table and the controlling macro. In summary, a custom menu has three basic elements:

Element	Effect
Controlling macro	Activates the menu-definition table.
Menu-definition table	Links each option to a macro.
Macros	Perform the various options contained in the menu. These macros are not limited to the menu options; they can run as normal macros without the menu.

Creating the Menu-Definition Table

A menu-definition table consists of five columns. In the first column, enter the names of the menu items. In the second column, enter the names of the command macros that correspond to the menu items in the first column. In the third (optional) column, enter the ⌘-*key* character combinations that you can use to invoke the macro command on the keyboard. In the fourth column, also optional, enter a message that appears in the status line when you select the menu option. In the fifth column, also optional, enter references to the custom help topics corresponding to the options. Figure 20.3 shows an example of a menu-definition table.

Notice several things about the example in figure 20.3. First, the labels in the first column are used exactly as shown for the menu items. If an option listed in this column has a corresponding entry in column 3, this entry also appears in the menu as the ⌘-*key* combination that runs the option from the keyboard. The hyphen character is used as a menu separation line to group menu items within a menu. This table produces the menu shown in figure 20.4 when activated by a controlling macro.

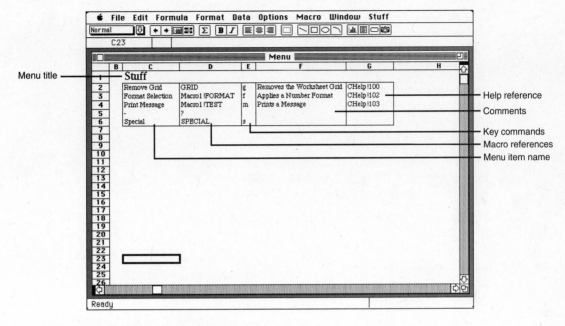

Menu title

Help reference
Comments
Key commands
Macro references
Menu item name

Fig. 20.3. *A typical menu-definition table.*

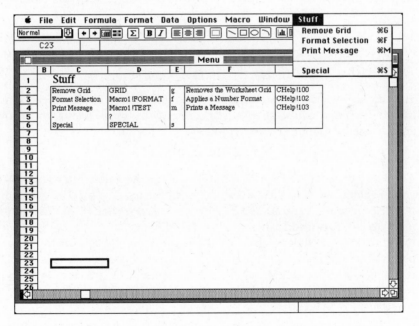

Fig. 20.4. *The menu produced by the menu definition table in figure 20.3.*

Also notice in the sample table that some of the macro names listed in column 2 are *external references*: the macros controlling these options are located on different macro sheets. The macro sheets must be open in order for these options to work.

The fourth column lists the on-line messages that appear in the status bar (at the bottom of the screen) when a menu is highlighted. If you omit the information in this column, the highlighted menu option simply will not display a status bar message.

The fifth column in this example shows how custom help topics are entered for each item in a menu. Complete details about using custom help are located in "Documenting and Custom Help," later in this chapter.

Finally, the menu's name appears above the first column. Excel uses this cell to identify the menu.

Creating the Menu Macro

After you create the menu-definition table, you can create the macro that activates the table by using three commands: ADD.MENU, ADD.BAR, and SHOW.BAR. The following sections provide details.

Adding a Menu to a Menu Bar

You can add a custom menu to any menu bar, including the four Excel menu bars and any new menu bar you create. Specify the menu bar to which you are adding the menu. The syntax follows:

=ADD.MENU(*bar_number, menu_table_range*)

Bar_number is the identification number of the menu bar you want. (Bars and their identification numbers are explained in the next section.) Remember that the menu bar does not have to be on-screen before you can add a menu to it. You can add a menu to the Graph menu bar, for example, when the standard worksheet menu bar is in view. When you activate the Graph menus, the new menu is present. The range reference *menu_table_range* contains the menu-definition table (the menu you are adding to the specified bar). Be sure to include the menu's title in the reference or use a name that has been applied to the range.

Note: If you add a menu to a bar now displayed on-screen, the menu appears as soon as you run the macro. Otherwise, you must show the menu bar after adding the menus to it.

Adding and Showing Menu Bars

To add a new menu bar to Excel, use the command ADD.BAR, which produces a menu bar containing only the Apple menu. This menu bar gets an identification number, which returns to the cell that contains the ADD.BAR command. When you add menus to this new bar, refer to the new bar's identification number by referring to the cell containing the ADD.BAR command. If the bar is not displayed already, use the SHOW.BAR command. Figure 20.5 shows an example.

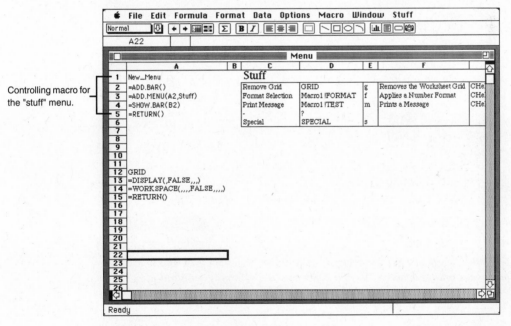

Fig. 20.5. Adding a menu to a newly created bar.

In figure 20.5, notice that the ADD.MENU command refers to the cell containing the ADD.BAR command. This reference is one way to refer to the added bar's identification number. The ADD.MENU command refers to the range named STUFF as the definition table. (Naming menu-definition tables is good practice, making it easier to create these macros.) Finally, use the SHOW.BAR command to display this new menu bar and its menu. The SHOW.BAR command should appear after the other commands to show the completed menu bar and its menus. If the SHOW.BAR command has no argument, the command displays the menu bar just created. You can display any other menu bar by making a reference to the bar's identification number.

To add menus to one of the Excel menu bars, use an ID number corresponding to the bar you want to use. Excel contains four menu bars with ID numbers 1 through 4 (see figs. 20.6 through 20.9). Two of the bars can have ID numbers 5 and 6 when the Short Menus command is active.

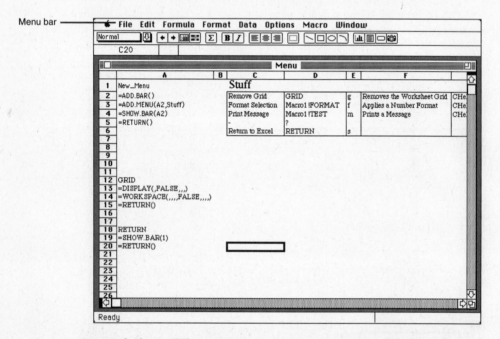

Fig. 20.6. *The Worksheet and Macro-sheet menu bar. ID = 1 when the Full Menus command is active; ID = 5 when the Short Menus command is active.*

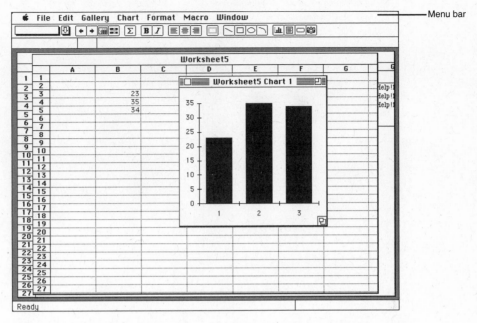

Fig. 20.7. *The Chart menu bar. ID = 2 when the Full Menus command is active; ID = 6 when the Short Menus command is active.*

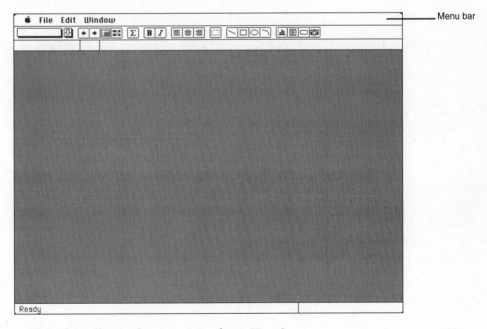

Fig. 20.8. *The Null menu bar (no active sheet). ID = 3.*

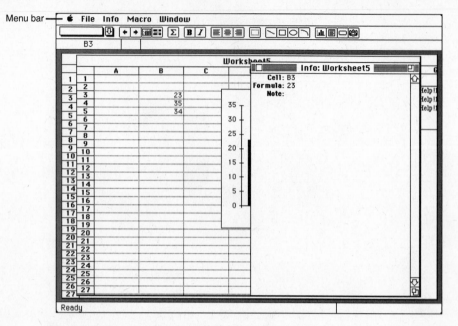

Fig. 20.9. *The Info menu bar. ID = 4.*

Noting Techniques for Menu Options

As you have seen, the controlling macro that activates custom menus, menu bars, or both is simple. Usually, a controlling macro contains only the two or three commands needed to display the bar and menus. The rest is up to the options inside the custom menus.

The following sections offer some ideas and techniques for options you can use in your custom menus and provide instructions for creating the macros that link to these options.

Deleting Menus and Menu Bars

To display a different menu bar at any time, create a macro that uses the SHOW.BAR command to display the bar. To return to the Excel menu bar, for example, run a macro that contains the command =SHOW.BAR(1). A common technique is linking this macro to one menu option on each custom menu bar. This option may be listed as Quit or Return to Excel.

Figure 20.10 shows an example of a Return to Excel macro. Remember that the menu-definition table that contains this option includes the name of this macro.

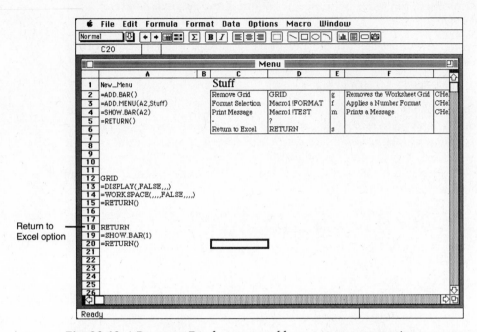

Return to
Excel option

Fig. 20.10. *A Return to Excel macro used by a custom menu option.*

If you do not include a Return to Excel option, the operator cannot use any of Excel's basic menu commands because he or she will be stuck in your custom menu bars. (You may purposely prohibit users from returning to Excel's commands to restrict their actions.) Your custom menus, however, must handle actions such as saving worksheets and quitting Excel. You therefore may add to one of your menus a Save option to run a macro containing the SAVE command. (For more details, see SAVE and QUIT in Appendix B.)

If you add a menu to an Excel menu bar, you may consider including an option in that menu that removes the menu itself, returning the menu bar to normal. This option may appear as

```
Remove This Menu
```

and will run a macro that contains the DELETE.MENU command. This command has the following syntax:

=DELETE.MENU(*bar_number,menu_name*)

Bar_number is the ID number of the bar containing the unwanted menu. The bar does not have to be displayed on-screen before you can remove a menu from it. (If you are removing a menu from a custom bar, *bar_number* should be a reference to the cell containing the original ADD.BAR command.)

Menu_name is the name of the unwanted menu (in quotation marks) on the specified bar. The command

=DELETE.MENU(1,"File")

removes the File menu from Excel's worksheet menu bar. (In this example, you do not want to remove this menu!) Instead of using names, you also can use menu numbers, which are counted from left to right on the bar. The Excel worksheet menu normally contains eight menus. Suppose that you have added a ninth menu to this bar. You can remove the new menu by using the command =DELETE.MENU(1,9).

> ### Tip: Using the ID Number of the Active Bar
> If you do not know a bar's ID number but do know that the bar is active, you can use the command GET.BAR to return the bar's ID number.

> ### Tip: Deleting Menu Bars
> Excel can accommodate 15 custom menu bars. If you exceed this limit, you may want to delete one or more bars to make room for new ones. You can delete a menu bar via the command DELETE.BAR. After you execute this command, you no longer can use the SHOW.BAR command to display this bar; instead, you must use the ADD.BAR command again.

Adding and Deleting Menu Options

To add a menu option, the option must first be defined somewhere, preferably in a menu-definition table. One way to do this is to define all menu options in the same menu-definition table. Options that you do not use all the time should appear at the bottom of the table. When you refer to the definition table in the ADD.MENU command, exclude the bottom cells from the range, thus excluding the unwanted options. Later, when you add an option to the menu, use the function

=ADD.COMMAND(*bar_number,menu_name,command_range_reference*)

Command_range_reference contains the added option—in this case, the range omitted from the original menu. The range does not have to be related to the original menu but can be a set of commands from a different menu-definition table. Avoid this practice whenever possible, however, because the procedure adds a considerable amount of confusion to the process of adding and removing menu options.

Where you enter the ADD.COMMAND and DELETE.COMMAND functions depends on the action that controls the addition or deletion of the option. In other words, you should add the menu option under certain circumstances. Often, selecting a different option (Option B) adds an option to a menu (Option A). In this case, the macro linked to Option B should contain the ADD.COMMAND function to control Option A.

> ***Note:*** Instead of adding and deleting menu options under certain conditions, consider using the enable/disable features of the menu options. These features are explained later in this chapter in the section "Disabling and Checking Menu Options."

You can add or delete menu options at any time. To delete an option, use the following command:

=DELETE.COMMAND(*bar_number,menu_name,command_name*)

Bar_number represents the menu bar containing the menu. *Menu_name* represents the menu that contains the unwanted option. This menu must be on the bar indicated in the *bar_number* argument. *Command_name* is the name of the option that you want to remove. The command

=DELETE.COMMAND(1,"File","Save")

for example, removes the File Save command from the worksheet menu bar. Notice that you enter the names as text strings.

The *menu_name* and *command_name* arguments can be the numbers of the menu and command instead. Menus and commands appear in numerical order. If you remove a menu or command, all subsequent numbers change to reflect the deletion.

Creating Toggle Menu Options

A common menu effect used in Macintosh applications is the toggle, which changes a menu option's name each time you select the option. Usually, menu options toggle between two items, such as Short Menus and Full Menus in Excel's Options menu. Using a toggle menu option eliminates the need for two different options and presents only the option that can be used at any given time. The very act of selecting the option makes its counterpart available.

You can add toggle capability to your custom Excel menus. You need some macro programming logic and the functions RENAME.COMMAND and SET.VALUE. You use the RENAME.COMMAND function twice to change the option's name twice, but the command name must be changed only when selected. The SET.VALUE function helps to determine the appropriate time to change the name by setting the values in certain cells. The macro uses these values to determine whether to rename the option. The syntax of the two functions follows:

=RENAME.COMMAND(*bar_number,menu_name,option_name,new_name*)

=SET.VALUE(*cell_reference,value*)

Figure 20.11 shows a macro that creates a toggle menu option.

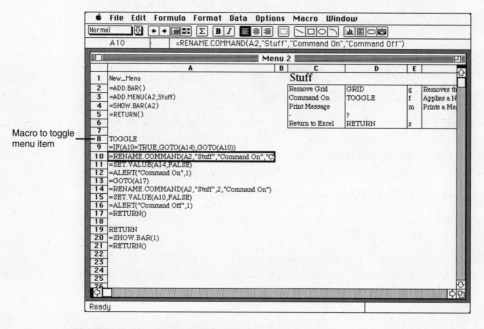

Macro to toggle menu item

Fig. 20.11. Creating a toggle menu option.

The macro Toggle has two main parts. The first part begins at cell A10 and changes the name of the option from Command On to Command Off. The second part begins at cell A14 and changes the option from Command Off to Command On. The function in cell A9 is the macro's decision-maker, deciding which of the two parts is used at any given time by looking at the value in cell A10. If this value is TRUE, the function in cell A10 has run—hence, the option's name is now Command Off. In this case, the macro branches to the second part (cell A14). If the value of A10 is FALSE, however, the function in A10 has not been run and the option's name is still Command On.

Finally, reset the values of A10 and A14 after each toggle with the SET.VALUE functions. Notice that these functions appear directly after the renaming functions. Finally, the ALERT commands represent any actions taken by the Command On and Command Off options. You can replace these commands with any other commands or use GOTO commands to branch the macro to other routines.

This limited example requires that the menu always start with the Command On option. A more sophisticated macro enables the option last selected to remain active, even after you quit Excel. You can design this kind of macro by adding commands that change the menu-definition table. Figure 20.12 shows the updated macro.

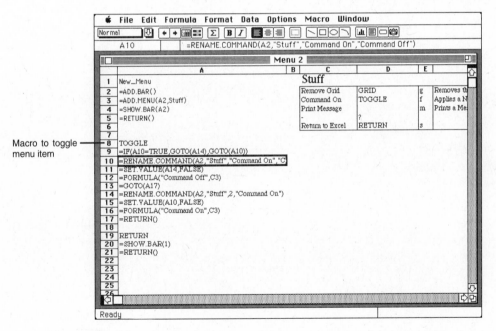

Macro to toggle menu item

Fig. 20.12. A toggle menu option that remains active after you quit Excel.

Disabling and Checking Menu Options

You can add or delete check marks for another menu-options technique. A check mark beside an option indicates that the option has been selected. When you select the option again, the check mark disappears. Often, checked options appear in groups within a menu. Controlling check marks is similar to controlling a toggle option. The macro logic stays the same (see fig. 20.13).

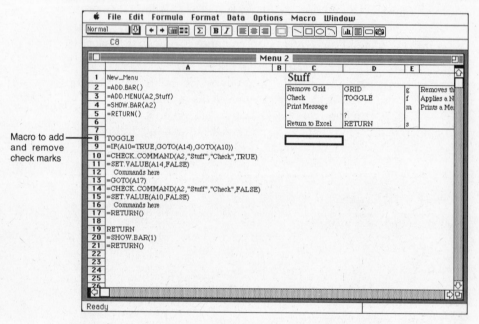

Fig. 20.13. Using check marks.

Disabling an option is much simpler than toggling a menu option. A disabled option, which appears in gray and cannot be selected, usually results from selecting some other option or performing some action. After the appropriate action has been taken, use the function ENABLE.COMMAND. The syntax follows:

=ENABLE.COMMAND(*bar_number,menu_name,command_name,state*)

State should be TRUE, which enables the command, or FALSE, which disables it.

Creating Custom Dialog Boxes

If you create custom menus, you also may need to create custom dialog boxes to go with them. You create and access custom dialog boxes the same way that you do custom menus. These dialog boxes have three parts:

- The *controlling macro*, which brings up the dialog box, is usually a custom menu item's macro. This macro activates the dialog box defined in the dialog-box definition table.

- The *dialog box definition table*, which contains values describing the dialog box and all its elements, can appear in any worksheet or macro sheet. When you select options from the dialog box (or make entries), Excel enters the results in a column of this table for reference by other macros.

- *Commands* responding to any controls that may be in the dialog box are usually part of the original controlling macro and appear directly after the command that produces the dialog box.

Bringing up a dialog box requires only one function: DIALOG.BOX. Any macro can issue this function, but most commonly you use the function in a macro that corresponds to a custom menu option or a button. The syntax of the function follows:

=DIALOG.BOX(*table_range*)

Table_range contains the dialog-box definition table. This range can be on any worksheet or macro sheet, but most commonly you enter the range on the macro sheet containing the custom menu and its option macros. An example of such a macro follows:

DIALOG

=DIALOG.BOX(DLG)

=RETURN

This macro refers to the dialog-box definition table named DLG. The following sections explain how to create dialog-box definition tables.

> **Tip: Avoiding Using Table Titles as Part of the Table Range**
> Do not use a table's titles in a table range reference; use only the range containing the items. Make sure that the first row is blank or contains values for the dialog box's location.

Creating a Dialog Box Definition Table

The dialog box definition table lists the elements contained in the dialog box. The table also controls the size, shape, and position of the box. Figure 20.14 shows a dialog box definition table, and figure 20.15 shows the dialog box the table creates.

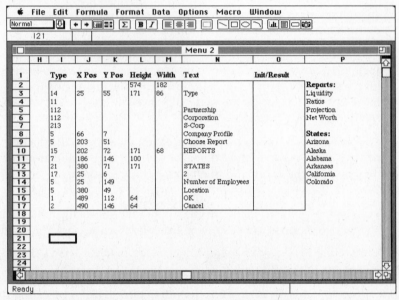

#	Type	X Pos	Y Pos	Height	Width	Text	Init/Result	
1	Type	X Pos	Y Pos	Height	Width	Text	Init/Result	
2				574	182			**Reports:**
3	14	25	55	171	86	Type		Liquidity
4	11							Ratios
5	112					Partnership		Projection
6	112					Corporation		Net Worth
7	213					S-Corp		
8	5	66	7			Company Profile		**States:**
9	5	203	51			Choose Report		Arizona
10	15	202	72	171	68	REPORTS		Alaska
11	7	186	146	100				Alabama
12	21	380	71	171		STATES		Arkansas
13	17	25	6			2		California
14	5	25	149			Number of Employees		Colorado
15	5	380	49			Location		
16	1	489	112	64		OK		
17	2	490	146	64		Cancel		

Fig. 20.14. A dialog box definition table.

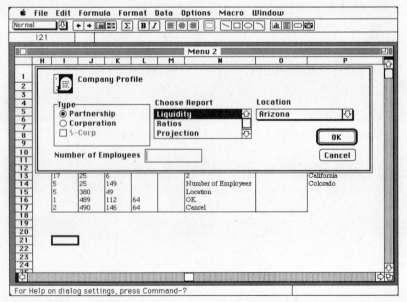

Fig. 20.15. The dialog box created by the table.

You can create a dialog box definition table in one of two ways: you can use the Dialog Editor or enter the table's values manually. The Dialog Editor program does most of the work in preparing the table and is the preferred method of creating dialog box tables. If you choose to enter the table's values manually, however, you should know something about the values in each column:

- *Type:* Specifies the type of each item. A complete list of items and their type numbers appears in the next section.

- *X Position:* Specifies the horizontal position of the upper left corner of the item. If you leave this column blank, Excel places the item.

- *Y Position:* Specifies the vertical position of the upper left corner of the item. If you leave this column blank, Excel places the item.

- *Width:* Specifies the item's width. If you leave this column blank, Excel chooses an appropriate width.

- *Height:* Specifies the item's height. If you leave this column blank, Excel chooses an appropriate height.

- *Text:* Specifies the text (if any) used for the item. Edit boxes do not have anything in this column; text boxes always have something in this column. If the @ character precedes a character in this box, @ becomes the keyboard command character for the item. If a button's text is "@Forget It," for example, pressing ⌘-F selects the button. If the item is a list box, this column should contain a reference to a range of cells that contains the entire list. This reference should be a range name or an R1C1-style range reference.

- *Init/Result:* Specifies the current settings in the dialog box. Excel updates this column as the settings change. If you enter information in this column, that information acts as default settings for the items. If the item is an edit box, this entry determines the current text in the box. If the item is a list box, this entry determines which choice in the list currently is selected. When a selection is made in the dialog box, the entry in this column updates to reflect the new selection. This column therefore contains the current settings selected in the dialog box at all times.

Each row in the table represents the settings for a different item, except the first row, which represents the settings for the dialog box itself. If this row is blank, Excel uses the default size, shape, and position. You can attach a custom help screen to this table by entering its name (as an external reference) in the first cell in the first row of the table. Details for creating custom help topics appear later in this chapter in "Documenting and Custom Help."

Note that you can give the dialog box a title by entering a text label into the Text column (sixth column) of the table's first row. This action not only adds a title to the dialog box, but also enables you to move the box by clicking on the title bar and dragging it to a new location. With movable dialog boxes, you also can click on the worksheet to enter cell references into the dialog box.

Using the Dialog Editor to Create the Table

Creating a dialog box is easy if you use the Dialog Editor program that comes with Excel. With this program, you can graphically build a dialog box and position the elements. Start the Dialog Editor program by opening the program's icon from the desktop. The program begins with a blank dialog box and three menus (see fig. 20.16). You do most of your work with the Item menu and the keyboard or mouse.

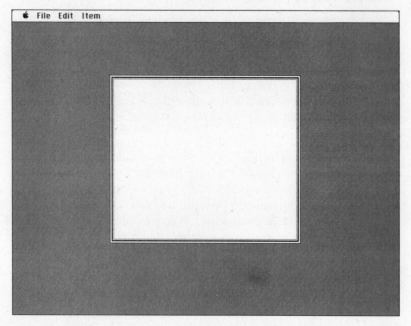

Fig. 20.16. The Dialog Editor.

To add an element to the dialog box, select the item from the Item menu. Most of these items offer several variations. The dialog box elements you can add appear in figure 20.17.

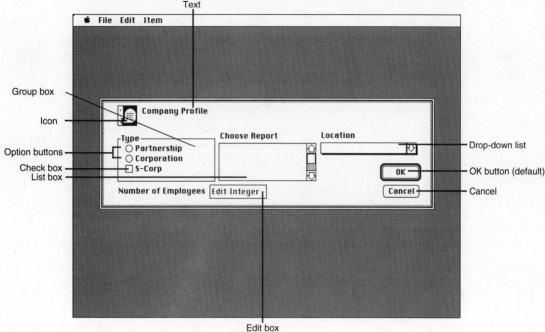

Fig. 20.17. Dialog box items.

Descriptions of the dialog box items follow:

- *OK and Cancel Buttons:* These buttons are standard on dialog boxes. Click on the OK button to enter your dialog box choices. Click on Cancel to cancel your changes. (You can change the names of these buttons, but their effects remain the same. To change the name, select the button and type the new name.)

  The OK button closes the dialog box and returns the value TRUE to the Init/Result column. The value FALSE then enters the Cancel button's Init/Result column. If you select the Cancel button, its Init/Result column gets the TRUE value and the OK button gets the FALSE value. You can design a macro that checks the Init/Result columns of these two buttons and responds accordingly. Details of these buttons follow:

Item	Type	Returns
OK (default)	1	TRUE/FALSE
OK (not default)	3	TRUE/FALSE
Cancel (default)	4	TRUE/FALSE
Cancel (not default)	2	TRUE/FALSE

- *Option Buttons:* Also called *radio buttons*, option buttons usually appear in groups. When option buttons are grouped, you can select only one button at a time. Option buttons are, therefore, useful for either/or choices.

  To create a group of option buttons, first add a group box by using the Group Box command from the Item menu. With the box still selected, press Return for each option button you want to add (or select the Button Option command from the Item menu for each option button). Excel makes these grouped buttons either/or options. You can change the name of an option button by selecting the button and typing the name you want or by typing the name immediately after the box appears.

  When you select an option button and click on the OK button, Excel returns the value TRUE to its Init/Result column, indicating that the option now is selected. You then can design a macro that takes the appropriate action based on this selection. Following are the details:

Item	Type	Returns
Option (grouped)	11	TRUE/FALSE
Option (not in group)	12	TRUE/FALSE

- *Check Boxes:* Similar to option buttons, check boxes usually imply and/or options. In other words, you can select one or more of the boxes at any time. You can group check boxes by creating the group box with the Group Box command from the Item menu, and then using the Button Check Box command from the Item menu for each box you want to add to the group. Make sure that you choose the group box first. Check boxes also can appear individually.

Item	Type	Returns
Check	13	TRUE/FALSE

- *Text:* Use the Item Text command to enter any text into the dialog box. Begin typing when you select the new text box. To add a second and subsequent text box, select any text and press Return.

Item	Type	Returns
Text	5	Nothing

- *Edit Boxes:* With an edit box, you can enter and edit text, integers, numbers, formulas, or cell references in the dialog box. Excel includes five types of edit boxes for these three types of entries. Each box permits only its own type of entry. Select the Edit Box command from the Item menu to add an edit box. You then can select the type of information allowed in the box.

When information appears in an edit box and you click on the OK button, Excel enters that information in the Init/Result column of the table. You can design a macro that uses that information for various purposes. When the dialog box appears, the edit box already contains the information in the Init/Result column. This information normally is the last thing entered in the box.

Item	Type	Returns
Text Edit box	6	Text in box
Integer Edit box	7	Integer in box
Number Edit box	8	Number in box
Formula Edit box	9	Formula in box
Reference Edit box	10	Cell or Range in box

- *Group Boxes:* Group boxes hold groups of items together in the dialog box. Option buttons and check boxes usually are found in group boxes, but you can place any items into a group box. To create a group box, select the Group Box command from the Item menu. To add a different item to the group box, select the group box and add the appropriate item from the Item menu; press Return to add more items of the same type. You can place existing items into a group by copying the items, highlighting the group box, and pasting the items.

Item	Type	Returns
Group box	14	Nothing

- *List Boxes:* List boxes display lists of options or files that you can select. When you select an item on the list and click on the OK button, the selected item returns to the Init/Result column of the definition table. You can build a macro using this information after clicking on the OK button. To specify the items in the list, enter the list of items into any worksheet or macro sheet range, and then refer to this range in the list box's Text column of the definition table. One good technique is to name the range and use the name in the table. When you display the dialog box, Excel reads the data in the indicated range and creates the list box with that data.

You can have a list box read a directory of files from the disk by entering the =FILES() function into the macro that brings up the dialog box. Do this before the DIALOG.BOX function is issued so that the FILES function can perform first. Enter the FILES function as an array range. In other words, when you enter the FILES function into the macro, select several cells in the same row (only a row of cells works), and then type =FILES() and press ⌘-Return. This procedure makes the FILES function an array function in the macro. Next, refer to this array range in the list box's Text column in the dialog definition table. (You can name the range and use the name.) Note that the number of cells in this array range determines the number of files read from the current directory.

Sometimes, list boxes are linked with edit boxes. In such a case, the edit box displays the item now selected in the list box. This box is called a *combination list box.*

Item	*Type*	*Returns*
List box	15	Selected item from list
Linked List box	16	Selected item from list
Drop-Down List box	21	Selected item from list
Drop-Down Combo box	22	Selected item from list

• *Directory Text:* This item displays the name of the current directory (folder). Directory Text is useful when you also have a list box that shows the files in the current directory.

Item	*Type*	*Returns*
Directory Text	20	Nothing

• *Icon:* You can insert one of several icons into your dialog box to make your dialog boxes match standard Macintosh boxes. After choosing this item, you can decide which icon you want.

Item	*Type*	*Returns*
Icon	17	Nothing

Moving and Resizing Items

To move an item to another location in the box, click on the box and drag the pointer. You also can use the keyboard to move an item by selecting the item with the Tab key and then moving the item with the arrow keys. To resize an item with the mouse, click on an edge and drag the pointer. To resize an item using the keyboard, select the item and use the Shift key with one of the four arrow keys to adjust the shape.

To change the size and shape of the dialog box, click the mouse on the bottom or right edge of the box. The pointer changes shape to indicate that you can click and drag the mouse to change the box. You also can click in the bottom right corner of the box and drag diagonally to change the position of that corner, thus changing the box's dimensions. You also can use the keyboard to change the size of the dialog box. To select the box, click the mouse button (or use the Select Dialog command from the Edit menu), and then press the Shift key with one of the four arrow keys.

Placing the Dialog Box into Excel

You cannot save a dialog box in the Dialog Editor program. Instead, store the dialog box's definition on the clipboard and paste the definition onto an Excel worksheet. Quit the Dialog Editor while your completed dialog box is in view. The program asks whether you want to save the dialog box to the clipboard. Select Yes. Next, enter Excel with the worksheet or macro sheet in view and use the Paste command from the Edit menu to paste the definition table into the worksheet at the current location of the pointer. Be sure to allow enough room for the table.

While the table is highlighted, use the Define Name command from the Edit menu to name the table. Use the Border command from the Format menu to add borders to the table.

Editing an Existing Dialog Box

You can edit a dialog box in Excel by changing the values in the various columns of the definition table. This task may not be easy. Instead, you may prefer to copy the table back into the Dialog Editor to modify the table. Highlight the entire table range and select the Copy command from the Edit menu. Next, move to the Dialog Editor and select the Paste command from the Edit menu. After you modify the dialog box, copy the box back into the worksheet, as described in the preceding section.

Acting on Dialog-Box Choices

The macro that brings up the dialog box normally acts on the choices made in a dialog box. Any macro, however, can access the values returned to the definition table, and when the macro runs, it can act on those values. By using the macro that brings up the dialog box, however, you can perform the desired actions as soon as you click on the OK button, because the macro still runs when the dialog box is in view. When you close the dialog box, the macro continues with the command just under the DIALOG.BOX function. The rest of the macro can interpret and act on the choices made.

Each edit box and control used in a dialog box returns something to the Init/Result column of the table. (What each item returns is discussed in the preceding sections.) Buttons return values of TRUE when the button has been selected and FALSE when the button has not been selected. You may have to test whether each button has been selected by using IF functions, such as the following:

=IF(O10="TRUE",ALERT("Button X pushed",1),GOTO(A14))

This function is entered in the macro that brings up the dialog box, under the function DIALOG.BOX. The function checks whether cell O10 contains the value TRUE. If the cell contains TRUE, meaning that the button has been selected, the message `Button x pushed` appears in an alert box. Otherwise, continue with the macro in cell A14; that cell continues the testing. You also may use the CHOOSE function to evaluate dialog box choices. (See Chapter 6.)

Creating Dynamic Dialog Box Items

Dialog boxes often include items that activate other items in the same dialog box. A particular option button, when selected, may activate several other option buttons or check boxes. When deselected, the option button deactivates those same buttons or check boxes. Such examples can be found throughout Excel.

Activating and deactivating dialog box items should be handled in the macro that brings up the dialog box. This macro must test for certain results from the dialog box, make changes to the dialog box items (activate or deactivate items), and display the dialog box again with the changes in place. To deactivate an item, add 200 to its item number in the table. A deactivated check box, for example, is item number 213.

Besides changing the item's number, you should set triggers in the dialog box. *Triggers* cause other items to activate or deactivate. Triggers can be any button item, and are established by adding 100 to their item numbers. To set a trigger, you can modify the dialog box definition table by adding 100 to the trigger items you want or by double-clicking on the item after you draw it in the Dialog Editor, and then choosing the Trigger box.

A *trigger* closes the dialog box and continues the macro that created it. The OK and Cancel buttons are natural triggers, but any item with 100 added to its item number also is a trigger. When the dialog box closes, Excel returns one of three values to the cell containing the DIALOG.BOX command: TRUE if you close the box with the OK button, FALSE if you close the box with the Cancel button, or the number of the trigger that closed the dialog box. The trigger number is the row on which the item is located in the table.

By examining the value in the cell containing the command DIALOG.BOX, you can act on the various conditions of the dialog box. You can deactivate items (add 200 to their numbers using the SET.VALUE command), activate items (subtract 200 from their numbers), or act on various choices or entries from the box. Generally, if a trigger closes a dialog box, reopen the dialog box as soon as you complete the necessary changes. This way, only the OK and Cancel buttons remove the box. Figures 20.18 and 20.19 show a macro that uses triggers to control dialog box items.

Figure 20.18 shows the controlling macro for the dialog box table in figure 20.19. (The actual dialog box created by this table is in fig. 20.17). The controlling macro activates the check box labeled S-Corp when the Corporation button is pressed, and it deactivates this check box when the Partnership button is pressed. Therefore, both the Partnership and Corporation radio buttons are triggers, as you can see from their item numbers in the table (items numbered 112 on the third and fourth lines of the table). Let's examine how the controlling macro makes this happen.

The macro is divided into segments, each taking care of a different action. The Partnership segment, beginning at cell A33, is used if the Partnership button is pressed. Its purpose is to deactivate the S-Corp check box and redisplay the dialog box. To activate the check box, the macro segment uses the command =SET.VALUE(I7,213). This command changes the item number of the check box in the table (cell I7) to the deactive value (item number 213 is a deactive check box). The macro segment then redisplays the dialog box by returning to cell A24, which is the original controlling macro that displays the dialog box. The process then starts all over again.

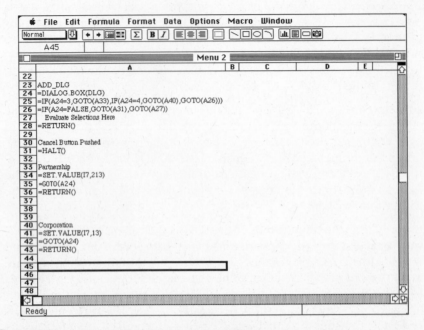

Fig. 20.18. *Controlling dialog box items with triggers.*

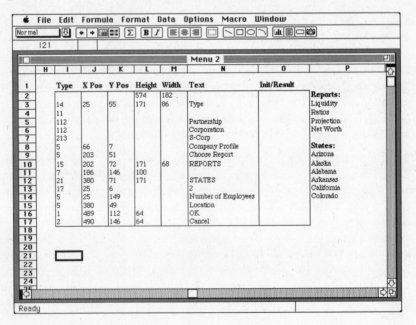

Fig. 20.19. *Using triggers to control dialog box items.*

The Corporation segment at cell A40 is similar. Its purpose is to activate the S-Corp check box and redisplay the dialog box. It uses the SET.VALUE command to change the check box item number back to 13, which is a normal check box.

The IF functions in cells A25 and A26 determine which items have been selected in the dialog box. Because the value of cell A24 will reveal which trigger or button was pressed in the box, the IF functions simply test for the possible values in this cell. In this case, the possible values are:

TRUE	The OK button was pressed.
FALSE	The Cancel button was pressed.
3	The Partnership button was pressed (trigger).
4	The Corporation button was pressed (trigger).

The Partnership and Corporation buttons have the values 3 and 4 because they are the third and fourth rows in the table (not including the headings or top row). This is simply how Excel identifies the triggers.

> *Note:* This macro is designed to show how the triggers and dialog box items are manipulated in the controlling macro. It is not a complete example because it does not currently test that the OK button was pressed. If the OK button is pressed, the macro should evaluate every value in the Init/Result column of the table to identify when items were selected and then act accordingly. These evaluations can be inserted into the macro at cell A27, or you can branch to another segment to perform these operations.

Using Error-Trapping Techniques

Errors generally occur when Excel does not accept an entry or when an entry prevents Excel from calculating an appropriate result. The functions HLOOKUP and VLOOKUP, for example, return an error when the lookup data cannot be found in the table. Anticipating the problem helps to trap such an error.

Suppose that a value is being calculated in cell B15. The formula may produce an error if the user enters an incorrect value somewhere else in the worksheet. Rather than present the error message in the cell, however, you can trap the error and produce a more useful message with a special error-trapping formula. The formula goes into a unique cell and may look like this:

=IF(ISERR(B15)=1,"Please check your entry and try again","")

Using the ISERR function with IF logic, this formula checks whether the value in cell B15 is an error. If an error exists, a message results.

Errors often occur while a macro runs. A user may enter the wrong type of information into a custom dialog box or input box and cause a macro-execution error. You can trap these errors to prevent the macro from halting, and then return to the input screen that caused the problem. Normally, Excel checks for errors in macros and presents a dialog box when an error occurs. This dialog box enables you continue the macro, halt the macro, or view the problem in the macro. This same error-checking is responsible for all kinds of alert messages throughout the program.

You can turn Excel's error-checking on or off by using the ERROR function in the following ways:

ERROR(FALSE)   Error-checking off

ERROR(TRUE)   Error-checking on

When error-checking is off, Excel skips macro errors and attempts to continue running the macro. Error-checking comes back on when the macro ends with the RETURN() function or when the macro encounters the ERROR(TRUE) function. You also can use this function to present custom error messages or specific error-invoked actions, such as returning to a dialog box, by specifying a macro to run when an error is encountered:

ERROR(TRUE,*macro*)

The *macro* argument is the name or cell reference of the macro you want to run when an error is encountered. This argument is used only when the first argument is TRUE. Note that this command eliminates all Excel error messages, including warnings to save your worksheet upon quitting Excel. If you want to eliminate macro error messages, but keep the regular program-alert messages, use the following syntax:

ERROR(2,*macro*)

If you use a macro reference with the ERROR command, you may want your custom error macro to present a message. Excel offers two commands for displaying messages on-screen. The ALERT command displays an alert dialog box containing any message. The user must click on the OK button in this dialog box before continuing. The syntax follows:

=ALERT(*text,type*)

Text is any message (enclosed in quotation marks) that you want displayed in the box. *Type* controls the type of alert box that is used. Entering 1 presents a Caution box (see fig. 20.20). Entering 2 presents a Note box (see fig. 20.21). Entering 3 presents a Stop box (see fig. 20.22).

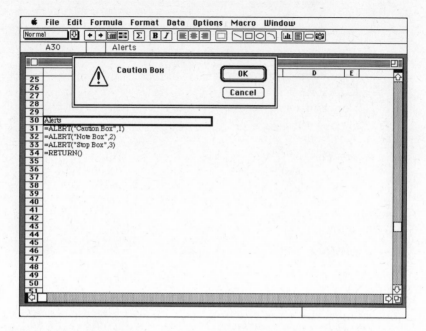

Fig. 20.20. *A Caution box.*

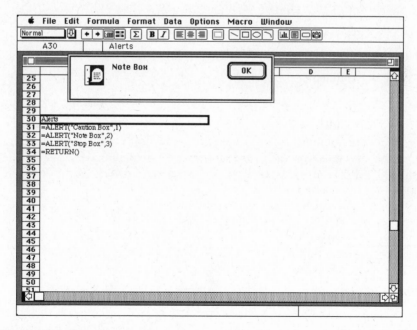

Fig. 20.21. *A Note box.*

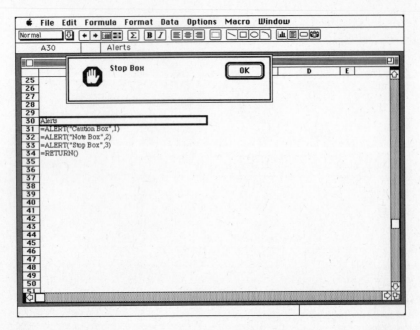

Fig. 20.22. *A Stop box.*

You also can display a message using the MESSAGE command in a macro. This command uses the status line to display your message and is useful when your message requires no response. The syntax follows:

=MESSAGE(*logical,text*)

The *logical* value must be TRUE or FALSE. If the value is TRUE, the message capability is turned on; if the value is FALSE, the message capability is turned off. When the message capability is off, the status bar returns to the normal Excel messages. You can use the MESSAGE command with the *text* value of "" (null) to turn the status line messages on and off without presenting your own message.

Be sure to turn on the normal message display again (using the MESSAGE(FALSE) command) after displaying custom messages. Otherwise, your custom message remains in view until you quit Excel.

> ***Tip: Test Your Macros***
> Many error-trapping needs can be found if you test your macros using various scenarios. Input unexpected values into input boxes and cells. See if the macro can handle these errors.

Using Add-In Macros

Add-in macros are commands or custom functions that become part of Excel itself. An add-in macro sheet is invisible and cannot be exposed with the Unhide command from the Window menu. Custom functions in the add-in macro sheet appear in the Edit Paste Function dialog box as though the functions are Excel functions. Also, command macros on the add-in sheet can be inserted into Excel's existing menus as though the macros are Excel commands. (This must be done in the macros themselves by inserting them into existing menus with the ADD.COMMAND command. See "Adding and Deleting Menu Options" earlier in this chapter.) In short, a user does not know a macro is running.

> *Note:* Excel provides several add-in macros that you can use at any time. Many of these have been explained in previous chapters. The Solver utility discussed in Chapter 8, for example, is an add-in macro. The What If and Worksheet Auditor features, also discussed in Chapter 8, are other add-in macros that come with Excel. Still more add-in macros can be found in the Macro Library folder. If the Macro Library folder does not appear on your system, you may not have installed it when you installed Excel. You can use the installation program to add these tools to your existing copy of Excel.

Also, the Close All command from the File menu does not affect add-in macro sheets, which remain open and active. You can close a macro sheet only if you include a Close option in it. This option should use the FCLOSE macro command to close the add-in macro sheet. You also can quit Excel to close an add-in. The Quit command from the File menu, however, does not ask you to save changes that may have occurred in the add-in sheet. If the add-in must be saved after it is used, then include a macro on the add-in that saves the sheet using the SAVE macro command. This macro should be applied to the sheet's *Auto_Close* macro.

You can save any macro worksheet as an add-in sheet. Just follow these steps:

1. Select the Save As command from the File menu to save the macro sheet.

2. Choose the options button.

3. Select the add-in option from the list of file formats.

4. Press Return.

5. Enter a name for the add-in and press Return again.

You can run an add-in macro in several ways. A summary follows:

- Double-click on the add-in icon to start Excel with the add-in active.

- Use the Open command from the File menu to open the add-in macro. The commands and functions provided by the macro activate as soon as you open the macro.

- Use an *Auto_Open* macro to open the add-in whenever a particular worksheet is opened.

- Place the add-in into the Excel Startup folder in the System folder. This procedure activates the add-in whenever you start Excel. (See the following section.)

If you want to access any of the add-in macros from a normal macro sheet, you can link the add-in macros to the normal sheet with the following type of reference:

=*Macro_name*()

This reference is the name of the macro as the name appears on the add-in macro sheet. Notice that the reference contains no external reference as you otherwise may expect. Because you cannot see the macros on this sheet, you must remember the macros' names. The exceptions are custom functions, which appear in the Edit Paste Function list.

To view or edit the macros on an add-in macro worksheet, you can open the add-in as a normal macro sheet. Select the Open command from the File menu and press Shift while double-clicking on the add-in's name. If you protected the add-in with a password, enter the password and press Shift while clicking on OK.

Using Start-Up Automation

As you know from Chapter 18, each worksheet has *Auto_Open* and *Auto_Close* macros that activate as soon as you open or close the worksheet. Excel provides an additional level of start-up automation, however. You can have worksheets, charts, macro sheets, add-ins, or workspace files appear as soon as you enter Excel. This level is especially useful for custom applications and add-ins.

To make a worksheet or other file appear automatically, move its icon into the Excel Startup folder, which appears in your Macintosh System folder.

You can move these files from their original folders by dragging the files into the Excel Startup folder.

> **Note:** If you are using System 7, the Excel Startup Folder will be located in the Preferences folder, which is in the System folder.

Also, if you move a template file (a worksheet saved as a template) into the Excel Startup folder, the file's name appears in the File New list, making locating and duplicating easier.

Documenting and Custom Help

You can add custom help screens to your custom menus and dialog boxes. Help screens act just like normal Excel help topics and can be accessed in the same ways. (See Chapter 3 for information about using Help.)

To create a custom help topic, open a new worksheet and enter the help topic in the following manner:

> *101 Comment
>
> *Help information here*

Each topic name should begin with an asterisk followed by an integer. You then can type a brief name or comment about the topic. Beneath this name, enter any help information you want to appear in the help screen. You can enter more than one help topic per worksheet by entering each topic in a new column using the format shown. Figure 20.23 shows an example.

Next, save this worksheet as a text file by using the Save As command from the File menu and choosing the Text option in the File Formats list. You now can refer to the help topics (by number) by including them in your custom menu tables and dialog box tables, as described earlier in this chapter. (See "Creating the Menu Definition Table.") Be sure to refer to the exact location of the file, using an external reference. For example, to link the help topic in Column A of figure 20.23 to a menu item, you enter the following reference into the menu definition table:

> (HELP!100

Custom help screens are useful for documenting custom menu options and dialog boxes, but you may want to provide help on using your custom worksheets. To provide help, you can include a button on the worksheet to bring up a text box or Info Sheet containing information about worksheet entries. If you use a text box, you can use toggle buttons to show and hide the text box. The following macro shows and hides the text box (note that the text box already is created and has the object number 1):

ShowBox

       HIDE.OBJECT("text 1",FALSE)

       RETURN()

HideBox

       HIDE.OBJECT("text 1",TRUE)

       RETURN()

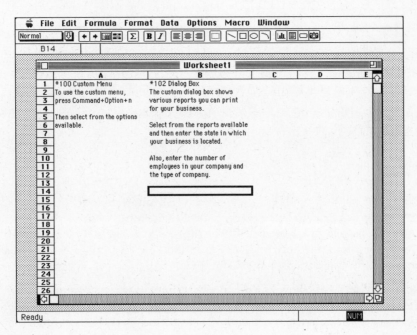

Fig. 20.23. *A custom help file.*

Attach these macros to the toggle buttons as described earlier in this chapter in the section "Toggle Buttons." Then, click on the button to display the text box; click again to hide the box.

Making Macros Faster and More Efficient

Often, macros can take quite a while to complete. Without some information, the user may not realize that anything is happening. One useful idea is to display messages throughout a macro's operation to keep the user informed of the macro's progress. Even a message that tells the user to "Stand By" can be helpful. Select key intervals in your macro and update the message.

Another idea is to keep the screen from continually redrawing itself during your macro's operation by issuing the command =ECHO(FALSE) at the beginning of the macro and =ECHO(TRUE) at the end. The screen does not change until the end of the macro.

To help speed up your macro, try turning Excel's automatic recalculation feature off. You can turn the feature back on at the end of the macro or leave the feature off and issue a =CALCULATE.NOW() command.

Summary

This chapter completes your education on macros and Excel. Although somewhat advanced, the chapter contains useful information for building custom applications in Excel. Apply as many of these ideas and techniques as you want. Here are some points to remember:

- You can use spreadsheet logic to toggle buttons.

- Use custom menus and dialog boxes to enhance the application.

- Menus are created from a menu definition table using the ADD.MENU command.

- Dialog boxes are created from a dialog box definition table using the DIALOG.BOX command.

- Use the Dialog Editor to help you create a dialog box definition table.

- The macro debugger helps you to locate errors in your macros. You can open this add-in utility by choosing the Open command from the File menu.

- You can create your own add-in utilities by saving them as add-ins with the File Save As command options.

Installing Excel

This appendix shows you how to get Excel up and running on your system. As you will see, installing Excel is simple and much of the work is done for you by the easy-to-use installation program. After you install Excel, you will be ready use the program and experiment with the examples provided in this book.

Noting System Requirements

When you purchase Excel, you should make sure that your system meets the requirements of the program. Essentially, Excel 3.0 requires that you have any Macintosh computer (except the old Macintosh 128 or 512), Version 6.02 or a later version of the Macintosh system, and Version 6.01 of the Finder. Excel cannot run under earlier versions of the system. You also need 1M of RAM, one 800K disk drive and one hard disk: these usually will be part of your system configuration. Excel requires from 1316K to 4181K of your hard disk, depending on how you install the program.

If you are running Excel under MultiFinder or System 7.0, you must have at least 2M of RAM.

Installing Excel

Before starting Excel, you should make a backup copy of each Excel program disk. Then, use the backup copy to install Excel on your system.

To install Excel, follow these steps:

1. Insert the Setup disk into the floppy drive. If the disk is not open and showing its contents in a window, double-click on its icon to open it.

2. Double-click on the Microsoft Excel Installer icon. A dialog box appears asking you to enter your name and organization (see fig. A.1).

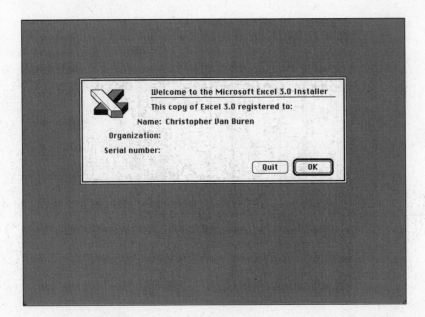

Fig. A.1. Entering your name and organization.

3. Enter your name and organization (if applicable) into the spaces provided. After you enter this information, it cannot be changed; the only way to alter it is to make a new copy of Excel from the original disks. You cannot avoid calling up this personalization dialog box, but you can pass up the dialog box without making

an entry. Doing so leaves the program unpersonalized. You then will be unable to personalize the program without making a new copy. Press Return when finished. The screen shown in figure A.2 appears.

You may not want to install the entire program if you are low on disk space. Using the dialog box check boxes, select the options you want and press Return. (You must, at least, install Microsoft Excel, the first item in the box.)

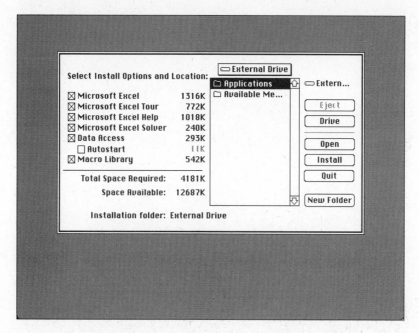

Fig. A.2. *The custom installation selections.*

4. Follow the instructions on-screen for swapping disks. When you finish, Excel presents a message telling you that you have completed the procedure, and you can begin using Excel.

B

Using Excel's Macro Commands

This appendix lists the macro commands available in Excel. Many of these commands duplicate the menu options with which you have become familiar. Others are the equivalent of mouse or keyboard actions. Still other commands are used especially for macros. The commands are listed alphabetically in this appendix.

> *Note:* Commands that mimic Excel menu options that display dialog boxes enable you to use the question mark syntax. When you add a question mark to the end of such a command, the macro presents Excel's dialog box. To bring up the File-Open dialog box, for example, you use the command OPEN?( ), which is the question-mark version of the OPEN macro command. Question mark versions are not listed separately in this appendix.

Command Listing by Category

To help you locate commands for specific purposes, a command listing is included. This listing groups commands according to their basic purpose. Commands that mimic the Edit menu options, for example, appear under the heading "Duplicating the Edit Menu Options."

To help you use the commands, some conventions are used in the argument names. Many names contain two or three words; these will always be separated by underlines, as in *type_of_link*. Remember that this is only one argument—commas are used to separate arguments. Also, many arguments end in either num or text, as in *type_num* and *name_text*. The *num* indicates that you should enter the argument as a number, and *text* indicates that you should enter the arguments as text, surrounded by quotation marks. The *logical* argument indicates that you should enter a value of TRUE or FALSE. Other argument names are words that help to remind you of the argument's purpose, as in *height%*.

Duplicating the File Menu Options

CHANGE.LINK(*old_link,new_link,type_of_link*)

CLOSE(*save_logical*)

CLOSE.ALL()

FILE.CLOSE(*save_logical*)

FILE.DELETE(*file_text*)

LINKS(*document_text,type_num*)

NEW(*type_num,xy_series*)

OPEN(*file_text, update_links, read_only, format, prot_pwd, write_res_pwd, ignore_rorec, file_origin*)

OPEN.LINKS(*document_text1,document_text2,..., read_only,type_of_link*)

OPEN.MAIL(*subject,comments*)

PAGE.SETUP(*head, foot, left, right, top, bot, heading, grid, h_center, v_center, orientation, paper_size, scaling*)

PAGE.SETUP(*head, foot, left, right, top, bot, size, h_center, v_center, orientation, paper_size, scaling*)

PRINT(*range_num, from, to, copies, draft, preview, print_what, color, feed*)

PRINT.PREVIEW()

QUIT()

SAVE()

SAVE.AS(*document_text,type_num, prot_pwd, backup, write_res_pwd, read_only_rec*)

SAVE.WORKSPACE(*name_text*)

Duplicating the Edit Menu Options

CANCEL.COPY()

CLEAR(*type_num*)

COPY()

COPY.CHART(*size_num*)

COPY.PICTURE(*appearance_num, size_num*)

CUT()

DUPLICATE()

EDIT.DELETE(*shift_num*)

EDIT.REPEAT()

FILL.DOWN()

FILL.LEFT()

FILL.RIGHT()

FILL.UP()

FILL.WORKGROUP(*type_num*)

INSERT(*shift_num*)

PASTE()

PASTE.LINK()

PASTE.SPECIAL(*paste_num,operation_num, skip_blanks,transpose*)

PASTE.SPECIAL(*rowcol, series,categories, replace*)

PASTE.SPECIAL(*paste_num*)

UNDO()

Duplicating the Formula Menu Options

APPLY.NAMES(*name_array,ignore, use_rowcol,omit_col,omit_row,order_num, append_last*)

CREATE.NAMES(*top,left,bottom, right*)

DEFINE.NAME(*name_text, refers_to,macro_type, shortcut_text, hidden*)

DELETE.NAME(*name_text*)

FORMULA.FIND(*text, in_num, at_num, by_num, dir_num, match_case*)

FORMULA.GOTO(*reference, corner*)

FORMULA.REPLACE(*find_text, replace_text, look_at, look_by, active_cell, match_case*)

GOAL.SEEK(*target_cell, target_value, variable_cell*)

LIST.NAMES()

NOTE(*add_text, cell_ref, start_char, num_chars*)

OUTLINE(*auto_styles, row_dir, col_dir, create_num*)

SELECT.LAST.CELL()

SELECT.SPECIAL(*type_num, value_type, levels*)

SHOW.ACTIVE.CELL()

Duplicating the Format Menu Options

ALIGNMENT(*type_num, wrap*)

APPLY.STYLE(*style_text*)

BORDER(*outline, left, right, top, bottom, shade, outline_color, left_color, right_color, top_color, bottom_color*)

BRING.TO.FRONT()

CELL.PROTECTION(*locked, hidden*)

COLUMN.WIDTH(*width_num, reference, standard, type_num*)

DEFINE.STYLE(*style_text, attribute_num, format_text*)

DEFINE.STYLE(*style_text, attribute_num, name_text, size_num, bold, italic, underline, strike, color, outline, shadow*)

DEFINE.STYLE(*style_text, attribute_num, type_num, wrap*)

DEFINE.STYLE(*style_text, attribute_num, left, right, top, bottom, left_color, right_color, top_color, bottom_color*)

DEFINE.STYLE(*style_text, attribute_num, aauto, apattern, afore, aback*)

DEFINE.STYLE(*style_text, attribute_num, locked, hidden*)

DEFINE.STYLE(*style_text, number, font, alignment, border, pattern, protection*)

DELETE.FORMAT(*format_text*)

DELETE.STYLE(*style_text*)

FORMAT.FONT(*name_text, size_num, bold, italic, underline, strike, color, outline, shadow*)

FORMAT.FONT(*name_text, size_num, bold, italic, underline, strike, color, outline, shadow, object_id_text, start_num, char_num*)

FORMAT.FONT(*color, backgd, apply, name, size, bold, italic, underline, strike*)

FORMAT.FONT(*color, backgd, apply, name_text, size_num, bold, italic, underline, strike, outline, shadow*)

FORMAT.MAIN(*type_num, view, overlap, gap_width, vary, drop, hilo, angle, gap_depth, chart_depth*)

FORMAT.MOVE(*x_pos, y_pos, reference*)

FORMAT.MOVE(*x_pos, y_pos*)

FORMAT.NUMBER(*format_text*)

FORMAT.OVERLAY(*type_num, view, overlap, width, vary, drop, hilo, angle, series_dist, series_num*)

FORMAT.SIZE(*x_off, y_off, reference*)

FORMAT.SIZE(*width, height*)

FORMAT.TEXT(*x_align, y_align, orient_num, auto_text, auto_size, show_key, show_value*)

HIDE.OBJECT(*object_id_text, hide*)

JUSTIFY()

MERGE.STYLES(*document_text*)

OBJECT.PROTECTION(*locked*)

PATTERNS(*aauto, apattern, afore, aback*)

PATTERNS(*lauto, lstyle, lcolor, lwt, lwidth, hlength, htype*)

PATTERNS(*bauto, bstyle, bcolor, bwt, shadow, aauto, apattern, afore, aback, rounded*)

PATTERNS(*bauto, bstyle, bcolor, bwt, shadow, aauto, apattern, afore, aback, invert, apply*)

PATTERNS(*lauto, lstyle, lcolor, lwt, tmajor, tminor, tlabel*)

PATTERNS(*lauto, lstyle, lcolor, lwt, apply*)

PATTERNS(*lauto, lstyle, lcolor, lwt, mauto, mstyle, mfore, mback, apply*)

PATTERNS(*type, picture_units*)

PLACEMENT(*value*)

ROW.HEIGHT(*height_num, reference, standard_height, type_num*)

SCALE(*cross, cat_labels, cat_marks, between, max, reverse*)

SCALE(*min_num, max_num, major, minor, cross, logarithmic, reverse, max*)

SCALE(*cat_labels, cat_marks, reverse, between*)

SCALE(*series_labels, series_marks, reverse*)

SCALE(*min_num, max_num, major, minor, cross, logarithmic, reverse, min*)

SEND.TO.BACK( )

UNGROUP( )

VIEW.3D(*elevation, perspective, rotation, axes, height%*)

Duplicating the Data Menu Options

CONSOLIDATE(*source_refs, function_num, top_row, left_col, create_links*)

DATA.DELETE( )

DATA.FIND(*logical*)

DATA.FORM( )

DATA.SERIES(*rowcol, type_num, date_num, step_value, stop_value*)

EXTRACT(*unique*)

PARSE(*text*)

SET.CRITERIA( )

SET.DATABASE( )

SET.EXTRACT( )

SORT(*sort_by, key_1, order_1, key_2, order_2, key_3, order_3*)

Duplicating the Options Menu Options

A1.R1C1(*logical*)

CALCULATE.DOCUMENT( )

CALCULATE.NOW( )

CALCULATION(*type_num, inter, max_num, max_change, update, precision, date_1904, calc_save, save_values*)

COLOR.PALETTE(*file_text*)

DISPLAY(*formula, gridlines, headings, zeros, color_num, reserved, outline, page_breaks, objects_num*)

DISPLAY(*cell, formula, value, format, protection, names, precedents, dependents, note*)

EDIT.COLOR(*color_num, red_value, green_value, blue_value*)

FREEZE.PANES(*logical*)

PRECISION(*logical*)

PROTECT.DOCUMENT(*contents, windows, password, objects*)

REMOVE.PAGE.BREAK()

SET.PAGE.BREAK()

SET.PRINT.AREA()

SET.PRINT.TITLES()

SET.UPDATE.STATUS(*link_text, status, type_of_link*)

SHORT.MENUS(*logical*)

STANDARD.FONT(*font_text, size_num, bold, italic, underline, strike, color, outline, shadow*)

WORKSPACE(*fixed, decimals, r1c1, scroll, status, formula, menu_key, remote, entermove, underlines, tools, notes, interface, menu_key_action*)

Duplicating the Windows Menu Options

ARRANGE.ALL()

HIDE()

NEW.WINDOW()

SHOW.CLIPBOARD()

SHOW.INFO(*logical*)

UNHIDE(*window_text*)

WORKGROUP(*name_array*)

Duplicating the Gallery Menu Options

COMBINATION(*type_num*)

GALLERY.AREA(*type_num,delete_overlay*)

GALLERY.BAR(*type_num,delete_overlay*)

GALLERY.COLUMN(*type_num,delete_overlay*)

GALLERY.LINE(*type_num,delete_overlay*)

GALLERY.PIE(*type_num,delete_overlay*)

GALLERY.SCATTER(*type_num,delete_overlay*)

GALLERY.3DCOLUMN(*type_num*)

GALLERY.3DLINE(*type_num*)

GALLERY.3DAREA(*type_num*)

GALLERY.3DPIE(*type_num*)

PREFERRED( )

SET.PREFERRED( )

Duplicating the Chart Menu Options

ADD.ARROW( )

ADD.OVERLAY( )

ATTACH.TEXT(*attach_to_num, series_num, point_num*)

AXES(*main_category,main_value,overlay_category,overlay_value*)

AXES(*x_main,y_main,z_main*)

DELETE.ARROW( )

DELETE.OVERLAY( )

EDIT.SERIES(*series_num,name_ref,x_ref,y_ref,z_ref, plot_order*)

FORMAT.LEGEND(*position_num*)

FORMAT.MOVE(*x_pos,y_pos*)

FORMAT.SIZE(*width, height*)

FORMAT.TEXT(*x_align,y_align,orient_num,auto_text,auto_size, show_key, show_value*)

GRIDLINES(*x_major,x_minor,y_major,y_minor,z_major,z_minor*)

LEGEND(*logical*)

MAIN.CHART(*type_num, stack, 100, vary, overlap, drop, hilo, overlap%, cluster, angle*)

OVERLAY(*type_num, stack, 100, vary, overlap, drop, hilo, overlap%, cluster, angle, series_num, auto*)

OVERLAY.CHART.TYPE(*type_num*)

SELECT.CHART()

SELECT.PLOT.AREA()

Duplicating Keyboard and Mouse Actions

ACTIVATE(*window_text, pane_num*)

ACTIVATE.NEXT()

ACTIVATE.PREV()

CANCEL.COPY()

CREATE.OBJECT(*object_type, ref_1, x_offset1, y_offset1, ref_2, x_offset2, y_offset2*)

CREATE.OBJECT(*object_type, ref_1, x_offset1, y_offset1, ref_2, x_offset2, y_offset2, text*)

CREATE.OBJECT(*object_type, ref_1, x_offset1, y_offset1, ref_2, x_offset2, y_offset2, xy_series*)

DATA.FIND.NEXT()

DIRECTORY(*path_text*)

FORMULA(*formula_text, reference*)

FORMULA.ARRAY(*formula_text, reference*)

FORMULA.FILL(*formula_text, reference*)

FORMULA.FIND.NEXT()

FORMULA.FIND.PREV()

FULL(*logical*)

HLINE(*num_columns*)

HPAGE(*num_windows*)

HSCROLL(*position, col_logical*)

MOVE(*x_pos,y_pos,window_text*)

SELECT(*selection,active_cell*)

SELECT(*item_text*)

SELECT.END(*direction_num*)

SIZE(*width, height,window_text*)

SPLIT(*col_split, row_split*)

TEXT.BOX(*add_text,object_id_text, start_num,num_chars*)

UNLOCKED.NEXT( )

UNLOCKED.PREV( )

VLINE(*num_rows*)

VPAGE(*num_windows*)

Outlining

DEMOTE(*rowcol*)

OUTLINE(*auto_styles, row_dir,col_dir,create_num*)

PROMOTE(*rowcol*)

SHOW.DETAIL(*rowcol, rowcol_num,expand*)

SHOW.LEVELS(*row_level,col_level*)

Controlling Macro Operation

ALERT(*message_text,type_num*)

ARGUMENT(*name_text,data_type_num, reference*)

ASSIGN.TO.OBJECT(*macro_ref*)

BEEP(*tone_num*)

BREAK( )

CALL(*register_ref,argument1,...*)

CANCEL.KEY(*enable,macro_ref*)

DISABLE.INPUT(*logical*)

ECHO(*logical*)

ELSE( )

ELSE.IF(*logical_test*)

END.IF()

ERROR(*enable_logical,macro_ref*)

FOR(*counter_text, start_num,end_num, step_num*)

FOR.CELL(*ref_name,area_ref, skip_blanks*)

FORMULA.CONVERT(*formula_text,from_a1,to_a1,to_ref_type, rel_to_ref*)

GOTO(*reference*)

HALT(*cancel_close*)

HELP(*file_text!topic_num*)

IF(*logical_test*)

INPUT(*message_text,type_num,title_text,default,x_pos,y_pos*)

MESSAGE(*logical,text*)

NEXT()

ON.DATA(*document_text,macro_text*)

ON.KEY(*key_text,macro_text*)

ON.RECALC(*sheet_text,macro_text*)

ON.TIME(*time,macro_text,tolerance,insert_logical*)

ON.WINDOW(*window_text,macro_text*)

RESULT(*type_num*)

RETURN(*value*)

RUN(*reference, step*)

SET.NAME(*name_text,value*)

SET.VALUE(*reference,values*)

STEP()

VOLATILE()

WAIT(*serial_number*)

WHILE(*logical_test*)

Creating Menus and Dialog Boxes

ADD.BAR(*bar_num*)

ADD.COMMAND(*bar_num,menu,command_ref, position*)

ADD.MENU(*bar_num,menu_ref, position*)

CHECK.COMMAND(*bar_num,menu,command ,check*)

CUSTOM.REPEAT(*macro_text, repeat_text, record_text*)

CUSTOM.UNDO(*macro_text, undo_text*)

DELETE.BAR(*bar_num*)

DELETE.COMMAND(*bar_num,menu,command*)

DELETE.MENU(*bar_num,menu*)

DIALOG.BOX(*dialog_ref*)

ENABLE.COMMAND(*bar_num,menu,command ,enable*)

GET.BAR( )

RENAME.COMMAND(*bar_num,menu,command ,name_text*)

SHOW.BAR(*bar_num*)

Manipulating Text Files

FCLOSE(*file_num*)

FOPEN(*file_text,access_num*)

FPOS(*file_num, position_num*)

FREAD(*file_num,num_chars*)

FREADLN(*file_num*)

FSIZE(*file_num*)

FWRITE(*file_num,text*)

FWRITELN(*file_num,text*)

Returning Values

ABSREF(*ref_text, reference*)

ACTIVE.CELL( )

DEREF(*reference*)

DOCUMENTS(*type_num*)

FILES(*directory_text*)

GET.CELL(*type_num, reference*)

GET.CHART.ITEM(*x_y_index, point_index, item_text*)

GET.DEF(*def_text, document_text, type_num*)

GET.DOCUMENT(*type_num, name_text*)

GET.FORMULA(*reference*)

GET.LINK.INFO(*link_text, type_num, type_of_link, reference*)

GET.NAME(*name_text*)

GET.NOTE(*cell_ref, start_char, num_chars*)

GET.OBJECT(*type_num, object_id_text, start_num, count_num*)

GET.WINDOW(*type_num, window_text*)

GET.WORKSPACE(*type_num*)

LAST.ERROR( )

NAMES(*document_text, type_num*)

REFTEXT(*reference, a1*)

RELREF(*reference, rel_to_ref*)

SELECTION( )

TEXTREF(*text, a1*)

WINDOWS(*type_num*)

Networking and Other Advanced Commands

APP.ACTIVATE(*title_text, wait_logical*)

CREATE.PUBLISHER(*file_text, appearance_num, size_num*)

EDITION.OPTIONS(*edition_type, edition_name, reference, option*)

EXEC(*program_text, background, minimum_size*)

EXECUTE(*channel_num, execute_text*)

INITIATE(*app_text, topic_text*)

OPEN.MAIL(*subject, comments*)

REGISTER(*module_text, procedure_text, type_text, function_text, argument_text*)

REQUEST(*channel_num, item_text*)

RESTART(*level_num*)

SEND.MAIL(*recipient, subject, return_receipt*)

SUBSCRIBE.TO(*file_text, format_num*)

UPDATE.LINK(*link_text, type_of_link*)

Command Listing in Alphabetical Order

The commands in this section are listed alphabetically. Because most of Excel's macro commands duplicate menu options, keyboard actions, or mouse actions, this chapter does not elaborate on the effects of the commands. To find more information on a command, turn to the corresponding menu command or action described earlier in this book. The primary purpose of this appendix is to list the commands available and to indicate the syntax required for each command.

> ***Note:*** This appendix lists the majority of Excel's macro commands, but not all of them. Many that are discussed at length in previous chapters, such as commands for creating custom menus, are not repeated here. Other commands were not included because they are esoteric or highly advanced.

For more information about macro arguments and cell references, see Chapter 19.

Many of these commands have a question-mark version of the same command, which brings up the Excel dialog box and thus makes the macro interactive. The question-mark versions usually are available for commands that duplicate menu options that bring up dialog boxes. If you use the question-mark version of a command, the arguments are optional, because you can select them from the dialog box that appears. If you use the arguments, Excel uses them as the dialog-box defaults.

A1.R1C1(*logical*)

Switches between the A1- and R1C1-style cell references on the active worksheet. Enter A1.R1C1(TRUE) to use A1 references or A1.R1C1(FALSE) to use R1C1 references.

ABSREF(*ref_text, reference*)

ABSREF returns the absolute reference of cells that are offset from a reference by a given distance. (See also OFFSET.)

Ref_text refers to a position relative to the cell in the upper left corner of the reference range; it tells Excel to move from one range of cells to another. The information must be in R1C1 style.

Reference denotes the range of cells at the starting point. *Reference* also can be an external reference.

ACTIVATE(*window_text, pane_num*)

Activates the specified window and a pane within the window, if applicable. Enter *window_text*, the name of the window to activate, as text with quotation marks or as an expression resulting in text. *Pane_num* is the pane within the window that you want to activate. Use any of the following values as the *pane_num*:

Value	Pane
1	Top pane if window is split horizontally Left pane if window is split vertically Top left pane if window is split two ways
2	Right pane if window is split vertically Top right if window is split two ways
3	Bottom pane if window is split horizontally Bottom left if window is split two ways
4	Bottom right pane if window is split two ways

ACTIVATE.NEXT( )

ACTIVATE.PREV( )

Activate the next and previous windows, respectively. Of course, more than one window should be open in order for these commands to work. These commands are the equivalents of the keyboard commands ⌘-M and ⌘-Shift-M.

ACTIVE.CELL( )

Gives the reference of the active cell in the selection as an external reference.

ADD.ARROW( )

Places a new arrow on the chart. You can remove the arrow by using the DELETE.ARROW( ) command.

ADD.OVERLAY( )

Adds an overlay chart to the existing chart. Adding an overlay causes the series to split between the overlay and the main chart. See also DELETE.OVERLAY( ).

ALIGNMENT(*type_num,wrap*)

ALIGNMENT?(*type_num,wrap*)

Equivalent to the Alignment command from the Format menu, the ALIGNMENT command aligns information in the current cell. Use any of the following values as the type argument:

Value	Alignment
1	General
2	Left
3	Center
4	Right
5	Fill

Enter TRUE or FALSE for the wrap argument, indicating whether you want to use word wrapping in the cell.

APPLY.NAMES(*name_array,ignore,use_rowcol,omit_col, omit_row,order_num, append_last*)

APPLY.NAMES?(*name_array,ignore,use_rowcol,omit_col, omit_row,order_num, append_last*)

Does the same thing that the Apply Names command from the Formula menu does: it replaces references and values in formulas with text names.

The arguments perform the same functions that appear in the check boxes in the Formula Apply Names dialog box. Descriptions of the arguments follow:

Argument	Enter
Name_array	The name you want to give the indicated reference or value.
Ignore	TRUE to create an Ignore Relative/Absolute check box.
Use_rowcol	TRUE to create a Use Row and Column Names check box.
Omit_col	TRUE to create an Omit Column Name if Same Column check box. (If you entered FALSE for *Use_rowcol*, Excel ignores this argument.)
Omit_row	TRUE to create an Omit Row Name if Same Column check box. (If you entered FALSE for *Use_rowcol*, Excel ignores this argument.)
Order_number	1 to list rows first or 2 to list columns first. (Indicates which range name appears first.)
Append_last	TRUE to replace the most recently defined names in addition to the names defined in Name_array. FALSE if you only want to replace the definitions listed in *Name_array*.

APPLY.STYLE(*style_text*)

APPLY.STYLE?(*style_text*)

Apply a previously defined style to the selected information, just as though you had chosen the Style command from the Format menu, selected a style, and clicked OK. For *Style_text*, enter the name of the style you want in quotes.

ARRANGE.ALL( )

Equivalent to the Arrange All command from the Window menu, arranges all open windows on-screen.

ATTACH.TEXT(*attach_to_num, series_num, point_num*)

ATTACH.TEXT?(*attach_to_num, series_num, point_num*)

Attach text to a chart object. For 2-D charts, use the values below to indicate what part of the chart you're labeling:

Value	Chart Element
1	Chart title
2	Value (y) axis
3	Category (x) axis
4	Series or data point
5	Overlay value (y) axis
6	Overlay value (x) axis

For 3-D charts, the *attach_to_num* values follow:

Value	Chart Element
1	Chart title
2	Value (z) axis
3	Series (y) axis
4	Category (x) axis
5	Series or data point

Enter values for *series_num* and *point_num* only if the *attach_to_num* is a series or data point.

AXES(*x_main,y_main,x_over,y_over*)

AXES?(*x_main,y_main,x_over,y_over*)

AXES(*x_main,y_main,z_main*)

AXES?(*x_main,y_main,z_main*)

Display or hide the value and category axis for the main chart and its overlay. Enter TRUE to show the item or FALSE to remove it. The first form is for standard charts and the second form is for 3-D charts.

BORDER(*outline,left, right,top,bottom, shade, outline_color,left_color, right_color, top_color,bottom_color*)

BORDER?(*outline,left, right,top,bottom, shade, outline_color,left_color, right_color, top_color,bottom_color*)

Create a border line at the top, left side, right side, or bottom of the active cell or range. The command also can outline the range or fill it with a shade. It also controls the color of each line. Enter a value from 0 to 7 for any of the arguments to create a line; omit an argument to leave it as is. Following is a list of these values:

Value	Specifies
0	No Border
1	Thin Line
2	Medium Line
3	Dashed Line
4	Dotted Line
5	Thick Line
6	Double Line
7	Hairline

BREAK( )

Breaks the flow of a FOR-NEXT, FOR.CELL-NEXT, or WHILE-NEXT loop and continues the flow of the macro with the cell following the NEXT command. In other words, it interrupts the current loop and continues with the macro. This is useful for stopping a loop if a certain condition is met. Combine this command with the IF command for control.

BRING.TO.FRONT( )

Brings the selected objects to the top of the other objects.

CALCULATE.DOCUMENT( )

CALCULATE.NOW( )

Emulate the Calculate Document and Calculate Now commands from the Options menu. These commands calculate the current worksheet.

CALCULATION(*type_num,iter,max_num, max_change, update,precision, date_1904,calc_save, save_values*)

CALCULATION?(*type_num,iter,max_num, max_change, update, precision, date_1904,calc_save, save_values*)

Correspond to the Calculation command from the Options menu and set various aspects of automatic recalculation for the worksheet. See Chapter 8 for details about these options. Descriptions of the arguments for these commands follow:

Argument	Description
type_num	Sets the calculation type as follows:
	1 Automatic
	2 Automatic except tables
	3 Manual
iter	Enter TRUE or FALSE to activate or deactivate the iterations option.
max_num	Enter a value representing the maximum number of iterations.
max_change	Enter a value representing the maximum amount of change.
update	Enter TRUE or FALSE to activate or deactivate the Update-Remote-References option, which is this argument's equivalent in the Calculation dialog box.
precision	Enter TRUE or FALSE to activate or deactivate the Precision-as-Displayed feature, which is this argument's equivalent in the Calculation dialog box.

Argument	Description
date_1904	Enter TRUE or FALSE to activate or deactivate the 1904 dating system.
calc_save	Enter TRUE or FALSE to activate or deactivate the Calculate before Save feature, which is this argument's equivalent in the Calculation dialog box.
save_values	Enter TRUE or FALSE to activate or deactivate the save external links feature.

CANCEL.COPY( )

Cancels the current copy operation and removes the marquee (highlighted box) surrounding the copied information. Using this command is similar to pressing ⌘-. after copying.

CANCEL.KEY(*enable,macro_ref*)

Disables the use of the Escape key (and ⌘-.) to interrupt a macro. This is useful for custom applications to prevent macros from being halted. Enter the command in one of the following ways:

CANCEL.KEY( )	Disables interruption
CANCEL.KEY(TRUE)	Enables interruption
CANCEL.KEY(TRUE,*macro_ref*)	Runs specified macro upon interruption

CELL.PROTECTION(*locked*, *hidden*)

CELL.PROTECTION?(*locked*, *hidden*)

Lock or hide the active cell. Enter TRUE to activate the option or FALSE to deactivate it. Omitting an option leaves the status unchanged.

CHANGE.LINK(*old_text,new_text, type_of_link*)

CHANGE.LINK?(*old_text,new_text, type_of_link*)

Set a new linked worksheet for the current worksheet. Equivalent to choosing the Links command from the File menu and selecting the Change option from the dialog box that appears. The variables *old_link* and *new_link* are the names of the old and new files, respectively. If you use the question mark form of this command, the Excel File Link dialog box appears.

CLEAR(*type_num*)

CLEAR?(*type_num*)

Clear data from the worksheet. The value should be the type of information you want to clear from the currently selected cell or range. Use one of the following values:

Value	Information Cleared
1	All
2	Format
3	Formulas
4	Notes

If you omit the *value* argument, Excel assumes the value 3 for the currently selected cell or range.

CLOSE(*save_logical*)

CLOSE.ALL( )

Remove the current window from the screen. Mimic the Close and Close All commands available from the File menu. If the *logical* variable is TRUE, Excel saves the document and closes it. If the variable is FALSE, Excel closes the document without saving it. If you omit the *logical* variable, Excel brings up a dialog box that asks whether you want to save changes made. CLOSE.ALL closes all unprotected worksheets.

COLOR.PALETTE(*file_text*)

COLOR.PALETTE?(*file_text*)

Enable you to share color palettes between various open documents, just like the Copy Colors From box in the Options Color Palette dialog box. For *file_text*, enter the name of the document containing the palette you want to copy.

COLUMN.WIDTH(*width_num, reference, standard,type_num*)

COLUMN.WIDTH?(*width_num, reference, standard,type_num*)

These commands change the column widths of the data specified in the reference field. For the *width_num* argument, enter the number of characters you want in each column. The characters are measured on the basis of the Normal cell style. Excel ignores this argument if the *standard* argument is TRUE or if a value is entered into the *type_num* argument.

For the *reference* argument, enter an external reference to an active worksheet or a set of columns expressed in R1C1 style. If you want Excel to use the standard width specified in the Format Column Width dialog box, enter TRUE in the Standard field. Excel will ignore any information in the *Width_number* field. Enter FALSE if you want Excel to use the width indicated in *Width_number*.

You can enter one of the following numbers for the *type_num* argument:

Number	Effect
1	Hides the selected column by setting the width to zero
2	Unhides the selected column by restoring the width to its previous value
3	Sets the selected column to the width of the longest data string in the column

COMBINATION(*type_num*)

Sets a combination chart for the currently active chart. Enter the combination chart number (as shown in the gallery produced by the Gallery Combination command) to set the chart. You also can use the question-mark version of this command to have Excel present the gallery choices.

CONSOLIDATE(*source_refs, function_num, top_row, left_col, create_links*)

CONSOLIDATE?(*source_refs, function_num, top_row, left_col, create_links*)

Consolidate data from several ranges in several worksheets into a single range on one worksheet. Type the complete data path for each source reference in quotes and list all source references in an array. To consolidate the ranges A5:B10 on worksheets named One and Two (which are located in the Data folder), for example, type this:

=CONSOLIDATE({"'Hard Drive:Data:One'!A5:B10",

"'Hard Drive:Data:Two'!A5:B10"},9,TRUE,TRUE)

Notice that double quotation marks surround each external reference in the array and single quotation marks surround the hard drive and folder path for each reference. This is required when your drive or folder references contain spaces. Finally, the entire array of two references is surrounded by braces {}.

For *function_num*, enter the number of one of the functions that follow to determine the calculation made upon consolidation:

Value	Calculation
1	AVERAGE
2	COUNT
3	COUNTA
4	MAX
5	MIN
6	PRODUCT
7	STDEV
8	STDEVP
9	SUM
10	VAR
11	VARP

The rest of the arguments in this command correspond to text boxes and check boxes in the Data Consolidate dialog box. If you want to turn on the item, enter TRUE; if not, enter FALSE.

COPY( )

Copies information in the selected cell or range. The CANCEL.COPY command removes the marquee after copying, which is the equivalent of pressing ⌘-. after using the Copy command.

COPY.CHART(*size_num*)

Does the same thing as COPY.PICTURE, if you leave out that command's appearance argument. Enter 1 if you want the chart copied as shown on-screen or 2 if you want the chart copied as shown when printed. This may involve a slight difference in the aspect ratio of the chart.

COPY.PICTURE(*appearance_num, size_num*)

Copies the active chart as a picture and places it on the Clipboard. Often, a chart on-screen looks different from the printed version. For both the appearance and size arguments, use one of the following two values to determine whether the copied chart will resemble the on-screen or printed version:

Value	Effect
1	Copies the chart as shown on-screen
2	Copies the chart as it would print on the printer

CREATE.NAMES(*top, left, bottom, right*)

CREATE.NAMES?

Creates names using data from the selected range. Enter TRUE or FALSE in any of these arguments to create a range name that uses the appropriate cells. *Top* uses the top row of the range, *left* uses the left column, *bottom* uses the bottom row, and *right* uses the right column.

CREATE.OBJECT(*object_type, ref_1, x_offset1, y_offset1, ref_2, x_offset2, y_offset2*)

CREATE.OBJECT(*object_type, ref_1, x_offset1, y_offset1, ref_2, x_offset2, y_offset2, text*)

CREATE.OBJECT(*object_type, ref_1, x_offset1, y_offset1, ref_2, x_offset2, y_offset2, xy_series*)

Insert a drawn object into a worksheet and create an ID number for the object. Generally, these commands are difficult to enter by hand and you should consider using the macro recorder to enter them. Use the first format for line art and pictures, the second for text boxes and buttons, and the third to embed charts that contain both art and text. Enter one of the following numbers to indicate the type of object you are creating:

Value	Object
1	Line
2	Rectangle
3	Oval
4	Arc
5	Embedded Chart
6	Text Box
7	Button
8	Picture

For *ref_1*, enter the cell in the upper left corner of the area the object is to occupy.

For *x_offset1*, calculate the distance from the upper left corner of *ref_1* to the upper left corner of the object. Enter this distance in points (1/72 of an inch). Do the same thing for *y_offset1*, which indicates the vertical distance between *ref_1* and the top of the object.

For *ref_2*, enter the cell in the lower right corner of the area the object is to occupy. (You don't need to include this information if you're creating a picture.)

For *xy_series*, enter a value from 0 to 3 to specify whether the first row or column of the chart that you are creating is to be used as a data series or series labels. This is only used when the object that you are creating is a chart and the first row or column could be used as labels or as a data series. Following are the values you can enter:

Value	Effect
0	Brings up the dialog box if the first row or column contains numeric values.
1 or omitted	Turns the first row or column into the first data series if it contains numeric values.
2	Turns the first row or column into category-axis labels if it contains numeric values.
3	Turns the first row or column into the x-axis values for an XY chart.

Note that when creating a chart or picture with this function, you must first copy the appropriate data to turn into a chart or picture. You do this with the COPY macro command.

CUT( )

Removes selected data and copies it to the Clipboard. Equivalent to the Cut command from the Edit menu.

DATA.DELETE( )

DATA.DELETE?( )

Delete records according to the current criteria range. Equivalent to the Delete command from the Data menu.

DATA.FIND(*logical*)

Finds a record in the database or exits from the find procedure. Enter TRUE to find records or FALSE to exit from the find procedure.

DATA.FIND.NEXT( )

DATA.FIND.PREV( )

Find the next and previous matching records in the database when performing a find operation. Equivalent to "flipping through" the records with the commands ⌘-F and ⌘-Shift-F.

DATA.FORM( )

Brings up the database data form for the currently set database.

DATA.SERIES(*rowcol,type_num,date_num, step_value, stop_value*)

DATA.SERIES?(*rowcol,type_num, date_num, step_value, stop_value*)

Enter a series of values into a range automatically. Equivalent to the Series command from the Data menu. Use these values for the following arguments:

Value	Represents
rowcol	
1	Rows
2	Columns
type_num	
1	Linear
2	Growth
3	Date
date_num	
1	Day
2	Weekday
3	Month
4	Year

Step_value is a number corresponding to the increment of the data series values. *Stop_value* is the maximum value allowed in the series. The command =DATA.SERIES(1,3,3), for example, enters a row of month names into the current selection. Notice that the stop and step values are not used in this example. Excel assumes 1 as the step value and stops at the last highlighted cell.

DEFINE.NAME(*name_text, refers_to, macro_type, shortcut_text, hidden*)

DEFINE.NAME?(*name_text, refers_to, macro_type, shortcut_text*)

Define a range name. For the *name* argument, enter the name you want as a text string. For *refers_to*, enter the address of the range as a normal external reference. Use !A1 to refer to cell A1 of the current worksheet. Use Worksheet!A1 to refer to cell A2 of an external worksheet. If you omit the *refers_to* argument, Excel uses the currently selected cell or range.

To name a formula or function, enter the information in quotation marks. If you are naming a macro, use the address of the first cell of the macro. Also, if you are defining a macro, enter the *macro_type* argument as one of the following:

Value	Macro Type
1	Function Macro
2	Command Macro
3	None (removes any current selection)

The *command_key* argument represents the command key used for the command macro. Enter this argument as a single-character text string. The *hidden* argument determines whether the name should be hidden or displayed; enter TRUE or FALSE accordingly.

DEFINE.STYLE(*style_text, number, font, alignment, border, pattern, protection*)

DEFINE.STYLE?(*style_text, number, font, alignment, border, pattern, protection*)

Create and change cell styles, just like the Define button in the Format Style dialog box. Enter the name you want to give the new style, followed by TRUE or FALSE values for the remaining arguments. TRUE activates the indicated format; FALSE causes Excel to ignore the instructions for that attribute. If all the selected cells have the same formatting, the default for all the arguments is TRUE; if there are different formats, the default is FALSE. You can omit all arguments except *style_text* to define a style based on the active cell.

DELETE.ARROW( )

Removes the selected arrow from the chart.

DELETE.FORMAT(*format_text*)

Removes a custom number format. Equivalent to the Delete option in the Format Number dialog box. Enter the format as a text string in the *format_text* argument.

DELETE.NAME(*name_text*)

Removes a range name from the list of active range names. Enter the name as the *name_text* argument.

DELETE.OVERLAY( )

Removes the overlay from the selected chart.

DELETE.STYLE(*style_text*)

Removes a style setting from a document, causing all the cells with the deleted format to return to the document's Normal style. Enter the name of the style to be deleted.

DEMOTE(*rowcol*)

DEMOTE?(*rowcol*)

Demote the highlighted information in an outline to the next lower level. Enter 1 (or no argument) to demote rows or 2 to demote columns.

DEREF(*reference*)

Displays the values of the indicated cell or range of cells. If *reference* is a range of cells, the array of cell values will appear. DEREF automatically converts relative references to absolute references.

DIRECTORY(*path_text*)

Sets the current directory for directory-sensitive macro commands, such as FILES. Enter the new directory path as a text string containing the complete path reference in quotation marks. Remember to surround the path with single quotation marks if drive or folder names contain spaces. For example, you could enter the following:

=DIRECTORY("'Hard Disk:Data:Excel'")

DISPLAY(*formulas, gridlines, headings,zeros,color_num, reserved,outline, page_breaks,object_num*)

DISPLAY?(*formulas, gridlines, headings,zeros,color_num, reserved ,outline, page_breaks,object_num*)

DISPLAY(*cell, formula,value, format, protection,names, precedents, dependents,note*)

Display or hide various elements on the worksheet. You use the first form of the command (or its question-mark version) with worksheets or macro sheets. Enter TRUE in any option that you want displayed; enter FALSE if you don't want the option displayed. Enter a value from 1 to 16 for the color option in order to select a color for the sheet. These arguments correspond to the check boxes on the Options Display dialog box.

You use the second form of the command with Info sheets. Enter TRUE to add an item to the Info sheet; enter FALSE to remove an item. The precedents and dependents options should have one of the following values:

Value	Option
0	None
1	Direct Only
2	All Levels

Use the question-mark form of this command with no arguments to display the Excel dialog box, as in DISPLAY?( ).

DOCUMENTS(*type_num*)

Gathers and displays an alphabetical list of all documents currently open on the desktop. Enter one of these numbers to indicate which types of documents should be listed:

Value	Lists
1 (or none)	All open documents except add-ins
2	Add-in documents only
3	All open documents

DUPLICATE( )

Creates a duplicate of the selected object.

EDIT.COLOR(*color_num, red_value, green_value, blue_value*)

EDIT.COLOR?(*color_num, red_value, green_value, blue_value*)

Enable you to create and add new colors to your 16-color palette. Enter a number form 1 to 16 to indicate which color box on the palette you want to replace with the new color. Set the values for red , green, and blue until you have the right shade. Enter values from 0 to 255 for each color.

After the new color is installed in the palette, any objects that appeared in the previous color automatically change to the new color.

EDIT.DELETE(*shift_num*)

EDIT.DELETE?(*shift_num*)

Remove the selected cells, rows, or columns from the worksheet and adjusts subsequent cells, rows, or columns to fill the space created. Equivalent to the Delete command from the Edit menu. The value should be one of the following:

Value	Effect
1	Shifts cells left
2	Shifts cells up
3	Deletes entire row
4	Deletes entire column

EDIT.REPEAT( )

Repeats the last action performed in your macro. Equivalent to the Repeat command from the Edit menu.

EDIT.SERIES(*series_num,name_ref, x_ref,y_ref,z_ref, plot_order*)

EDIT.SERIES?(*series_num,name_ref, x_ref,y_ref,z_ref, plot_order*)

Enables you to change the data displayed in a chart. Enter the number of the series you want to change into the *series_num* argument. If you leave this blank, Excel creates a new series. Enter the names for the series and axis labels into the *name_ref*, *x_ref*, *y_ref*, and *z_ref* arguments. Change the position of the series by entering a position number as the *plot_order* argument. (All arguments can be cell references.) Each of these arguments corresponds to the choices in the Edit Series dialog box.

ENABLE.COMMAND(*bar_num,menu, command,enable*)

Controls which custom menu commands are available to the user. (Disabled commands are dimmed on the menu, and aren't available.) Enter the ID number for the menu bar, the name of the menu, and the name of the command. Finally, enter TRUE to enable the command , or FALSE to disable it. ENABLE.COMMAND does not work on built-in menus.

EXTRACT(*unique*)

EXTRACT?(*unique*)

Extract data from the active database according to the active criteria settings. Enter TRUE to extract unique records only; enter FALSE to extract all matching records.

FILE.CLOSE(*save_logical*)

Closes an entire document. Enter TRUE if you want to save the file before closing or FALSE if you don't want to save the file. If you don't enter TRUE or FALSE, a dialog box appears, asking if you want to save the file.

FILE.DELETE(*file_text*)

FILE.DELETE?(*file_text*)

Remove a file from disk and are equivalent to the Delete command from the File menu. The *file_text* argument is the file that you want to remove. Excel searches the current directory for the specified file. The question-mark version of this command brings up the Excel dialog box, in which you can specify the file to delete. Your specification can use wild cards to select files.

FILES(*directory_text*)

Compiles a horizontal list of all the files names in the indicated folder—up to 255 items. This command is useful for creating a list of file names with which you want your macro to work.

FILL.DOWN( )

FILL.LEFT( )

FILL.RIGHT( )

FILL.UP( )

Fill a range of cells with information contained in the first cell of that range.

FILL.WORKGROUP(*type_num*)

FILL.WORKGROUP?(*type_num*)

Fill all the worksheets in the workgroup with information in the active worksheet's selection. Note that you first must define a workgroup from several open files. This is equivalent to the Edit Fill Workgroup command. The *type_num* argument can be one of the following:

Value	Effect
1	Fills all information from the current selection
2	Fills only the formulas from the current selection
3	Fills only the formats from the current selection

**FORMAT.FONT(*name_text, size_num,*
bold, italic, underline, strike, color, outline, shadow)**

FORMAT.FONT?(*name_text, size_num,bold ,italic, underline, strike,color,outline, shadow***)**

FORMAT.FONT(*color,backgd ,apply,name_text, size_num, bold ,italic, un derline, strike,outline, shadow***)**

FORMAT.FONT?(*color,backgd ,apply,name_text, size_num, bold ,italic, underline, strike,outline, shadow***)**

FORMAT.FONT(*name_text, size_num,bold ,italic, underline, strike, color,outline,shadow,object,object_id_text, start_num, char_num***)**

FORMAT.FONT?(*name_text, size_num,bold ,italic, underline, strike,color,outline, shadow,object_id_text, start_num, char_num***)**

Apply a font, size, and style to the selected cell or range. Equivalent to the Font command from the Format menu. The first version of the command applies to worksheets and macro sheets. The version containing the arguments color, background, and so on applies to charts. The third version applies to text boxes. Omitting an argument altogether chooses the standard font and styles for the current selection. You can use both versions with the question-mark form to bring up the Excel dialog box. For example, =FORMAT.FONT?( ) brings up the dialog box with the standard font and styles selected.

Enter TRUE or FALSE in the style arguments to turn them on or off, respectively. The *name_text* argument is the name of the font entered as a text string. The *size_num* argument should be a valid point size entered as a number. The *color* argument should be a value from 0 to 8, representing the color you want for the font. The value 0 tells Excel to select the color automatically. *Background* values can be any of the following:

Value	Background
1	Automatic
2	Transparent
3	White Out

The *apply* argument applies the font selection to all like elements in the chart. Enter TRUE or FALSE as the value of this argument.

The *start_num* argument is used for text boxes and determines the starting character (counted by number from the first character in the box) to be formatted. Enter a number from 1 to the number of characters in the box. If this argument is omitted, Excel assumes the first character in the box.

The *char_num* argument is used for text boxes and determines the number of characters affected by the formatting. Enter a value indicating the number of characters following the *start_num* character that you want to format.

FORMAT.LEGEND(*position_num*)

FORMAT.LEGEND?(*position_num*)

Control the position of the legend. Use one of the following values to specify the position:

Value	Position
1	Bottom
2	Corner
3	Top
4	Right
5	Left

FORMAT.MAIN(*type_num, view, overlap, gap_width, vary, drop, hilo, angle, gap_depth, chart_depth*)

FORMAT.MAIN?(*type_num, view, overlap, gap_width, vary, drop, hilo, angle, gap_depth, chart_depth*)

Format a chart according to your specifications, and are equivalent to the Main Chart command from the Format menu. Start by entering the type of chart:

Value	Chart
1	Area
2	Bar
3	Column
4	Line

Value	Chart
5	Pie
6	XY (scatter)
7	3-D Area
8	3-D Column
9	3-D Line
10	3-D Pie

For *view*, enter a number from 1 to 4 to indicate which of the chart views you want for the chart. These numbers correspond to the dialog box choices for each of the 10 chart types. Depending on the chart type you select, the view number selects one of its views. (Not all 10 chart types offer four different views.)

Overlap is the percentage of overlap (from –100 to 100) that you want to have between columns. A positive number enables you to cover the specified column or bar with an adjacent column or bar; a 100% overlap completely covers the column or bar. A negative number separates the columns by a percentage of the largest distance available. Enter 0 if you want the columns to be adjacent, with no overlap or distance between them.

Gap_width is the space between bar or column groupings, expressed as a percentage of the bar or column width. Enter a number from 0 (for no gap) to 500.

Vary, *drop*, and *hilo* correspond to the Vary by Categories, Drop Lines, and Hi-Lo Lines check boxes. Enter TRUE to turn on these options or FALSE to turn them off.

Gap_depth and *chart_depth* apply to 3-D charts only. *Gap_depth* indicates the depth of the gap in front of and behind a bar, column, line, or area, expressed as a percentage of the specified item, from 0 to 500. *Chart_depth* indicates the visual depth of the chart, expressed as a percentage of the width of the chart, from 20 to 2000.

FORMAT.MOVE(*x_pos,y_pos*)

FORMAT.MOVE?(*x_pos,y_pos*)

Move a chart object (the selected object) to another area of the chart window. The *x_pos* and *y_pos* values indicate the object's distance from the upper left corner of the screen.

FORMAT.NUMBER(*format_text*)

FORMAT.NUMBER?(*format_text*)

Choose a numeric format for the selected cell or range. Enter the number format as a text string, as in

=FORMAT.NUMBER("#,##0.00").

FORMAT.OVERLAY(*type_num,view,overlap,width,vary,drop, hilo, angle, series_dist, series_num*)

FORMAT.OVERLAY?(*type_num,view,overlap,width,vary,drop, hilo,angle, series_dist, series_num*)

Format an overlay chart according to your specifications, and are equivalent to the Overlay Chart command from the Format menu. Start by entering the type of chart:

Value	Chart
1	Area
2	Bar
3	Column
4	Line
5	Pie
6	XY (Scatter)

For *view*, indicate which of these three data views you want:

	View 1	View 2	View 3
Area	Overlapped	Stacked	Stacked 100%
Bar	Side-by-side	Stacked	Stacked 100%
Column	Side-by-side	Stacked	Stacked 100%
Line	Normal	Stacked	Stacked 100%
Pie	Normal		
XY (Scatter)	Normal		

Overlap is a percentage of overlap (from –100 to 100) that you want to have between columns. A positive number enables you to cover the specified column or bar by an adjacent column or bar; a 100% overlap enables you to cover the column or bar entirely. A negative number separates the columns by a percentage of the largest distance available. Enter 0 if you want the columns adjacent, with no overlap or distance between them.

Width is the space between bar or column groupings, expressed as a percentage of the bar or column width. Enter a number from 0 (for no gap) to 500.

Vary, *drop*, and *hilo* correspond to the Vary by Categories, Drop Lines, and Hi-Lo Lines check boxes. Enter TRUE to turn on these check boxes, or FALSE to turn them off.

Angle is the number of degrees (from 0 to 360) at which the first slice in the pie chart should begin. The default is 50 degrees.

Series_num corresponds to the First Overlay Series box in the Format Overlay dialog box. Enter the number of the first series in the overlay. The default is 1.

FORMAT.SIZE(*x_off,y_off, reference*)

FORMAT.SIZE?(*x_off,y_off, reference*)

Specify the size of the selected chart or object in measurements relative to a cell on the worksheet. The *x_off* argument is the width in points from the cell specified in reference to the right side of the object. The *y_off* argument is the height in points from the cell specified in reference to the bottom of the object. *Reference* is the cell for which these measurements are relative.

FORMAT.SIZE(*width, height*)

FORMAT.SIZE?(*width, height*)

Specify the size of a selected chart or object. Enter a value (in points) for the object's width and height.

FORMAT.TEXT(*x_align,y_align,orient_num,auto_text, auto_size, show_key, show_value*)

FORMAT.TEXT?(*x_align,y_align,orient_num,auto_text, auto_size, show_key, show_value*)

Format text on the chart. Specify each of its arguments according to the following list:

- *x_align:* Enter a value to represent the horizontal alignment:

Value	Alignment
1	Left
2	Center
3	Right

- *y_align:* Enter a value to represent the vertical alignment:

Value	Argument
1	Left
2	Center
3	Right

- *orient_num:* Enter a value from 0 to 3 to determine the orientation of the text:

Value	Orientation
0	Horizontal text
1	Vertical text
2	Vertical Upward
3	Vertical Downward

- *vertical_text:* Enter TRUE to make the text appear vertically; otherwise, enter FALSE or omit the argument.

- *auto_text:* Enter TRUE to make the text orientation automatic; otherwise, enter FALSE.

- *auto_size:* Enter TRUE to make the text size automatic; otherwise, enter FALSE.

- *show_key:* Enter TRUE to show the key of the selected attached text.

- *show_value:* Enter TRUE to show the value for an attached text label.

FORMULA(*formula_text, reference*)

Enters data—in the form of a text string, a number, or a formula—into a cell of the worksheet. The result is the same as if you typed it from the keyboard.

Formula_text is the information you want entered. You should enter this argument as a text string or an expression resulting in a text string. The *reference* is the cell into which you want to enter the data. If you omit this argument, Excel uses the active cell.

Excel deciphers whether your formula text entry is a number, formula, or text string. Excel uses the same criteria for making this decision as it does when you type data from the keyboard. Anything beginning with an equal sign is a formula; anything beginning with an alphabetic character (except range names) is a text string, and so on. If the cell receiving this data already contains information, Excel replaces that information with your new entry.

FORMULA.ARRAY(*formula_text, reference*)

FORMULA.ARRAY(*formula_text, reference*)

Enters a formula into a range of cells as an array formula. This is similar to entering a formula by pressing ⌘-Return. Enter the desired formula as the *formula_text* argument (surrounded by quotation marks) and the range reference for the array as the reference argument. Enter the reference as a text string in R1C1 format. Be sure to include the equal sign in the formula text entry.

FORMULA.FILL(*formula_text, reference*)

Similar to the FORMULA command. Using FORMULA.ARRAY is similar to typing a formula into the first cell of a range and pressing ⌘-Return to enter the formula, but FORMULA.ARRAY creates an array formula. Using FORMULA.FILL is similar to typing a formula into the first cell of a range and pressing Option-Return to enter the formula. This action duplicates the entry for the entire range.

FORMULA.FIND(*text, in_num, at_num, by_num, dir_num, match_case*)

FORMULA.FIND?(*text, in_num, at_num, by_num, dir_num, match_case*)

Search for the text specified in text. The variables *in_num*, *at_num*, *by_num*, and *dir_num* should be values of 1 or 2, which represent the following:

Value	Represents
in_num	
1	Formulas
2	Values
3	Notes
at_num	
1	Whole
2	Part
by_num	
1	Rows
2	Columns
dir_num	
1	Next
2	Previous

The *match_case* argument determines whether Excel should match upper and lower-case letters or not. Enter TRUE or FALSE accordingly.

FORMULA.FIND.NEXT( )

FORMULA.FIND.PREV( )

Find the next and preceding cells matching the find criteria after you use the Find command from the Data menu (or the equivalent macro command). Equivalent to pressing ⌘-H or ⌘-Shift-H.

FORMULA.GOTO(*reference,corner*)

FORMULA.GOTO?(*reference,corner*)

Mimic the Goto command from the Formula menu. Equivalent to the SELECT macro command. For the reference, enter the address of the cell or range to select. You also can enter a range name or an R1C1-style reference entered as text. The corner argument, when TRUE, causes the reference to appear in the upper left corner of the screen. This is useful for predicting accurately what the screen will look like when you use this command.

FORMULA.REPLACE(*find_text, replace_text, look_at, look_by, active_cell, match_case***)**

FORMULA.REPLACE?(*find_text, replace_text, look_at, look_by, active_cell, match_case***)**

Replace information in the worksheet with information of your choosing. The *find_text* argument is the text you want to replace. The *replace_text* argument is the replacement text. You can use wild cards in these specifications. The *look_at*, *look_by*, and *active_cell* arguments should be one of the following values:

Value	Represents
look_at	
1	Whole
2	Part
look_by	
1	Rows
2	Columns
active_cell	
TRUE	Replaces the current cell
FALSE	Replaces the entire file

The *match_case* argument determines whether Excel should match upper- and lowercase characters; enter TRUE or FALSE accordingly.

FREEZE.PANES(*logical***)**

Freezes the panes of a split-screen display. Equivalent to the Freeze Panes command from the Options menu. Enter TRUE to freeze the panes or FALSE to unfreeze them.

FULL(*logical***)**

Mimics the window zoom box in the upper right corner of a window. If *logical* is TRUE, the window expands to its full size. If *logical* is FALSE, the window shrinks to its modified size.

GALLERY.3D.AREA(*type_num***)**

GALLERY.3D.AREA?(*type_num***)**

GALLERY.3D.COLUMN(*type_num***)**

GALLERY.3D.COLUMN?(*type_num***)**

GALLERY.3D.LINE(*type_num***)**

GALLERY.3D.LINE?(*type_num***)**

GALLERY.3D.PIE(*type_num***)**

GALLERY.3D.PIE?(*type_num***)**

GALLERY.AREA(*type_num, delete_overlay***)**

GALLERY.AREA?(*type_num, delete_overlay***)**

GALLERY.BAR(*type_num, delete_overlay***)**

GALLERY.BAR?(*type_num, delete_overlay***)**

GALLERY.COLUMN(*type_num, delete_overlay***)**

GALLERY.COLUMN?(*type_num, delete_overlay***)**

GALLERY.LINE(*type_num, delete_overlay***)**

GALLERY.LINE?(*type_num, delete_overlay***)**

GALLERY.PIE(*type_num, delete_overlay***)**

GALLERY.PIE?(*type_num, delete_overlay***)**

GALLERY.SCATTER(*type_num, delete_overlay***)**

GALLERY.SCATTER?(*type_num, delete_overlay***)**

Set the type of chart for the active chart window. The *type_num* argument represents the respective chart type number, as shown in the gallery. (The gallery is available when you use the Gallery menu options; it shows the available chart types.) To see these numbers, use the corresponding menu command. You also can use the question-mark version of these commands to have Excel display the gallery for you. The *delete_overlay* option should be TRUE or FALSE. TRUE applies the gallery selection to the main chart and removes any overlay that is present. FALSE applies the gallery selection to the overlay or main chart—depending on which is selected.

GET.CELL(*type_num, reference*)

Views location, content, or formatting information on the cell in the upper left corner of the indicated reference. Enter one of the following numbers to specify what kind of information you want; then enter the range of cells for which you want information:

Value	Information
1	Absolute reference of the upper left cell, expressed as text
2	Row number of the top cell
3	Column number of the far left cell
4	Type
5	Contents
6	Formula in the cell, in A1 or R1C1 format
7	Number format of the cell
8	Cell alignment:

	1	General
	2	Left
	3	Center
	4	Right
	5	Fill

Value	Information
9	Left border style of the cell:

	0	No border
	1	Thin line
	2	Medium line
	3	Dashed line
	4	Dotted line
	5	Thick line
	6	Double line
	7	Hairline

Value	Information
10	Right border style (using the same numbers described in the Value 9 entry)
11	Top border style (using the same numbers described in the Value 9 entry)
12	Lower border style (using the same numbers described in the Value 9 entry)
13	Cell pattern, expressed as a number from 0 (no pattern) to 18. The patterns are numbered according to the Format Patterns dialog box.
14	Cell lock on: TRUE or FALSE
15	Hidden cell: TRUE or FALSE
16	Column width, expressed in characters
17	Row height, expressed in points
18	Font name
19	Font size
20	Bold text: TRUE or FALSE
21	Italic text: TRUE or FALSE
22	Underlined text: TRUE or FALSE
23	Strikethrough text: TRUE or FALSE
24	Font color, expressed as a box number from the 16-color palette
25	Outlined cell: TRUE or FALSE
26	Shadowed cell: TRUE or FALSE
27	Page break status:
	0 No break
	1 Row
	2 Column
	3 Row and column

Value	Information
28	Row level
29	Column level
30	Active cell is in summary row: TRUE or FALSE
31	Active cell is in summary column: TRUE or FALSE
32	Sheet name
33	Cell is formatted to wrap: TRUE or FALSE, 0 if automatic
34	Left border color, expressed as a palette color number or 0 if automatic
35	Right border color, expressed as a palette color number or 0 if automatic
36	Top border color, expressed as a palette color number or 0 if automatic
37	Bottom border color, expressed as a palette color number or 0 if automatic
38	Foreground color shade, expressed as a palette color number or 0 if automatic
39	Background color shade, expressed as a palette color number or 0 if automatic
40	Cell style

GET.CHART.ITEM(*x_y_index, point_index, item_text*)

Yields the horizontal or vertical position of a point on a chart. For the *x_y_index* argument, enter 1 to get the horizontal coordinate or 2 to get the vertical coordinate.

The *point_index* argument is a number indicating the point on the chart. If the indicated item is anything other than a data line, use these values to indicate chart position:

Value	Position
1	Lower or left (default)
2	Upper or right

If the *item_text* argument is an area in an area chart or a rectangle, use these values:

Value	Position
1	Upper left
2	Upper middle
3	Upper right
4	Right middle
5	Lower right
6	Lower left
8	Left middle

If *item_text* is an arrow, use 1 to indicate the arrow shaft or 2 to indicate the head.

If *item_text* is a pie slice, the values are as follows:

Value	Position
1	Outermost counterclockwise point
2	Outer center point
3	Outermost clockwise point
4	Midpoint of the most clockwise radius
5	Center
6	Midpoint of the most clockwise radius

GET.DEF(*def_text,document_text, type_num*)

Gets the text name that defines a specific area, value, or formula in a document. For the first argument, enter a cell reference, range reference (R1C1-text style) value, or formula. Next, enter the name of the worksheet or macro sheet that the *def_text* data appears in. If no worksheet is specified, Excel assumes that it's the active sheet. Finally, enter one of the following values to indicate which types of names you want returned:

Value	Names Returned
1 or none	Normal names only
2	Hidden names only
3	All names

GET.DOCUMENT(*type_num,name_text*)

Gives you specific information about a document. Enter one of the 44 type values that follow to get the information you want; then enter the name of the document that you are inquiring about. If you don't enter a document name, Excel will get information about the active document. The values you can enter follow:

Value	Information
1	Document name (text only)
2	Document path name
3	Document type:

	1	Worksheet
	2	Chart
	3	Macro sheet
	4	Info window is active

Value	Information
4	Have changes been made to this document since it was last saved? (TRUE = yes)
5	Is document read-only? (TRUE = yes)
6	Is the file protected? (TRUE = yes)
7	Is the document protected? (TRUE = yes)
8	Are the document windows protected? (TRUE = yes)

Values 9 through 12 apply only to charts:

Value	Information
9	Main chart type:

	1	2-D Area
	2	2-D Bar
	3	2-D Column
	4	2-D Line
	5	2-D Pie
	6	2-D xy (Scatter)
	7	3-D Area

Value	Information
8	3-D Column
9	3-D Line
10	3-D Pie
10	Overlay chart type (uses the same value numbers as the Value 9 entry)
11	Number of series in main chart
12	Number of series in overlay chart

All the values that follow apply only to worksheets and macro sheets (except 34 through 37 and 40). These values also apply to charts:

Value	Information
9	Number of first used row
10	Number of last used row
11	Number of first used column
12	Number of last used column
13	Number of windows
14	Calculation mode:
1	Automatic
2	Automatic, except tables
3	Manual
15	Is iteration enabled? (TRUE = Yes, FALSE = No)
16	Maximum number of iterations
17	Maximum change between iterations
18	Is remote reference updating enabled? (TRUE = Yes)
19	Is Options Calculation dialog box set to Precision as Displayed? (TRUE = Yes)
20	Is document set to 1904 Date System in Options Calculation dialog box? (TRUE = Yes)
21	Names of the four default fonts
22	Sizes of the four default fonts

Value	Information
23	Which of the four default fonts are bold? (Expressed as a four-item logical array. If font 2 is bold, for example, the array reads FALSE, TRUE, FALSE, FALSE.)
24	Which of the four default fonts are italic? (Expressed like those in the Value 23 entry.)
25	Which of the four default fonts are underlined? (Expressed like those in the Value 23 entry.)
26	Which of the four default fonts are struck through? (Expressed like those in the Value 23 entry.)
27	What colors are the four default fonts? (Stated in color numbers 1-16)
28	Which of the four default fonts are outlined? (Expressed like those in the Value 23 entry.)
29	Which of the four default fonts are shadowed? (Expressed like those in the Value 23 entry.)
30	Consolidation references for the worksheet listed in a horizontal array as text entries. If your worksheet has no consolidation references in the Formula Consolidate dialog box, this returns to NA.
31	Function used in the current consolidation, expressed as a number from 1 to 11.
32	Status of check boxes in Data Consolidate dialog box. The first cell represents the Top Row check box; the second cell represents the Left column check box; the third cell is the Create Links to Source Data check box.
33	Is Recalculate before Saving turned on? (TRUE = Yes; 0 = Automatic setting is active)
34	Is document read-only recommended? (TRUE = Yes; 0 = Automatic setting is active)
35	Is document write-reversed? (TRUE = Yes; 0 = Automatic setting is active)
36	Who has current write permission for the document?
37	File type, as displayed in the File Save As dialog box. See SAVE.AS for file type numbers.

Value	Information
38	Is Summary Rows Before Detail turned on? (TRUE = Yes)
39	Is Summary Columns to Right of Detail turned on? (TRUE = Yes)
40	Is Create Backup File turned on? (TRUE = Yes)
41	Which objects are displayed?
	1 All objects displayed
	2 Placeholders for pictures and charts
	3 All objects hidden
42	All objects in the sheet, expressed as a horizontal array
43	Is Save External Link Values turned on? (TRUE = Yes)
44	Are the document objects protected? (TRUE = Yes)

GET.FORMULA(*reference*)

Provides the formula entered into the cell indicated in the reference argument. This formula is returned as a text string, as in "=A5*25".

GET.NAME(*name_text*)

Yields the reference associated with the name that you have specified as the *name_text* argument. Enter the desired range name in quotation marks. Excel returns the reference that appears in the Define Name dialog box for the name that you enter. The reference is returned as text.

GET.OBJECT(*type_num,object_id_text,start_num,count_num*)

Provides information about a worksheet object, such as a chart, text box, rectangle, and so on. This information is useful when your macros need to manipulate or edit objects that already exist on the worksheet. Enter the desired object number (or name and number) as the *object_id_text* argument. If this number is omitted, Excel uses the currently selected object. The arguments *start_num* and *count_num* are used only for text boxes (using a *type_num* value from 12 to 21). They enable you to specify the exact text in the box for which you want information. *Start_num* is the starting character and *count_num* is the number of characters beyond *start_num*.

Following are the type numbers you can specify to determine the type of information returned about the object:

Number	Type of information
1	Type of object:

    1   line

    2   rectangle

    3   oval

    4   arc

    5   chart

    6   text box

    7   button

    8   picture

2	Is the object locked? (TRUE = Yes)
3	Layer on which the object appears.
4	Cell address directly under the upper left corner of this object.
5	Horizontal distance (in points) from the upper left corner to the lower right corner.
6	Vertical distance (in points) from the upper left corner to the lower right corner.
7	Cell address directly under the lower right corner of the object.
10	Name of the macro attached to the object (returned as text) or FALSE if no macro is attached.
11	Relationship to worksheet:

    1   Moves and sizes with cells

    2   Moves with cells

    3   Does not move or size with cells

The following type numbers are for text boxes only:

| 12 | Text inside the text box from the indicated *start_num* position for the indicated number of characters in the *count_num* argument. Text is returned in quotation marks. |

Number	Type of information
13	Font name (as text) of the text indicated by *start_num* and *count_num*.
14	Font size of all the text indicated by *start_num* and *count_num*.
15	Is text bold? (TRUE = Yes)
16	Is text italic? (TRUE = Yes)
17	Is text underlined? (TRUE = Yes)
18	Is text formatted with strikethrough? (TRUE = Yes)
19	Is text outlined? (TRUE = Yes)
20	Is text shadowed? (TRUE = Yes)
21	A number indicating the color of the text.
22	A number indicating the alignment of the text:
	1 left
	2 right
	3 center
23	A number indicating the vertical alignment of text:
	1 top
	2 bottom
	3 center
24	A number indicating the orientation of the text:
	0 horizontal
	1 vertically stacked
	2 vertical upward
	3 vertical downward
25	Is box automatically size? (TRUE = Yes)

The following type values are for all objects:

Number	Type of information
26	Is object visible? (TRUE = Yes)
27	Border type:

Number	Type of information
	0 custom
	1 automatic
	2 none
28	Border line style indicated as a number from 0 to 8
29	Border line color indicated as a number from 0 to 16
30	Border line weight indicated as a number from 0 to 4
31	Type of fill pattern used:
	0 custom
	1 automatic
	2 none
32	Object fill pattern indicated as a number from 1 to 18.
33	Fill pattern foreground color indicated as a number from 0 to 16.
34	Fill pattern background indicated as a number from 0 to 16.
35	Arrowhead type used on a line:
	1 narrow
	2 medium
	3 wide
36	Arrowhead length used:
	1 short
	2 medium
	3 long
37	Arrowhead style used:
	1 no head
	2 open head
	3 closed head
38	Does the object have rounded corners? (TRUE = Yes)
39	Does the border have a shadow? (TRUE = Yes)

GOAL.SEEK(*target_cell*,*target_value*, *variable_cell*)

GOAL.SEEK?(*target_cell*,*target_value*, *variable_cell*)

Calculate the values needed to reach a specific goal. Equivalent to the Goal Seek command from the Formula menu. You can get detailed information on using Formula Goal Seek, and its three options, in Chapter 8.

GOTO(*reference*)

Changes the flow of the current macro. The macro branches to the reference indicated as the reference argument. This should be a reference to a cell in the current macro sheet or an external macro sheet. See examples in Chapter 19.

GRIDLINES(*x_major*,*x_minor*,*y_major*,*y_minor*, *z_major*,*z_minor*)

GRIDLINES?(*x_major*,*x_minor*,*y_major*,*y_minor*, *z_major*,*z_minor*)

Add major and/or minor grid lines to the category and value axes of the active chart. Enter TRUE to add the grid lines or FALSE to remove them.

GROUP( )

Creates a single object from a group of selected objects, so that you can manipulate them together as one. This command yields the group name.

HIDE( )

Hides the current window but leaves it open.

HIDE.OBJECT(*object_id_text*, *hide*)

Hides or displays objects. The *object_id_text* argument is the object's number specified as a text string and surrounded in quotation marks. The *hide* argument can be TRUE to hide the object or FALSE to display it. Use the GET.OBJECT command to determine an object's ID number.

HLINE(*num_columns*)

HPAGE(*num_windows*)

HSCROLL(*position,col_logical*)

Scroll the active window horizontally. HLINE scrolls the window by the specified number of columns, horizontally. Using this command is identical to using the scroll arrows of the active horizontal scroll bars. HPAGE scrolls the window by the specified number of pages, or screens—an action identical to clicking in the horizontal scroll bar. Use a positive number to represent movement to the right and a negative number to represent movement to the left. HCSCROLL scrolls the window by percentage or column number. Here are some examples:

=HLINE(65)	Scrolls the active window 65 columns to the right
=HPAGE(-5)	Scrolls the active window five screens to the left.
=HSCROLL(22,TRUE)	Scrolls to column 22

INSERT(*shift_num*)

INSERT?(*shift_num*)

Inserts cells, rows, or columns, based on the selection. The argument, which represents how to shift existing data, should be one of the following:

Value	Effect
1	Shifts cells right
2	Shifts cells down
3	Shifts entire row
4	Shifts entire column

JUSTIFY()

Justifies a column of text and is equivalent to the Format Justify menu command.

LAST.ERROR()

Provides the reference of the cell in which the last macro sheet error occurred.

LEGEND(*logical*)

Adds or removes the legend from the active chart. Enter TRUE to add the legend or FALSE to remove it.

LINKS(*document_text,type_num*)

Returns, to a cell or range of cells, the names of all worksheets linked to the worksheet specified by *document_text*. If you omit the name, Excel assumes the active worksheet. Enter one of the following values for the *type_num* argument to determine what information will be returned:

1   Microsoft Excel Link

2   DDE Link

3   Incoming NewWave Link

4   Outgoing NewWave Link

5   Publishers

6   Subscribers

One way to use the command is to highlight a range in the macro and enter the LINKS command as an array entry (press ⌘-Return) into that range. The range will contain the names of files linked to the specified file. If there are five files linked to the worksheet, for example, be sure to highlight at least five cells in the range; otherwise, the command will fill the specified number of cells in the range and stop. You now can refer to this array range in commands that expect an array or range for a value. You may, for example, present these names in a custom list box by referring to this range in the dialog-box definition table.

Another way to use the command is as a parameter for a command that expects an array as its argument. An example is the OPEN.LINKS command:

=OPEN.LINKS(LINKS("Spreadsheet"))

This formula opens all documents linked to the worksheet named SPREAD-SHEET. You use the LINKS command to get the names of the linked files as an array.

LIST.NAMES( )

Pastes a list of names into the worksheet range, beginning at the current cell. This feature is useful for listing available range names in a custom list box.

MAIN.CHART(*type_num, stack, 100, vary, overlap, drop, hilo, overlap%, cluster, angle*)

MAIN.CHART?(*type_num, stack, 100, vary, overlap, drop, hilo, overlap%, cluster, angle*)

Control various aspects of the main chart. The question-mark version brings up the Excel menu and eliminates the need for the arguments. The arguments are defined as follows:

Argument	Enter
type_num	A value representing the chart type, including the following:
	1 Area
	2 Bar
	3 Column
	4 Line
	5 Pie
	6 Scatter
stack	TRUE to stack the chart; otherwise, enter FALSE
100	TRUE to create a 100% value chart
vary	TRUE to activate the Vary by Categories option or FALSE to deactivate the option
overlap	TRUE to overlap the series markers in the chart. This argument works with the *overlap%* argument listed later.
drop	TRUE to add drop lines to the chart or FALSE to remove them
hilo	TRUE to add high-low lines to the chart or FALSE to remove them
overlap%	The percentage value for the overlap of the series markers
cluster	The percentage value for the cluster spacing of series markers
angle	The angle (in degrees) of the first pie slice for a pie chart

If any of these arguments does not apply to the currently selected chart, Excel ignores it.

MERGE.STYLES(*document_text*)

Brings all the styles from an outside document and merges them into the current document. Enter the name of the document containing the files to be merged.

MOVE(*x_pos,y_pos,window_text*)

MOVE?(*x_pos,y_pos,window_text*)

Moves a window to another screen location—an action equivalent to dragging on the window's title bar. The arguments *x_pos* and *y_pos* represent the horizontal and vertical positions of the upper left corner of the window. These positions are measured in points (a point is 1/72 inch) from the upper left corner of the screen. The argument *window_text* is the name of the window that you want to move. If you omit this argument, Excel moves the active window.

NAMES(*document_text,type_num*)

Lists alphabetically all the defined names within a document and presents them in a horizontal array. NAMES is similar to LIST.NAMES, but NAMES places the list of names in the macro sheet instead of the active worksheet.

Enter the name of the document you want to create the list for, followed by one of these values:

Value	Lists
1	Normal names only
2	Hidden names only
3	All names

NEW(*type_num,xy_series*)

NEW?(*type_num,xy_series*)

Mimic the New command from the File menu by opening a new worksheet. The *type_num* argument is a number representing the type of worksheet to open, according to the chart that follows (if you use the question-mark version, the familiar File New dialog box appears):

Value	Type Worksheet
1	Worksheet
2	Chart
3	Macro sheet
4	International macro sheet
"name"	Template name

When opening a chart, enter the *xy_series* argument as one of the following:

Value	Effect
0	Displays dialog box with options
1	First row or column used as the first data series
2	First row or column used as category labels
3	First row or column used as category axis values for scatter chart

NEW.WINDOW( )

Creates a new window for the active window. The two windows display the same file but can be operated independently.

NOTE(*add_text, cell_ref, start_char, num_chars*)

NOTE?( )

Insert, remove, or change a note attached to a cell. To add a new note (or replace an existing note), use the *text* and *cell_reference* arguments only. The *text* argument is the information you want to enter into the note, and *cell_reference* is the cell whose note you want to use. To remove a note, omit all the variables, as in =NOTE( ). To add information to an existing note, include the *start_character* and *count_character* arguments. The *start_character* is the character location in the note where you want to begin inserting the new text information. If this value is larger than the number of characters in the note, Excel inserts the new information at the end of the note. The *count_character* determines how many characters you want to replace with the new text. Some examples of the NOTE command follow:

Command	Effect
=NOTE()	Removes the note at the current cell.
=NOTE(,!A1)	Removes the note attached to cell A1 of the current worksheet.
=NOTE("This is it",!A1)	Adds the note *This is it* to cell A1 of the current worksheet. If a note exists, Excel replaces it.
=NOTE("This is it",!A1,9999)	Adds the note *This is it* to the end of the existing note attached to cell A1.

OBJECT.PROTECTION(*locked*)

Locks or unlocks a selected object. Enter TRUE if you want Excel to lock the object; enter FALSE if you want the object unlocked.

OPEN(*file_text, update_links, read_only, format, prot_pwd, write_res_pwd, ignore_rorec, file_origin*)

OPEN?(*file_text, update_links, read_only, format, prot_pwd, write_res_pwd, ignore_rorec, file_origin*)

Similar to the Open command from the File menu. The *file_text* argument is the name of the file that you want to open, entered as a text string. This should be the entire directory path. The *update_links* argument can be one of the following:

Value	Effect
0	Updates no references
1	Updates external references
2	Updates remote references
3	Updates external and remote references

The *read_only* variable controls whether the document can be changed (enter FALSE or omit the argument) or just viewed (enter TRUE). The *format* variable is useful when you open text files. Use one of the following values:

Value	File
1	Opens text file as a tab-delimited file
2	Opens text file as a comma-delimited file

Prot_pwd corresponds to the Password box; enter a password in quotation marks. The *write_res_pwd* argument is the password for write restriction. The *ignore_rorec* should be TRUE or FALSE to enable or disable the read-only recommendation. The *file_origin* argument should be one of the following values to indicate the type of file:

Value	File
1	Macintosh
2	Windows (ANSI)
3	DOS or OS/2

You can omit the argument to indicate the current system (Macintosh). Refer to the Password Protection dialog box to match these arguments with dialog box choices.

OPEN.LINKS(*document_text1, document_text2,..., read_only, type_of_link*)

OPEN.LINKS?(*document_text1, document_text2,..., read_only, type_of_link*)

Open all documents specified. You should enter the named document as text strings or as a range reference to a range containing a list of text strings. You also can use the LINKS command to generate a list of names for this command. The *logical* argument should follow all names or references and determines whether the opened documents are read-only (TRUE) or read and write (FALSE). For *type_of_link*, indicate the link type by entering one of these six values:

Value	Link Type
1	Excel link
2	DDE link
3	Incoming NewWave link
4	Outgoing NewWave link
5	Subscriber
6	Publisher

OUTLINE(*auto_styles, row_dir, col_dir, create_num*)

Creates a new outline. The first three fields correspond to the Automatic Styles, Summary Rows below Detail, and Summary Columns to Right of Detail check boxes in the Formula Outline dialog box. Enter TRUE to turn on the check box or FALSE to turn it off. For *create_num*, enter these values:

Value	Effect
1	Creates an outline with current settings
2	Applies outlining styles to selected item

OVERLAY(*type_num, stack, 100, vary, overlap, drop, hilo, overlap%, cluster, angle, series_num, auto*)

OVERLAY?(*type_num, stack, 100, vary, overlap, drop, hilo, overlap%, cluster, angle, series_num, auto*)

Controls the format of the overlay chart. For details about these arguments, see MAIN.CHART.

OVERLAY.CHART.TYPE(*type_num*)

Sets the chart type for the overlay chart (if one exists). Use the following values to specify the chart type:

Value	Chart
1	None (no overlay)
2	Area
3	Bar
4	Column
5	Line
6	Pie
7	Scatter

PAGE.SETUP(*head, foot, left, right, top, bot, heading, grid, h_center, v_center, orientation, paper_size, scaling*)

PAGE.SETUP?(*head, foot, left, right, top, bot, heading, grid, h_center, v_center, orientation, paper_size, scaling*)

PAGE.SETUP(*head, foot, left, right, top, bot, size, h_center, v_center, orientation, paper_size, scaling***)**

PAGE.SETUP?(*head, foot, left, right, top, bot, size, h_center, v_center, orientation, paper_size, scaling***)**

This command has two versions: the first is for worksheets and macro sheets, and the second is for charts. These commands are equivalent to the Page Setup command from the File menu. The arguments *head* and *foot*, which you must enter as text, print a header and footer. The arguments *left*, *right*, *top*, and *bot* control the margins of the printed page. These arguments represent the size, in inches, of the margins. The arguments *head* and *grid* control whether the worksheet headings and grid lines print with the data. Enter TRUE to print these elements or FALSE to keep them from printing. Omitting an argument leaves the option as it was last set. The *size* argument indicates the size of a chart as follows:

Value	Chart Size
1	Screen size
2	Fit to page
3	Full page

The *h_center* and *v_center* arguments are equivalent to the Center Horizontally and Center Vertically check boxes in the File Page Setup dialog box. Enter TRUE to turn the centering on and FALSE to turn it off. *Orientation* can be 1 (Portrait) or 2 (Landscape). *Paper_size* determines the type of paper used. Enter a value from 1 to 26 to choose a paper size.

PARSE(*text***)**

PARSE?(*text***)**

Break up a text sting by placing individual elements into separate cells. Each space in the original string creates a new cell.

PASTE( )

PASTE.LINK( )

PASTE.PICTURE( )

PASTE.PICTURE.LINK( )

Paste information from the Clipboard into the worksheet at the pointer location. The PASTE.LINK command is useful for creating automatic external references.

PASTE.SPECIAL(*paste_num,operation_num, skip_blanks, transpose*)

PASTE.SPECIAL?(*paste_num, operation_num, skip_blanks, transpose*)

PASTE.SPECIAL(*rowcol, series, categories, replace*)

PASTE.SPECIAL?(*rowcol, series, categories, replace*)

PASTE.SPECIAL(*paste_num*)

PASTE.SPECIAL?(*paste_num*)

Emulate the Paste Special command from the Edit menu. Use the first version when pasting information from one worksheet into another. Use the version containing the arguments *rowcol*, *series*, *categories*, and *replace* when pasting from a worksheet into a chart. You should use the command version containing *paste_num* as the only argument when you paste from a chart into a chart. Descriptions of the arguments follow:

Argument	Description
paste_num	Represents the type of information to print. Use one of the following:
	1 All
	2 Formulas
	3 Values
	4 Formats
	5 Notes

Note: Options 4 and 5 do not apply to the third version of the PASTE.SPECIAL command.

operation_num	Specifies the operation to perform when pasting. Use one of the following:

Argument	Description
	1 None
	2 Add
	3 Subtract
	4 Multiply
	5 Divide
skip_blanks	Determines whether to skip blank cells when pasting. Enter TRUE to skip blanks; otherwise, enter FALSE.
transpose	Determines whether to transpose data when pasting. Enter TRUE to transpose; otherwise, enter FALSE.
rowcol	Determines whether rows or columns are pasted as categories in the chart. Use a 1 to specify rows or a 2 to specify columns.
series	Enter TRUE to specify the first column of each row as the text for data series or FALSE to use the first row of each column as the data series.
categories	Enter TRUE to specify the first column of each row as the text for the categories or FALSE to use the first row of each column as the text for the categories.
replace	Enter TRUE to add new categories to the existing chart categories. Enter FALSE to replace the existing categories.

Remember that the question-mark versions of commands bring up the Excel dialog box associated with the command.

PATTERNS(*aauto, apattern, afore, aback*)

PATTERNS?(*aauto, apattern, afore, aback*)

PATTERNS(*lauto, lstyle, lcolor, lwt, bwidth, blength, btype*)

PATTERNS?(*lauto, lstyle, lcolor, lwt, bwidth, blength, btype*)

PATTERNS(*bauto,bstyle,bcolor,bwt, shadow,aauto, apattern,afore,aback, rounded*)

PATTERNS?(*bauto,bstyle,bcolor,bwt,shadow,aauto, apattern,afore,aback, rounded*)

PATTERNS(*bauto,bstyle,bcolor,bwt, shadow,aauto, apattern,afore,aback, invert,apply*)

PATTERNS?(*bauto,bstyle,bcolor,bwt, shadow,aauto, apattern,afore,aback, invert,apply*)

PATTERNS(*lauto,lstyle,lcolor,lwt,tmajor, tminor,tlabel*)

PATTERNS?(*lauto,lstyle,lcolor,lwt,tmajor, tminor,tlabel*)

PATTERNS(*lauto,lstyle,lcolor,lwt,apply*)

PATTERNS?(*lauto,lstyle,lcolor,lwt,apply*)

PATTERNS(*lauto,lstyle,lcolor,lwt,mauto, mstyle,mfore,mback,apply*)

PATTERNS?(*lauto,lstyle,lcolor,lwt,mauto, mstyle,mfore, mback,apply*)

PATTERNS(*type, picture_units*)

PATTERNS?(*type, picture_units*)

Correspond to the Patterns command from the Format menu. Like its menu equivalent, the PATTERNS command comes in many forms, depending on the item selected. The following is a description of each form, its arguments, and the selected items to which it applies:

If the selection includes a chart, plot area, legend , text label, area (of an area chart), or bar (of a bar chart), use the form

PATTERNS(*bauto,bstyle,bcolor,bwt, shadow,aauto,apattern, afore,aback,invert,apply*)

If the selection includes a chart grid line, high-low line, drop line, or lines on a picture chart, use the form

PATTERNS(*lauto,lstyle,lcolor,lwt,apply*)

If the selection includes a data line (on a line chart), use the form

PATTERNS(*lauto,lstyle,lcolor,lwt,mauto,mstyle,mfore,mback,apply*)

If the selection includes a chart arrow or line objects, use the form

PATTERNS(*lauto, lstyle, lcolor, lwt, hwidth, hlength, htype*)

If the selection includes worksheet cells, use the form

PATTERNS(*aauto, apattern, afore, aback*)

If the selection includes worksheet objects (except lines), use the form

PATTERNS(*bauto, bstyle, bcolor, bwt, shadow, aauto, apattern, afore, aback, rounded*)

Descriptions of the arguments follow:

Argument	Enter
aauto	An area setting:
	0 Set by user
	1 Automatic
	2 Invisible
aback	A number from 1 to 16 to choose the background color for the pattern.
afore	A number from 1 to 16 to choose the foreground color for the pattern.
apattern	A number from 1 to 18, corresponding to the patterns available in the Format Patterns dialog box.
apply	TRUE to apply the settings to all like elements.
bauto	Border setting:
	0 Set by user
	1 Automatic
	2 None
bcolor	A color style selection from 1 to 16. These values correspond to the color selections in the Format Patterns dialog box.
bstyle	A border style selection from 1 to 8. These values correspond to the border styles in the Format Patterns dialog box.

Argument	Enter
bwt	A border weight value from 1 to 4, corresponding to the weight values in the Format Patterns dialog box.
blength	A value to set the length of the arrow head:
	1 Short
	2 Medium
	3 Long
htype	A value to set the type of arrow head:
	1 No head
	2 Open head
	3 Closed head
hwidth	A value to set the width of the arrow head:
	1 Narrow
	2 Medium
	3 Wide
invert	TRUE to invert a value if that value is negative. This entry corresponds to the Invert if Negative box in the Format Patterns dialog box. FALSE returns the option to normal.
lauto	Line setting:
	0 Set by user
	1 Automatic
	2 Invisible
lcolor	A color style selection from 1 to 16. These values correspond to the color selections in the Format Patterns dialog box.
lstyle	A border style selection from 1 to 8. These values correspond to the border styles in the Format Patterns dialog box.
lwt	A border weight value from 1 to 4, corresponding to the weight values in the Format Patterns dialog box.

Argument	Enter
mauto	A value to set the marker style:
	0 Set by user
	1 Automatic
	2 None
mback	A number from 1 to 8 to set the background color for the pattern.
mfore	A number from 1 to 8 to set the foreground color for the pattern.
mstyle	A value from 1 to 7 to set the marker type. These values correspond to the marker types in the Format Patterns dialog box.
rounded	TRUE to round the corners of the object.
type	Controls picture charts. Type one of the following values:
	1 Stretched pictures
	2 Stacked pictures
	3 Stacked and sized pictures
picture_units	A value representing the value (in y-axis scale units) you want each picture in a picture chart to be. The *type* argument must be 3 if you use this argument.
shadow	TRUE to include a shadow or FALSE to remove it.
tlabel	A value to set the position of the tick labels:
	1 None
	2 Low
	3 High
	4 Next to axis
tmajor	A value to set the major tick mark style:
	1 None
	2 Inside

Argument	Enter
	3 Outside
	4 Cross
tminor	A value to set the minor tick mark style:
	1 None
	2 Inside
	3 Outside
	4 Cross

PLACEMENT(*value*)

Enter one of the following values to indicate the placement method used to attach the selected object or objects to the cells beneath them:

Value	Placement Method
1	The object should be moved and sized with the cells
2	The object should move with the cells but retain its original size
3	The object is free-floating and is not affected by the movement and sizing of the cells

PRECISION(*logical*)

Equivalent to the Precision as Displayed check box of the Options Calculation command. Enter TRUE to check the box (to enable the option) or FALSE to uncheck the box (to disable the option).

PREFERRED( )

Sets the current chart to the preferred format, which is established with the SET.PREFERRED command.

PRINT(*range_num, from, to, copies, draft, preview, print_what, color, feed*)

PRINT?(*range_num, from,to,copies,draft,preview, print_what, color, feed*)

Equivalent to the Print command from the File menu. The arguments are identical to the various buttons and check boxes found in the File Print dialog box. The range should be one of the following values:

Value	Option
1	Print all
2	Print from...

If you enter the value 2, the *from* and *to* arguments become active; otherwise, Excel ignores them. You can omit these arguments if you want. *From* and *to* should be numeric values representing a page range. *Copies* should be a numeric value representing the number of copies you want to print.

You should omit the *draft* argument, but leave in the comma as a placeholder. This argument is not recognized by the Macintosh; Excel includes the argument to make Excel for the Macintosh compatible with Excel for the PC. The following is an example showing the fifth argument as the placeholder comma:

=PRINT(2,3,3,1,, FALSE,1,TRUE,1).

The *preview* argument should be TRUE if you want to print a preview and FALSE if you want to print normally. The *print_what* argument represents the type of information to print:

Value	Information to Print
1	Sheet (the worksheet and values)
2	Notes (cell notes)
3	Both

You should omit the *print_what* argument when you print a chart. The *color* argument should be TRUE if you want to print in color and FALSE if you want to print in black and white. The *feed* argument should be one of the following for dot-matrix printers:

Value	Type of Feed
1	Continuous feed
2	Cut sheet

When printing from a non-Apple printer (or a printer that is not compatible with Apple printers), use the question-mark form of the PRINT command. This form presents the standard Print dialog box, from which you can make selections.

PRINT.PREVIEW( )

Shows on-screen the page breaks and setups of the active file so that you can check them before printing. Equivalent to the Print Preview command from the File menu.

PROMOTE(*rowcol*)

PROMOTE?(*rowcol*)

Promote the selected outline rows or columns to a higher level. Similar to the Promote button. Enter one of these values:

Value	Effect
1	Promote rows
2	Promote columns

PROTECT.DOCUMENT(*contents,windows, password ,objects*)

PROTECT.DOCUMENT?(*contents,windows, password ,objects*)

Equivalent to the Protect Document command from the Options menu. Enter TRUE or FALSE as the value of the contents, windows, and objects arguments. TRUE protects; FALSE unprotects. Use FALSE in both options to remove protection entirely. If a password is required to unprotect the file, enter it as a text string in the password argument.

QUIT( )

Quits Excel and displays the Save dialog box if files need saving. Equivalent to the Quit command from the File menu.

REFTEXT(*reference,a1*)

Converts the given reference into an absolute reference, in text form. Enter TRUE if you want an A1-style reference or FALSE if you want an R1C1-style reference.

RELREF(*reference, rel_to_ref*)

Tells you the distance (in rows and columns) that one cell is from another. The reference is returned as a text-style R1C1 reference indicating the number of rows and columns the reference argument is offset from the *rel_to_ref* argument. Enter any cell or range for both arguments. For example, you can enter

=RELREF(C5,B4)

for a return of R[1]C[1]. The result indicates that C5 is one row and column higher than B4. You should enter the arguments as absolute A1-style references for best results.

REMOVE.PAGE.BREAK( )

Removes the page breaks relative to the pointer's position.

ROW.HEIGHT(*height_num, reference, standard_height, type_num*)

ROW.HEIGHT?(*height_num, reference, standard_height, type_num*)

Set the height of rows in the worksheet. Enter the height (in points) as the *height_num* argument. The *reference* argument specifies which row(s) to change and should be entered as an external reference or as an R1C1-style reference entered as text. If *reference* is omitted, Excel assumes the current selection. The *standard_height* argument should be TRUE or FALSE. A value of TRUE causes each row to be sized according to the height of the fonts in that row. For *type_num*, enter 1 to Hide, 2 to Unhide, and 3 for Best-Fit. These are equivalent to the three buttons in the Format Row Height dialog box.

RUN(*reference, step*)

RUN?(*reference, step*)

Run a macro specified by the reference argument. This argument should be a valid macro name entered as a text string; the starting address of a macro, entered as an external reference, as in =RUN(!A1); or an R1C1-style reference entered as a text string. For *step*, enter TRUE to run the macro in single-step mode or FALSE to run the macro at regular speed.

SAVE( )

SAVE.AS(*document_text,type_num,prot_pwd ,backup, write_res_pwd , read_only_rec*)

SAVE.AS?(*document_text,type_num,prot_pwd ,backup, write_res_pwd , read_only_rec*)

The SAVE command saves the document or, if not previously saved , brings up the standard Save dialog box. The SAVE.AS command saves the file in the current directory under the *document_text* name. Equivalent to the Save and Save As commands from the File menu. The *type_num* variable represents the file type you want to save the file as. Use any of the following:

Type Value	Type Description
1	Normal Excel
2	SYLK
3	Text
4	WKS
5	WK1
6	CSV
7	DBF2
8	DBF3
9	DIF
10	Reserved
11	DBF4
12	Reserved
13	Reserved
14	Reserved
15	WK3
16	Excel 2.x
17	Template
18	Add-in macro
19	Macintosh text

Type Value	Type Description
20	Windows text
21	OS/2 or DOS text
22	CSV (Macintosh)
23	CSV (Windows)
24	CSV (OS/2 or DOS)
25	International macro

The *prot_pwd* argument is any password to protect the document. The *backup* argument should be TRUE if you want to make a backup as you save and FALSE if you want to forgo the backup. Enter a *write_res_pwd* if you want to restrict the file to read-only status unless the password is supplied. (If the file is for open access, leave this field blank.) Enter TRUE for *read_only_rec* if you want to save the file as read only recommended or FALSE to save it normally.

Use the question-mark form of the SAVE.AS command to save the document to a different directory or to enable the user to provide his own name and type for the document. For example, =SAVE.AS?() brings up the standard dialog box for your selections.

SAVE.WORKSPACE(*name_text*)

SAVE.WORKSPACE?(*name_text*)

Save the workspace of the open files and create a workspace file. For more details about these files, refer to Chapter 7. Enter the name of the workspace file as the *name_text* variable.

SCALE(*cross, cat_labels, cat_marks, between, max, reverse*)

SCALE?(*cross, cat_labels, cat_marks, between, max, reverse*)

SCALE(*min_num, max_num, major, minor, cross, logarithmic, reverse, max*)

SCALE?(*min_num, max_num, majorminor, cross, logarithmic, reverse, max*)

SCALE(*cat_labels, cat_marks, reverse, between*)

SCALE(*series_labels, series_marks, reverse*)

SCALE(*min_num,max_num,major,minor,cross,logarithmic, reverse,min*)

This command controls the scale of the axes in a chart. To control the category axis on any chart except a scatter (xy) chart, use the following form:

SCALE(*cross,cat_labels,cat_marks,between,max, reverse*)

To change the value axis of a chart, use this form:

SCALE(*min_num,max_num,major,minor,cross,logarithmic, reverse,max*)

To change the category axis of a 3-D chart, use the following form:

SCALE(*cat_labels,cat_marks, reverse,between*)

To change the series (or depth) axis of a 3-D chart, use this form:

SCALE(*series_labels, series_marks, reverse*)

To change the value axis of a 3-D chart, use this form:

SCALE(*min_num,max_num,major,minor,cross,logarithmic, reverse,min*)

Explanations of the arguments used in the commands follow:

Argument	Enter
cat_labels	Number of categories that should appear between tick labels
cat_marks	Number of categories that should appear between tick marks
cross	Value at which the category axis crosses the value axis
major	Value for the major-unit scale
max_num	Maximum value for the value axis
min_num	Minimum value for the value axis
minor	Value for the minor-unit scale
series_labels	Number of series between tick labels (default = 1)
series_marks	Number of series between tick marks (default = 1)

The arguments that follow may be omitted if you want to leave the option unchanged from its last setting:

Argument	Enter
between	TRUE to make the category axis cross between categories; otherwise, enter FALSE.
reverse	TRUE to display categories in reverse order; otherwise, enter FALSE.
max	TRUE to cause the indicated axis to cross at the maximum category; otherwise, enter FALSE.
logarithmic	TRUE to set a logarithmic scale; otherwise, enter FALSE.

SEARCH(*find_text, within_text, start_num*)

Yields the character number at which the searched-for character or text string is found. Enter the text you want to find (including wild-card characters, if needed), followed by the name of the document in which you want the search to occur. *Start_num* is the character number in the document at which the search should begin. The default is 1.

SELECT(*selection, active_cell*)

SELECT(*object_id_text, replace*)

SELECT(*item_text*)

This command selects elements of a worksheet, chart, or object, depending on which form you use. To select cells in a worksheet, use the following form:

SELECT(*selection, active_cell*)

When used with a worksheet, this command selects the worksheet cell or range specified by the selection variable. If the selection is a range of cells, you can make any cell in the range the active cell by entering its address as the *active_cell* variable. The *active_cell* should be one of the cells in the selection.

You can specify the selection as a cell or range on the current worksheet, using the form !A5 or !A5:B6. You can, of course, make this reference an external one by including the window name, such as Worksheet1!A5:B6. You also can refer to a named range, as in !Sales (for the current worksheet) or Worksheet1!Sales (for an external worksheet named WORKSHEET).

Alternatively, you can make the selection relative to the active cell by entering the argument as an R1C1-style reference entered as a text string. The command

=SELECT("R1C2:R3C3","R1C3")

for example, highlights the range B1:C3 and makes the active cell C1. You also can use the entry "RC" to represent the active cell and move the pointer relative to that cell with entries like the following:

=SELECT("RC[1]")   Moves the pointer one column to the right

=SELECT("R[-3]C[2]") Moves the pointer three rows up and two columns to the right

To select elements of a chart, use this form:

SELECT(*item_text*)

When used with a chart, the SELECT command selects the chart element specified by the *item_text* argument. Use any of the following entries to specify the item text:

item_text	*Specifies*
Chart	Entire chart
Plot	Plot area
Legend	Legend
Axis 1	Main chart's vertical (value) axis
Axis 2	Main chart's horizontal (category) axis
Axis 3	Overlay chart's vertical (value) axis
Axis 4	Overlay chart's horizontal (category) axis
Title	Chart title
Text Axis 1	Main chart's value axis title
Text Axis 2	Main chart's category axis title
Text *n*	*n*th text added to the chart
Arrow *n*	*n*th arrow added to the chart

Be sure to enter the argument in quotation marks.

To select objects, use the following form of the command:

SELECT(*object_id_text, replace*)

When used with objects, the SELECT command selects the object(s) specified in the *object_id_text* argument. This should be the name and number of the object(s), such as "Oval 2", "Arc 1", or "Oval 5, Arc 1, Line 1". Be sure to enter the references as text strings surrounded by quotation marks. You can use the GET.OBJECT or SELECTION command to determine the number of the selected object. The *replace* argument determines whether the new selections are added to existing selections. Enter FALSE to keep previously selected items selected or TRUE to unselect them before selecting the new items.

SELECT.CHART( )

SELECT.LAST.CELL( )

Selects the cell at the intersection of the last occupied row and column. Equivalent to the Select Special Last Cell command from the Formula menu.

SELECT.PLOT.AREA( )

Select the chart and plot area, respectively.

SELECT.END(*direction_num*)

Selects the cell at the edge of the range in one of four directions:

Value	Direction
1	Left
2	Right
3	Up
4	Down

SELECT.SPECIAL(*type_num,value_type, levels*)

SELECT.SPECIAL?(*type_num, value_type,levels*)

Select the information indicated by the variables. Equivalent to the Select Special command from the Formula menu. The following is a list of each possible value:

Value	Information
type_num	
1	Notes
2	Constants
3	Formulas
4	Blanks
5	Current region
6	Current array
7	Row differences
8	Column differences
9	Precedents
10	Dependents
11	Last cell
12	Visible cells only (outlining)
13	All objects
value_type	
1	Numbers
2	Text
4	Logical values
16	Error values
levels (applies to type number 9 or 10 only)	
1	Direct only
2	All levels

SELECTION( )

Provides the reference or object name of one or more selected objects. This is useful for determining object numbers for other macro commands. Multiple object selections are returned as a string of several items, separated by commas.

SEND.MAIL(*recipient, subject, return_receipt*)

SEND.MAIL?(*recipient, subject, return_receipt*)

Works with Microsoft Mail Version 2.0 or higher to send the active document to the designated recipient. Enter the recipient's name (or an array of several names) as quoted text, followed by the message's subject (a title or file name). If you want a return receipt, enter TRUE for the final argument.

SEND.TO.BACK( )

Places the indicated window or other object behind all other open windows on the desktop.

SET.CRITERIA( )

SET.DATABASE( )

SET.EXTRACT( )

Set the current criteria, database, and extract ranges, respectively. Be sure to select the range you want before using these commands.

SET.PAGE.BREAK( )

Sets a page break at the position of the pointer.

SET.PREFERRED( )

Sets the preferred chart type to match the selected chart. Equivalent to the Set Preferred command from the Gallery menu. If you use the PREFERRED command after using the SET.PREFERRED command, Excel duplicates the chart you set with this command.

SET.PRINT.AREA( )

Activates the selected range as the current print area. If only one cell is selected, the command removes the print area.

SET.PRINT.TITLES( )

Activates the selected range as the titles range for printouts. First, select the range of cells, and then use this command as you would use the Set Print Titles command from the Options menu.

SHORT.MENUS(*logical*)

Enter TRUE as the argument to have Excel display short menus. Enter FALSE to have Excel display full menus.

SHOW.ACTIVE.CELL( )

Scrolls the screen view until the active cell is showing. Identical to the keyboard command ⌘-Backspace. This feature is useful when the pointer has been scrolled out of view.

SHOW.CLIPBOARD( )

Displays the contents of the Clipboard in a new window.

SHOW.DETAIL(*rowcol, rowcol_num, expand*)

Creates a button that expands or collapses the specified detail. For *rowcol*, enter one of these values:

Value	Operates on
1	Rows
2	Columns

Rowcol_num is the R1C1 number designating the row or column you want to expand or collapse. Enter TRUE to expand the detail or FALSE to collapse it.

SHOW.INFO(*logical*)

Displays the Info window. Enter TRUE to activate the Info window. If the Info window is active and the *logical* value is FALSE, Excel activates the document linked to the Info window.

SHOW.LEVELS(*row_level,col_level*)

Shows the indicated number of levels and columns in an outline. Enter the number of row levels and column levels that you want to display.

SIZE(*width, height, window_text*)

Changes the size of the active window, just like dragging the size box in the lower right corner of any Macintosh window. Enter the width and height of the window (in points) and the name of the window to be sized.

SORT(*sort_by,key1,order1,key2,order2, key3,order3*)
SORT?(*sort_by,key1,order1,key2, order2,key3,order3*)

Equivalent to the Sort option from the Data menu, this command sorts the selected range of cells. The *sort_by* argument can be either of the following values:

Value	Specifies
1	Rows
2	Columns

Enter the address of the cell representing the first key field as the *key1* argument. This address should be an external reference or an R1C1-style reference entered as text. The *order1* argument should be either of the following values:

Value	Specifies
1	Ascending
2	Descending

You also can add a second and third key, as well as an *order3* argument.

SPLIT(*col_split, row_split*)

Splits the window to create panes—comparable to dragging the split-window marker with the mouse. Indicate the column on which you want to split the sheet by typing its numeric value as the *col_split* variable. Indicate the row on which you want to split the sheet by entering its value as the *row_split* argument. The following are examples:

Argument	Effect
=SPLIT(5,0)	Splits the window vertically at column 5
=SPLIT(5,3)	Splits the window horizontally at row 3 and vertically at column 5

STANDARD.FONT(*font_text, size_num, bold, italic, underline, strike, color, outline, shadow*)

Sets the standard font for the entire worksheet. The arguments are identical to those of the FORMAT.FONT command.

TABLE(*row_ref, column_ref*)

TABLE?(*row_ref, column_ref*)

Create a new table from the input values and formulas defined in a worksheet. Equivalent to the Table command from the Data menu. Enter the reference for the one cell that serves as the row input for the table, followed by the one cell that serves as the column input.

TEXTREF(*text, a1*)

Converts *text* references to absolute a1 or R1C1-style references. Enter the text reference to be converted. For *a1*, enter TRUE for an A1-style reference or FALSE for an R1C1-style reference.

UNDO( )

Revokes your last action. Identical to the Undo command from the Edit menu.

UNGROUP( )

Breaks a grouped object into its parts, enabling you to manipulate each object separately. Similar to the Ungroup command from the Format menu.

UNHIDE(*window_text*)

Brings into view a hidden window. For the *window_text* argument, enter the window name as a text string.

UNLOCKED.NEXT( )

UNLOCKED.PREV( )

Move the current cell to the next or preceding unlocked (that is, unprotected) cell in the sheet, respectively. These commands are equivalent to using the keyboard commands Tab and Shift-Tab.

UPDATE.LINK(*link_text,type_of_link*)

Updates a link to another document, enabling you to get new information from supporting files. Enter the full path name of the link as a quoted text string; then enter one of the following four link types:

Value	Link Type
1	Excel link
2	DDE link
3	Not available
4	Outgoing NewWave link

VIEW.3D(*elevation, perspective, rotation, axes, height%*)

VIEW.3D?(*elevation, perspective, rotation, axes, height%*)

Present a new view of a 3-D chart.

Elevation is the viewing elevation of the chart, expressed in –90 degrees (directly beneath) to 90 degrees (directly above). The default setting is 25 degrees.

The *perspective* argument is a number between 0% and 100%, indicating how close you are to the chart. A higher number yields a closer view. The default is 50%.

Rotation is the orientation of the chart around the z axis, expressed from 0 to 360 degrees. The default is 30.

The *axes* argument determines whether the chart's axes are locked in the window plane or rotate with the chart. Enter TRUE to lock the axes or FALSE to enable the axes to rotate. If the chart is 3-D, the default value is FALSE; if the chart is not 3-D, the default value is TRUE.

VLINE(*num_rows*)

VPAGE(*num_windows*)

VSCROLL(*position, row_logical*)

Scroll the active window vertically. VLINE scrolls the window vertically by the specified number of rows. Using this command is similar to using the scroll arrows of the active vertical scroll bar. VPAGE scrolls the window by the specified number of pages, or screens—an action similar to clicking in the vertical scroll bar. Use a positive number to represent downward movement and a negative number to represent upward movement. VSCROLL scrolls the window by percentage or row number. Enter the number of the row you want to scroll to, or a percentage number or fraction indicating the vertical location in the document. For *row_logical*, enter TRUE to scroll to the row position or FALSE to scroll to the vertical position indicated by the fraction position. See also HLINE and HPAGE.

WINDOWS(*type_num*)

Yields the names of all the open Excel windows, including hidden ones. The names appear as a horizontal list. The three possible argument values follow:

Value	Effect
1	Lists all windows except add-in documents
2	Lists add-in documents only
3	Lists all documents

WORKGROUP(*name_array*)

Creates a new workgroup. Enter the text names of all the open, unhidden worksheets and macro sheets you want to include in the new group. (You cannot include charts, however.) If you leave the argument field blank, Excel recreates the most recently created workgroup. If this is the first workgroup created during the current Excel session, all open and unhidden worksheets and macro sheets are collected into one workgroup.

WORKSPACE(*fixed, decimals, r1c1, scroll, status, formula, menu_key, remote, entermove, underlines, tools, notes, interface, menu_key_action*)

WORKSPACE?(*fixed, decimals, r1c1, scroll, status, formula, menu_key, remote, entermove, underlines, tools, notes, interface, menu_key_action*)

Equivalent to the Workspace command from the Options menu. Its arguments correspond to the dialog box options in that command. Enter TRUE or FALSE to activate or deactivate the option. For the *underlines* argument, enter one of the following values to control how the keyboard indicator keys are displayed:

Value	Display
1	Underlines on
2	Underlines off
3	Automatic

C

Excel Command Guide

Menu Commands and Procedures

Table C.1
Opening and Closing Worksheets

Description	Command	Key
Open New File	File New	N
Open Existing File	File Open	O
Close File	File Close	W
Save File	File Save	S
Save File under Different Name	File Save As	
Save File under Different Format	File Save As	
Save Workspace	File Save Workspace	
Delete Files from Disk	File Delete	
Quit Excel	File Quit	Q

Table C.2
Printing

Description	Command	Key
Determine Page Setup	File Page Setup	
Begin Printing	File Print	P
Select Print Area	Options Set Print Area	
Set Titles for Page	Options Set Print Titles	
Set Manual Page Break	Options Set Page Break	

Table C.3
Editing Data

Description	Command	Key
Move Data	Edit Cut (then Paste)	X
Copy Data	Edit Copy	C
	Edit Fill Right	R
	Edit Fill Down	D
	Edit Fill Left	Shift-R
	Edit Fill Up	Shift-D
Copy Data into Workgroup	Edit Fill Workgroup	
Paste Data	Edit Paste	V
	Edit Paste Special	Shift-V
Paste Data from other Worksheet	Edit Paste Link	
Remove Data	Edit Clear	B
Insert Cell	Edit Insert	I
Delete Cell	Edit Delete	K
Name Cells and Ranges	Formula Define Name	L
	Formula Create Names	
Add or Edit Cell Note	Formula Note	
View Note	Formula Note	
	Window Show Info	

Table C.4
Finding Data

Description	Command	Key
Go to Specified Cell	Formula Goto	G
Find Specific Data	Formula Find	J
Replace Data	Formula Replace	
Find Specific References	Formula Select Special	
Display Active Cell	Formula Show Active Cell	

Table C.5
Entering Data

Description	Command	Key
Accept Entry	Return Enter	
Cancel Entry	Esc ⌘-.	
Repeat Previous Entry	Edit Repeat	
Insert a function name	Formula Paste Function	
Insert a Name	Formula Paste Name	
Protect Cells from Entry	Format Cell Protection (then Options Protect Document)	
Create a Series of Numbers or Dates	Data Series	

Table C.6
Formatting

Description	Command	Key
Specify Number Formats	Format Number	
Align Data	Format Alignment Toolbar Buttons	

continues

Table C.6 *(continued)*

Description	Command	Key
Change Fonts	Format Font	
Change Row Height	Format Row Height	
Change Column Width	Format Column Width	
Justify a Column of Text	Format Justify	
Sort Rows	Data Sort	
Wrap Text in a Cell	Format Alignment	
Change Cell Pattern and Color	Format Patterns	
Add Borders & Lines	Format Border	

Table C.7
Using Databases

Description	Command	Key
Show Database Form	Data Form	
Find Data in Databases	Data Find	F
Extract Records	Data Extract	E
Delete Records	Data Delete	
Establish Database Range	Data Set Database	
Establish Criteria Range	Data Set Criteria	
Establish an Extract Range	Data Set Extract	

Table C.8
Using Windows and Panes

Description	Command	Key
Freeze Panes	Options Freeze Panes	
Create New Window for Active Worksheet	Window New Window	

Description	Command	Key
Display Worksheet Information	Window Show Info	
Arrange Windows On-Screen	Window Arrange All	
Show Contents of Clipboard	Window Show Clipboard	
Hide Active Window	Window Hide	
Show Hidden Windows	Window Unhide	
Show Help Window	Window Help	

Table C.9
Using Objects

Draw Object	Toolbar Tools
Change Object Patterns and Borders	Format Patterns
Format Text Box or Button Font	Format Font
Change Text Alignment in Button or Text Box	Format Text
Move Object to Front	Format Bring to Front
Move Object to Back	Format Send to Back
Group Several Objects	Format Groups
Change Object/Worksheet Relationship	Format Object Placement

Table C.10
Using Charts

Description	Command	Key
Change Chart Type	Gallery *Type* Format Main Chart	
Set Custom Chart Type	Gallery Set Preferred	

continues

Table C.10 *(continued)*

Description	Command	Key
Add Text to Chart	Chart Attach Text	
Add Arrow to Chart	Chart Add Arrow	
Display Legend	Chart Add Legend	
Hide Legend	Chart Delete Legend	
Add Axes	Chart Axes	
Remove Axes	Chart Axes	
Add Grid Lines	Chart Gridlines	
Remove Grid Lines	Chart Gridlines	
Make Combination Chart	Chart Add Overlay	
Remove Overlay Chart	Chart Delete Overlay	
Select Chart	Chart Select Chart	A
Select Plot Area	Chart Select Plot Area	
Recalculate Chart	Chart Calculate Now	
Format Any Chart Element	Format Patterns (after selecting element)	
Change Fonts in Chart	Format Font (after selecting text)	
Change Text Orientation	Format Text (after selecting text)	
Change Axis Scale	Format Scale (after selecting axis)	
Edit Series Positions and Data	Chart Edit Series	
Change 3-D Chart Perspective	Edit 3-D View	

Table C.11
Performing Miscellaneous Actions

Description	Command	Key
Reset Linked Worksheets	File Links	
Change Worksheet	Options Display	
Display	Options Worksheet	
Change Calculation Procedure	Options Calculation	
Calculate the Document Now	Options Calculate Now	
Display Short Menus	Options Short Menus	
Display Long Menus	Options Long Menus	
Activate Num Lock		
Toggle	Shift-Clear	
Cancel Action	Esc, ⌘-.	
Edit Formula	⌘-U	
Close Window	⌘-F4 ⌘-W	
Restore Window	⌘-F5	
Move to Next Window	⌘-F6 ⌘-M	
Move to Preceding Window	⌘-Shift-F6 ⌘-Shift-M	
Maximize Window	⌘-F10	
Move to Next Pane	F6	
Move to Preceding Pane	Shift-F6	
Activate Menu	F10 or /	
Outline Worksheet	Formula Outline	

Table C.12
Using Macros

Description	Command	Key
Record a Macro from Scratch	Macro Record	
Run an Existing Macro	Macro Run	
Start Macro Recorder for Existing Macro Sheet	Macro Start Recorder	
Set Macro Record Area on Macro Sheet	Macro Set Recorder	
Change Relative/Absolute References in Recorded Macros	Macro Relative Recorder	

Command Equivalents

Table C.13
File Menu Equivalents

Key Combination	Function
F11	New Chart
Shift-F11	New Worksheet
⌘-F11	New Macro Sheet
⌘-N	New (shows dialog box)
F12	Save As
⌘-Shift-S	Save As
Shift-F12	Save
⌘-S	Save

Key Combination	Function
⌘-F12	Open
⌘-O	Open
⌘-Shift-F12	Print
⌘-Q	Quit

Table C.14
Edit Menu Equivalents

Key Combination	Function
⌘-Y	Repeat
F1	Undo
⌘-Z	Undo
F2	Cut
⌘-X	Cut
F3	Copy
⌘-C	Copy
F4	Paste
⌘-V	Paste
⌘-Shift-V	Paste Special
⌘-B	Clear
⌘-Shift-C	Copy Picture
⌘-K	Delete
⌘-I	Insert
⌘-D	Fill Down
⌘-R	Fill Right
⌘-Shift-R	Fill Left
⌘-Shift-D	Fill Up

Table C.15
Formula Menu Equivalents

Key Combination	Function
Shift-F3	Paste
⌘-F3	Define Name
⌘-L	Define Name
⌘-Shift-F3	Create Name
F5	Goto
⌘-G	Goto
Shift-F5	Formula Find
⌘-J	Formula Find
F7	Find Next
⌘-H	Find Next
Shift-F7	Find Previous
⌘-Shift-H	Find Previous
Shift-F2	Note
⌘-Shift-N	Note
⌘-Shift-O	Select Notes
⌘-*	Select Current Region
⌘-/	Select Row Differences
⌘-Shift-/	Select Column Differences
⌘-[	Select Direct Precedents
⌘-Shift-[	Select All Precedents
⌘-]	Select Direct Dependents
⌘-Shift-]	Select All Dependents
⌘-Shift-B	Bold
⌘-Shift-I	Italic
⌘-Shift-P	Plain

Key Combination	Function
⌘-Shift-U	Underline
⌘-Shift-W	Shadow
⌘-Option-O	Border Outline
⌘-Option-←	
⌘-Option-→	
⌘-Option-↑	
⌘-Option-↓	Add Border to Side
⌘-~	General Format
⌘-!	0.00 Format
⌘-@	*h:mm* AM/PM Format
⌘-#	*d-mmm-yy* Format
⌘-$	$#,##0.00;($#,##0.00) Format
⌘-%	0% Format
⌘-^	0.00E+00 Format

Table C.16
Data Menu Equivalents

Key Combination	Function
⌘-F	Find Next
⌘-Shift-F	Find Preceding
⌘-E	Extract

Table C.17
Options Menu Equivalent

Key Combination	Function
⌘-=	Calculate Worksheet

Table C.18
Window Menu Equivalents

Key Combination	Function
⌘-F2	Show Info Window
⌘-?	Help
Shift-F1	Help

Table C.19
Chart Menu Equivalent

Key Combination	Function
⌘-A	Select Chart

Table C.20
Shortcut Keys for Moving the Pointer and Selecting

Key	Key Only	⌘-	⌘-Option-*
↑	Up One Cell	Up One Block	Top Border
↓	Down One Cell	Down One Block	Bottom Border
←	Left One Cell	Left One Block	Left Border
→	Right One Cell	Right One Block	Right Border
Home	Beginning of Row	Cell A1	
PgUp	Up One Screen	Left One Screen	
PgDn	Down One Screen	Right One Screen	
Space Bar	Select Column		

Key	Shift-	⌘-Shift-	In Charts (key only)
↑	Extend One Cell Up	Extend One Block Up	Select Next Class
↓	Extend One Cell Down	Extend One Block Down	Select Preceding Class

Key	Key Only	⌘-	⌘-Option-*
←	Extend One Cell Left	Extend One Block Left	Select Next Item
→	Extend One Cell Right	Extend One Block Right	Select Preceding Item
Home	Extend to Column A	Extend to Cell A1	
PgUp	Extend One Screen Up	Extend One Screen Left	
PgDn	Extend One Screen Down	Extend One Screen Right	
Space Bar	Select Row	Select Worksheet†	

Note: To extend the selection, press F8 before pressing the movement key. Press F8 again to end the extended selection. To cancel the extend-selection operation, press Cancel.

* See also ⌘-Option-O

† Also ⌘-A

Index

Symbols

T

Free Catalog!

BUSINESS REPLY MAIL

First Class Permit No. 9918   Indianapolis, IN

Postage will be paid by addressee

11711 N. College
Carmel, IN 46032

NO POSTAGE
NECESSARY
IF MAILED
IN THE
UNITED STATES

BUSINESS REPLY MAIL

First Class Permit No. 9918   Indianapolis, IN

Postage will be paid by addressee

11711 N. College
Carmel, IN 46032